M. RAY LOREE, B.A., University of Manitoba, Ph.D., University of Chicago, is Professor of Educational Psychology at the University of Alabama. He previously taught at Louisiana State University and formerly held positions as Coordinator of Evaluation and Guidance, Oklahoma City Schools, and public school teacher and administrator in schools in Manitoba, Canada. Professor Loree has written extensively in his field and is the editor of *Educational Psychology*, published by The Ronald Press Company.

PSYCHOLOGY

OF

EDUCATION

M. RAY LOREE

UNIVERSITY OF ALABAMA

THE RONALD PRESS COMPANY · NEW YORK

Library of Congress Catalog Card Number: 65–15107

PREFACE

The major purpose of this text is to help the student develop and apply psychological concepts, principles, and theories in dealing with educational problems. In effect, this is a bringing to bear of scientific method on problems in education. With this in mind, three strategies have been adopted in this text:

1. Discussions of psychology as a science and the research methodologies of psychology are introduced in Chapter 1. Examples of how the psychologist may use theories of behavior in studying individual behavior are presented in Chapter 2.
2. Considerable space is devoted throughout the text to detailed descriptions of research studies so that the student will have concrete examples of the way psychologists study behavioral problems.
3. Both educational and psychological problems are analyzed in terms of stimulus, organismic, and response variables in the hope that students, in thinking about any instructional problem, will develop a predisposition to ask the question: "What are the crucial stimulus, organismic, and response variables?"

To be effective, instruction needs to be geared to certain characteristics of the learner (the organismic variable). Chapters 2–5 are primarily concerned with "The Learner."

Chapters 6–9 are concerned with the "Teaching-learning Process" with emphasis upon what the teacher does to promote learning (the stimulus variable).

While there are general principles of learning that are applicable to all forms of learning, the procedures that the teacher follows in guiding different kinds of learning do vary. Chapters 10–13 consider separately psychological materials relevant to the teacher's task of guiding the student to the attainment of different kinds of educational objectives (the response variable).

The materials presented in Chapters 2–13 are most clearly relevant to the following major tasks of the teacher: defining objectives, selecting learning experiences, organizing learning experiences, and guiding the learning process in the classroom. Chapter 14 is focused upon another task of the teacher, i.e., evaluating the effects of instruction.

The learner reacts as a total person in any learning situation. Hence, any analysis of the learner may leave the impression that he is much more compartmentalized than he really is. The final chapter of this book, Chapter 15, discusses the individual as a total person.

The Appendix contains a "self-teaching" unit on statistical concepts and is particularly pertinent as background material for Chapters 4 and 14.

A student must do more than read about educational psychology in order to learn to analyze instructional problems in psychological terms. The student must interact with the material he reads. To encourage this interaction, learning exercises are interspersed within each chapter throughout the text. By also including answer cues at the end of each chapter, the text is, in effect, semiprogrammed.

Materials contained in this text have been pretested in both undergraduate and graduate level courses in educational psychology at the University of Alabama. I wish to acknowledge the many constructive suggestions and encouragement received from many graduate students and from my colleagues—Robert Bills, Lewis Blackwell, Fain Guthrie, Beverley Holaday, Kenneth Parsley (author of Chapter 15), and Frederick Westover. Any text reflects the influence on its author of others. As a graduate student at the University of Chicago, my thinking about curriculum and educational problems became greatly influenced by Ralph W. Tyler. This influence is reflected at several points in this book. I gained an appreciation for thorough analysis in working with Benjamin S. Bloom, first as a graduate assistant and later as one participant in developing the *Taxonomy of Educational Objectives*. The conviction that a course in educational psychology should stress psychology in order to contribute most effectively to a teacher-preparation program grew out of daily interaction with former colleagues in the department of psychology at Louisiana State University.

Gratitude is expressed to the many publishers who generously have given permission to quote from copyrighted works. Finally, special grateful acknowledgment is tendered to my wife, Ellen Loree, for her encouragement and patience, and for assuming major responsibility for typing and proofreading the entire manuscript.

M. RAY LOREE

University, Alabama
February, 1965

CONTENTS

1 THE NATURE OF EDUCATIONAL PSYCHOLOGY 1

Educational Psychology Defined, 1. Psychology as a Science, 2. Psychological Research, 6. The Educational Process, 25. Guiding Learning, 30. Summary, 36. Answer Cues, 37.

2 OBSERVING AND INTERPRETING INDIVIDUAL BEHAVIOR 39

Reinforcement Frame of Reference, 41. Phenomenological Frame of Reference, 52. Psychoanalytic Frame of Reference, 56. Summary, 68. Answer Cues, 70.

3 DEVELOPMENT 71

Constitutional Determinants of Development, 72. Cultural Basis of Development, 78. Nature-Nurture, 95. Principles of Development, 98. Summary, 105. Answer Cues, 106.

4 APTITUDE TESTING 108

Aptitude Testing in the School, 108. Intelligence Tests, 113. Interpreting Test Scores, 127. Differential Abilities, 141. Summary, 147. Answer Cues, 148.

5 EMOTIONAL AND SOCIAL DEVELOPMENT . . . 150

Emotional Development, 153. Social Development, 169. Summary, 189. Answer Cues, 190.

6 GENERAL NATURE OF LEARNING 193

School Learning, 195. The Learning Process, 199. Guiding Learning, 210. Summary, 217. Answer Cues, 218.

v

7 GUIDING LEARNING 220

Research on Teaching Methods, *221*. Classroom Social Climate, *235*. Anxiety, *243*. Summary, *253*. Answer Cues, *254*.

8 MOTIVATION 257

Drives, *257*. Needs, Goals, and Competence, *259*. Achievement Motivation, *266*. Social Motives and Incentives, *274*. Summary, *287*. Answer Cues, *289*.

9 TRANSFER, PERCEPTION, AND RETENTION . . . 291

Transfer, *291*. Perception, *304*. Retention, *315*. Summary, *326*. Answer Cues, *328*.

10 ACQUIRING INFORMATION AND
MOTOR SKILLS 330

Acquiring Information, *331*. Psychomotor Learning, *345*. Summary, *353*. Answer Cues, *354*.

11 ACQUIRING CONCEPTS 356

Concepts as Categories, *356*. Experimental Study of Concept Attainment, *359*. Concepts as Explanations, *363*. Piaget's Stages of Development, *366*. Factors Affecting Concept Attainment, *374*. Teaching Concepts, *380*. Summary, *385*. Answer Cues, *387*.

12 THINKING 389

Mediating Cognitive Processes, *389*. Forms of Thinking, *398*. Summary, *419*. Answer Cues, *419*.

13 AFFECTIVE LEARNING 422

The Nature of Attitudes, *422*. Learning Attitudes, *434*. Summary, *457*. Answer Cues, *459*.

14 EVALUATION OF LEARNING 462

Characteristics of a Good Test, *462*. Teacher-Made Achievement Tests, *470*. Standardized Achievement Tests, *499*. Summary, *503*. Answer Cues, *505*.

15 PERSONALITY AND ADJUSTMENT 508

Personality Theories, *508*. Adjustment, *519*. The Teacher's Role in Adjustment in the Classroom, *534*. Research in Personality, *536*. New Problems for Personologists, *538*. Summary, *539*. Answer Cues, *540*.

Appendix: STATISTICAL CONCEPTS 545

Methods for Describing Data, *545*. Measures of Central Tendency, *548*. Partition Values, *549*. Dispersion of Scores, *550*. The Normal Distribution, *553*. Types of Scores, *557*. Correlation, *563*. Tests of Significance, *570*. Answer Cues, *574*.

REFERENCES 577

NAME INDEX 605

SUBJECT INDEX 613

PSYCHOLOGY
OF
EDUCATION

THE NATURE OF EDUCATIONAL PSYCHOLOGY

The six-year-old has learned much even before his first day of formal education. He has learned to walk; he has learned to approximate tolerably well adult standards of eating; he has discovered that words have meaning and has built up a vocabulary of about 2,500 words; and he has made at least a beginning in that complex art of relating himself to other people. These represent but a few of the many learning achievements of the six-year-old.

Obviously, the six-year-old would continue to learn in succeeding years even if he never attended school. Doubtless many rich learning experiences would fall his lot during his many school-free days. Yet our society has decreed that the six-year-old will go to school and attend regularly for a period of years. The school is expected to provide a better education than the child would obtain out of school. Schools are expected to structure educational experiences so that the child attains with efficiency valued educational objectives.

EDUCATIONAL PSYCHOLOGY DEFINED

In developing effective strategies to promote efficient learning, educators search through the literature of many disciplines for research findings, theories, and ideas that have relevance to the diverse problems of the school. Educational psychology is one of education's major foundation areas of knowledge. *Educational psychology may be defined as that branch of the science of psychology that draws from and contributes to the general field of psychology: research findings, psychological concepts, principles, theories, and techniques that are relevant to the task of guiding the educative process.*

The content of educational psychology is delineated, first, by the fact that educational psychology is a branch of psychology. Psychology is the science of the behavior of living organisms. The content of educational psychology is part of that larger body of knowledge concerning behavior that constitutes the content of psychology. The content of educational psychology is delineated, second, by the purposes of the school and other educative agencies, and the problems encountered in achieving those purposes.

The educational psychologist assumes two major roles:

1. The *practitioner* role. As a practitioner, the educational psychologist brings to bear psychological research findings, concepts, principles, theories, and techniques to the solution of concrete educational problems. The educational psychologist is assuming a practitioner role when he endeavors to interpret the behavior of the individual child, or when he evaluates a teaching practice in terms of what he knows about the psychology of learning, or when he develops a psychological testing program for a school.

2. The *scientist* role. As a scientist, the educational psychologist conducts research that adds to the body of knowledge known as psychology.

The two roles of the educational psychologist are by no means clearly differentiated. The problems that the educational psychologist tackles in his scientific role often stem from the problems he encounters in his practitioner role. And the educational psychologist in his practitioner role brings to bear the same way of thinking and scientific methodologies that he employs in his scientific role.

The basic orientation of this text is that the most valuable contribution that psychology can make to the prospective teacher is a way of analyzing and thinking about educational problems. This way of analyzing and thinking about educational problems is, in effect, an application of the scientific method to the problems of education. The scientific method through which the psychologist conducts research can serve as a useful model for the teacher in tackling the diverse problems of education. It is appropriate, therefore, that we examine in some detail the relationship of psychology as a science to the role of the teacher.

PSYCHOLOGY AS A SCIENCE

The investigative techniques of the psychologist are restricted by the fact that psychology is a science. Many of the commonly held beliefs about human behavior, such as, "The shape of the head is a reliable index of a person's intelligence," "Red-headed people are by nature more temperamental than other people," "Long slender hands usually indicate an artistic nature," and "A person who is slower than average in learning usually remembers better than average," are rejected by psychologists because they are not generalizations arrived at through the scientific study of behavior. What may be regarded today as the content of psychology is that body of knowledge about the behavior of living organisms that has been attained by investigative methods consistent with the basic beliefs and operating conceptions of science.

Science

Science refers primarily to those systematically organized bodies of accumulated knowledge concerning the universe which have been derived exclusively through techniques of objective observation. The content of science, then, consists of data. These are acquired, checked, and verified by techniques of observation and measurement. The data are organized within various schemes or systems of interrelated conceptual propositions. [Lachman, 1960, p. 13.]

Science is empirical. Knowledge is acquired through first-hand observation rather than through authority or solely through reasoning processes. This means for the scientist that an acceptable answer to the question "What is the evidence?" must be based upon data obtained through direct observation. No psychologist's *opinion* on such a question as "Can college students learn more effectively when they study in groups than when they study independently?" is acceptable scientific evidence. Nor would logical reasons for or against independent study constitute scientific evidence. *Only data obtained through direct observation constitute scientific evidence.*

Often a question asked the scientist is so broad that no single empirical test can provide an adequate answer. Scientists need to conduct numerous experiments in order to probe various facets of a single broad question. For example, the question of group versus independent performance really includes many questions. Lorge *et al.* (1958) list 74 references in a survey of studies done in the years 1927–1958 contrasting the quality of group performance and individual performance. These 74 studies were not just repeated efforts to obtain an answer to a single question. Lorge and his associates note that in the many studies surveyed, the types of groups, tasks, and criteria of performance varied from one study to another. Hence the various studies answer somewhat different questions. In answering the single broad question of the comparative merits of group versus independent study, the scientist would consider as evidence all studies that included careful descriptions and measurements of the individuals and groups included in an experiment, the types of tasks upon which they worked, and the criterion measure of group and individual performance.

Learning Exercises[1]

1. What is wrong with this definition: "Psychology is the study of the mind, including its private thoughts, wishes, fears, and attitudes"?
2. In what respect does a telephone directory meet the criteria of a science listed by Lachman? In what respect does it fail to meet the criteria?
3. Would readings of scientific instruments constitute scientific data even though, without the instruments, the phenomena measured are unobservable?
4. An answer to the question "Can students' ability to solve arithmetic problems be developed better by students working individually or in groups?" would require more than one research study. Why?

Certain ideals are of paramount importance to the scientist. These ideals are reflected in the ways the scientist conducts his work. Lachman (1960, pp. 27–54) lists seven operating concepts of science. Lachman's list is relevant to the role performance of a teacher in two respects. First, the list of operating concepts of science helps to define for the teacher what can be expected and what cannot be expected from scientific research. Second, some of the operating concepts reflect ideals that are common to the role of the scientist and to the role of the teacher. Following are five of the operating concepts of science included in Lachman's list.

A. The conception of *amorality*.

Science is neither moral nor immoral. It is amoral. "The scientist in his professional capacity does not specify the moral implications of his data" (p. 39).

This means that the teacher must not expect from science answers to the questions "What is good?" or "What is bad?" The teacher may wish to consider research data in arriving at a

---

[1] Learning through reading is facilitated when the reader interacts with the materials he reads. To encourage this interaction process, "Learning Exercises" are interspersed throughout each chapter. The learning exercises are made up of questions that are relevant to the immediately preceding discussion. Thus learning exercises 1–4 are pertinent to the preceding discussion on pages 1 to 4. At the end of each chapter "Answer Cues" are listed for each learning exercise. It is suggested that the reader think through answers to each set of learning exercises before checking the answers that the author had in mind. For many of the learning exercises, the reader will be able to develop more comprehensive answers than those briefly sketched in the Answer Cues.

value judgment. But research data, in and of itself, does not supply a value judgment.

B. The conception of *objectivity*.

". . . the scientist must remain impersonal, impartial, and detached in making observations and in interpreting data . . ." (p. 41).

Obviously, this is an equally important ideal for the teacher in performing such tasks as assigning grades, observing and interpreting the behavior of the "naughty" and the "good" child, and in assessing the effectiveness of his own teaching.

C. The conception of *caution*.

The methods of the scientist must be characterized by meticulous caution. Hypotheses must be clearly formulated; the design of an investigation must be carefully thought through; the collection of data, the statistical analysis of data, the interpretation of the data, and the verification of data—all must be carried out with painstaking vigilance.

The net result of such painstaking efforts on the part of the scientist may be an advance in knowledge. For the teacher, the net result of equally careful planning and teaching may be a desirable development of an individual child.

D. The conception of *skepticism*.

"The scientist maintains a highly critical attitude, preferably an overcritical attitude, an attitude of suspicion, toward the data of science as well as toward other 'data.' He continually regards the data of science as provisional and tentative, never as complete, final or absolute . . ." (p. 43).

The teacher constantly is bombarded with recommendations on how to teach. Often the teacher is told that a certain recommendation is based upon scientific evidence. It is important for the teacher to recognize that scientific evidence is provisional and tentative; that recommendations need to be examined carefully before adoption and, if adopted, the teacher needs to maintain a critical attitude concerning the recommended practice and his effectiveness in implementing the recommendation. For the teacher, the conception of skepticism is operational when he remains willing to critically evaluate new ideas and when he critically examines the effectiveness of his current practices.

E. The conception of *theory construction and utilization*.

". . . within the field of science at any time there are many blank intervals, many uncharted, even unexplored areas. The scientist attempts to coalesce or unite temporarily the unexplored or partially explored regions with the relatively more definitely known regions, by proposing theories amalgamating both . . . The theory provides a tentative scheme or plan of the otherwise uncharted areas and thereby furnishes an orientation. Furthermore, theories indicate or suggest directions for further investigation . . ." (pp. 45–46).

Theories are not proven or disproven. A theory is built upon a delimited set of data and is made consistent to that set of data. In psychology, there are a number of theories of learning and theories of personality that have stimulated research effort. However, in the opinion of the author there is no single present-day psychological theory that is sufficiently comprehensive to encompass all the research data relevant to all educational problems. The teacher may find ideas worth considering within a number of psychological theories. In Chapter 5, an effort will be made to illustrate how different psychological theories serve to direct the observations of the teacher to different facets of a behavioral problem.

Learning Exercise

5. Below are listed four statements. A scientist speaking in his professional capacity might make some of these statements but not others. Which of the statements might a scientist make? Which of the statements would not be made by a scientist? Indicate for each statement which one of Lachman's operating conceptions of science is relevant.
   (a) Divorce is immoral.
   (b) Learning theories have value in that they suggest directions for further research efforts.
   (c) Research data have proved conclusively and for all time that heredity is more important than environment in shaping development.
   (d) A scientist makes his data support any hypothesis he wishes.

PSYCHOLOGICAL RESEARCH

Psychologists deal with three types of variables in their study of behavior. These are:

1. *Stimulus:* the source of energy that affects a sense organ—what the behaver is responding to in a situation.
2. *Organism:* the behaver and, more particularly, the characteristics of the behaver that predispose him to respond to the stimulus in a certain way.
3. *Response:* the activity, movement, answers, or unobserved glandular secretion that occurs when an organism is stimulated.

Stimulus Variables

The word "stimulus" refers to any antecedent circumstance that evokes a response. Food may function as a stimulus to evoke a salivation response. A teacher's frown may be part of a pattern of stimuli that quiets a boisterous boy in a classroom. The turning of a traffic light from green to red serves as a stimulus for most motorists to stop their cars at a street intersection. The questions teachers ask their pupils in the classroom usually evoke responses. When they do, the questions asked are stimuli. A stimulus is usually, but not always, directly observable and external to the organism. However, the stimulus may be within the organism, as when a muscle movement causes pressure on certain end organs.

The stimulus variables in psychological experiments are rarely simple. In studies of psychophysical relationships, the limits of the intensity of physical stimuli that separate seeing from not seeing, hearing from not hearing, and tasting from not tasting have been extensively investigated, as have the smallest differences in stimuli that can be detected by individuals. Even for these psychophysical experiments in which the stimulus variable appears to be relatively simple, Skinner (1953, p. 131) points out that "what appear to be simple sensory reactions often depend upon variables in the fields of conditioning, motivation, and emotion." In life, responses are evoked usually by complex patterns of stimuli rather than a single simple stimulus.

Organismic Variables

No one stimulus evokes identical responses in all people. Nevertheless, some stimuli can be identified that elicit roughly equivalent responses in most people. For example, an electric shock administered to a finger usually elicits a hand-withdrawing response. However, for many situations encountered in life, the response elicited depends in part upon certain characteristics of the behaver. The responses made by a bright school girl to an algebra problem differ from those made to the same problem by a less intelligent girl. In this case intelligence is an organismic variable of importance in predicting a response. A picture of an architecturally beautiful young lady in attractive bathing attire frequently elicits qualitatively different responses from males than from females. In this example the sex of the behaver is an organismic variable of importance in predicting a response. Usually, it is necessary to know something about certain characteristics of the behaver in order to predict what responses he will make in a given situation. In many studies in psychology, comparisons are made of people of different characteristics. The characteristics that are varied in such studies are referred to as *organismic variables.*

An organismic variable arises out of some way in which organisms may be classified. The classification may be made on the basis of observations and measurements of physical or physiological characteristics such as height, weight, and age. Classifications may be made on the basis of the condition of the organism, such as the degree of hunger, thirst, or fatigue. Whenever possible, the researcher obtains quantitative measurements of the condition of the organisms. Thus, the hunger of an animal may be measured in terms of number of hours of food deprivation. Fatigue may be quantified in terms of the number of hours the subjects included in a study have been working on some task immediately prior to the time of the experiment. In many experiments, a classification is made on the basis of some psychological characteristic or of some differentiating feature of the individual's past or current experiences. Thus, level of educational attainment, degree of job satisfaction, political affiliation, socioeconomic level, record of law violations, size of school attended—all of these may be organismic variables. When individuals are included in a research study and are classified on the basis of prior observations of performance or responses, it is convenient to regard such classification as an organismic variable. Thus, in conducting an experiment to find out which of two teaching methods is superior, a researcher may introduce an organismic variable in his experimental design by seeking answers to two questions: (1) "Which method is superior for very intelligent pupils?" and (2) "Which method is superior for less-intelligent pupils?" Intelligence, in such a study, may be regarded as an organismic variable, even though the classification of intelligent versus less intelligent is based upon a previously obtained response measure.

Response Variables

There are many kinds of responses. Swinging a golf club is a response. Answering a question is a response. A pupil working on a test is making a series of responses. When we speak, look, write, laugh, or cry, we are making responses. *Any muscular or glandular process that depends upon stimulation is a response.*

The stimulus or stimuli eliciting the response are not always easy to identify. Skinner (1938) has pointed out that there are two types of responses: (1) *respondent,* and (2) *operant.* Respondents are directly elicited by stimuli. The salivary response of a dog at the sight of food is an example of respondent behavior. The stimulus (food) serves as a cue to touch off a specific response (salivation). The term "operant" emphasizes the fact that the behaver *operates* upon the environment to produce consequences. Turning on the ignition key in a car produces the consequence of starting the car. Turning on an ignition key, opening a door, writing a letter, and reading a book are all examples of operant behavior. While certain antecedent conditions have led up to each act, the stimuli are not readily identifiable. The response is identified by its effect on the environment rather than by the stimuli that evokes the response. In the school situation, the emotional responses elicited by such words as "holiday," "A," "F," "mathematics," and "test" are respondent behaviors. The series of responses a pupil makes in preparing for a test are operant behaviors.

In psychological research, the response variable may be simple responses such as knee jerks, pupillary responses, and respiratory changes. More typically in research of interest to the educational psychologist, the behavior investigated is much more complex. Performance on achievement or aptitude tests, interest or personality inventories, and ratings on such complicated behaviors as aggression, cooperativeness, leadership, or creativity are more typical of the response variables to be found in research reports of interest to the educator. Ordinarily, the researcher endeavors to obtain some objective measurement of the response variables he investigates. Thus, number of words typed per minute might be used as a measure of typing ability.

The task of assessing the relative merits of two or more instructional methods is extremely difficult, yet the task is of crucial importance to the educator. The stimulus variable (the method of instruction) often extends over several weeks or months. The response variable is some measure of learning. But educators are interested in many kinds of learning, and therefore a number of measures of learning are usually required. It may be found that the method of instruction that appears to be effective in teaching students factual information does a poor job in developing desirable attitudes. For example, the students in an English class may learn the plot of *King Lear* thoroughly but also learn to hate Shakespeare. The question "Do students learn more efficiently in small discussion classes than in large lecture sessions?" is really many questions. Under which instructional arrangement do the students acquire information more efficiently? Which arrangement is better to develop students' problem-solving abilities? Under which arrangement is it easier to develop desirable attitudes, interests, and appreciations? Obviously, each type of educational objective focuses upon a different response variable and hence requires a different measure of student attainment.

Learning Exercise

6. Classify each of the following into stimulus, organismic, and response
   variables:
   (a) Knee jerk
   (b) Intensity of light
   (c) Age
   (d) Methods of presenting a lesson
   (e) Achievement test scores
   (f) Urban or rural residency
   (g) Number of years' education completed by father and mother
   (h) Music played while students study
   (i) Length of material to be memorized
   (j) Speed of reading

The Methods of Psychology

The methods of psychological investigation are adapted to achieve
three major purposes of the science of psychology. These purposes are:
(1) the description and classification, (2) the prediction, and (3) the explanation of behavior. Methods of collecting data have been developed to facilitate the description and classification of behavior. These
methods involve the use of mechanical and electronic instruments, the
use of tests, interviews, rating scales, self-reporting inventories, sociometric techniques, and many other devices. The prediction of behavior
is made possible as a result of an understanding of the relationship
between various psychological variables. Experimentation is a major
but not the only method used by the psychologist to achieve this purpose. Correlational, cross-sectional, longitudinal, and clinical studies
are also methods used by the psychologist, and will be discussed later
in this chapter. The problem of explanation in psychology is that of
identifying *what* variables and determining *how* these variables affect
the phenomena in which we are interested. From many research
studies, principles and theories are generated for the purpose of explaining behavior.

Often, an *intervening variable* may be used in explaining behavior.
An intervening variable has been defined as "any variable that is functionally connected with a preceding and a following variable" (English
and English, 1958, p. 579).[2] *Hunger* is an intervening variable. It is

---

[2] Throughout this text, the term "intervening variable" will be given this broad
general meaning. No distinction will be made between "intervening variable,"
"hypothetical construct," and "intervening process variable." The term "mediating
process" will be used when attention is focused upon a description of the operation
of the intervening variable within the individual.

inferred from observation of certain antecedent conditions (i.e., food deprivation) and the behavioral consequences (i.e., eating). Thus:

FOOD DEPRIVATION ⟶ HUNGER ⟶ EATING

Such terms as "intelligence," "interest," "attitude," "appreciation," "habit," "motivation," "perception," and "memory" are intervening variables. They are unobservable, but they can be defined in terms of some preceding antecedent condition and a following behavioral consequence. They cannot be measured directly. However, they may be inferred from the responses of the behaver in specific situations. Thus, when Johnny is given a series of problems that he solves correctly, we may infer that Johnny is intelligent. We may even operationally define intelligence in terms of the procedures followed in obtaining Johnny's test score. Then the test would provide an indirect measurement of the intervening variable, "intelligence."

The Experiment in Psychology

The experimental method in psychology in its simplest form consists of (1) manipulating a stimulus variable, (2) while holding all other variables constant, (3) in order to test whether and how some preselected response variable is affected.

The variable that is manipulated or changed as the experimenter sees fit is called the *independent variable*. The variable upon which the effects of the changes are observed is called the *dependent variable*.

In many experiments, only two groups are employed. Each group is subjected to a different treatment. As frequently one of the treatments is the usual set of conditions, the group receiving this usual treatment is referred to as the *control group*. The group given the more unusual treatment is referred to as the *experimental group*.

In the experimental method, some specific stimulating condition is an independent variable. The *task* that the subjects of the experiment are called upon to perform may be varied in some way (e.g., memorizing poems of varying lengths), and the effects on a response variable (e.g., time required to memorize) are observed. Or the *method* by which a task is performed may be varied (e.g., memorizing by parts versus memorizing by wholes), and variations are observed in the response measure. Or some feature in the *environmental* context in which the task is performed may be varied (e.g., memorizing while music is playing versus memorizing without music), and the effects on the dependent variable are observed. In each case, the stimulus variable is manipulated by the experimenter and a response measure is obtained. Research studies of this type are called S→R type studies.

S→R **Studies.** Many precepts are expressed in S→R form. For example, the dictum "Spare the rod and spoil the child" suggests that failure to inflict physical punishment on a child (stimulus variable) results in the child behaving in ways that are considered undesirable by adults (the response variable). Similarly, a relationship between a stimulus and a response variable is suggested in many familiar quotations, such as "Absence makes the heart grow fonder," "When the cat's away the mice will play," "Necessity is the mother of invention," "Practice makes perfect," and many others.

The teacher in the classroom conducts an S→R experiment when he tries out a new method of instruction and compares the performance of children who are exposed to the new method of instruction to the performance of children instructed by the old method. Conclusions regarding the relative effectiveness of the two methods are justified if all other variables affecting performance are controlled.

A series of experiments reported by McKeachie, Pollie, and Speisman (1955) illustrate a number of features of S→R type experiments. The experiments were designed to compare the test performance of college students who were given an opportunity to write comments about their objective examination questions to the performance of students who were given no such opportunity. In one of the experiments, the instructions provided at the beginning of the test for the experimental group contained the words: "Feel free to make any comments about any items in the space provided" (p. 93). The test instructions for the control group omitted this provision for student comments. In this study, the experimental group performed significantly better than the control group.

Note in the above experiment that the stimulus variable is the set of instructions to a test. This stimulus variable was manipulated or varied in two ways: (1) provision for student's comments to objective-type test items, and (2) no provision for comments. Hence, the stimulus variable is the independent variable within the experiment. The experimental requirement of holding all variables constant would necessitate that the conditions under which the test was taken be identical for the two groups except for the inclusion or exclusion of an opportunity for students to comment on test items. Also, presumably the abilities of the two groups of students were comparable so that any differences in performances of the experimental group and the control group might be attributable to the stimulus variable. The dependent variable is a response variable—the scores obtained by the students in the two groups on the test. The experiment may be represented as follows:

S (independent variable) ————→ R (dependent variable)

Test instructions: Test performance

1. Opportunity to comment
   (experimental group)
2. No opportunity to comment
   (control group)

The experiment of McKeachie *et al.* reported above illustrates one way in which experimental problems originate. The first step in experimentation is that of stating a problem. The problem may take the form of what Underwood (1949) describes as the "I-wonder-what-would-happen" type. A college instructor might ask the question, "I wonder what would happen to students' performance on a final examination *if* I awarded high grades at mid-semester." The instructor is really posing a question of whether quality of grades awarded at mid-semester is an effective stimulus variable, i.e., will influence the response variable—student performance on a final examination. Underwood notes that the "I-wonder-what-would-happen" type of problem is supplanted by an "I'll-bet-this-would-happen" type of problem as more facts are accumulated within a science. The experiment of McKeachie *et al.* is of this "I'll bet" type.

The concept of anxiety attracted the attention of a number of psychologists during the late forties and on into the fifties. Consistent with research findings was the basic assumption of McKeachie *et al.* that "such a high degree of anxiety is mobilized by classroom tests that the students' performance is adversely affected" (p. 93). The investigators theorized that this occurred because students begin a test with some anxiety and that this anxiety increases as they encounter questions that are too difficult or too ambiguous for them to answer. The investigators reasoned further that if the anxiety generated by the failing of items could be diminished in some way, test performance should improve. From this point, the investigators formulated the hypothesis that "Students who are encouraged to write comments about test items on their answer sheets will make higher test scores than students who have no opportunity to make comments" (p. 93). Experimental procedures were designed to test this hypothesis, and the results of the experiments thereafter conducted supported the hypothesis.

The series of studies conducted by McKeachie *et al.* illustrate a number of characteristics inherent in psychological research. Results of the first experiment supported the hypothesis that students given an opportunity to write comments on objective test questions would score higher than students who had no such opportunity. But research findings are of no value in a science if they cannot be verified. Therefore, the experiment was repeated three times. Comparable results were obtained. Because the results of the experiment did not directly test the investigators' theory about discharge of anxiety, a number of additional experiments were planned. This too is typical of research. Even a theory restricted in scope to the relationship of test anxiety to student test performance needs to be translated into testable hypotheses that often require not one but several experiments. After the first experiment, McKeachie and his associates conducted a number of experiments designed to better understand how encouraging students to write comments on an objective examination improved their test scores. One experiment was designed to test the following three hypotheses:

1. Students' performances on a test will be improved if they are permitted to write their feelings about test items, but are not permitted to write explanations, as compared to students who have no opportunity to write comments.
2. Students' performances on a test will be improved if they are permitted to write explanations to their answers, but are not permitted to write their feelings, as compared with students who have no opportunity to write comments.
3. Giving students the opportunity to write comments affects their scores on items succeeding the item which is commented on rather than on the item upon which comments were made.
   [McKeachie *et al.*, 1955, pp. 94–95.]

Three groups of students were administered a test. Instructions for one group invited the students to state their *feelings* concerning any question—its fairness, clarity, importance, triviality, etc. Instructions for a second group gave students an opportunity to state their *explanations* of how they arrived at an answer for any questions on the test that seemed to need explanations. Instructions for the control group provided no opportunity to make comments. Results of this experiment were somewhat surprising. No significant differences were found between the test scores of the three groups given different instructions. Apparently, instructions that restricted students' comments to either feelings or explanations dissipated the effect of permitting any type of comment. However, Hypothesis 3 was supported. The groups given an opportunity to write comments performed significantly better than the control group on the *last half* of the test. A repetition of the experiment by the investigators and by others (Calvin *et al.*, 1957) yielded comparable results. McKeachie *et al.* point out that their findings fit in with their theory that tension is built up in students throughout a test and that the opportunity to comment serves to reduce the increasing tension.

An experiment may be conducted in a laboratory or in a natural setting. It is of primary importance in any experiment to control all factors likely to affect the dependent variable except the one factor that is manipulated. This can be done most adequately in the laboratory. Further, psychological laboratories can be equipped to measure with precision many stimuli and response variables. However, for varying reasons, many problems of interest to the psychologist are not amenable to laboratory research. Fortunately, laboratory research and research conducted in a natural setting may supplement each other. Exploratory research in a natural setting may provide tentative conclusions that later can be tested more rigorously in the laboratory by more controlled experiments. And often the generalizations stemming from laboratory research need to be tested in natural settings.

Learning Exercises

7. What intervening variable is involved in the experiments of McKeachie et al.?
8. Why is it necessary to conduct classroom experiments to verify conclusions reached through laboratory research?

S→O→R Studies. In S→O→R problems, a stimulus condition is varied in two or more ways, and the differential effects on a response variable are observed for subjects that are classified into two or more categories. For an experiment in education, the method of instruction might be varied (stimulus variable). With each method, pupils of varying levels of ability (organismic variable) may be included in the study. Then some measure of achievement (response variable) might be obtained in order to observe how students of varying levels of ability have learned under each method of instruction. As a teaching machine experiment will be used to illustrate the S→O→R type of study, perhaps a little background information on the teaching machine is in order.

The label "teaching machine" is unfortunate for the simple reason that it is not the machine that teaches. The machine is a device through which teaching is done. The function of the machine is comparable to that of the movie projector that shows an educational film, and the instructional "program" presented by the "teaching machine" is comparable to the educational film presented by the movie projector. A "teaching machine" may be any kind of device through which information and a series of problems or questions are presented to a student, and, after giving the student an opportunity to answer the question, informs the student in some way (usually immediately after his response) whether or not his answer is correct. The information and the series of problems or questions on a unit of instruction are referred to as a *program,* and the process of constructing a program is referred to as *programming.* Much of the experimentation on the teaching machine in recent years has been of the S→R or S→O→R type, with certain characteristics of the *program* constituting the stimulus variable.

Size of step is one characteristic of a teaching machine program that has been investigated. A *small step* program includes many items on a relatively small amount of instructional material. Supposedly little effort is required by the student to answer a particular item because items are sequenced in such a way as to make it easy to proceed from one item to another. A *large step* program contains fewer items. More effort is required by the student to complete a learning session because the student is constantly encountering fresh material. Items related to concepts previously covered are eliminated from the program.

A study conducted by Shay (1961) on the relationship of intelligence to size of item step on a teaching machine program is illustrative of the S→O→R type study.

Shay constructed three programs to cover a fourth-grade unit in Roman numerals. A *large step* program contained 103 items; a *medium step* program, 150 items; and a *small step* program, 199 items. Thus, the stimulus condition was varied in three ways. Ninety fourth-grade pupils were divided into three groups on the basis of a pretest on Roman numerals and group intelligence test scores. A third of the children were above average in intelligence (I.Q. over 109); one-third, average (I.Q. 93–109); and one-third, below average (I.Q. below 93). Thus, in effect, the fourth-grade classes were divided into nine groups in order to obtain all possible combinations of ability level and size of step in the teaching machine program. The apparatus used to teach the children Roman numerals was arranged so that a green or red light would light up to inform the pupil of his success immediately after he attempted each question in the program. The training program consisted of 50 items a day on consecutive school days until the pupil had completed the whole program. Performance measures (the response variable) consisted of a posttraining test made up of old and new items, total posttraining test scores, total errors, and time required to complete the program.

The results of Shay's experiment indicate that at *all* levels of ability, as size of step decreases, there is an accompanying increase in both posttest score and time to complete the program. As might be expected, pupils of greater ability outperform pupils of lesser ability. Shay's experiment, thus, appears to support the position that it is not necessary to provide more than one program for pupils of varying initial abilities.

Learning Exercises

9. In the Shay $S_x \to O_y \to R_z$ experiment (pages 16–17) in which the step size is varied for above-average, average, and below-average students,
   (a) What are the independent variables?
   (b) What are the dependent variables?
10. In the series of experiments conducted by McKeachie *et al.* (pages 12–15), in which college students commented on test questions, did any one of the studies include an organismic variable? If so, which one?

The Differential Method

In the differential method, some characteristic of the behaver is the independent variable. Subjects included in the research study are classified according to some criterion such as delinquent versus nondelinquent; emotionally disturbed versus normal; or children of different ages, grades, or sex.

Studies conducted by the differential method usually can be classified as O→O type or O→R type studies.

O→O Studies. An O→O study is concerned with the relationship between two organismic variables. The relationship between height and weight of boys could be studied to find out the degree to which variations in height are accompanied by variations in weight. In such a study, height may be thought of as one organismic variable, and weight as a second organismic variable. Literally thousands of O→O type studies are possible because of the large number of ways it is possible to classify people. For example, a social scientist might be interested in finding out whether the incidence of juvenile delinquency varies in different socioeconomic classes. For such a study, a classification of children on the basis of the socioeconomic status of their homes is one organismic variable, and the presence or absence of a court record is a second organismic variable. Thus:

O (Socioeconomic status) ─────────→ O (Delinquency)

   1. Upper   1. Court record
   2. Middle   2. No court record
   3. Lower

O→R Studies. "Ministers' sons are likely to turn out badly." "An only child is generally spoiled." "Brunettes are naturally more passionate than blondes." These are but a few of the convictions held by some people about the relationships between organismic and response variables. It is commonplace for people to predict the behavior of individuals of a particular religion, race, nationality, or nearly any other classification into which people may be divided. In so doing, a person's behavior is predicted from knowledge of some characteristic of the behaver.

O→R studies are concerned with the relationship between an organismic variable and a response variable. A study reported by Campbell and Horrocks (1961) illustrates one form of an O→R study. The Minnesota Teacher Attitude Inventory was administered to 127 teachers in training and to their parents. Comparisons were made of the attitude scores obtained by five groups: (1) daughters, (2) sons, (3) all students, (4) mothers, and (5) fathers. These five groups constitute the organismic variable in this study. The response variable is the attitude test score. Thus:

O ─────────→ R

   1. Daughters   Scores on the Minnesota Teacher Attitude
   2. Sons   Inventory
   3. All students
      i.e., (1) + (2)
   4. Mothers
   5. Fathers

Some of the reported results of the study were: (1 the closest agreement in attitude test scores was between mothers and fathers; (2) mothers and fathers tended to be more authoritarian than their children of either sex; (3) daughters tended to be more permissive than sons in their concept of teacher-pupil relationships; and (4) students tended to identify attitudinally with the parents of the same sex.

Experts in subject-matter areas often make use of O→R type of research findings in building curricula. For example, texts in physical education report the findings of O→R studies relating age to measures of motor abilities, and studies relating age to play interests (Jones, Morgan, and Stevens, 1957; Kraus, 1957).

Many psychological problems do n permit experimental manipulation because of moral or ethical considerations. For such problems, the researcher may try to locate subjects who in their life situation are treated in ways that would not be permissible in the psychological laboratory. A study by Sears *et al.* (1953) is illustrative. Sears and his associates wished to investigate the relationship between the amount of punishment received by a child and the amount of his subsequent dependent and aggressive behavior. Obviously, the researchers would be ill-advised to bring children into the psychological laboratory and systematically vary in intensity and frequency the physical punishments administered to the children. So instead the researchers located preschool-aged children and classified them on the basis of the punitiveness of their parents. Then differences in dependent and aggressive behavior of these children were observed in nursery school activities. The study by Sears *et al.* resembles an experimental study in all respects except that the experimenters did not have control of any stimulus variable. Therefore, the differential method was employed in which a characteristic of the subjects for the study (children of parents of varying degrees of punitiveness) replaced a stimulus variable (varying the physical punishment administered in the laboratory) as the independent variable.

Learning Exercise

11. Buswell (1922) recorded on motion picture film the eye movements of pupils from the first grade through the Senior year in high school. He then determined for each grade level the average number of fixations per line, the average duration of the fixation, and the average number of regressions per line. Is Buswell's study of the O→R type or of the S→O→R type?

Longitudinal and Cross-Sectional Approaches

Longitudinal and cross-sectional approaches are used in studies focused upon the course of development. They are conducted to answer questions such as: "How do the interests of children change with age?" and "What is the average speaking vocabulary of children at different ages?" Longitudinal and cross-sectional studies employ the differential method but do so for the purpose of understanding the course of development. In the cross-sectional approach, *different* children are studied at different ages; in the longitudinal approach, the *same* children are studied at different ages. The cross-sectional studies involve less time because the researcher does not have to wait for the children to grow older in order to observe changes in their behavior. The longitudinal approach permits an appraisal of the interrelations among developmental processes.

The Clinical Method and the Clinical Case Study Approaches

Some of our knowledge about human behavior has come from the observations of psychologists who work with individuals who have problems. The boy who is doing poorly in school may be brought by his parents to the psychologist in order to find out why. A teacher may refer a boy who is a behavior problem in school, and the psychologist may spend a number of sessions with the boy in an effort to understand his behavior. The methods used by the psychologist in order to understand and possibly help solve the problems of an individual are called *clinical methods*. These methods may entail the use of tests of various kinds, including intelligence, achievement, interests, and personality tests. Clinical methods may utilize interview data obtained from the child himself, his parents, and from other people important in the life of the child. Information concerning the child's early development may be obtained by the clinician for the purpose of understanding the child's present problems. When therapeutic treatment is given by the clinician over an extended period of time, notes are made in order to trace the child's progress.

The *case study* approach involves procedures similar in many respects to those of the clinical approach. In both, attention is focused on one individual—usually an individual with a problem. The teacher or social worker making a case study gathers extensive information about the child's developmental background—his physical growth and health history, and his past and present educational achievement. Information on his past behavior is obtained through interviews and available records. Information is obtained on the home, family, and neighborhood in which the child lives in order to assess environmental influences. The child is observed in natural settings over a period of time.

The intensive study of one individual over an extended period of time does provide data that permits the prediction of the behavior of that *one* individual. After all, a wife predicts the behavior of her husband, a college student predicts the behavior of his friend, and a pupil the behavior of his teacher—all on the basis of prior observations.

What we are interested in here, however, is how useful the somewhat more systematic procedures followed in the clinical method and the case study are in yielding generalizations that hold true for many people. As scientific tools, both the clinical method and the case study lack the rigorous controls and often the precision of measurement that are possible in the experimental method. Interpretation of the mass of data obtained is frequently highly subjective. However it should be noted that much of our knowledge in clinical and abnormal psychology and in psychoanalysis is based on intensive studies of the individual. The clinical method may take the form of an R→O type research.

R→O Studies. In R→O studies, the responses of the behaver are related to some organismic variable. We encounter R→O type inferences almost daily. Some person is judged to be a Communist, an atheist, or a member of some group or other on the basis of what he says or does. More informed judgments are made by clinical psychologists and psychiatrists in classifying the mental illness of a patient on the basis of what the patient says or does. One research area where examples of R→O type research may be found is in the validation studies of certain psychological tests. A research study designed to determine whether scores on a test could differentiate "normals" from clinically diagnosed "neurotics" would constitute an R→O type research.

Predictive Studies

The prediction of behavior is one of the major purposes of the science of psychology. The use of psychological tests is one means through which the psychologist predicts behavior. In order to find out how well a particular psychological test predicts some later performance, it is necessary to conduct an R→R type study.

R→R Studies. R→R type studies are concerned with the relationships between two response variables. When a teacher administers an intelligence test and predicts from the test results that a pupil will do well in school, the teacher is basing his prediction on the belief that performance on the intelligence test (R_x) is related to some measure (R_y) of the pupil's performance in school.

In the many R→R studies in which intelligence test scores (R_x) are used to predict later academic achievement (R_y), the correlations usually run between about .30 and .70. Table 1–1 illustrates how the obtained relationships may be translated into an expectancy table. The table is based on the administration of the Ohio State University Psychological Examination to 920 freshmen at Ohio State University. The entries in Table 1–1 show what proportion of students, whose test scores lie in each decile range, may be expected to earn point-hour ratios of at least 1.00, 1.50, 2.00, 2.50, and 3.00. Thus, from the table it may be seen that the chances that a student who scores in the lowest tenth of his class on the psychological test will keep off probation (point-hour ratio = 1.50) are only a little better than even (.55), and that he has but one chance in a hundred of earning a 3.00 average or better. Table 1–1 illustrates the fallibility of the predictions made on the basis of the findings of R→R studies. The student who scores in the top tenth of his class on the predictive test may find himself on probation at the end of his first semester in college, and the student who scores in the lowest tenth of his class on the predictive test may earn honors during his first semester. Level of motivation, acquired study habits, past learning, and other factors may upset the prediction for an individual student.

Numerous research studies have been conducted to determine how well various psychological tests predict some later behavior of individuals. These are all R→R types studies. Neither the predicting measure nor the measure of what is predicted need necessarily be a psychological test. Mechanical or electronic devices, rating scales, inventories, interviews, or any other means through which it is possible to secure accurate observation and measurement of the behavior concerned may be used.

TABLE 1–1

Expectancy Table for Freshman Achievement

O.S.U. Psychological Test		Probability of Earning a Point-Hour Ratio of at Least:				
Decile	Raw Score Range	1.00 (D Av.)	1.50 (Probation)	2.00 (C Av.)	2.50	3.00 (B Av.)
Highest	114–150	100	99	93	74	42
Ninth	102–113	100	98	89	65	33
Eighth	92–101	100	97	84	56	25
Seventh	83–91	99	94	77	46	18
Sixth	75–82	98	91	69	37	12
Fifth	66–74	97	86	60	28	8
Fourth	56–65	95	81	51	21	5
Third	48–55	93	73	41	15	3
Second	39–47	89	65	32	10	2
Lowest	Less than 39	83	55	24	6	1

Adapted from Bingham (1951), based on data supplied by G. B. Paulsen.

Learning Exercise

12. For each question listed below, indicate the type of research study that would be required in seeking an answer to the question. (Indicate the type in terms of S, O, and R; e.g., S→R.)
    (a) Do children who are classified as urban children perform better on intelligence tests than children classified as rural children?
    (b) Do students' scores on a musical aptitude test predict grades in a music course?
    (c) What value has recitation for classroom learning as measured by end-of-course grades? Would spending relatively more time reciting than reading be a better method of study than that of spending relatively more time reading than reciting?
    (d) Are children who have a court record (i.e., delinquents) taller and heavier than non-delinquent children?
    (e) Is praise for good work in the classroom as motivating for boys as it is for girls? *Increase in work output* may be used as a measure of motivation.

Explanation in Psychology

Psychological explanations of human behavior are encountered daily in our present-day culture. The novelist, the advertising executive, the baseball manager, and the man on the street explain psychologically the behavior of a Lothario, an unsuspecting consumer, a ball player, or a mother-in-law utilizing the psychological and psychoanalytic terminology that has infiltrated our daily vocabulary. Even newspaper columnists dispense gems of psychological wisdom on, of all things, boy-girl relationships.

Much of what passes as psychological explanation is merely name calling. To explain an individual's behavior as "instinctive," or due to "paranoic" tendencies, or due to an "inferiority complex" may sound impressive, but it is not informative. The teacher who attributes John's lack of effort in an eighth-grade classroom to laziness is really explaining John's behavior only in terms of the behaviors that define "laziness." What we have here is something like this:

1. Laziness may be defined as a lack of effort.
2. John lacks effort.
3. Therefore, John's lack of effort may be explained by his laziness.

This is merely explaining observed behavior (lack of effort) by giving it a name (laziness).

Let us explore the nature of explanations in psychology by examining further the case of John, an eighth-grade pupil. An examination of the school records reveals that John obtained an I.Q. score of 140 on an intelligence test administered while he was in grade 6. His marks in grade 8 are mediocre, mostly C's and D's. John is what is defined as an "underachiever." How can we explain John's performance? To explain by name-calling, we would say that John is obtaining lower grades than might be expected from a boy of his abilities because he is an underachiever. This would merely be saying that John is underachieving because he is an underachiever. Additional study of John's case uncovers the following facts that better explain John's underachieving behavior:

1. John is in poor physical health and appears to tire quickly as the school day progresses.
2. John missed many days of school in grade 7 when concepts, important to the understanding of eighth-grade work, were taught.
3. John is left out of the play activities of the other boys in the class even though he appears to want to join their activities.

The above facts may constitute an explanation of John's underachievement *providing* the following principle is true: All boys who are in poor physical health and tire easily in school, and who have missed important work in their previous school year, and who are not accepted into peer groups they strive to join underachieve in school. Note carefully that, for purposes of illustration, we are making the questionable assumption that the above principle is true.

We are now in a position to give at least a rough idea of the characteristics of explanation in psychology. An explanation states the circumstances or antecedent conditions that control some behavior and describes the relationship of the behavior to the controlling conditions. Thus, the basic problem in explaining behavior is that of identifying *what* variables and describing *how* these variables affect the behavior under consideration. In our example, the interaction of health, adequacy of past learning, and peer-group acceptance were postulated as the variables affecting underachieving behavior. The postulated relationship was that when all three were poor, underachieving occurred.

The principle outlined above to explain underachieving is crude in a number of respects. First, it is deficient in that no mathematical relationship is indicated between measures of the antecedent conditions and measures of underachievement. It is not clear from the statement of the principle how bad the physical health has to be, how much absenteeism from school there must be, and how poor the peer-group

370.15 L885p
c.1

relationship must be in order to result in x amount of underachievement. Many of the explanatory principles in physical sciences may be reduced to a mathematical formula; not so in the social sciences.

Second, our principle lacks generality. It attempts to explain only underachievement in school. This is but one small segment of human behavior. As a science progresses, principles that explain many phenomena supplant principles that explain few. And principles are combined into theories in order to attain even greater generality.[3]

To explore all the complexities of the explanatory attempts prevalent in psychology today is beyond the scope of this text. The basic point to be noted in the foregoing brief discussion is that explanation in psychology involves an *exact description* of the relationship between a behavior and the antecedent conditions that control the behavior.

THE EDUCATIONAL PROCESS

In our society, schools are assigned major responsibility in guiding the education of children. The teacher encounters five major tasks in discharging this responsibility. These are:

1. Establishing the goals or objectives of instruction;
2. Selecting appropriate learning experiences for groups of students and for the individual student;
3. Organizing the learning experiences;
4. Guiding the learning process in the classroom; and
5. Evaluating the outcomes of instruction.

Defining Educational Objectives

The educational objectives of the school have undergone several marked changes since the beginning of the century. One major change has been in the conception of educational objectives. In 1900 the dominant educational psychology was based on the theory of formal discipline. Based on faculty psychology, this theory states that memory, judgment, imagination, and other traits are faculties of the mind that can be disciplined through academic exercise. Historically, specific subjects were considered superior to others as exercises of a particular faculty. The results of many research studies conducted during the early part of the century failed to support this theory, and psychologists began to conceive of learning as the acquisition of patterns of

[3] Underwood, among others, points out that there is little agreement as to the meaning or the function of a "theory." Underwood uses the term in the sense of a "system of ideas or facts (no matter how small the system) when this system allows for deduction" (Underwood, 1957, pp. 178–79).

behavior. Educational objectives are now stated in terms of the changes sought in pupil behavior.

The scope of educational psychology has widened with the increasing range of objectives accepted by the American school. To a considerable extent, as Tyler (1957) has pointed out, curriculum changes have occurred as a result of changing demands of American society on the school. The rapid change in technological development and social life requires a continually increasing level of education on the part of our youth. As a result, an increasing proportion of children continue their formal education for longer periods. The school of today is expected to contribute to the personality and character development of the child. Indeed, the school is called upon to assume many responsibilities formerly assigned to the home, church, and neighborhood. Tyler writes:

> The educational needs of today and the immediate future are greater than ever before. American education has done an amazing job in getting almost all children and youth in school and providing schools for this immense number. The schools have been astoundingly successful in building confidence on the part of the public in the capabilities of education in building our civilization. The time has come, however, to recognize realistically the magnitude of the job, to identify the objectives which the schools can best attain, to encourage the home, the church and other institutions to undertake the tasks appropriate to them, to devise learning experiences clearly relevant to the school's proper objectives and to work out an organization of the curriculum which aids the students in attaining a high level of educational competence. These steps still lie ahead of us. [Tyler, 1957, p. 94.]

Many value judgments are involved in assessing the worth of any set of educational objectives, and the findings of psychology are not directly applicable in making value judgments. However, the findings of psychology often are pertinent to answering two questions that the teacher needs to raise in considering any educational objective. These questions are: (1) Is the educational objective possible of attainment? and (2) For what grade level is the educational objective most appropriate?

Some educational objectives may be highly worthy and yet either impossible to attain or attainable only through a heavy concentration of teaching time and effort. A knowledge of the psychology of personality may aid the teacher in deciding whether or not an educational objective is really calling for an almost impossible change in personality structure. A knowledge of developmental psychology should aid the teacher in forming realistic expectations concerning the behavioral changes that are feasible at different age levels. A knowledge of the changing interests and concerns of children may be of value in identifying the most appropriate grade level for particular educational objectives.

Selecting Learning Experiences

A "learning experience" constitutes an interaction between the learner and his environment. Consequently, in a strict sense, the teacher does not select learning experiences. The teacher does try to structure the classroom situation in such a way as to stimulate learning experiences. The problem of providing learning experiences is the problem of structuring stimuli so that they will evoke a series of student responses leading to the attainment of defined educational objectives. In the not too distant past, the teacher accomplished this task through the medium of a limited number of techniques—lecturing, reading, homework assignments, drill, and the use of tests. The pupil was expected by home and community to learn well; and the teacher was expected to persuade, exhort, or coerce any unwilling participants in this learning adventure. Today, the number of techniques has increased and includes a vast array of audio-visual aids, class discussions of many forms, individual and group projects, teacher-pupil planning of activities, and teaching machines, to mention a few.

Literally thousands of "learning experiments" have been conducted by psychologists. Many experiments have been conducted in the psychological laboratory, where the learning tasks are almost invariably much simpler than the learning tasks set for children in the classroom. Hence, the teacher will rarely find evidence within purely psychological research on the relative merits of various methods of teaching a particular academic subject. Nevertheless, many experiments may be found that are related to the nature of motivation and perception in learning, the conditions that maximize retention and transfer of learning, the role of practice in learning, and many other facets of the learning process. Certain learning principles have emerged from the multitude of experiments. It is these principles that constitute the major contribution of psychology to the teacher's task of selecting learning experiences. The teacher, in planning a program of instruction, may utilize principles of learning as criteria in evaluating the relative merits of alternative instructional plans.

Organizing Learning Experiences

The purpose of organizing learning experiences is to maximize the total learning resulting from many separate learning experiences. Learning experiences are organized over a period of time. This the teacher does in deciding what to teach first, what second, what third, and so on, and when to review. Usually, some principle is applied in ordering the several learning experiences into an effective sequence. In mathematics, the principle may be to begin with the simple and proceed to the more complex, or to proceed from the concrete to the abstract. In history, the teacher and textbook author customarily impose a chronological order on historical events. Universities impose an organization of learning experiences by making one course a prerequisite for a more advanced course.

Learning experiences may be organized horizontally as well as over a period of time. Learning in one subject may supplement the learning that takes place in another subject so that the student sees relationships between what is learned in the two subjects.

Very little attention has been given to the development of principles of organizing learning experiences in the classroom during this century. Older principles such as proceeding from the known to the unknown, from the easy to the difficult, and from the simple to the complex remain the major guides. Possibly new principles for organizing learning experiences may emerge from teaching machine experiments. Experimenting with teaching machines programming does force the experimenter to direct his attention to the ordering of items.

Guiding Learning in the Classroom

In observing a classroom in operation, it is not possible to see the educational objectives, the learning experiences, and the organization of learning experiences that have been planned by the teacher (or by the teacher and students). The plans cannot be seen, although the nature of the plans may be inferred from the observable on-going activities in the classroom. The teacher's role in the classroom is comparable in many respects to that of the artist. And the quality of artistry will differ from teacher to teacher. Some teachers explain ideas to pupils better than do other teachers. Some teachers are more sensitive than others to cues indicating whether or not pupils are grasping the ideas that are presented. Some teachers are more successful than others in establishing healthy relationships with pupils. The verbal responses that some teachers make in evaluating the work of pupils serve to motivate pupils to do better; other teachers generate resentment.

Often it requires but a short period of observation of a teacher in action to note instances where psychological principles are artistically applied. Unfortunately, with some teachers, instances where psychological principles are unintelligently violated also may be observed.

Much in the general field of psychology is applicable to the diverse tasks performed by the teacher. But the successful application of psychological principles, theories, and techniques in the classroom requires both artistry and wisdom on the part of the teacher.

Evaluating the Outcomes of Instruction

Evaluation is a process of determining to what extent the educational objectives are being realized by an instructional program. A complete evaluation program would provide pre- and postinstruction measurements on the student attainment of all objectives in a curriculum. In addition, retention measures are needed to determine the permanency of learning. Teacher-made and standardized achievement tests ordinarily constitute a major part of an evaluation program. But a variety of evaluative techniques, many of which are not paper-and-pencil tests, are needed to assess the development of interests, attitudes, appreciations, motor skills, and habit patterns.

Where possible, the achievement of students is expressed quantitatively. The present-day teacher needs to understand a number of statistical and measurement concepts as well as to become familiar with various evaluative techniques. The teacher also needs to develop some skill in the construction of achievement tests. Hence, the subject matter included in "psychological tests and measurements" constitutes an important portion of educational psychology.

Learning Exercise

13. For which one of the five major tasks of the teacher is each one of the following research studies designed to provide pertinent information?
    (a) The faculty in Albert High School is debating about what kind of guidance program they should introduce in their school. There is a difference of opinion as to whether students need to know more about the kinds of employment available in their own community. In order to decide whether the school should teach occupational information, a test is constructed and administered to students in the school to see how much vocational information has been acquired without benefit of school instruction.
    (b) The faculty in Brown High School already has a guidance program and teaches vocational information. A test is constructed and administered to the students in order to study the school's success in teaching vocational information.
    (c) The faculty at Charles High School plan an experiment designed to find out whether a lecture method or a project method is a better way of teaching vocational information.

(d) The first two units of a group guidance course given at Donald High School deal with (1) a study of self, and (2) a study of the world at work. The faculty plans a study to find out which unit should be taught first.

GUIDING LEARNING

In guiding the learning of children, the modern teacher can choose from a variety of instructional techniques. The task of choosing wisely would be greatly simplified if research findings supplied definitive answers to questions such as: "Are teaching machines effective?" "Should television be used in the school as a media of instruction?" "Do students learn better by working in groups than by working individually?" "Does learning progress better when the teacher and pupils cooperatively plan the goals of instruction?" "How effective is the 'core curriculum' as a means of integrating the content of various subject-matter areas?" "Are projects in which students plan and carry out many different activities a more effective way of promoting learning than the read-recite procedure?"

Unfortunately, research findings do not provide definitive answers to questions of the type listed above. A teaching method that is effective for one teacher may be ineffective for another teacher. Further, a teaching method that is effective for some of the children in a classroom may be ineffective for others. It is of limited value to the teacher to know that research has shown that teaching method A is *on the average* superior to teaching method B. It is of more value to the teacher to know what makes one method of teaching more effective than another. The important question to raise is: "What variables determine the effectiveness of an instructional technique?" These variables may be classified into (1) stimulus or learning experience variables, (2) organismic variables, and (3) response variables.

The following outline constitutes one way of organizing the variables that are relevant to the effectiveness of an instructional method.

Stimulus Variables

A. Method Variables.

1. METHOD OF INSTRUCTION.

a) Motivation. Children are motivated to learn and hence learn better under some methods of instructions than others. As will be pointed out in Chapter 8, the child may be stimulated to learn by a wide variety of motives.

b) Teacher guidance. Some methods of instruction are superior to others because of *what the teacher does* to guide learning. "What the teacher does" includes explanations of ideas and processes; selection of learning materials (books, films, programs for teaching machines, etc.); and selection and organization of other learning experiences (group work, class discussions, field trips, etc.). The teacher sets up learning situations in which the student can acquire the information (perceptions, facts, concepts, ideas, etc.) that is necessary to the attainment of an educational objective.

c) Practice. Some methods of instruction are superior to others because the student is afforded a better opportunity to practice the responses implied in an educational objective, or because the practice sessions are more judiciously arranged.

d) Reinforcement. Practice alone does not establish a desired response. Some feedback concerning the adequacy of the learner's response is necessary. Reinforcement may be thought of as knowledge of results that brings some satisfaction to the learner.

2. TASK. Two methods of instruction may be identical and yet differ in effectiveness because of differences in the tasks or activities that children are called upon to perform. Children learn better when the tasks they are called upon to perform are *interesting, meaningful,* and of an appropriate *length* and *difficulty* level.

B. Environmental Variables. The formal education of a child takes place within a limited time period in history—a period of war or peace; of prosperity or depression; of international, national, community, or family turmoil or tranquility; and within an ever-changing technology, the products and by-products of which may either stimulate or disrupt the child's educational progress. It is evident that a multitude of events in the larger world of the child can influence his development. Within the school itself, characteristics of the child's physical environment—the quality of the school plant, books available in the library, supplies and teaching aids available, the seating arrangement in the classroom, the noise level in the classroom, etc.—also can affect learning efficiency. And as we shall see later the school environment of the child is made up of a complex pattern of interpersonal relationships. Finally, the quality of teacher-pupil relationships constitutes an important factor contributing to the effectiveness of a pupil's learning.

The net effect of all environmental factors is to create an emotional climate that either facilitates or hinders school learning. One child may be emotionally and socially adjusted to the school situation, and hence free to devote a reasonable proportion of his total energy output to the attainment of educational goals. For another child, the pressures of the environment to better his status position may absorb all of his energies. Striving for educational goals may be in harmony or disharmony with the behavioral norms of the student body. The atmosphere in one classroom may be characterized as stimulating, with pupils encouraged to interact with the subject matter learned and to plan some of their own learning activities. In another classroom, the atmosphere may be characterized as restrictive, with pupils apparently trying to discover what the teacher wants. In still another classroom, the atmosphere may be characterized as apathetic, with pupils passively resisting the educational program of the school. In short, environmental factors play a large part in determining the effectiveness of the learning that takes place in any classroom.

Learning Exercise

14. Two science teachers use the same text and make the same assignments to their classes. Initially, the two classes are equal in ability and in achievement on a pretest on science. After instruction, one class does much better on the science test administered to both classes.

     Which of the variables discussed in the preceding section might account for the differences in performances between the two classes? Which variables probably did not account for the difference?

Organismic Variables

Organismic variables may be conveniently classified into two broad categories:

A. *Characteristics of the learner,* e.g., intelligence level, age, sex, socioeconomic class, etc.

B. *Mediating processes,* e.g., remembering, perceiving, thinking, experiencing, anxiety, frustration or stress, etc.

A. Characteristic of the Learner. The method of instruction that is effective for one student may not be effective for another student. Some students are brighter than others and hence are more efficient learners. Some students have more thoroughly mastered the previous subject matter that is prerequisite to an understanding of new material. Some students are more highly motivated than others. The characteristics of the learner that make a difference in his learning efficiency are often discussed in educational literature under the heading of "readiness."

What constitutes "readiness" varies with each school learning. A student's success in any learning task depends upon the developmental status of those aspects of his total development that are relevant to the task to be learned. The factors of importance in learning to read are not exactly the same as those relevant to learning arithmetic. For all school learning, the readiness of the student to profit from instruction is dependent upon:

1. The maturity and quality of his physical and mental equipment;
2. His perception of the learning situation as a means of meeting his needs and attaining his goals; and
3. The adequacy of his past learning as a preparation for the learning situation.

A useful question to raise for any educational objective is: "Why does the learner not exhibit, prior to instruction, the behavior described in the educational objective?" Often it is possible to formulate an answer to this question in terms of one or more of the following kinds of deficiencies: (1) the learner is *irregular* in the behavior; (2) the learner lacks needed *information;* and (3) the learner lacks *perceptual* or *cognitive* abilities and skills.

1. IRREGULARITY DUE TO LACK OF MOTIVATION. For some educational objectives, the learner has available, prior to instruction, the response pattern described in the educational objective. Learning consists of regularizing or making more consistent the response pattern. For example, the educational objective "The child is becoming used to washing his hands before eating . . ." (Kearney, 1953, p. 56) implies that the child already knows how to wash his hands before eating and sometimes does. Learning for this objective consists of regularizing an already established response pattern. The child knows what he is supposed to do. The instructional problem is mainly one of motivating the child.

2. LACK OF INFORMATION. For many educational objectives of the school, the responses to be learned are not initially possessed by the learner, at least not in the response pattern desired. The teacher needs to supply *information* to the learner in order to facilitate learning.

3. LACK OF PERCEPTUAL AND COGNITIVE ABILITIES AND SKILLS. For many educational objectives, the inability of the learner to make the to-be-learned response prior to instruction may be for reasons other than deficiencies in motivation and information. For example, a pupil may fail to solve an arithmetic problem even though he tries and seems

to have all the information needed. A pupil may know a number of laws in trigonometry and yet be unable to apply them in solving practical problems. Or a pupil may know the position of keys on a typewriter and yet be unable to type rapidly and accurately. Many educational objectives involve the learning of complex response patterns that are not initially in the repertoire of the learner. If the learner is *unable*, even when he tries, to supply the complex behavior pattern prior to instruction, then his failure cannot be attributable to a lack of motivation. And failure cannot be attributable to lack of information if the learner is supplied with all the information he needs. The learner needs to develop perceptual and cognitive abilities in order to produce the to-be-learned response.

Learning Exercise

15. Identify the initial deficiencies of the learner (motivational, informational, or perceptual-cognitive) for each of the following learning incidents:
    (a) A girl who infrequently volunteers to tell a story before her first-grade classmates by the end of the year volunteers quite frequently.
    (b) The children in Miss Smith's class were much more frequently courteous at the end of the year than they were at the beginning of the year, even though Miss Smith did not give "lectures" in courtesy.
    (c) Mr. Brown gave a test to his biology class that covered factual material in a chapter that the pupils had taken up in class. After the pupils had an opportunity to read the chapter, Mr. Brown gave the test again. The pupils did much better on the second test.
    (d) Mary in studying for a test in grammar memorized definitions of parts of speech. She did quite poorly on the test, which required her to recognize parts of speech. After special coaching in recognizing parts of speech, Mary was able to do much better on a retest.

B. Mediating Processes. Terms such as "intelligence," "perception," "motivation," "drive," "hunger," "fear," "anxiety," "set," "conflict," "stress," etc., frequently are encountered in explanations of behavior. Such terms represent processes occurring within the organism and interacting between the presentation of a stimulus and the occurrence of a response.

An understanding of the nature of perceptual, motivational, cognitive, and affective mediating processes is of particular importance to the educator. The arithmetic teacher who strives to discover how a pupil arrives at an answer to a problem is focusing attention on cognitive mediating processes. The high school counselor who tries to understand how a pupil perceives himself and his environment and what goals are of importance to him is directing attention to perceptual, cognitive, and motivational mediating processes. Knowledge of the nature of mediating processes should help the teacher to assess the potential value of various instructional methods for different educational objectives.

Response Variables

A method of instruction that is effective for imparting information may be ineffective for developing problem-solving abilities or for changing attitudes. Different types of educational objectives call for different instructional procedures. There are many possible ways of classifying educational objectives. One rough classification is:

A. Cognitive objectives—knowledge, concepts, and problem-solving skills
B. Affective objectives—attitudes, values, interests, and appreciations
C. Psychomotor skills—handwriting, typing, physical education activities, painting, etc.

While all learning involves some cognitive, affective, and behavioral aspects, many educational objectives may be regarded as primarily cognitive, affective, or psychomotor. Some educational objectives, however, involve a complexity of behaviors (e.g., learning to assume responsibility for the safety of others) and may be classified as "action patterns" or "competencies."

Planning Instruction

The teacher needs to consider stimulus, organismic, and response variables in planning instruction. One way of structuring the complexity of variables involved in an instructional problem is:

Stimulus	Organismic	Response
A. Method variables	A. Characteristics of the learner	A. Cognitive
1. Method of instruction	B. Mediating processes	B. Affective
a) Motivation		C. Psychomotor
b) Teacher-guidance		D. Action pattern
c) Practice		
d) Reinforcement		
2. Task		
a) Length		
b) Difficulty		
c) Meaningfulness		
B. Environmental context variables		

In order to assess the potential effectiveness of a method of instruction, it is necessary to raise questions such as: (1) "Is the planned method of instruction likely to motivate students?" (2) "Are adequate teacher-guidance procedures included within the method?" (3) "Does the method provide the right kind of practice for students?" (4) "Does the planned instruction provide appropriate reinforcements for students as they learn?" (5) "Are the tasks that the students are called upon to perform of appropriate length and difficulty and are they meaningful?" (6) "Is the method of instruction geared to the abilities and needs of all members of the class and does it provide for individual differences within the class?" (7) "Will the method of instruction actually change the individual so that he is able to perceive, think about, and feel about his environment and himself in a new way?" and (8) "Does the method of instruction develop the particular cognitive, affective, and psychomotor response patterns that are incorporated within the educational objectives of the school?" The purpose of this text is to present materials from the subject matter of psychology that will aid the student in arriving at answers to questions such as the above.

SUMMARY

Educational psychology is that branch of psychology concerned with the educative process. Hence, an understanding of the nature of educational psychology involves some appreciation of the characteristics of both psychology and the educative process.

Psychology is the science of behavior. As a science, its investigative methods are consistent with certain basic beliefs and operating conceptions of science. Psychology is empirical. Knowledge about behavior is acquired through systematic observation.

Psychologists deal with three types of variables: stimulus, organismic, and response. Psychological research involves studies of relationships between various combinations of these variables. Thus in an S→R study, some task, method, or environmental condition is varied; and the effect of the variation on some response measure is observed.

The methods of psychology are adapted to achieve three major purposes: (1) the description and classification; (2) the prediction; and (3) the explanation of behavior. A variety of means, such as tests, rating scales, and electronic instruments, have been developed in order to describe and classify behavior where possible data are quantified through some kind of measurement. The experimental method is the major but not the only method used by psychologists in predicting behavior. Explanation in psychology is achieved through exact descriptions of the variables that affect the behavior under consideration.

The content of educational psychology is delimited by the kinds of problems encountered in guiding the educative process. Guiding the educative process may be analyzed into the following five different tasks: (1) defining educational objectives, (2) selecting learning experiences, (3) organizing learning experiences, (4) guiding the learning process in the classroom, and (5) evaluating the outcomes of instruction.

The major contribution that psychology can make to the teacher is a way of thinking about educational problems. This way of thinking is, in essence, a scientific approach in which the teacher attempts to identify the variables that are crucial in a particular educational problem.

Answer Cues

1. Psychology deals with observable behavior. Private thoughts, wishes, etc., become of concern to psychology only when expressed in some way.

2. Meets criteria: systematic organization; objective observation. Fails: lacks system of interrelated conceptual propositions; lacks measurement.

3. Yes. The measurements themselves are directly observable. (Psychological test results are directly observable.)

4. Tasks, types of group and individuals, and criteria of performance—all could be quite different from one study to another.

5. (a) No—A. (b) Yes—E. (c) No—D. (d) No—B.

6. (a) R. (b) S. (c) O. (d) S. (e) R. (f) O. (g) O. (h) S. (i) S. (j) R.

7. Anxiety.

8. Because variables other than the experimental variable may be operative within the classroom.

9. (a) Size of item step, and intelligence levels. (b) Various performance measures.

10. No.

11. $O \rightarrow R$.

12. (a) $O \rightarrow R$. (b) $R \rightarrow R$. (c) $S \rightarrow R$. (d) $O \rightarrow O$. (e) $S \rightarrow O \rightarrow R$.

13. (a) Establishing objectives. (b) Evaluation. (c) Selecting experiences. (d) Organizing experiences.

14. The task variable and important parts of the organismic variable are controlled—i.e., they are the same for both classes—and hence would not likely contribute to the difference. Also, the response variable is controlled because both classes took the same test. Possibly the method of instruction variable—ways of motivating students, the teacher's explanations, and the

kind of reinforcement provided—accounted for the difference. Or possibly the environmental variable—i.e., the emotional climate of the classroom—contributed to the difference.

15. (a) Motivational. (b) Motivational. (c) Informational. (d) Perceptual-cognitive.

2

OBSERVING AND INTERPRETING
INDIVIDUAL BEHAVIOR

Psychology as a science seeks to obtain general descriptions of behavior. In so doing, much of the uniqueness of the individual is lost. For example, growth curves of height and weight represent the average growth of many children and do not quite describe the growth of one particular child. Each child is unique in the way he develops, in his mental equipment, in his social and emotional behavior, and in his total personality. But if science seeks general descriptions of phenomena and the individual is unique, then what use is a science of behavior in interpreting individual behavior?

There are two answers to this question. First, while it is true that each child is unique in many ways, it is equally true that each child is similar to other children in many ways. Hence, a generalization such as "Aggression is an indication of some sort of frustration" may hold true for all children even though both what frustrates and the form that aggression takes may vary from child to child. Thus, some psychological generalizations may suggest what to look for in observing the individual child, and lead to the formulation of tentative hypotheses in interpreting the behavior of the child. A second answer to the question is that each child's personality, while differing from that of any other child, has its own internal consistency (Lecky, 1945). What motivates Sammy may differ from what motivates Joe, but if we observe Sammy over a period of time, we may begin to see consistencies in Sammy's behavior. It should be added that the consistency of an individual's behavior is rarely obvious. Rather, the consistency rests in some psychological characteristic of the individual's life style. Thus, Sammy may have a strong need to express his independence, to do things in his own way. Sammy's behavior may appear inconsistent until this need-for-independence facet of Sammy's personality is recognized. In summary, even though each individual is unique, a science of behavior has potential value in interpreting behavior because individuals are similar as well as different, and because there is a consistency in the behavior of an individual from day to day.

In this chapter, the position is taken that observing and interpreting behavior in the classroom is an improvable skill, and that practice by the teacher in bringing to bear certain psychological frames of reference on what is observed is one way in which this skill can be improved.

By *frame of reference* we mean a constellation of interrelated concepts which constitutes a systematic approach to the analysis of certain types of problems. Thus, a geologist in observing rocks brings to bear a geological frame of reference which results in different observations than those made by a non-geologist. To use a psychoanalytic frame of reference in observing and interpreting behavior would entail noticing behaviors that were meaningful within a set of concepts that could be subsumed under the term "psychoanalysis." To use the frame of reference of the cultural anthropologist would result in focusing attention on behaviors that could be compared and contrasted with behaviors found in different cultures. It is evident from a number of research studies in perception that a person brings to bear some frame of reference in observing an event even though he may be unaware of the influence of his frame of reference.

In this chapter, three major frames of reference—that of reinforcement learning theory, the phenomenological, and the psychoanalytic—will be discussed briefly and their possible uses in observing classroom behavior will be examined. A fourth frame of reference—the developmental—will be discussed in Chapter 3.

Learning Exercises

1. Which laws would be useful in observing and interpreting individual behavior:
   (a) Laws describing consistencies in the behavior of a single individual; and/or
   (b) Laws describing the regularities in the behavior of all individuals?
2. On which would we tend to focus our attention in observing, from an "ideals of democracy" frame of reference, a class planning a unit in Civics:
   (a) The subject matter content discussed; or
   (b) Characteristics of the planning process?

REINFORCEMENT FRAME OF REFERENCE

Learning is defined in Hilgard and Marquis (Kimble, 1961) as *a relatively permanent change in behavior potentiality which occurs as a result of reinforced practice.* In this definition, "reinforced" is used in an empirical sense. Certain events are termed "reinforcers" when they tend to increase the probability that the to-be-learned response will be repeated when the stimulus situation recurs. The following classroom incident illustrates the meaning of reinforcement.

Each day, Miss Brock, a second-grade teacher, asks members of her class to come to the front of the room and tell the class any interesting little happening that they have experienced lately. Jim, age eight, rarely volunteered. One day Jim did volunteeer. The class listened attentively to Jim's story and laughed at one amusing part of the story. Miss Brock noticed on subsequent days that Jim volunteered more frequently.

1. In this classroom incident, Miss Brock asking members of the class to come to front of room is the *stimulus situation;*
2. To volunteer is one *to-be-learned response;*
3. The class listening attentively and laughing at one amusing part of the story is the *event that reinforced;* because
4. Jim volunteered more frequently on subsequent days, i.e., the probability of volunteering has increased.

When a student tries out a new method of studying for an examination and obtains an "A" grade, then the "A" grade is a reinforcer *if* the student later tries out again his new method of studying. For a teacher who tries out a new teaching method on her class, the interest and the learning progress of the class would constitute a reinforcer if the teacher later tries out the same or similar method under similar circumstances.

Many events may serve as reinforcers of behavior patterns, and an event that is a reinforcer for one individual may not be a reinforcer for another individual. In observing and interpreting individual behavior from a reinforcement frame of reference, attention is focused on identifying the class of events that reinforce an individual's behavior. We turn now to a discussion of a number of concepts developed by learning theorists that may be subsumed under the heading of a *reinforcement frame of reference.*

Classical Conditioning

In classical conditioning experiments, a kind of substitute learning occurs. Ivan Pavlov, a Russian physiologist, noticed that the mere sight of food was sufficiently a substitute for the taste of food itself to cause dogs in his laboratory to salivate. He proceeded to induce dogs to salivate in response to various stimuli such as the sound of a tuning fork, bell, or metronome. Pavlov conducted his experiment in a sound-proof room and in other ways rigorously controlled experimental conditions. A dog was lightly harnessed and trained to stand quietly on a table. Prior to the experiment, a minor operation was performed in which the salivary duct of the dog was diverted to the outside of the cheek. A small glass funnel was cemented over the opening of the cheek to collect the saliva. The experimental procedure consisted of striking a tuning fork and a few seconds later presenting meat powder. The meat powder was delivered mechanically to the dog, while the experimenter observed through a glass window from an adjoining room. After combining the tone and the food on a number of trials, the dog salivated at the sound of the tuning fork—before the food was presented. Additional trials resulted in a strengthening of the salivary response, i.e., increasing the flow of saliva. Diagrammatically, a typical Pavlov experiment may be represented thus:

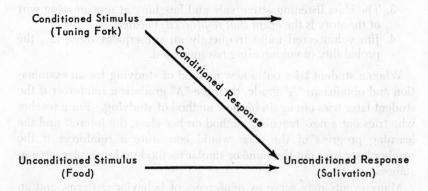

The food which was capable of eliciting the salivation response at the beginning of the experiment was named the *unconditioned stimulus* (UCS). The salivation response to the food (UCS) was named the *unconditioned response* (UCR). The learned response, i.e., salivation at the sound of the tuning fork is referred to as a *conditioned response* (CR).

Classical conditioning experiments have been conducted that have utilized a variety of stimuli: light, an air puff, electric shock, and many other stimuli of like simplicity. Outside of the psychological laboratory, many life situations fit the classical conditioning model. Kimble and Garmezy (1963) report the following illustrative incident.

Two small country boys who lived before the day of the rural use of motor cars had their Friday afternoons made dreary by the regular visit of their pastor, whose horse they were supposed to unharness, groom, feed and water and then harness again on the departure. Their gloom was lightened finally by a course of action which one of them conceived. They took to spending the afternoon of the visit retraining the horse. One of them stood behind the horse with a hay-fork and periodically shouted "Whoa" and followed this with a sharp jab with the fork. Unfortunately, no exact records of this experiment were preserved save that the boys were quite satisfied with the results. [Pp. 135–36.]

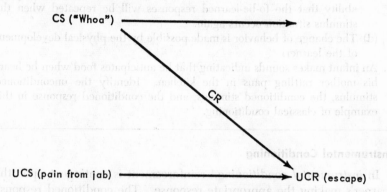

Pearson (1954) reports a case that illustrates how classical conditioning may operate to affect children's attitudes toward school subjects.

A ten-year-old boy did well in all his school subjects except mathematics. In this subject he persistently failed. Careful study of his mathematics revealed that he did all arithmetical processes correctly regardless of their difficulty if the number 3 was excluded. He consistently made errors in the simplest computations when the number 3 was included. In the first grade the teacher had become provoked with him because of his slowness in learning to write a 3. She hit him over the hands many times to force him to form it properly. As a result he associated the number 3 with pain and so could not use it in his computations. [P. 33.]

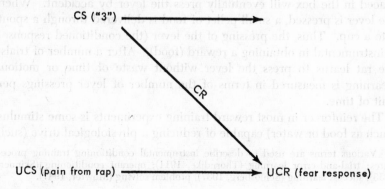

Learning Exercises

3. Which of the following is a necessary characteristic of *learning* as defined by Hilgard and Marquis?
   (a) The change in behavior is *desirable*.
   (b) The learner responds with some regularity to a stimulus situation in a different way than he formerly did.
   (c) The consequences of the learner's responses serve to increase the probability that the to-be-learned responses will be repeated when the stimulus situation occurs again.
   (d) The change of behavior is made possible by the physical development of the learner.
4. An infant makes sounds indicating that he anticipates food when he hears his mother rattling pans in the kitchen. Identify the unconditioned stimulus, the conditioned stimulus, and the conditioned response in this example of classical conditioning.

Instrumental Conditioning

In *instrumental conditioning*,[1] reinforcement is contingent upon the learner's making the appropriate response. The conditioned response is *instrumental* in obtaining reinforcement. There are a number of types of instrumental conditioning experiments, including: (1) reward and secondary reward training; (2) avoidance training; (3) escape training; and (4) omission training.

Reward and Secondary Reward Training. In reward training experiments, a reward such as food is given when the learner makes the appropriate response. The Skinner box (Skinner, 1938) is one of the best reward training situations. The box is large enough to confine a small animal. A lever is located at one end of the box. A hungry rat placed in the box will eventually press the lever by accident. When the lever is pressed, a small pellet of food is delivered through a spout into a cup. Thus, the pressing of the lever (the conditioned response) is instrumental in obtaining a reward (food). After a number of trials, the rat learns to press the lever without waste of time or motion. Learning is measured in terms of the number of lever pressings per unit of time.

The reinforcer in most reward training experiments is some stimulus (such as food or water) capable of reducing a physiological drive (such

[1] Various terms are used to describe instrumental conditioning training procedures: trial-and-error learning (Thorndike, 1911); operant conditioning (Skinner, 1953); success learning (Schlosberg, 1937); problem solving (Mowrer, 1947).

as hunger or thirst). According to one view, reinforcement is explained in terms of need reduction, drive reduction, or drive-stimulus reduction.[2] The reinforcer re-establishes the equilibrium of the organism. There are, however, many situations where the reinforcer stimulates the organism rather than reduces a need or drive. Sexual stimulation, certain tastes, odors, tactile stimuli, and sounds may be reinforcing. In the school situation, we find students repeating response patterns (such as attending a football game) where the reinforcement has been excitement rather than tension reduction.

In secondary reward training, the reward derives its reinforcing value from prior conditioning in which it has been associated with a primary reward. Wolfe's (1936) experiment with chimpanzees illustrates secondary reward training. The experiment was in two parts. In the first part of the experiment, the chimpanzees were trained to place tokens in the slot of a vending apparatus. The tokens were small red, blue, and brass disks, similar to poker chips. The chimpanzee received a reward of two grapes if he put a red token in the vending machine, one grape for a blue token, and no reward for a brass token. From a pile of tokens, the trained chimpanzee selected the red tokens to place in the machine, then chose the blue tokens, and ignored the brass tokens. Up to this point, the experiment followed a simple reward training procedure. In the second part of the experiment, after the reward value of the tokens had been established, the chimpanzees were taught a series of complicated tasks in which the only reward received for a correct response was a token. Note in this second part of the experiment the reward of tokens derived its reinforcing value from prior association with the primary reward—grapes.

Other Types of Instrumental Conditioning. Numerous experiments, many of which have been conducted with animals, demonstrate that reward is not the only stimulus condition or consequence that reinforces a response. In *avoidance training,* the conditioned response

[2] Chapter 9 in Hilgard and Marquis (revised by G. A. Kimble, 1961) contains an excellent discussion on the "Mechanism of Reward."

The terms "drive" and "need" are defined differently by different psychologists. N. E. Miller (Miller and Dollard, 1941) conceives of needs as an environmental lack or excess needed to be corrected for biological survival (e.g., need for water). Drive, for Miller, is conceived as a strong stimulus that impels action. Any stimulus can become a drive if it becomes sufficiently strong. Faint music in the distance has little drive value; blaring music has considerably more. Reinforcement is conceived by Miller as drive-stimulus reduction.

The various theories on the nature of reinforcement (with their supporting experimental evidence) may be of relevance to the educator to the extent that they yield promising hypotheses regarding the characteristics of reinforcers that can be provided by the teacher in the classroom.

prevents the occurrence of a painful stimulus. In *escape training*, the conditioned response is followed by the termination of a painful stimulus. In *omission training*, a positive reinforcer (reward) occurs if the organism does *not* make some particular response.

The application of avoidance, escape, and omission training to child rearing practices presents many difficulties. Sometimes what we think is rewarding to a child is really punishing and vice versa. Also, in complex learning the child may not perceive accurately what aspect of his behavior has led to reward or punishment. With these cautions in mind, we can think of numerous life illustrations of each type of conditioning.

Avoidance training, i.e., preventing a painful stimulus. During the process of growing up we learn to recognize many danger signals and discover responses that avoid painful consequences. The eighth-grade boy has somehow or other acquired a rather ingenious pain-avoidance technique when he presents his father with an unsatisfactory report card with the remark, "Here's my report card, Dad, and also one of yours that I found in the attic."

Escape training, i.e., terminating a painful stimulus. All the ways we learn to lessen both physical and psychological pain may be explained in terms of escape training. The daydreams of the adolescent permit him to escape from the unpleasant present. The adolescent girl returns to her dolls when she does not receive an invitation to the school dance. We also learn, by trial and error, effective means of reducing physical pain.

Omission training, i.e., getting a reward by not making a particular response. A child learning to handle money is one example of omission training. By not spending his money on trivial purchases, the child has the money available to purchase a much-desired article.

Learning Exercise

5. Each of the events described below illustrates a type of conditioning. For each event, identify: (1) the type of reinforcement illustrated; (2) what has been reinforced; and (3) what is the reinforcer.
   (a) In grade 1, Mike often failed to say "Please" when he asked for something, but the teacher smiled at Mike whenever he did say "Please." After a few months, Mike regularly said "Please" whenever he asked for something.
   (b) Twice, in the first week of the school year, Percival, age twelve, caused a disturbance in class. On both occasions, the teacher became angry and scolded Percival. As the school year progressed, Percival

caused a disturbance in class more frequently and the teacher continued to scold him.

(c) Mary stated to some friends at the beginning of her junior year in high school that English and History were her best subjects. On her first English theme she received an "A" grade. Later she was overheard to remark to friends that English was her best subject.

(d) A tenth-grade class learns that, if a sufficient number of class members protest about the length of a burdensome homework assignment, the teacher will reduce the length of the assignment.

(e) Alice becomes discouraged when her teacher criticizes her school work. She reduces her feelings of unhappiness by seeking the company of friends who are also experiencing difficulty with their school work.

Other Learning Concepts

Five other learning concepts have emerged from classical and instrumental conditioning experiments:

1. Reinforcement
2. Experimental extinction
3. Spontaneous recovery
4. Generalization
5. Discrimination

Reinforcement. Classical conditioning occurs merely by pairing the unconditioned and conditioned stimulus. In Pavlov's experiment, the flow of saliva tended to increase as the appearance of food (UCS) regularly followed the sound of the tuning fork (CS). The two country boys increased the strength of the conditioned response of the parson's horse by regularly following the "Whoa" by a sharp jab with the hayfork. The first-grade teacher reinforced the fear response when she repeatedly hit the boy over the hands for forming the number 3 improperly.

In instrumental conditioning, the conditioned response is usually acquired gradually. Reward or the fulfillment of an expectancy constitutes the reinforcement. The volunteering of the second-grade boy to speak before the class was reinforced by the class's listening attentively to the boy when he did volunteer. In instrumental conditioning, any stimulus condition that will maintain or strengthen the conditioned response constitutes reinforcement. Experimentally, the strength of the conditioned response is customarily measured in any of five ways: (1) *probability of occurrence*—a strong conditioned response is likely to occur every time the stimulus condition is present; (2) *number of oc-*

currences in a period of time; (3) *magnitude of response—*e.g., the subject runs faster; (4) *latency—*or the time interval between the onset of the conditioned stimulus and the onset of the conditioned response; and (5) *resistance to extinction—*i.e., how long the conditioned response persists when it is not reinforced.

Extinction.   Conditioned responses become weaker unless they are reinforced.   The Pavlovian dog will not salivate at the sound of a tuning fork for the remainder of his life.   The parson's horse will eventually not bolt at the sound of "Whoa" if the hay-fork stimulus is consistently omitted.   Both of these conditioned responses gradually become weaker when they are not reinforced.   This weakening of the conditioned response as a result of continued presentation of the conditioned stimulus without reinforcement is known as *extinction.* Some conditioned responses are more resistant to extinction than are others.   Apparently, the fear response of the boy who was rapped over his hand by his first-grade teacher for failure to make a number 3 properly persisted for years even though, presumably, succeeding teachers did not reinforce the fear response.

In instrumental conditioning, extinction occurs when the conditioned response is repeatedly non-rewarded.

Learning Exercise

6. The advice is often given to ignore temper tantrums in young children. The frequency of temper tantrums might be expected to increase if any kind of attention to the child while having the tantrum is _____.

Spontaneous Recovery.   Extinction does not destroy a conditioned response.   The Pavlovian dog salivates immediately after the first sounding of the tuning fork on the day following the extinction series.   A period of rest is all that is necessary for the reappearance of the conditioned response.   In instrumental conditioning as well as in classical conditioning, a seemingly extinguished response reappears after a time interval with no intervening reinforcement.   The slot machine addict may leave the machine after a number of non-rewarded trials, only to return another day to try his luck again.   The golfer who quits his game in exasperation on one day returns to play the next day.   This recovery of the conditioned response without intervening reinforcement is known as *spontaneous recovery.*

Generalization. An organism conditioned to respond to one particular stimulus will also respond to other similar stimuli. In the Pavlov experiment, the dog will respond to the sounds emitted from tuning forks of different pitches from that initially used in training. The closer the pitch of a tuning fork is to that of the tuning fork originally used, the stronger is the conditioned response. This ability of different but similar stimuli to evoke a conditioned response is known as *stimulus generalization.* Sometimes our initial reaction to a new acquaintance may be explained in terms of stimulus generalization. If in the past we have experienced happy relationships with children of foreign extraction, we tend to initially react favorably with other children of foreign extraction.

Generalization may occur with responses as well as stimuli. *Response generalization* is said to occur when a stimulus that has come through training to elicit one response will also elicit, without additional training, a related response. Examples of response generalization are encountered daily. The responses "Thank you," "Thanks," "I appreciate that," or even a smile may be equally appropriate responses when a person has performed a small favor for us.

In Chapter 9, we shall see that transfer of learning is possible because of the phenomena of stimulus generalization and response generalization. Every response can be elicited, not just by one stimulus, but by a class of similar stimuli. And every stimulus elicits, not just one response, but one of a class of responses.

Discrimination. By reinforcing one stimulus and not reinforcing a similar stimulus, it is possible to secure a conditioned response to only the reinforced stimulus. The dog that has been conditioned to salivate to the sound of a particular tone also will salivate to other tones. However, if the dog is reinforced only when the conditioned tone is presented and never with any other tone, the dog eventually will salivate to the sound of the conditioned tone and not to any other tones.

Discrimination is well illustrated in a child's learning of language. Parents may be delighted when the young child first says the word "Da-Da" at the sight of the father. Later, the parents are disappointed when the child says "Da-Da" at the sight of other male figures. Eventually, the child learns to discriminate between the various male figures in his life and reserves the response "Daddy" for only one particular male.

Relevance of Reward Training to School Learning. Reinforcement learning theories have been disappointing to many educators in that they do not explain all that we would like to know about classroom learning. For example, there is no simple direct application of reinforcement learning theory that answers the question, "How do we present an algebra lesson so that students will follow our explanation and understand algebraic processes?" Even psychologists who are thoroughly versed in reinforcement learning theory sometimes encounter difficulty in communicating ideas to students. But the teaching-learning process involves more than just "teacher explains—student understands." The teacher guides the learning process and in so doing can reward and hence reinforce those student responses that represent progress toward defined educational objectives.

What are the appropriate rewards that can be arranged by the teacher in the classroom? The question will be explored more fully in later chapters. For our present discussion, it is pertinent to note that what is rewarding to one student may not be rewarding to another student. Praise from the teacher may be rewarding to one student but not to another. Peer approval has different reinforcing value from one student to another. For the student striving to attain academic goals, knowledge of results is reinforcing. For example, the student having successfully worked a problem in geometry is reinforced merely by knowing that he has worked the problem correctly. Thus, observing individual behavior from a reinforcement frame of reference includes noticing individual differences between students in what constitutes reward.

We know that a potential reward condition has served as a reinforcer only if we have evidence that a response has been strengthened. To illustrate:

An elementary school pupil makes many mistakes in addition because he fails to copy down neatly the numbers to be added. He tends to get correct the questions in which he has copied down the numbers more carefully. He begins to copy down the numbers more carefully and obtains more correct answers. Over a period of days, he improves noticeably in the care he takes in copying down numbers.

In this illustration, an activity (copying down numbers correctly) has been reinforced by knowledge of results (i.e., knowledge that correct answers have been obtained). We have reason to believe that knowledge of results has served as a reinforcer because the copying-down-numbers-neatly response has increased in frequency.

Feelings of students, or at least the overt expression of feelings, may be reinforced in a classroom. For example, in a civics class discussing racial relations, one student may express a strong feeling against school integration. Other students may indicate approval of the first student's feelings. If, in subsequent discussions there is an increase in the frequency or intensity of the expressed feeling against school integration, then the approval of the other students would appear to have served as a reinforcer.

The way events turn out may confirm or challenge a person's self concept. The college student who thinks of himself as an "A" student reinforces this self concept when he obtains "A" grades.

Observing and interpreting individual behavior from a reinforcement frame of reference involves raising a series of questions as one observes. For example, in observing a school class in session over a period of days, questions such as the following might be raised:

1. What pupil activities is the teacher reinforcing? How?
2. What kind of interactions between pupils are being reinforced? How?
3. What appear to be effective reinforcers for different members of the class?
4. In what ways are individuals in the class having a particular self concept reinforced?
5. What motives and feelings are being reinforced? How?
6. How may past reinforcements explain present behaviors of individuals in the class?

Learning Exercises

7. Which concept—reinforcement, experimental extinction, spontaneous recovery, stimulus generalization, response generalization, or discrimination —is exemplified in each of the following:
   (a) A teacher devises a new method of explaining fractions to her class. The class is successful in solving fraction problems. Subsequently, the teacher continues to utilize her new method of explaining fractions.
   (b) A child reacts unfavorably to his new teacher who resembles his disliked aunt.
   (c) A child learns to distinguish "b" from "d."
   (d) A child varies his response when he receives a gift, sometimes saying "Thank you," sometimes saying "Thanks," etc., but always making some appropriately courteous response.
   (e) The adolescent outgrows preadolescent ways of behaving that are no longer appreciated by his age mates.
   (f) A child quarrels with his playmate, but returns the next day to again enjoy playing with him.
8. Which of the following exemplifies reinforcement of a *self concept?* Which exemplifies reinforcement of a *feeling?* Which exemplifies reinforcement of a *motive?*

(a) John considers himself a good student. He obtains high grades.
(b) Bill wants to become a professional ball player. He hits a home run in an important game.
(c) John loves Mary. Mary loves John.

PHENOMENOLOGICAL FRAME OF REFERENCE[3]

The point of view that is now called phenomenology is very close to what the average person on the street would call a "common sense" point of view of behavior. The vocabulary of the phenomenologist does not include terms such as "Oedipus complex," "anal character," and "phallic symbol," that appear to the average man to be shrouded with an aura of ghostology. Largely lacking also from the phenomenologist's vocabulary are technical terms of comparable abstractness to "retroactive inhibition," "disinhibition," and "interoceptive conditioning." Much of the terminology of the phenomenologist in describing behavior is familiar to a person who has lived in the American culture for several years, and the units of behavior that are described by the phenomenologist are the same units that are customarily employed in everyday conversation.

Phenomenologists stress that, in order to understand an individual's behavior in a situation, it is necessary to understand the *meaning* of that situation to the individual behaver. And two individuals may attach entirely different meanings to identical experiences. This may be illustrated at a baseball game where two persons see a batter strike out. For the one individual, the batter struck out because he was a poor hitter. For the second individual, the batter struck out because the pitcher was a good pitcher. The phenomenologist argues that specifying precisely the nature of the stimulus condition rarely provides a basis for predicting individual behavior because each individual attaches different meanings to any given experience. It becomes necessary therefore to understand how the individual perceives the world about him in order to understand that individual, and in order to predict how he will behave in a given situation.

The Perceptual Field

Combs and Snygg (1959) state as their basic postulate that: "All behavior, without exception, is completely determined by, and pertinent to, the perceptual field of the behaving organism (p. 20). By

[3] The author is indebted to Dr. Fain Guthrie for his help in writing this section on the phenomenological frame of reference.

perceptual field, Combs and Snygg mean "the entire universe; including himself, as it is experienced by the individual at the moment of action" (p. 20). Note that the assumption is made that a person behaves in terms of what his experiences mean to him at the moment of behavior. This means, for example, that if a person sees something black coiled under a bush, the person's first reaction may be to get a hoe or something else and try to kill it, or else to run from it. When the person gets the hoe and comes back, the fact that the object turns out to be a black water hose coiled up under the bush is of no importance in interpreting his initial behavior. The important fact is what this experience meant to the person at the time he behaved. Thus, the perceptual field may or may not correspond to physical reality.

The perceptual field in any given instance may exclude much of one's physical surroundings. As you now read this page, you may, for the moment, be quite unaware of many objects in your immediate surroundings. For the moment, such objects are not part of your perceptual field, although as you glance about you, you will immediately bring some of these objects into your perceptual field. Objects not in your physical surroundings may be part of your perceptual field. If you were to think about some event that occurred yesterday, you would bring immediately into your perceptual field objects that are not now physically present. In short, the perceptual field is an individual's personal and unique field of awareness.

Organization of the Perceptual Field. The individual is not equally aware of all parts of his perceptual field. There is a *figure-ground* character to the organization of an individual's perceptual field at any moment. As a person reads a book, the major focus of attention (i.e., the figure) is the printed page and the ideas therein. He may at the same time be dimly aware of other people in the room and background music (i.e., the ground).

An individual's perceptual field is continually changing. One event succeeds another event in rapid succession. Further, because of learning, an individual's perception of the same phenomena changes. A high school boy who is enjoying in his Physics class a unit on electricity may perceive an electrical apparatus in a new way. Learning, for the phenomenologist, is this process of progressive *differentiations* from the more-general perceptual field. New meanings are attached to what is observed.

The fact that an individual's perceptual field is constantly changing does not mean that it is unorganized. Quite the opposite. Each individual's unique past experiences have given him a unique set of meanings that are brought into play in each new experience. At any time that the individual has to make a decision, at any time that he has to act, he acts in terms of the meanings available to him. The person will take into his perceptual field things that are consistent with this set of unique meanings. For example, college students and alumni watching their team on the football field somehow or other see unsportsmanlike conduct only on the part of players of the opposing team. That a member on one's own college football team is a "dirty" player is not usually a part of the unique set of meanings available to college students and alumni. Hence, when a member of one's own college team is accused by others of an unsportsmanlike act, we tend to interpret the act differently. *The perceptual field strives to maintain itself, not to be destroyed.*

In Chapter 9, we will examine further the influence of affective processes on perception. We shall see that the perceptual field is organized in such a way as to satisfy the individual's needs. People tend to see what they wish to see.

Self Concept

Each individual has had a multitude of discrete perceptions of self. The organization of all the ways an individual has of seeing himself is called by Combs and Snygg the *phenomenal self*, i.e., the self of which one is aware. A person perceives himself as possessing certain physical characteristics, character and personality traits, and abilities. These many perceptions of self vary widely in their importance to an individual. Combs and Snygg reserve the term "self concept" for those perceptions of self that are of central importance to the individual. Diagrammatically, the complete phenomenal field of the individual may be represented by a series of concentric circles.

The large circle encompasses the complete phenomenal field. The part of the phenomenal field that includes all perceptions of self is represented by a smaller circle and labeled the phenomenal self. The central core of the phenomenal self that is of great importance to the individual is labeled the self concept.

An individual becomes greatly concerned when the turn of events seems to challenge an important concept of self. If an elementary school girl seems almost heartbroken when she obtains less than 100 per cent on a spelling test, a tentative inference may be made from this observational data that a part of this girl's self concept is the idea "I am an excellent speller." In the same classroom, another pupil might accept with equanimity his poor performance in spelling on test after test. Evidently, the notion that "I am a good speller" is not

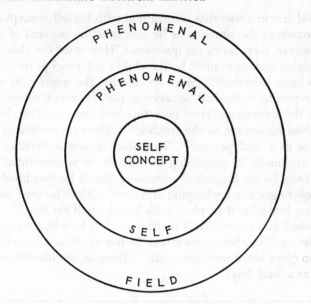

a part of this pupil's self concept. For this pupil striking out at a crucial point in a championship baseball game would be a shattering experience if an important part of his self concept is "I am a good hitter and can deliver in the pinch."

Each individual wants to defend and enhance his self concept. In attempting to defend and enhance his self concept, the individual learns those things that have personal meanings to him, he rejects those things that tend to destroy his perceptions of self, and he structures the world in terms of how it is necessary for him to structure the world. For the girl who perceives herself as an excellent speller, learning each day's spelling lesson is of importance to her. She will not abandon easily the idea that she is an excellent speller even in the face of contradictory evidence. Rather, she will find extenuating circumstances for her errors that will permit her to defend her self concept. And she will include "spelling competency" in what she considers to be a worthy person.

Observing Behavior

The phenomenal psychologist insists that noting how the child acts constitutes but a beginning step in observing and interpreting the behavior of a child. The important question to raise is: "How must the child feel in order to do what he is doing?" Phenomenology insists that a person always does what seems best to him at the time of acting.

The child acts in a way that is consistent with his self concept and with the demands of the situation as he sees it at the moment of behavior. The observer, then, raises the questions: "How must the child perceive the situation and what must be the child's self concept for him to behave as he is behaving?" More specifically, the teacher, in observing and interpreting individual behavior in the classroom, raises questions such as the following: "How does this little boy see the classroom?" "How does he see me as the teacher?" "Does he see me as a 'good' person or as a 'bad' person?" "How does he see arithmetic?" "Does he see arithmetic as something he can do or as something he can't do?" "Does he see English as something that, if he gets involved in it, it is likely to get him a whipping at home?" "Does he see Charlie over there as a boy who, if he plays with him, he will get hurt?" "Does he see baseball as a game, that if he tries to play, he will get laughed at?" "Does he see his father as one whom he has to please all the time, or as one who gives him encouragement?" "Does he see himself as a 'good' boy or as a 'bad' boy?"

Learning Exercises

9. From a phenomenological point of view, an object that is within our physical environment but of which we are unaware is not within our

   _____ _____.

10. Is the perceptual field of an individual restricted to concrete objects?
11. Two individuals enter a room in which people are listening to classical music. Individual A's attention is immediately concentrated on the selection of music played. Individual B's attention is directed to one of his friends in the audience. Explain, in terms of figure-ground relationships, the difference in the organization of the perceptual fields of individuals A and B.
12. The term used by phenomenologists to describe the process of discovering new facets in an observed phenomenon is _____.
13. A young lady joins a group in a game of bowling. She bowls poorly and her friend tells her that she is a poor bowler. She readily agrees and is not in the least offended. How would the phenomenologist explain the young lady's reaction?

PSYCHOANALYTIC FRAME OF REFERENCE

Modern child psychology is greatly influenced by the writings of Sigmund Freud, the founder of psychoanalysis. Psychoanalysis may be considered as a theory of personality dynamics that places great emphasis upon the influence on the individual of unconscious motivation, and as a developmental theory that is concerned with the historical origins of personality. Freud believed that all behavior is lawful, and that even the apparently inconsequential slips of the tongue, dreams, gestures, word associations, etc., of an individual provided important cues to that individual's personality. Hence, observing from a psychoanalytic frame of reference involves noticing many aspects of an individual's behavior that are not considered of significance from other psychological points of view. It also involves attaching quite different interpretations to an individual's behavior than would be the case from other frames of reference.

Personality Structure

Freud considered personality to have a structure consisting of three parts: the *id,* the *ego,* and the *superego.*

The Id. The function of the *id* is to gratify instinctual urges. It is guided by the *pleasure principle,* seeking pleasures through the release of tensions and the avoidance of pain. It is primitive, irrational, and almost wholly unconscious. The id is asocial, amoral, and demands gratification of needs regardless of consequences. The id is present at birth. The ego and the superego develop from the id as the child matures.

The Ego. A young child's environment does not meet all his demands. While the mother meets many of his urges, she denies other urges. The function of the *ego* is to cope with *external* events in such a way that needs will be met efficiently, and to deal with *internal* events by gaining control over the unbridled demands of the id. The ego is governed by the *reality principle.* The ego seeks pleasure but does so more wisely and effectively than the id. The ego is the executive branch of the personality structure that endeavors to maintain harmony in the relationship between the id, the superego, and the reality world.

The Superego. The *superego* corresponds roughly to the conscience. In the course of development, the child is restrained by his parents in his attempts to satisfy certain urges, no matter how strong the urge. The parent condemns as "wrong" stealing, destructiveness, and many forms of aggression. The external restraints are eventually internalized so that the child may reach a stage of development where he will go into a store and refrain from stealing because it is "wrong." Thus, the superego may condemn as wrong some things that the ego might otherwise do to satisfy the demands of the id. In addition, the superego has the positive function of keeping the person behaving in ways consistent with the ideals formed in childhood.

Peck and Havighurst (1960), in an intensive longitudinal study of 34 children, identified four levels of superego functioning.

1. The first consisted of a collection of harsh, crude, inconsistent "Don'ts," that are punitive but ineffective in guiding and controlling behavior in a morally sound way. Like the immature child who is subjected to constant scolding from his parents, the individual with this kind of conscience experiences vague, uncomfortable feelings that more or less curb his urges even though he has not any firm convictions of "right" and "wrong."
2. A second kind of conscience takes the form of *rule conformity*. The individual strives to adhere to the standards of "respectable others." Some rules are internalized and so the individual is not able to greatly change his code without experiencing feelings of guilt. However, behavior is modelled after authority figures, and the individual seeks for the approval and support of authority figures.
3. A third kind of conscience consists of a firmly organized body of internalized moral rules that operate quite independently of other people's opinions. The individual with this kind of conscience has early learned what is "right" and "wrong," and once this is learned, it is not modified throughout life. In the Peck and Havighurst study, adolescents with this kind of conscience seemed to have a good deal of hostility to be controlled, and so their principles appeared to be mostly a series of "Don'ts." They seemed to be emotionally incapable of questioning their consciences or examining rules in terms of some larger moral purposes. Absolute rules governed their behavior.
4. A fourth kind of conscience consists of a firm set of internalized moral principles, but these principles can be subjected to rational questioning and testing. Thus, the superego is not decompartmentalized from the ego. Interaction with ego results in constant growth of the superego and strengthening of the ego. In describing the individual with this type of functioning, Peck and Havighurst write:

He strongly feels that the best way to live is to give others as much consideration as himself, as often as possible. Finally, he checks each new situation alertly to see who is involved, how any given action will affect them, and governs his behavior accordingly because he wants to. It is difficult to find in such a system any fixed, important body of compartmentalized principles which could be called a superego as sharply distinct from the ego. [P. 101.]

Ego Span. The fourth level of conscience as described by Peck and Havighurst has something in common with the concept of "ego span" as described by French (1937) and Josselyn (1948). The function of the ego is not merely arbitrating between the demands of the id and the demands of the superego. It is rather finding solutions to life problems that satisfy both the demands of the id and the demands of the super-ego. Thus, the high school girl who has an important examination scheduled a week hence, and also an important social event scheduled on the week end before the examination, might look ahead and so arrange her work schedule in order to adequately prepare for the examination and yet find time to attend the social event. The super-ego says to her: "Study. Your parents expect you to do well in school. Don't let anything interfere with your studies." The id says to her: "Go to the dance. You will have fun. Your boy friend expects you to go, and you will win much admiration if you go." The ego says: "If I plan my work well this week, I can prepare for the test and still go to the dance."

The term "ego span" refers to the range or span of life problems for which the ego can work out solutions that satisfy the demands of both the id and the superego. From this viewpoint, the emotionally mature individual is not the one with the strong superego. A strong superego may place demands that are impossible to attain (e.g., "It is sinful even to think about sex"). When this occurs, we may have an extremely anxiety-ridden individual constantly suffering from feelings of guilt. The emotionally mature individual is one who has come to terms with the culture in which he lives. The emotionally mature individual is neither the individual who throws off the shackles of culturally imposed restraints, nor the blind, conforming, inhibited individual who denies all his needs. Rather, the emotionally mature individual has internalized the moral teachings of the culture. He wishes to follow, and is able to follow, his ideals and do so in ways that are satisfying. The emotionally mature individual is the individual with a wide ego span.

The ego span is not static nor inflexible. Under the best of conditions, i.e., when everything is going smoothly, it is capable of broad functioning. When things go wrong, or when the pressures of life become too great, the ego span contracts. The individual who is under great stress is not able to solve problems that normally would cause him little difficulty. But individuals differ in their capacity to withstand frustration and stress. The weak ego has a narrow span under the best of conditions and readily narrows under minor pressures. The emotionally mature individual has a relatively strong ego with a wide ego span that is resistant to contractions under conditions of frustration and stress.

Learning Exercises

14. What aspect of a person's personality structure is expressed when he acts impulsively without regard for remote consequences?
15. What is the reasoning aspect of a person's personality structure?
16. To what aspect of personality structure can we attribute feelings of guilt?
17. Four adolescents who did not habitually use profane language were asked, "Why not?" Order the following responses according to Peck and Havighurst's four levels of superego functioning:
    (a) "Nice people don't swear."
    (b) "I just haven't any urge to swear. I guess it's because my parents taught me that it is wrong."
    (c) "My mommy told me not to swear."
    (d) "Swearing is offensive to many people. As a general principle, I try not to be needlessly offensive to others."
18. Why would we ordinarily expect ego span to increase with age?

The Developmental Process

Freud viewed the human being as an energy system. The basic energy, called *libido,* energizes any kind of activity, but its natural expression is sexual. Freud considered almost any impulse to receive pleasure as an expression of libido, and hence sexual. In the course of an individual's development, the libido goes through a number of phases, called psychosexual stages. The expression of libidinal energy is different at each stage, and each stage is conceived as having particular significance for personality development. For Freud, psychosexual development is like biological growth that would take place for each individual regardless of specific environmental conditions. An attempt within psychoanalysis to take into account the adjustments to the environment required at each stage of development has been made by Erikson (1959).

The Oral Stage. During the oral stage, the most important source of gratification for the infant is from stimulation of the oral areas—the mouth, lips, and tongue. Libidinal pleasure is derived from sucking at the mother's breast and on other objects such as the thumb, fingers, toes, nipple, etc. During the early oral phase, the infant develops a desire to incorporate objects in the mouth, as though to make the object a part of himself. In this early oral stage, the infant is passive and receptive. During the later oral stage, when the child acquires teeth, the infant encounters frustration brought about by the eruption of the teeth. The infant enters a biting stage, which is interpreted by psychoanalysts as attributable to an aggressive desire to retaliate and destroy. Weaning brings with it further frustration and a new ambivalent relationship to the mother. The child experiences both friendly and hostile feelings toward the mother.

Psychoanalysts insist that the oral period is tremendously important to the development of the personality structure of the child. According to Erikson (1950, 1959), the child encounters his first psychosocial crisis during this period, i.e., of developing either *a basic trust or a basic mistrust* of the world. The amount of trust developed from the earliest infantile experiences depends upon the quality of the maternal relationship. Mothers create a sense of trust in their children through a combination of sensitive care of the infant's needs guided by a set of prohibitions and permissions that provide for the infant a consistency, continuity, and sameness of experience. The infant's first social achievement, according to Erikson, "is his willingness to let the mother out of sight without undue anxiety or rage, because she has become an inner certainty, as well as an outer probability" (1950, p. 219). A crucial testing of the relationship between inside and outside occurs during the suffering experienced during teething. The pain from within is not alleviated by the outer friends.

The adult who has developed this basic trust is one who has faith that situations will never become more than can be managed. He approaches situations with an expectancy that some good can eventuate through his own efforts. His interactions with people are marked by an absence of unrealistic suspicions. In situations that do not work out well, he is willing to try new approaches. He has differentiated those situations where he needs to depend on others from those situations where he must assume responsibility.

The insistence of psychoanalysts on the importance of the oral stage has stimulated much research on the relationship between infant feeding practices in the home and the later personality characteristics of the child. Some of this research will be discussed in Chapter 3.

The Anal Stage. The oral stage of development merges into and overlaps with the anal stage. Pleasure is derived through both holding in and through elimination. It is in this area that the child first most

clearly demonstrates mastery of his own impulses. Toilet training thus
becomes the medium through which the child's emerging ego (self-
control), his instinctual drives, and the demands of the outside world
come into conflict. For the psychoanalyst therefore, the techniques of
toilet training are seen as contributing importantly to personality development. Munroe (1955) writes:

> The child must give up his narcissistic omnipotence. If he can identify
> happily with the mother and accept her requirements as his own, the
> emerging pride in his personal mastery of instinctual impulses can be con-
> structively directed toward socially acceptable regulation. His own sense
> of achievement is enhanced by parental praise. On the other hand, if he is
> forced to *give up* his self-determination out of fear, whether of direct
> chastisement or severe loss of love, his inner determination tends to develop
> *in opposition to the outside world.* The upshot may be anxious effort at
> compliance, not from a shared interest in regulation but from fear of
> authority. Or there may be defiance instead. Or, most common of all, a
> mixture of the two. [P. 197.]

The psychosocial crisis that occurs during this period, according to
Erikson (1950, 1959), is that of *autonomy versus shame and doubt.* Autonomy is attained through the *gradual* attainment of self-control (not
parental control). If the outer control is too rigid or the training is too
early, the child develops a lasting sense of doubt and shame.

The Phallic Stage. About the fourth year, and continuing to approximately age six, libidinal energy appears to become more concentrated
on the genital zone. This period when the child finds erotic pleasure
mainly in the sexual organs themselves is called the phallic stage.
Developing during this stage is the Oedipus complex—the boy's sexual
interest in his mother, and the girl's interest in her father. The child
develops strong ambivalent feelings toward the parent of like sex, and,
as the parent is considered omnipotent, feelings of anxiety are generated. These feelings of anxiety are alleviated by the child's identifying with the parent of like sex. The parent's commands and image
become *introjected,* i.e., incorporated into the child's own psyche. The
child's views of parental attitudes are incorporated as his own, and
musts and must-nots come from within. The superego is formed.

Erikson calls the psychosocial crisis occurring during this period
(from about ages four to six) as *initiative versus guilt.* Increased ability
of the child to move around plus increased mastery of language permit
the child to take initiative in establishing interpersonal relationships.
In Erikson's words, the preschool child is "on the make." The child
selects social goals, seems to enjoy competition in attaining those goals,

and thrives on the pleasure of conquest. The boy does this "making" by head-on attack; the girl, by making herself attractive and endearing.

The resolution of the Oedipus conflict and the development of the superego may result in a too harsh sense of guilt over the goals sought. The conscience of the child *can* be primitive, cruel, and uncompromising. Later, conflicts over initiative may result in a self-restriction that stunts the individual's expression and development of thought and feelings.

The Latency Period. The latency period begins at about age six and continues until puberty. During this period, the sexual urges of the child are repressed. Energy is directed toward consolidating the relationships between ego, superego, and id as the child acquires new knowledge and skills and establishes new relationships to his peers. The child develops feelings of affection, especially toward children of his own sex. Parents are seen more objectively, and peers may even, on occasion, replace parental influence. According to Freudian theory, the energies of the child during this period are directed toward activities that serve as substitutes for activities once associated with libidinal urges. The child's curiosity about sex, for example, is extended to curiosity about how things work, and about the world around him. According to Freudian theory, the sexual curiosity would not extend to other realms if it had not been earlier frustrated and punished. But if the sexual curiosity had been too harshly punished, then during puberty, the child might repress curiosity because it would be too anxiety provoking.

Erikson (1950, 1959) describes the psychosocial crisis of the latency period as one of *industry versus inferiority*. The major problem of the child during this period is to become industrious and to attain competency through industry. In all cultures, at this period, children receive some systematic instruction. Failure to solve this problem leads to the development of a sense of inadequacy and inferiority. Erikson points out that formal education has tended to make one of two errors. Either the school is made a grim adult world in which the child is expected to develop self-restraint, a sense of duty, and do what he is told to do, or the school is made an extension of the play-world of the preschool child. Erikson criticizes both trends thus:

The first trend, if carried to the extreme, exploits a tendency on the part of the preschool and grammar-school child to become entirely dependent on prescribed duties. He thus learns much that is absolutely necessary and he develops an unshakable sense of duty; but he may never unlearn again an unnecessary and costly self-restraint with which he may later make his own life and other people's lives miserable, and in fact spoil his own children's natural desire to learn and to work. The second trend, when carried to an extreme, leads not only to the well-known popular objection that children do not learn anything any more but also to such feelings in children as are expressed in the by now famous remark of a metropolitan child who apprehensively asked one morning: "Teacher, *must* we do today what we *want* to do?" Nothing could better express the fact that children at this age *do* like to be mildly but firmly coerced into the adventure of finding out that one can learn to accomplish things which one would never have thought of by oneself, things which owe their attractiveness to the very fact that they are *not* the product of play and fantasy but the product of reality, practicality, and logic; things which thus provide a token sense of participation in the real world of adults. [1959, pp. 83–84.]

Erikson argues that both play and work make unique contributions to the development of the child during this period, and that the good teacher learns how to alternate play and work, games and study, so that in play the child has an opportunity to think through difficult experiences and, in effect, master experiences; and in work the child, through his industry, develops the pleasure of work completion.

Adolescence. The oral, anal, and phallic stages of development, taken together, are called the pregenital period. Sensual feelings, during the pregenital period, arise from self-stimulation. After the interruption of the latency period, sexual instincts begin to develop in the direction of other people. The adolescent begins to be attracted to members of the opposite sex. This final stage of development is called the genital stage.

Erikson contends that the major problem that the adolescent must work through is that of developing a sense of *ego identity*. In puberty and adolescence, the sameness and continuity in the previously learned patterns of relationships to others is distorted. Faced with a physiological revolution within himself, the adolescent becomes preoccupied with how he appears to others as compared with what he feels he is. He must cultivate new skills and new roles that permit a congruence between his changing self concepts and his changing self ideal. "The sense of ego identity, then, is the accrued confidence that one's ability to maintain inner sameness and continuity (one's ego in the psychological sense) is matched by the sameness and continuity of one's meaning for others." (Erikson, 1959, p. 89.)

The danger at this stage is *identity diffusion*. Erikson writes:

In general it is primarily the inability to settle on an occupational identity which disturbs young people. To keep themselves together they temporarily overidentify, to the point of apparent complete loss of identity, with the heroes of cliques and crowds. On the other hand, they become remarkably clannish, intolerant, and cruel in their exclusion of others who are "different," in skin color or cultural background, in tastes and gifts, and often in entirely petty aspects of dress and gesture arbitrarily selected as *the* signs of an in-grouper or out-grouper. It is important to understand (which does not mean condone or participate in) such intolerances as the necessary *defense against a sense of identity diffusion,* which is unavoidable at a time of life when the body changes its proportions radically, when genital maturity floods body and imagination with all manners of drives, when intimacy with the other sex approaches and is, on occasion, forced on the youngster, and when life lies before one with a variety of conflicting possibilities and choices. Adolescents help one another temporarily through such discomfort by forming cliques and by stereotyping themselves, their ideals, and their enemies [1959, p. 92.]

Fixation and Regression. It should be re-emphasized that the various stages of development are not completely distinct one from another. Libidinal satisfaction is not obtained exclusively from one region during any one stage. Nor are the psychosocial crises resolved once and for all in one stage of development. One stage merges into the next and the problems associated with a given stage tend to persist to some extent. Normally, a person progresses gradually and continuously from one stage to another. Sometimes, however, progress comes to a halt and a person remains at one stage. When this occurs in psychological growth, we say that the person has become *fixated.*

Fixation may occur because an individual experiences excessive satisfaction at one stage and hence is reluctant to move on to the next stage. Apparently, some deprivation and frustration is necessary to spur the individual to surrender the old and familiar in order to obtain the new and unfamiliar. The mother who gives in to the infant's protests at weaning is not providing the deprivation necessary for the child to move on to the next stage. The preschool child who finds complete satisfaction in the home may be reluctant to attend school. For college students, possibly the examination system generates sufficient frustration so that they willingly abandon the coziness of college life for the forbidding world of work.

Fixation may result from excessive frustration as well as excessive gratification. The infant requires a considerable amount of gratification of oral needs. If the infant's oral needs are too severely frustrated, then oral demands are likely to continue long past the normal period of renunciation. The adolescent seeking independence and constantly being denied opportunities to do things his own way may become fixated at the adolescent stage of development. According to Hartmann *et al.* (1947), normal development is stimulated by a large amount of indulgence combined with a small amount of frustration.

Hall (1954) lists three dangers that may contribute to the fixation of the individual at an immature level. These dangers are insecurity, failure, and punishment. The three dangers may be illustrated by the elementary school child who remains "tied to his mother's apron strings" rather than striving to gain peer-group acceptance. If the child is *insecure,* he may fear that he has not the *abilities* needed to participate actively in the activities of his peer group. Fear of *failure* may be due to the child's being apprehensive of ridicule for his unsuccessful efforts. Fear of *punishment* may take many forms. To behave in ways acceptable to the peer group may be too threatening because the child knows his mother would not approve. He may be afraid that by behaving in ways that are not approved by his mother he will lose her love and he is not sure that his new friends will compensate for this loss.

After reaching a certain stage of development, a person reacts to frustration and failure encountered by retreating to an earlier level. This is called *regression.* A child experiencing unhappiness may regress to more infantile behavior; e.g., temper tantrums, bed-wetting, etc. The high school girl who fails to attract the attention of a boy she admires may return to playing with her dolls. Rarely is the regression complete. Part of the energies of the person find outlet in the immature behavior and part in more mature activities.

Defense Mechanisms

The ego may cope with problems by distorting reality. This distortion is an unconscious process and is called a *defense mechanism.* Fixation and regression are examples of defense mechanisms. *Repression* is one defense mechanism that is central in psychoanalytic thinking. Repression is the keeping of some unacceptable thought, urge, wish, or painful experience out of consciousness. This is not done consciously. It is not the same thing as putting something out of mind. A traumatic event may be too painful to an individual to recall. The ego defends the organism by repressing the memory of the painful event. In Chapter 15 the various defense mechanisms will be discussed more extensively.

Observing from a Psychoanalytic Viewpoint

We have but sketchily discussed a few psychoanalytic concepts. However, enough has been said to suggest a few of the ways a teacher might utilize psychoanalytic concepts in observing the behavior of children.

1. Psychoanalytic points of view concerning the importance of the early developmental history of the child to his present personality status should help the teacher differentiate between what characteristics of the child are modifiable and what are not modifiable. A teacher would never be so unrealistic as to expect a child to grow one foot in height in twenty-four hours just because she told him to do so. A teacher would be equally unrealistic to expect the child who mistrusts others to become trustful of others overnight just because she told him to do so. The tendency of a child to be aggressive, or to be dependent, or to be outgoing, or shy and lacking in confidence, or the child's ability to control his own behavior—all these characteristics are examples of behavioral styles with a long developmental history. Such characteristics are not easily modifiable, and often the task of the teacher is to help the child find socially acceptable ways for expressing his basic personality characteristics.

2. A psychoanalytic point of view focuses attention on the over-all adjustment of the child. In observing from a reinforcement frame of reference, the observer may focus attention on any overt behavior of the child. In observing from a phenomenological frame of reference, the observer concentrates on how the child perceives himself and how he perceives his environment. From a psychoanalytic point of view, the observer concentrates his attention on forms of behavior indicative of the child's over-all adjustment. Attention may be focused more specifically upon behaviors related to a problem of particular importance in one developmental period (e.g., Erikson's industry versus inferiority psychosocial crises of the latency period).

3. A psychoanalytic point of view emphasizes that emotional maturity is not merely a matter of learning to conform. Hence, the progress of the child in becoming emotionally mature cannot be judged merely by observing how nicely he behaves. Emotional maturity may better be defined in terms of ego span. The child learns for an increasing number of life problems ways of behaving that are both personally satisfying and culturally approved.

4. In observing from a psychoanalytic frame of reference, one becomes acutely aware of the importance of unconscious motivation.

Learning Exercises

19. Identify the psychosexual stage in which each of the following is of central importance to the development of a healthy personality:
    (a) Gaining self-control without loss of self-esteem
    (b) Self-understanding
    (c) Developing confidence in the dependability of the environment

(d) Constructing, creating, accomplishing, mastering
(e) Self-direction
20. Match the concept in Column A to the definition or descriptive characteristic in Column B.

Column A	Column B
1. Libido	(a) Process through which superego is formed
2. Introjection	(b) Inability to settle on an occupational identity
3. Identity diffusion	(c) Basic energizer of any kind of activity
4. Fixation	(d) A return to a happier stage of development
5. Regression	(e) May occur because of no deprivation or frustration
6. Repression	(f) Keeping out of consciousness

SUMMARY

The characteristics of the observer, including his knowledge and concepts about phenomena observed, contribute importantly in determining what is observed. The term "frame of reference" is used in this chapter to denote a set of interrelated concepts which influence the observation and interpretation of an event. Three psychological frames of reference are discussed: reinforcement, phenomenological, and psychoanalytic.

A *reinforcement* learning theory frame of reference focuses attention on how *changes* in the behavior of the individual occur. Learning, from a reinforcement point of view, is explained in terms of classical and instrumental conditioning. We tend to repeat those responses that are reinforced. Historically, it is possible to identify three main explanations of reinforcement: (1) substitution, (2) effect, and (3) expectation.

Substitution explanation—the establishing and strengthening of the conditioned response by presenting the unconditioned stimulus shortly after presenting the conditioned stimulus. Classical conditioning experiments may serve as models for this type of reinforcement.

Effect explanation—Thorndike (1911) originally proposed the law of effect, which states in essence that responses that have satisfying consequences are strengthened, and those followed by discomfort or annoyance are weakened. Later, formulations of the law of effect make use of such terms as "drive reduction" or "tension reduction," rather than "satisfying," "discomfort," and "annoyance." *Reward* and *escape* training appear to fit well the effect explanation of reinforcement.

Expectancy explanation—reinforcement consists of a confirmation of an expectancy. When the learner perceives the significance of various features of the stimulus situation, he formulates expectations of the consequences of his response. When the consequences are what he expects, reinforcement is said to take place. In the expectancy explanation of reinforcement, behavior is considered to be *purposeful*. The expectancy explanation of reinforcement seems particularly appropriate in explaining *avoidance* and *omission* training experiments.

Observing individual behavior from a phenomenological frame of reference involves an effort to understand the *meaning* of a situation to the individual behaver at the moment of action. It is assumed that the behaver constantly tries to maintain and enhance his self concept. Changes in behavior occur as a result of a change in the behaver's phenomenological field. The phenomenological field includes all phenomena of which the behaver is aware in his present and past physical fields. It includes perceptions and concepts of self as well as perceptions of the environment. The phenomenological field is *reality* for the behaver. The behaver's past experience becomes relevant in observing only to the extent that it sheds light on the unique set of meanings that the behaver attaches to each new experience.

Information concerning the child's early developmental history becomes of importance in observing and interpreting individual behavior from a psychoanalytic point of view. The personality structure of an individual is viewed as consisting of three parts: the id, the ego, and the superego. Emotional maturity develops as the ego span of the individual expands and is strengthened. For an increasing number of life's problems, the individual learns ways of behaving that satisfy both the demands of the id and the superego.

The human being is viewed as an energy system, and the basic energy is called *libido*. In the course of development, the libido goes through a number of psychosexual stages. According to Erikson, the child experiences identifiable psychosocial crises in each psychosexual stage. Thus, in the latency period (from about age six to puberty) the child's major problem is *industry* versus *inferiority*. Through both play and work the child strives to prove to himself that he is a worthy, competent individual.

Unconscious motivation plays a large part in psychoanalytic theory. The behaver, for example, is not aware that his behavior is fixated at an immature level because of insecurity, fear of failure, or fear of punishment. The ego may distort reality in order to maintain the equilibrium. But this distortion is not a conscious process.

In observing from a psychoanalytic point of view, attention is focused on the over-all adjustment of the child.

Answer Cues

1. Both.

2. (b).

3. (b), (c).

4. UCS—food; CS—rattling pans; CR—the infant's anticipatory behavior.

5. (a) Secondary reward training; to say "Please"; smile. (b) Secondary reward training; causing a disturbance; teacher's anger. (c) Classical conditioning; liking of English; the "A" grade (association of English with pleasantness). (d) Avoidance learning; protesting behavior; reduction in length of assignment. (e) Escape training; seeking out friends who also are experiencing difficulties; reduction of feelings of unhappiness.

6. Reinforcing.

7. (a) Reinforcement. (b) Stimulus generalization. (c) Discrimination. (d) Response generalization. (e) Experimental extinction. (f) Spontaneous recovery.

8. (a) Self concept. (b) Motive. (c) Feeling.

9. Phenomenological or perceptual field.

10. No. For example, concepts of self may be included.

11. For individual A, the music constitutes *figure* and the people in the audience constitute *ground*. For individual B, his friend constitutes figure, and all else is ground.

12. Differentiation.

13. "I am a good bowler" is not part of the young lady's self concept.

14. Id.

15. Ego.

16. Superego.

17. From lowest to highest level: (c), (a), (b), (d).

18. With increased experience, the person has opportunity of discovering ways of behaving that satisfy both id and superego.

19. (a) Anal. (b) Adolescence. (c) Oral. (d) Latency. (e) Phallic.

20. 1c, 2a, 3b, 4e, 5d, 6f.

3

DEVELOPMENT

Developmental psychology is concerned with the psychological changes that occur with increasing age, and with the many conditions affecting the course of human development. The teacher endeavors to influence favorably the developmental process through selecting and structuring educational experiences that are appropriate to the child's developmental status. If all children were the same, this task of gearing educational experiences to developmental status would be relatively simple. But the teacher in the classroom is confronted with pupils varying in physical, intellectual, emotional, social, and personality characteristics. The teacher therefore needs to observe the developmental status of each individual child in the classroom. One child may learn slowly, another quickly; one child concentrates well on his lessons, another is easily distracted; one child appears happy and is well adjusted to his peers and to the demands placed upon him by the school, another child appears unhappy, is quarrelsome, and rebels against the demands of the school. In a multitude of ways, the children in one classroom differ. And a mere cataloguing of the ways in which the children differ serves no useful purpose. Observation needs to be systematic. The teacher needs to know what to look for in observing the behavior of the individual pupil and how to interpret observational data. Can we find in the field of developmental psychology facts and concepts that can be utilized by the teacher in more systematically observing the individual child? The answers to the following two questions provide one such promising frame of reference:

1. *What are the determinants of behavior?* To what extent does heredity limit the possibilities of the school in forwarding the development of children? Are, for example, personality traits modifiable? Must some desirable behavioral changes await maturation? To what extent does environment shape the individual?

An understanding of the extent to which constitutional and environmental factors determine the behavior of the individual should aid the teacher in discriminating between those behaviors of pupils that are modifiable and those that are not.

2. *What is normal development?* From birth onward the question "Am I normal?" is asked by the child, and the question "Is the child normal?" is asked by parent and teacher. The concept of normality has several meanings. Absence of pathology, socially acceptable behavior, average development, behavior typical of the average child, behavior indicative of good personal adjustment, or even ideal forms of behavior—any one of these may constitute the criterion of normality. Sometimes the expected behavior is what is considered as normal. The important point is that in observing and interpreting behavior, one or more criteria of normality is usually employed. Sometimes the criteria are unrealistic, as when the first-grade teacher expects her pupils to sit quietly in their seats all day without some chance for physical activity. The literature on developmental psychology contains a wealth of information on "normal" development and behavior. This information has potential value to the teacher in observing and interpreting individual behavior.

In this chapter, we will seek answers to three questions:

1. What is the constitutional basis for development?
2. What is the cultural basis of development?
3. What principles of development may be utilized in interpreting the developmental status of the normal child, and in predicting his later development?

CONSTITUTIONAL DETERMINANTS OF DEVELOPMENT

Today, there is considerable agreement among scientists concerning the contribution of nature and nurture to development. Both the contribution to development of heredity and maturation and the contribution of environment are recognized. Heredity sets a limit on the potential attainment of an individual. Maturation determines *when* optimum development can take place. Environment determines to what extent potential development is realized. In brief, development occurs as a result of an interaction between constitutional and environmental factors.

Heredity

The life of an individual begins when a *sperm cell* from the father unites with an *ovum* or egg from the mother to form a fertilized egg, called a *zygote*. Each of these germ cells (sperm and ova) contains 23 pairs of long threadlike bodies, called *chromosomes*. Each chromosome is made up of chains of chemical units, known as *genes*,[1] which are the bearers of heredity. Each gene has its own place in the chain and its distinctive function in inheritance. The action of many genes is required to produce a single inherited trait.

The child receives 46 chromosomes, half or 23 from each of his parents. The 46 chromosomes in the germ cell seem to divide at random. In all, the number of combinations of 23 chromosomes that could be derived from 23 pair is 2^{23} or 8,385,108. Thus, a human male can produce over 8 million genetically different sperms; and any one of these 8 million chromosome combinations in the sperm might unite with any one of the 8 million chromosome combinations in the ovum to form a single zygote. In addition, through a phenomenon known as *crossing-over*, genes from one chromosome occasionally exchange places with genes from another chromosome, thus, further increasing tremendously the number of different possible combinations. Except for identical twins formed from the same ovum and the same sperm, identical inheritance is not conceivable. Dobzhansky (1956, p. 56) estimates that the number of possible combinations of human genes with their possible mutations as "vastly greater than the number of atoms in the entire universe." Obviously, only an infinitesimal fraction of the possible gene combinations is, or ever can be, realized anywhere in the world. It should be added that the mechanics of heredity insure similarity as well as individual differences because whatever combination of chromosomes comprises the zygote, nothing can be there that was not contributed by one or the other parent.

In general, only physical or physiological characteristics are inheritable. These include structure of body and many physical peculiarities; normal fingers and toes; blood type; color of hair, skin, and eyes; amount of hair, and whether curly, kinky, or straight; normal or abnormal vision; color blindness; shape of ear and characteristics of structure of ear affecting hearing; blood pressure; allergies; lung structure that is susceptible or resistant to tuberculosis; etc. In addition, many characteristics are attributable to a combination of hereditary and environmental influences. Among such characteristics are health and vigor; mentality; stoutness or slenderness; and susceptibility to and immunity from various diseases.

---

[1] Some geneticists find it convenient to replace the term "gene" by the chemical components of the chromosome in developing a more penetrating analysis of the hereditary process. The chromosome has been shown to be composed mainly of protein and deoxyribonucleic acid (DNA). For these geneticists, it is the DNA molecules arranged in long chains that contain the hereditary materials. (See Gamow, 1955; Taylor, 1960.) However, the term "gene" is still widely used.

Before the beginning of the century, the conclusion was reached that acquired characteristics are not inheritable. This conclusion is still believed to be true. Genes are not changed during the course of living. A mother who plays a musical instrument or listens to classical music during pregnancy does nothing for the musical aptitude of the unborn child. College degrees and any improved intellectual functioning derived therefrom are not inheritable. Acquired appreciation of beauty and acquired morality or immorality are not directly inheritable from father and mother to son and daughter. The father who learns to become an alcoholic does not biologically transmit his learned craving to his children. This does not mean that the acquired characteristics of the parent do not influence the development of the child. The child may develop traits that are similar to his parents because of the environment provided by the parents.

Learning Exercises

1. Match the term in Column A to the descriptive phrase in Column B:

Column A
1. Chromosome
2. Gene
3. Zygote
4. Dominant gene

Column B
(a) Fertilized egg produced by union of sperm cell and ovum
(b) Long threadlike bodies in germ cell
(c) Bearers of heredity
(d) Determiner of physical characteristics in offspring

2. If you were asked the following questions in a high school biology class, what answers would you give to each question?
   (a) If a married Caucasian couple move to a tropical climate, would their children be born dark complexioned?
   (b) Do children who are born out of wedlock inherit a more delicate constitution than legitimate children?
   (c) Is musical ability inherited?

Maturation and Readiness

With the passage of time, certain developmental changes occur within the child that are primarily due to heredity. The child grows larger, and in time his body proportions change. Myelinization of nerves leading from the bladder and rectum occurs, and with this change the child is ready for toilet training. Changes occur with age in the functioning of the endocrine glands. During adolescence, increasing amounts of sex hormones and adrenal androgens are produced that stimulate the development of the reproductive organs. The term "maturation" refers to such developmental changes—anatomic, physiologic, and chemical—that are due to heredity and will occur with the passage of time within a normal environment. Note that the "normal environment" is conceived as permitting or supporting development rather than determining development. Olson (1959) expresses the relationship between maturation, nurture, and development in the form of an equation:

$$\text{Maturation} \times \text{Nurture} = \text{Development}$$

Olson delineates the role of maturation thus:

The term *maturation* refers to the unfolding of a design which is essentially hereditary in origin. Maturation is frequently thus confined to sequences and patterns which are innate and over which no external influence has any power. Maturation includes the fact that the nervous system often anticipates a new function; that is, the environment does not create the function. The progression is assured by internal factors and the environment supports the changes but does not generate them. . . . [P. 17.]

The concept "maturation" is of importance to the educator when considered in relationship to the concept "learning." Learning is a process through which a change of behavior or level of performance occurs as a result of training or experience. Most behavioral changes are due to an interaction between maturation and learning. Maturation is of importance in determining *when* a child is ready for a particular learning experience, but the child has to have the training or experience in order to learn. Thus, to learn to walk, the child must have adequate bone and muscle development (largely maturation) plus the experience of trying to walk (learning).

It is not possible to hurry the acquisition by the child of certain motor skills, particularly during the first two years. This is well illustrated in a study reported by Gesell and Thompson (1941). Identical twins (designated as twin T and twin C) were given training in climbing a small staircase consisting of four treads and a platform that formed the fifth tread. At the age of 46 weeks, neither twin was able to place a foot or a knee on the first tread while the experimenter held both of a twin's hands. Twin T was given a daily 10-minute practice period on the stairs. At the end of six weeks, twin T could climb the steps in about 25 seconds, while twin C was able only to put his left knee on the first tread. Then twin T's training was stopped, and a week later twin C began a two-week training period (from ages 53 to 55 weeks). In these two weeks, twin C was able to climb the stairs as well as twin T who had had six weeks of training. One week later when the twins were 56 weeks old, their performances on the steps were practically equal. Thus, the *two* weeks of training starting at age 53 weeks for twin C resulted in as much progress as the six weeks of training starting at age 46 weeks for twin T.

For the school-aged child, maturation is one of three factors determining the *readiness* of the child for any specific learning task. The degree of success the child has encountered before entering school in acquiring information, mastering concepts, and developing intellectual skills is a second factor determining the readiness of a child for his first year in school. For each successive grade, the pupil's success in learning is dependent in part on the adequacy of his past learning. A third factor determining readiness is the child's motivation. Children, like adults, work harder at tasks they perceive as means to meeting their needs and attaining their goals.

Children entering the first grade differ in their readiness to profit from instruction. A study conducted by Donnelly (1935) illustrates the extent of differences in the success of children in acquiring a basic sight vocabulary during their first year in school. Donnelly constructed a test of 150 primary-grade-level words. The test was administered individually to 389 pupils in seven first-grade classrooms in Massachusetts. At the end of a nine-month period of instruction, some pupils could recognize all 150 words; others could recognize none. The most proficient 10 per cent of the pupils did better after *three* months' instruction than the least proficient 10 per cent of the pupils after *nine* months.

Flanagan (1964) reports that the Project TALENT survey of 440,000 high school students revealed that 25 to 30 per cent of ninth-grade students know more about many school subjects than the average twelfth-grade student, and that the top 5 per cent of the students in a grade can learn the English meanings of twice as many foreign words as the average student can in the same study time.

As a result of studies indicating that many children experience difficulty in learning to read during the first grade, an effort has been made to identify the factors involved in reading readiness. Some of the factors are (1) mental age, (2) vision, (3) hearing, (4) health and vigor, (5) emotional adjustment, (6) adjustment to school, (7) desire to read, and (8) background of experience and learning. It may be noted that factors dependent upon maturational processes are included in the above list, but past learning and motivational factors are also included.

There is some evidence that less training is required for the more mature child to reach a given level of proficiency. Wood and Freeman

(1932) conducted an experiment in typing in the first five grades of an elementary school. After one year of practice, fifth-grade children were typing at better than twice as many words per minute as the children in grade 2. The experiment went on for two years. It was found that children with two years of typing were typing no faster than children of the same grade who had only one year of typing experience.

Dunkel and Pillet (1957) compared the performance in French of elementary school pupils and college freshmen. After three years' instruction in French, the elementary school pupils were somewhat behind the level achieved by college freshmen after one term. However, about 43 per cent of the elementary school children would have passed the freshman test in French reading, and about 80 per cent would have passed a test in aural comprehension.

Research studies such as the Wood and Freeman and the Dunkel and Pillet studies are of the O→R type. For such studies, the organismic variable is usually age or grade level, and the response variable is some measure of achievement. There is no stimulus variable in these studies, as the method of instruction is not varied.

It is well to recognize the limitations of the findings of readiness research of the O→R type. First, the findings of a single readiness research study hold true only for the particular method of instruction employed in the study. This means that we should regard as tentative recommendations as to the age or grade level for teaching children the concepts and skills of any subject in the curriculum—even when the recommendations are based upon readiness research. Newer and improved methods of instruction may make it possible to teach certain skills to children at a much earlier age than is now customary. There have been numerous reports in recent years of children, aged two to five, learning to read, write, and spell (Tyler, 1964; Pitman, 1963) and of children in the lower primary grades learning mathematical processes that are usually taught in the high school (Bruner, 1960, 1964a).

A second limitation of the findings of readiness research of the O→R type is evident when we turn our attention to the response variable. It is possible for the child to learn undesirable but unmeasured responses as well as desirable skills during the course of instruction. Tyler (1964) cautions:

Too little is known about these attempts to teach young children more "complex" ideas and skills for us to be able to assess them in any realistic sense. However, even if it be demonstrated that young children can learn this or that "advanced" process, we should still need to decide whether it is desirable and appropriate for them to do so. Sociologically, we may ask whether this is the best way for children to spend their time and energy.

Intellectually, we may ask whether this is the most suitable preparation for future intellectual activities. Emotionally, we may ask whether "early" systematic instruction in reading, mathematics, or what have you, will have a harmful effect upon motivation, or upon personal and social behavior . . . instruction can be introduced prematurely; it can as truly be delayed unduly. Soft sentimentality may be damaging to the personality; so, too, may exces sively high expectations and requirements. [Pp. 223–24.]

Learning Exercises

3. What research evidence reported above supports each of the following generalizations?
   (a) Developmental rate remains uniform within very wide limits of encouragement and training.
   (b) Less training is required by the more mature child to reach a given level of proficiency.
4. Cook (1948) has pointed out that from a random group of six-year-olds entering the first grade, 2 per cent of them may be below the average four-year-old in general intelligence, and 2 per cent above the average eight-year-old. A four-year range in general intelligence may be expected for the remainder of the group. By the time the six-year-olds reach the sixth grade, this range may be expected to increase from four years to about eight years. In the light of these facts, what individual differences in readiness may be expected within a single classroom?

CULTURAL BASIS OF DEVELOPMENT

The human infant could not survive if he were completely dependent upon his natural resources. In all cultures, infants are nursed, subjected to restrictions for their own protection, and provided with care and training. The precise child care practices vary from culture to culture. The Balinese mother, for example, feeds the child when he is flat on his back and helpless. Despite the child's discomfort, the mother forces food into the baby's mouth until he is stuffed. In the light of this practice, it is understandable that the Balinese view eating as something unpleasant. If the Balinese eats in public, he consumes his food rapidly and eats as though the process was something of which to be ashamed (Bateson and Mead, 1942). It is interesting to note a parallel in our own culture in toilet training, commonly begun too early and continued too harshly. Possibly the furtive behavior practiced with toilet habits is a product of early experience.

As we discuss the cultural basis of development, let us keep two questions in mind: (1) "What aspects of the culture exert an impact on the individual?" and (2) "What behaviors, percepts, and motives of the individual are modified by the culture?" The first question focuses attention on the stimulus variable; the second question directs attention to mediating processes and response variables.

Culture

The term "culture" encompasses "the pattern of all those arrangements, material or behavioral, whereby a particular society achieves for its members greater satisfactions than they can achieve in a state of nature" (English and English, 1958, p. 133). It includes all the learned behaviors shared by most members of a society and handed down from one generation to another. Studies by cultural anthropologists have yielded a wealth of information on ways in which the beliefs, attitudes, values, arts, morals, laws, and customs vary from one culture to another. The language, religion, ethics, family unit, housing, governmental organization, and social stratification—to name but a few categories—vary from culture to culture.

Cultural Norms. Cultural norms serve as standards even for judging the body appearance, face, voice, and personality of others. In our culture, for example, considerable agreement exists among males as to the ideal body proportions for young ladies; and marked deviations from this cultural ideal are observed and characterized with words such as "skinny" or "fat." In Central Africa, beauty is almost equated with obesity. At puberty, the girl is placed in the "fatting house" and fed with sweet and fatty foods, sometimes for years. Her period of seclusion ends with a parade in all her corpulent grandeur, followed by her marriage to her proud bridegroom (Benedict, 1934). In our culture, much folklore has developed about the face and its expression, the voice and a person's manner of speaking, and the amount of bodily activity (Henry, 1949). Facial features may be described as "sharp"; voices as "shrill"; and a person as "restless." Each description implies some deviation from a cultural norm.

"Goodness" in our culture is a very complex concept. The task of building the structure of goodness in the child is regarded as the principal task of the parent in the formative years. Goodness usually means conforming to the wishes of adults. But every situation in our culture has different goodness demands: goodness at home is not the same as goodness at school; goodness on the playground is not the same as goodness at church; goodness in one socioeconomic class may deviate somewhat from goodness in another socioeconomic class; goodness at one age level is not always the same as goodness at another age level; and goodness for mother is sometimes different from goodness for father.

Basic Personality Structure.   There is general agreement that culture is of importance in shaping the life style of an individual.   There is less agreement among social scientists as to *how* important culture is. Kardiner (1945), for example, views the cultural surroundings as *the* determinants of the personality growth pattern.   He has developed the concept of the *basic personality structure,* which he defines as "that personality configuration which is shared by the bulk of the society's members as a result of the early experiences which they have in common" (pp. vi–viii).   The process is conceptualized thus:

1. Cultural tradition determines what lessons the parents will teach the child, and how the lessons are taught.
2. Different cultures have different lessons to teach and different ways of training the child.
3. A lasting effect upon the child's personality is exerted by his early experiences.
4. Therefore, similar experiences will tend to produce similar personalities within a culture.

The amount of research on basic personality structure is extensive. Much of this research pertains to relationships between early child rearing practices, such as where the child sleeps, whether he is breast-fed or not, when he is weaned, how toilet training proceeds, and how he is punished, and personality characteristics.   Sears and Wise (1950), for example, studied the relationship between age of weaning and the degree to which the infant gave indications of emotional disturbance. They found a tendency for the child who was weaned later to show more emotional disturbance.   That this might not be true for all cultures is suggested by a cross-cultural study reported by Whiting and Child (1953).   Material on the same variables, i.e., age of weaning and emotionality, was collected from a sample of 37 societies scattered throughout the world.   They found that, between cultures, late weaning was associated with less emotionality.   As may be seen from Fig. 3–1, the age of weaning was much later for the 37 societies investigated by Whiting and Child than for the children in Kansas City.

The concept of a basic personality structure is reflected in many studies of national character (Inkeles and Levinson, 1954).   One of the difficulties in studies of national character is that culture does not follow national lines alone.   Races, religions, occupations, social classes, and geographic regions within a nation cut across national boundaries.

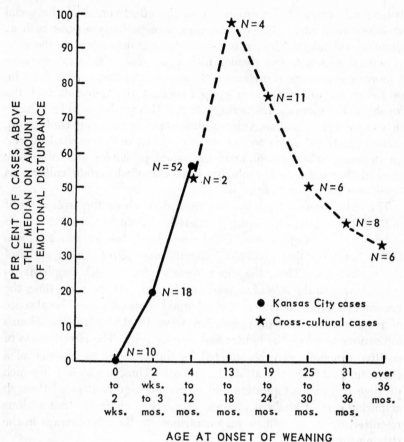

Fig. 3–1. Relation Between Age at Onset of Weaning and Amount of Emotional Disturbance Shown by Child. Comparable data from 80 individual children from Kansas City (Sears and Wise, 1950) and from 37 societies (Whiting and Child, 1953) are presented. (From J. W. M. Whiting, "The Cross-cultured Method." In Gardner Lindzey (ed.), *Handbook of Social Psychology*, 1954, vol. I, p. 525, Addison-Wesley, Reading, Mass.)

Yet it is a fact that people in different nations live under different social systems. Further, the appropriate behavior patterns for individuals performing different roles, such as father, older sibling, teacher, and employee, differ somewhat from nation to nation. More important are the internation differences in the system of *social sanctions*—the rewards and punishments meted out to group members by other individuals and the group at large for adherence to or departure from the behavioral norms of the group. Too, the effectiveness of the social sanctions may vary. The effectiveness of negative sanctions such as shaming, ridicule, or charges of wrong-doing is dependent on the individual's readiness to feel shame, ridicule, or guilt. Dicks (1952) notes a more-than-average readiness on the part of the Russian "to share in, or be aware of, offences in oneself against the demands and the loyalty to the group." Dicks suggests that this readiness to feel shame may explain the Russians' vulnerability to public shaming, confessions, and recantations. Differences between cultures in the emphasis placed on shaming, ridiculing, or involving moral principles are sufficiently marked that some anthropologists have classified certain cultures as "guilt" or "shame" cultures.

The effectiveness of positive sanctions depends on the aspirations of individuals to attain the rewards offered. While in all cultures individuals aspire to attain rewards of some kind, Inkeles and Levinson (1954) point out that psychological traits may affect the strengths of the aspirations. Thus, the Sioux society places much emphasis on achievement in the role of warrior and hunter. At the same time, the presence of large amounts of undischarged aggression plus the absence of negative sanctions on aggression serve to strengthen the Sioux's aspirations to adopt the hunter and warrior role. The effectiveness of positive sanctions may be affected by the presence or absence of a character trait that helps attain the reward. Thus, in a society in which prestige is a major aspiration and where prestige is attained through acquiring certain kinds of physical property, a character trait such as retentiveness or miserliness may contribute to the effectiveness in the striving for prestige.

Learning Exercises

5. How is the concept "culture" similar in meaning to the concept of a "basic personality structure"? How is it different?
6. Billy, age eight, beats Tom in a fistfight, thus earning a new respect from his classmates. Percival informs the teacher about Billy and Tom's playground battle, thus earning the scorn of the other members in the class. Identify an example of positive sanctions and an example of negative sanctions in this drama.
7. Erikson (1950) contends that American behavior in a group is characterized by an emphasis on the principle that there accrue to each group member "claims for future privileges on the basis of one's past concessions." Erikson sees this pattern arising out of the American family life where each member is regarded as having rights and interests equally

to be protected. Assuming this characterization of the American family pattern is correct, what parallels do you see in the operation of the American political structure?

Group Membership

Membership in various subgroups, as well as in the larger culture, affects the behavior of an individual and often an individual's basic personality structure. The subgroup may vary in size from groups composed of all people of the same religion, sex, occupation, social class, or geographic region to smaller groups of one's fraternity or sorority, informal cliques, clubs, gangs, or the small (but tremendously influential) family unit. Each group establishes its own set of behavioral norms—the way members of the group are expected to behave in certain situations. Each group works out a system of social sanctions through which the individual member is rewarded for adherence to and punished for deviation from the group norms. The term "reference group" is used by social psychologists to define a group with which an individual identifies, or with which he would like to be identified. A reference group serves as a yardstick in judging which aspirations, values, beliefs, and behavior patterns are commendable and which are not. The reference group also serves the individual in evaluating his own worth. The fact that each individual belongs to several groups contributes to individual differences in personality. That it may lead also to conflict is demonstrated daily. For example, the adolescent may experience conflict as a result of differences between the social norms of his family and those of his peer group.

Learning Exercise

8. James Horton became part of a teen-age gang while in grade 7. In grade 9, members of the gang, in search of "kicks," began "borrowing" cars after school hours. One day members of the gang met with a serious accident. The car they had "borrowed" was wrecked, and James along with other members of the gang faced court charges. Several members of the gang, including James, came from good families where they had been taught to respect property and never to steal. How might the terms *"group norms," "reference groups,"* and *"social sanctions"* be used in providing one possible (and partial) explanation of James's behavior?

Role and Status

A *role* has been defined as "a patterned sequence of learned *actions* or deeds performed by a person in an interaction situation" (Sarbin,

1954, p. 225). An individual during the course of one day may assume many roles. Thus, a girl in school assumes the role of *student;* between periods chatting with another student, she may assume the role of *friend;* returning home she assumes the role of *daughter;* and later attending a dance with her date, she may assume the role of *sweetheart.* It is not difficult to appreciate the fact that the learned actions or deeds that are appropriate to one role are not appropriate to another role. Quite different skills, behaviors, and personality characteristics are expected for different roles.

The numerous roles assumed by an individual frequently conflict. To study or to attend a fraternity party may constitute a role conflict situation for the college student, particularly if an important test is scheduled in the near future. It may prove useful to examine what Allport (1961) refers to as "four meanings of role" in order to obtain some basis for predicting how our student would resolve his "study or party" conflict:

1. Role-Expectations. Role expectations are located in the social system of which the student is a part. How is the student expected to fulfill his role as a fraternity member by (*a*) his instructor, adviser, academic dean, etc,; (*b*) his fraternity brothers; (*c*) his family; and (*d*) other important reference groups?
2. Role-Conception. Each individual defines his role in his own way, and the way a person defines his role may or may not correspond to the role expectations of society.
3. Role-Acceptance. There are students who accept their roles as students and others who rebel against their roles as students. There are fraternity members who fully accept their roles as fraternity members and others who do not.
4. Role-Performance. Role performance depends upon all the foregoing conditions—what the expectations from each role are, how the student conceives his roles, and how he accepts each role.

Each role has certain status conditions associated with it that are determined by the particular group or culture. *Status* refers to the position of the individual in the prestige system of his society. We will now examine how the social structure of the school affects the individual student.

Social Structure of a School

Each classroom evolves, as the school year progresses, into a miniature society that includes a set of behavioral norms; a system of social sanctions; and a variety of roles such as classmate, member of the football team, president of the class, student, president of the debating club, and teacher.

Students and the teacher in a class form role expectations; i.e., each class member expects each role in the class to be performed in a particular way. Each individual forms conceptions of his own particular roles, and each individual varies in the degree to which he accepts or rejects his roles.

The influence of interpersonal relationships on adolescent behavior is well illustrated in one intensive study of the social structure of a suburban high school (called Wabash School) in a midwestern community (Gordon, 1957). Gordon presents evidence indicating that at Wabash the individual student obtained status primarily through (1) grade placement (i.e., seniors tended to have higher status than freshmen; and (2) academic grades (i.e., the higher the grade point average, the higher the status). However, academic grades were not a pure measure of scholastic achievement. Attitude and conduct of the student were taken into consideration in assigning grades. Gordon suggests that social class factors, the status position of the student in the school's organizations, and even the attractiveness of physically mature girls seemed to influence the grades assigned by some teachers. An upward trend in grade average was noted between grade 9 and grade 12. While this is explainable in part because poorer students dropped out of school, Gordon notes a second factor: ". . . the adaptation students made to teachers as they assimilated the student lore which defined, 'what teachers expect,' 'how to pass,' and 'how to get a grade.' Apparently, we need a distinction between *grade achievement*, grades assigned on the basis of technical competence, and *grades attained* as a result of the manipulation of the grade givers" (p. 37).

Student organizations at Wabash provided a structure for status striving. More prestige was attached to some organizations than others. The top five prestige organizations, as rated by the students, were (1) student assembly, (2) varsity basketball, (3) varsity football, (4) honors society, and (5) cheer leaders. The bottom five prestige organizations were (1) roller skating club, (2) outdoor club, (3) pencil pushers (creative writing), (4) riding club, and—the lowest in the hierarchy—(5) knitting club. There is some evidence in the Gordon study that teachers did not fully realize the potentials of the student organizations. One eleventh-grader expressed herself thus:

Many of the students who are chosen by the teachers to be on Yearbook or Bugle and many of the Student Assembly committees were very mischosen. . . . There are a lot of kids who really want to be on these things but the teachers just get in a rut and choose the same people year after year just because they don't want to be bothered with showing somebody new how things run. They pick up the same bunch of kids for everything and they don't do as good a job because they know that they will get chosen the next year anyway so why should they worry. So I guess your school success is based on how many clubs and committees you have beside your picture in the Yearbook. [Pp. 64–65.]

The informal organization at Wabash was found to parallel the formal student organization. A prestige hierarchy of cliques existed in each of the eight grade-sex divisions of the high school. For example, five large cliques among grade 12 boys were identified. These were, in order of their social prestige, (1) the athletic crowd, (2) the music and club activity crowd, (3) the dating crowd, (4) the "brainy" crowd, and (5) the hunting and fishing crowd. Economic status was one but not the sole factor of importance to a student's status in the informal organization. Personality factors, physical prowess, dating success, and clothing were among the other factors related to status.

Behavioral Norms and Social Sanctions. Students high in general social status at Wabash were found to be influential in administering positive and negative social sanctions and in setting standards. The "big wheel" at Wabash was usually a senior, an athlete, a member of a prestige clique, successful in dating, a member of many prestige student organizations, and having plenty of clothes. With respect to meeting the expectations of the dating pattern, Gordon observes:

The boy who successfully dated for a major social function was concerned with conformity to the following expectations:

1. *The girl:* She must be asked in the proper manner, the appropriate time in advance. . . .
2. *Transportation:* The car was essential . . . "Walking is for birds and freshmen."
3. *Money:* ". . . The complete date involved going to some approved place into the city where expenditure of money was necessary."
4. *Behavior:* Behavior tended to be labelled with clichés. Approved behavior was "rite," "neat," "george," and "okay." Disapproved behavior was "fruit," "drippy," or "clyde" . . .
5. *Where to go after the dance?* The social function was not the important topic of discussion the next day but, "Where did you go afterwards?" "When did you leave the dance?" "What time did you get home?"
6. *Time of arrival at the party:* "Big wheels" arrived and left at the correct time. . . . The party began and ended with the arrival and departure of the pattern setters.
7. *Interaction at parties was limited largely to dates and cliques:* There was much inhibition about mixing. One didn't dance till certain groups were on the floor. "Cutting in" was not approved. [Pp. 126–27.]

The application of negative sanctions by a "big wheel" is illustrated in the following comment of a grade 12 boy: "Vance keeps everyone else in line on dress. He is always making fun of someone else's clothes. He'll say, 'Look at that guy's socks. Is he a 'fruit?' You gradually get on to what to wear. I gradually became aware . . ." (Gordon, 1957, p. 121.)

Rebellion or Conformity? Coleman (1961), in a study of student bodies in eleven high schools, reports findings that parallel those of Gordon. The schools in Coleman's study were carefully selected to reflect a wide range of differences in size of community and social backgrounds of the students. In all schools, the importance for boys of being a "star athlete" and for girls of being an "activities leader" was greater than being a "brilliant scholar."

Coleman interprets his findings as evidence that adolescent and adult educational goals are in conflict, and that the modern adolescent looks increasingly to each other for psychological support and social reward rather than to his parents, teachers, and other adults. Havighurst and Neugarten (1957) offer an alternative interpretation. These writers suggest that at the present time in the United States, there is an emphasis upon "getting along," and that: "the adolescent who stresses the importance of popularity may be reflecting directly the values of the adult" (p. 136). Other writers too have noted a trend toward conformity, a desire for a cozy togetherness and an avoidance of conflict. Friedenberg (1959) views adolescence as a period of self-definition in which youth strives to discover who he is, what he feels and believes, what he can do, and what he wants to become. In accomplishing this task, the adolescent must become independent and differentiate himself from the culture. This process necessarily entails conflicts. But society increasingly stresses the ideal of conformity. Individuality is not valued. Conflicts are feared as disturbances by parents and teachers rather than valued for their growth potential. Under these conditions, argues Friedenberg, it is becoming increasingly difficult for the adolescent to define himself through conflict with society.

Social Class

Results from a host of investigations of the social class structure of a number of American communities point to the pervasive influence of class membership on the behavior of individuals. While differences in social status range along a continuum with imperceptible gradations from person to person, psychologists and sociologists have been able to identify in various communities investigated the presence of from three to six distinct classes. Each class is marked off from other classes by differences in privileges and disprivileges, differences in value systems, and differences in behavioral styles of living. While in theory each American is free to associate with whomever he chooses, in practice association between members of different classes somehow or other is subtly restricted. For example, West (1945) found in the community he studied that church, clubs, and other organizations were status-bound units, even though in many everyday activities, males crossed stratification lines. Mills (1951) in a study of marriages in one community found that people tend to choose marriage mates from their own social class.

Measuring Social Class. A number of scales have been devised to measure the social status of an individual. Warner and his associates (1949) have developed the Index of Status Characteristics that has been found to correlate highly with social class participation and family reputation as evaluated by the community. As the scale is relatively

TABLE 3–1
Primary Rating Scales of Four Status Characteristics

OCCUPATION (original scale)	SOURCE OF INCOME
1. Professionals and proprietors of large businesses	1. Inherited wealth
2. Semiprofessionals and smaller officials of large businesses	2. Earned wealth
3. Clerks and kindred workers	3. Profits and fees
4. Skilled workers	4. Salary
5. Proprietors of small businesses	5. Wages
6. Semiskilled workers	6. Private relief
7. Unskilled workers	7. Public relief and non-respectable income
HOUSE TYPE (original scale)	DWELLING AREA
1. Large houses in good condition	1. Very high; Gold Coast, North Shore, etc.
2. Large houses in medium condition; medium-sized houses in good condition	2. High; the better suburbs and apartment house areas; houses with spacious yards, etc.
3. Large houses in bad condition	3. Above average; areas all residential, larger than average space around houses; apartment areas in good condition, etc.
4. Medium-sized houses in medium condition; apartments in regular apartment buildings	
5. Small houses in good condition; small houses in medium condition; dwellings over stores	4. Average; residential neighborhoods, no deterioration in the area
6. Medium-sized houses in bad condition; small houses in bad condition	5. Below average; area not quite holding its own, beginning to deteriorate, business entering, etc.
7. All houses in very bad condition; dwellings not intended originally for homes	6. Low; considerably deteriorated, rundown and semislum
	7. Very low; slum

Adapted from Warner et al. (1949, p. 123). Reproduced by permission.

simple and easy to apply, it may serve to make more concrete the meaning of various social class groupings. Table 3–1 presents one edition of this scale. For the occupation and house-type categories, the original scales rather than the revised scales are included in Table 3–1. For more precise information regarding the application of the scales as well as an understanding of the rationale underlying the assignments of ratings, see Warner *et al.* (1949, chap. 9).

To obtain a single numerical rating on the scale for an individual, the numerical value accorded in each category is multiplied by an assigned weight value. The rating for occupation is multiplied by 4; the ratings for source of income and the weighting for house type are each multiplied by 3; and the rating for dwelling area is multiplied by 2. The following hypothetical case is illustrative:

Status Characteristic	Rating	Assigned Weight	Rating Weight
Occupation	6	4	24
Source of Income	5	3	15
House Type	5	3	15
Dwelling Area	4	2	8
		Total	62

Once a total score is obtained, the social class equivalent may be obtained by consulting Table 3–2. Note that, for the above example, a score of 62 places an individual in the upper-lower class.

TABLE 3–2

Social Class Equivalents for I.S.C. Ratings for Old Americans, Jonesville

Weighted Total of Ratings	Social Class Equivalents
12–17	Upper Class
18–22	Upper Class probably, with some possibility of Upper-Middle Class
23–24	Indeterminate; either Upper or Upper-Middle Class
25–33	Upper-Middle Class
34–37	Indeterminate; either Upper-Middle or Lower-Middle Class
38–50	Lower-Middle Class
51–53	Indeterminate; either Lower-Middle or Upper-Lower Class
54–62	Upper-Lower Class
63–66	Indeterminate; either Upper-Lower or Lower-Lower Class
67–69	Lower-Lower Class probably, with some possibility of Upper-Lower Class
70–84	Lower-Lower Class

From Warner *et al.* (1949, p. 127). Reproduced by permission.

It should be noted that the population for any given community would rarely, if ever, be distributed evenly throughout the six class levels. Warner (1949, p. 14) presents the following percentages for his six class scales based upon studies of communities in New England:

Upper-Upper	1.4%
Lower-Upper	1.6%
Upper-Middle	10.0%
Lower-Middle	28.0%
Upper-Lower	34.0%
Lower-Lower	25.0%

Learning Exercise

9. According to Warner's I.S.C. scale, to what social class would a dentist belong whose source of income was fees, who lived in a medium-sized house in good condition in one of the better suburbs of a city?

Class Consciousness. Certain factors in American life tend to minimize class consciousness. First, upward social mobility is possible through such means as acquiring wealth, entrance into a prestige occupation, higher education, or marriage. To move into the upper-upper class is difficult in many communities because of the importance attached to "old families," i.e., families who have occupied prestige positions in the community for generations. Mobility is facilitated by the acquisition of wealth if accompanied by the "right" kind of house in the "right" neighborhood with the "right" furniture, and, above all, the "proper" set of behaviors. Education, particularly at the lower end of the class scale, facilitates social mobility. A second important factor minimizing class consciousness is the verbally subscribed set of democratic ideals concerning the equality of man. Davis, Gardner, and Gardner (1941) in studying the social perspectives of the social classes in the deep South found that individuals classified as lower-lower class tended to perceive themselves as "People just as good as anybody."

While individuals in the American culture do not tend to perceive people in higher classes as their superiors, they do perceive people in lower classes as their inferiors. Davis and his associates (1941, p. 19) report that the people in his middle class categories tended to perceive lower class people as a "No 'count' lot." People in the upper-lower class, while perceiving themselves as "Poor but honest folk," perceived people of the lower-lower class as "Shiftless people."

People in the lower classes apparently are conscious that people in higher classes tend to regard themselves as superior. Davis *et al.* report that lower-middle class people characteristically view people in the upper-middle class as "People who think they are somebody." And the lower-lower class sees the upper-lower class as "Snobs trying to push up" (Davis *et al.*, p. 19). As we shall see later, this aspect of class consciousness constitutes a troublesome part of the social class problem facing the school.

Most people are not able to identify with accuracy their own social class status (or, at least, they classify themselves differently than would a sociologist). In 1940, *Fortune* magazine questioned many people to find out what class they would claim to belong to—upper, middle, or lower. Only 8 per cent placed themselves in the lower class (as compared to 59 per cent on the basis of Warner's classification), while 79 per cent identified themselves as middle class.

Social Class Behavioral Differences. How do children from the various social classes differ in behavioral characteristics? Obtaining an answer to this question is of particular importance to the educator because of the fact that most teachers cherish middle class values; and, as Martin and Stendler (1959) point out:

> Middle-class teachers may try to teach the virtues of thrift, nonaggressiveness, care of property, respect for authority, cleanliness, and getting ahead to children who come from families with quite different values. They may teach their pupils that "nice" people don't swear, whereas the child from the slums may count among his friends and relatives many with a rich and pungent vocabulary. [P. 354.]

Davis (1948), in his book on the influence of social class on learning, found systematic differences between classes in their attitudes toward education. Middle and upper class parents typically have a favorable attitude toward education and reward their children for academic achievement. Lower-lower class parents are much less favorably disposed to the school. Davis found that the child from the lower-lower class home is taught by his peers to regard school as a trap, and to circumvent tasks imposed by school. Lower class children find contradictions between the teachings of home and school. A somewhat better attitude exists with upper-lower class parents who view education as a means of vocational preparation, although not believing in the intrinsic value of education for its own sake.

There are class differences in the educational and vocational goals set by parents for their children. Characteristically, upper and middle class parents expect their children to go to college. Upper-lower class parents feel that their children should finish high school but not neces-

sarily college and have lower vocational goals for them than those of
the parents in the higher classes. This is reflected in a study by Hollingshead (1949). Adolescents in a midwestern community (Elmtown)
were classified into five social classes: Class I, II, III, IV, and V. As one
part of the study, adolescents were asked to list the occupation they
wished to follow. Only 7 per cent of the children from the lowest
social class (Class V) listed business and professional occupations as
compared to 77 per cent of the children from the two highest social
classes (Classes I and II). Of importance to planners of school guidance programs is Hollingshead's finding that 41 per cent of the children
from the lowest social class had not made a vocational choice. Only 3
per cent of the children from the two highest social class groups
reported that they were undecided as to a vocational goal.

It is generally found that children of higher social classes do better
on intelligence tests than do children from the lower classes (Neff,
1938). This may be due to an intellectual superiority (on the average)
of the higher status children. However, there are non-intellectual
factors that may explain, at least in part, the differences in performance.
Many intelligence tests are highly verbal in content and hence would
tend to favor the higher social classes. Social class differences in test-
taking motivation may be an additional factor favoring higher social
class children. Middle class parents expect their children to do schoolwork well. Lower class parents do not characteristically exert such
social pressure on their children. Hence, for many lower class children,
taking an intelligence test may be just another school imposed task that
need not entail any great effort.

It should be stressed, however, that there are many exceptions to
these generalizations. The intellectual stimulation of the home is more
important than the particular social class to which a child belongs.
Bloom (1964) refers to the various stimulating factors in the home as
"environmental *process* variables" and distinguishes such variables from
"environmental *status* variables" such as age, socioeconomic status, and
parents' education. Wolf (1963) found a correlation of +.76 between
measures of environmental process variables and I.Q. This compares
with correlations of about +.40 or below that have been found between
intelligence and environmental status measures.

Social class differences have been found in the grades assigned to
high school students. In the Hollingshead study, over 50 per cent of
the grades assigned to adolescents in Classes I and II were high (85
to 100 per cent) as compared to about 8 per cent for adolescents in
Class V. A much higher percentage of the lowest class children failed
(23 per cent) than did the highest class of children (3 per cent). Hol-

lingshead reports that, although intelligence was found to be associated significantly with class position, the degree of association was not high enough to account either for the concentration of failures in Class V or for the high grades assigned in Classes I and II.

Some research evidence indicates that overt expressions of aggression and feelings of hostility are more likely to be tolerated and even encouraged in the lower class than in the middle class home (Davis, 1941, 1948). This does not mean that the middle class child is without strong aggressive feelings. Sanford *et al.* (1943) found that aggressive needs frequently were evident in the fantasy stories told by middle and upper class preadolescents in taking the Thematic Apperception Test. Yet, according to the teacher's reports, these same preadolescents infrequently expressed aggression overtly.

A number of studies have pointed to social class differences of children in their attitude toward authority (e.g., Dolger and Ginandes, 1946; Meltzer, 1936). Although there is much variability within each class, middle class children manifest pleasant, accepting, and respecting attitudes toward their parents; and most frequently are neither overly dependent nor hostile to their parents. Lower class children entertain more feelings of hostility (mixed with love) and tend to view authority as unreasonable and severe. In Meltzer's study, the most variability in attitude toward parents was found in upper class children. They expressed the most feelings of both rejection and overdependency.

A number of studies indicate that standards of acceptable sexual behavior vary from one class level to another. Kinsey *et al.* (1948) report that among lower class boys, premarital intercourse is regarded as natural, inevitable, and desirable. Upper and middle class boys are restrained by a belief that premariatal intercourse is sinful. Half of the lower class males and only 10 per cent of the higher status males in Kinsey's sample reported that they had engaged in intercourse by age fifteen. In contrast, masturbation and petting to a climax are regarded more with disfavor by lower class boys than by boys of higher status. Somewhat comparable conclusions in the relationship of social class status to sex mores are reported in a number of other studies (e.g., Hollingshead, 1949; Kirkendall and Osborne, 1949).

Social Class and the School Environment. In the Hollingshead Elmtown study, about 58 per cent of his sixteen-year-old boys and girls belonged to Class IV and Class V. These two classes correspond roughly to the lower class groups in other studies. Hollingshead reports that Class IV members are conscious of their inferior status, resent the attitudes of the higher classes, and avoid contact with those who are lower. A Class IV girl described the school situation as follows:

Frankly, for a lot of us, there is nothing here, but just going to classes, listening to the teacher, reciting, studying and going home again. We are pushed out of things. There is a group of girls here who think they are higher than us. They look down on us. . . . I'd like to be in school activities and the school plays, and things like that, but they make us feel like we're not wanted. . . . [Hollingshead, 1949, pp. 202–3.]

Teen-agers are strongly influenced by the opinion of their peers. Meek writes: "We have long realized that boys and girls during this period care more about what their friends or gang or clique think than about what either their parents or teachers think" (1940, p. 43). This does not mean that a lower class child strongly influences the behavior of a middle class child just because the two are in the same classroom. Influence is exerted primarily through intimate associates such as members of the same clique or best friends.

Hollingshead found in his study that cliques were formed along class lines. Analysis of 1,258 clique ties revealed that about 3 out of 5 were between boys and girls of the same prestige class, 2 out of 5 were between boys and girls belonging to adjacent classes, and only 1 out of 25 were between adolescents belonging to classes twice removed from one another.

The influence of social class on friendship formation is even more strikingly evident in the Hollingshead study. Each boy and girl was asked to name his best friend. In every case, the listed best friend was a member of the same clique of the person who listed him. Further, 78 per cent of the girls and 71 per cent of the boys listed as their best friend a person who belonged to the same social class as they did. No Class I or II boy or girl listed as his best friend a boy or girl in Class IV or V. No Class III boy or girl and less than 3 per cent of the Class IV adolescents listed a boy or girl in Class V as their best friend.

Dating in Elmtown reflected the clique pattern. Sixty-one per cent of the daters belonged to the same social class, 35 per cent belonged in an adjacent class, and 4 per cent were separated by one intervening class. Girls particularly faced strong pressure from their peers to avoid dating boys from a lower social class. Boys were somewhat more willing to date girls from lower classes, although when they did they were suspected of sex exploitation.

Many lower class pupils are socially rejected not only by their higher status classmates, but by school authorities as well. Hollingshead, in discussing family influence on the assignment of grades, states:

It is believed widely in Classes IV and V, and to a somewhat less extent in Class III, that the grades a student receives are determined by the position of his parents in the social structure rather than by his ability or his industriousness. This belief is not without foundation, as is generally the case when one encounters a persistent belief illustrated by one story after another, over a number of years of questionable grading practices in relation to the children of prominent families. [P. 181.]

Resentment was general among lower class students over the way disciplinary matters were handled in the Elmtown school. Violation of the rules of the school by Class I and II students were excused with little or no punishment. The same violations were punished harshly when committed by a Class IV or V student.

Learning Exercises

10. Some psychologists contend that the major motivation is to maintain and enhance his self concept. How do the study by Davis *et al.* and the *Fortune* magazine survey (see section on "Class Consciousness") support this point of view?
11. Classify each of the following according to whether it is more typical in the lower or the middle class:
    (a) Virtues of thrift and respect for authority stressed in the home
    (b) More favorable attitudes toward education
    (c) Many contradictions between teachings of home and school
    (d) More children choose professions as a future career
    (e) Less motivation in taking tests
    (f) Express aggression openly
    (g) Masturbation regarded with disfavor
    (h) Extensive participation in school extracurricular activities

NATURE-NURTURE

There have been numerous studies of the effects of heredity and environment upon intelligence and personality. Some of the earliest studies traced family histories in order to demonstrate that certain traits ran in families. Sir Francis Galton (1869), for example, identified a large number of eminent men in England and then determined what proportion of their relatives were eminent. He found a much higher incidence of eminence among the relatives of the eminent than would be expected by chance. Similarly, an unusually high percentage of musicians may be found in five generations of the Bach family, seemingly pointing to the inheritance of musical talent (Sandiford, 1938).

Bad qualities, too, seem to run in families. In one genealogical survey of 750 members of the Jukes family, covering seven generations, it was found that the family had cost New York State over a million and a half dollars through crime, pauperism, and vice (Dugdale, 1877). In another study, the descendants of Martin Kallikak, a Revolutionary soldier, were studied. Kallikak mated illicitly with a feeble-minded girl, and later with a girl of normal intelligence. Several cases of feeble-mindedness were found among the descendants of the first union, while none were found from the second union.

None of the above studies adequately differentiates the effects of heredity from the effects of environment. The son of an eminent man lives in a different environment and has different opportunities than the average child. The criminal and the destitute are apt to provide their children with an inferior environment. Either heredity or environment, or both, could account for the findings in each study.

Evidence pointing to the influence of heredity or development may be found in studies of family resemblances. Table 3–3 presents data from Newman et al. (1937) and Burt and Howard (1956), demonstrating that the correlations obtained from measures of stature and of intelligence of pairs of relatives conform fairly well to what might be expected on the basis of Mendelian principles of heredity.

TABLE 3–3
Blood Relationship and Correlations Between
I.Q.'s and Between Statures

	Height	I.Q.
Identical twins*	.93	.88
Fraternal twins*	.64	.63
Between siblings†	.54	.51
Between parents and children†	.51	.49
Between grandparents and grandchildren†	.31	.34
Between uncles (or aunts) and nephews (or nieces)†	.29	.35
Between first cousins†	.24	.29

* Newman et al., 1937.
† Burt and Howard, 1956.

In the light of these studies, the conclusion that intelligence test scores as well as stature are determined in large part by heredity seems inescapable. Certain limitations to the conclusions that can be drawn for both studies need to be pointed out. Neither study established a relationship between intelligence and heredity—only a relationship between heredity and whatever was measured by the "intelligence tests" used. Also, the relationship would be expected to change somewhat if the intellectual quality of environment had been varied systematically. To illustrate, Newman *et al.* (1957) located 19 identical twins that had been separated in infancy. The correlation between I.Q.'s of the identical twins reared apart was .77 (still quite high even though lower than the .88 for identical twins reared together). For the eight pairs of twins for which the differences in educational advantages were greatest, the differences in I.Q. ranged from 7 to 24 points. For the remaining pairs of twins, with less differences in educational advantages, the differences in I.Q.'s for the most part were quite small.

The twin-study method of investigation has provided evidence that physical features such as eye and skin color, shape of face, shape of nose, etc., and anatomical traits such as height, weight, hand length, etc., depend heavily upon heredity. In the case of anatomical traits, non-hereditary influences such as nutrition and exercise are of importance also. Physiological traits, such as blood pressure, pulse rate, breathing rate, salivation, perspiration, and age at first menstruation, have been found to be influenced by heredity (Jost and Sontag, 1944; Stern, 1949). Twin-studies have produced evidence that identical twins were more similar than non-identical twins in the ages when they could first sit up or walk. Kallman (1946; 1953) has used the twin-study method in investigations of the role of heredity in mental disorders. Kallman's findings suggest that genetic factors may predispose individuals to certain mental disorders.

How Heredity and Environment Influence Behavior

Anastasi (1958) points out that research on the heredity-environment question has gone through two phases: (1) investigations as to *which* type of factor, heredity or environmental, is responsible for individual differences in a given trait; and (2) investigations designed to discover *how much* of the variance of a trait could be attributed to heredity and how much to environment. From many research studies, it has now become apparent that the proportional contribution of heredity to the variance of a given behavioral trait will vary under different environmental conditions. Both heredity and environment contribute to all behavior traits, and the extent of their respective contributions cannot be specified for any given trait. Hence, a much better question to ask, according to Anastasi, is *how* do heredity and environmental factors influence behavior?

Environmental conditions can do much to modify the effects of some hereditary factors on behavior. Thus, hereditary deafness may lead to intellectual retardation as a result of interference with normal social and language development and schooling. Or the hereditary handicap may be offset by appropriate adaptations of instructional procedures. A disease experienced by a child who has inherited a susceptibility to that disease may result in an intellectual and social handicap for the child due to an interruption in his schooling. Or a concentration of the child's energies on intellectual pursuits rather than athletic and social functions may result in outstanding intellectual development. General body build is strongly influenced by hereditary factors. The child who is endomorphic in our culture may become maladjusted due to the way other children react to him. Or the child may be able to adjust successfully to his body build. The mere fact that a physical characteristic is inherited does not lead inevitably to a single behavioral consequence.

In summary, physical and physiological traits are strongly influenced by hereditary factors, although they may be modified by environment. Behavioral traits, whether they be of an intellectual, motor, emotional, or social variety, can be explained *only* in terms of interactions between hereditary and environmental factors.

Learning Exercises

12. What is the major weakness of the *family history* method as a means of determining the influence of heredity on development?
13. From the discussion on "Nature-Nurture," what do you consider as acceptable evidence that (a) heredity and (b) environment influence intelligence test performance?

PRINCIPLES OF DEVELOPMENT

The problem of what constitutes normal development is very real both for parent and teacher. Parents and teachers may become worried about the developmental progress of a child even when development is normal. And sometimes parents and teachers are not sufficiently alert to danger signals indicating unsatisfactory development. Literally thousands of studies involving observation of children do provide a wealth of data that do answer many questions concerning normal development. Developmental psychologists have attempted to reduce some of this data to a relatively few generalizations. These generalizations, termed "principles of development," have some value to parent and teacher in assessing the present developmental status of an individual child and in forming realistic expectations concerning his future development. In this section, attention is focused on these principles of development.

Continuity and Sequence of Growth

Growth is a continuous process, and the unfolding of the pattern of growth is a part of what is inherited. The organism interacting in a normal environment develops in a gradual orderly sequence from one stage to another. What occurs at one stage serves as a foundation for subsequent stages.

The general direction of growth is in (1) a cephalocaudal, or head to foot, direction; and (2) in a proximodistal, or center to periphery, direction. Thus, the development of the upper part of the body precedes the development of the lower extremities (cephalocaudal direction). And development proceeds from a shoulder to fingers, hip to toes direction (proximodistal). The direction of growth in structure is paralleled by the development of functional changes. The infant gains control of the upper parts of his body prior to control of the lower parts and is able to coordinate gross arm movements prior to coordination of finger movements.

Developmental direction is also from the general to the specific. When an attractive object is placed above an infant while on his back, the infant appears to attempt to grasp it with all parts of the body —bouncing up and down and waving his arms and legs. This generalized body movement is eventually replaced with specific arm movements with the superfluous leg and body movements dropping out from the total response pattern. A parallel may be noted at later levels of development in the acquisition of a motor skill. A child learning to swim appears to bring into play all muscles of the body in a wildly uncoordinated fashion. Later, the unnecessary generalized body movements are replaced by well-coordinated specific movements of the appropriate body parts.

The orderly sequence of development is to be found not only in growth and development of body structure and function, but extends even to areas of character and personality development. "Each child sits before he stands; he babbles before he talks; he fabricates before he tells the truth; he draws a circle before he draws a square; he is selfish before he is altruistic; he is dependent on others before he achieves dependence on self" (Gesell and Ilg, 1943). For most children, it is possible to make some predictions on "what comes next."

Development does not proceed at an even pace. In height, for example, growth is relatively rapid during infancy and early childhood. It is slower but constant in middle childhood, spurts prior to puberty, and then slackens during adolescence. Gesell and Ilg (1943) have pointed out that development proceeds in a spiral fashion, rather than onward and upward. Progress is made in a particular line of development, followed by a period of no apparent development, or even a regression to a prior stage of development. In learning to walk, the young baby may revert to creeping for a time before proceeding to a higher level of skill in walking. In language development, after the child has learned to speak a few words, the child may make no progress for a few months during a period in which the child is focusing his energies on learning to walk. A similar phenomena frequently occurs during school years. Progress in school work may come to a standstill while the child is working through some other developmental problem.

Individual Differences

Children differ in rate of growth. As Bayley (1956) has stated, "It is a rare child who follows the same course in all of the observed variables through all of his growth." Growth of structures and functions for different individuals proceed at different rates and reach maturity at different times. A child may be fast growing at one period and slow growing at another period.

Individual differences in the process of becoming sexually mature illustrate well the extent of variation in growth patterns. Stolz and Stolz (1951) report a range of at least five and one-half years in the age at which adolescence begins for boys and at least four and one-half years at which it ends. A comparable range has been reported in the range of ages at which adolescence begins for girls (Courtis, 1933).

There are definite differences in the growth patterns between boys and girls. In general, boys are taller than girls at age ten; but girls are taller than boys at ages eleven, twelve, and thirteen, after which boys again forge ahead of girls. The greatest gain in weight for girls, on the average, is between ages eleven and thirteen; whereas the greatest gain for boys is between fourteen and fifteen. The onset of puberty occurs about two years earlier for girls than for boys.

Individual differences in the rapid bodily changes occurring during adolescence is frequently a cause of worry to both boys and girls. As Malm and Jamison (1952) point out:

The boy who stays small and immature much longer than the others, the boy whose external genitalia are very immature, whose pattern of pubic-hair distribution is not like that of most of the boys, the girl who doesn't menstruate until she is seventeen or eighteen—all of these can understandably ask themselves: "Am I normal?" Such may also be the question with the boy whose body contours are somewhat feminine. [P. 108.]

The fact that some boys and girls mature earlier than do others is of relevance to the problem of social and personal adjustment during the adolescent years. The early maturing girl and the late maturing boy encounter particularly difficult adjustments. Sheer size of the early maturing girl makes her conspicuous among her age-mates and creates problems in social adjustment. The late maturing boy is not only conspicuous because of his smaller size, but his lack of size and strength puts him at a disadvantage in competitive athletics. Complicating the adjustment problem is the fact that to be accepted by one's age-mates becomes increasingly important during adolescence.

Evidence that age of maturing is a factor in the adjustment of some boys may be found in a study reported by Jones and Bayley (1950). Sixteen early maturing boys and sixteen late maturing boys were selected out of a group of 90 cases in an urban public school system. On the average, the physically advanced and the physically retarded boys were separated by about two years in skeletal age, even though of the same chronological age. Observations and ratings were obtained on the social behavior of the boys at different intervals from ages twelve to seventeen. Jones and Bayley summarized their findings thus:

Those who are physically accelerated are usually accepted and treated by adults and other children as more mature. They appear to have relatively little need to strive for status. From their ranks come the outstanding student body leaders in senior high school. In contrast, the physically retarded boys exhibit many forms of relatively immature behavior; this may be in part because others tend to treat them as the little boys they appear to be. Furthermore, a fair proportion of these boys give evidence of needing to counteract their physical disadvantage in some way—usually by greater activity and striving for attention, although in some cases by withdrawal. [P. 146.]

Cumulative Effect of Experience

Tennyson once wrote, "I am a part of all that I have met." Decades later, developmental psychologists expressed the same principle in more prosaic language. An experience at one age influences the later behavior of an individual. Even where maturation is primarily responsible for growth, nutritional deficiencies and poor health conditions can affect adversely the developing organism. Each event of significance in the life of the child changes the child to some extent. A chain of events adding up over a period of months to a rejection of the child by his parents is likely to result in an unhealthy personality development.

At school, poor instruction in arithmetic at an early grade level may make later progress in arithmetic more difficult. "Getting off on the wrong foot" in our relationship with another individual makes it increasingly difficult later to establish good relationships with that individual. In short, experiences have a cumulative effect.

This does not mean that each individual is a fragile creature that can be shattered by one unfortunate experience. Quite the reverse, both the body and the personality have marvelous recuperative powers. A healthy child living in a favorable environment where his health needs are met and where he is secure in the love of his parents can withstand many rebuffs. Under such circumstances, parents or teachers may be unwise in their dealings with the child on occasion without causing irreparable damage.

Interaction of Aspects of Development

A change in any one aspect of a child's development can affect his development in other areas. Thus, an impairment of a child's physical health may affect his intellectual, emotional, and social development. The field of psychosomatic medicine provides illustrations of the effects of emotional disturbances on physical health. Richards (1951) provides case study material on a boy over a seven and one-half year period that shows a close correspondence between the child's intelligence test performance and the child's current life situation. During periods when things were going well for the child at home and school, his intelligence test scores were relatively high. During periods when disturbing elements were present at home and school, intelligence test performances were lower. Richards quite properly points out that no generalizations can be made on the basis of a single case. Nevertheless, Richards' findings are consistent with the findings contained in case studies made by psychologists and teachers.

In our culture, particularly, physical growth and development affect total development. At all ages and for both sexes, physical attributes are an important means of gaining approval. The boy in elementary and secondary school who is skillful in competitive sports wins admiration from his peers. For the female, beauty is a social asset.

Critical Events and Periods in Development

All events in an individual's life have not equal significance. Certain events stand out and exert a disproportionate impact on total development. The first day at school, a prize won in a contest, the first date, graduation from high school, and many others become memorable events. An unexpected success or failure may have a pervasive effect upon a child's later development. Combs and Snygg (1959) relate how an unexpected success in a street fight changed dramatically a boy's self concept and subsequent behavior. The boy, Peter, was shy, retiring, and particularly fearful of a gang of boys in his neighborhood. One day the gang caught up with Peter and began tormenting him. The leader of the gang knocked him down and sat on his chest. When the gang leader threatened to kill him, Peter in a fit of terror threw the leader off, pounced on him, and began beating his head in the ground. Peter relented only after the leader begged for mercy. Peter was led off the field a hero by the other members of the gang. The respect accorded Peter from his new found friends, the loss of his fear, and the new confidence in himself changed Peter to an active boy who got into more mischief, much to the puzzlement of his teacher.

Not only may a single event become especially significant to the development of an individual, but certain periods in the development of the individual are of critical importance to a particular form of development. For example, the first year the child is in school is of particular importance in learning to get along with age-mates. Havighurst (1953) has used the term "developmental task" to denote "a task which arises at or about a certain period in the life of the individual, successful achievement of which leads to his happiness and to success with later tasks, while failure leads to unhappiness in the individual, disapproval by society, and difficulty with later tasks." Thus, the child who is reasonably successful in learning to get along with his age-mates in his first year in school has made a good beginning in learning social skills and is free to expend some of his energy in attaining other forms of development. The child who is unsuccessful stands out against other more successful children in his class and finds it increasingly difficult to attain social skills even when he expends a disproportionate amount of time and energy trying to gain acceptance from his peers. Similarly, adolescence is a period of crucial importance in learning new relations with age-mates of both sexes. The boy who learns these new social skills at the same time as his friends is excused for his social ineptitudes because they are to be expected at his stage of development. The boy who is unsuccessful in learning new relations with his age-mates is left behind his peers and finds it increasingly difficult to attain the required social skills in later years.

Some developmental tasks, according to Havighurst, arise mainly from physical maturation; others arise primarily from the cultural pressures of society; while still others arise out of the personal values and aspirations of the individual. Learning to walk is an example of a task that becomes crucial only when maturation of bones, muscles, and nerves has reached a point where success in learning to walk is possible. Havighurst lists "learning to behave acceptably toward the other sex" as another example of a task arising mainly from physical maturation. In contrast, learning to read is a task imposed on the child by our society; while the task of selecting and preparing for an occupation is one in which personal values and aspirations of the individual play a large part.

Havighurst has listed developmental tasks for six periods of development: infancy and early childhood, middle childhood, adolescence, early adulthood, middle age, and later maturity. Examples of developmental tasks for these age levels are as follows:

Infancy and early childhood: learning to take solid foods; to talk; to control elimination; to distinguish right and wrong.

Middle childhood (roughly age six to twelve): learning physical skills; building wholesome attitudes toward oneself as a growing organism; learning to get along with age-mates; learning the appropriate sex role; learning to read, write, etc.; developing concepts necessary for everyday living; developing conscience; achieving personal independence; developing attitudes toward social groups and institutions.

Adolescence: accepting one's physique; achieving a masculine or feminine social role; achieving emotional independence of parents and other adults; achieving assurance of economic independence; selecting and preparing for an occupation; preparing for marriage and family life; developing intellectual skills; desiring and achieving socially responsible behavior; acquiring a set of values and an ethical system as a guide to behavior.

Learning Exercise

14. Match the developmental data in Column B to the principle of development listed in Column A.

Column A	Column B
1. Orderly sequence of development	(a) Growth spurt prior to puberty
2. Proximodistal direction of development	(b) Slow maturing boy encounters social adjustment problems
3. Growth proceeds at an even pace	(c) Home influences on personality development
4. Individual differences	(d) A child crawls before he walks
5. Cumulative effects of experience	(e) Importance of learning to get along with age-mates during ages six to twelve
6. Interaction of aspects of development	(f) Gross muscles of the arm develop before finer muscles of the fingers
7. Critical periods of development	(g) Early and late maturers

---

SUMMARY

A number of generalizations derived from developmental psychology may serve as a useful framework in observing and interpreting the behavior of the individual child. These are:

1. The present developmental and behavioral status of the child has come about as a result of interaction between hereditary and environmental forces. All things are not possible for all children. Heredity does impose limitations. Yet under proper environmental influences, children of widely varying hereditary characteristics can affect satisfactory adjustments. In brief, heredity determines the potentials of development; but it neither guarantees the realization of a child's potentials nor condemns the child to an unsatisfactory development.

2. What is impossible for the child at one age may become possible at a later age. With the passage of time and a fairly normal environment, maturational processes readies the child for more advanced learning experiences.

3. Within a single culture, there is some agreement and some disagreement as to what is "good," "proper," "correct," "desirable," etc. The area of disagreement as to standards or norms is reduced within subgroups of a culture, such as social classes, religions, clubs, cliques, or gangs, or the individual family unit. Thus, the behavior of the individual child is influenced by (a) the culture as a whole (through lessons taught by parents who represent the culture), and (b) by an increasing number of reference groups each with its own set of behavioral norms.

4. As the child develops, he learns different *roles*—son, friend, pupil, etc. Each role has its own set of appropriate behaviors. How a child performs a role depends upon (a) the expectations of individuals or groups of importance to the child, (b) the accuracy of his perception of how he is expected to perform the role, and (c) the degree to which he accepts the assigned role.

5. The behavioral norms and the assigned roles of children from different social classes vary.

6. Certain principles of development are of value in assessing present developmental status and in anticipating future development. These are:

a) There is an orderly sequence of development that permits some accuracy in predicting, at least in part, "what comes next."

b) Children differ in rates of growth. Yet even though variations in growth rates are to be expected, they may constitute a source of worry to the child.

   c) Experience has a cumulative effect. Hence, we sometimes need to look to the past to explain and understand the present in the life of the child.

   d) All aspects of development interact. Unsatisfactory school work may be due to disturbances or worries in other aspects of a child's development.

   e) There are critical events and critical periods in the development of the child. A single event can affect the course of a child's development. At different age levels, there are particular developmental tasks that the child needs to master in order to forward his complete development.

Answer Cues

1. 1b, 2c, 3a, 4d.

2. (a) No—sun would not affect genes of parents. (b) No. (c) Only to the extent that musical ability is attributable to certain physical characteristics such as ear structure, long fingers, etc.

3. (a) Gesell and Thompson's study—each twin learned to climb stairs only when mature enough to learn. (b) The Wood and Freeman study on typing and the Dunkel and Pillet study on learning French.

4. A wide range in readiness for any learning may be expected in any classroom due to differences in maturational level, past learning, and motivation.

5. Both terms encompass learned behaviors, attitudes, and values handed down from one generation to another. The term "culture" is broader, including both materials and behavioral arrangements. Attention is directed to *differences* in the lessons taught in different cultures in describing the basic personality structure of the various cultures. (Additional distinctions may be made between these two concepts.)

6. Positive sanction—the respect accorded Billy for winning the fight; negative sanction—the scorn accorded Percival for tattling.

7. In general, the emphasis on individual rights. Erikson points out a similarity in the unwritten but firm rule of Congress that no important bloc shall be voted down on matters touching upon its vital interests. The support of the bloc may be needed in supporting future legislation of interest to other groups. Paralleling the way Congress settles a controversy to a point of majority concurrence, the solution of problems within a family is often a compromise of the interests of family members.

8. Part of the *group norm* is to search for excitement and to participate in the activities of the gang even though an element of danger is involved. For James, the gang is a *reference group*. *Social sanctions* would be applied by members of the gang—positive sanctions for participating and negative sanctions for non-participation in gang activities.

9. $4 + 9 + 6 + 4 = 23$. Either upper or upper-middle class.

10. Individuals even in the lowest classes do not perceive themselves as "inferior." Individuals perceive themselves as "superior" to those of lower

socioeconomic status.   Individuals tend to overestimate their socioeconomic status.

11. Middle: (a), (b), (d), (h).   Lower: (c), (e), (f), (g).

12. Either heredity or environment, or both, can account for the findings of such studies.

13. Heredity: the substantial relationship between intelligence test scores of identical twins reared apart.   Environment: the lesser relationship between I.Q. scores for identical twins who experienced radically different educational advantages.

14. 1d, 2f, 3a, 4g, 5c, 6b, 7e.

4

APTITUDE TESTING [1]

Schools today make extensive use of psychological tests designed to measure the learning potential of students. Such tests are classified as *aptitude* tests. An aptitude test designed to measure general mental abilities is customarily referred to as an *intelligence* test, or (when used in a school setting) an *academic aptitude* test. In addition to tests constructed to measure general mental abilities, we have numerous tests to measure more specific abilities. For example, a mechanical aptitude test is a test that attempts to measure the kinds of abilities needed to acquire knowledge and skills in mechanics. Similarly, tests of clerical aptitude, artistic aptitude, musical aptitude, scientific aptitude, law aptitude, and algebra aptitude—each focuses on measuring a few specific abilities of importance for a particular kind of learning.

The major distinction between aptitude tests and achievement tests rests in the purposes of the tests. The purpose of aptitude tests is to predict some future performance. This prediction is made on the basis of an assessment of the abilities needed for future success. The purpose of achievement tests is to measure *past* learning. Both aptitude and achievement tests attain their purpose through some assessment of the *present* status of the person tested. The constructor of the aptitude test has endeavored to fashion a predictor of future performance and has not been primarily concerned, as has the achievement test constructor, with sampling the content of a particular course or area of study. However, the test user may employ a test labeled an achievement test as one basis for predicting future performance.

APTITUDE TESTING IN THE SCHOOL

In order to understand better some of the ways psychological tests are used in the school, let us visit the office of Mr. Garth Thompson,

[1] Students who have not been introduced to statistics may find it profitable to study the materials contained in the Appendix before reading Chapter 4.

mathematics instructor at Rosedale High School, and review with Mr. Thompson some of the results of the high school fall testing program.

Two of the tests used in the fall testing program at Rosedale were the School and College Aptitude Test (SCAT), and the Sequential Test of Educational Progress (STEP). SCAT is an academic aptitude test yielding three scores: Verbal, Quantitative, and Total. STEP is an achievement test battery with separate tests on Mathematics, Reading, Writing, Listening, Social Studies, Science, and Essay. Mr. Thompson was particularly interested in the performance of the transfer students in grades 10, 11, and 12, for whom he had insufficient information to assess their aptitudes. He jotted down the following notes on two transfer students in his grade 12 class:

> Roger Stanton—local percentiles on SCAT: Verbal 90, Quantitative 95, Total 97. Local percentiles on STEP: Mathematics 85, Reading 80, Writing 75, Listening 90, Social Studies 70, Science 95, Essay 50.
>
> Previous school record: a high B average on his work in grades 9, 10, and 11; mostly A's in mathematics and science and B's and an occasional C in social studies and English.
>
> Roger appears to be a promising candidate to join Bob Wrenn, Tom Knoll, and Amy Jacks for the advanced projects in mathematics.
>
> Mary Smith—local percentiles on SCAT: Verbal 65, Quantitative 45, Total 52. Local percentiles on STEP: Mathematics 40, Reading 60, Writing 80, Listening 68, Social Studies 64, Science 48, Essay 60.
>
> Previous school record: A's and B's in English, B's in social studies and French, C's in science, and C's and D's in mathematics.
>
> Although the difference in performance on Verbal and Quantitative scores on SCAT might well be attributed to chance, Mary apparently has encountered difficulty in her mathematics courses in high school. Her performance in the Quantitative on SCAT and the Mathematic section of STEP suggest that she has the ability to be successful in the grade 12 mathematics course. Will need to find out source of Mary's difficulty in mathematics.

Mr. Thompson noted that a number of his students in each grade performed quite differently than he had expected. Mike Janckewitz, for example, scored the equivalent of the 10th percentile in the Verbal and at the 50th percentile on the Quantitative portions of SCAT. Yet last year Mike had done exceptionally fine work in mathematics and was the only member of the class to solve some difficult problems in mathematics. Mr. James, the science teacher, had been quite enthusiastic over a science project Mike had completed; and Miss Reynolds, the English teacher, reported that Mike had improved considerably in English and had earned a C in her course. Mike's performance on SCAT certainly appears to underestimate his innate intelligence level, although possibly his SCAT scores are realistic predictors of how well Mike would perform in college. However, it is extremely doubtful whether Mike will go on to college. It had taken the combined efforts of Coach Butler and Mr. Thompson to persuade Mr. Janckewitz to allow Mike to remain in school and complete his high school education.

Jean Scott, one of the top grade 11 students, scored at the 40th percentile on the SCAT and was correspondingly low on the various STEP subtests. Mr. Roberts, the school counselor, pointed out that Jean's mother had instituted divorce proceedings during the summer vacation and that this fact might well explain Jean's disappointing performance in the fall testing program.

Mr. Thompson noted that some other good students scored lower than he expected on SCAT. These students were possibly "overachievers," i.e., students who were making a near maximum use of the abilities they possessed in their schoolwork. Mr. Thompson was not surprised that certain C students in each grade performed exceptionally well on SCAT. He had suspected that these students were not working up to capacity. He was surprised to find Bill Clark in grade 10 among the underachievers. He had attributed Bill's ordinary performance in mathematics to ordinary ability. Yet Bill's performance on SCAT was among the best of the tenth-grade students.

Mr. Thompson checked the record of Chester Dyson. Mr. Robert Dyson, Chester's father, was one of the most successful architects in the city and for a number of years had planned a career in engineering for Chester. On previously administered academic aptitude tests, Chester had scored extremely high. However, on the Differential Aptitude Tests, Chester had scored at the 99th percentile in Verbal Reasoning and Language Usage and between the 75th and 95th on the other subtests. Mechanical Reasoning was his lowest score. On the Kuder Preference Record, his lowest measured interest was in the mechanical area. Chester was rated as the most outstanding twelfth-grade student in English and among the best students in social studies and French. He was a good student but not among the top five in mathematics and science. Mr. Thompson noted that Chester did somewhat better on the Verbal than on the Quantitative portions of SCAT. Also, Chester's pattern of test scores on STEP was consistent with the school staff's previous assessment of his relative strengths and weaknesses.

Mr. Thompson studied carefully the records of the ninth-grade class. Most of these students were in their first year at Rosedale High School. Mr. Thompson planned to make use of the test results on SCAT and on the mathematics section of STEP as an initial basis for grouping his ninth-grade class. At a mathematics workshop at the State University, remedial instruction material for ninth-grade mathematics had been programmed for use with teaching machines. Also, Mr. Thompson wished to try out with teaching machines some programmed material at a more advanced level with some of the better students in his class.

Purposes Served by Tests of Academic Aptitude

The SCAT test used in the Rosedale High School is one of the many group academic aptitude tests currently on the market. Following are some of the purposes that various academic aptitude or intelligence tests are designed to serve:

1. Identifying the student who is average, advanced, or retarded in the abilities needed for planned instruction and thus providing information necessary in order to gear instruction to the ability level of the student.
2. Identifying the over- and underachiever through comparing a student's abilities as measured by an academic aptitude test with his achievement in school courses.
3. Forming class groups of students of fairly similar levels of ability. Some school systems organize classroom groups by ability levels, while in other school systems many teachers form small groups within a class for certain purposes of instruction.
4. Guiding a student toward appropriate academic and vocational goals. At the junior and senior high school levels as well as at the college level, students have decisions to make as to the curriculum to enter, the courses to enroll in, and often a vocation to work toward. Academic aptitude test performance becomes one source of data in reaching such decisions.
5. Interpreting school progress to the student's parents, so that they may become realistic in assessing the student's present academic performance and in planning for his future academic and vocational goals.
6. Comparing students' verbal and non-verbal abilities. A student's poor academic performance may be due primarily to a low general intellectual ability, or it may be due to certain inadequacies in his past school learning. For example, the student who is deficient in reading ability, and who scores much higher on a non-verbal than on the verbal section of an aptitude test, may be capable of benefiting from appropriate remedial reading

instruction and may improve his academic achievement in all subjects as a result of an improved reading ability.

7. Understanding the pattern of mental abilities. Academic aptitude is a complex concept. The concept "intelligence" is even more complex. Two individuals may obtain the same total score on an academic aptitude test and yet have quite different subscores. Various academic aptitude tests differ in the number and names of subscores. For the SCAT test, we have seen that three scores may be obtained: Verbal, Quantitative, and Total. Some other tests attempt to yield an assessment of a variety of mental factors. For example, in the California Short-Form Test of Mental Maturity, seven subtests may be grouped to give scores on Logical Reasoning, Numerical Reasoning, and Verbal Concepts; or the seven subtest scores may be combined to yield a Language and a Non-Language score. The manuals for tests that yield a large number of subscores usually point out that understanding the pattern of mental abilities is of importance to the teachers.

The extent to which tests of academic aptitudes may be useful to the classroom teacher is dependent largely upon how well the teacher understands the nature of academic aptitude tests and how well the teacher applies his knowledge about psychological tests in interpreting test scores. In order to interpret test results, the teacher should understand: (1) What the test he is using actually measures; (2) How accurately the test measures what it sets out to measure; and (3) What future performances the test scores predict and how much confidence can be placed in such predictions.

The balance of this chapter attempts to supply background information of use to the teacher in interpreting aptitude test scores.

Learning Exercise

1. The ways a teacher uses test results reflect his educational beliefs. Identify from the case study material a way Mr. Thompson used test results that seems to reflect either his *agreement* or his *disagreement* with each of the following statements:

   (a) Learning experiences in mathematics should be the same for all students within a single grade level.

   (b) Test results may reveal that certain students are capable of better work in school.

   (c) Emotional disturbance may interfere with a student's performance on an aptitude test.

   (d) School grades are useless in assessing a student's aptitudes.

INTELLIGENCE TESTS

A teacher, in interpreting intelligence test scores of pupils in his class, may make inferences about the quality of the intelligence of each class member. What does a teacher mean when he comes to the conclusion that one member of his class is more intelligent than another member? Let us examine some of the possible meanings that may be given to the construct "intelligence."

The Nature of Intelligence

Psychologists have defined intelligence in a variety of ways. Some definitions focus attention on the ability to adapt to one's environment as the key characteristic. Other definitions stress ability to learn as the distinguishing feature. Still others equate intelligence to the capacity to do abstract or symbolic thinking. The first point we may note then is that various definitions of intelligence presented by psychologists differ in the essential characteristic that defines intelligence.

Second, we may note that intelligence may be conceived either as an innate potential or as learned behavior. Hebb (1949, p. 294) has pointed out that the word "intelligence" has two valuable meanings: One is (a) an *innate potential,* the capacity for development, a fully innate property that amounts to the possession of a good brain and a good neural metabolism. The second is (b) the functioning of a brain in which development has gone on, determining an *average level of performance or comprehension* by the partly grown or mature person.

Hebb's distinction of the two meanings of intelligence is of importance in assessing the effects of environment on intelligence. Intelligence, conceived as an innate potential, cannot be improved by providing a superior environment. Individual differences in intelligence can be explained in terms of differences in heredity. Intelligence, thought of as a *functioning* of a brain, is manifested by those behaviors that we classify as intellectual. These behaviors include the use of sets of symbols, such as language and number, and the use of concepts and generalizations in problem situations. These intellectual behaviors are learned. They are amenable to the environmental influences of the culture in which we live (Hunt, 1961).

A third facet that needs to be considered in examining the construct "intelligence" is whether intelligence is conceived as a single general ability or as a number of distinctively different abilities. Are there different kinds of intelligences, and is it possible for a person to have much of one kind and not so much of another kind of intelligence? This question has been of interest to psychologists from the very beginning of the intelligence testing movement.

The first intelligence tests of this century were constructed to yield a single score to represent the level of an individual's intelligence. Later, some psychologists began to conceive of intelligence as a number of mental abilities. A number of theories emerged about the nature and organization of mental abilities. E. L. Thorndike of Columbia University postulated a neurological basis of intelligence with literally billions of potential neural bonds or connections between stimuli and responses. All of a person's responses to specific stimuli were supposedly established as a result of practice and learning. Intelligence was conceived by Thorndike as the arithmetical sum of a series of varied and unrelated abilities. While for Thorndike intelligence was made up of many, many specific abilities, he did provide for a rough grouping into three classes: (1) abstract—the ability to handle symbols, (2) mechanical—the ability to manipulate things, and (3) social—the ability to be effective with people.

A British psychologist, C. Spearman, advanced a two-factor theory of intelligence. As a result of factor analysis studies, Spearman came to the conclusion that intelligence was made up of a general mental factor (g factor) and specific factors (s factors). The g factors would be brought into play in all kinds of intellectual tasks. Intellectual tasks, differing in nature, would require certain abilities specific to the task, in addition to general mental ability. Thus, the reason a student performs at a high level in all subjects might be attributable to a high general mental ability. The reason he performs relatively higher in one subject than another might be attributable to the presence of greater specific factors for one subject than for the other.

A third effort to explain the organization of intelligence was made by L. L. Thurstone of the University of Chicago. Thurstone (1938) also using a factor analysis method came to the conclusion that intelligence could be best accounted for by postulating seven primary mental abilities. These are: (1) number, (2) word fluency, (3) verbal meaning, (4) memory, (5) reasoning, (6) spatial perception, and (7) perceptual speed. These were termed by Thurstone as primary mental abilities. While at first Thurstone saw no need to postulate a general factor, his later studies seemed to indicate a need for a general factor in addition to his group factors.

Guilford (1959) has developed what may be considered as a fourth major formulation of the organization of intelligence. Guilford divides intellectual abilities into a small group of *memory* abilities and a larger group of *thinking* abilities. Thinking abilities are subdivided into three categories: *cognitive* abilities, *productive* abilities, and *evaluative* abilities. Cognitive abilities involve the discovery of information and the rediscovery or recognition of information. Productive abilities involve the use of information. Evaluative abilities involve a checking operation utilized whenever it is necessary to ascertain the adequacy of things cognized or produced. Productive abilities are further subdivided into *convergent* thinking and *divergent* thinking. Convergent thinking proceeds toward a one right answer to a problem. Divergent thinking proceeds in different directions as a person explores a variety of aspects of a problem presented. (See Fig. 4–1.)

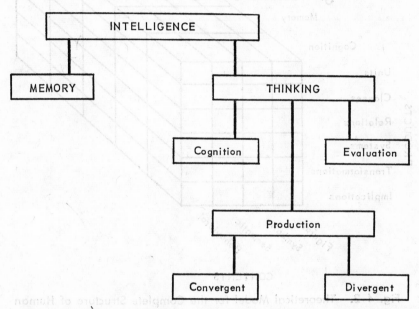

Fig. 4–1. Main Categories in "Operations" Dimension of Intellectual Abilities. (From *Personality* by J. P. Guilford. Copyright 1959. McGraw-Hill Book Co. Used by permission.)

A second dimension in Guilford's theoretical model for the structure of the human intellect is the kind of contents involved. Four components of contents are: (1) *figural*—visual or auditory forms or even the form of patterns of felt movement; (2) *symbolic*—letters, numbers, sounds, words, or sentences that represent elements; (3) *semantic*—meaningful verbal material; (4) *behavioral*—ability to infer the perceptions, thoughts, feelings, attitudes of others from their behavior.

The third dimension in Guilford's model is the kind of *products* involved in an operation. Guilford postulates six kinds of products upon which the intellect may operate. These are: (1) *units,* (2) *classes of units,* (3) *relations between units,* (4) *patterns or systems,* (5) *transformations,* and (6) *implications.*

In all, the five kinds of *operations,* four kinds of *content,* and six kinds of *products* yield a total of 120 abilities or cells. (See Fig. 4–2.)

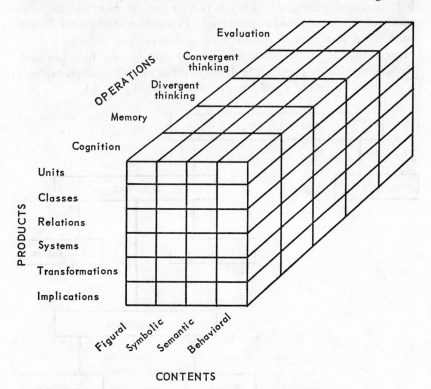

CONTENTS

Fig. 4–2. Theoretical Model for the Complete Structure of Human Intellect. (From *Personality* by J. P. Guilford. Copyright 1959. Mc-Graw-Hill Book Co. Used by permission.)

Guilford (1964) questions the belief in a *g* factor in intelligence. From factor-analytic studies involving more than 7,000 correlation co-efficients, Guilford found a substantial number (17 to 24 per cent) of correlations that could be considered to be zero. Each test used by Guilford was designed to measure one unique ability. Guilford attributes the demonstration of a *g* factor in previous studies to the lack of variety and the factorial complexity of the tests used.

Learning Exercises

2. Do the studies of identical twins reared apart (see Chapter 3) provide evidence that both of Hebb's meanings of intelligence are reflected in intelligence test scores? Explain.

3. Which of the following is most readily explained in terms of (1) a general mental ability (*g* factor)? (2) group factors (primary mental ability)? (3) specific factors?
   (a) Johnny has difficulty in expressing himself fluently but learns arithmetic easily.
   (b) Betty learns quickly in all school subjects.
   (c) Bill finds it difficult to learn some portions of his arithmetic but experiences no difficulty on other parts of his arithmetic.

Stanford-Binet

From its very beginning, the intelligence testing movement has involved the measurement of the kind of intelligence required for school success. At about the turn of the century in France, the Paris school authorities were concerned with the problem of identifying pupils who were not sufficiently mentally developed to profit from the instruction provided in the Paris schools. Binet and an associate named Simon worked on the problem and in 1905 published a test consisting of 30 separate tests or items arranged in ascending order of difficulty.

The practical question that Binet and Simon asked themselves was: What abilities are required to do schoolwork? The test developed tapped a variety of functions with particular emphasis upon verbal comprehension, judgment, and reasoning.

In 1908 and 1911, revisions of the original test were made. In the 1908 revision, tests were grouped into age levels from three-year-olds to age thirteen. The concept *mental age* was introduced. Average test performances for groups of children of successive chronological age levels were computed. The performance of any given child then could be equated to such average performances. For example, if a ten-year-old passed the test commonly passed by the average eleven-year-old, then he was assigned a mental age of 11. In the 1911 revision, additional items were added at a number of age levels, and the scale was extended to the adult level.

The work of Binet and Simon early attracted the attention of American psychologists. In 1910, L. M. Terman at Stanford University began experimenting with the Binet Scale and in 1916 produced the Stanford Revision of the Binet Scale. In 1937, Terman and Merrill replaced the 1916 test with Forms L and M of the Stanford-Binet. The latest revision in 1960 combines the best tests of the 1937 revision into a single Form L-M.

The Stanford-Binet tests are grouped into age levels ranging from age II to superior adult. From ages II to V, the test is organized into half-year intervals. Between V and XIV, the age levels are in yearly intervals. Above the XIV age level are Average Adult and Superior Adult levels I, II, and III. Each age level is made up of six tests, except the Average Adult level, which contains eight tests.

The tests included for each age level were selected so as to be of appropriate difficulty for the average child of that age level. They cover a wide variety of mental abilities and appear to tap different abilities at different age levels. Tests involving apparatus and pictures are included in the earlier levels. More reasoning-type tests appear at the later levels. Thus, the meaning of the term "intelligence" changes from one level to another.

In administering the test, the examiner begins at a level where the child is likely to succeed and proceeds to give all tests at succeeding levels until the child fails on all tests for a level. The highest level at which the child passes all tests is designated as the child's *basal age*. A credit (usually two months of mental age) is assigned for each test passed by the child in the levels above his basal age. These credits are added to the basal age to obtain the child's mental age. For example, a child:

Passed all tests at 8-year level = 8 years (basal age)
Passed 4 tests at 9-year level = 8 months
Passed 3 tests at 10-year level = 6 months
Passed 0 tests at 11-year level = 0 months
Mental Age = 9 years, 2 months

In the 1937 Stanford-Binet, a ratio I.Q. could be obtained by dividing a child's mental age by his chronological age and multiplying by 100. Thus, in the example above, if the child's chronological age was 8 years, 4 months, then his I.Q. would be:

$$\frac{110 \text{ months}}{100 \text{ months}} \times 100 = 110$$

In the 1960 revision of the Stanford-Binet, ratio I.Q.'s are replaced by deviation I.Q.'s. These deviation I.Q.'s are standard scores[2] with a mean of 100 and a standard deviation of 16. The disadvantage of ratio I.Q.'s is that they are not comparable from one test to a second test when the standard deviations of the two tests vary. Thus, a child scoring one standard deviation above the mean on two intelligence tests, one of which had a standard deviation of 12 and the second, a standard deviation of 20, would have I.Q.'s on the two tests of 112 and 120, respectively. In the 1937 Stanford-Binet, the standard deviations

[2] See the Appendix for a discussion of standard deviation and standard scores.

are fairly comparable for most age levels. However, the standard deviations do fluctuate from a low of 13 at the six-year level to a high of 21 at the two-and-a-half-year level. The introduction of the deviation I.Q. in the 1960 form insures a statistical comparability of I.Q. scores from one age level to another.

Wechsler Intelligence Scales

In 1939, the Wechsler-Bellevue Intelligence Scale was published. The materials and tasks included in this test were selected on the basis of their appropriateness for adults. Subsequently, the Wechsler-Bellevue test was replaced by the Wechsler Adult Intelligence Scale (WAIS) and the Wechsler Intelligence Scale for Children (WISC).

The Wechsler scales are organized into a series of subtests of various types. The subtests are combined into a Verbal Scale and a Performance Scale. Deviation I.Q.'s in which the mean has been set at 100 and the standard deviation at 15 may be determined for the Verbal Scale, the Performance Scale, and for the Full Scale.

The separate Performance Scale I.Q. may have diagnostic value for individuals with verbal or cultural handicaps. A person who learns English late in life or who has had a very limited education may encounter difficulty on a verbal test of intelligence. In one study of Verbal-Performance discrepancies on the WISC (Seashore, 1951), occupational group differences were found to be small and statistically insignificant except that in the professional and semiprofessional category, a greater proportion of children obtained higher Verbal than Performance I.Q. The discrepancies for rural children and children from lower socioeconomic levels were not statistically significant, although there was some tendency to obtain higher I.Q.'s on the Performance than on the Verbal Scale.

Other Individual Tests

The Stanford-Binet and the Wechsler scales incorporate somewhat different definitions of intelligence even though certain general abilities contribute largely to the total scores on both tests (Cronbach, 1960, pp. 195–97). The shifting definition of what constitutes intelligence can be further illustrated by examining other individual tests. The Draw-a-Man Test, for example, evaluates the intelligence of the child from ages five to fifteen by the quality of a drawing of a man. Tests for infants place heavy emphasis on sensorimotor development. The California First-Year Mental Scale (ages one to eighteen months), for example, includes a list of behaviors such as reaches for ring, lifts cup up by handle, and makes tower of two cubes. The age in months at which each development is normally found is indicated.

Learning Exercises

4. A child, aged ten years, five months, performed as follows on the Stanford-Binet:

> Passed all tests at 7-year level
> Passed 5 tests at 8-year level
> Passed 2 tests at 9-year level
> Passed 1 test at 10-year level
> Passed 0 tests at 11-year level

   (a) What is his *basal age?*
   (b) What is his I.Q.?

5. How do the subtests provided on the Wechsler scales differ from the Stanford-Binet subtests?

Group Tests of Intelligence

Typically, schools use group tests rather than individual tests to assess the abilities of pupils. The abilities measured by group tests appear to be fairly comparable to the abilities measured by individual tests. Group tests permit an economy of time as many children can be tested at one time. Much less training is required in order to adequately administer, score, and interpret the results of a group test than is required for an individual test. The major advantage of the individual test is that it provides the examiner a much better opportunity to observe the child as he takes the test. The child who is emotionally disturbed, ill, confused by the directions of the test, or poorly motivated can be much more readily detected when tested individually. Aptitude tests attempt to measure what a person *can* do. Therefore, invalid results are obtained when conditions prevail that interfere with an individual's performance.

Group tests may be classified according to age levels. Primary-level group tests usually are designed for children in kindergarten and the first two or three grades of elementary school. No reading or writing is required of the children for primary-level tests. Pictures and diagrams make up the test items. Oral instructions include demonstrations and practice exercises to make sure the child understands the tasks he is required to do. The youngest age level at which it is practical to test children in groups is the kindergarten and first-grade level. For these early ages, considerable individual attention is required to insure that the children follow directions. Hence, groups of no more than about 12 children can be tested effectively at one time.

It is possible to include more written material in tests for the elementary school (grades 3 or 4 through 8), high school, and college levels. Various group tests for these levels differ considerably in content and organization. Some tests are of the "omnibus" variety. In an omnibus test, a vocabulary item may be followed by an arithmetic reasoning item, followed by a spatial relationship type item, etc. The items are usually arranged in order of difficulty. The ability of the student is represented by a single score. Other tests yield several scores in order to reflect intraindividual differences in primary mental abilities. One of the most common practices is to organize test material so as to obtain a measurement of "verbal" and "non-verbal" abilities. Performance on a verbal test is dependent in part upon the reading ability of the child and has been found to be a good predictor of ability of the child to do typical schoolwork. Non-verbal tests are usually pictorial or numerical in content. While non-verbal tests do not predict academic achievement as well as verbal tests, they do give an estimate of the ability of the child who is lacking in ability to read. Non-verbal tests do require the child to understand the spoken language. In this respect, non-verbal tests may be distinguished from "non-language" tests, which require no language, either written or spoken. Non-language tests are of value in assessing the abilities of children with language handicaps, such as the deaf, the speech defective, the illiterate, and children living in homes where the English language has been poorly mastered.

There are no group tests that clearly dominate the field as the Binet and Wechsler dominate the field of individual tests of general intelligence. The following section will describe a number of tests that are widely used in schools. The tests selected to discuss are not necessarily the best tests available. The "best" test for a particular classroom depends upon the objectives for which the test is used as well as some practical considerations such as the amount of time and money available.

Pintner-Cunningham Primary Test. This test covers the kindergarten, grade 1, and the first half of grade 2. It is a part of the Pintner General Ability Tests, Verbal Series, which extends through the college freshman level. The Pintner-Cunningham Primary test is available in three equivalent forms: A, B, and C. Each form consists of the following subtests:

1. *Common Observation:* The child marks all pictures of objects in a set that fit some category, such as all things that Mother uses when she sews her apron (Fig. 4–3, row 1).
2. *Aesthetic Differences:* The child marks the prettiest of three drawings of the same object, such as a house (Fig. 4–3, row 2).
3. *Associated Objects:* The child marks the two things that belong together in a row of pictures, such as a hat and a coat (Fig. 4–3, row 3).
4. *Discrimination of Size:* The child marks the items of clothing that are the right size for the individual pictured. For each article of clothing—shoes, hat, gloves, etc.—one is too large, one is too small, and one is the right size.
5. *Picture Parts:* A series of pictures of increasing complexity is shown. These contain children, animals, toys, and other objects. The same objects are shown outside the picture, mixed in with other objects. The child marks the objects outside the picture that appear in the picture.
6. *Picture Completion:* For each incomplete picture, the child locates and marks the correct missing part among several parts presented.
7. *Dot Drawing:* The child copies drawing by joining dots (as shown in Fig. 4–3, row 4).

A total raw score is obtained by adding scores on each subtest. The mental age corresponding to any raw score may be obtained by consulting a table of age norms. A ratio I.Q. may then be obtained by dividing by the chronological age. A procedure for obtaining deviation I.Q.'s is also provided in the test manual.

Otis Quick-scoring Mental Ability Tests. This series includes three batteries: Alpha, for grades 1 to 4; Beta, for grades 4 to 9; and Gamma, for high school and college.

Alpha consists of 45 items. Each item contains four pictures or diagrams such as the following:

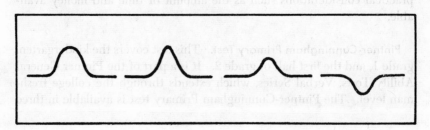

1. Common Observation

2. Aesthetic Differences

3. Associated Objects

4. Dot Drawing

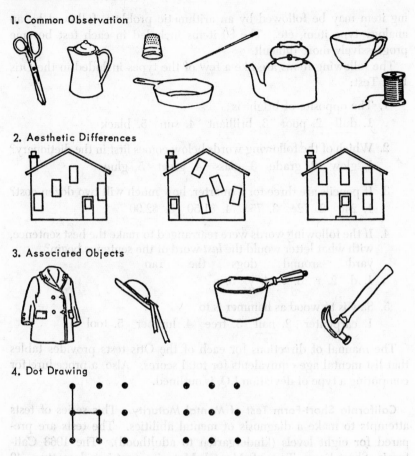

Fig. 4–3. From *Pintner-Cunningham Primary Test: Form A.* Copyright 1923, 1938 by Harcourt, Brace & World, Inc., New York. All rights reserved. Reproduced by permission.

The 45 items are administered under two sets of directions: "non-verbal" and "verbal." For the non-verbal part, the child uses a dark colored crayon and is directed to draw a line through the one picture that is not like the other three. Twelve minutes are allowed to complete the 45 items. Next, for the verbal part, the child uses a light colored crayon, and oral directions are given for each item. For the item above, the administrator reads: "Mark the one of the lines that bends up which is farthest from the one that bends down." Five seconds working time is allowed for each item.

The Beta and Gamma tests consist of a variety of types of items and are presented in a spiral omnibus arrangement. Thus, a verbal reasoning item may be followed by an arithmetic problem, followed by an analogy type item, etc. The 80 items included in each test become progressively more difficult.

The following items are like a few of the types included in the Otis Beta Test:

1. The opposite of bright is
   1. dull 2. poor 3. brilliant 4. sun 5. black

2. Which of the following words below comes first in the dictionary?
   1. glow 2. grade 3. glass 4. greet 5. glue

3. If pencils are three for a quarter, how much will two dozen cost?
   1. 24¢ 2. 72¢ 3. 75¢ 4. $1.50 5. $2.00

4. If the following words were rearranged to make the best sentence, with what letter would the *last* word of the sentence begin?
   yard   around   dogs   the   ran
   1. d 2. r 3. t 4. y 5. a

5. Saw is to wood as hammer is to
   1. carpenter 2. nail 3. tree 4. lumber 5. tool

The manual of directions for each of the Otis tests provides tables that list mental age equivalents for total scores. Also, a procedure for computing a type of deviation I.Q. is outlined.

California Short-Form Test of Mental Maturity. This series of tests attempts to make a diagnosis of mental abilities. The tests are prepared for eight levels (kindergarten to adulthood). The 1963 California Short-Form Test of Mental Maturity requires less than 40 minutes testing time. The test yields language, non-language, and total scores from which mental ages, I.Q.'s, standard scores, and percentiles can be derived. Separate scores may be obtained for each of four areas: memory, logical reasoning, numerical reasoning, and verbal concepts. However, the four "factor" scores should be interpreted with caution as the subtests are short and hence provide only rough measures. The test as a whole assesses ability to solve problems involving verbal, numerical, and pictorial materials.

The Lorge-Thorndike Intelligence Tests. This series of tests includes five levels that cover a range from kindergarten to college freshman. The lowest two levels do not involve reading, although they do require comprehension of oral language. Level 3 (grades 4 to 6), Level 4 (grades 7 to 9), and Level 5 (grades 10 to 13) provide a verbal and non-verbal battery. The verbal battery is made up of subtests named Word Knowledge, Sentence Completion, Verbal Classification, Verbal Analogies, and Arithmetic Reasoning. The non-verbal battery is entirely pictorial, diagrammatic, or numerical and includes the subtests Figure Analogies, Figure Classification, and Number Series. Both verbal and non-verbal batteries were designed to measure abstract intelligence, defined by the authors as "the ability to work with ideas." The non-verbal tests were included to provide a better basis for assessing the abstract intelligence of the retarded reader.

The correlations between the verbal and non-verbal tests cluster around .65. Thus, there is much in common in what is measured in the two series, and differences in scores on verbal and non-verbal will not be significant for the majority of pupils. However, the authors report that in about 25 per cent of cases, the two tests will yield I.Q.'s differing by as much as 15 points.

Scores for these tests are expressed as deviation I.Q.'s with a mean of 100 and a standard deviation of 16. Age, grade, and percentile norms are also given; and median I.Q.'s for children from high, average, and low socioeconomic levels are reported.

School and College Ability Tests (SCAT). SCAT includes five levels covering a range from grade 4 through the college sophomore year. The tests have been developed to "aid in estimating the capacity of a student to undertake the academic work of the next higher level of schooling." The test for each level yields three scores: Verbal, based on Part I, Sentence Understanding, and Part III, Word Meaning; Quantitative, based on Part II, Numerical Computation, and Part IV, Numerical Problem Solving; and Total, based on all four parts.

Following are sample items from Form 2A (grades 10, 11, and 12):

Part I. *Sentence Understanding:* Select the missing word by deciding which one of the five words *best* fits in with the meaning of the sentence.
The shortage of wage labor in the farming districts (   ) the invention of labor-saving devices.
    A. delayed   B. threatened   C. determined
   *D. quickened   E. characterized

Part II. *Numerical Computations:* Work each problem in your head or on a piece of scratch paper. Then select the correct answer from the five suggested answers.
$$.7 - .007 =$$
A. .603   *B. .693   C. .697   D. .707   E. None of these

Part III. Word Meanings: Pick the word or phrase whose meaning is closest to the word in large letters.

CASUAL

A. uncertain *B. offhand C. quiet D. rude E. sly

Part IV. Numerical Problem Solving: Work each problem in your head or on a piece of scratch paper. Then select the correct answer from the five suggested answers.

How much more do 800 three-cent stamps cost than 150 two-cent stamps?

A. $2.10 B. $6.50 C. $8.00 *D. $21.00 E. $27.00

SCAT differs from previous tests discussed in this chapter in that the authors did not attempt to provide a measurement of intelligence. The test items are restricted to school-related abilities. Test results are intended to serve as an aid in planning and guiding the learning experiences of students. Any suggestion that the SCAT may be used as a means of assessing the total intellectual resources of the testee is carefully avoided in the test manual.

Each of the five levels of SCAT are expressed on a common scale, thus permitting comparisons of performances from one level to another. Scores also may be converted to percentiles for the appropriate grade. The *Manual for Interpreting Scores* includes instructions for recording obtained scores with a *percentile band* rather than a single percentile. The percentile band covers a distance of approximately one standard error of measurement up and down from the student's percentile rank.

Learning Exercises

6. What is an advantage of:
   (a) An individual test over a group test?
   (b) A group test over an individual test?
   (c) A non-verbal test over a verbal test?
7. Match a descriptive phrase in Column B to a test named in Column A.

Column A	*Column B*
1. Pintner-Cunningham Primary Test	(a) A spiral omnibus test, grades 4–9
2. Otis Beta	(b) Designed particularly to predict school success
3. SCAT	(c) Separate verbal and non-verbal tests available for grade 4 and above
4. Lorge-Thorndike	(d) Subtests contain rows of pictures. Child marks pictures of objects in a row that fit some category.

INTERPRETING TEST SCORES

Some normative frame of reference is necessary in order to interpret any individual test score. In this section, we will examine how intelligence test scores are distributed, growth curves of intelligence, factors affecting performance, the reliability and stability of test scores, and finally the predictive value of scores.

Distribution of Intelligence

The distribution of the I.Q.'s in the 1937 sample of the Stanford-Binet is shown in Table 4–1. The mean of the distribution is 101.8, and the standard deviation is 16.4.

TABLE 4–1

Distribution of 1937 Stanford-Binet Standardization Group

I.Q.	Per Cent	Classification
160–169	0.03	
150–159	0.2	Very superior
140–149	1.1	
130–139	3.1	Superior
120–129	8.2	
110–119	18.1	High average
100–109	23.5	Normal or average
90–99	23.0	
80–89	14.5	Low average
70–79	5.6	Borderline defective
60–69	2.0	
50–59	0.4	Mentally defective
40–49	0.2	
30–39	0.03	

SOURCE: L. M. Terman and Maud A. Merrill, *Stanford-Binet Intelligence Scale* (Boston: Houghton Mifflin Co., 1960), p. 18. Reproduced by permission.

The classification labels attached to various ranges of I.Q.'s represent convenient means of describing test performance. They are not intended to categorize the total intellectual functioning of individuals. Some individuals of I.Q. 160 fail to distinguish themselves, whereas other individuals who score somewhat lower do become outstanding in intellectual pursuits. Some individuals of I.Q. 60 are able to earn their own living, whereas other with higher performance are apparently intellectually unable to do so. Despite limitations, classification levels of intelligence are of use in forming tentative judgments on how well an individual may be expected to perform in his intellectual endeavors. Also, classification labels do not misleadingly suggest a precision of measurement as do single I.Q. scores.

The children in any school classroom differ widely in mental ability. In one study of a freshman class in the high school of a large city, a range of more than 10½ mental age years is reported (Johnson, 1937). Ninth-grade pupils in a school may vary from a mental age equivalent of the average fourth-grade pupil to a mental age equivalent of the average college senior.

Growth Curves

From the very beginning of the intelligence testing movement, the method adopted for selecting test items insured that intelligence test performance would improve with age—at least up to the early teen ages. Age differentiation was one of the major criteria in the selection of test items in the original Binet scales and in subsequent revisions of the scales. In the development of the 1937 Stanford-Binet, for example, test items were discarded that were not passed by an increasing percentage of children at successive age levels. Hence, we can examine studies reporting growth curves of *intelligence test scores*, but we are on tenuous grounds when we make inferences from such studies concerning the growth of *intelligence*.

Figure 4–4 portrays results that are typical of a number of studies on the relationship of intelligence test performance to age.

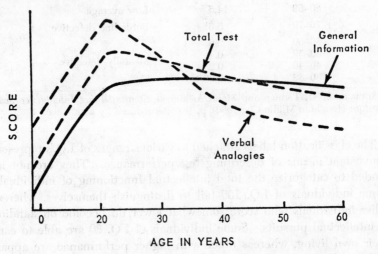

Fig. 4–4. Scores on an Intelligence Test and on Subtests Plotted Against Age. (From Jones and Conrad, 1933.)

The following generalizations can be made on the basis of several studies:

1. Intelligence test performance improves steadily with age up to early adolescence and then improves at a slower rate.
2. Many studies indicate that intelligence test performance reaches its peak by late adolescence or the early twenties, and then a slow but steady decline begins. However, there is some evidence (Bayley, 1955; Owens, 1953) that test scores continue to rise at least until age fifty. This seems to be particularly true for gifted persons (Bayley and Oden, 1955).
3. Some studies indicate that the rate of decline varies with the nature of the test materials. Wechsler's standardization data on the WAIS show the average Performance score reaching a peak at about age twenty-two and then dropping off rapidly, while the average Verbal score rises until about age thirty and then declines gradually (Wechsler, 1955). Note that in Fig. 4-4 little or no decline occurs in General Information, whereas considerable loss occurs in Verbal Analogies.

Even these generalizations may require modification sometime in the future as we learn how to provide children with a more stimulating intellectual environment.

Factors Affecting Performance

The evidence presented in Chapter 3 on the nature-nurture controversy supports the conclusion that intelligence test performance is influenced by both heredity and environment. In addition, performance on an intelligence test is affected by a person's emotional and physical condition at the time he is tested, his motivation and interests, and the physical and emotional conditions in the testing room (light, heat, noise, teacher, etc.). Further, because different abilities are measured by different intelligence tests, a person may perform better on one intelligence test than on another. Thus, an individual's performance on an intelligence test needs to be interpreted in the light of both permanent and temporary characteristics of the individual and the nature of the measuring instrument. In this section, the factors affecting performance will be examined more specifically.

Physiological Factors. Much is yet to be learned about the physiological basis of intelligence. Certain physiological conditions such as microcephaly, mongolism, and cretinism have been shown to be related to mental deficiency. But only about 20 per cent of the mentally defectives suffer from such conditions. For the bulk of the total population, little relationship has been found between physiological measurements and intelligence test scores. No appreciable relationship has been found between head size, brain weight, or height of forehead. Only a slight positive relationship exists between height and weight and intelligence test scores, with considerable overlap in the distributions of test scores.

Racial and National Differences. Psychologists have conducted extensive investigations to determine the extent, if any, of racial differences in mental ability. There are a number of research pitfalls in such studies. First, there is the problem of defining "race." Skin color is the most convenient and frequently employed criterion for classifying people into different races. Yet pigmentation of the skin differs in amount rather than in kind from person to person. However, because anthropologists have not succeeded in identifying a clearly superior criterion for distinguishing races, comparisons of performance of races on intelligence tests have been made on skin-color groups. A second difficulty is that of identifying racial groups composed of individuals who genetically are not mixed with another racial group. The problem of racial mixture has been largely ignored in the many investigations of racial differences.

Data on intelligence collected during World War I and World War II indicate that there are racial differences in intelligence. During World War I, the Army Alpha, a verbal test, and the Army Beta, a performance test, were administered to draftees. Table 4–2 summarizes the findings (Yerkes, 1921). Total score possible for the Alpha was 212; for the Beta, 118.

Table 4–2 reveals both regional and racial differences. The regional differences in test performance was not restricted to the Negro draftees. The northern white averaged higher than the southern white; and the median Army Alpha scores for Negroes from Pennsylvania, New York, Illinois, and Ohio were higher than the median Army Alpha scores for whites from Mississippi, Arkansas, Kentucky, and Georgia.

TABLE 4–2

Intelligence Test Scores by Region and Race

Group	Median Alpha Score	Median Beta Score
White, native-born	58.9	43.4
Northern Negro	38.6	32.5
Southern Negro	12.4	19.8

Interpretation of research findings on racial differences is complicated by the fact that both hereditary and environmental factors are reflected in intelligence test scores. It is conceivable that differences may be attributable to innate factors. It is much more likely that differences are due to inequalities in the average intellectual environment experienced by the two races (Pettigrew, 1964). Research conducted by Klineberg (1935), and Lee (1951) have been interpreted as evidence that an improvement in educational opportunities can result in an increase in I.Q. scores. In Lee's study, Southern-born Negro children were tested in successive years after they had moved to Philadelphia. The longer the children remained in the Philadelphia schools, the greater was the increase in I.Q. scores. Thus, 182 of these children entering grade 1A averaged 86.5. Tested again when in grade 2B, the average was 89.3. In grade 4B, the average was 91.8; and in grade 6B, 93.3.

Possibly the most significant finding from the many comparative studies that have been conducted is the fact that I.Q. scores for Negro and white overlap considerably. Although research evidence indicates that Negro children score lower on the average than white children on intelligence tests, many white children score lower than the average Negro child, and many Negro children score higher than the average white child.

Studies on intelligence test performance of immigrants to United States and their children show, in general, a superiority of northern over southern European stock. There is some basis for attributing this superiority to "selective immigration" rather than to innate differences. When a non-language test was used to test a sample of Danes and Italians in their own country in Europe, no difference was found in the intellectual levels; whereas Danish-Americans performed significantly higher than Italian-Americans (Franzblau, 1935).

Socioeconomic Class Differences. Many studies have established a relationship between I.Q. and socioeconomic levels (Tyler, 1956). On the average, children classified as belonging to the upper socioeconomic levels do better on intelligence tests than do children from the lower levels. This holds true, not only in the United States, but in other countries such as England and Russia (Johnson, 1948). The results of the many studies do not clarify whether the differences in test performance are attributable to heredity or environment. It may be that persons with greater innate potentials tend to gravitate to occupations requiring more intelligence. However, there is some evidence that present-day intelligence tests tend to discriminate against individuals in the low socioeconomic levels. Davis (1951) reports an extensive study in which a number of intelligence tests were administered to pupils in a city in a midwestern state. The percentage of pupils passing each item in the several tests was computed for both a high and a low socioeconomic group. A much higher proportion of upper class children than lower class children passed items such as the following:

A symphony is to a composer as a book is to what?

A. paper   B. sculptor   C. author   D. musician   E. man

For some other items, pupils from the low socioeconomic group did just as well as the pupils from the upper class group. Also of importance to the test interpreter is the possibility that middle class children try harder to do well on tests than do lower class children. Some of the findings of Eells (1951) and his associates appear to give credence to this possibility of motivational differences between classes.

The multiplicity of studies showing the relationships of racial, national, and social class differences to performance on intelligence tests, plus studies showing adverse effects of intellectually deprived environments on test performances, should serve to prompt caution in interpreting intelligence test scores. The I.Q. scores of children who come from other than white, middle class urban homes are particularly difficult to interpret. Test performance may very well underestimate innate potential. Yet the lower scores may predict accurately later academic achievement because the verbal deficiencies that contribute to the low scores may also be a factor contributing to a later unsatisfactory achievement in school.

Personality and Emotional Factors. Self-confidence, the willingness to persist in school-like problem-solving tasks, the extent of anxiety produced in taking a test—these and many other personality and emotional factors affect test performance. Richards (1951) reports a longitudinal study of intellectual development in which one boy was administered a form of the Stanford-Binet over a seven and one-half year period. Four trends were apparent in the boy's I.Q. curve: a rise of 11 points from ages three to five; a drop of 13 points from five to six; a rise of 25 points from six to eight; and a drop of 18 points from eight to ten. Observational and test data obtained during the period revealed a close correspondence between the emotional climate of home and school and the rising or falling of the boy's I.Q. Drops in the I.Q. corresponded to periods in the home when business worries prevented the father from devoting much time to his son, and in the school when formal and disturbingly restrictive disciplinary conditions prevailed. Increases in the I.Q. corresponded to periods that were happier for the boy in both home and school.

The test interpreter needs to be alert to the possibility that personality or emotional factors may affect the performance of an individual on a test. One advantage of the individual test over the group test is the increased opportunity that the examiner has to detect any signs that the child taking the test is emotionally disturbed.

Reliability and Stability of Intelligence Test Scores

The research on the reliability and stability of intelligence test scores can be organized so as to answer a number of questions of practical concern to the teacher.

First, there is the question of accuracy of a single measurement. If a child is tested today and he obtains an I.Q. of 110, what is his I.Q. likely to be if he is retested a few days later with a parallel form of the same test? When the accuracy of the 1937 Stanford-Binet I.Q. was checked by comparing Form L and Form M, I.Q.'s of seven-year-olds obtained a few days apart correlated about .91 (Terman and Merrill, 1937, p. 47). Even with this degree of reliability, the average shift in I.Q. from form to form is substantial:

5.9 points for I.Q. 130
5.1 points for I.Q. 100
2.5 points for I.Q. below 70

Children obtaining an I.Q. of 130 on one form shifted as much as 12 or 14 points higher or lower when tested with a second form of the Binet a few days later.

We can obtain a rough estimate of how much shift to expect in a child's I.Q. score for any test for which we know the reliability coefficient and the standard deviation by applying the formula to obtain the standard error of measurement (see Chapter 14):

$$S_m = S_t\sqrt{1 - r_{11}}$$

where S_m is the standard error of measurement
S_t is the standard deviation of test scores
r_{11} is the reliability coefficient

Suppose our test has a reliability of .91 and a standard deviation of 16 points. Then:

$$S_m = 16\sqrt{1 - .91} = 16\sqrt{.09} = 4.8 \text{ or about 5 points}$$

Thus, for a child who obtained an I.Q. of 110, the chances are about two in three that his "true" score lies somewhere between 105 and 115.

A second question that may be raised concerns the comparability of I.Q. scores from two different tests administered at approximately the same time. Here we might expect some divergence in performance for a number of reasons. Because the two tests tap somewhat different mental abilities, we could expect some differences in performance. The norms for each test will have been established on different standardization groups. Non-comparability of norms could occur due to different proportions of bright, average, and dull pupils included in the standardization groups. Differences in the sizes of the standard deviations would result in a given I.Q. on the two tests varying in meaning. Knezevich (1946) reported the scores obtained by 28 high school students who were administered the Henmon-Nelson test and then one month later the California Test of Mental Maturity. The I.Q. scores averaged about 5½ points higher on the Henmon-Nelson than on the California test. Differences in I.Q. points for the 28 students were as follows:

    0–5 points differences for 11 students
    6–10 points differences for 8 students
    11–15 points differences for 4 students
    16–20 points differences for 3 students
    More than 20 points differences for 2 students

Finally, we may raise questions concerning the long-term stability of I.Q. scores. Will children who obtain I.Q. scores above average at age eight tend to be above average three, four, or five years hence; and will children below average tend to remain below average? In short, is the I.Q. constant? The research evidence on this question can be summed up as follows: For the majority of children, the I.Q. scores will remain roughly comparable over a period of years providing the tests are properly administered and scored. Tests given before the age of six years predict poorly, and the accuracy of prediction decreases somewhat as the interval between testings is increased. In one study (Honzik, Macfarlane, and Allen, 1948), the I.Q.'s of a group of children were measured at intervals from the time they were two until they were eighteen. Some large shifts in I.Q. were noted (in one case, 55 points), but tests given at ages eight or nine were found to correlate .88 with tests given at age ten and .86 at ages fourteen or fifteen.

There is some evidence that schooling affects intelligence test performance. Lorge (1945) retested 131 young men who had been tested

20 years previously and found a relationship between test scores and highest grade completed in school. Groups were formed on the basis of comparability of original scores, and then each group was subdivided according to the highest grade in school completed. Matched on the basis of initial scores, the young men with more schooling tended to do better on the retesting than those with less schooling. In all, there is sufficient evidence concerning changes in the level of intellectual functioning of children to question seriously the previously held assumptions of a "fixed intelligence" and a "predetermined development of intelligence" (Hunt, 1961).

Intelligence and School Success

Why do some students earn better grades in school than other students? It is not difficult to think of a number of reasons. Some students work harder than others. Some students have better work and study habits. Mastery of foundation courses makes it easier for some students to do well on more advanced courses. Intelligence level may also be related to educational achievement. Probably most of the variations in the grades obtained by the students in any one class is due to an interaction of motivation, study and work habits, past learning experience, and intelligence, plus certain chance factors associated with the students' performances and the instructor's grading.

In view of the number of factors that can affect educational achievement, it is not surprising to discover that the correlations between intelligence test scores and grades in school is not particularly high. For the many studies conducted at the high school level, most of the reported correlations range from about .30 to .80 (Super, 1949). At the college level, the correlations are a bit lower—.20 to .70. Applying the coefficient of determination (r^2), we have then only 9 to 64 per cent of the variability in high school grades related to intelligence test scores, and only 4 to 49 per cent of college grades.

The differences in the correlation between test scores and grades found in various studies is probably due to differences in the range of ability levels of the students included in each study. Not much of the differences in course achievement can be attributable to differences in intelligence levels, if all students are about equal in intelligence. In such a case, the correlation will be negligible. If, on the other hand, students vary widely in intelligence levels, and are much alike in other factors related to course achievement, then the correlation between intelligence and grades is likely to be high.

Intelligence test scores predict grades in some subjects better than in others. The following correlations between Form L of the Binet intelligence test scores and grades of tenth-graders in various subjects are illustrative (Bond, 1940):

Reading comprehension	.73
Reading vocabulary	.79
Reading speed	.43
English usage	.59
History	.59
Spelling	.46
Biology	.54
Geometry	.48

It is not uncommon to find reports of correlations in the high .70's and the .80's between intelligence and standardized achievement test scores (Cronbach, 1960). Why do intelligence test scores predict academic achievement as measured by a standardized battery better than academic achievement as measured by teachers' grades? Probably for two main reasons: First, the achievement tests are more reliable and more objectively scored. To the extent that this is the reason, intelligence test scores could be expected to provide an improved prediction of teachers' grades when (1) the quality is improved of the examinations that serve as criterion scores, and (2) when teachers' grading procedures are improved. A second reason is that teachers' grades are based on achievement over material specifically taught within a course, whereas standardized achievement tests are not so clearly geared to the subject matter taught by any one single teacher. The boy or girl who is quick to learn, who remembers material taught two or three grades back, and who picks up knowledge from many sources, *but* who does not strive strenuously to attain high grades in the courses in which he is presently enrolled may do well on an intelligence test and do relatively better on a standardized achievement test than on school tests. The boy or girl who is slower to learn, who does not remember particularly well material taught in previous grades, *but* who does strive diligently to do well in school may perform only at the average level on an intelligence test and a general standardized achievement test even though he is currently doing "A" work in school. Whatever the reasons may be, intelligence test scores usually are in closer agreement with standardized achievement test scores than with teachers' grades.

For a counselor in a high school, an intelligence test score is far from perfect as a predictor of an individual student's success in college.

This is well illustrated by the data supplied by Hartson (1941, 1945) on Oberlin College. Hartson found that while some students with Otis I.Q. equivalents of less than 100 manage to graduate, 65 per cent of the entering freshmen who were below 110 failed academically. This would mean that 35 per cent of the students below 110 were successful. To predict academic success at Oberlin for the student below 110 would involve searching for legitimate reasons for expecting him to belong to the 35 per cent group of successful students.

Identifying the Gifted and the Retarded

Does a teacher require intelligence test results in order to estimate the academic potential of his pupils? Research evidence does not provide an unequivocal "Yes" or "No" answer to this question. Possibly, some teachers can estimate fairly accurately while others cannot. Gronlund and Whitney (1958) asked 26 fourth-grade teachers to make judgments of the intelligence of their pupils. The median correlation of teachers' ranking of their pupils and a measured intelligence test score was .70 for boys and .76 for girls. The interquartile range for boys was .11; for girls, .14.

Gibbons (1938) has noted a tendency of teachers to underestimate the intelligence of superior students and to overrate dull pupils. Lewis (1943) reports a study involving 45,000 elementary school children in grades 4 to 8 in 455 schools in 36 states. For one phase of the study, pupils with an I.Q. rating of 145 or more were selected. This represents an achievement of about one in a thousand in ability as measured by the Kuhlman-Anderson test. Of these very superior children, Lewis reports only one boy in five and two girls in five were rated by their teachers as being *precocious* or *mentally quick*. Two of the group were designated by their teachers as being *dull* or *mentally sluggish*.

The Lewis study constitutes evidence that teachers often do not recognize the gifted child. This may be due in part to the many prevalent misconceptions about the gifted. The popular stereotype of the gifted child is one who is small in stature, intense in nature, wearing glasses, and very poorly emotionally and socially adjusted. Research evidence does not lend support to this characterization of the gifted child.

The most extensive research studies of gifted children was made by Terman and his associates (1925, 1947, 1954). In the 1920's, 1,500 elementary and high school pupils of I.Q.'s of 140 and above were located. For this select group, extensive data was obtained with respect to their physical measurement, achievement, and behavioral characteristics. Principal results are stated by Terman as follows:

Children of I.Q. 140 or higher are, in general, appreciably superior to un-selected children in physique, health, and social adjustment; markedly superior in moral attitudes as measured either by character tests or by trait ratings; and vastly superior in their mastery of school subjects as shown by a three-hour battery of achievement tests. In fact, the typical child of the group had mastered the school subjects to a point about two grades beyond the one in which he was enrolled, some of them three or four grades beyond. Moreover, his ability as evidenced by achievement in the different school subjects is so general as to refute completely the traditional belief that gifted children are usually one-sided. [Terman, 1954, p. 223.]

Terman's follow-up studies of his group of gifted children indicate that the group as a whole has marked up impressive accomplishments. Several, by the time they were thirty, were nationally and inter-nationally known. Novelists, short-story writers, poets, a sculptor, a gifted musical composer, and several scientists were included in the group. A number of the gifted children did not live up to their promise. With a few exceptions, intellectually creative productivity was found to be confined to the males.

Terman concluded: "The data reviewed indicates that, above the I.Q. level of 140, adult success is largely determined by such factors as social adjustment, emotional stability, and drive to accomplish" (Terman and Oden, 1940, p. 84).

Intelligence tests can be of some value in identifying the mentally retarded. However, teachers need to exert extreme caution in inter-preting a low intelligence test score. A child may perform poorly on an intelligence test for many reasons extraneous to his capacity to learn. It is true that children who score relatively low on an intelligence test usually do experience difficulty with schoolwork. However, as pointed out by Tyler (1948), the adoption by the school of more appropriate educational objectives and better means of attaining objectives could result in a revised definition of the characteristics associated with suc-cess in school. Then pupils who are now classified as non-educable on the basis of their intelligence test performance may, with more appro-priate teaching methods, become educable.

Predicting Vocational Attainment

As might be expected, people in some occupations do better on in-telligence tests than people in other occupations. Harrell and Harrell (1945) report scores on the Army General Classification Test of 18,782 white enlisted men in the Army Air Force, classified according to their civilian occupations. Data for just a few of the occupations reported by Harrell and Harrell follow:

Civilian Occupation	Number of Cases	Mean Score	Standard Deviation	Range of Cases
Accountant	172	128.1	11.7	94–157
Clerk-Typist	468	116.8	12.0	80–147
Machinist	456	110.1	16.1	38–153
Laborer	856	95.8	20.1	26–145

The data illustrates both the difference in average performance by occupation and the extensiveness of the overlap in scores among occupations.

The difficulty of anticipating future occupational status is demonstrated in a follow-up study conducted by Cantoni (1955) on 97 high school boys. A number of measurements, including the Kuhlman-Anderson Intelligence Tests, were administered to the boys in 1943. Ten years later, the occupations of these boys were ascertained. A higher proportion of boys with higher intelligence test scores were located in the higher status occupations. Thus, about 57 per cent of the boys scoring 105 and above on the intelligence test were located in business and the professions, as compared to about 28 per cent of the boys scoring below 90. When the boys were classified on the basis of their high school average, contrasts are greater. For the boys scoring above 105 with better than a 2.5 grade point average, 80 per cent were located in business and the professions as compared to 20 per cent of the boys scoring below 90 on the intelligence test and below a 1.5 grade point average. Even though the number of cases is small in the various categories in Cantoni's study and only a rough method of classifying occupational status was employed, the difficulty of predicting future occupational status for any one boy is well illustrated.

Ghiselli (1955) has made a comprehensive survey of the many studies investigating the relationship of intelligence test scores and occupational proficiency. Average validities for group intelligence tests between both proficiency during training period and worker's actual performance on the job vary widely from one type of occupation to another. For certain occupations such as agricultural workers, bench workers, and assemblers, the correlations are usually below .20. Higher correlations (usually from about .35 to .50) are found for managerial and professional occupations as well as for some of the highly skilled workers.

Learning Exercises

Following are test scores on intelligence and reading tests, and the academic rank in class for Miss Lang's sixth grade:

Pupil	Chron. Age (Yrs.–Mos.)	Binet M.A.	Binet I.Q.°	Lorge-Thorndike Non-Verbal I.Q.	Rank in Class	Reading Comprehension Grade Level
Ada	10–5	15–2	140	135	4	12–6
Ben	11–8	15–9	130	128	2	12–0
Cal	11–5	13–0	111	126	14	5–6
Dave	10–5	12–6	116	111	10	7–6
Eve	10–10	12–6	112	114	12	7–0
Fred	11–9	12–1	101	120	15	5–6
Gay	11–4	12–1	104	97	16	6–6
Hal	11–8	12–9	107	105	9	6–9
Ivy	11–5	16–0	134	122	1	11–0
Joe	11–6	12–0	102	116	20	6–0
Kay	10–10	13–11	124	117	8	10–6
Lil	11–0	13–10	121	120	7	9–0
May	11–7	13–1	110	118	17	9–4
Nora	10–11	13–11	123	126	5	8–10
Ora	11–8	12–6	105	95	13	6–10
Phil	11–10	12–0	100	105	18	6–8
Quin	11–6	13–1	111	117	19	6–4
Reg	12–0	15–7	125	119	6	9–4
Sam	11–5	13–3	113	115	11	8–2
Tom	11–2	10–9	95	96	21	6–1
Una	11–8	10–11	93	90	23	5–2
Vera	12–1	11–8	96	120	3	10–5
Walt	12–11	11–0	92	91	22	5–1
Xi	12–9	11–0	87	95	24	3–6
Yo	13–4	10–0	77	80	25	3–0

° Based on the Pinneau Revised I.Q. Tables (Terman and Merrill, 1960, pp. 257–335).

Learning exercises 8–15 are based on the above distributions.

8. How would a distribution of the Binet I.Q. scores differ from that of Table 4–1?

9. What is the range of Stanford-Binet mental ages in Miss Lang's class?

10. Assuming that the I.Q. scores held constant over a period of three years, who would make the greater gain in mental ages—Ben or Una?

11. Xi and Yo are the sons of an immigrant to the United States. Their parents speak English poorly. How would you interpret their Binet scores?

12. Would a distribution of intelligence test scores, such as found in Miss Lang's class, be more likely to be found among middle or among lower socioeconomic group children?

13. Vera is obtaining "A" grades in school. When she took the Binet test, she was emotionally disturbed. How would you interpret her score?

14. If Phil were tested three times with the Binet, two of his three scores might be expected to fall between _____ and _____. (Assume $S_m = 5$.)

15. Miss Lang jotted down some questions opposite the names of certain students. Name the students for which each of the following questions seem appropriate:
(a) Does this "very superior" student need more challenging work?

(b) Would the "high average" (or "superior") boy benefit from remedial reading instruction? (Three boys.)

(c) Is this "high average" girl not working up to capacity because of lack of interest?

DIFFERENTIAL ABILITIES

The idea that intelligence is composed of many abilities directed the energies of psychologists into new avenues of research. Efforts were made to determine the particular abilities required for success in different occupations and academic curricula. Initially, psychologists proceeded in a piecemeal fashion. Separate tests of mechanical, clerical, verbal aptitudes, etc., were constructed; and many of these tests are still found useful as aids in providing vocational guidance. Later, psychologists used a statistical technique known as "factor analysis" in order to more systematically sort the abilities of man. Two types of differential abilities have grown out of this later effort. In the first type, the factors identified are conceived as pure, basic, or primary mental abilities of the individual. Factors were given names such as "memory," "perceptual ability," and "inductive reasoning." The California Test of Mental Maturity, previously discussed, is one example of this type of test. In the second type of test, the separate abilities measured are much more complex and represent identifiable skills required for a number of occupations or for the learning of different academic subjects. The tests are designed to measure such abilities as "mechanical reasoning," "clerical speed and accuracy," and "language usage." The Differential Aptitude Test is an example of this second type of test.

Various tests have been developed to measure the separate abilities of man. Before proceeding to a discussion of these various aptitude tests, let us examine the meaning of the term "aptitude." An *aptitude* may be defined as "a condition or set of characteristics regarded as predictive of an individual's ability to acquire with training some knowledge, skill, or set of responses." Note in this definition that there is no assumption that aptitudes are hereditary. A low score on an aptitude test may mean only that the individual has not had as yet the experiences necessary to prepare him for some specific training program. For example, a low score on a reading readiness test (one kind of aptitude test) is not interpreted by a primary grade teacher as evidence that the child cannot learn to read. Rather, the low score is interpreted to mean that certain experiences need to be provided the child to develop the subskills necessary for the child to profit from formal instruction in reading. In a similar fashion, when a high school student obtains a low mechanical aptitude test score, it does not mean that the student is incapable of ever benefiting from instruction in courses related to mechanics. Possibly the low score may be due to relatively little opportunity in the past for the student to work with mechanical things. If such be the case, it would be theoretically possible to provide training experiences that would develop the mechanical aptitudes of the student in much the same way as experiences to develop reading readiness are provided to first-grade pupils who score low on a reading readiness test. Unfortunately, we do not know as much about how to provide experiences to develop mechanical aptitude as we know concerning the development of reading readiness. In addition, it is not so imperative that everyone develop mechanical aptitudes. Other aptitudes may serve as substitutes.

It should be noted that in the definition of aptitude given above, there is no assumption that aptitudes are not inherited. If we can identify physiological characteristics of the individual, such as the possession of a good brain and a good neural metabolism, then it would appear that heredity would be of importance in the developmental status of the aptitude. The low reading readiness test score or the low mechanical aptitude test score may be largely attributable to innate factors rather than to a lack of opportunity to develop the aptitude.

Differential Aptitude Tests

The Differential Aptitude Tests (Bennett, Seashore, and Wesman, 1959) were designed to measure abilities that would be useful in many academic and vocational areas. The tests are intended primarily for boys and girls in grades 8 to 12. Following are: (1) the name of each test in the battery; (2) the ability that the test authors are endeavoring to measure; (3) a test item example, *or a brief description of the type of items included;* and (4) some of the academic and occupational fields listed by the test authors as examples of areas where the ability tested is needed for success.

1. *Verbal Reasoning:*

> *Designed to measure:* Ability to understand concepts framed in words.

> *Test item example:*[3]

> . . . . . is to water as eat is to . . . . .

[3] Most test item examples on pages 142–145 are drawn from the practice exercises of the DAT. Reproduced by permission. Copyright 1947, © 1961, The Psychological Corporation, New York, N.Y. All rights reserved.

1. continue 2. drink 3. foot 4. girl
A. drive B. enemy C. food D. industry

The student is required to combine the appropriate number and letter. In this case the answer is 2C.

> *Fields where ability is needed:* High-level occupations where complex verbal relationships and concepts are important. College.

2. *Numerical Ability:*

> *Designed to measure:* Understanding of numerical relationships and facility in handling numerical concepts.

> *Test item example:* What *one* number can replace *both* question marks?

$$\frac{3}{?} = \frac{?}{48}$$

A 1
B 10
C 25
D 100
*E None of these

> *Fields where ability is needed:* College curricula requiring quantitative thinking, such as mathematics, physics, and engineering. Many occupations at varying levels: bookkeeper, statistician, shipping clerk, carpentry, tool making.

3. *Abstract Reasoning:*

> *Designed to measure:* Ability to perceive relationships in abstract figure patterns.

> *Test item example:*

Problem Figures   Answer Figures

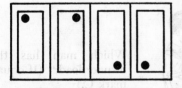   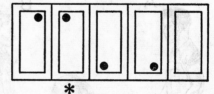

*

The four Problem Figures make a series. The student is required to find which one of the Answer Figures would be next, or the fifth one in the series.

> *Fields where ability is needed:* In curricula, professions, or vocations that require perceptions of relationships among things rather than among words or numbers.

4. *Space Relations:* Ability to deal with concrete materials through visualization.

Test item example:

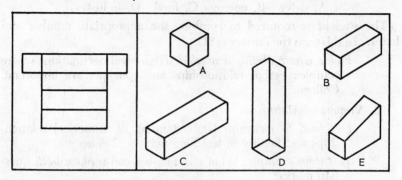

A pattern that can be folded is shown at the left, and five figures are shown at the right. The student is required to select the figures that can be made from the pattern shown. In the above, C and D are correct both in shape and size.

> *Fields where ability is needed:* College curricula or occupations requiring ability to visualize objects in three dimensions. Such fields as drafting, dress designing, architecture, art, die-making, and decoration.

5. *Mechanical Reasoning:* Reasoning in the mechanical field and understanding of mechanical and physical principles in familiar situations.

   Test item example:

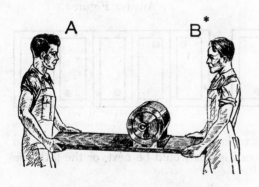

Which man has the heavier load? (If equal, mark C.)

Each item consists of a picture and a question about the picture.

> *Fields where ability is needed:* Academic curricula requiring understanding of the principles of common physical forces. Physical science field and certain technical fields. Occupa-

tions such as carpenter, mechanic, maintenance man, assembler, etc.

6. *Clerical Speed and Accuracy:* Speed and accuracy with simple number and letter combinations.

Test item example:

Test Items					Answer Sheet				
v	AB	AC	AD	AE	F	v	AC	AE	AF	AB	AD
w	aA	ab	BA	Ba	Bb	w	BA	Ba	Bb	aA	aB

Each item contains five combinations of letters and/or numbers. One combination is underlined. The student is required to find the one combination on the separate answer sheet that is the same as one which is underlined in the test item. The test is composed of two parts, each part containing 100 items. The student is allowed three minutes to work on each part.

Fields where ability is needed: Occupations such as filing, coding, and stockroom work.

7. (a) *Language Usage—Spelling:* Ability to distinguish between correct and incorrect spelling of words that occur frequently in everyday vocabulary and that are frequently misspelled.

Test item example:

Example		Sample of Answer Sheet	
W. man		Right	Wrong
		|X|	| |
X. gurl		Right	Wrong
		| |	|X|

7. (b) *Language Usage—Sentences:* Ability to distinguish between good and bad grammar, punctuation, and word usage.

Test item example:

Example	Sample of Answer Sheet
Ain't we/ going to the/	A B C D E
A B	|X| | | | | | | |X|
office/ next week/ at all.	
C D E	

Student is required to identify errors.

Fields where ability is needed: A basic skill in many vocations, including stenography, journalism, proofreading, and advertising.

The manual accompanying the DAT includes percentile and standard score norms for boys and for girls for each grade from 8 to 12 inclusive. Reliability of each test is high. Differences in interest performance of ten units of standard score may be regarded as significant with reasonable confidence. Literally thousands of validity studies on the DAT have been conducted. Most of these studies have been concerned with the prediction of high school and college achievement. Many of the validity coefficients are high. There is evidence that the Verbal Reasoning and the Numerical Ability tests provide the best combinations of DAT scores to predict future academic performance. For example, grade 9 scores in DAT VR + NA predicted Total Scores on the Essential High School Content Battery taken in grade 12 to the extent of $r = .80$ for boys and .70 for girls (Bennett, *et al.*, 1959).

Use of Multiple Aptitude Tests

The use in the schools of multiple aptitude test batteries such as the DAT, the Flanagan Aptitude Tests (1953–1959), or the Guilford-Zimmerman Aptitude Survey (1947–1956) presents many problems. Testing time is long and the costs are relatively high. The time consumed in scoring and interpreting is great. Parents and students all too frequently expect the counselor, on the basis of test results, to provide a prescription of what academic or vocational program the student should enter. This is never possible. Success in any academic or vocational field is dependent upon much more than is measured by the tests. At best, the test results merely provide data from which a competent counselor may obtain significant clues that need to be taken into account by the student in arriving at his own academic or vocational decision.

In addition to multiple aptitude test batteries, there are numerous types of specific aptitude tests commercially available, including tests of motor ability, art aptitude, musical aptitude, spatial visualization, and aptitudes for a variety of academic courses and specific professions.

Learning Exercise

16. Percentile scores for three eleventh-grade students on the DAT were as follows:

	Mary	Sue	Bill
AR (Abstract Reasoning)	95	75	88
NA (Numerical Ability)	80	65	95
AR (Abstract Reasoning)	80	85	90
SR (Space Relations)	70	90	95
MR (Mechanical Reasoning)	65	50	90
CSA (Clerical Speed and Accuracy)	80	70	60
LU. Sp. (Language Use: Spelling)	96	70	80
LU. Sc. (Language Use: Sentences)	94	75	84

On the basis of these scores *alone,* for which of the three students would each of the following decisions appear to be appropriate?

(a) To major in physics in college
(b) To major in English in college
(c) To prepare for a dress designing career

SUMMARY

So called "intelligence tests" may be more accurately thought of as "academic aptitude" tests. They can serve a number of purposes in the school. Academic aptitude test results aid the teacher in (1) forming realistic academic expectations for each member of the class and gearing instruction to the student's ability level, (2) identifying the over- and underachiever, (3) grouping students of comparable ability levels for instructional purposes, (4) guiding students to appropriate vocational and academic goals, (5) interpreting school progress of the student to his parents, (6) differentiating between the student who is failing because of a lack of intellectual resources from the student who is failing because of inadequate academic background, and (7) understanding the pattern of the student's mental abilities.

The teacher in interpreting intelligence test scores needs to keep clearly in mind the distinction between intelligence conceived as an innate potential and intelligence as a measure of learned behavior. The approach to assessing the intellectual resources of the student is influenced by whether the teacher conceives of intelligence as a single characteristic or as a number of mental abilities.

Some notion of what is measured by intelligence may be obtained by examining a number of individual and group intelligence tests. From such an examination, it becomes evident that the specific abilities measured vary from one test to another and, indeed, vary from one age level to another. Most intelligence tests are highly loaded with verbal materials, although portions of some tests attempt to measure other abilities. Most, but not all, intelligence tests yield an I.Q. score. The present trend is to obtain deviation I.Q. scores (which are really standard scores) rather than ratio I.Q.'s. The number of scores obtainable differ from one intelligence test to another. The temptation to obtain as many scores as possible from one testing is tempered by the need to have each score reliable. Finally, intelligence tests differ in the degree to which the test items resemble the tasks pupils are called upon to do in school.

In interpreting test scores, it is necessary to have some frame of reference in mind. Test scores may be assessed in the light of knowledge of how intelligence test scores are distributed throughout the whole population and how test performance changes with age.

A number of cautions need to be observed in interpreting any single test score. Factors relative to performance include physiological factors, race, nationality, and socioeconomic status. Additional caution is required in interpreting a test score of an individual who does not come from a white, urban, middle class home. Personality and emotional factors can have a temporary and a fairly long-term effect on the quality of performance of an individual on an intelligence test.

In general, present-day intelligence tests are reasonably reliable, and for most individuals fairly stable over long periods of time. However, intelligence test results, at best, are rough measurements; and small differences in performance from one testing period to another are to be expected.

Intelligence test scores predict school success best. Even here, other variables such as motivation, past learning, and study skills need to be taken into account to maximize accuracy of prediction. Although there is evidence that teachers can predict quite well intelligence levels of their pupils, the literature provides much evidence that teachers often estimate intelligence poorly, particularly of the gifted. Our knowledge of what may be expected from the gifted has been extended by a number of studies, notably those of Terman and his associates.

Intelligence tests are associated with vocational attainment, much as we might expect. What is surprising is the extent of overlap in intelligence test performance existing between certain "intellectual" and "non-intellectual" occupations. Some relationship does exist between intelligence test performance of boys while in high school and their later occupational attainment. The relationship is greater when high school grade average also is taken into account.

A number of tests designed to measure specific aptitudes are available. During the past two decades, aptitude test batteries have been built that provide a means of comparing the relative strengths and weaknesses in an individual's abilities.

Answer Cues

1. (a) Disagree. Plan to put Roger Stanton in advanced project group. Plan to use programmed learning for remedial group. (b) Agree. Bill Clark's performance on SCAT. (c) Agree. Jean Scott. (d) Disagree. Mr. Thompson searched for consistencies between school performance and aptitude test performance.

2. Yes. High correlation of I.Q. of twins reared apart attributable to innate potential. The fact that this correlation was lower than for twins reared together attributable to the influence of environment.

3. (a) Group. (b) General. (c) Specific.

4. (a) 7 years. (b) 80.

5. Subtests combined on the Wechsler to yield a Verbal, a Performance, and a Total Score. The Binet subtests are arranged by age levels and yield a single estimate of an I.Q.

6. (a) Examiner has better chance to observe the child and note signs indicating that the child is not performing up to capacity. (b) Easier to administer and score. More than one child can be tested at one time. (c) Can estimate ability of child who has a reading difficulty.

7. 1d, 2a, 3b, 4c.

8. Higher proportion of high I.Q.'s.

9. Six years.

10. Ben. There is a greater growth rate for higher I.Q.'s.

11. Probably underestimations of their innate potential.

12. Middle.

13. Probably an underestimation of her innate ability and her usual functional ability.

14. 95 to 105.

15. (a) Ada. (b) Cal, Fred, Joe. (c) May.

16. (a) Bill. (b) Mary. (c) Sue.

5

EMOTIONAL AND SOCIAL DEVELOPMENT

The school in our society has been delegated a major responsibility for advancing the knowledge and intellectual abilities and skills of children. The children who make up the population of a school are individuals in the process of working through various emotional and social problems. Hence, the members of the faculty of any school, whether they like it or not, are faced with the fact that their school is a kind of laboratory within which children develop emotionally and socially. The importance attached to non-academic objectives may vary from teacher to teacher. However, even the strictly academically oriented teacher soon discovers that intellectual development does not occur apart from other aspects of development.

In order to obtain some preliminary notion of the nature of a teacher's problems arising out of the course of social and emotional development of children, let us visit Miss Rainbird, a teacher of English at Bolton High School.

The football season had reached a climax at Bolton High with Bolton meeting defeat in the semifinals for the state championship. Miss Rainbird along with other faculty members welcomed the end of an interlude during which an increasing proportion of the student body apparently relegated the achievement of academic goals to a position of minor importance. Pep rallies, extra band practices, and a prevailing atmosphere of excitement had distracted many students from their studies. Miss Rainbird decided to spend a Saturday afternoon in the school's guidance office reviewing information about characteristics of individual pupils in her tenth-grade class. Miss Rainbird's approach to her self-imposed task was guided by convictions that: (1) the study of English could contribute importantly to the total development of each pupil she taught; and (2) her understanding of the developmental problems of each pupil could help her conduct her English classes in such a way as to contribute to the academic progress and to the emotional and social development of each pupil. Here is some of the information Miss Rainbird gathered on a few of the members of the tenth-grade class.

Mervyn D. Wright. Mervyn is the son of H. D. Wright, the most influential citizen in Bolton. Mervyn's great grandfather was one of the earliest settlers in the Bolton community. His grandfather founded the Wright Paper Mill, and Mervyn's father has built up the company to its present prosperous status. Mervyn is well above average in intelligence, a leader in social activities in the tenth-grade class, and a member of the football team. His academic record is fairly good but by no means outstanding. Mervyn has not displayed the driving energy that characterizes his father. During his junior high school years, Mervyn was a bit of a disciplinary problem. One of Mervyn's ninth-grade teachers had noted in his cumulative record folder that "Mervyn apparently feels that he is above the rules of the school." Another teacher had noted that Mervyn seems to work most effectively when given a project that permits freedom of expression.

June Blake. June is the daughter of Mrs. Abigail Blake, a moderately wealthy widow in Bolton. June is dominated by her mother who chooses both her clothes and her friends. June is not permitted to date or to wear make-up. Her hair is plaited in two long braids. June is overweight. Apparently, in junior high school years, June acquired the nickname "Piggy." One time when June ventured an opinion in class, a few of her classmates began making sounds suspiciously like "Oink! Oink!" June rarely participates in class discussions. Given an assignment, June speaks to the teacher after class to make certain that she understands thoroughly what she is expected to do. June's grades are excellent.

Joe Miller. Joe is a late maturer, and is called "Shorty" by his classmates. His father is a clerk in a small grocery store. Joe's cumulative record folder indicates that he obtained an I.Q. of 128 on an intelligence test administered at the beginning of grade 7. Yet he obtained a score equivalent to only 92 on a test administered in grade 10. In elementary school and the first year of junior high school, Joe was mischievous, daring, and constantly seeking attention from his peers. He seemed fairly happy up until the end of grade 7 and gained a fair degree of acceptance from other boys in his class. Increasingly, after grade 7, Joe's boisterous and clowning behavior failed to achieve recognition from important boys in his class. The girls who were dating the "big shots" in his class treated him with disdain. Lately, Joe has lost some of his boisterousness. He seems now to be sullen and unhappy. His grades, which were once fairly good, are progressively becoming worse.

Ann Spence. Ann's academic record is among the best in the tenth-grade class, although recently Ann seems to have lost interest in school-work and her grades have slipped somewhat. Ann's father is an accountant at the Wright Paper Mill. Ann is well liked by her class-mates and was elected treasurer of her class. Outside of school, Ann has been active in church work. During grade 9, Ann became very interested in boys and presently is going steady with Tom Dixon, a grade eleven boy who is a star on the football team.

Jack Wrenn. Jack is about a year older than most of his classmates. He is a big lad, a member of the football team, of average intelligence, and has a poor academic record. His father is one of the leading real-tors in Bolton. Jack owns his own sports car and has got into some trouble for speeding violations. He dates frequently, often with girls whose reputations are poor, and is reported to constantly boast about his sex conquests. Jack has evidenced little interest in his schoolwork.

Bill Stanton. Bill is a bright boy and is doing outstanding work in science and mathematics. He and his classmate Dale Thompson are inseparable. Both are members of the school's science club, but are not interested in other school extracurricular activities. Bill has been obtaining grades of B in English and social studies, and is not strongly motivated to work up to capacity in subjects that seem to him unrelated to science. Bill's father is a pharmacist, and has encouraged Bill in his science interest.

Mary Balzick. Mary is the eldest daughter in a family of ten. Her father, Mike Balzick, is a laborer at the railroad freight yard. He is reportedly a thoroughly dependable worker. The Balzick family are regular church-goers and have won the reputation in Bolton of being good solid folk. Mary works hard at her schoolwork and has been able to maintain almost a B average, despite the fact that she has been working nights in a restaurant as a waitress. Mary is regarded by the faculty as a wholesome but somewhat quiet girl. Most of her class-mates are friendly toward her although she is not invited to the round of informal parties planned by a group of girls in the tenth-grade class. Earlier in the semester when the class was casting parts for a play, someone suggested, "Let's make Mary the scullery maid." Mary seemed to fight back tears and was absent from school the next two days.

Ronald Trice. Ronald is the son of a noted physician. His older brother is said to be one of the most brilliant students ever to attend Bolton High, and has since won a number of academic honors at the state university. Ronald's academic record has been good but not outstanding. He usually works diligently at his studies. However, there are spells when he seems to give up and do very little work. Examinations are particularly stressful for Ronald. A number of times he has completely "blown up" on mathematics and science tests.

The very brief sketches of pupils in Miss Rainbird's tenth-grade class illustrate the uniqueness of the emotional and social problems to be found in any classroom. The general nature of emotional development and of social development are the major themes to be considered in this chapter.

EMOTIONAL DEVELOPMENT

Such phenomena as fear, anxiety, anger, disgust, grief, jealousy, joy, affection, and sympathy may be classified as emotions. Subjectively, an emotion may be described as a complex feeling state—a stirred-up state of the organism—accompanied by certain physiological changes in the body and an impulse to act. More objectively, we may describe emotional behavior in terms of: (1) the characteristics of the stimuli or situations that evoke a particular emotion (the stimulus variable), (2) the physiological changes occurring when the emotion is experienced (the organismic variable), and (3) the overt response pattern to the experienced emotion (the response variable).

The Differentiation of Emotions. The early conclusion reached by Watson (1919) that the newborn infant displays three "unlearned" emotions—love, fear, and anger—has not been supported by later research findings. Bridges (1930, 1932) advances a theory that the various emotions develop through a process of differentiation. Bridges reports that the following sequence of development characterizes the emotional behavior of the infant:

At birth and the first few weeks of life.	*Undifferentiated excitement.* To any internal or external intense stimulation the infant responds with uncoordinated movements of the whole body.
At about three months.	The two emotions *delight* and *distress* are differentiated from the parent emotion, excitement. Distress is shown to certain disturbing stimuli

	and is characterized by responses such as muscle tension, interference in breathing, and crying. Delight is expressed to a different set of stimuli and is characterized by responses such as relaxation of tension, free random movements, and cooing.
At about six months.	The emotion of distress is further differentiated into *anger, disgust,* and *fear.* In general, aggressive responses are made to anger-provoking stimuli, while avoidance or withdrawing responses are made to fear-provoking stimuli.
At about twelve months.	The emotion of delight is further differentiated into *elation* (in response to objects and events) and *affection* (in response to people).
At about the age of eighteen months.	*Jealousy* has been differentiated from distress, and differential responses have developed between *affection for adults* and *affection for children.*
At about twenty-four months.	The emotion *joy* may be distinguished from the general emotion of delight.
By the time the child is five years of age.	*Shame, anxiety, disappointment,* and *envy* have been differentiated from the distress-type emotion, and the emotion *hope* has been differentiated from delight.

Learning Exercise

1. Arrange the following positive and negative emotions in order of their appearance, as observed by Bridges:
   (a) Delight, joy, elation, affection for children
   (b) Distress, jealousy, shame, anger

The Problem of Observing Emotional Behavior in the School. The scientific study of emotions is made difficult by virtue of the fact that emotions are so complex and because of the fact that an emotional state is not directly observable—it can only be inferred from some observed behavior. Lindsley (1951) and, more recently, Arnold (1960) review several studies in which the organic and physiological changes occurring with emotion have been measured through the use of special procedures and recording devices. While the data from these studies probably add up to the soundest advance that psychologists have made in their study of emotions, the data do not have a direct bearing on the educator's problem of fostering the healthy emotional development of children.

Once an emotion is experienced by a child, the teacher cannot modify the physiological changes that accompany it. The teacher can do two things to modify emotional behavior. He may modify a child's perception of certain emotion-provoking situations. And he may modify a child's overt response pattern to the experienced emotion. A teacher modifying a child's perception of policemen so that the sight of a policeman no longer elicits the emotion of fear exemplifies the first type of constructive education of the emotions. A teacher or parent training a child to refrain from striking another child every time he becomes angry exemplifies the second type. Often the teacher's task of modifying emotional behavior involves a combination of both types of procedures. For example, the child who experiences fear when called upon to give a speech before his classmates may be aided in developing the skills needed to perform this task, and then, as a result of a succession of success experiences, the child may modify his perception of the feared task.

In order to understand the effects of emotion on the total behavior of an individual, it is useful to identify two dimensions of emotion. An emotional experience may involve varying degrees of *pleasantness* or *unpleasantness*. Joy, for example, is usually pleasant while fear or anger is unpleasant. However, the classification of emotions into the pleasant emotions and the unpleasant emotions is complicated by a second dimension of emotional behavior, i.e., *intensity*. Mild fears, for example, may be pleasant or even exhilarating and sought after. People seek experiences that generate a mild form of fear when they ride a roller coaster or attend a horror or suspense movie. Intensity is thus a second dimension of an emotional experience. The effects of mild emotions may differ from the effects of severe emotions. Mild fears, mild anxieties, and mild frustrations may motivate, may alert the individual to perceive cues in a problem-solving situation, and, in general, may integrate behavior. Severe emotions may interfere with cue perception and result in a disintegration of behavior.

Learning Exercises

2. In what two ways might a person modify the emotional behavior of a child who fears water?
3. Whether or not an emotion serves to organize behavior or to disorganize behavior depends upon what dimension of emotions?

Fear

The emotion of fear is elicited from a situation that is perceived by a person as threatening to his well-being. For a situation to be perceived as threatening, the individual must experience some doubt as to the adequacy of his available responses to cope with it. The two-year-old child who wanders onto a busy thoroughfare may not experience fear even though he is in great danger. The danger must be perceived before the fear is experienced. The mother watching a car narrowly miss running over her child experiences fear because she perceives the danger and is helpless to do anything about it.

The mature individual is aware and can report upon some of his reactions to an emotional experience. Shaffer (1947) provides data on the symptoms of fear reported by aviators who had just returned from combat missions. Some of the symptoms reported along with the percentage of the 4,504 aviators reporting each symptom were: pounding heart and rapid pulse (86 per cent); muscles very tense (83 per cent); easily irritated (80 per cent); dryness of throat and mouth (79 per cent); cold sweat (79 per cent); butterflies in stomach (69 per cent); sense of unreality (65 per cent); need to urinate frequently (65 per cent); trembling (53 per cent); feeling weak or faint (41 per cent).

There are many changes that occur throughout the body when the individual experiences an emotion (Lindsley, 1951). These changes are regulated in a complex fashion by the central nervous system, by the autonomic nervous system, and by the endocrine glands. Psychologists and physiologists have encountered difficulty in differentiating among various emotions. Different intense emotions produce similar disturbed states in the organisms. Differential reactions in anger and fear have been measured by a number of physiological indicators (Ax, 1953). One interesting finding of the Ax study is that the measures where the greater physiological responses occurred for fear may be explained in terms of the action of adrenalin; whereas those where the greater response occurred for anger are explainable in terms of the actions of adrenalin plus noradrenalin.

The overt response to any one experienced emotion may vary. One person experiencing fear may "freeze" so that he is incapable of action; another individual may run away; and still another may try out some response pattern that appears to have some likelihood of successfully coping with the feared situation. Emotions such as rage, fear, and disgust are usually classified as disintegrative emotions, particularly if the emotion is intense. However, as Hebb (1949) has pointed out, the disintegration "is often *incipient* or *potential* and likely to be successfully averted by the aggression or avoidance of the subject" (p. 241). The disintegration of behavior may take the form of a narrowing of perception so that the person does not perceive the cues he needs in order to deal with a danger. Or the disintegration may take the form of a breakdown of learned response patterns, as when a person panics in deep water and loses his swimming skill.

We can summarize our discussion on the nature of the emotion of fear in terms of stimulus, organism, and response variables, thus:

S	O	R
A threatening situation or one that may be perceived as such	1. Processes (a) Perception of threat (b) Conscious feelings; pounding heart, tensions, etc. 2. Physiological changes; galvanic skin response, heart responses, changes in blood chemistry, etc.	1. Integrative (a) Flight (b) Constructive aggression 2. Disintegrative (a) Narrowing of perception (b) Disorganization of response patterns

Learning Exercise

4. A child is excessively fearful of being ridiculed by other children.
   (a) What organismic process variables of the child might be modified? How?
   (b) What integrative response patterns might the child learn to cope with his (her) fear?
   (c) How might the child's fear interfere with his (her) ability to function well in a social situation?

Sources of Fear. The kinds of situations that frighten children change with age. This is to be expected in view of the role played by learning in the acquisition and elimination of fears. A situation becomes fearful only after the child has learned to perceive it as threatening. And after the child has learned responses that successfully cope with the situation, it ceases to be fearful.

EARLY CHILDHOOD FEARS. Jersild and Holmes (1935) have studied the relative frequencies of fears in response to various situations for children from birth to six years of age. In one study, parents recorded during a period of 21 days situations in which their children displayed fear. The number of fears reported declined after age two. For the two-year-old, the average number of fears reported per day was about six, whereas for the four- to five-year-old group, the average was about two. The decline in fears was particularly marked for concrete immediate situations such as: noise; strange objects, situations, and persons; falling; and danger of falling. An increase in number with age was reported for fears of the less tangible, such as fear of imaginary creatures, the dark, and being alone. The over-all decline in fears may be attributable in part to a learned inhibition to express fears openly, and in part to the fact that the less tangible fears are more likely to be expressed in privacy with no one present to observe.

From the many studies of fears of the preschool child, a number of distinct categories of fears can be identified. Jersild (1954) lists the following categories of early-appearing fears: (1) noise and loss of support; (2) other sensory stimuli (any sudden, intense, abrupt stimulus); (3) fear of the unfamiliar; (4) fear of animals; (5) fear of darkness; and (6) fear of solitude and separation. While it is possible to identify certain common characteristics in the fears of all preschool children, it is important to note that many individual differences exist in the fears displayed by different children. The conditions that produce individual differences in the fears of children will become evident when we examine how fears are learned and how they are eliminated.

Trends in Fears of Older Children. As the child grows older he is able to recognize the potential danger in an increasing number of situations. At the same time, he has acquired the skills to deal with situations that formerly evoked fear responses. Baldwin (1955, p. 152) points out that, "The difference between mature and immature manifestations of fears is that the mature person identifies the source of the fear-producing stimuli and directs behavior away from the danger."

The changes that occur in the fears of children with age do not entirely move in the direction of increased realism. In a study by Jersild, Markey, and Jersild (1933), 398 children, aged five to twelve years, were asked to describe their fears and the worst thing that had ever happened to them. The most frequently mentioned fears fell into the category of "contact with, or activities of, or dangers from supernatural agents, ghosts, witches, corpses, mysterious agents or events." Not so surprising is the fact that none of the children mentioned as a "worst actual happening" any event that fell in this category. The second largest cause of fear was "attack or danger of attack by animals." While 12.8 per cent reported a fear within the animal category, only 1.8 per cent reported it as an actual worst happening. On the other hand, only 12.8 per cent reported fears of bodily injuries, while 72.7 per cent reported such injuries as actual worst happenings.

A number of irrational fears develop in children concerning their progress in school. In a study of Jersild, Goldman, and Loftus (1941),

53 per cent of 1,124 children indicated on a checklist that they sometimes or often worried about not being promoted, although the promotion policies of the schools the children attended were such that only about 1 per cent of the children would not be promoted.

Studies of adolescent fears reveal:

1. A continuation and even an increase in fears centered on the school, such as fear of tests, school grades, oral reports and recitations, teachers, and report cards (Liss, 1944; Anastasi *et al.*, 1948; Noble and Lund, 1951; Angelino *et al.*, 1956).
2. Fears of a social nature such as fears of parental and/or peer disapproval or ridicule, fears of social situations, fears of loss of prestige, fears of loss of affection or love, fears of being placed in an embarrassing situation, and fears of being discriminated against as a member of a minority group (Means, 1936; Anastasi *et al.*, 1948; Noble and Lund, 1951; Malm and Jamison, 1952).
3. Fears among boys of adult responsibilities, possibly, according to Fleege (1945), aggravated by oversolicitous parents and teachers who have prolonged the boys' dependency.
4. Fears relating to self such as poverty, death, serious illness, being physically incapacitated, getting and holding a job, sex inadequacy, marriage, and moral crises (Hurlock, 1955).
5. An over-all decrease in the number and intensity of fears as the individual learns that many of his erstwhile fears are groundless. However, considerable individual differences exist in the fears of adolescents with many of the earlier fears, such as fears of animals and fear of the dark, persisting for some adolescents.

Learning Exercises

5. For which of the following might you expect an increase in a display of fear from age two or three to age six or seven?
   (a) Fear of loud noises
   (b) Fear of falling
   (c) Fear of ghosts
6. A child learns certain fears in school, some of which are realistic and some, unrealistic. What is the difference between a realistic and an unrealistic fear? Give an example of each.

How Fears Are Learned. Emotional learning differs in important respects from cognitive and motor learning. It is possible to consciously direct one's energy to such tasks as learning the capitals of European countries or learning to bend glass. In contrast, learning to appreciate music, to cherish democracy, to hate tyranny, to fear lightning—all emerge as by-products of our activities or experiences. A child does not try to learn to fear giving a speech in front of his class-mates. The fear is acquired as a result of the child's perceiving the speech-situation as threatening to his attainment of quite other goals. Maintaining peer acceptance may be of importance to the child, and the speech to be given may be feared because he foresees possible ridicule from his classmates. The child may perceive the task of giving a speech as something that he ought to be able to do, but lacks confi-dence in his speech-making ability. Motivation is clearly involved in the child's task of giving a speech, but just as clearly, the motive is not to acquire fear. The fear emerges as a complex resultant of the child's past experiences, his perception of the situation, his perception of him-self, and the child's motives.

The oft-quoted experiment reported by Watson and Raynor (1920) illustrates how emotional reactions may be acquired through *classical conditioning*. The subject of the experiment was an eleven-month-old boy, Albert. Albert, at the beginning of the experiment, liked animals such as rats, rabbits, cats, and dogs. Albert did exhibit fear responses when he heard a very loud noise. The experimenter conditioned the infant by first presenting a tame laboratory white rat, and then striking an iron bar with a hammer. After a number of pairings of these stimuli, Albert exhibited clear signs of fear of the rat. The instant the rat was presented alone, Albert began to cry and crawl away as fast as possible. Diagrammatically, the experiment may be presented thus:

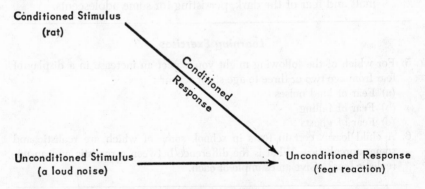

The Watson and Raynor experiment also illustrates how a learned fear may generalize to other similar stimuli. Albert's learned fear of the white rat generalized to other furry objects such as rabbits, a fur neckpiece, and even Santa Claus' whiskers. As noted in Chapter 2, such a phenomenon is referred to as *stimulus generalization*. Many of our irrational fears—fear of enclosed spaces, fear af elevators, fear of water, etc.—probably have their origins in some early experience in which pain was paired with some stimuli (object or situation), thus inducing fear of the stimuli that generalized to similar stimuli.

Learning Exercise

7. How can a teacher teach children to fear him by using classical conditioning procedures? (*Hint:* unconditioned stimulus = pain; unconditioned response = fear response; conditioned stimulus = teacher.)

That a learned fear may function as a drive is illustrated in an experiment conducted by Miller (1948). The experimental apparatus consisted of two adjoining compartments, one of which was painted white and the other black. (See Fig. 5–1.) A door that could be raised or

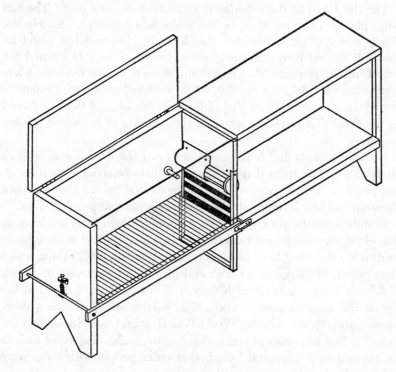

Fig. 5–1. Apparatus Used by Miller to Study Acquisition of Fear in Rats. (From Miller, 1948.)

lowered separated the two compartments. On the floor of the white compartment was a grill through which an electric shock could be applied. The first part of the experiment consisted of placing white rats, one at a time, in the white compartment. The door between the two compartments was raised so that the rats could roam freely between the two compartments. No preference was shown by the rats for either compartment. The second part of the experiment consisted of applying electric shocks to rats placed in the white compartment. The door between the two compartments was raised, thus permitting the rats to escape from the painful stimulus. The acquisition of this escape response can be explained as follows:

> drive—electric shock
> cue—door
> response—running through door to black compartment
> reward—escape from shock

The third part of the experiment resembled the first part. The rats were placed, one at a time, in the white compartment. No electric shock was applied. However, the door was lowered but could be raised if the rat turned a wheel arrangement. The rats learned the wheel-turning response, thus permitting them to escape from the white compartment. Apparently, the white compartment had become a feared situation in the first part of the experiment, and the fear served as the drive that served to motivate the learning of the wheel-turning response.

Possibly parents and teachers do not need the evidence of Miller's study to convince them that fear may motivate behavior. An interesting problem is what happens to fear-motivated good behavior when the source of fear is removed. We shall examine that problem later.

Imitation constitutes a second way through which fears are learned. The child who sees his mother cringe during an electrical storm is likely to develop the same fears as his mother. Hagman (1932) interviewed the mothers of 70 preschool boys and girls about their own and their children's fears. A fairly high degree of resemblance was found between the fears of mother and child, particularly concerning dogs, insects, and storms. During World War II, John (1941) found that the extent of fear responses of young children to an alarming event such as an air raid was influenced by whether older people with them were calm or displayed terror.

Third, fears may be acquired because of an *unpleasant consequence of goal-directed behavior*. The boy who falls from a tree that he is climbing may subsequently fear high places. Pupils who obtain lower grades than they expect on examinations are apt to fear later examinations. The child who tries some new activity and is ridiculed for his efforts or suffers physical pain may become fearful of all new activities. As a result, such a child later may be classified by others as timid.

Certain organismic and environmental conditions are conducive to the acquisition of fears. A person who is in ill health or fatigued is more susceptible to fears than one who is healthy and rested. Because fears involve perceiving a threat, maturation is of importance to the learning of fears. Bright children acquire fears earlier than less-bright children. In the study conducted by Jersild and Holmes (1935), a correlation of .53 was found between intelligence and the number of fears of children aged 24 to 35 months.

The particular fears a child has will depend to a considerable extent upon his unique past history, including the kinds of experiences encountered by the child in school. The child who has been treated harshly or unfairly by some teacher, the child who has experienced bitter disappointment concerning his examination performances, and the child who has been embarrassed or humiliated before his classmates—all may develop fears centered around their school life. Similarly, the characteristics of the home environment contribute to the kinds of fears a child learns. The child who is unsure of the love of his parents, or the child who sees his family breaking up, is likely to develop fears concerning his relationships to others. The child who is constantly pressed by his parents to excel but never quite lives up to his parents' expectations is likely to develop fears of failure. According to Jersild (1954), the child who is severely punished by his parents may develop a tendency to be anxious in at least three ways. He may feel abandoned or rejected. He may develop excessive feelings of guilt. Or he may develop hostile feelings toward his parents and become afraid of his hostile impulses. In countless ways, home and school provide a unique environment for each child. Some of the fears a child learns are related to the failures of home and school to provide a secure environment that adequately meets the needs of the child.

Methods of Modifying Fears. It should be noted at the outset that some fears have self-preservative value. Some fears serve to mobilize energy and put a person on the alert in face of real danger. These are not the fears that parents and teachers wish to modify. Fear behavior of a child needs modification under two sets of circumstances. First, where the child sees danger where there is no danger. Second, where there is some danger, but the danger can be averted by some appropriate behavior. Hence, to modify fear behavior of a child it is necessary to change his perception of a fear-provoking situation and/or modify his response patterns to the fear-provoking situation.

Following are some of the ways parents, teachers, and psychologists attempt to modify children's fears.

1. *Talk.* Explaining to the child that there is nothing to fear may help when the child's fear is actually groundless. Explanations are effective to the extent that they change the child's perceptions of the feared situation. Unfavorable verbal reactions of others when a child displays fear may result in the child's learning to "hide" his fears without modifying the experienced fear, and may do more harm than good.

2. *Example.* The example of others may help a child change his perception of a feared situation and, in addition, may aid him in developing the responses needed to avert injury.

3. *Experimental extinction.* Fear of an activity (such as going into water or patting a dog) is reinforced when the consequences of participating in that activity are painful. When no disastrous consequences result from the child's participating in the feared activity, the fear response may be gradually extinguished. A considerable amount of skill and patience is required of the parent or teacher in order to reduce fear through experimental extinction.

4. *Counter-conditioning.* A conditioned fear (such as Albert's fear of white rats in the Watson and Raynor study) may be gradually eliminated by association of the feared object with something pleasant. For example, an ice cream cone (unconditioned stimulus) may be associated with white furry objects (conditioned stimulus). Again, considerable skill is required in eliminating fears by the counter-conditioning method.

5. *Teaching the skills needed to cope with the situation.* The child who is afraid of water loses his fear once he has learned to swim well. The pupil afraid to give a speech before his classmates may experience much less fear once he has developed skill in speaking *and has experienced success in giving speeches before his classmates.*

Learning Exercise

8. The following describes how several methods were employed in overcoming a small boy's fear of dogs.

> Ever since John was bitten by a large dog at age 4, he has been afraid of dogs. His parents buy a small, lively puppy. The parents play with the puppy while John is in the same room enjoying a candy bar. They coax John to come and pat the puppy while John's father holds it. The puppy

wags its tail. John's mother explains that the puppy wags
its tail because it likes to be patted by John. After a few
days, John thoroughly enjoys playing with the puppy.

(a) How did the parents use "example" as a method of overcoming John's
fear?
(b) How did they use "experimental extinction"?
(c) What one incident in the above describes a beginning of a "counter-
conditioning" procedure?

Anger

Anger is a response to a threatening or a frustrating circumstance.
In anger, the tendency is to move against or attack the source of disturbance even if the source of anger is oneself. The intensity of the
anger response ranges from a mild expression of irritation to a violent
temper tantrum. Whether anger permits a mobilization of energy
making possible effective behavior or results in a disorganization of
behavior depends upon the intensity of the emotion. As previously
noted, the physiological and visceral components of anger are difficult
to differentiate from other emotions.

Changes with Age in Sources and Expressions of Anger. The circumstances that elicit anger responses change with age simply because
what is threatening or frustrating at one age may not be so at a later
age. As the child learns to deal effectively with the problems he
encounters, the frustration generated by those problems is reduced
and hence the tendency to experience anger is reduced. And as the
child learns that certain types of anger responses are not effective, and
can be, indeed, punished (e.g., physically attacking another person), he
learns to substitute more socially permissible expressions of anger.
Hence, behavior is modified in two ways: (1) situations previously perceived as frustrating or threatening are no longer so perceived, either
because the situations are more accurately appraised or because effective responses have been learned to cope with the frustrating or threatening situation; and (2) more socially permissible response patterns
have been discovered as ways of expressing the felt anger.

Because what elicit anger responses no longer do so at a later age
does not mean that the incidence of experiencing anger decreases with
age. New problems supplant old problems. Ricketts (1934) studied
the crying of preschool children during anger episodes over a two-year
period. In the home, conflicts over toilet and dressing routines were
major sources of anger. In nursery school, conflict over playthings was

the major source of anger. Between the ages of three and four, the total number of anger outbursts decreased and the mode of expressing anger tended to change from kicking, striking, struggling, and crying to that of fussing and scolding.

The developmental changes that occur in both the sources and expressions of anger are well documented in a now-classic study conducted by Goodenough (1931). The cooperation was obtained of the mothers of 45 children (most of whom were at the preschool age). The mothers kept daily records of anger incidents that occurred over a period of from one to four months, noting the time, place, immediate cause, and duration of an outburst as well as the behavior exhibited. In this way, records of more than 1,800 anger incidents were obtained. Nearly 70 per cent of all the incidents fell into three categories: (1) conflicts over routine physical habits (over 20 per cent), (2) conflicts with authority (nearly 20 per cent), and (3) problems of social relationships (nearly 30 per cent). During the second year of age, the first two conflict categories included over 50 per cent of the anger outbursts. In children between the ages of three and four, problems of social relationships became the major source of anger, and accounted for nearly 45 per cent of all outbursts. Goodenough classified the direction of anger outbursts into three categories: (1) undirected anger (e.g., holding breath, kicking randomly, screaming), (2) motor or verbal resistance (e.g., resisting being held, verbal refusal of a request), and (3) motor or verbal retaliation (e.g., biting or verbal scolding). Goodenough found that with increasing age there was a decrease in undirected anger and an increase in directing anger against something or someone.

Studies are lacking at the school-age levels comparable to the Goodenough study. As the child spends an increasing proportion of his time outside the home, it is to be expected that problems in social relationships outside the home will become an increasing source of anger. In a study of junior high school pupils, Hicks and Hayes (1938) found the following sources of anger, in order of frequency: being teased; being treated unfairly; a sibling taking their property or imposing on them; things not being right; people being sarcastic; and people being bossy.

Problems originating in the home continue to be sources of anger throughout the school years. Block (1937) found that 71 per cent of a sample of junior and senior high school pupils indicated that they were disturbed by having the mothers hold a brother or a sister up to them as a model of behavior. Items relevant to desires for independence, nagging, and restrictions were also checked many times.

At all ages, organic factors such as illness, fatigue, and hunger can increase a child's susceptibility to anger. Goodenough (1931) found an increased frequency of anger outbursts for children suffering from temporary conditions of poor health such as colds, digestive disturbances, minor accidents, and bowel movement irregularities. Also, in Goodenough's study, it was found that a higher incidence of anger outbursts occurred from 11–12 in the morning and from 5–6 in the afternoon than for any other hours.

Environmental circumstances that made children more susceptible to anger in the Goodenough study included: the presence of many adults or older siblings in the family; visitors; older persons being critical, overanxious, uncertain, or nagging on small matters; a concern for the moral goodness or badness of the child's behavior disregarding its appropriateness from a developmental or situational point of view; inconsistency in discipline; and the child's past experience of getting his own way by displaying anger.

Jersild (1954) has noted the varieties of forms of expression taken by anger and hostility as a child grows older. From undirected expressions of anger such as screaming and kicking, the child learns to direct his anger at the object of his wrath. But the child is under strong societal pressure to refrain from attacking physically another person who makes him angry. So the child learns substitutes for physical attack such as: verbal aggression (e.g., calling names, assertions of superiority, and, later, tattling, gossip, or slander); teasing; swearing; expressing hostility in fantasy and play; displaced hostility (e.g., taking anger out on a younger brother); cruelty to animals or to persons who cannot retaliate; prejudice; antisocial acts (e.g., truancy, sexual promiscuity, juvenile delinquency); self-inflicted punishment; externalization (e.g., a boy hostile toward his teacher perceives the teacher as hostile toward him and thus justifies his grievances against the teacher); feeling abused (e.g., perceiving other people as unfair, dishonest, and against him).

Modifying Anger Responses in Children. Not all feelings of anger or even expressions of anger are bad. We would hope that a child or an adult would be angry at injustice, cruelty, or deceit. Under certain conditions, the angry response, or at least a feeling of anger, is healthy.

Anger is inappropriate when the individual perceives a situation as threatening or frustrating when the situation actually is not or need not be. It is inappropriate when small frustrations lead to inordinate feelings of anger or when the mode of expressing the felt anger is unsuitable. Anger responses are modified as the individual learns to perceive no-threat where previously he perceived threat; when he learns responses that enable him to cope successfully with situations that previously frustrated him; and when he learns more socially acceptable ways of expressing his felt anger.

What can the teacher do to aid the child gain control over anger? Research provides no definitive answer to this question. However, the following suggestions are at least consistent with some research findings:

1. *The teacher can provide children with opportunities to work together to achieve common purposes.* Research evidence supplied by industrial and social psychologists supports the conclusion that working together to achieve a common purpose brings about a harmony of interests to which even self-interest will be subordinated (see, for example, Homans, 1950). Many of the thwartings of the school-age child occur in his relationship with his peers. Projects in which children work together toward common purposes not only reduce conflicts but afford opportunities to improve their perceptions of the behavior of others.

2. *The teacher can reinforce the child when he behaves constructively in a thwarting situation.* A study conducted by Keister and Updegraff (1937) demonstrates that nursery school children can be taught to react constructively to frustration. Children who responded initially to puzzle problems in an immature manner (e.g., destructive behavior, emotional outbursts, etc.) were trained over a six-week period with similar problems.[1] The problems were presented in order of difficulty so that the children would experience success in their early attempts. With the more difficult later problems, the child needed to persevere to attain success. He was encouraged to do so and his perseverance was reinforced by eventual success. At the end of the training program, the children were given problems similar in nature to their initial problems. It was evident that the behavior of children after training was remarkably different from their behavior prior to training. They persisted longer in attempting to solve the puzzle problem. Anger responses, such as destructive behavior and crying, disappeared.

3. *The teacher can be consistent and fair in his classroom disciplinary measures.* Unfairness ranks high as a source of anger. If the response that is tolerated on one occasion is punished on another occasion, the child is cheated in his efforts to come to terms with his environment.

4. *The teacher can communicate his respect for the pupil as an individual even though at times he may express disapproval for the behavior or the performance of the pupil.* Anger and aggressive re-

[1] For one of the training situations, pictures from interesting story books were cut out, mounted on plywood, varnished, and cut into puzzles. The experimenter read the story to the child until she reached a part that was illustrated by one of the pictures. She then stopped and asked the child to put the puzzle together before continuing the story. Four picture-puzzle books of increasing difficulty were prepared with each book containing from four to six pictures.

sponses to frustration constitute learned defenses of the pupil who lacks confidence in himself and the pupil who feels rejected. The teacher who perceives each of his pupils as a worthy individual and can communicate this feeling of respect to the student provides the kind of emotional climate conducive to the learning of more constructive responses to frustration.

5. *The teacher can provide opportunities for the pupil to express his emotions.* Mental hygienists stress the need for the individual to give expression to his emotions. One important element in one theory of counseling—client-centered counseling—centers upon the counselor's providing the kind of permissive atmosphere that permits the counselee to express verbally his feelings to the counselor without fear of being rejected. A method of treating emotionally disturbed children known as play therapy attempts to create play situations in which the child may safely, and without condemnation, express feelings of hostility and other emotions that are usually denied expression. In many areas of the school program, teachers can provide opportunities for children to express their feelings.

Learning Exercises

9. What angers the two-year-old may not anger the four-year-old. Why?
10. Why does a child change his way of expressing anger?
11. A child becomes very angry when he is teased. His parents instruct him to stay away from other children who tease him. What limitations are there to the parent's solution of the child's problem?
12. Which is the more desirable: (a) to teach children that it is wrong to feel angry; or (b) to help children express anger constructively?

SOCIAL DEVELOPMENT

The child at birth does not attach meaning to social stimuli. Even the mother's smile initially has no meaning to the infant. By the time the child enters school, he has learned much about how he is expected to behave in group situations, and this social learning continues during his school years. This process of becoming a social being is known as *socialization.* More precisely, socialization is "the process whereby a person (especially a child) acquires sensitivity to social stimuli (especially, the pressures and obligations of group life) and learns to get along with, and to behave like, others in his group or culture" (English and English, 1958). *Social development* refers to the sequence of continuous changes that the child goes through in this process of becoming a social being.

The child beginning school at age six faces awesome social adjustment problems. From a home where the parents have been the central adult figures, the child is shepherded to a strange room in a strange building where a strange adult called the teacher tells him what to do. In his home, he was relatively free to play as he wished; in this strange classroom, he finds his freedom of movement much more restricted. At home, a few neighboring children made up his play group; at school, he is surrounded by many, many children whom he has never seen before. He is to find out that there are right and wrong ways of behaving in the classroom and on the school playground. And he has had all of six years of living as an experiential background for his many social adjustment problems.

Possibly no teacher is so deserving of admiration and respect as the competent primary grade teacher. Her task is extremely complex and exacting. Hereditary and environmental factors have combined to insure that each child is unique. The homes of some children provide love and security; other homes do not. Some children have had much opportunity to play with other children of their own age; other children have had little opportunity. Some children attend nursery school or kindergarten; others do not. The social behaviors taught within each home differ, and as a result, one child may appear to be friendly, aggressive, and independent while another child may appear to be polite, shy, and dependent.

The teacher in this strange new world of the first-grade child is to become extremely important. The teacher who is patient, kind, accepting, and concerned can create the classroom atmosphere conducive to the total development of the child. The teacher who is impatient, sarcastic, and rejecting can stunt, or at least retard, the development of the child.

While all first-grade pupils are different in many respects, in other respects they are the same. Learning the give-and-take of social life among other children is a developmental task for all the children. During his first years at school, the child learns much concerning how to treat friends, how to play fair in games, and how to approach adults. In short, he learns a set of social habits that he will continue to use throughout his life. Havighurst (1950, p. 19) maintains that "the 9 or 10-year-old already shows what he will be like, socially, at 50." Hence, it is particularly important during the first three grades of school for the teacher to devote time and energy to the problem of guiding the social development of each child.

Learning physical skills necessary for ordinary games is one major means through which a child gains and maintains status among his peer group. This is particularly true for boys. The peer group rewards the boy who excels in physical skills and punishes with disdain or indifference the boy who lacks skill. This poses a difficult problem for the elementary school teacher. The problem is partially solved through providing a varied physical education program because different boys excel at different games and most boys find they can perform tolerably well in some games. For boys who seem unable to acquire adequate skill in any game, the problem becomes one of finding another area of competency (e.g., some intellectual attainment) that will command the respect of his peers. The important point is that gaining peer acceptance is a vital need of most elementary school children. Any help the teacher can give the child in learning how to meet this need will contribute to the child's total development.

Learning Exercise

13. Name two developmental tasks of major importance to the six- to nine-year-old.

The Home

In the discussion in Chapter 3 on the "cultural basis of development," it was noted that cultural traditions determine in large part what lessons parents will teach the child and how the lessons are taught. For this reason, American children who enter school at age six have learned many of the same lessons, and some of these lessons differ from the lessons taught in other cultures. Yet, while there are many similarities in the behavior of six-year-olds in America, there are also many differences. Children differ in their attitudes toward adults. One child may view adults as helpful and friendly; another child may have learned to fear adults, or at least, not to trust them. Children differ in their attitudes toward themselves. One child learns to be dissatisfied with himself, and frequently wishes he were like someone else; another child develops a high degree of self-acceptance. Children differ in their conceptions of their many roles. In the presence of an adult, one child expresses himself freely and confidently; another child has learned that children should remain quiet unless spoken to. One child learns to relish competition and to strive to be first in all of his endeavors; another child shuns competition. In countless ways, six-year-olds differ, and, to a considerable extent, these differences are attributable to the lessons taught in the home.

Emotional Climate of the Home. Parents have long been sensitive to the fact that they are judged by the way their children behave. Eyebrows are lifted at the minister's little son who swears, and the slightest misdemeanor of the son of the town's target of gossip is greeted with the judgmental question, "What can you expect?" A number of psychologists have become interested in studying the relationship between certain characteristics of the home and the personality characteristics and behavior of the child. One approach to this problem has been that of examining the effects on the young child of various emotional climates of homes. In this approach, an effort is made to determine the types of child behavior associated with the rejecting home, the overprotective home, the democratic home, the autocratic home, etc.

Various investigative techniques have been employed by different researchers in their study of home atmosphere, and the information sought about parent-child relationships has varied from one study to another. Nevertheless, some agreement has emerged from various studies as to the basic dimensions of parent-child interaction that exert an impact on the behavior of the child. In two of the most extensive studies conducted (Baldwin *et al.*, 1945, 1949; and Sears *et al.*, 1957) *warmth* was found to be a major dimension of parent behavior influencing the child. Homes rated high on warmth are characterized as child centered with the mother devoted to the child, approving rather than disapproving of his behavior, offering him more rewards, providing him with more guidance, and finding ample time to play with the child. Sears and his associates found that lack of warmth on the part of the mother was associated with feeding problems, bed-wetting, and over-aggressiveness. The possibility that physical punishment by a warm, affectionate parent is more effective than by a cold, hostile parent is suggested by some of Sears's data. The following answer of one mother to an interviewer's question suggests that the real punishment to the child is the painful thought that the mother does not love him.

I. "How does he act when you spank him—does it seem to hurt his feelings or make him angry, or what?"
M. "It hurts his feelings. I think Billy feels you don't love him then—that's how it affects him. He'll come back to you and say, 'I love you, Mummy.'"
I. "How do you react to this?"
M. "Oh, I give him a hug; I love him, too. I've told him and Jean, if I get very cross and spank and say something cross to them that, 'Even though I'm very cross, I still love you.' I tell them to remember that when I'm cross." [Sears, Maccoby, and Levin, 1957, p. 334.]

The study by Sears and his associates is based upon standardized interviews with 379 mothers of five-year-old children. Data was obtained in the interviews concerning the development of the conscience of the child. Conscience development was then related to various child-rearing practices. Two characteristics of the mother appeared to interact to forward the development of the conscience: warmth of the mother toward the child in conjunction with the withdrawal of love when the child behaves wrongly. Table 5–1 shows the relationship.

TABLE 5–1

Relationship of High Conscience to the Mother's Warmth and Her Use of Withdrawal of Love

	Percentage of Children Rated High on Conscience
Mother relatively cold, and:	
Uses withdrawal of love fairly often	18%
Uses little or no withdrawal of love	25
Mother relatively warm, and:	
Uses withdrawal of love fairly often	42
Uses little or no withdrawal of love	24

Source: R. R. Sears, Eleanor Maccoby, and H. Levin, *Patterns of Child Rearing* (Evanston, Ill.: Row, Peterson & Co., 1957), p. 388.

Psychoanalytic theory suggests that the sixth year is a critical year for conscience development. Most of the five-year-olds in Sears's study appear to have made some progress in conscience development. The largest percentage of the children (38 per cent) in this study were rated: "Moderate conscience development. May not confess directly, but look sheepish; seldom denies." However, 13 per cent of the children were rated as providing "no evidence" of conscience and 28 per cent were rated "little evidence" of conscience. Only 3 per cent of the children received ratings of "strong conscience," while 17 per cent were rated "considerable" conscience.

Learning Exercise

14. (a) Were *most* of the children of mothers who were rated "relatively warm" and "uses withdrawal of love fairly often" rated high on conscience?

   (b) Does Sear's data indicate that the child of seven is more apt to have developed a strong conscience if his relatiosnhip to his mother is "warm" and the mother uses "withdrawal of love" for his misdemeanors?

Baldwin (1949) studied the nursery school behavior of children from homes rated on three variables—warmth, democracy, and indulgence.[2] Children from homes rated high on democracy were rated as active and socially outgoing (hostile and domineering as well as friendly). These children occupy favored status position in the group, a reflection of their success in bossiness. And they are rated high on activities demanding intellectual curiosity, originality, and constructiveness. The effects of the warmth variable on nursery school play behavior is difficult to assess from Baldwin's data as most of the homes rated high on democracy were also rated high on warmth. The warmth variable appears to contribute less to aggressive, bossy, and attention-gaining behavior. It also contributes less to original, constructive, and outgoing leadership behavior. The effects of the indulgence variable are, in general, opposite to those of the democracy variable, with the following two specific effects: physical apprehension, and lack of skill in muscle activities.

Baldwin, Kalhorn, and Breese (1945) found a relation between types of homes and the changes of the child's I.Q. over a three-year period. The largest gains in I.Q., amounting to from eight to ten points, occurred in homes characterized by warmth, freedom of exploration and acceleratory pressure from the parent. A deliberately accelerating parent attempts to teach the child activities that are challenging. I.Q. changes of children from rejecting and possessive homes were found to be insignificant.

Certain interpersonal orientations of the child become established early in life and tend to persist in later years. The child who learns in his early home life to be outgoing, active, and positive in his attitudes to others tends to maintain this interpersonal orientation (Emmerich, 1964).

Peck (1958) studied the relationship between certain characteristics of family emotional and regulatory patterns and elements in the personality structure of the adolescent as measured by teacher ratings, test scores, and clinician's ratings. Thirty-four adolescents were tested each year from age ten to eighteen and their parents interviewed. Among the findings were:

---

[2] In the home obtaining a high rating on the "democracy" syndrome, the mother is able to justify clear policies to guide the behavior of the child, and these policies are democratically administered. The mother satisfies rather than thwarts the curiosity of the child, and tends to approve rather than disapprove of the child's behavior. Behavior is guided by suggestion rather than coercion and few restrictions curb the freedom of the child.

The home rated high on "indulgence" is child centered and the mother is devoted to the child. But the mother babies the child, is overprotective, and anxious for his welfare. The contact of the child with his mother is extensive and intense.

1. The adolescent's ego strength (i.e., emotional maturity, personal integration, autonomy, rationality of behavior, and accuracy of social and self-perception) and the adolescent's willingness to conform to societal expectations were related to consistency, mutual trust, and mutual approval experienced within his family.
2. Superego strength (i.e., the presence of an effective behavior-guiding conscience) was mainly related to the regularity and consistency of family life.
3. Generalized friendliness and spontaneity were associated with a lenient, democratic family atmosphere. Some friendly children were found to have weak egos and weak superegos. These children were found to come from inconsistent and irregular families.
4. Hostility with guilt concerning inner impulses tended to be associated with severely autocratic, untrusting, and disapproving parents.

Peck's findings are, in general, in agreement with those of an earlier study conducted by Radke (1946), although different research techniques were used. In Radke's study, mothers and fathers of 43 children attending nursery school or kindergarten filled out a questionnaire and were interviewed concerning their disciplinary practices and how they exercised parental authority. Data on the behavior of the children were obtained through teachers' ratings, interviews with the children, doll play sessions, and pictorial projective tests. Children from the more democratic homes compared to those from the more autocratic homes were more emotionally stable, more popular, more considerate of others, more sensitive to praise and blame, and less quarrelsome.

Radke (1946) has summarized the findings of a number of studies on the kinds of child behavior commonly associated with different types of homes. Table 5–2 presents excerpts from her summary.

Two very general conclusions may be drawn from the extensive research on the relationship between characteristics of the home and the behavior of the child. First, desirable child behavior characteristics tend to be associated with homes that provide the child with ample love; that are harmonious, calm, happy, and compatible; where discipline is strict and consistent; and where parents play with the child. Second, it is *not* possible to infer with accuracy the characteristics of a child's home from observations of his behavior. It may be noted from Table 5–2 that the aggressiveness of the child is associated with diverse types of homes: the rejective home, the overprotective home, the inharmonious home, and the home that is defective in discipline.

TABLE 5–2
Effects of Various Types of Homes on Child Behavior

Type of Home	Type of Child Behavior Associated with It
Rejective	Submissive, aggressive, adjustment difficulties, feelings of insecurity, sadistic, nervous, shy, stubborn, non-compliant
Overprotective, "babying"	Infantile and withdrawing, submissive, feelings of insecurity, aggressive, jealous, difficult adjustment, nervous
Dominating parent	Dependable, shy, submissive, polite, self-conscious, uncooperative, tense, bold, quarrelsome, disinterested
Submissive parent	Aggressive, careless, disobedient, independent, self-confident, forward in making friends, non-compliant
Inharmonious	Aggressive, neurotic, jealous, delinquent
Defective discipline	Poor adjustment, aggressive, rebellious, delinquent, neurotic
Harmonious, well-adjusted	Submissive, good adjustment
Calm, happy, compatible	Cooperative, superior adjustment, independent
Child accepted	Socially acceptable, faces future confidently
Parents play with child	Security feelings, self-reliant
Giving child responsibilities	Good adjustment, self-reliant, security feelings

Adapted from *The Relation of Parental Authority to Children's Behavior and Attitudes* by Marian J. Radke (Institute of Child Welfare Monograph No. 22). The University of Minnesota Press, Minneapolis. Copyright 1946 by the University of Minnesota.

Learning Exercise

15. On the basis of the studies on the home reviewed in this chapter, evaluate each of the following statements:
    (a) A child from a democratic home may be difficult to manage in the classroom.
    (b) A child from a warm, democratic home is likely to be highly creative.
    (c) Parental pressure to achieve may result in an increase in the child's measured I.Q.
    (d) A consistent, stable home life is conducive to the development of a conscience.
    (e) It is apparently very easy for homes to contribute to the development of aggressive behavior.

Measuring Social Acceptance

A number of techniques have been devised to study social acceptability. Some commonly used devices are:

1. *Sociometric techniques.* These techniques, originated by Moreno (1934), are used to elicit positive and/or negative responses about each member of a group by all other members of the group. In a school setting, members of a classroom may be asked to write down the names of one, two, or more children whom they prefer as a playmate, as a seatmate, as a party guest, or as an associate in some other specific situation. The children's choices may be diagrammed to form a sociogram as in Fig. 5–2.

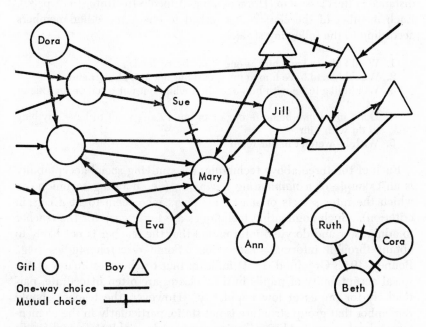

Fig. 5–2. A Portion of a Sociogram Showing Choices for Nine Seventh-Grade Girls.

Ordinarily, a complete classroom is diagrammed. However, Fig. 5–2 illustrates some of the kinds of information concerning social structure that may be gleaned from a sociogram. Two *cliques* may be noted. Ruth, Cora, and Beth form a closed clique. They neither choose other class members nor are chosen by others. Mary is a *star*. She is chosen by six girls and one boy. Mary is also the center of a clique that includes Sue, Jill, Ann, and Eva. This clique is more open. Mary, Eva, and Sue are chosen by other girls in the class and Eva chooses one girl outside of the clique. Dora appears to be an *isolate* as she is not chosen by any member of the class. A number of mutual choices may be noted.

2. *Guess Who.* In the "Guess Who" technique, brief descriptions of

various types of children are listed and the pupils are asked to write the names of classmates who most nearly fit each description. Included are statements such as, "Who is it that is always bossing other children?" and "Who is always friendly and helpful especially toward those younger than himself?"

3. *Social Distance Scale.* This technique was originally designed to measure various degrees of social acceptability of national and racial groups (Bogardus, 1925). It has been adapted for measuring social distance in the classroom (Horace Mann–Lincoln Institute, 1947, p. 30). Each member of the classroom is asked to check the other members according to the following scale:

1. Would like to have him as one of my best friends
2. Would like to have him in my group but not as a close friend
3. Would like to be with him once in a while but not often or for long at a time
4. Don't mind him being in our room but I don't want to have anything to do with him
5. Wish he weren't in our room

Each of the three above techniques for studying social acceptability is an example of a *nominating technique* (i.e., a rating technique in which the rater selects or names his peers who seem to fit a certain criterion). Such nominating techniques are fairly easy for the teacher to administer and do yield information that the teacher is not likely to obtain through informal observation. Some research studies (e.g., Bonney, 1947; Gronlund, 1951) indicate that teachers' estimates of the social acceptability of pupils in their classes are often inaccurate, particularly for pupils of low popularity. However, the teacher should remember that group structure is not static, particularly in the elementary school years. Also, a sociogram merely yields information on what children are selected. The non-selected child may be actively rejected, or ignored, or accepted but not as a close friend. Further, a sociogram yields no information concerning the reasons for a child's selection or rejection. Other devices such as anecdotal records are needed in order to understand factors underlying the social structure of a class.

4. *Anecdotal records.* A teacher in his daily work observes many incidents that are of significance in understanding the various children in his classroom. Written reports of informal teacher observations of pupils have been called *anecdotal records*. A collection of anecdotal records for one pupil may help the teacher understand the child's unique personality. Students of psychological measurement have noted a number of features of a "good" anecdotal record:

1. It describes a specific event with sufficient concrete detail to give the event meaning.
2. It avoids statements that evaluate the behavior of the child as good or bad, desirable or undesirable, acceptable or unacceptable.
3. It describes events that relate to the child's total development, usually events that are typical of the child's behavior and that set him off as unique from other children.
4. It focuses attention on the behavior of the child rather than on the teacher's reaction to the behavior.
5. Interpretative or evaluative statements of the teacher are separated from descriptions of events (sometimes interpretations are placed within parentheses).
6. Events that illustrate a child's progress toward school goals (that cannot be assessed by more objective methods) are included as well as events depicting adjustment problems.
7. Incidents are reported that shed light on how the child perceives others and how he perceives himself.

Learning Exercise

16. Criticize the following statements found in anecdotal records of teachers:
    (a) Bill was a nuisance today. He didn't pay attention in class and distracted other children who were trying to work.
    (b) Tony and Jack quarreled over who was to bat first in a ball game. Tony always seems to want to have his own way.
    (c) Ruth is a new girl in class. I think she is a bad-mannered child.
    (d) Robert obtained the highest mark on the mid-semester arithmetic examination.

Developmental Trends

The task of the teacher would be much less complex if it were possible to delineate the social behaviors to be expected from children at different age levels. Such a behavioral description is not possible. Individual differences exist in the social behavior of children at any given age level. Hence, a description of the typical or characteristic social behavior of children at a particular age may not accurately portray the behavior of an individual child. Further, social development, like other forms of development, is marked by "anticipation and regression." Thus, in observing the play activities of a group of eleven-year-old boys over a period of time, we may on one occasion see them playing "cops and robbers" (which is more typical of the play interests of the seven- or eight-year-old), and on another occasion see the boys participate enthusiastically in some organized sport (which typically becomes an all-absorbing play interest for the thirteen- or fourteen-year-old). Hence, a listing of children's play characteristics for a particular age level contains some activities that are also characteristic for later ages (Gesell *et al.*, 1946, 1956).

Despite the difficulties inherent in the task of describing the social behavior of children at different age levels, it is possible to identify a number of developmental trends in social development.

Increase in Social Interaction. As the child grows older, there is an increase in his tendency to seek social interaction with other children. This tendency is reflected in the slowly changing play activities of the child. The interest of the six- or seven-year-old in playing in the sand pile by himself or alongside of another child is gradually replaced by interest in group games and participation in organized clubs such as the Cub Scouts and the Brownies. Again we can note the fact that old interests die slowly. The twelve-year-old boy may maintain his interests in hide-and-seek and running games, in climbing trees and building tree forts, at the same time as his newer interests emerge in baseball, football, and all kinds of other sports. The twelve-year-old girl may continue her interest in doll play while developing new interests in sewing for herself, phoning friends, and visiting friends overnight.

As children interact with one another, they accumulate experiences that permit the development of sympathetic behavior. A child who knows what it is like to feel embarrassed is in a position to perceive another child as embarrassed and experience feelings of sympathy. Murphy (1937), in a study of nursery school children, aged two to four years, observed that the older children manifested sympathy to a wider range of distress situations. The preschool child may be led through sympathy to aid another child in distress. The sympathetic behavior may quickly dissipate if the reactions of the injured child conflict with his own desires. Wright (1942) found that among eight-year-old boys altruistic behavior was directed toward other boys whom they perceived as generous and from whom they could earn social approval. Thus, the increased incidence with age of sympathetic behavior should not be interpreted as a development toward selfless behavior. Interaction with other children permits an increased ability to perceive when another is in distress. The sympathetic response may be, at least in part, a means of gaining social approval.

Increased social interaction brings with it opportunities for increased conflicts between children. One rather surprising finding in studies by

Murphy (1937) and Jersild and Markey (1935) is that aggressiveness and sympathy seem to go together—at least among preschool children. In both studies, the outgoing, gregarious, aggressive child who participated in all social activities tended to exhibit more sympathetic behavior than his less socially responsive peer.

Improved Perception of Self and Others. A child's self concept as well as his perceptions of others is influenced by his interpersonal relationships. A child who is liked, approved, and respected by his parents, teachers, peers, and other significant persons is apt to develop attitudes of acceptance of self and others. A child who is rejected and belittled by significant others is likely to develop unfavorable attitudes toward self and others.

Some evidence that children improve with age in their ability to perceive accurately the attitudes of others toward them may be found in a study reported by Dymond et al. (1952). Groups of second- and sixth-grade children were asked to make up stories about a series of pictures they were shown. The stories told were scored for empathy (i.e., sensitivity to the feelings and attitudes of others). Sixth-graders were found to express more opinions than the second-graders concerning the thoughts and feelings of persons in the picture. As the higher empathy scores of the sixth-graders might be attributable to superior verbal ability rather than greater sensitivity, a second measure of social insight was administered. Each child was asked to write down the names of other members in his class with whom he would like to sit, invite to a party, and be with in a variety of situations. Then each child was asked to judge the extent to which he was liked or disliked by each other member of his class. In this way, a measure was obtained of the accuracy of each child's perception of how well he was regarded by each of his classmates. The children who had scored high on the empathy test were found to be more accurate in their perceptions on how they were regarded by their classmates. The accuracy of perception of the sixth-graders was found to be greater than that of the second-graders.

Learning Appropriate Sex Role. Our society exerts strong pressures to induce boys to behave like boys (or like men) and girls to behave like girls (or preferably like young ladies). At birth, boy babies are supplied with blue blankets and girl babies with pink blankets. Dolls, nursing kits, and toy household appliances are regarded as proper toys for girls. Guns, baseballs, and anything that makes a loud noise are regarded as boys' toys. The process of learning the appropriate sex role proceeds through life and the person who does not learn the appropriate sex role fails to win respect from others. Even the non-conformist finds it expedient to behave in a sex-appropriate manner and reserves his defiance of the authority of society to more rewarding battlegrounds.

In America, the mother and father of the child are his two principal socializing agents. For the boy, when the father-son relationship is good, the boy is likely to identify with the father and model his be-havior after him. The girl finds a model in her mother while the father serves as a reinforcer of her femininity. As learning an appropriate sex role occurs through the child's identifying with a parent, anything in the home that interferes with the identification process can also inter-fere with the learning of the sex role. Broken or inharmonious homes, or unfavorable parent-child relationships, may retard the child's sex-role learning.

Sex differences in behavior may be found even among nursery school children. Hattwick (1937) obtained ratings on 60 observable behavior characteristics for several hundred nursery school children, aged two to four-and-a-half, and found statistically significant differences be-tween boys and girls for 27 characteristics. The behaviors that boys were rated as doing more frequently were: breaking toys; grabbing toys; being hard to reason with; ignoring requests; laughing and jumping around excessively; rushing into danger; handling sex organs; leaving tasks incomplete; tenseness at rest; and wasting time at rou-tines. The behaviors that girls were rated as doing more frequently were: avoiding risk; avoiding play with others; bossing; criticizing others; crying easily; fearing strange places; fearing high places; jeal-ousy; misrepresenting facts; refusing food; shrinking from notice; stay-ing near adults; sucking thumb; twisting hair; telling fanciful stories; and seeking praise.

By the time children enter school at age six, they have developed a sufficiently clear concept of their sex role as to prefer playmates of their own sex (Koch, 1956, 1957). Throughout the elementary school years, sex-appropriate behaviors are reinforced, and sex-inappropriate behav-iors are punished by a child's peers. Often, little is left for the teacher to do in aiding children learn their sex roles except to accept boys behaving like boys and girls behaving like girls.

During the adolescent period, a new developmental task emerges— that of establishing new relations with age-mates of the opposite sex. Many ways of behaving that were appropriate in the preadolescent period become inappropriate during adolescence. Older adolescents in addition to the parents are likely to serve as models as the adolescent works out his daily interpersonal problems.

Learning Exercise

17. What can children learn on the playground during a recess period that may contribute to their social development?

Sex Problems.   In our culture, the adolescent is confronted with many conflicting and confusing attitudes toward sex.   For many people, the term "immorality" means violation of the sex code; but sex is also portrayed as a forbidden delight.   Chastity is considered a virtue by religious faiths and by many adults; but an adolescent peer group may regard premarital sexual intercourse as normal and desirable.   Sex is not to be talked about; but it is constantly talked about in the communications media.   As a result of all this confusion, even the natural sensation of sex excitement may elicit in the adolescent extreme feelings of guilt.

Accurate information concerning sex experimentation between boys and girls is difficult to obtain.   Findings of various research studies vary.   Apparently, more adolescents from the lower socioeconomic levels than from the middle and upper levels engage in sex activity.   A smaller percentage of boys who eventually obtain a college degree have premarital intercourse than do adolescents who obtain less education. In a study of 4,600 unmarried men at a military induction center, Hohman and Shaffner (1947) found that less than one-eighth of the men who did not finish grade school were virgins as compared to about one-third of college men.   In a study of college students, Ehrmann (1952) found between 35 and 40 per cent of the males and about 10 per cent of the females indicated that they had had sexual intercourse on a date. Ehrmann attributes the discrepancy between male and female percentages to the fact that the majority of the men students' dates were not with coeds.

Masturbation is a common problem particularly among boys because: (1) the practice is almost universal (Ross, 1950; Kinsey, 1948; Ramsey, 1943); and (2) the belief is widespread that it results in some kind of physical, mental, moral, or social damage (Pullias, 1937).   There is no scientific evidence that masturbation is the cause of any abnormality.   However, belief in the ill effects and the feelings of guilt engendered may produce anxiety and interfere with healthy development.

Homosexuality, i.e., the experiencing of sexual pleasures from physical association between members of the same sex, may be a matter of more serious concern.   In the Kinsey study, about 25 per cent of the adolescents and adults questioned about their adolescent sex experiences reported that they had indulged in homosexual relations (Kinsey *et al.*, 1953). For many adolescents, this may represent passing experimentation. For others, the practice may continue into adulthood.

A number of studies reveal that many adolescents obtain sex information from unreliable sources. One questionnaire study of 392 college men indicated that 45 per cent of the young men reported that they obtained their sex information in bull sessions with the gang (Peterson, 1938). Only 10 per cent reported the father as a source.

The problem of providing adequate sex information to children and adolescents is perplexing, and the role that the school should play is controversial. The suggestion that the school should offer special "sex education" courses has been met with strong opposition. Recommendations have been made that sex education materials be integrated into various courses in the curriculum (Kirkendall, 1944). However, the assumption that all would be well if only the adolescent received the "right" sex information is open to serious question. Frank (1944), among others, has pointed out the crucial role of the parents as the adolescent learns a new set of masculine or feminine behaviors. With respect to the girls' development, Frank writes:

The girl especially is susceptible to this family drama and to the father's relation to herself. She needs the father's overt approval and outspoken admiration of herself as a young woman, to help her to clarify and accept her feminine role, especially to be a woman in "a man's world." If the father ignores her or continually criticizes her, or if he demands that she achieve something—school grades, social or other prestige, and similar signs of success—in order to gain and hold his approval, then she may find it difficult to accept the feminine role. From clinical records there are indications that some of the young girls who are involved in sex delinquencies and who have venereal infections are individuals who have never accepted, indeed have rejected, the female and feminine role. They are likely to be daughters from families where the mother has been of little importance, receiving little or no respect from her husband, often a cowed, submissive wife; moreover, these girls have never enjoyed approval or admiration from their fathers and so have never developed any feeling of being a woman with a sense of their own dignity or worth as a woman. Consequently they have no difficulty in playing the role of sex object, offering themselves freely to any casual male, calculatingly cool and deliberate. They have little sex interest and are passive if not frigid. To speak of them as the victims of passion, or weak-willed individuals who could not resist sex temptation, is to misunderstand completely their conduct and their feelings. By exercising power over men, some are getting revenge for the years of humiliation they have suffered as girls under dominant fathers and contemptuous brothers. [Frank, 1944, pp. 244–45.]

Learning Exercise

18. Evaluate each of the following statements:
    (a) Girls should be taught that "no nice girl is interested in sex."
    (b) Adults should not talk about sex to adolescents because to do so stimulates the sexual desires of the adolescent.
    (c) There are many motivations for sexual expression that are basically not sexual.

Achieving Independence. In our culture, the child is expected to become increasingly independent. However, we live in an interdependent society. Hence, independent behavior is expected from the individual in some situations and dependent behavior in other situations. Even adults are daily dependent upon the services of the electrician, policeman, doctor, etc. For the child, the situations calling for independent behavior are continuously changing. At one age level, the child is expected to depend upon parental guidance in many situations, and is rewarded for so doing. Gradually and unsystematically, the child is expected to unlearn his former behavioral patterns for one situation after another and to rely upon his own resources. For the growing child, it sometimes appears that he is expected to be dependent in situations where he wants independence and is expected to be independent where he wants to be dependent.

Children show wide variability in both their dependent and independent tendencies. At birth, the infant is dependent upon his mother for survival. During the first year of life, the mere presence of the mother acquires reward value and the child becomes emotionally dependent upon the mother. Thus, dependency is a learned drive that finds expression first in hugging, kissing, and clinging to the mother, and later in a more extensive set of behaviors that involve the seeking of help, attention, and the approval of others. The strength of this learned drive will vary from child to child. Research evidence seems to indicate that certain child-rearing practices—such as the rigidity of feeding schedules, the severity of weaning, the kind and severity of punishment, overprotectiveness, and rejection—affect the strength of the child's dependence tendencies.[3]

Independence is also learned. As the child matures, he is increasingly able to meet his own needs through his own efforts. He learns to walk, climb, jump, carry things, and control his environment in

[3] See Robert Watson, *Psychology of the Child* (New York: John Wiley & Sons, Inc., 1959), pp. 244–52, 408–23, for a succinct analysis of the research findings on the determinants of dependence and independence tendencies.

numerous ways. As a result of meeting his own needs through independent action and the praise attained from parents for doing things for himself, independence itself becomes a drive.

The important point for teachers to realize is that both dependence and independence drives are learned. The teacher may wish that independence was not of such importance to one pupil in his class and that another pupil was not so dependent. But the teacher can do little to modify the drives themselves. All that the teacher can do is to aid the pupil express the drive in a socially desirable manner.

Training for, and encouragement of, independent behavior increases independence. Fales (1944), in studying a group of nursery school children, recorded the number of times the children refused help in putting on and taking off their wraps. Then, children of one group were given training in taking off their wraps and later compared to children in a second group who were not so trained. The trained group increased greatly in the percentage of refusals of help in taking off their wraps (i.e., they expressed independence) as compared to the untrained group. In another study, Fales praised and thus encouraged one group of children for their independence efforts while another group was not praised. The praised group increased in independence. Thus, training and encouragement fosters independent behavior in activities where the child's abilities are not sufficiently well developed as to give him confidence.

Learning Exercise

19. In the Fales studies, is there any evidence that the researchers increased the nursery school children's *drive* for independence or reduced their dependence *drive*? What prediction would you make about the dependence-independence behavior of the children in the Fales study if they were confronted with a new task that required abilities that they had not fully developed?

Independence is of particular importance to the adolescent. As the child attains adult physical status, former parental restraints become increasingly frustrating. Bolstered by the mores of his peer group, the adolescent struggles to extend the area of situations in which he makes decisions independent of his parents. The adolescent wishes to choose his own clothes, friends, and recreational activities, and to plan time spent on study and recreation as he himself sees fit. Parents also expect more adult-like behavior. But parents tend to expect the adolescent to assume the adult's responsibilities while the adolescent wishes to exercise the adult's privileges.

The struggle of the adolescent for emancipation from the home ordinarily takes place within a home atmosphere in which parent and adolescent love each other. On a questionnaire of family problems, four out of five of a sample of about 1,500 Georgia and Michigan high school boys and girls indicated that they viewed the home as "a place where I share life with people dear to me" (Williams, 1949). On the same questionnaire, many specific complaints against their parents were registered by the adolescents. Punke (1943) found in one survey that social life and money were the sources of over half of the family quarrels reported by 989 adolescent boys and 1,142 adolescent girls.

Attaining Social Acceptability. To be able to get along with others is a highly prized quality in American society. In order to be successful in many occupations, it is necessary to be able to work effectively with others. And for most occupations, this social skill has some importance. Parents are proud when their children get along well with others and become worried when they do not. In America, "friendliness" rates high on a scale of desirable personality characteristics and the man without friends is often pitied. It is not surprising therefore that the American public made a book entitled *How to Win Friends and Influence People* a best seller; that a number of American social scientists direct their research energies to the study of group dynamics and social status; and that the American school strives to aid children to learn to get along well with others.

Psychologists have identified a number of qualities that appear to be associated with social acceptance among children. At the preschool level, social compliance—i.e., the capacity of the child to quickly adapt his behavior to the social demands of a situation—was found in one investigation to be most highly related to children's judgments of popularity status (Lippitt, 1941). Dunnington (1957) found high-status preschool children to interact verbally with other children more frequently than lower-status children. McCandless and Marshall (1957a, 1957b) found that preschool children who seemed to be highly dependent on adults tended to be low in social status.

At the elementary school level, some additional qualities have been noted. The child who is socially aggressive and friendly and who enters enthusiastically into social activities continues to be popular, while the quiet, shy child with few expressive interests remains low in popularity status (Northway, 1943, 1944; Bonney, 1943). However, the child who is noisy, boastful, and rebellious tends to become unpopular. The popular boy or girl is more likely to conform to the group norms and be sensitive to the feelings of others (Northway, 1943, 1944; Dymond *et al.*, 1952).

Bonney (1944) found among school children in grades 3 to 5 that social success is positively related to the socioeconomic status of their parents. It is not clear, however, whether the popularity can be attributed to the socioeconomic factor or to other factors (such as intelligence level) that tend to be associated with socioeconomic status. It has been found that the qualities that make for popularity vary from one socioeconomic level to another.

Pope (1953) studied the social behavior values of 400 California children, averaging 12 years in age, and divided equally into two socioeconomic groups. One group came from lower-lower class homes; the other from the upper-middle and lower-upper classes. The reputation of each child among his peers was secured on each of 25 traits and traits were identified that were associated with popularity. Distinct differences in the traits contributing to popularity were found between socioeconomic classes and between sexes. The aggressive, belligerent, and domineering boy assumed a leadership role among the lower group boys. Among the upper group boys, skill in competitive games earned prestige but domineering behavior made a boy unpopular. Among both groups of girls, the "little lady" who is friendly, tidy, and a good student was widely accepted. However, the upper socioeconomic "little lady" was found to be more vivacious and more likely to go out with boys. Among the lower group, rowdy, talkative, and aggressive girls went out with boys in the lower group more than did quieter girls.

Children may be popular at one age and not at a later age. Kuhlen and Lee (1943) investigated changes in the characteristics of socially accepted and socially unaccepted boys and girls in grades 6, 9, and 12. Some differences in traits were noted. The unaccepted boy and girl in the sixth grade tended to be characterized as "restless." At the twelfth-grade level, "restlessness" was characteristic of the popular boy and girl. "Talkativeness" and "bossiness" were not associated with popularity at the sixth grade but they were by the twelfth grade. To act older than one's age characterized the popular boy and girl in the sixth and ninth grades, but not the popular twelfth-grade boy, and was more likely to be characteristic of the unpopular twelfth-grade girl.

Slow maturing boys and girls may encounter changes in their social status. Approval from peers is more likely to be forthcoming for the child who keeps pace with his age-mates in physical development. During adolescence, a new set of social skills is required to gain popularity and many of the previously admired skills are no longer appropriate. The slow maturing boys and girls may be ignored in the new social activities, particularly if they persist in maintaining their earlier interests and behavioral characteristics. Jones and Bayley (1950) found a tendency for late maturing boys to do just this. They were more childish, giggly, restless, and bossy, and did not learn to dance or carry on a conversation with a girl.

Learning Exercise

20. Why might a child who is popular at one age be unpopular at a later age; and a child who is popular with one group of children be unpopular with another group of children?

SUMMARY

Emotional behavior can be described in terms of: (1) the characteristics of situations that evoke an emotion; (2) the physiological changes that occur when the emotion is experienced; and (3) the ways in which the emotion is expressed. Emotional behavior is learned. There is evidence of some consistency in the order of appearance of emotions from one child to another. Mild emotions may serve to motivate the child. Intense emotions may serve to disrupt the behavior of the child. The task of the school in fostering healthy emotional development is twofold: (1) modifying the perceptions of children of emotion-provoking situations; and (2) modifying the ways that children express their emotions.

Fear is provoked by a situation that is perceived as threatening and for which the child has not an adequate response. Different intense emotions produced similar, but not identical, disturbed states in the organism. Individual differences exist in the overt responses to intense emotions, although to some extent an individual can learn to avoid the disintegrative effects of intense emotions. The sources of fear change with age. The preschool child is fearful of concrete immediate situations that threaten bodily harm. As the child acquires skills to cope with these situations, new fears arise, sometimes of things that may occur in the more distant future. At all ages, many of the fears of children are irrational. Fears may be acquired through classical conditioning, through imitation, or as a result of unpleasant consequences of goal-directed behavior. Adults attempt to modify children's fears in a number of ways. Teaching a child the skills needed to cope with a situation is one of the most effective means of modifying fears. Counter-conditioning and experimental extinction are, for certain situations, effective means of modifying fears but are more difficult to manage.

Like fear, the sources of anger and the modes of expressing anger change with age. New frustrations supplant old frustrations. The conflicts over toilet and dressing routines are supplanted by conflicts over playthings, which in turn are supplanted by conflicts over social relationships. Behaviorally, temper tantrums are supplanted by verbal aggression, displaced hostility, and antisocial acts. The incidence of anger is affected by the child's physical health. Home and school can aid the child to gain reasonable control over anger by being fair, treating the child with respect, providing opportunities for children to work together to achieve common goals, reinforcing constructive behavior to thwarting situations, and by providing children with opportunities to express their emotions in a socially acceptable way.

Both home and school are laboratories within which the child acquires social skills, and the emotional climate of both home and school greatly influence the socialization process. Research on the type of child behavior associated with various types of homes reveals quite complex relationships. It is difficult to generalize from the findings of the many studies beyond stating that the home that is not inharmonious and in which the child is loved and respected as an individual and is firmly and consistently disciplined is a home favorable to the child's healthy social development.

A number of techniques have been developed to study the social acceptance of a child. Sociometric techniques such as the sociogram, "Guess Who," and social distance scale are discussed in this chapter. Anecdotal records provide a means to the teacher of observing the development of a child over a period of time. Some questions the teacher may keep in mind in recording incidents that are crucial to the social development of the child are:

1. Are the play activities of the child contributing to his social development? Are his play interests appropriate to his age level?
2. Are his interactions with other children leading to the development of sympathetic behavior?
3. Is the child improving in his perceptions of self and others?
4. Is the child learning an appropriate sex role?
5. Is the child accepted by his peers?
6. Is the child finding in the school the satisfying social and emotional experiences needed as a background for working through perplexing sex problems?
7. Is the child increasingly attaining socially responsible independence?

Answer Cues

1. (a) Delight, elation, affection for children, joy. (b) Distress, anger, jealousy, shame.

2. Modify the child's perception that water is threatening. Modify the child's overt response patterns in water.

3. Intensity.

4. (a) Perception of threat. Any procedure that would modify the child's perception of ridicule as threatening. (b) Flight. Walk away from or ignore ridiculing situation. Fight back verbally. (c) Through narrowing of perception—i.e., not noticing elements in a social situation ordinarily noticed. Confused disorganized responses.

5. (c).

6. Realistic—what is feared has a strong chance of occurring. *Examples:* Being called upon in class to give an oral report; fears of a social nature. Unrealistic—little likelihood of the occurrence of what is feared. *Examples:* A good student fearing failure; fear of ghosts.

7. By inflicting pain, the teacher can teach the child to fear him. This, of course, is undesirable (see discussion on "Punishment" in Chapter 8).

8. (a) Parents playing with the puppy. (b) John pats dog and is not bitten. (c) Parents play with puppy while John enjoys candy bar.

9. Situations no longer frustrating either because they are more accurately perceived or because effective responses have been learned to deal with the situation.

10. Adopts ways that work better or are more socially acceptable.

11. The child would not have an opportunity to learn effective responses to teasing nor to learn to perceive "teasing" as non-threatening.

12. Constructive, or at least non-destructive, expressions of anger is the better. A child will experience anger. To teach the child that this is wrong can lead to unhealthy feelings of guilt.

13. Learning to get along with age-mates. Learning physical skills needed for ordinary games.

14. (a) No. Only 42 per cent. (b) Yes. The highest percentage in Table 5–1 is 42 per cent.

15. (a) Baldwin's study. May be hostile and domineering. (b) In the Baldwin study, the warmth variable did not contribute to originality. (c) Yes. At least this was true in the study by Baldwin *et al.* (d) Yes—according to Peck's study. (e) According to studies summarized by Radke: aggressiveness is associated with the rejective home, dominating parents, submissive parents, the inharmonious home, and the home with poor discipline. According to Baldwin's study, the democratic home also can develop an aggressive child.

16. (a) Not sufficiently specific. Focuses attention on teacher's reaction to Bill (a nuisance). (b) Evaluative statement not separated ("Tony . . . want[s] . . . own way"). (c) Does not describe a specific event. Evaluates behavior (bad-mannered). (d) This merely reports a more objective measure and hence adds no new information.

17. Interests appropriate to their age and sex; sympathetic behavior; an improved perception of self and others.

18. (a) Danger of generating feelings of guilt. (b) Adolescents obtain much sex information from their peers. (c) For the girl, to gain an acceptance as a female that has been denied her in family life.

19. No evidence of increase of drive. Prediction would depend upon the degree of similarity of the new task to the old task. If the child perceived the new task as one he was unable to perform, then dependent behavior would be predicted.

20. The characteristics that contribute to popularity vary with age and socioeconomic class.

6

GENERAL NATURE
OF LEARNING

The stimulus, organismic, and response variables that need to be taken into account by the teacher in guiding learning have been discussed briefly in Chapter 1. In this chapter, we will examine more closely the range of educational objectives found in the modern school in order to appreciate all that the educator has in mind when he uses the term "learning." Second, we will look at learning from a reinforcement learning theory point of view in order to explore some of its relevancies and limitations to school learning. Finally, we will discuss the learning experience variable in order to search for principles that may serve as guides to the teacher in selecting and organizing learning experiences.

Learning may be defined as *a relatively permanent change of behavior that occurs as a result of experience or practice.* Let us examine this definition.

First, it should be remembered that some changes of behavior occur for reasons other than experience or practice. Some changes of behavior occur as a result of maturation. Some occur as a result of fatigue. Changes in behavior may occur because of a change in the level of motivation of the individual. None of these changes can be considered as learning. According to our definition, only changes occurring as a result of experience or practice may be considered as learning.

Second, note that there is no assumption implicit in the definition concerning the desirability or correctness of the acquired change of behavior. Thus, a person can learn to misspell a word. A person can learn to be an alcoholic. Any change of behavior that occurs as a result of experience or practice is regarded as learning, whether or not the change is correct or wrong, good or bad.

Third, it should be noted that our definition does not specify clearly what it is that is learned. Does learning consist of newly acquired overt response patterns? Or does learning consist of changes occurring within the organism with the overt responses merely an expression of the changed organism? Psychologists who have studied learning from a purely stimulus-response orientation have greatly expanded our knowledge of the learning process. Reinforcement learning theory, discussed in Chapter 2, has been developed largely through the experiments conducted by stimulus-response psychologists. In recent years, however, there has been an increased emphasis by psychologists on mediating processes. J. McV. Hunt (1961) traces the development of this renewed emphasis and shows how several lines of investigations are coalescing to radically revise concepts of the brain and its functioning. Hunt states:

. . . stimulus-response methodology (as distinct from stimulus-response theory) has been rediscovering "mind," or at least has been rediscovering that something important is going on between the ears. The new "mind," however, is quite different from the old one. Where the old one consisted of footloose faculties, the new "mind" consists of "hypothetical constructs" or "intervening variables" which are tied both to the history of the organism's interaction with the environment and to its observed response characteristics. . . . [P. 8.]

Psychologists, working within the framework of stimulus-response methodology, have contributed to filling in the vacuum between the presentation of a stimulus and the occurrence of a response. Early, Hunter (1912, 1918, 1924) argued that some kind of *symbolic process* needed to be postulated to explain complex maze learning of animals. Hull (1930, 1952) advanced the idea that one response could have a stimulus value and lead to further responses. This concept of *pure stimulus acts* has been elaborated by Miller and Dollard (1941) and given the label "response-produced cues." For Tolman (1932) and Krechevsky (1932), these mediating processes are central to learning. Tolman conceives of learning as the formation of *expectancies;* that is, what the learner learns is essentially an expectation of the consequences of his response. The response made is merely an acting out of this expectancy. In a similar vein, Krechevsky uses the term "hypotheses" to describe these central mediating processes.

Osgood distinguishes between *stimulus objects* (Ṡ), which are capable of eliciting instrumental response sequences *without* any mediational process, and signs ([S̲]), which elicit mediating processes. For Osgood (1953), learning consists of two types: "(a) modifications in the mediation process elicited by a particular stimulus pattern (e.g., the buzzer sound must come to mean 'danger'; it must be perceived in a different way); or (b) modification in the instrumental sequence elicited by a particular mediator (e.g., the buzzer still signifies 'danger,' but something other than running must be done)" (pp. 403–4). Osgood's view thus constitutes a rapprochement between stimulus-response theory and the cognitive theories of Tolman and of Krechevsky. For Osgood, both mediating processes and instrumental responses are learned.

Learning Exercises

1. Identify an example of a *pure stimulus act* in the following:

   John's reminiscing about mother's apple pie served as a stimulus for the further act of ordering apple pie at a restaurant.

2. What would Tolman say was learned in the following?

   Since Betty's parents began giving her one dollar for each A on her report card, Betty hurried home after she received a report card to show her parents her A's.

3. Find an example of *sign learning* in the following:

   Bill learned that his teacher usually smiled when she handed a pupil a report card containing very good grades.

SCHOOL LEARNING

The modern school attempts to promote different kinds of learning. This becomes evident from statements of educational objectives formulated by various educational committees. Educational objectives cover a wide range of *content*. The content of educational objectives may be organized in terms of subject-matter areas, e.g., English, mathematics, social studies, science, music, and home economics. Or the content of educational objectives may be classified areas of living. For example, the Mid-Century Committee on Elementary Education identifies nine broad areas of elementary school learning (Kearney, 1953). These are: (1) physical development, health, body care; (2) individual social and emotional development; (3) ethical behavior, standards, values; (4) social relations; (5) the social world; (6) the physical world; (7) esthetic development; (8) communication; and (9) quantitative relationships.

The educational objectives of the school can be classified into behavioral as well as into content categories. The handbook *Taxonomy of Educational Objectives; Cognitive Domain* (Bloom, 1956a) classifies intellectual-type objectives into six categories. Following are brief descriptions of the six categories with examples of objectives based on the content of this text.

1. *Knowledge*—the recall of facts, concepts, principles, theories, etc.
   Example: to be able to list the nine areas of elementary school learning set forth by the Mid-Century Committee.
2. *Comprehension*—the understanding of facts, concepts, ideas, etc. at a level. The learner is able to glean the meaning of material communicated to him and make use of the material without necessarily relating it to other material.
   Example: to understand the meaning of reinforcement learning concepts (such as classical conditioning, extinction, and discrimination) sufficiently well so that you can explain each concept in your own words and give original examples of behavior that illustrate each concept.
3. *Application*—to make use of principles, generalizations, rules of procedure, etc., in solving some problem or performing some intellectual task.
   Example: to be able to apply statistical concepts in comparing the end-of-the-course test performances of two random samples of students who were taught the same subject matter by two different methods.
4. *Analysis*—the breakdown of a communication into its elements or parts and see the relationship between the parts.
   Example: to scan a chapter of a text in order to find out how the materials presented in the chapter are organized, the major topics treated, and relationship of the subtopics to the major topics.
5. *Synthesis*—putting together information and ideas to form some original communication.
   Example: to be able to plan a unit of instruction for a particular teaching situation, utilizing the principles of learning described in this chapter.
6. *Evaluation*—judging the value of a communication, theory, plan, etc., in terms of some criteria.
   Example: after thinking through a set of criteria by which to judge the value of a psychological theory or frame of reference to be able to evaluate the comparative usefulness to a teacher of the following frames of reference: phenomenological, reinforcement, psychoanalytic.

The categories of the cognitive domain are organized in order of complexity. The more complex behaviors include the simpler behaviors. Thus, knowledge is necessary to achieve a comprehension objective; knowledge and comprehension are involved in the attainment of an application-type objective; etc.

Learning Exercise

4. Classify each of the following objectives according to the major categories included in the cognitive domain taxonomy:
   (a) Becoming familiar with a range of types of literature
   (b) The ability to make use of the laws of trigonometry in solving practical problems
   (c) Skill in comprehending the interrelationships among the ideas in a passage
   (d) The ability to plan a unit of instruction for a particular teaching situation
   (e) The ability to grasp the meaning of social science data presented in graphical form
   (f) The ability to apply esthetic standards to the choice and use of the ordinary objects of the everyday environment

---

A second handbook, A *Taxonomy of Educational Objectives: Affective Domain* (Krathwohl, Bloom, and Masia; 1964), classifies what is sometimes referred to as *emotional learning* objectives into five categories:

1. *Receiving*—willingness to receive or attend to certain stimuli.
   Examples: paying attention and listening carefully when others speak; listening for rhythm in poetry or prose read aloud; increases in sensitivity to human need and pressing social problems.
2. *Responding*—the child becomes sufficiently involved to be willing to participate or even seek out an activity and gain satisfaction from it.
   Examples: willingness to comply with health regulations; acquaints himself with significant current events through reading and discussion; enjoys self-expression in music.
3. *Valuing*—has accepted certain beliefs, attitudes, values, and ideals as his own. These values, attitudes, etc., are internalized to an extent that they influence behavior with some consistency.
   Examples: desires to develop ability to speak and write more effectively; examines opposing viewpoints on controversial issues before forming opinions about them; devoted to the ideals of democracy.
4. *Organization*—conceptualizes and organizes his internalized

values into an interrelated system and eventually an integrated system.

Examples: begins to form judgments as to the responsibility of society for conserving human and material resources; regulates amount of rest in accordance with the demands of his activities.

5. *Characterization by a Value or Value Complex*

This final category really includes two levels. At the first level, the valuing as described in category 3 has become so much a part of the individual that it consistently influences his behavior. The behaver experiences no conflict in a wide range of situations for which the values are relevant. He has developed a *generalized set* to behave in a way that is consistent to the values he holds. And ways of behaving that are consistent to the value he holds can be said to *characterize* his behavior.

At the second level, the organization of a value system as described in category 4 has become so much a part of the individual that the value complex consistently influences his behavior. The fully internalized and consistently organized system of values becomes a philosophy of life for the individual.

Examples: full acceptance of objectivity and systematic planning as basic methods of arriving at satisfactory choices; has developed a consistent philosophy of life.

The categories of the affective domain are ordered according to the degree of *internalization* involved. Thus, the category *receiving* involves merely a relatively passive willingness to attend to different stimuli. Increasingly, the later categories involve behavior that becomes an essential part of the individual and of more importance in his total life style.

Learning Exercise

5. Classify each of the following objectives according to the major categories included in the affective domain taxonomy:
   (a) Notices the esthetic in art objects displayed in an art class
   (b) Desires to attain optimum health
   (c) Personal and civic life is regulated by a code of behavior that is based on ethical principles and is consistent with democratic ideals
   (d) Increased appetite and taste for what is good in literature
   (e) Develops a loyalty to one's group without forming antagonistic attitudes toward other desirable groups

---

Some educational objectives can be classified under a third major category—*competency* or *action pattern* domain. The various psycho-motor skills that the school seeks to develop belong in the competency domain. Any educational objective that is primarily focused upon the development of an action pattern or a habit belongs in the competency domain. Some examples are:

"He is able to conduct meetings, address the chair, make motions, and elect officers." (Kearney, 1953, p. 108.)

"Believes in the conservation of human and natural resources, practices it, and supports programs and organizations concerned with this national problem." (French, 1957, p. 203.)

"He habitually assumes responsibility for the safety of others, group cooperation, audience courtesy, sportsmanship in games, and courtesy in the use of language." (Kearney, 1953, p. 77.)

"He is able to skim quickly. He can select appropriate titles for paragraphs that are read or written." (Kearney, 1953, p. 106.)

Objectives in the competency domain may include cognitive or affective components and indeed may constitute descriptions of overt responses that are indicative of the attainment of cognitive and affective objectives.

Our discussion up to this point has been designed to illustrate the wide varieties of behavioral changes that teachers in the modern school seek to bring about in children. Psychologists, in their study of learning, have conducted experiments involving a much narrower range of behavioral changes. The psychologist, after defining learning, has attempted to identify *what* variables affect learning and *how* each variable affects learning. From the findings of literally thousands of learning experiments, a number of learning theories have been advanced.

THE LEARNING PROCESS

In Chapter 2, a number of reinforcement learning concepts are discussed. Before advancing to additional concepts, it might be profitable for you to reread the section on "Reinforcement Frame of Reference" in Chapter 2. The following "Learning Exercises" may aid you in your review.

Learning Exercises

6. A puff of air in a person's eyes ordinarily elicits a blinking response. In an experiment, the sound of a buzzer is followed by a puff of air in the

subject's eyes. After buzzer and air puff have been paired a number of times, the subject blinks at the sound of the buzzer (before the puff of air is administered).

(a) According to our definition, has learning taken place?

(b) What type of conditioning has occurred?

(c) Identify the unconditioned stimulus, the conditioned stimulus, and the conditioned response.

(d) Once the eye-blink response to the buzzer has been established, what would reinforce this response?

(e) Suppose the conditioned response was not reinforced for a number of trials, what would take place?

(f) Suppose after extinction has taken place, the subject was given a rest period, and then returned to the experiment. If on the first trial, the conditioned response occurred, what would we call this reoccurrence (without intervening reinforcement) of the conditioned response?

(g) If the conditioned response occurred to the sound of the buzzer that emitted a different tone, what concept would be demonstrated?

7. Mr. Harper, an eighth-grade teacher, disliked and treated coldly his aunt who had very large ears. On the first day of school, he found himself treating very coldly a girl in his class who had very large ears. What concept is exemplified in Mr. Harper's behavior?

8. Helen *becomes flustered* when *she is laughed at*. One day Helen was *called upon to give a speech*. She did and was laughed at by her classmates. After this Helen becomes flustered just as soon as she is called upon to give a speech.

In this example of classical conditioning, the UCS, CS, and CR are in italics. Identify each.

9. For each of the incidents described below, identify the type of instrumental conditioning that is exemplified.

(a) In a tenth-grade social science class, Mr. Watson often invites discussion on controversial social issues. When a member of the class attempts to define more precisely the problem presented, or points out the need for more information before a conclusion is reached, Mr. Watson listens carefully and briefly points out the merit of the student's comment. As the year progresses, more and more responses occur of the type "Let's look at the problem carefully before reaching a conclusion."

(b) Mr. Jones also presents problems to his English class, but he is extremely critical of all comments made by the students and makes sure they are "put straight." As the year progresses, participation in class discussion decreases.

(c) Bill feels keenly disappointed every time he receives a low grade in a school subject. His painful feelings of inadequacy are somehow reduced if he criticizes his sister's behavior. No one in Bill's family, including Bill, can understand why at report time Bill becomes very critical of his sister.

A wide range of complex processes are involved in human learning. And, as we have seen, the different kinds of changes of behavior that the school seeks to bring about in children cover a large portion of the whole range of human learning. Psychologists, in their study of the learning process, have searched for concepts, principles, and theories that hold true for all forms of learning. Dollard and Miller (1950) maintain that four fundamental factors are important in all learning. These factors are: *drive, cue, response,* and *reinforcement.*

Drive

The concept drive, as used by Dollard and Miller, is roughly equivalent to motivation. For learning to take place, the learner must *want* something. What is wanted may be relief from some internal disequilibrium. Hunger, thirst, sex, and pain are examples of unlearned or *primary* drives. Any stimulus can become a drive if it is sufficiently strong. Soft music has little primary drive function. Blaring music has more drive function. A drive then is a state of tension, and the individual experiencing the tension is impelled to do something to reduce the tension.

For the most part, our society protects its members from experiencing the full strength of primary drives. Hunger and thirst are satisfied before they become extremely painful. *Secondary* or *learned* drives therefore become relatively more important in human behavior. The emotions fear, anger, anxiety, and disgust are examples of learned drives; and the reduction of these emotions are *learned* or *secondary reinforcements.* Money is a good example of a secondary reinforcement, with the need for money functioning as a learned drive. In school learning, learned drives, such as the need to achieve, are ordinarily of more importance than primary drives.

Cue

A drive impels a person to respond. Cues determine what particular response is made and when and where that response is made. In a school classroom, the end-of-the-period bell functions as a cue for pupils to move away from their seats. Internal and external stimuli may have both drive and cue value. The intensity of the stimuli determines its drive value. The quality of the stimuli determines its cue value. A person when hungry makes food-seeking responses. Thus, hunger has a cue value as well as a drive value. The intensity of the hunger determines its drive value. The fact that the person is experiencing hunger rather than thirst or some other state of disequilibrium determines the cue value of the internal stimulus.

The teacher in a classroom has both drive value and cue value for the pupils. The teacher's announcement of a forthcoming test may function as the stimulus to elicit feelings of anxiety for some of the pupils. For these pupils, the announcement has drive value. To the extent that pupils make "test-preparation" responses, the announcement also has cue value.

Response

A clearly defined educational objective identifies the responses students are expected to learn in certain defined situations. Thus, for the objective "paying attention and listening carefully when others speak," "when others speak" roughly defines the situations encompassed by the objective. The response expected to be learned is "paying attention and listening carefully." The objective implies that a pupil in the classroom is expected to learn to notice the cues "teacher speaking" or "classmate speaking in a discussion," and attach a listening response to such cues.

The ease with which a response can be learned depends upon the initial tendency for the cue to evoke the desired response. For the "listening" objective described above, the pupil must first make the listening response before it can be reinforced. If the pupil does listen fairly frequently when others are speaking, then the teacher has the opportunity to reinforce the listening response so as to increase its frequency of occurrence. Some clues as to how the teacher can reinforce desired responses of pupils may be found later in this chapter in the discussion on "Conditioning of Verbal Behavior."

Reinforcement

Repetition does not necessarily strengthen the tendency for a response to occur. Some reinforcement is necessary. Food and water are frequently used as reinforcers in experiments with animals. When the animal in an experiment makes the desired response, food is forthcoming. On subsequent trials, the animal increasingly makes the response that results in the reward. In the classroom, reinforcers other than food and water usually are regarded as more appropriate. As we shall see presently, the experiments conducted by some psychologists in recent years on conditioning of verbal behavior have considerable classroom applicability.

Learning Exercise

10. When Alice enters grade 1, she is able to count but is not able to answer the question "How much are four and three?" By the end of the school

year, Alice is able to supply the answer "seven" to this question and do many other simple addition problems. Alice enjoys school. She wants to please her teacher and her parents, and so she strives to learn the right answers to the questions her teacher asks. While learning to add, Alice tries one answer after another to the questions asked. She tries counting blocks; she asks her neighbor; she looks in the book; or she guesses. But through all this trial and error learning, Alice feels happy when she gets the right answer and her teacher is pleased. Alice's parents, too, are pleased as Alice slowly but surely gains mastery over the number combinations.

Identify the *drive, cue, response,* and *reinforcement* from the above account of Alice learning to add four and three.

Conditioning of Verbal Behavior

The importance of giving the learner specific and immediate knowledge of the results of his efforts has long been established (Wolfle, 1951). In some learning situations, the learner knows whether he has made an error immediately after he has made a response. A diver who lands on his stomach on a dive from the high board needs no one to inform him that he has done something wrong. However, for most oral and written responses that a student makes in school, there is no such "built-in" knowledge of results. The student needs to be informed as to the adequacy of his oral and written responses. Signs of approval such as a nod, a smile, or such words as "Right!" or "Good!" may become reinforcers of desired responses.

Research evidence indicates that reinforcement occurs even when the learner is not aware that certain of his responses are being reinforced (Krasner, 1958). Greenspoon (1954) asked subjects, tested individually, to say all the words they could think of. For one group in the experiment, a red light was made to go on every time the subject named a plural noun. For a second group, a tone was sounded when the subject named a plural noun. The output of plural nouns for these two groups was significantly greater than it was for three other groups that were not reinforced for naming plural nouns, and none of the subjects were able to verbalize the relationship between the reinforcers (light and tone) and the kind of responses they were giving. They were apparently unaware that an increasing proportion of the words they were saying were plural nouns.

A highly generalized class of responses of individuals may be reinforced without the subject's awareness. Verplanck (1955) reports a study in which statements of *opinion* occurring during conversation were reinforced through the experimenter either paraphrasing or agreeing with each opinion statement. All the subjects so reinforced increased in their rate of verbalizing statements of opinion. Twenty-one out of 24 subjects, who were not reinforced for opinion statements, decreased in their output of such statements. The students in the experiments were not aware that statements of opinion were reinforced.

Quite complex verbal skills, such as those involved in participating in a group discussion, can be improved through the use of verbal reinforcement. Loree and Koch (1960) divided each of four educational psychology classes into six panel discussion groups, each of which was composed of four members. Each group conducted a panel discussion at the beginning of the semester and, on a matched topic, at the end of the semester. The experimental instructional conditions in the interval between the initial and final panel discussions were varied between classes. For two classes, designated as the *control non-practice groups,* no additional panel discussion practice was provided. For one class, designated as the *experimental practice groups,* panel participants were given practice in conducting panel discussions but were given no opportunity to hear a playback of a tape recording of their panel discussion. For the fourth class, designated as the *experimental reinforced groups,* practice was provided; and the participants later met to hear a playback of the panel discussion. During the playback, the instructor stopped the recording whenever a panelist used a good panel discussion technique. The instructor then commented on the good technique. It was found that significant gains were made by the "reinforced groups." The initial mean of the six reinforced groups was 70.5; the final mean was 103.5. Gains for the discussion groups in the other three classes were in no case more than 3 points greater than the initial means. The groups that had practice without reinforcement did no better than the groups that had no practice.

Learning Exercises

11. Miss Drew, an English teacher, requires her students to write many themes during a semester. Miss Drew assigns a letter grade for each theme completed but does not comment on strong and weak features of each theme.

    In what way is Miss Drew's procedure an inadequate means of providing knowledge of results?

12. Miss Blake sometimes provides class time for her pupils to work on problems in mathematics. During this time, Miss Blake helps students individually. When she sees a student has worked a problem correctly, she informs him at once that his answer is right.

    What merit can you see in Miss Blake's procedure of providing knowledge of results?

13. A college class plots to manipulate the behavior of an instructor. When

the instructor moves toward one corner of the classroom, the members of the class pay close attention to the instructor's lecture. Attention is maintained just as long as the instructor moves toward or stands in the corner of the room. When the instructor makes no movement toward the corner of the room or moves away from the corner, the class is inattentive. After a number of class sessions, the instructor finds himself, for some reason he does not understand, delivering his lecture from one corner of the room.

(a) What is the reinforcer in the above incident?

(b) In what respect is the reinforcement in the above incident similar to the reinforcement in Greenspoon's and Verplanck's studies?

14. The teaching procedure of Miss Drew (the English teacher mentioned in Learning Exercise 11) is most comparable to the instructional procedure of what groups in the Loree and Koch study?

15. What kind of analysis would a teacher first need to make in order to develop "scientific attitudes" of students through reinforcement?

Principle of Successive Approximation

We have noted that the ease with which a response can be learned depends upon the initial tendency for the cue to evoke the desired response. For some educational objectives, there is some tendency for the pupil to give a "correct" response to an appropriate cue. For example, a child may be courteous in some situations occasionally, but not always. By reinforcing courteous behavior of the child when it occurs, the initial tendency of the child to be courteous may be strengthened. In other situations, a child may rarely be courteous. Learning would indeed progress very slowly if the teacher were forced to await the appearance of this rare response in order to provide reinforcement. Fortunately, through example and through verbal communication, the situations calling for courteous behavior and what constitutes courteous responses can be made clear. Much social learning occurs through imitation (Miller and Dollard, 1941), and a child may learn to try out the desired responses at the suggestion of respected adults.

For many educational objectives, there is no initial tendency for a pupil to give a correct response to a cue. For the child entering grade 1 who cannot read, there is no initial tendency for the child to read a page from a book. However, the language and concept development of the average first-grade child is such as to partially ready the child to learn to read. Upon this foundation, the primary teacher builds further language skills. She plans situations in which listening is well motivated. She reads stories aloud. She both exhibits and encourages good speech patterns. She encourages interests in written language by printing on the chalkboard what children dictate to her. She helps the children to notice separate sounds in words. She provides practice in seeing the differences in printed letters and printed words such as the difference between *b* and *d*, and *turn* and *torn*. She provides practice in observing the relationship between the letter form and the sound of the letter. These and other learnings constitute a part of establishing reading readiness. And reinforcement is not reserved for the final desired response, i.e., reading the printed page. Reinforcement is provided to develop each subskill needed in order to learn to read. The teacher utilizes the *principle of successive approximations*, i.e., reinforcing responses that represent progress toward the attainment of the ultimate desired responses even though they are not themselves the ultimate responses desired.

Skinner (1953) describes a simple experiment that illustrates the shaping up of response patterns through reinforcing successive approximations. In the Skinner experiment, a pigeon is placed in a box where its behavior may be observed through a one-way screen. The pigeon can be fed by using a small food tray that is operated electrically. The behavior to be developed is that of raising the head above a given height. A scale is pinned on the far wall of the box in order to observe the height of the pigeon's head. Initially, the experimenter observed the height at which the head of the pigeon is normally held. Then a line on the scale is selected that is reached only infrequently by the pigeon. Whenever the pigeon's head comes up to this height, it is rewarded with food. Almost immediately there is a change in the frequency with which the head is raised up to the line. Also, the pigeon, on occasions, raises its head higher than the rewarded height. The experimenter next selects a second and higher height on the scale and reinforces the pigeon only when the head is raised up to this new height. Again there is a change in the frequency with which the head is raised up to the new line, and again the pigeon occasionally raises its head above the rewarded height. The experimenter continues the procedure of selecting higher and higher points on the scale until the pigeon's posture has changed so that the top of the head seldom falls below the line that was first chosen.

In Skinner's experiment, the behavior developed—raising the head high—is extremely simple compared to the complexity of responses involved in reading. Just being able to discriminate between a *b* and a *d* is a behavior at least as complex as raising the head. And reading involves numerous discriminations of this kind. Notwithstanding differences in the complexity between animal and human learning, Skinner's experiment does suggest that *learning is facilitated through rein-*

forcing a level of performance that is higher than the learner's normal level, even though it is lower than the level we wish to ultimately develop.

Learning Exercise

16. How might a fourth-grade teacher utilize the principle of successive approximations in developing the reading ability of her pupils (assuming she knew the reading difficulty level of a large number of books and the reading interests of her pupils)?

Continuous and Partial Reinforcement

Reinforcement may be continuous or partial. Reinforcement is continuous when a previously rewarded response is reinforced every time that it subsequently occurs. Reinforcement is partial when reinforcement of the previously rewarded response is frequently omitted during learning.

Much of our learned behavior has been shaped up by partial reinforcement. Friendly responses to others are frequently but not always reinforced by the reciprocal friendly responses of others. The mother often but not always rewards with a smile her child for saying "please" and "thank you." An elementary school child writes down neatly the number of an addition problem, and his care is frequently but not always reinforced by obtaining the correct answer. We learn to "play the percentages." We learn to expect certain consequences to sometimes follow certain responses.[1] While research suggests that conditioning is usually somewhat poorer under partial reinforcement conditions than it is under continuous reinforcement, research also indicates that responses learned under partial conditions are more *resistant to extinction* than are responses learned under continuous reinforcement conditions (Kimble, 1961, pp. 160–64).

---

[1] What reinforces may be viewed as a confirmation of an expectation rather than as something that reduces a tension. Possibly both concepts of the nature of reinforcement are of value to the teacher in his effort to find ways of reinforcing desired response patterns of pupils. For our purposes, reinforcement is viewed as any consequence of a response that increases the probability of the response recurring under similar conditions.

There are a number of theories of extinction that may be used to explain this research finding. Chapter 10 in Gregory A. Kimble's revision of Hilgard and Marquis' *Conditioning and Learning* (1961) contains a discussion of the various theories. The effectiveness of partial reinforcement probably varies according to the proportion of reinforced trials, the degree of motivation of the learner, the magnitude of the reward, the specificity of the response leading to the reward, and other factors.

Learning Exercises

17. In learning to drive, a person learns to step on the brake pedal in order to stop the car. Assuming the brakes are in order, is this an example of learning through continuous or through partial reinforcement?
18. Occasionally, Mary brushes her hair carefully before going to school. Sometimes when she does this, one of her friends compliments her on the appearance of her hair. Mary gradually develops the habit of brushing her hair each morning before going to school. Is this an example of continuous or of partial reinforcement?

Habit-Family Hierarchy

In instrumental learning, the response to be learned must occur before it can be reinforced. Instrumental conditioning is therefore a process of increasing the strength of a response tendency. The response to be learned is already in the behavior repertory of the learner.

The concept of *habit-family hierarchy*, developed by Hull (1934), is useful in understanding the instrumental conditioning process. At the beginning of training in an instrumental conditioning situation, the learner has a variety of responses at his disposal. All the responses that the learner might make in a particular situation form a *habit-family*. As the response tendencies vary in strength, the learner is more likely to make some responses than others. All the responses in the habit-family form a hierarchy, ordered according to strength. Initially, in the learning situation, the strongest response tendency is most likely to be elicited. If, on the first trial, this response is not reinforced, then the response tendency will be weakened. Through successive non-reinforcement, the incorrect responses become weaker. *Extinction* takes place even though part of the strength of the non-reinforced is recovered between trials (*spontaneous recovery*). When the response to be learned does occur and is reinforced, its strength is increased. Learning the correct response is thus a process of raising the correct response to the dominant position in the habit-family hierarchy.

The following hypothetical incident may serve to illustrate, in simplified form, the concept of habit-family hierarchy and its relationship to instrumental learning.

A five-year-old boy is playing with toys alongside his four-year-old sister who is playing with other toys. Suddenly the boy wants one of his sister's toys. He attempts to take the toy from his sister. The sister attempts to hold on to her toy. On similar occasions in the past, the brother has responded in one of five ways: (1) physical attack on his sister, (2) verbal attack, (3) appeal for outside arbitration in his favor, (4) playing with the toy cooperatively with his sister, and (5) withdrawal. While the particular response made by the brother seemed to be influenced by how he felt and how he felt toward his sister at the time, physical attack was his most frequent response. The next most frequent response was verbal attack. The most desirable response— cooperative play—appeared to be the fourth strongest response tendency. The five responses together in order of their frequency of occurrence constitute a habit-family hierarchy.

Suppose that this play situation occurs on a number of occasions and that parents can control the reinforcement of the different competitive responses. Suppose further we assume that (1) the response with the greatest over-all response tendency occurs on each occasion, (2) both parent approval and satisfaction in play constitute reinforcement for the boy, and (3) non-reinforcement is insured by the parents who make sure that the boy does not get the toy by making any undesirable responses. Consistent with reinforcement learning theory, we might expect something like the following to occur.

On Occasion 1, the boy tries physical attack. When this does not work (is non-reinforced), the strength of this response tendency is reduced and other responses will be tried. As the cooperative play is low in the hierarchy, this response may not occur for some time as the boy alternates between the three strongest response tendencies. Eventually through the extinction process (i.e., the weakening of the response tendency through non-reinforcement), the cooperative play response may rise temporarily to the top of the hierarchy and make its appearance. If this does occur and the cooperative play response is reinforced, then the probability is increased of its recurrence on a similar situation in the future. This does not mean that on Occasion 2 the cooperative play response will be the first response of the boy. Extinction is not a process of destroying response tendency. Through spontaneous recovery, a portion of the strengths of responses 1, 2, and 3 will be recovered. Probably the physical attack response will be the first response on Occasion 2 to make its appearance. Eventually, however, the cooperative play will become the predominant response in the habit-family hierarchy.

The above illustration admittedly is oversimplified. The development of desirable behavior patterns in children is by no means a simple or a mechanical process. Rarely has the teacher or parent a full knowledge of what consequences serve to reinforce a behavior of a child. Even less frequently can the parent or teacher completely control a

series of learning situations so that desired responses are reinforced and
undesired responses are not reinforced.

Learning Exercise

19. When John is given a homework assignment, he usually responds in one
of the following ways:

    (a) He puts off the assignment as long as he can and then does it hur-
riedly.

    (b) He gets hold of a friend's work and copies it.

    (c) He sets aside sufficient time and then does the assignment well.

    (d) He does not do the assignment.

What additional information do we need in order to arrange the above
"habit-family" into a "habit-family hierarchy"?

GUIDING LEARNING

Five major tasks are involved in guiding the learning of children:
(1) defining educational objectives, (2) selecting learning experiences,
(3) organizing learning experiences, (4) guiding the learning process in
the classroom, and (5) evaluating the outcomes of instruction. In this
chapter, we have examined the range of educational objectives found
in the modern school. Clearly, the kinds of learning experiences provided for students need to vary. In later chapters, we will examine
psychological research that is relevant to the teacher's tasks of selecting
and organizing learning experiences for particular kinds of learning:
psychomotor, cognitive, and affective. In this chapter, we are concerned with identifying the variables and searching for principles that
apply to the selection of learning experiences for all kinds of educational objectives.

Learning Experience Variables

A *learning experience variable* is a characteristic or a complexity of
characteristics of experiences that, if varied, makes a difference on the
effectiveness of learning. Thus, when we say that *motive-incentive
appeal* is a learning experience variable, we mean simply that the
effectiveness of learning varies with the motive-incentive appeal of the
learning task. To say that *difficulty* is a learning experience variable
implies that the difficulty of the learning task makes a difference on
how well learning progresses. *Methods of instruction* (e.g., lecture
method versus discussion method) may be considered a learning ex-

perience variable, although a complexity of characteristics are involved in all instructional methods.

Learning experience variables may be viewed as stimulus variables just as long as no implication is made that it is possible to identify a particular stimulus in an event that is solely responsible for a behavior. The total environmental field or situation of the behaver contains a multitude of *potential* stimuli, some of which become *effective* stimuli as a result of the organism interacting with its environment.[2]

Learning experience variables may be conveniently discussed under two headings:

1. Method Variables—including the nature of the tasks that the *pupil* is called upon to learn as well as variations in the ways the *teacher* presents and arranges the tasks; and
2. Environmental Variables—the environmental conditions under which learning occurs.

Method Variables

Literally thousands of educational research studies have been designed to assess the effectiveness of various teaching methods. A few areas of research interest to the educator are:

1. Relative effectiveness of lectures and student discussions
2. The effectiveness of television, movies, radio, and other audio-visual aids
3. Education geared to students' interests versus more traditional education
4. Relative effectiveness of various methods of teaching reading, arithmetic, and other academic subjects
5. The value of homework
6. The effective use of tests

The term "area of research" is appropriate for each of the above topics. Many specific research problems could be formulated under each topic. Certainly no simple pat answer can be given as to the educational effectiveness of television or any other instructional technique. The effectiveness of any instructional technique may vary with different kinds of educational objectives. Television, for example, may be a promising instructional tool for imparting information and may have possibilities (under certain conditions) for changing people's attitudes. But television may be limited in its value as a means of developing problem-solving abilities. The effectiveness of any instructional

[2] Green (1962, pp. 26–32) presents a brief but cogent analysis of the problems of defining "stimulus."

method is also dependent upon certain characteristics of the learner, e.g., age. In the final analysis, any instructional method can best be evaluated in terms of its effectiveness in bringing about desired changes in pupil behavior. Nevertheless, it is still profitable to raise the question "What characteristics of the method contribute to its effectiveness?" It is possible to classify method variables in terms of the factors involved in the learning process. Thus:

1. Motivation (Drive): Some methods of instruction may be better than others because the tasks that the pupils are called upon to perform are of greater interest to them, and hence they work harder. Or the method includes techniques for arousing motivation.
2. Teacher-Guidance (Cue): Teaching may be superior because the teacher provides the right kind of guidance (explanations, demonstrations, visual aids, etc.) at the "right" time and in the "right" amounts as the pupil attempts to perform the learning task.
3. Practice (Response): Learning may be superior because practice is focused upon crucial aspects of the learning task. The amount of practice is sufficient, and practice sessions are organized in ways that facilitate learning.
4. Reinforcement: A method may be superior because it permits the use of appropriate reinforcers and these reinforcers can be applied or programmed so that they efficiently shape up the desired pupil behavior.

1. Motivation. The educational objectives quoted in this chapter represent adult views on what children need to learn. They do not always reflect the child's view of what he needs to learn. The extent to which children should choose their own educational goals and plan their own learning activities has long been a matter of controversy among educators. Many educators reject the idea of complete domination of classroom learning by either teacher or pupils and point out that many educational objectives can be attained most efficiently through the cooperative planning of teachers and pupils. The teacher begins the school year with an over-all plan of what the children are expected to learn. Within the framework of this plan, many opportunities for teacher-pupil planning arise. There is some research evidence that people become more highly motivated when given an opportunity to participate in planning their own activities. The important point is that tasks vary in their motive-incentive appeal to children. Children tend to work harder on tasks that are consonant with their goals. Hence, the procedures through which tasks are

chosen may be considered as a method variable affecting pupil motivation.

Frequently, the teacher is faced with the problem of stimulating interest of children in a new learning activity. Teachers use a variety of techniques to stimulate the initial motivation of pupils. Learning activities are selected that both appeal to children and lead to the attainment of educational objectives. This does not mean that the activities selected must be of a play variety. Children are curious and desire to learn. Children like to create and construct. They like to master what they set out to learn and particularly derive pleasure when they can make use of what they learn. And many children, particularly from middle class homes, desire to make good grades. In Chapter 8, the learned needs of children are discussed. We might expect that techniques to stimulate interest would be effective to the extent that they are consonant with the needs of children. For the present, we may note that techniques to create an initial desire on the part of the pupil to learn a task vary in their motive-incentive appeal.

2. Teacher-Guidance. For most learning tasks, some sort of teacher guidance is needed to promote efficient learning. In considering the role of the teacher in guiding pupil learning, three major questions arise: (*a*) *What* kind of guidance is needed? (*b*) *When* should the guidance be provided? and (*c*) *How much* guidance should be provided? The answer to each of these questions may vary according to the nature of the task to be performed, the kind of learning measured, and certain characteristics of the learner.

Teacher-guidance may take the form of verbal or written explanations, demonstrations, the use of audio-visual materials, assignments, class discussions through which the contributions of class members lead to a clarification of difficulties, or some form of pupil activities (excursions, projects, shop work, painting, etc.). The kind of teacher-guidance that is most appropriate depends largely upon the kind of educational objective involved.

3. Practice. Efficiency of learning is by no means solely dependent upon the quality of teacher-guidance. What the learner practices is of even greater importance. *Practice* has been defined as "the occurrence of a specifiable response or group of responses in the presence of a specifiable stimulus situation" (English and English, 1958). On the basis of this definition, all learning activities—reading, writing a term paper, participating in a discussion, memorizing, playing basketball, etc.—may be regarded as practice.

Considerable attention has been given in the literature on learning to the subject of *distribution of practice*. Should practice on a task be *massed* (i.e., total practice time concentrated in lengthy practice sessions), or should practice be distributed (i.e., total practice time broken up into short practice sessions). Are long practice periods in working arithmetic problems superior to more numerous short practice periods? Is it better to practice on the piano for three hours once a week or for one-half hour for six days per week? Hovland (1951) in reviewing the literature on distribution of practice reports that for both verbal and motor learning, a majority of studies (but not all) have found some form of distributed practice superior to massed practice. Of course, the terms "massed" and "distributed" are relative terms. The length of practice sessions and the length of intervening rest periods vary widely from one study to another.

A number of factors have been identified that favor distributed practice. The repetition of the same response pattern over and over may lead to fatigue and a consequent lowering of performance level. Hull (1943) has explained this lowering of performance by the concept of "reactive inhibition"—a negative drive state similar to fatigue. As effort is exerted in repeating a response, inhibition to repeat that response builds up. This inhibition dissipates with rest. Hence, distributed practice sessions permit the maintenance of high-level performance. The concept of reactive inhibition helps to explain the improvement of performance often occurring after a period of no practice. In motor learning, this phenomenon whereby improvement takes place after a period of no practice is called *reminiscence*. This explains why the baseball player hits surprisingly well on the first day of spring practice, why the golfer makes some fine shots after a layoff period, etc. Another major advantage of distributed practice rests in the fact that motivational level can be maintained more easily over short practice sessions. Prolonged practice sessions can easily result in lower motivation and consequently less efficient learning.

The most efficient distribution of practice periods varies according to the kind of task to be learned. Some tasks require a "warming-up" period in which the learner becomes oriented to the requirements of the task (e.g., writing a term paper). For such complex tasks, the practice sessions need to be sufficiently long so that full work efficiency can be attained and continued until there is a decrement in work efficiency. For a complex motor task, the initial practice sessions need to be sufficiently long and frequent to enable the learner to thoroughly understand the nature of the task and to acquire some rudimentary skill. In one study in which college women were taught to play billiards under a variety of practice schedules, the most effective schedule turned out to be one in which practice sessions were one day apart for a few sessions, and then spread out over increasingly longer intervals. The massing of the early sessions permitted the learning of the basic skills sufficiently thoroughly to prevent forgetting, and the spreading out of the later sessions was conducive to the correction of a manageable number of error responses.

Whether it is better to learn by *wholes* or by *parts* is a second problem concerning practice that has long attracted the attention of psychologists. In memorizing a poem or in learning a complex motor task, the learner may choose either to learn the task as a whole or to break up the task into parts, which he learns separately and integrates later. Again this problem is complicated by the large number of ways that the learning task and the characteristics of the learner may vary, as well as variability in what is considered a *whole* and what is considered a *part*. McGeoch and Irion (1952), in reviewing a number of studies on this problem, point out a number of factors to be considered in judging the potential effectiveness of whole and part methods of practice.

1. Part methods are advantageous since material is divided into easier-to-learn units; and, as we have seen, efficiency in learning is affected by the length of the task to be learned.
2. Whole methods are advantageous in that no time is lost in connecting and seeing the relationship between previously learned smaller parts.
3. There is some evidence that the whole method is relatively more effective for the more intelligent learner.
4. The whole method gains in its relative effectiveness when the learner practices with both methods.
5. The whole method gains in effectiveness when practice is distributed rather than massed.
6. Although research findings are not entirely clear concerning the influence of the meaningfulness of the material to be learned, there is some reason to believe that the whole method works better than the part method for meaningful materials.

4. Reinforcement. Practice by itself does not result in learning. The learner must know during practice whether he is making a correct or an incorrect response. This point is sometimes overlooked in teaching. The English teacher who assigns innumerable themes that are never corrected is unlikely to see improvement in the writing skills of his students. Some kind of reinforcement is necessary to effect a change in behavior, and *knowledge of results* constitutes an effective form of reinforcement for much school learning. Experimentally, *immediate* knowledge of results has been shown to effect an improvement to a greater degree than *delayed* knowledge of results. One of the main arguments of advocates for the use of teaching machines to present programmed learning is that the learner can be provided mechanically with immediate and sufficient knowledge of results.

The level of motivation of the learner to achieve educational goals may vary over a period of time as a result of the kind of reinforcements provided. A pupil may work diligently at the beginning of a semester only to decrease his efforts later. Therefore, the teacher has the problem of sustaining as well as initiating motivation. Part of the changes in motivational level may be attributable to the environmental context in which the learning takes place. Extracurricular activities of pupils often constitute stiff competition to the pupils' academic goals. Part of the change in motivational level may be attributable to some change in the learner, such as a temporary illness. But changes in the motivational level of pupils also appear to be affected by certain aspects of the instructional methods of the teachers. Does the teacher praise or criticize the achievement of pupils? Does the pupil experience success or failure from his efforts? Does the teacher rely upon rewards or punishments to motivate pupils? Do pupils compete or cooperate with each other in performing tasks? The research findings on the effects of praise versus reproof, success versus failure, competition versus cooperation, reward versus punishment are of common interest to psychologist and educator.

Learning Exercises

20. John and Henry take five college courses. John reserves one evening a week to study each subject. Henry studies each of his five subjects each evening. Which of the two is massing practice?
21. For his course in typing, John practices for three hours one evening a week. What concept best explains each of the following occurrences?
    (a) There is a rapid rise in the level of John's performance during his first ten minutes of practice.
    (b) After an hour of practice, John takes a coffee break; and after returning to his typing, his level of performance improves considerably.
    (c) John's level of performance deteriorates during his last hour of practice.
22. Henry studies for three hours continuously, memorizing chemistry formulas. He takes twenty minutes per day learning terminology in zoology. For which course is his study procedure the more effective?
23. In studying history, Henry customarily scans a chapter to find out the

main topics treated and then reads to fill in details. John reads the chapter paragraph by paragraph, testing himself at the end of each paragraph to see if he knows its content.

(a) Evaluate Henry's method of studying history.
(b) If Henry's study method worked for him, what would be your guess about his intelligence level?
(c) What desirable feature do you find in John's method of studying history?

SUMMARY

The modern school is concerned with many different kinds of learning. Compared to the older-type school, the modern school appears to be more concerned with:

1. Knowledge and understanding of immediate value to the child;
2. A wider range of areas of development (e.g., social, emotional, ethical, and esthetic);
3. A greater variety of behaviors (e.g., interests, attitudes, and action patterns); and
4. Intellectual problem-solving abilities such as the ability to apply knowledge.

Learning theories developed by psychologists are based, for the most part, upon much simpler forms of learning than those occurring in the classroom. Nevertheless, concepts subsumed under different theories of learning have some value in suggesting partial explanations for much classroom learning. The applicability of some reinforcement learning concepts, such as classical and instrumental conditioning, reinforcement, extinction, spontaneous recovery, generalization, discrimination, verbal conditioning, partial reinforcement, and the principle of successive approximations have been briefly explored up to this point.

For Dollard and Miller (1950), four fundamental factors are important in all learning. These are:

1. Drive—the learner must *want* something.
2. Cue—the learner must *notice* something.
3. Response—the learner must *do* something.
4. Reinforcement—the learner must *get* something.

The teacher's task of guiding the learning process in the classroom is indeed complex. The teacher needs to take into consideration three types of variables: (1) learning experience or stimulus variables, (2) organismic variables, and (3) response variables.

Both the method of instruction and the environmental context within which learning occurs constitute parts of the learning experience variable. One method of instruction may be superior to another because of:

1. Greater *motivation* of pupils
2. More effective *teacher-guidance*
3. More effective provision for *practice*
4. More appropriate use of *reinforcements*

Answer Cues

1. John's reminiscing about mother's apple pie.

2. The *expectancy* of receiving a dollar for each A.

3. The teacher's smile is a sign standing for "good grades are on the report card."

4. (a) Knowledge. (b) Application. (c) Analysis. (d) Synthesis. (e) Comprehension. (f) Evaluation.

5. (a) Receptivity. (b) Valuing. (c) Characterization. (d) Responding. (e) Organization.

6. (a) Yes. A change of behavior has occurred. (b) Classical. (c) UCS —air puff; CS—buzzer; CR—eye-blink to CS. (d) The air puff following the sound of the buzzer. (e) Extinction. (f) Spontaneous recovery. (g) Stimulus generalization.

7. Stimulus generalization.

8. UCS—she is laughed at; CS—called upon to make a speech; CR—becomes flustered.

9. (a) Secondary reward training. (b) Avoidance training. (c) Escape training.

10. *Drive:* wanting to please teacher and parents. *Cue:* discriminating between the question "How much are four and three?" and other questions. *Response:* varying responses and finally giving the response "seven." *Reinforcement:* reduced tension as Alice sees that she has pleased her teacher (or parents).

11. Knowledge of results should be specific.

12. Where possible, knowledge of results should be *immediate*.

13. (a) Receiving attention. (b) Reinforcement occurs even when the learner (the instructor) is not aware that certain of his responses are being reinforced.

14. The experimental practice groups.

15. Define behaviorally what is meant by scientific attitudes so that "scientific attitude"–type responses may be recognized and reinforced when they occur.

16. By encouraging pupils to read books of interest to them and of a reading difficulty level just a little greater than the books they customarily read.

17. Continuous. The car stopping constitutes the reinforcement.

18. Partial. The compliment is probably the reinforcer.

19. The strength of each response tendency, i.e., the frequency of occurrence of each of the four response tendencies.

20. John.

21. (a) Warmup.   (b) Reminiscence.   (c) Reactive inhibition.

22. Zoology.

23. (a) Good; Henry's whole method is particularly effective when practice is distributed.   (b) Probably reasonably high intelligence; the whole method is relatively more effective for the more intelligent learner.   Or possibly average intelligence but through practice, he has made the whole method effective for him.   (c) Self-testing—giving him knowledge of results.

7

GUIDING LEARNING

In guiding the learning of children, the modern teacher can choose from a variety of instructional techniques. The task of choosing wisely would be greatly simplified if research findings supplied definitive answers to questions such as: "Are teaching machines effective?" "Should television be used in the school as a media of instruction?" "Do students learn better by working in groups than by working individually?" "Does learning progress better when the teacher and pupils cooperatively plan the goals of instruction?" "How effective is the 'core curriculum' as a means of integrating the content of various subject-matter areas?" "Are projects in which students plan and carry out many different activities a more effective way of promoting learning than the read-recite procedure?"

Unfortunately, research findings do not provide definitive answers to questions of the type listed above. We shall see later in this chapter that modern methods of teaching are generally found to be more effective than older methods. But a teaching method that is effective for one teacher may be ineffective for another teacher. Further, a teaching method that is effective for some of the children in a classroom may be ineffective for others. It is of limited value to the teacher to know that research has shown that teaching method A is *on the average* superior to teaching method B. It is of more value to the teacher to know what makes one method of teaching more effective than another. The important question to raise is "What variables determine the effectiveness of an instructional technique?" In Chapter 1, these variables are classified into (1) stimulus or learning experience variables, (2) organismic variables, and (3) response variables. This chapter is primarily concerned with the stimulus variable in that it focuses attention on the teacher's role in promoting learning.

The problem of employing research as a tool for developing better teaching procedures will be examined in this chapter. Two research strategies will be illustrated. First, we will examine the strategy of comparing two general teaching approaches, each approach having multiple characteristics (e.g., modern versus traditional education). Second, we will discuss programmed learning as an example in which the teaching method variable is more definitely specified.

The study of the effectiveness of a teaching method requires a clear specification of the characteristics of the method that contributes to its effectiveness. We need to know also the kinds of learning for which a method is effective. The effectiveness of a teaching method also depends upon certain characteristics of the environment in which learning takes place. Therefore, as a second major theme in this chapter, we will discuss the classroom social climate and how it affects learning.

RESEARCH ON TEACHING METHODS

A strong case can be made for the proposition that the educational experiment is the only means of settling disputes regarding educational practice. Yet the direct contributions to educational practice from controlled experimentation have been disappointing. A large number of factors can influence the effectiveness of any teaching procedure. Campbell and Stanley (1963) point out:

. . . we should not expect that "crucial experiments" which pit opposing theories will be likely to have clear-cut outcomes. When one finds, for example, that competent observers advocate strongly divergent points of view, it seems likely on a priori grounds that both have observed something valid about the natural situation, and that both represent a part of the truth. [P. 173.]

Then vs. Now Studies

American schools have always been subjected to a barrage of criticism. A Citizens' Committee in Madison, Wisconsin, after visiting some classrooms, reported: "Almost universal lack of distinct articulation, proper pronunciation and correct spelling" (quoted by Brown, 1959). The report is dated 1901.

Such criticisms have prompted efforts on the part of school people to conduct "Then vs. Now" studies in which the academic performance of pupils of an earlier period is compared with pupils of today. Tests that have been administered to groups of children of a previous generation are administered to a new generation of children. Almost invariably the present-day children outscore the children of a previous era. Each successive generation appears to be learning more subject matter than did past generations. For example, in one study conducted by the California Test Bureau (and reported by Shane, 1959), reading and arithmetic test scores made by 230,000 pupils before and after 1945 were reviewed. It was found that the average child's reading, mathematics, and language usage scores on the same tests improved by 12 per cent over a ten-year period. Bloom (1956b) compared the performance of high school seniors in 1943 and 1955 on the General Educational Development Tests. A representative 5 per cent of all the public schools in the country were included in both the 1943 and 1955 testings. Bloom found that the 1955 seniors outperformed the 1943 seniors on all tests—English, social studies, science, and mathematics.

It is important to remember that the multitude of "Then vs. Now" studies are not experiments. A large number of factors could explain the progressive improvement of children on tests from one generation to another, and the studies themselves provide no clues as to what these factors may be. The studies do suggest that there is little merit in the notion of returning to the past for models of teaching procedures. Better, we should place our hope in continued experimentation as a vehicle of improving the efficiency of the educative process, while at the same time continue to critically examine the basic values underlying our educational objectives.

Learning Exercises

1. In what respects does Bloom's study provide a sounder basis than studies involving only a few classrooms for concluding that the school did a better job in 1955 than in 1943?
2. What factors can you think of that might account for Bloom's findings?

Traditional vs. Modern Experiments. It is not necessary to go back to the achievement records of children of earlier generations in order to compare traditional and modern methods of teaching. Many teachers have not embraced newer approaches to teaching. The teaching procedures found in some of today's classrooms do not differ markedly from the teaching procedures of 50 years ago.

It is necessary to identify the differentiating characteristics of traditional and modern education in order to make comparisons. This is easy to do for certain practices (e.g., use of television), but quite difficult to do for other practices (e.g., attention paid to the interests of the child). Obviously, the modern school has resources that were not available in the schools of the past. But good teachers of previous decades incorporated many "modern" practices in their teaching. Consequently, some of the characteristics that have been identified as differentiating the modern from the traditional school represent "changes in emphasis" or "more teachers following a practice" rather than innovations. Keeping the above limitations in mind, we can identify some of the differences between traditional and modern approaches to teaching as follows:

1. *A wider range of techniques are used in the modern school to motivate children to learn.* Learning activities are frequently organized into "experience units" rather than "subject-matter units"—particularly at the elementary school level, but often too at the secondary school level. Experience involves an interaction of the individual with a situation. To insure interaction, learning activities are organized around the purposes of the learner. The teacher formulates broad educational objectives in advance, but the pupils and teacher plan together activities that are consonant to the attainment of the educational objectives. The activities planned are not restricted to listening to the teacher, reading what the teacher prescribes, and completing the writing assignments of the teacher. The pupil finds in school an opportunity to participate in many activities that are in line with his own interests. In the modern school, it is generally recognized that the student should derive satisfaction from a learning experience.

2. *A greater variety of learning experiences are provided in the modern school.* In the traditional school, the educational objectives for an academic subject can generally be summarized as "mastery of the content of the one textbook prescribed for the course." The student is expected to memorize the main facts contained in the text. To attain the objective of the course, the student reads the text, listens to the teacher, and recites.

The educational objectives of the modern school cover a wide range of behaviors. The student is still expected to learn facts, but he is also expected to think about the meaning of the facts he learns. He is expected to develop his problem-solving abilities, to interpret data, to apply principles, to interact and criticize ideas he encounters, and to be creative. The modern school is also expected to develop desirable attitudes, interests, and appreciations in the student. Psychomotor educational objectives are also found in the modern school.

Because a student must have experiences that give him a chance to practice the kind of behavior implied by an objective, we find a wide range of learning experiences in the modern school. Newer technological developments—motion pictures, television, and other audiovisual aids; automated teaching devices; language laboratories—are utilized. Students in the modern school work in groups, carry on class discussions, work on projects, take field trips, make extensive use of the library, participate in interest-group clubs, and carry on their own student government. A wide range of learning experiences becomes necessary to attain the wide range of educational objectives.

Because of the increased recognition of the importance of individual differences, the modern school attempts to gear instruction to the needs and abilities of the individual student in a variety of ways. Through the use of tests and other evaluative techniques, an attempt is made to assess the needs and abilities of the student. Extended curriculum offerings permit the high school student to select subjects suited to his own needs. The elementary school teacher gears instruction to the needs of the pupil through forming special ability or interest groups and by making individualized assignments.

3. *A more comprehensive evaluation of student progress characterizes the modern school.* Some kinds of tests have always been used in American schools to evaluate student progress. With the development of new testing techniques, a wider range of evaluation devices are used to evaluate the progress of today's pupil. More emphasis is placed on measuring the pupils' ability to solve problems, and this emphasis is being increasingly reflected in the newer standardized tests. It is more generally recognized that the total development of the individual child should be studied, and a variety of techniques (anecdotal records, home visitation, attitudes, and interest scales, etc.) are used for this purpose. Evaluation is thought of as a continuous process that serves multiple purposes.

Many difficulties are encountered in conducting research designed to determine the comparative merits of traditional and modern education. There is, in the first place, the difficulty of deciding what are the major differentiating characteristics of modern and traditional education. No two efforts by writers to identify the major differentiating characteristics yield identical results. In the second place, it is certainly not possible to identify classrooms that exemplify all the characteristics of modern education, and it is probably not possible to find a classroom exemplifying all the characteristics of traditional education. Despite these difficulties, the research findings of comprehensive comparative studies are fairly consistent. Wallen and Travers (1963) conclude from an examination of "activity" versus "traditional" studies covering a period of over 30 years that:

In the early grades, students in the progressive curriculum tend to perform somewhat below expectation in reading and arithmetic but overcome their inferiority by about sixth grade; they tend to be average or somewhat superior throughout their school years in achievement areas involving language usage; when moving up to junior high school, they suffer no handicap in dealing with a more traditional curriculum; when compared on tests designed to measure work skills, organizing ability, ability to interpret information, and civic beliefs, they score higher but often not significantly so; they tend to be better informed on current affairs and they tend to be rated higher by high school teachers and independent observers on such dimensions as initiative, work spirit, and critical thinking. In summary, the findings indicate no important differences in terms of subject-matter mastery and a superiority of the progressive students in terms of the characteristics which the "progressive school" seeks to develop. [Pp. 473–74.]

Learning Exercise

3. Which of the following is more characteristic of "traditional education" than of "modern education"?
   (a) Teacher does all the planning
   (b) Instruction geared to individual differences
   (c) One text with all students reading the same page at the same time
   (d) A read-recite routine of covering the subject matter of a course

---

Limitations of "Then vs. Now" Experiments. There are a number of limitations to keep in mind in assessing the findings of "Then vs. Now" experiments. The "experimental" students included in a study may differ initially from the "traditional" students with respect to variables related to achievement. The teacher method experimental variable may be confounded by additional characteristics of the teaching method that are not controlled in the experiment. The environmental context in which learning takes place may not be the same for the experimental and the traditional groups. The very fact that an experiment is being conducted may inspire both teachers and students in the experimental group to greater efforts. The findings of the experiment must be restricted to the kinds of achievement that are measured. When the teaching methods under consideration differ in a multiplicity of characteristics, it is not possible in a simply designed experiment to isolate the effects of any single characteristic. In short, "Then vs. Now" experiments (like all experiments on teaching methods) are limited to the extent that relevant stimulus, organismic, and response variables are inadequately controlled in the experimental design.

What conclusions may be drawn from the research on teaching methods? Wallen and Travers (1963) observe:

. . . teaching methods have not been designed systematically in terms of what is known about the learning process but rather have been products of other trends in thinking. The conditions which most commonly generate teaching methods are unlikely to produce patterns of teaching behavior markedly more effective than those that have been produced in the past. A

consequence of this is that research on teaching methods bears little resemblance to scientific research which systematically builds up knowledge
of a particular phenomenon. . . . It does not follow, however, that one
cannot look to research for help on these matters in the future. There is no
question but what educational research has, in the past, been extremely helpful on such specific issues as appropriate word difficulties for beginning
reading books. Further, educational research shows signs of entering a new
and more sophisticated era; the old "shotgun" studies, useful as they may
have been in their time, are giving way to studies formulated in such a way
as to provide clear-cut evidence on sharply defined problems. [Pp. 484–
85.]

Learning Exercise

4. From Wallen and Travers' point of view, which of the following is the
   more likely to contribute to an advance in teaching methodology?
   (a) Well-defined studies on one small aspect of a teaching method con-
       ducted with adequate control of all variables
   (b) Broad comparative studies of two or more teaching methods that con-
       tain numerous characteristics

Wallen and Travers' criticisms seem particularly valid when one
attempts to draw conclusions about the effectiveness of an ill-defined
general teaching approach for all types of learning. More sharply
defined problems become possible when the teaching method is more
clearly defined and is generated from research on the learning process
(e.g., programmed learning). The balance of this section deals with
programmed learning.

Programmed Instruction

In this age of automation, the machine has taken over the work of
man for one job after another. It is little wonder that many educators
react with dismay to the idea of teaching machines in the classroom.
The educator visualizes a man-sized robot teacher directing the work
of little children and replacing the warm, human teacher in the classroom. The slow progress in the mechanization of the classroom is
probably largely due to the fact that the educator places so high a value
on the personal interaction between the teacher and the pupils. But
the use of teaching machines in the classroom does not mean that the
human teacher is no longer needed, any more than does the use of
motion pictures in the classroom. The teaching machine is another
instructional tool for the human teacher. A research problem is that of
assessing the educational value of this tool.

Some Early Devices. The teaching machine is not wholly new. The slide projector and the phonograph are two examples of instruments that have long been used to present information to the learner. Machines were developed to teach spelling and logic in the nineteenth century (Stolurow, 1961).

The earliest concentrated effort to develop mechanical devices to relieve the teachers of some of their functions was made by Sidney Pressey (1926). The early teaching machines developed by Pressey were really testing devices. In his earliest model, a series of questions and multiple-choice answers were mounted on a revolving drum. Each question could be viewed through a window in a shield covering the drum. Four keys, corresponding to the four alternatives in the multiple-choice item, were arranged on the right-hand side of the drum. When the student pressed the right key, the drum revolved and presented a new question. If the student pressed the wrong key, the drum would not revolve. The student then would try again until he selected the correct response to the question. The machine kept a record of the number of wrong responses made.

Learning Exercise

5. The stimulus presented to the student is controlled for both a slide projector and for a Pressey-type machine. What additional control is attained in a Pressey teaching device?

Modern Teaching Machines. Pressey's testing devices did not stimulate much research interest. Almost 30 years elapsed before the idea of teaching machines in the classroom captured the imagination of educators. In 1954, B. F. Skinner, a highly esteemed psychologist, published a provocative article entitled "The Science of Learning and the Art of Teaching." Skinner argued that the teacher could not personally provide all the needed reinforcements required to shape up complex behavior patterns for each individual child in the classroom. Skinner estimated that between 25,000 and 50,000 situations require reinforcement to shape up efficient mathematical behavior of children in the first four years of school.

Skinner and his associates have designed a number of teaching machines. A *program* is first made covering the material to be taught. The program is divided into *frames*. Each frame provides some information, asks a question, and provides space for the student to construct an answer. The program is stored in the machine on circular paper disks, paper tape, cards, sheets, or film. In one simple machine, the frames appear to the learner through a window to the left, and he writes his answer to a question on a separate paper tape which appears at a window to the right. When a knob is turned, the student's written answer is covered up by a transparent plastic and the correct answer is exposed beside his answer. The student then turns the knob and goes on to the next question.

More than 100 different teaching machines or similar devices have been developed, varying considerably in complexity. Some teaching machines present information to the student both in visual and auditory form. One example of an audio-visual teaching machine is a language-training device developed at the Center for Programmed Instruction in New York City. In this apparatus, the student sees words, sentences, and pictures projected on a small screen, and hears the instructor's voice over a set of earphones. The student makes the required oral and written response, pushes a button to hear the correct oral response, and then another button to display the correct written response.

Adaptive machines have been constructed to allow for changes in the sequence of presentation of the frames of a program. Rath, Anderson, and Brainerd (1959) adapted the International Business Machine digital computer, model 650, to teach binary arithmetic. The problem to be solved by the learner is presented on a typed copy through the program in the computer. The learner types his answer which is transmitted to the computer for checking. As soon as the learner makes a mistake in the process of working a problem, the computer types "wrong," and presents a new problem adjusted to the learner's capacity as revealed by the number of specific errors the learner has made on that particular phase of the program. Thus, the subject matter presented is constantly modified in keeping with the learner's skill level and rate of learning.

Skinner-type machines call for programs in which the student constructs answers to questions posed. Crowder (1960) has developed a programming procedure in which the student is given material to learn in small logical units; then given a short multiple-choice test over the material covered; and the results of the test are used to determine what next unit shall be presented to the student. The student who performs well on a unit is ready to go on to more advanced material. The student who performs poorly needs some additional instruction and practice exercises over the initial material. Programs in which the sequence of frames presented are the same for all learners are called *linear programs*. Programs in which the sequence of frames vary for different learners are called *branching programs*. Obviously, the type of machine required for a branching program will differ from that required for a linear program.

As we have noted, complex computer teaching systems have been devised for branching programs. However, a branching program can be presented without a machine. In the *scrambled book* method, developed by Crowder (1960), the first frame is presented on the first page of the book, but from this point on, the learner does not follow a numerical sequence of pages. The learner might be directed to page 10 if he selects one answer, or to page 18 if he selects another answer. If he chooses a wrong answer, he is directed to return to page 1 and make another choice. After making a correct choice, the student is directed to another page in the book where new information is presented and a new question is posed. In this way, the student proceeds back and forth throughout the book until he completes the program.

Learning Exercises

6. Which is the larger unit of instruction: a program or a frame?
7. Which type of program is designed to take care of individual differences in the amount of instruction needed?
8. Is the "scrambled book" program an example of a linear or an example of a branching program?

Characteristics of Programmed Instruction. The effectiveness of instruction provided through the medium of the teaching machine depends primarily upon the quality of the program rather than the quality of the machine. The machine exists only to provide instruction that has the following characteristics:

1. A relatively small amount of information is presented to the student at one time. A question is asked that almost all students are likely to answer correctly. Thus, both the information provided and the questions asked are geared to the "readiness" of the learner.

2. After the student responds to a question, he is *immediately* informed whether his response is right or wrong. This type of feedback or reinforcement is intrinsic to the task performed.

3. Each successive frame in a program constitutes a *small step* so that the student will not be likely to make errors as he works through the program. This principle of gradual progression serves not only to make the student correct as often as possible, but it also serves to shape up efficiently complex behavior.

4. To insure 90 to 95 per cent correct student responses to a frame, a technique called *fading* or *vanishing cues* is employed. When informa-

tion is presented for the first time, the student is provided with maximum cue support. Often the student merely has to copy a significant term from the information provided in the frame. In succeeding frames, the cueing is gradually reduced.

5. Each student works individually on a program at his own pace. In this way, programmed instruction is geared to individual differences in the learning rates of students. As we have previously noted, branching programs permit adjusting the number of frames in a program according to the ability of the learner.

Learning Exercise

9. What characteristics of programmed instruction are missing in the following instructional procedures?

> An algebra teacher explains how to factor trinomials. She then gives the class some very easy trinomials to factor. The students work the examples; turn in their work; the teacher corrects the work; and turns it back to the students the next day. The students did correctly, on the average, 75 per cent of the questions.

Experimental Findings on Programmed Instruction. Programmed instruction has been compared with conventional methods of instruction at every educational level and with various academic subjects (Lumsdaine and Glaser, 1960). It has been compared most often with the normal classroom procedure in which the teacher's lectures are supplanted by textbook reading. Lumsdaine (1963) points out the limitations on generalizability of such evaluative studies. All that is demonstrated is that a particular program (that is probably not representative of all programmed material) is more or less efficient than the instruction provided by a particular teacher (who also is probably not representative of all teachers) for a particular kind of learning. In short, the relative quality of the programmed instructional material and the teacher's instructional methods need to be considered in evaluating studies that compare the effectiveness of programmed instruction to conventional instruction. A poorly constructed teaching machine program is likely to be less effective than the instruction provided by a skillful teacher; and a well-constructed program is likely to be more effective than the instruction provided by an inadequate teacher.

COMPARISONS WITH CONVENTIONAL INSTRUCTION. Many studies have compared programmed and conventional instruction. Silberman (1962), in his review on programmed instruction, cites several studies in which programmed instruction has been shown to be superior to conventional instruction, but other studies showed no significant difference in learning between conventional and programmed groups. Many studies report that their programmed instruction required less training time.

The findings of some research studies are indeed encouraging. Porter (1959) reports a study in which experimental groups of second-grade and sixth-grade pupils learned spelling by machine instruction much better than did matched control groups of children taught in a more conventional manner. Children in the experimental group worked at their desks on programmed material in spelling with a simple mechanical teaching machine for 22 out of the 34 weeks of spelling instruction. The same words were taught to the control group children. For both the second- and sixth-grade groups, spelling achievement as measured by standardized achievement tests was significantly superior for the experimental groups. The children with the machines mastered the subject matter in less than one-third the usual time. Porter found no relationship between intelligence test scores and achievement in the experimental groups, but did find a significant relationship in the control groups. In studies conducted by other investigators, however, superior students did better than less able students on tests given at the completion of programmed materials (e.g., Lane, 1963). To check whether the superior performance of the experimental groups was attributable to the novelty of working on machines, Porter compared achievement on the first versus the second half of the machine-taught lessons. No significant difference was found. Following is a sample of Porter's program material.

1. Underline these words: *thunder, steady, soaked, frightened*
   I hadn't gone half-way when thunder rolled and rain came down in a steady pour. I was soaked. I made a dash for an old horse shed. And there was Wolf. Crouching in the shadow, he looked so like a wolf that for a moment he frightened me.

   frightened   steady   thunder   soaked

2. Circle the word that rhymes with *ready:*
   thunder   steady   pour   soaked

   steady

3. Circle the word that means *firm, regular,* or *not shaking:*
   steady   thunder   umbrella   southern   sweeping

   steady

4. Write the missing letters:
   Then rain came down in a s_ea_y pour.

   steady

5. Write the missing letters; they are all the same:

Ragged clouds were sw_ _ping the south_rn sky.

sweeping   southern

6. Write the missing letters:

Without thinking of an umbre_ _a, I set out.

umbrella

7. Write the missing letters:

Half-way to the store thu_ _er rolled.

thunder

8. Write the missing letters:

Then rain came down in a s_ea_y pour.

steady

9. Write the missing letters:

Brushing, moving quickly, s_ee_ing.

sweeping

[Porter, 1959, pp. 86–87.]

Learning Exercise

10. How is the *fading technique* applied by Porter in teaching how to spell the word "steady"?

Providing Knowledge of Results. The provision of knowledge of results is not always crucial in machine instruction. Moore and Smith (1961) conducted an experiment in which experimental groups of sixth-grade pupils worked on Porter's spelling program. A control group worked on the same program with the correct answer omitted after each item. Over a period of four weeks, the control group performed better on weekly tests and a final posttest than did the experimental group. The differences between the groups were not statistically significant but were consistently in favor of the control group that received no *immediate* knowledge of results.

It is difficult to interpret Moore and Smith's findings. Is the provision of knowledge of results not crucial to the effectiveness of self-instructional materials? An examination of Porter's spelling program reveals that knowledge of results is provided *eventually* in that the spelling words to learn are repeated from item to item. For Porter's program, knowledge of results may be thought of as *built in* to the program. The inclusion of the correct response after each item may be *overcueing*.

Research findings on the value of providing immediate knowledge of results with programmed material are scanty and ambiguous (Krumboltz, 1961). Using a programmed textbook, Meyer (1960) found that groups given immediate knowledge of results learned significantly more than a group that received no immediate knowledge of results. Krumboltz and Weisman (1962b) varied the percentage of frames in which the answers to questions were provided. Answers were provided to all frames in the programs of one group of students; to 67 per cent of the frames in the program of two other groups of students; to 33 per cent of the frames for two more groups; and no answers were provided for a sixth group. The investigators constructed the six variations of a programmed textbook on how to interpret educational test results and administered the program to 121 college students. As soon as each subject finished his program, he took a 50-item completion-type test. The investigators found that students in groups receiving the most knowledge of results made fewer errors in completing their programs. However, there were no significant differences among groups in their performance on the criterion test.

Learning Exercises

11. Reinforcement appears to serve two functions. One is to provide information or feedback, and the other is to sustain effort. How might you explain why providing knowledge of results in some programmed learning experiments has not led to improved learning?
12. Would the omission of knowledge of results in a program mean that that learner receives no reinforcement in working through the program?

Response Modes. In a number of studies, the kind of response the student is required to make in a program has been varied. Two questions that have been investigated are:

1. Are programs in which students are required to construct a response better than programs in which students respond to multiple-choice test questions? Most studies indicate that students learn about equally well with both types of programs (Silberman, 1962). However, Fry (1960) in a program in Spanish found the constructed response superior, although as in other studies, a greater amount of training time was required.

2. Can a student learn as much just by reading a program without making any overt responses? Apparently, it is possible, although the

conditions required to make it possible have not been clearly identified. Silberman (1962) cites a number of studies in which the covert response was found more efficient than the overt response and another group of studies in which the covert response was found to be equally efficient. These studies employed very short programs. We do not know whether the covert response would continue to be more efficient with longer programs. Also, Goldbeck (1960) found learning-material difficulty to be a variable. The covert response was found to be more efficient for easy material but less efficient for the more difficult levels. There is also the question of whether students retain material as well when they are not required to make an overt response. Krumboltz and Weisman (1962a) obtained superiority of the overt response on a criterion test that was delayed two weeks, but found no difference on a posttest given immediately after the completion of the program.

Learning Exercise

13. Previously, we have discussed mediating processes. Are mediating processes overt or covert responses?

Size of Step. Experiments comparing small-step and large-step programs, generally but not always, have demonstrated the small-step program to be superior although it takes longer. More research is needed to determine the crucial variables that need to be taken into consideration in determining the optimum-size step of a program.

Branching vs. Linear Programs. Teaching machines should permit the construction of programmed materials geared to the abilities and past learning of the learner. One means of adapting programs to individual differences is through construction of a *branching* program. In a *linear* program, all students work through an identical set of frames. In a branching program, some of the frames can be eliminated for the brighter student and remedial exercises included for the slower learner. However, research studies have not as yet demonstrated that branching programs are superior to linear programs (Silberman, 1962).

Learning Exercise

14. How is it possible for two competent researchers to investigate the same problem and obtain different results?

What are the possibilities of improving classroom instruction through the use of programmed learning? It is much too early to provide a definitive answer to this question. At present, programmed learning does not appear to be an educational breakthrough comparable to the invention of printing—as the early enthusiasts claimed. But neither does it appear to be a teaching fad that should quickly disappear from the educational scene. Future research may more clearly delineate: (1) the kinds of school learning amenable to programming; (2) the qualities in a program that make it effective; and (3) the ways that programmed learning can be most effectively coordinated with other forms of instruction. Perhaps, as Pressey (1963) suggests, the learning theory underlying programmed learning needs modification, and programs need to be constructed to conform to different principles of learning. Programmed learning does offer opportunities for educators to study the learning process in the classroom under better than usual controlled conditions. In all, when we take into consideration the short time that researchers have worked on identifying the crucial variables in programmed learning, an attitude of cautious optimism toward programmed learning seems justified.

CLASSROOM SOCIAL CLIMATE

Progress in learning is affected by the quality of interpersonal relationships existing within the classroom. These relationships may be warm or cool, tense or relaxed, antagonistic or cohesive, friendly or hostile. The classroom constitutes a miniature social structure, and students may expend much energy in striving to attain prestige within the school's social structure. One factor determining whether desirable social (and academic) learning occurs in the school is the quality of the relationships between the teacher and the pupils.

Teacher-Pupil Relationships

The characteristics of teacher-pupil interpersonal relationships may be described in terms of a number of dimensions. The emotional quality of the relationships is certainly one important dimension affecting progress in learning. The relationships may be described in terms of whether the teacher and the pupil *like* or *dislike* each other; whether *respect* or *disrespect* characterizes the relationship; whether *tension* or *relaxation* seems to prevail in the classroom; and whether *fear* and *anxiety* or a *feeling of security* are experienced by teacher and pupils as a result of their interactions. These and other emotions may stem from the kind of interactions between pupils and the teacher. Because the emotions themselves are not observable, it is difficult to obtain an accurate description of the emotional characteristics of a classroom. It is necessary to obtain data that sheds light on how pupils feel toward their teacher and how the teacher feels toward his pupils.

We do have some research evidence, particularly at the elementary school level, on the teacher-characteristics liked by pupils. In these studies, the terms "friendly," "fair," and "encouraging" frequently occur as teacher-characteristics liked by pupils. A study conducted by Leeds (1954) in which he compared the behavior traits of best-liked and least-liked teachers of fourth-, fifth-, and sixth-grade pupils in South Carolina and Pennsylvania communities is illustrative. Some of the reasons given by the pupils for liking the teachers were:

> "Because she is always friendly to pupils."
> "She is patient and kind."
> ". . . not a boss."
> ". . . interested in my hobby."
> "Because she is helpful. I can take my problem to her. She understands. She is pretty (that helps out a lot)."
> ". . . because she is fair and I feel free to ask her anything."
> [Leeds, 1954, p. 34.]

Some of the undesirable behavioral traits that differentiated the ten best-liked teachers from the ten least-liked teachers in the Leeds study were: "failure to praise," "scolds pupils a lot," "often bossy," "becomes angry at pupils' failure to understand," and "talks too much." Yet, undesirable behaviors were attributed to even the best-liked teachers. For example, about 34 per cent of the pupils checked the item "Scolds a pupil in front of other pupils" for the best-liked teachers. However, 86 per cent of the pupils checked this item for the least-liked teachers.

A second way in which teacher-pupil interrelationships may be described is in terms of a *harmony-disharmony* dimension. Harmony would seem likely to prevail to the extent that:

1. The goals of instruction in the classroom are acceptable to both the teacher and the pupils;
2. The learning experiences selected are palatable to both teachers and pupils; and
3. The teacher performs his teacher role in ways consonant with the hopeful expectations of the pupils, and the pupils perform their pupil roles in ways consonant with the hopeful expectations of the teacher.

Teacher-pupil planning, under certain conditions, may be an effective means of attaining harmony. It would seem reasonable to expect that the goals of the pupils and the goals of the teacher would come closer together if the responsibility for planning goals and activities were shared by the teacher and pupils. Not always, however. The teacher is often expected by the pupils to provide leadership in defining educational goals and in deciding the most effective, instructional means of attaining those goals. The failure to find morale high in the "democratic" groups in experiments involving military groups, business groups, and college classes (Berkowitz, 1953; Guetzkow *et al.*, 1954; Hemphill, 1949; McCurdy and Lambert, 1952; Wispe, 1951) possibly is attributable to a dissonance between the leader's role performance and the role the leader was expected to play by group members. In the classroom situation too, the possibility exists that teacher-pupil planning procedures will not result in harmony if such procedures are perceived by pupils as an inadequate performance of the teacher-role.

Thirdly, teacher-pupil interrelationships may be viewed as varying along a *stimulative-restrictive* dimension.[1] The control pattern of the teacher may be such as to stimulate the pupils to explore a wide range of possible responses in a learning situation. Or the teacher's control pattern may restrict the learner to discovering the specific response that the teacher wants. One might expect that the following descriptions of teacher behaviors listed by Flanders (1960) would stimulate the pupils to explore alternative responses in the classroom:

(a) accepts, clarifies, and supports the ideas and feelings of pupils
(b) praises and encourages
(c) asks questions to stimulate the pupil's participation in decision making
(d) asks questions to orient pupils to school work or to the topic of discussion. [P. 204.]

In contrast, one might expect a restriction in the range of pupil responses where the teacher criticizes or deprecates the efforts of the pupil to cope with a learning problem, or the teacher who tells the pupil precisely how to perform a task. Pupils in the classroom of the restrictive teacher learn to search for the one right answer and the one correct way of performing a task. Pupils in the classroom of the stimulating teacher learn to search for alternative responses or ways of performing tasks. Of course, all teachers stimulate at times and all teachers restrict at other times. The ratio of stimulation to restriction, nevertheless, may vary from one classroom to another.

Either a stimulating or a restrictive classroom atmosphere may emerge from nearly any teaching procedure or teacher control pattern. Some lecturers manage to stimulate students to explore further the ideas and

[1] This dimension corresponds roughly to Flanders' (1960) *indirect* or *direct* teacher influence dimension, and partially to Anderson and Brewer's (1946) *integrative-dominative* dimension.

unresolved issues that they present. Other lecturers manage to restrict the activity of students to understanding and possibly memorizing the materials presented. Some classroom discussions stimulate students to explore ideas and carry out a variety of activities. Other classroom discussions restrict the students to trying to guess what answers the teacher wants. Teacher-pupil planning would seem to provide pupils with opportunities to explore. Yet the stimulus value of the verbal exchanges that take place within teacher-pupil planning sessions vary widely. While some degree of permissiveness in the classroom is essential if students are to make exploratory responses, we cannot say that the more permissive the teacher is, the greater his stimulus value. What teacher-behavior variables are of importance in creating a stimulating or a restricting classroom atmosphere is a question that is only partially answered by research findings.

Learning Exercises

15. Would a classroom in which pupils and the teacher liked and respected each other, and in which the pupils experienced no anxiety, be conducive to academic learning?
16. How could there be disharmony in the relationship between teachers and pupils if the teacher allowed the pupils to do whatever they wished?
17. In which case could a restrictive control pattern be more easily justified:
    (a) Teaching a practical First Aid course; or
    (b) Teaching creative writing?

Authoritarian-Democratic Studies. Should a teacher be democratic in a classroom or should he be authoritarian? Texts in education, industrial management, and counseling discuss these two styles of leadership under a variety of labels: teacher-centered versus learner-centered; dominative versus integrative; employer-centered versus employee-centered; therapist-centered versus client-centered; etc. In education, research studies comparing the two styles of leadership have been conducted over a span of nearly two decades. Let us examine some of the research findings.

The classic series of experiments on democratic-authoritarian leadership was conducted by Lewin, Lippitt, and White.[2] In one study, four clubs of ten-year-old boys were organized and provided with three styles of leadership: authoritarian, democratic, and laissez faire. Every six weeks, each of the four groups had a new leader with a different

---

[2] There are a number of reports on this research; e.g., Lewin, Lippitt, and White (1939), Lewin (1939), Lippitt and White (1958).

style of leadership. Each club had three leaders during the course of five months. In the authoritarian style of leadership, all policies were set by the leader; steps to be followed for each activity were dictated by the leader one at a time; the work tasks and work companions were assigned by the leader; and the leader praised or criticized each member personally for his work. In the democratic style of leadership, policies emerged as a result of group discussion; general steps to be followed in an activity were sketched and alternative procedures suggested; members chose their own work patterns and divided up their tasks; and the leader was objective rather than personal in his praise and criticism. In the laissez-faire type of leadership, the group had complete freedom to do whatever it pleased—materials were supplied and then the leader stayed out of the activities. Each of the four leaders played the role of autocrat and the role of democratic leader at least once. Results of this and similar-type experiments in the series were:

1. The least amount of aggression, interpersonal hostility, and the highest morale was found in groups with democratic leaders.
2. The greatest productivity occurred in groups with autocratic leaders, although the democratic groups maintained their work better when the leaders left the room.
3. Laissez-faire groups were low in both morale and productivity.

It is tempting to conclude from the Lewin, Lippitt, and White study that maximum learning is fostered in a democratic, student-centered classroom. But research evidence does not justify such a sweeping generalization. A great deal depends upon the kind of educational objective measured. Stern (1963) in reviewing 34 studies concludes, "In general, it would appear that the amount of cognitive gain is largely unaffected by the autocratic or democratic tendencies of the instructor" (p. 426). Stovall (1958), in reviewing 27 studies which compared lectures versus class discussions, found that the balance of evidence slightly favored the lecture as a means of imparting knowledge, but the discussion method was superior for developing higher-level cognitive skills and in changing attitudes, values, and behavior patterns. Possibly even these generalizations should be assessed cautiously.

Anderson (1959) has reviewed 49 experimental studies in which authoritarian leadership has been compared to democratic leadership with respect to (1) productivity and (2) morale. In educational research, productivity is assessed by some measure of learning. Morale has been assessed in terms of the satisfaction a group derives from its work or its success in progressing toward its goals.

Relevant to productivity, Anderson found 11 studies reporting greater learning for learner-centered (democratic) groups, 13 studies that showed no difference, and 8 that found teacher-centered (authoritarian) methods to be better. Anderson concludes that: "The evidence available fails to demonstrate that either authoritarian or democratic leadership is consistently associated with higher productivity" (p. 212).

Anderson finds a somewhat clearer picture with respect to the effects of the two types of leadership on morale. Twenty-one studies plus an unspecified number of doctoral dissertations are listed that find high morale associated with democratic leadership. Included in these studies are fraternities, sororities, boys' clubs, grade school classes, therapy groups, and temporary groups. But higher morale in democratic groups was not found in seven studies involving military groups, business groups, and college classes. Anderson suggests the following explanation for some of the discrepancies in the research findings:

Democratic leadership is associated with high morale when a primary group goal is social as in the case of the recreational and fraternal groups, or emotional catharsis, as in the case of the therapy groups. Morale is higher under authoritarian leadership, however, in groups which are primarily committed to some task goal rather than a social-emotional goal. [P. 204.]

Research on democratic-authoritarian leadership illustrates some of the pitfalls encountered when an effort is made to classify the behaviors involved in highly complex interpersonal relationships into a few ill-defined categories. The difficulties are compounded when moralistic labels such as "democratic" and "authoritarian" are attached to the categories, and the researcher appears to be trying to discover whether "virtue" is, after all, more rewarding than "sin."

Learning Exercise

18. How is it possible that the 32 studies on the relative productivity in learner-centered and authoritarian classrooms (reviewed by Anderson) should have such diverse findings?

Discipline

Teacher-pupil relationships in a classroom are likely to be influenced by the kind of disciplinary measures adopted by the teacher. The term "discipline" in a classroom means different things to different people. To one person, a well-disciplined classroom is one in which the teacher imposes his will upon unwilling pupils by aggressively punishing a pupil for any misdemeanor. To another person, a well-disciplined classroom is one in which pupils and teacher work cooperatively, willingly, and constructively toward educational goals. From both points of view, an absence of misbehaviors in the classroom is one indication of good discipline. However, observing from the first image of a well-disciplined classroom, we focus attention on how the teacher handles the misbehaviors that occur in the classroom; whereas, with the second image as a reference, we are more interested in observing the effects of all of the teacher's interactions with pupils on the learning of the pupils.

How does a teacher's method of handling the misbehaviors of one child influence the later behavior of that child and of other children who witness the disciplinary action? This is indeed a complex question. Disciplinary actions can vary in so many ways. The perceptions of the disciplinary action of both the deviant child and other children witnessing the disciplinary action vary. Personality characteristics of the children in the classroom may be an important factor influencing the efficiency of any one disciplinary action. Much research is needed on classroom management. In the meantime, it is necessary to guard against overgeneralizing from present research evidence. Certainly, it is not possible at the present time to provide the teacher with a neat set of rules for maintaining discipline.

Kounin, Gump, and Ryan (1961) review a number of studies related to the teacher's methods of handling misbehaviors in the classroom. In one experiment, an instructor's admonition of a college student for coming in late to class with the added threat that "this cannot help but affect my evaluation of you and your grade" resulted in an increase in classroom tension and the lowering of students' judgments of the instructor's helpfulness, likeability, freedom from authoritarianism, and fairness. A number of other experiments conducted at the kindergarten, elementary school, and high school levels show a relationship between a teacher's "desist-technique" and both the deviant and witnessing children's attitudes toward the teacher.

The prestige of the disciplined child and how he reacts to a desist-technique influence his classmates' perception of the disciplinary incident and their attitudes toward the teacher. Gnagey (1960) found that when high prestige members of a fifth-grade class submitted quietly and politely to a disciplinary action, the other members of the class tend to be less disrupted from their schoolwork, rate the disciplinary action as fair, and rate the teacher as "more capable of handling kids." More disruption and lower ratings were given the teacher in the classroom where the high prestige deviant reacted to the disciplinary action in a defiant manner.

One study conducted by J. J. Ryan (reported in Kounin *et al.*, 1961) indicates that certain characteristics of a pupil influence his reactions to his teacher's management of deviancy in the classroom. Highly motivated children tend to respond constructively to desist-techniques. Children poorly motivated tend to be disrupted by disciplinary incidents. The child who likes his teacher tends to judge his teacher's desist-techniques as "fair," while the child who dislikes his teacher tends to judge the same desist-technique as "unfair." Once a child has developed a liking or a disliking for his teacher, he tends to perceive and judge the behavior of his teacher in ways consistent with his attitude.

In general, rough disciplinary measures fail to produce desired results. In one study (Kounin and Gump, 1958), 406 incidents involving the desist-techniques of 26 kindergarten teachers were analyzed. When the teacher clarified for a deviating child how he was expected to behave, the deviating child and the other children in the classroom tended to conform to the teacher's wishes. The teacher who responded angrily when a child misbehaved tended to disturb other children in the class. Overt signs of fear and anxiety and an interference with the constructive activities of the children were noted after a teacher had dealt roughly with a deviant child, but no effect of the roughness on "conformance or nonconformance" was observed. In a study of first-graders, Kounin and Gump (1961) noted the same disrupting tendencies in the classes of punitive teachers. In addition, more aggressive behavior occurred among the pupils in classes of punitive teachers than in the classes of non-punitive teachers.

Learning Exercise

19. In one classroom during the showing of a science film, a boy highly regarded by his classmates said aloud, "Hey, is this film about over?" The teacher, who was new to the class, directed the boy to leave the classroom and report to the principal. On leaving the room, the boy said, "Yes ma'am, I'm sorry." In another classroom, the identical incident occurred, but in leaving the room, the high prestige boy said belligerently: "I'll leave the room, but I won't go to the principal's office. The heck with you!"

    (a) On the basis of Gnagey's study, what predictions would you make concerning the relative amount of work disruption in the two classrooms, and the judgment of the children as to the fairness and competency of the two teachers?

    (b) On the basis of Ryan's research what characteristics of the pupils in the two classrooms might influence their reactions to the teacher's desist-technique?

(c) Suppose the teacher meted out much more severe punishment for deviant behaviors of this kind. On the basis of the research of Kounin and Gump, what predictions would you make concerning the effect of such severity on the behavior of the children?

ANXIETY

Is the anxiety level in the classroom an important variable influencing learning? The announcement of a forthcoming test appears to raise the anxiety level of students. Other teaching procedures such as an assignment of a speech also seem to generate anxiety. Some students appear to become more easily apprehensive than others, and some teachers seem to generate more anxiety than others. The disciplinary measures used by the teacher may be one source of anxiety. Some teachers seem to be better able than others to handle constructively the anxieties of students.

In this section, we will explore the effects of anxiety on school performance. First, we need to examine more closely the meaning of the term "anxiety" and some of the ways that are available for measuring anxiety.

The Meaning of Anxiety

Anxiety and fear have much in common. Both are responses to threat, and the physiological changes accompanying both emotions are similar. The major distinction between the two emotions rests in the clarity of an individual's perception of just what is threatening him. A small boy understands quite well why he is afraid when a big bully threatens to punch him. He is less able to explain vague feelings of apprehension that he experiences concerning the quality of his schoolwork. Anxiety refers to a pervasive state of apprehension and of painful uneasiness concerning some impending disaster. The source of the anticipated disaster is not well defined. As anxiety is a tension state, it serves as a drive. But because the precise nature of the danger is not recognized, the appropriate tension-reducing response cannot be rationally determined.

Several theories have been advanced concerning the nature and genesis of anxiety. A number of theories emphasize the child's feeling of helplessness in adequately relating himself to people who are of importance to him, thus leading to a disorder in his relationship to himself. The theory of anxiety presented by Horney (1937, 1942, 1945, 1950) is illustrative.

According to Horney, anything that disturbs the security of the child in relation to his parents (such as rejection, overprotection, harsh punishment, inconsistent treatment, etc.) may produce basic anxiety. Horney defines basic anxiety as "the feeling a child has of being isolated and helpless in a potentially hostile world" (Horney, 1945, p. 41). Various strategies are developed by the anxious, insecure child in an effort to cope with his basic anxiety (Horney, 1937). He may become hostile and aggressive and develop a neurotic need for power over others. He may strive excessively for the affection, approval, or admiration of others. He may develop a neurotic ambition for personal achievement or constantly strive for perfection. Or he may withdraw from relationships with others, and strive for self-sufficiency and independence. Any one strategy may become predominant and take on the force of a drive or need. Horney refers to these needs as "neurotic" because they are an irrational solution to the child's basic problem.

Experimental psychologists have attempted to explain anxiety in terms of a reinforcement learning theory frame of reference. Based upon laboratory experiments, the learning theorist attributes anxiety to the pairing of a neutral stimulus—the conditioned stimulus with some unconditioned noxious stimulus. The previously described experiment of Miller (see pages 161–162) is illustrative of the type of laboratory research that has generated explanations of anxiety in terms of conditioning concepts. In common with theories of anxiety advanced by psychoanalysts, learning theorists conceive anxiety as a premonition of injury or pain, and ascribe drive properties to a learned anxiety. However, as pointed out by Kimble (1961, p. 444) conceptions of anxiety based upon laboratory research overemphasize the importance of fear of objective situations.

Freud (1926) recognizes three types of anxiety: *reality* anxiety; *neurotic* anxiety; and *moral* anxiety. It has been reality anxiety, i.e., fears of real dangers such as physical harm or economic privation, that the experimental psychologist has been able to study in the laboratory. Neurotic anxiety is the fear that antisocial, sexual, or aggressive urges will get out of hand and prompt the person to do something for which he will later be punished. According to Freudian psychology, the symptoms of neurotic anxiety are found in free-floating anxiety, phobias, and panic. Moral anxiety is fear of the conscience. The fear is again of punishment. But the person with the highly developed conscience experiences feelings of guilt or shame because even the urges to behave in ways that are contrary to his moral upbringing generate moral anxiety.

Learning Exercises

20. To which of Freud's three types of anxiety does Horney's "basic anxiety" most closely correspond?
21. Margaret becomes emotionally disturbed when she takes a test.
    (a) Which of Freud's three types of anxiety does Margaret experience?
    (b) How might reinforcement learning concepts be used to explain how Margaret acquired test-anxiety?

The Measurement of Anxiety

The study of anxiety has been stimulated in recent years by the construction of the Manifest Anxiety Scale (Taylor, 1953). The scale was designed as a means of differentiating general drive level of subjects. The scores on the scale are assumed to be related to emotional responsiveness, which in turn contributes to drive level (Taylor, 1956). The Manifest Anxiety Scale has been widely used in studies investigating the differential performance of high and low anxiety groups on both simple and complex learning tasks. Experimental evidence tends to support the conclusion that classical conditioning can be affected more rapidly with the more-anxious individuals. There is some evidence indicating that the performance on learning tasks deteriorates under stress conditions to a greater degree for anxious students than for non-anxious students (Gordon and Berlyne, 1954; Lucas, 1952).

The Manifest Anxiety Scale has been modified for use with fourth-, fifth-, and sixth-grade children by Castaneda, McCandless, and Palermo (1956). A total of 42 anxiety items are included in what the authors call the *Children's Manifest Anxiety Scale* (CMAS). The level of anxiety is obtained by summing the number of "Yes" responses to items such as the following: "It is hard for me to keep my mind on anything." "I feel I have to be best in everything." "I blush easily." "I worry most of the time." "My feelings get easily hurt." "I get angry easily." An additional 11 lie scale items are interspersed with the anxiety items. The following are illustrative: "I am always good." "I never get angry." "I never lie." In one study, McCandless, Castaneda, and Palermo (1956) found some tendency for the more-anxious children to be less popular with their peers. McCandless and Castaneda (1956) found that the more-anxious children averaged lower in school achievement than the less-anxious children. Wirt and Broen (1956) investigated the relation of the Children's Manifest Anxiety Scale to the concept of anxiety as used in the psychological clinic. The CMAS was administered to 505 fourth-, fifth-, and sixth-grade children in Minnesota public schools and 34 children from the same grades who had been referred to the Child Study Department. CMAS scores did not differentiate between the two groups. Nor was a positive relationship found between anxiety as rated by teachers or by psychologists after diagnostic study and CMAS scores. Wirt and Broen conclude that the CMAS measures something different than the clinical concept of anxiety. They speculate that the CMAS probably measures "willingness to say deviant things about the self" or "test-taking attitude."

The lack of relationship between CMAS scores and the ratings on anxiety of psychologists and teachers may be interpreted in many ways. That a given test yields scores that are not in agreement with the judgments of clinicians and teachers is not a devastating criticism of the test. The process of establishing the validity of any test usually requires many research studies in order to determine what behavior the test does predict. In recent years, numerous investigations have explored psychological and behavioral correlates of various anxiety scales, including the CMAS. For example, one finding in a study by Smock (1958) is that high manifest anxiety as measured by the CMAS is associated with perceptual rigidity, i.e., the inability to perceive things differently even when the objective conditions have changed.

Sarason and his colleagues have conducted extensive research on test anxiety with elementary school children. Their book (Sarason, Davidson, Lighthall, Waite, and Ruebush, 1960) contains an excellent review of the literature on anxiety as well as summaries of their own research findings over a period of years. They have developed two anxiety scales: a General Anxiety Scale for Children (GASC) and a Test Anxiety Scale for Children (TASC).

The following items are illustrative of the 34-item general anxiety scale: "Do you sometimes worry about whether other children are better looking than you are?" "Do you sometimes worry about whether your body is growing the way it should?" "Do you worry when you are home alone at night?" "Do you worry about whether your father is going to get sick?" "Do you worry that you might get sick in some accident?" "Are you afraid of spiders?" In order to detect the child who, consciously or unconsciously, provides false information about himself 11 "lie items" are interspersed throughout the scale. Examples of lie items are: "Have you ever been afraid of getting hurt?" "Has anyone ever been able to scare you?"

The Test Anxiety Scale for Children consists of 30 questions. The first 18 questions are related to a variety of types of school performances such as answering questions in class, not understanding work presented, missing schoolwork through sickness, etc. Examples of such items are: "When the teacher is teaching you about reading, do you feel that other children in the class understand her better than you?" "When the teacher says she is going to find out how much you have learned, does your heart begin to beat faster?" The last 12 items are directly related to test-taking, and include items such as: "Are you afraid of school tests?" "While you are taking a test do you usually think you are doing poorly?"

Relationships of Measures of Anxiety to Other Variables

Before discussing research findings on the relationships between scores on various anxiety scales and other variables, it may be useful to clarify the relevancy of such research to the problems encountered by the classroom teacher. Sarason *et al.* (1960) state:

> From the outset it was our hope that the results of our research would enable us in the future to apply our procedures to three very important practical problems: (1) to pick out those children whose school performance suffers because of disabling personality factors; (2) to pick out those children whose early school performance appears adequate but whose later school performance will reflect personality disturbance; and (3) to determine the ways in which the classroom situation can be used to help those children who have disabling reactions and attitudes toward school. [1960, p. 263.]

The authors point out that these purposes have not as yet been realized. Yet the research progress that has been made should serve to alert the teacher to the fact that anxiety in the classroom is a teaching problem, should serve to provide some insight into the nature of the problem, and possibly to provide some clues as to constructive ways of dealing with the problem.

Anxiety and Intelligence. A number of studies have investigated the relationship between intelligence test performance and anxiety scale scores. The data from most of these studies support the conclusion that anxiety interferes with intelligence test performance, i.e., children scoring high on an anxiety scale tend to score lower on an intelligence test than do children who score low on the anxiety scale. Sarason *et al.* (1960) report negative correlations ranging from $-.229$ to $-.297$ between I.Q.'s derived from group intelligence tests and TASC scores for children in grades 3, 4, 5, and 6.

The negative correlation between intelligence test performance and measures of anxiety does not, by itself, justify a conclusion that anxiety interferes with intelligence test performance. The possibility exists that less intelligent children in our culture tend to become highly anxious. However, the data from two studies cast doubt on this interpretation. Zweibelson (1956) hypothesized that the correlation between scores of fifth-grade pupils on the TASC and the Davis-Eells games would be significantly lower than between TASC and the Otis intelligence tests. The Davis-Eells games are not presented to children as tests and hence are not as likely to generate feelings of anxiety. Zweibelson's hypothesis was confirmed. The correlation between TASC and the Davis-Eells games was −.14 as compared to a correlation between TASC and Otis Beta of −.28, and Otis Alpha of −.24. In a later study, Lighthall *et al.* (1959) administered the Otis Alpha to pupils when they were in grades 2 and 4; the Otis Beta to pupils when they were in grades 5, 6, and 7; and the Davis-Eells games when pupils were in grades 5 and 7. TASC scores were available for all pupils, so that gains of high anxiety pupils could be compared to gains of low anxiety pupils on the various intelligence tests. Beta gains from grades 5 to 7 were greater for the low anxiety group. And on the Davis-Eells games, the high anxiety children gained significantly more than did the low anxiety children. Thus, both the Zweibelson and the Lighthall studies lend support to the conclusion that anxiety interferes with test performance and suggest the possibility that test performance of high anxiety pupils will improve if the test administrator is successful in reducing the anxiety-provoking features of the test situation.

Learning Exercises

22. In a classroom in which the teacher generated a great deal of anxiety, would you expect the performance on learning tasks of an anxious student to deteriorate more than that of a non-anxious student?
23. How might it be possible for a highly anxious student to obtain a "low anxiety score" on the CMAS?
24. How do Sarason's tests resemble and how do they differ from the CMAS?
25. Do Zweibelson's and Lighthall's research support the conclusion that anxiety impairs the intellectual development of high anxiety children? Give reasons for your answers.

Anxiety and Problem Solving. The relationship of anxiety to problem-solving processes is complicated because of the numerous variables that can enter into the problem-solving process. Under certain conditions, mild anxiety seems to facilitate problem-solving; under other conditions, anxiety interferes with problem-solving. Both the complexity and the nature of the problem to be solved are apparently important variables. Castaneda, Palermo, and McCandless (1956) conducted a study in which elementary school children were chosen on the basis of extreme scores in the CMAS, the children with high scores being the high anxiety group, and the children with low scores being the low anxiety group. The apparatus used involved five electrical push buttons that could turn off five lights of different colors. The experimenter could actuate any single light and set any single push button so that depressing it turned off the light. The task of the child was to learn the five separate light combinations, some of which were easy and some more difficult. It was found that the high anxiety group performed better than the low anxiety group on the simple learning tasks but did more poorly on the more complex tasks.

Gaier (1952) reports significant relations between anxiety (measured by the Rorschach test) and achievement of college students. High anxiety students surpassed others on test items measuring knowledge of specific information (rho = .34). But they did relatively poorly on problem-solving test items involving analysis, application, or synthesis (rho = −.48; −.61; −.42).

In a study by Barnard et al. (1961) it was found that high anxiety third-grade children expressed more negative feelings than did low anxiety children in evaluative interviews in which the children were told that they were later to be tested. The pervasiveness of the anxiety feelings generated by the interview was such that negative feelings were expressed even in response to questions such as "Tell me about your best friend" or "Tell me something that made you very happy." High anxiety children who had obtained comparable TASC scores but who were interviewed in a friendly, permissive atmosphere showed much less tendency to express negative feelings to questions designed to elicit positive feelings. And no instances of extreme negative affective statements were made to positive "pull" questions by low anxiety children interviewed under evaluative conditions. Another finding of the Barnard study is that the responses of the high anxiety children were less comprehensible than those of the low anxiety children.

Under certain conditions, the high anxiety child outperforms his low anxiety peer on problem-solving tasks. We have previously described the study by Castaneda et al. (1956) in which the high anxiety child did better than the low anxiety child on simple tasks although not on the more difficult tasks. Sarason et al. (1960) have postulated that the conditions of the problem-solving task that facilitate learning for the high anxiety child include: (1) the absence of an evaluative or testlike factor in the situation; (2) that the task permits the child to gratify dependency needs; and (3) that the task be such that it can best be solved by

the cautious problem-solver. The study comparing the performances
of the high anxiety children on the David-Eells games and the more
testlike Otis test is relevant to the first condition. A study conducted
by Ruebush (1960) supports the ideas that tasks calling for cautiousness
and tasks that are structured to meet children's dependency needs
facilitate performance for high anxiety children.

In the Ruebush study, a child is shown a drawing of a figure and
then, after the figure is removed, the child is asked to find the figure in
a more complex drawing. The child was instructed that he could ask
to look at the simple figure as many times as he wished and that the
time taken up in so doing would not count in his score. Further, if he
makes a mistake, he will be so informed and he can continue his search
for the simple figure that is embedded in the more complicated one.
The instructions are thus formulated to convey to the child the idea that
the examiner is there to help him, hence, presumably gratifying the
child's dependency needs. The subjects for the study were 48 sixth-
grade boys. The boys were divided into six groups on the basis of
performances on the TASC and performance on the Otis Beta Intelligence Scale. Each child participating in the study was given a chance
to identify a number of embedded figures varying in complexity of
design. Results were scored in two ways: the total number of figures
identified and the amount of time required to do so. The high anxiety
children were superior to the low anxiety children on both scores, although the superiority was limited to the middle and low intelligence
level groups. A "cautiousness" score was obtained by dividing the
number of times a boy asked to see the simple picture by the number
of "wrong" guesses. It was found that: (1) high anxiety boys obtained
higher cautiousness scores, and (2) cautious boys solved more figures.

In a later study conducted by Waite and reported in Sarason *et al.*
(1960) two types of tests were employed. In one of the tests, the
subjects were under pressure to work quickly. In the second test, there
was no pressure to hurry; the examiner was more likely to be perceived
as supportive rather than demanding; and the child needed to be cautious rather than impulsive. In this study, the hypothesis that low
anxiety children would do better on the first test was confirmed.

Learning Exercises

26. On which school task—memorizing mathematical formulas or working
    mathematical problems—would you expect the high anxiety student to
    do relatively poorly?

27. What difficulty might a music teacher encounter in teaching music appreciation to high anxiety students just prior to an announced test?
28. For what type of occupation might it be desirable to have high anxiety employees?

Anxiety and School Learning

According to Anderson (1950) all human behavior is based on the avoidance of anxiety. The child who wants to do well in his schoolwork attends school, is attentive in class, does homework assignments, and studies for tests, not only in order to do well, but also to avoid the anxiety engendered by any expectation of failure. In the process of working toward a goal, the experiencing of some anxiety is normal and serves as a spur to work harder to achieve the goal. The teacher in motivating children to achieve educational goals arouses anxieties in children. The teacher in his role of maintaining discipline in the classroom and in helping children to learn to assume responsibilities is arousing normal anxieties in most children. And this normal anxiety facilitates learning.

The teacher also assumes the role of anxiety reducer as he aids children in seeing how educational goals can be achieved and provides children with success experiences. To the extent that the teacher provides a reasonable amount of freedom and yet manages the classroom so that the pupil knows what is expected of him and what is not permitted, the teacher is likely to have a classroom atmosphere that is secure and conducive to reducing anxieties.

Teachers differ considerably in their ability to handle children's anxieties. Davidson and Sarason (1961) report a study in which three second-grade classrooms were observed daily over a period of four months in order to determine the relationship of scores on the Test Anxiety Scale for Children to a variety of personality and behavioral characteristics of children. The teacher was found to be a prime variable. Clinicians assigned a positive or negative rating to observers' notes on incidents relevant to the teachers' handling of children's dependence, cautiousness, fear of failure, motivation, failure and success, behavioral problems (shyness, anxiety, aggression), and instances in which the teacher expressed strong emotions on value judgments. One teacher described by the observers as authoritarian, punitive, and rejecting of needs to be independent or cautious received 64 positive ratings and 223 negative ratings. A second teacher described by observers as one who showed acceptance of all children, though not all behavior, and who focused attention on the academic achievement and improvement of the children, received 283 positive ratings and 44 negative ratings. With such wide differences in the abilities of teachers to handle anxiety in the classroom, the problem of studying the relationship of anxiety to school learning is made very difficult. We know some anxiety is conducive to learning. We also know that too much anxiety interferes with learning. And we have just noted that teachers differ in their skills in handling anxiety. Hence, whether the high or low anxiety child performs the better in school may depend, in part, upon who his teacher is.

A number of studies have reported a negative relationship between anxiety and school achievement. McCandless and Castaneda (1956) found negative correlations between anxiety and school achievement scores in 25 out of the 30 computed for fourth-, fifth-, and sixth-grade boys and girls on the Iowa Every Pupil Test and the Children's Manifest Anxiety Scale. However, only 13 of the 25 negative correlations were statistically significant and 10 of these were for the sixth-grade level. Arithmetic computation appeared to be the subject most susceptible to the effects of anxiety. This finding is consistent with one of Haggard's (1957) that: "The high arithmetic achievers could express their feeling freely and without anxiety or guilt" (1957, p. 397). Lynn (1957) found that, among English school children, anxiety is positively correlated with reading attainment but not with arithmetic. Allison and Ash (1951) experimented in the use of films with college students and raised the anxiety of students by telling them that the test to follow a film and based on its content would indicate whether they belonged in college. An improvement of test scores followed the experimental raising of anxiety.

On the basis of evidence received so far, it appears that anxiety results in a greater mobilization of effort and hence may lead to more efficient learning. Too much anxiety, however, may interfere with the learning process, possibly due to "narrowing our perceptual field" as Combs and Snygg (1959) contend. Hence, in school tasks where the pupil needs to think of and choose between data relevant to the solution of a problem, increased anxiety may result in poor problem-solving. And it appears that the amount of interference resulting from any given anxiety-provoking situation will differ from child to child, with some children better able to withstand the effects of stress than other children.

Learning Exercise

29. How might a teacher constructively aid the high anxiety child who is experiencing difficulty in arithmetic?

SUMMARY

The modern teacher has numerous instructional techniques from which to choose. An instructional method that is effective for one type of educational objective (e.g., imparting information) may not be effective for another type of educational objective (e.g., changing attitudes). Therefore, the kind of change in pupil behavior that the teacher is attempting to effect should be kept in mind in selecting learning activities. Once this is determined, we may ask why the learner does not now behave in the way described in the educational objective. Is it information the learner needs? Is it practice in noticing the right cues? Is it practice in processing information? The answers to questions such as these should suggest an appropriate teaching technique. And the answers to these questions may vary for different pupils in the classroom. Choosing an appropriate instructional technique involves choosing learning tasks that are meaningful, interesting, and at an appropriate level of difficulty for the learner. It involves the problem of: (1) motivating the pupil, (2) providing the opportunities for cue recognition, (3) providing practice, (4) reinforcing the appropriate behavior when it occurs, and (5) providing an environment favorable to learning.

Research on teaching methods does indicate that the modern school is providing a better education than that provided in previous decades. But a more systematic research procedure is needed to insure that teaching procedures constantly improve. Experiments of limited scope, designed to answer well-defined problems, are needed.

Through programmed instruction, it may be possible to more thoroughly examine the teaching-learning process. A program of instruction that may be presented through some kind of "teaching machine" does provide more control over the stimulus variable and the kind of responses required of the learner. On the stimulus side, the relative merits of linear versus branching and scrambled book programs, and large-step versus small-step programs have been investigated as well as a number of techniques for sequencing the frames of a program.

On the response side, constructed responses have been compared to multiple-choice responses and overt responses to covert responses. Also, the importance to learning of immediate knowledge of results has been investigated with school-like tasks. While there appears to be little likelihood that a revolution in teaching technology will come about in the immediate future through the use of teaching machines, research on programmed instruction does hold promise of advancing our knowledge of how children learn in the classroom.

How well children learn depends, in part, upon the environmental context in which the learning takes place. The quality of the teacher-pupil relationships is an important part of the total environmental context. Teacher-pupil interpersonal relationships may vary with respect to their emotional quality, the degree of harmony or disharmony between pupils and teachers, and the extent to which the teacher serves to stimulate or restrict the activities of pupils.

Research on the stimulative-restrictive dimension of teacher-pupil relationships has been given unfortunate labels such as authoritarianism versus democratic, learner-centered versus teacher-centered, etc. And the set of specific teacher behaviors subsumed under each label undoubtedly varies from one study to another. Within a classroom, there are many occasions when the teacher focuses attention on helping the student acquire correct responses (i.e., restrictive) and other occasions when the teacher tries to stimulate the student to explore many avenues of thought.

The problem of discipline in the classroom can best be thought of positively as one of motivating students to learn. The child misbehaves when the child is not motivated to learn. The kind of "desist-technique" employed by the teacher will then affect the social and emotional climate in the classroom. The child respects firm and fair disciplinary actions. Rough disciplinary measures fail to produce desirable results.

Teachers vary in the amount of anxiety they provoke in children. The effects of anxiety are not universally bad. Mild anxiety may facilitate certain kinds of learning, while too much anxiety interferes with the learning process. The task of the teacher in controlling anxiety level is complicated by the fact that children vary in their susceptibility to feelings of anxiety and in their ability to work efficiently while experiencing anxiety.

Answer Cues

1. A representative sample of all schools is used in the Bloom study. In studies involving only a few schools, the students and the teachers included might not be representative of the nation as a whole.

2. Better teachers in 1955 than during World War II; more favorable environmental climate for learning; better teaching methods, etc.

3. (a), (c), (d).

4. (a).

5. Control of student responses.

6. A program.

7. Branching.

8. Branching.

9. Relatively large amount of information provided before students responded. No *immediate* knowledge of results. Steps not sufficiently small to attain 90 to 95 per cent correct.

10. The pupil underlines "steady" in frame 1; copies "steady" in frames 2 and 3; and fills in missing letters in frames 4 and 8.

11. The learner may not need the knowledge of results because his answer looks right to him. Possibly the process of looking at his answer and judging whether it is right has some learning value.

12. No. Possibly just completing a job may be reinforcing.

13. Covert.

14. This may easily occur, particularly when the variables that influence performance have not been clearly identified. An important variable (i.e., some characteristics of the learner or some additional characteristic of the learning situation) may not be controlled in an early experiment. Later, when the uncontrolled variable is identified, researchers design their experiments so as to control the effects of the variable.

15. It should be. Pupils would not be distracted from learning by the emotional quality of the interpersonal relationship. However, the pupils in striving to learn would probably generate some anxiety, but this anxiety would be task oriented and hence should facilitate learning.

16. Teacher might not be fulfilling expected roles.

17. (a) In teaching First Aid, the teacher probably would want the pupils to learn *a* correct way of treating an injury.

18. The specific teacher leadership behaviors subsumed under the terms "learner-centered" and "authoritarian" probably varied from study to study, as the characteristics of the learner, the learning tasks, and the measures of learning probably also varied from study to study.

19. (a) More disruption in the classroom and lower ratings of the teacher who was defied. (b) The academic motivation of the pupil might be expected to influence whether or not the incident distracted him from his work. His liking for the teacher might be expected to influence his judgment of the fairness of the teacher. (c) More severe punishment might be expected to produce more aggressive behavior in the pupils and more emotional disturbance.

20. Neurotic anxiety.

21. (a) Reality anxiety. (b) By classical conditioning. Test-taking, which was originally a neutral situation for Margaret, became associated with unpleasantness.

22. Probably. There is some evidence that anxious students do not withstand stress as well as non-anxious students.

23. By not answering truthfully the items on the CMAS or by answering on the basis of a faulty perception of self.

24. Both GASC and CMAS are measures of general anxiety for children. Both include lie scale items. TASC is focused on anxiety concerning school tasks.

25. No. The stress of taking a test interferes with the intellectual functioning of high anxiety children. However, on measures of intellectual

functioning under non-stressed conditions (e.g., Davis-Eells Games), high anxiety children actually attained greater gains in intellectual development than did low anxiety children.

26. Problem solving.

27. Negative feelings of high anxiety students generated by the anticipation of a test.

28. Occupations requiring painstaking detail work; requiring accuracy; where speed is not the prime consideration; and dependency needs are met.

29. Give freedom to children to express their anxieties about arithmetic. Work patiently with the child in developing the arithmetic skills needed to reduce anxiety. Gear the problems assigned the child to his ability so that he can experience success; then gradually increase difficulty up to a reasonable standard.

8

MOTIVATION

There is no magical set of rules that will enable the teacher to deal effectively with the diverse motivational problems encountered in the classroom. The teacher must rely on his professional judgment based upon his knowledge of how motivation initiates and sustains behavior. Psychologists in their study of motivation have been concerned with three broad questions: (1) Why does a person become active? (2) Why does a person act one way rather than another? and (3) How do you get a person to change his behavior in some desirable direction? (Hunt, 1960). This chapter is concerned with these questions.

To obtain an answer to the first question—"Why does a person become active?"—we will need to examine the concept of "drive."

The concepts "needs," "goals," and "competence" will be helpful in studying the second question, "Why does a person act one way rather than another?"

The third question—"How do we get a person to change his behavior in some desirable direction?"—is most clearly relevant to the teacher's problem of initiating, directing, and sustaining motivation. This problem varies from one child to another. Research findings on "achievement motivation" help to identify some of the characteristics of the learner associated with motivation to perform school tasks. But, for all children, the social environment influences motivation. The final portion of this chapter contains discussions on the influences of "praise" and "reproof," "rewards" and "punishments," and the "group" on a child's motivation.

DRIVES

The motivational basis for some behavior can be explained neatly in terms of "drive-reduction." The term "drive" refers to a physiologically imbalanced state of the organism that impels the organism to action.

The imbalanced state of the organism may be attributable to a tissue need or deficit, e.g., hunger or thirst. Or the imbalanced state of the organism may result from a strong external stimulus such as an electric shock, intense light, or loud noise. In either case, the organism is impelled to activity until a response is found that reduces the drive. Thus, central to the drive-reduction theory of motivation is the idea that some disequilibrium of the organism leads to activity, and this activity tends to persist until equilibrium is re-established. Further, the responses that lead to drive-reduction are learned and thus lead to later economical pursuit of goals.

The type of drives discussed above are called *primary drives*. They are unlearned. A person does not learn to be hungry, thirsty, or to experience pain; although the responses elicited by the hunger, thirst, sex, and other drives are modified as a result of experience. Thus, a person *learns* to like or dislike a particular food, and learns to eat in a socially approved manner even though the motivational basis for the behavior is an unlearned primary drive.

Through conditioning, stimuli other than those that initially aroused activity come to serve as substitutes in initiating activity. Thus, originally the internal stimulation resulting from food deprivation may be considered as a primary hunger drive, and this drive will initiate and maintain activity. Later the sight, smell, or the sounds of food being prepared may come to function as a drive. Learned drives of this kind are referred to as *secondary* or *acquired* drives. The experiment conducted by Miller (1948) outlined in Chapter 5 is illustrative of how drives may be learned. Initially, the primary drive, *pain*, was sufficient to activate the rat in Miller's experiment. But after the pain from an electric shock was experienced by the rat in a white compartment, the white compartment came to serve as a substitute stimuli for the electric shock. A secondary drive, *fear*, was acquired. In a comparable manner, according to drive-reduction theory, other drives and needs (need for affection, need for approval, and so forth) are built upon primary drives.

Some research evidence points to motivating conditions that do not fit so neatly into a drive-or-need-reduction theory of motivation. For example, Butler and Harlow (1957) have demonstrated that monkeys can learn to make discriminations when the only reward for their learning activity is that of being able to explore their environment (an *exploratory* drive). Kagan and Berkun (1954) and Hill (1956) have presented evidence pointing to an *activity* drive. In Hill's experiment, rats that were confined and thus deprived of activity become, when released, more physically active than rats that were not so confined.

Berlyne (1960) postulates that conceptual conflict arouses a *curiosity* drive. The conflict is reduced by the acquisition of knowledge. Berlyne's concept of conceptual conflict is similar to concepts advanced by Festinger (1957). Festinger uses the term "cognitive dissonance" to denote a conflict between two cognitive elements (beliefs, evaluations, perceptions). When dissonance is present, there is a drive toward its reduction.

A number of psychologists (e.g., White, 1959; Hunt, 1960; Young, 1961) object to the use of the term "primary drive" (or even "drive") as applied to exploration, curiosity, and the like. Young (1961, p. 56) writes:

Primary drives, like hunger and thirst, have internal, organic origins; they rest upon observable tissue conditions. Secondary drives, by contrast, originate externally; they are environmental determinants. Viewed from this angle, play, manipulation, exploration, curiosity, and similar forms of behavior are *secondary* until they have been shown to have observable bases or origins within the tissues.

White (1959, pp. 300–301) lists three characteristics of the orthodox conception of a drive: "(a) there is a tissue need or deficit external to the nervous system which acts upon that system as a strong persisting stimulus; (b) this promotes activity which is terminated by a consummatory response with consequent reduction of need; (c) the reduction of need brings about the learning which gradually shapes behavior into an economical pursuit of suitable goal objects." White argues that so-called drives such as exploring, activity, curiosity, and variety fail to meet these criteria.

NEEDS, GOALS, AND COMPETENCE

Needs

In observing individuals in different situations, we sometimes note consistencies in their behavior. One child seeks help from others in any task he performs. In characterizing the behavior of this child, we may say that he has strong *dependency* needs. Another child wants to do any task he is given "in his own way." We may characterize this child as one with a strong need for *independence*. Still another child devotes much of his energies to gaining the favor of his classmates. We may characterize this child as one with a strong need for *peer approval*. The term "need" is used to denote some inferred common characteristics of the motivational basis for the behavior of an individual. We cannot see a need. We infer its presence from our observations of an individual. The concepts "need" and "drive" are sometimes used synonymously; although by using the term "need," we may avoid the problem of the physiological basis of motivation.

Psychologists have provided a number of classifications of the various needs of people. The lists of needs vary in length. Combs and Snygg (1959) have postulated one basic need—*the need for adequacy*. According to Combs and Snygg, each individual develops a self concept that includes perceptions of what one is like physically, morally, socially, and how one is able to perform in numerous situations. To meet the need for adequacy, the individual must be able to maintain and enhance his self concept. From a phenomenological point of view, as presented by Combs and Snygg, people are never unmotivated. A child who does not seem to want to learn arithmetic does not see arithmetic achievement as a means of self-enhancement. Hence, the problem of motivating this child is a problem of changing his perception of himself so that he sees arithmetic achievement as necessary to meeting his need for adequacy.

Maslow (1954) lists the basic needs as physiological needs, safety needs, belongingness and love needs, esteem needs, and the need for self-actualization (i.e., to realize one's potentialities). For Maslow these needs form a hierarchical order. Higher-order needs do not operate to motivate the individual until the lower-order needs are minimally satisfied. Maslow postulates in addition a cognitive need—the desires to know and to understand—and aesthetic needs.

Murray (1938) listed 12 viscerogenic (i.e., physiological) and 28 psychogenic needs. Murray's need system has been made the basis of a number of measurement approaches to motivation. Table 8–1 contains a list of Murray's psychogenic needs grouped arbitrarily into five broad functions. A number of the needs could be classified under more than one function.

TABLE 8–1

Murray's Classification of Psychogenic Needs

A. Needs associated with acquiring and retaining inanimate objects
  1. *Acquisition:* to gain possessions and property
  2. *Conservation:* to collect, repair, clean, preserve things
  3. *Retention:* to retain possession of things; to hoard; to be frugal, economical and miserly
B. Achievement striving needs
  4. *Achievement:* to overcome obstacles; to exercise power; to accomplish the difficult
  5. *Construction:* to organize and build
  6. *Superiority:* to excel, receive recognition
  7. *Cognizance:* to explore, ask questions, satisfy curiosity

8. *Orderliness:* to arrange, organize; put away objects; to be tidy and precise
9. *Play:* to relax, seek diversions, have fun

C. Prestige and esteem needs
   10. *Recognition:* to receive praise, commendation, respect
   11. *Exhibition:* to attract attention; to excite, amuse, stir, shock, thrill others
   12. *Inviolacy:* to prevent depreciation of self-respect; to maintain psychological distance
   13. *Avoidance of inferiority:* to avoid failure, shame, humiliation, ridicule
   14. *Defensiveness:* to defend against blame or belittlement; to justify one's actions
   15. *Counteraction:* to refuse admission of defeat by restriving and retaliating
   16. *Blame avoidance:* to avoid blame, ostracism, or punishment by being obedient and conventional
   17. *Abasement:* to comply, accept punishment, apologize, confess, atone

D. Needs associated with power relationships to others
   18. *Dominance:* to influence or control others
   19. *Deference:* to admire and willingly follow a superior
   20. *Similance:* to agree, imitate, identify with others
   21. *Autonomy:* to resist influence; to strive for independence
   22. *Contrariness:* to be unique; to act unconventionally; to take opposite sides

E. Needs associated with emotional and social relationships to others
   23. *Affiliation:* to form friendships and associations; to greet, join, and live with others
   24. *Rejection:* to be discriminating; to snub, ignore, or exclude
   25. *Aggression:* to attack or injure another person
   26. *Nurturance:* to nourish, aid, or protect the helpless
   27. *Exposition:* to give information; to demonstrate, explain, interpret, lecture
   28. *Succorance:* to be dependent; to seek aid, protection, sympathy

SOURCE: Murray (1938). In the interest of communicating, the original terminology of Murray has been changed for some of the needs. Also, the definitions for the terms have been condensed.

Even Murray's extensive list of needs may easily be extended. From factor analysis studies, Guilford (1959) and Cattell (1957) identified many needs that closely resembled Murray's needs. Some quite different needs were also found, e.g., exploration, curiosity, persistence of effort, willingness to withstand discomfort in order to achieve a goal, need for a soft environment, need to conform, moral compulsion (honesty), risk taking and adventure, variety, and need for discipline.

The difficulties inherent in the use of "needs" as units of motivation stem from the fact that motives for an individual are concrete, unique, and multiple, and represent the present (not the past) state of the organism. A variety of needs may find expression in any one act, and the same act performed by another individual may reflect a different constellation of needs. Allport (1961) points out that "The past is not important unless somehow it can be shown to be dynamically active in the present" (p. 220). A boy coming from a home in which he is rejected and abused may turn out to be a criminal, or he may resolve his conflicts and supplant earlier hostile motives with others that permit him to come to terms with society. To explain the fact that changes are constantly taking place in the motives of an individual and to account for the concrete uniqueness of personal motives, Allport (1937, 1960, 1961) has formulated the *principle of functional autonomy*. Acquired drives that are learned originally as a means to an end (for example, working to acquire food) may become ends in themselves (working itself becomes a source of satisfaction and is functionally autonomous from its original motive—acquiring food). Functional autonomy, according to Allport (1961, p. 229), "refers to any acquired system of motivation in which the tensions involved are not the same as the antecedent tensions from which the acquired system developed."

Goals

Goals represent end states sought by an organism. To obtain an A in a course one is taking, to win an election, to become a lawyer, to be invited to a party, to get out of an assigned task—all are examples of goals. For any particular act, a person may have *multiple goals*. A student working on a term paper may have as goals: to obtain a good grade; to learn more about a topic in which he is interested; to win the approval of parents, teachers, or classmates; to become a lawyer; and so forth. In turn, each goal may be related to one or more needs. Goals may be *immediate* or *distant*. While immediate goals are usually more influential than goals that cannot be realized until the distant future, children as they mature become increasingly influenced by distant goals. Distant goals tend to become effective motivators as the individual sees clearly the intermediate goals that must be achieved in order to reach the distant goal. As Allport (1955) points out, it is better to plan toward a kind of continual "becoming" than toward a final goal.

For Miller, Galanter, and Pribram (1960), understanding behavior involves understanding the process through which an individual plans an activity. A "plan" includes some over-all "strategy" as well as numerous specific detailed "tactics." The nature of the plan is determined by what Miller *et al.* call the "image"—which is the total knowledge of an individual including all of his previously worked out plans, his present goals, and his values. In the execution of a plan, a constant feedback occurs in which the operations performed are checked against the requirements of the image. One phase of the operation of a plan will persist until congruity is attained between the "image" and the obtained results, or else fatigue and other conditions call for some revision of the plan.

For the classroom teacher, Miller *et al.*'s system of analysis suggests two possible explanations of the behavior of the student who "lacks motivation." First, the apparent lack of motivation may be real in the sense that the student's personal goals match poorly the educational goals of the school. A second possibility is that the student merely lacks efficient plans to achieve the educational goals of the school. But the detailed thought processes that occur as a student executes a plan—to solve an arithmetic problem, for example—are not visible to the teacher. How, then, can a teacher obtain information on the adequacy of a student's planning processes? One approach that has been suggested by Miller *et al.* and others is to have a student "think aloud" as he works through a problem. Bloom and Broder (1950) tried this approach in a study in which "good" and "poor" problem-solvers thought aloud while working on examination-type problems. One finding was that the method of approach to each problem (the plan) of the poor problem-solvers was inadequate even when the poor problem-solvers had all the information needed to solve a problem. Further, Bloom and Broder found that it was possible to improve the problem-solving strategies of the poor student.

Learning Exercises

1. Which of the following fit in well to a drive-reduction theory of motivation:
   (a) A rat learns to fear a room that is painted white. The rat previously had received electric shocks in the white compartment. Later, without benefit of shock, the rat learned how to escape from the white compartment. (See Miller's experiment described in Chapter 5, pp. 161–162.)
   (b) Harlow, Harlow, and Meyer (1950) demonstrated that well-fed monkeys will learn to take apart a puzzle with no other reward than the privilege of unassembling it.
   (c) In Wolfe's secondary reward training experiment (see Chapter 2, p. 45), chimpanzees were rewarded only with tokens that they had previously learned could be used to obtain grapes from a vending machine.
   (d) Bexton, Heron, and Scott (1954) paid college students 20 dollars a day to do nothing. For 24 hours a day, the students lay on a comfortable bed. Eyes, ears, and hands of the students were shielded to minimize a stimulus variation. The students developed an overwhelming desire for variation, and few were able to endure the sameness of their comfort for more than two or three days.
2. John is greatly disturbed when he receives only a B grade in mathematics

but is not disturbed over the D he obtained in French. How would Combs and Snygg explain John's behavior?

3. From which need theory could you most confidently predict that John's schoolwork would suffer if he were suddenly rejected socially by his classmates?

4. Which of Murray's psychogenic needs is most clearly exemplified in each of the following statements?
   (a) It is important to Dave to get grades better than any other student in his class.
   (b) Tom is the show-off in the class.
   (c) Mary finds her chemistry course difficult but challenging and works hard to master the subject matter.
   (d) Bill only works effectively if he is allowed to do things his own way.
   (e) Alice's sympathies are easily aroused by people in trouble.
   (f) Jack likes to tie tin cans to cats' tails.

5. What concept is illustrated in the following incident:
   Mary first was motivated to study chemistry because it was difficult and challenging. Later she began to find chemistry easy for her, but she continued to work hard on chemistry because she liked it.

6. Hal was assigned a term paper in his high school English class. Identify from the following: (1) the distant goal, (2) the more immediate goal, (3) the "image," and (4) the "plan."
   (a) To complete a term paper on "space travel" in two weeks.
   (b) To become a journalist.
   (c) To search for books on "space" in the library, to set aside one hour each night to work on the term paper, to discuss the topic with Dad, to check criticisms received on his last term paper, etc.
   (d) The term paper should be about 3,000 words. It should be well organized, interesting, and clearly written. It should not have errors in spelling or grammar. A bibliography should be included.

Competence

Motives may be conveniently classified into two categories. In the first category, we find the drive- or need-reducing motives. The organism seeks food, water, oxygen, etc., in order to correct some deficiency or lack. The tissue deficiencies that stimulate the organism—hunger, thirst, sex, and the like—we call *primary drives*. Some other drives and needs appear to be learned through conditioning. For example, fear may be acquired as a drive through associating pain with some previously neutral stimulus. It may be that some psychological needs are acquired in a comparable fashion. At any rate, all the drives and needs in our first category have one common characteristic; i.e., the organism strives to reduce the level of stimulation. Hunger pangs constitute too high a level of stimulation. Hence, the organism strives to *reduce* this level. Feelings of anxiety constitute too high a level of stimulation, and so we find the organism striving to reduce the level and reestablish homeostasis.

For the second category, we find the organism striving to *increase* stimulation. We seek mild excitement. We avoid monotonous situations. Leuba (1955) has proposed that there is an optimum level of stimulation for the organism (varying at different times), and that learning occurs as the organism strives to attain this optimum level. Sometimes the stimulus level is too high (e.g., fear), and we strive to reduce the level; sometimes the stimulus level is too low (e.g., boredom), and we seek to increase the level. We are attracted to the novel and hence explore and manipulate our stimulus field. The child at play and in the classroom needs frequent novelty in the stimulus field in order to maintain his interest. Yet a stimulus field that is too foreign to the past experiences of the child does not evoke his interest. Hebb (1949) in exploring the neurological correlates of learning suggests that sustained interest occurs most readily from a stimulus field characterized by "difference-in-sameness." This means that the child is most likely to be interested in something for which he has some degree of familiarity, but which also has some element of novelty.

The distinction between stimulus-reduction motives and stimulus-increase motives is somewhat similar to the distinction made by Woodworth (1958) between "need-primacy" theories of motivation and a "behavior-primacy" theory. Woodworth's *behavior-primacy* theory holds that "all behavior is directed primarily toward dealing with the environment." For Woodworth, dealing with the environment includes more than overt responses to stimuli. Memory and thought processes also constitute ways of dealing with the environment. Organic drives break into the flow of dealing-with-the-environment activities; but the basic motivation, for Woodworth, is that of producing effects upon the environment without any immediate service to an aroused organic need.

White (1959) proposes that all the kinds of behavior that have to do with effective interaction with the environment be considered under the general heading of *competence*. Competence includes all forms of capabilities and skills, such as: ". . . grasping and exploring, crawling and walking, attention and perception, language and thinking, manipulating and changing the surroundings, all of which promote an effective —a competent—interaction with the environment" (White 1959, pp. 317–18). Competence, argues White, is a motivational concept in that (1) the behavior that leads to the acquired ability or skill is directed, selected, and persistent; and (2) because it satisfies an intrinsic need to

deal with the environment. White gives the name "effectance motivation" to the motivational aspect of competence and subsumes under this
term such "drives" or "needs" as curiosity, manipulation, mastery,
achievement, and novelty. For White, effectance motivation is more
persistent than organic drives even though it is not so intense. To
quote White: "Putting it picturesquely, we might say that the effectance urge represents what the neuromuscular system wants to do when
it is otherwise unoccupied or is gently stimulated by the environment"
(p. 321).

ACHIEVEMENT MOTIVATION

Some of Murray's psychogenic needs appear to belong in White's
effectance motivation category, e.g., achievement and construction.
Originally, Murray's need system was advanced as a basis for a program of research. Over the years, however, only a few of Murray's
needs have received extensive research attention. The most extensive
efforts have been directed to Murray's achievement motive. A method
of measuring this motive has been developed by McClelland and his
associates (1953). The procedure is that of showing the subject a series
of four ambiguous pictures and then requiring the subject to write a
story about each picture. For example, one picture in the standard
series is that of an adolescent boy seated in a classroom with a book in
front of him. The boy is looking away from the book. To insure
completeness of plot, four questions are posed to the subject. These
are: "What is happening?" "What has led up to this situation?"
"What is being thought?" "What will happen?" The stories told by
the subject are then scored for "achievement imagery." A carefully
defined scoring system has been worked out in which plus scores are
assigned to statements such as "He is determined to get a good grade."
Eleven categories of need-achievement imagery are delineated—including statements about something done to attain an achievement goal, an
anticipation of successful attainment of a goal, overcoming obstacles,
positive affect attached to an achievement-directed activity, and some
unique accomplishment.

McClelland reports several experiments showing that achievement-
need scores are related to at least some aspects of the achievement
motive. For example, Lowell (1952) divided a group of 40 college
students into two groups on the basis of performance on the achievement motivation test. Following this test, the subjects were given a
20-minute scrambled word test in which they were to find as many
common words as possible from scrambled words such as WTSE (e.g.,

west, stew). The subjects were given a booklet containing ten pages, each containing 24 scrambled words. They were allowed two minutes to work on each page. Table 8–2 reveals that for successive four-minute periods, the high n-achievement students tended to increase their work output, whereas the low n-achievement students tended to remain at their initial performance level.

TABLE 8–2

Mean Output of Scrambled Words per Four-Minute
Periods for High and Low n-Achievement Students

		Four-Minute Periods				
	1	2	3	4	5	Total
High n-achievement						
($n = 19$)	19.6	22.7	23.4	23.1	24.9	113.7
Low n-achievement						
($n = 21$)	19.4	20.2	21.2	20.0	19.9	100.8
Mean difference	0.2	2.5	2.2	3.1	5.0	12.9

Adapted from McClelland *et al.* (1953, p. 230).

Several studies have shown that, on the average, subjects with high need-achievement scores perform better than subjects with low scores when an expectancy is aroused that good performance on an assigned task will be accompanied by a feeling of personal accomplishment (Atkinson and Reitman, 1956). When, however, there is no reason to expect any form of reward for good performance, low need-achievement subjects apparently are motivated just about as much as high need-achievement subjects. A study conducted by French (1955) is illustrative. French used a modified form of McClelland's measure of motivation to identify high and low need-achievement subjects among 90 male students in an Air Force Officer Candidate school. The officer candidates were then divided into three experimental groups with 15 high- and 15 low-scoring need-achievers in each group. Each of the three experimental groups then took a simple digit-letter code test under a different instructional condition. Thus:

Group 1—the "relaxed group": the experimenter merely sought the cooperation of the subjects for his research study.

Group 2—the "task-motivated group": the subjects were told that the test to be given was related to general intelligence, and their performances could affect their future career.

Group 3—the "extrinsically motivated group": the subjects were offered a reward extrinsic to the task, i.e., permission to leave the testing room for the five men making the highest scores.

As shown in Table 8–3, the high need-achievement officer candidates did relatively better when the task to be performed was presented as one of importance to their future careers. For low need-achievement officer candidates, apparently the extrinsic reward of leaving the testing room was the strongest incentive.

TABLE 8–3

Performance Scores of High and Low Need-Achievers on a
Substitution Task Under Three Achievement Motivation Levels

Instructions Designed To Induce Motivation Level		Means and Standard Deviations of Performance Scores	
		High n-Achievement	Low n-Achievement
1. Relaxed	Mean	17.7	15.4
	S.D.	16.6	17.7
2. Task motivation	Mean	29.8	16.7
	S.D.	16.3	14.2
3. Extrinsic-goal motivation	Mean	18.2	22.5
	S.D.	15.5	14.3

Adapted from French (1955).

Whether or not praise motivates a student may depend upon whether the praise received is for something the student considers to be of importance. Praise for working well with others may motivate the student who considers getting along with others to be of great importance. For the student with a strong need to achieve, praise for effective work is more apt to be motivating. An experiment conducted by French (1958) is relevant. French obtained measures for both the need to achieve and the need to affiliate on airmen at Lackland Air Force Base. One part of French's study involved a total of 32 men with high achievement and low affiliation motivation scores. These men were formed into groups of four. A like number of groups were formed of men who scored high in affiliation and low in achievement motivation. Each of the several groups was given the task of piecing together 20 phrases or short sentences into a little story. Each subject was given five cards with one phrase or sentence on each card. The task of the group was to work out the proper order of the cards to form a story. This was to be done wholly through discussion and without showing each other their cards or writing anything down. One-half of the groups (designated as the "Task Feedback" groups) were interrupted from their task by the experimenter when they were halfway through the time allotted. The experimenter praised these groups for their efficiency and drew attention to the good practice they were utilizing, e.g., trying to rough out possible plots and making use of grammatical cues. The remaining groups (designated as the "Feeling" groups) were similarly interrupted. The experimenter praised these groups for how well they were working together and commented upon specific ways in which their behaviors contributed to group harmony, e.g., giving everyone a chance to contribute and praising good suggestions. Following the interruption, the groups continued to work on their stories. The stories of all groups were then scored for completeness and accuracy. The average performance scores for the eight groups included for each experimental condition were as follows:

Achievement-motivated; Task-Feedback	......	M 40.5; Range 36–45
Achievement-motivated; Feeling-Feedback	.....	M 29.3; Range 25–37
Affiliation-motivated; Task-Feedback	....	M 29.1; Range 24–36
Affiliation-motivated; Feeling-Feedback	....	M 38.4; Range 30–45

Thus, the groups of men who were high in *achievement* and low in affiliation motivation tended to perform better when given *task*-relevant feedback, while the men high in *affiliation* and low in achievement motivation tended to perform better when they were praised for the friendly *feelings* they displayed.

Home Background and Achievement Motivation

How is it that some students score high and some low on a test designed to elicit motivation fantasy? Are the differences in the ways children are treated by their families a factor in achievement motivation? Research evidence is beginning to shed some light on the relationship between parent behavior and achievement motivation. Winterbottom (1958) studied the relationship between the strength of *n*-achievement scores of 29 eight-year-old boys and the independent and mastery training these boys received as reported by their mothers. Achievement motivation scores were obtained from the stories told by the boys in response to verbal cues.[1] In an interview, mothers were asked to check from a list of twenty training *demands* the things she wanted her child to learn by the age of ten and the approximate age she thought her child should have learned the behavior. Some of the training demands included in the list were:

To know his way around his part of the city so that he can play where he wants without getting lost

[1] Lowell (1950) first employed the technique of *verbal cues* rather than picture cues to elicit achievement stories. The verbal cues (such as: "A mother and her son—they look worried" and "Brothers and sisters playing—one is a little ahead") served as suggestions for stories. Winterbottom used verbal cues because she found that some young children find it difficult to give imaginatively rich stories to pictures in the four-minute time allotted.

To try hard things for himself without asking for help
To make his own friends among children his own age
To do well in competition with other children; to try hard to come
out on top in games and sports

In addition, the mother responded to a list of 20 training *restrictions;*
e.g., "Not to fight with children to get his own way." Information was
also obtained on the ways in which mothers rewarded "good" behavior
and punished "bad" behavior.

The main results of Winterbottom's study indicate that the mothers
of boys with strong achievement motivation differ from the mothers of
boys with weak achievement motivation in that:

1. They make more demands before the boy reaches the age of
   eight for independent behavior and mastery of tasks. By age
   seven, the mothers of sons with high *n*-achievement expect 60
   per cent of the demands checked to be learned, as compared to
   33 per cent for mothers of sons with low *n*-achievement. By age
   eight, mothers of sons with high *n*-achievement, on the average,
   say they require 11.7 of the 20 listed skills learned, as compared
   to 6.1 skills for mothers of sons with low *n*-achievement—almost
   twice as many.
2. They evaluate their son's accomplishments higher and are more
   rewarding. Mothers of high *n*-achievement sons tended to consider their sons above average in the skills implicit in the list of
   20 demands and reported more physical affection as reward for
   fulfilling demands than mothers of low *n*-achievement boys.
   However, no significant differences were found between the
   mothers of high and low *n*-achievement boys in the use of punishment for unfulfilled demands.
3. The total number of restrictions made through age seven is
   greater, but the total number of restrictions made through age
   ten is less. Mothers of sons with high *n*-achievement apparently
   stress early independent achievement. The child is urged to
   master a skill early (e.g., "to know his way around the city"), is
   restricted until he does (e.g., "not to play around the home"),
   and then is left alone.
4. The number of demands they make through age seven exceeds
   the number of restrictions.

The average number of demands and restrictions required below and
above age eight by mothers of boys with high and low *n*-achievement
scores are shown in Table 8–4.

Utilizing behavioral rating scales as a means of appraising achievement motivation level, Crandall and his associates have embarked on a

TABLE 8-4

Average Number of Demands and Restrictions by Mothers of High and Low n-Achievement Boys

	Mothers' Demands		Mothers' Restrictions	
	Age Seven and Below	Age Eight and Above	Age Seven and Below	Age Eight and Above
Sons with high n-achievement	11.7	7.4	8.8	4.5
Sons with low n-achievement	6.1	12.1	5.8	9.6

Adapted from McClelland *et al.* (1953).

series of studies of children from ages three to eight. Crandall, Preston, and Rabson (1960) found that the amount of achievement effort shown in free activity in nursery school is greater for children whose mothers reward approval seeking and achievement efforts. For these age levels (three to five), independence training was not found to be related to achievement effort.

McClelland *et al.* (1953) found that high n-achievement male college students tend to perceive their fathers as unfriendly and unhelpful more so than low n-achievement college students. Yet the reverse is true for boys in high school. High n-achievement high school boys perceive their fathers the same as those with low n-achievement. There are a number of possible explanations for this reversal. First, we should remember that a boy's perceptions of his father's behavior need not be reliable. The high n-achievement college student may be trying to establish his own independence, and his father's efforts to help him may be misconstrued as unfriendly interference. The low n-achievement college student may be happy to remain dependent upon his parents.

Rosen and D'Andrade (1959) studied parents' behavior while watching their sons attempt to solve problems provided by the experimenters. Mothers of high n-achievement boys became highly involved, set high expectations of excellence, met good performance with warmth, and poor performance with disapproval. The fathers of high n-achievement boys put less pressure on their sons than did fathers of low n-achievement boys. Strodtbeck (1958) also found higher achievement motivation where the mother who subscribed to achievement values dominated the home. Kagan and Moss (1959) have also provided data pointing to the relationship of the mother's behavior to achievement fantasy. Early maternal concern with achievement increased both achievement fantasy and I.Q. gain in girls.

Social Class and Achievement Motivation

Rosen (1958) in a study of 120 high school sophomore boys from two large public high schools in Connecticut found a relationship between n-achievement scores and the socioeconomic status of the boys' parents. Rosen's group was stratified into five socioeconomic classes on the basis of the occupation, education, and residence of the major wage earner in the family. The highest status group was labeled "Class I"; the lowest, "Class V." Achievement motivation was measured by McClelland's method of eliciting achievement imagery stories from pictures. The boys' stories were then scored, and the boys scoring above the median in achievement imagery were treated as high need-achievers and those below the median, as low need-achievers. The percentages of boys classified as high need-achievers from the various socioeconomic levels were found to be as follows:

Classes I and II ($n = 30$) 83%
Class III   ($n = 30$) 43%
Class IV   ($n = 30$) 30%
Class V   ($n = 30$) 23%

Rosen also administered a "value orientation" inventory in order to identify the boys who held values that were conducive to getting ahead in our society. Achievement-oriented values were defined as those that reflected:

1. The idea that it is possible to manipulate one's physical and social environment so as to attain one's life goals
                    rather than
the idea that "when a man is born the success he is going to have is in the cards."

2. The idea that planning and sacrifice are worthwhile in order to obtain future gain
                    rather than
the idea of enjoying the present and letting the future take care of itself.

3. The idea that one must be individualistically oriented in one's outlook of life even to the extent of being willing to move away from one's family in order to achieve life goals
                    rather than
the idea that "nothing in life is worth the sacrifice of moving away from your parents."

A scale of 14 items was constructed that reflected the several values implicit in the above "ideas." This scale was administered to all 120 boys, and each boy indicated his agreement or disagreement to each

statement. The scale was then scored for achievement value orientation. Scores above the median were designated as High Achievement
value scores. The percentages of boys from each socioeconomic class
obtaining High Achievement value scores were:

Classes I and II 77%
Class III 70%
Class IV 33%
Class V 17%

Douvan (1956) has provided research data showing that lower class
children vary from situation to situation in achievement motivation,
whereas middle class children's achievement motivation tends to remain the same at least in school-like situations. The teacher, therefore,
usually is confronted with a more difficult task in motivating lower class
children to work hard at their school work.

Learning Exercises

7. White (1959), in discussing an experiment involving exploratory behavior, states: "Such behavior can be most readily conceptualized by
   admitting that under certain circumstances reinforcement can be correlated with an increase in arousal or excitement rather than a decrease"
   (p. 301). Which of the following may be classified as "stimulus-increase"
   motives?

   (a) Curiosity   (d) Hunger
   (b) Anxiety   (e) Effectance
   (c) Mastery

8. In Lowell's Scrambled Word Task, the high n-achievement group
   showed a mean gain in output from the first to the last four-minute
   period of 5.32 words (S.D. = 3.89), while the low n-achievement groups
   showed a gain of only 0.43 (S.D. = 4.81).

   From the above data, does it appear that one or more of the low
   group made a greater gain in output than one or more of the high group?
   (Note the standard deviations for each group.)

9. On the basis of the data presented in Table 8–3, why would you say that
   it is *not* safe to assume that all people who obtain a high n-achievement
   score will be motivated to good performance when given a task that is
   worthwhile performing?

10. What does French's study (re task and feeling feedback) suggest for the
    classroom teacher who is trying to motivate pupils?

11. Two restrictions included in Winterbottom's list were: "Not to leave
    clothes around or untidy," and "Not to be sloppy at the table." No
    significantly different numbers of mothers of high and low n-achieving
    sons reported these two restrictions for age eight or above; but at age

seven and below, the difference is significant. Based on Table 8–4, would you expect more mothers of the high than of the low *n*-achievement boys to make these restrictions for their sons at age seven or below?

12. In what respect is there a difference between the research findings of Winterbottom and Crandall *et al.*?

13. Assuming that high *n*-achievement is necessary in order to climb the socioeconomic ladder, would you expect most children from Class V homes to raise their status?

SOCIAL MOTIVES AND INCENTIVES

The social environment is an important source of many motives. Goals are set in a social context. Significant others spur on an individual to achieve goals or restrain him from acting in a disapproved manner. In this section, some of the influences on motivation of the social environment will be considered.

Praise and Reproof

Can a teacher motivate a child better through praise or through reproof? No simple answer to this question is possible. The relative effectiveness of praise and reproof varies with the personality of both teacher and child as well as the degree of original motivation of the child and the total social setting.

In an early experiment, Hurlock (1924, 1925) compared the effects of praise and reproof on 106 fourth- and fifth-grade pupils. The children were divided on the first day of the experiment into four equivalent groups on the basis of their performance on a simple addition test. Similar 15-minute tests were then given on four more days. The four groups took the test under different motivational conditions. Children in a *control* group, placed in a separate room, were given no information on how well they had performed on the previous day's test. On each of the final four testing sessions, the children in the *praised* group were named and commended for the excellence of their work the previous day and were urged to continue the good work. Children in the *reproved* group were also named and scolded for their poor work, careless mistakes, and failure to improve. Whether a child received praise or reproof depended upon the groups to which he was assigned —not upon his actual performance. The children in the *ignored* group received neither favorable nor unfavorable recognition, although they did hear other children praised or reproved.

On the second day of the experiment, both the praised and the reproved groups did better than the other two groups; but on subsequent
days, the performance of the reproved group declined. At the end of
the experiment, the praised group was significantly better than all other
groups. Other differences between groups were not highly significant
(see Fig. 8–1).

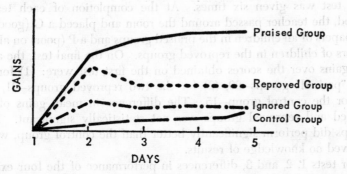

Fig. 8–1. Gains in Average Scores on Arithmetic Tests Under Different Motivating Conditions. (Adapted from Hurlock, 1925.)

Reproof does not always lower motivation. Nor does praise always
increase motivation. Rosenfeld and Zander (1961) obtained data from
a questionnaire given to 400 boys in the tenth grade. Part of the results
of this study parallel those of Hurlock's. Students tend to ignore or
oppose a teacher's influence when they receive disapproval for adequate performance and tend to be amenable to a teacher's influence
when rewarded for good performance. But the results of the study
indicate that disapproval for inadequate performance does not seem to
lower motivation. Nor does indiscriminate reward given regardless of
the adequacy of the performance increase motivation.

A study made by Thompson and Hunnicutt (1944) provides evidence
that the relative effectiveness of praise and reproof is dependent on
personality factors. Fifth-grade pupils were given a personality test
that yielded introversion-extroversion scores. Two groups of introverts
and two groups of extroverts were formed. Praise was given to the
children in one of the groups of extroverts and one of the groups of
introverts for their performance on a number cancellation test. Reproof was given to the children in the other introvert and extrovert
groups. Children in another *control* group were given neither praise
nor reproof. Thus, in effect, five groups of children were formed:

1. Introvert-praised group
2. Extrovert-praised group

3. Introvert-reproved group
4. Extrovert-reproved group
5. Control group

The test given to the children in each of the five groups consisted of a long series of random numbers, e.g., 8740237657 . . . The task of the children was to see how many 7's they could cross out in 30 seconds. This test was given six times. At the completion of each testing period, the teacher passed around the room and placed a G (good) on the papers of all children in the praised groups and a P (poor) on all the papers of children in the reproved groups. On the final test, the average gains over the scores obtained on the first test were: (1) for the two "praised" groups—20, (2) for the two reproved groups—21, and (3) for the control group—15. The difference in mean gains of the praised and reproved groups was not statistically significant. Both groups did perform significantly better than the control group, which received no knowledge of results.

For tests 1, 2, and 3, differences in performance of the four experimental groups were not statistically significant. However, for tests 4, 5, and 6, the cumulative effect of praise and reproof began to result in clear-cut differences in the performances of the four groups. The pupils classified as extroverts, i.e., confident, outgoing pupils, who received reproof did significantly better than the extroverts receiving praise. Criticism spurred these pupils on to greater efforts. The opposite was true for the less-confident, retiring introvert pupils. The introvert pupils receiving praise performed significantly better than the introvert pupils receiving reproof. Encouragement for the non-confident pupil increased his work output.

Reward and Punishment

Reward. What constitutes reward varies from person to person. In the classroom, reward often takes the form of various recognitions of achievement: grades, prizes, stars, and so forth. Rewards may also take the form of privileges or being excused from distasteful tasks. Social rewards take the form of approval, acceptance, or affection from others. A reward is typically pleasant and satisfying.

Punishment too may take a variety of forms. Physical punishments, withdrawal of privileges, the assignment of unpleasant tasks, and withdrawal of affection are inflicted by parents, teachers, and other authoritative figures to show disapproval of a behavior and to prevent its recurrence in the future. Punishments are typically unpleasant and sometimes even painful.

In assessing the value of rewards in fostering learning, it is useful to distinguish between extrinsic and intrinsic rewards. Rewards are *extrinsic* to the extent that they bear an artificial relationship to the learning to be achieved. A money prize for obtaining an A grade, or even the A grade as the reward attained through long unenjoyable hours of study with no further satisfaction derived from the course material learned are examples of extrinsic reward. *Intrinsic* rewards, on the other hand, are more closely related to the task performed. The reward of satisfaction from taking good pictures following the study of photography and the enjoyment of dancing after learning to dance are examples of intrinsic rewards.

Extrinsic rewards are effective. A multitude of reinforcement learning studies attest to the effectiveness of rewards in fostering learning. But unfortunate by-products may accrue when the rewards for learning are totally extrinsic to the learning to be achieved. Money prizes and grades as rewards for learning may interfere with a student experiencing the simple joy of learning. Something is amiss when a major in English on completion of her degree requirements remarks: "Thank God that's over. I'll never read another book again." Harlow (1953) reports a study in which monkeys persisted in solving certain kinds of manipulative puzzles even when not receiving a food reward for solutions, while monkeys that were given a food reward ceased their manipulation of the puzzles once they had obtained their reward. An extrinsic reward can interfere with a potential intrinsic reward.

Punishment. It is commonly believed that punishment is a necessary ingredient to good upbringing of children and that the absence of punishment results in unruly behavior. By *punishment* is meant some painful or unpleasant stimulation inflicted intentionally upon another. Often, punishment is administered to show disapproval of a behavior and to prevent its recurrence in the future. For a child, punishment may consist of spanking, verbal reproof or correction, deprivation of something wanted, or ridicule. Punishment and the threat of punishment are techniques employed by parents and teachers in order to control the behavior of children.

For many years, psychologists have been interested in studying the effectiveness of punishment as a means of controlling behavior. Much of the research and thinking has been influenced by the views of the late E. L. Thorndike. As a result of a number of experiments on both animals and humans, Thorndike reached the conclusion that punishment was not an effective means of weakening a response tendency. In one experiment, Thorndike (1932) gave a multiple choice Spanish vocabulary test to students who were unfamiliar with Spanish. For each Spanish word in the test, five English words were suggested. If the student guessed the correct response, the experimenter said "Right" (reward). If the student guessed the incorrect alternative, the experimenter said "Wrong" (punishment). On a later testing, it was possible to see if students provided the rewarded or the punished responses more frequently than might be expected on the basis of chance. Thorndike found that the effect of saying "right" apparently did increase the response tendency to repeat the initially given response. The effect of saying "wrong" rather than weakening actually had a small strengthening effect. Although there has been some criticisms of Thorndike's experimental methods in his work on punishment (Stephens, 1934), later experimentation has continued to cast doubts on the effectiveness of punishment as a means of controlling behavior.

Estes (1944), in a series of experiments, investigated the effect of punishment on the bar-pressing response of rats in a Skinner box. First, rats learned the bar-pressing response in order to get food. Then one group of rats was sometimes given an electric shock for pressing the bar, while another group was never shocked. When both positive and negative reinforcements were omitted, both groups persisted in pressing the bar. The punished rats pressed the bar less frequently at first, but soon were pressing it just as frequently as the non-punished rats. Punishment apparently temporarily weakened the bar-pressing response, but did not eliminate it.

The fact that punishment only temporarily weakens a behavior tendency does not mean that punishment has no value. It means rather that punishment alone is not enough. During the interval when the undesired behavior tendency is weakened, a parent or teacher has the opportunity to teach the correct behavior. Then, when the undesired behavior tendency does return to full strength, the desired behavior tendency may, by that time, be of greater strength than the undesired behavior tendency.

Punishment is of value too when it is an inevitable and immediate but unexpected consequence of an act. A child who touches a hot stove does not strive to touch the stove again. But this is quite different from punishment by a mother for stealing a cookie. Here, rewarding consequences are possible if the child can escape detection.

Punishment may be informative. The corrections on a student's composition paper may be considered as punishment in that they constitute criticisms and lower the student's grade. But they also are informative to the student who wants to do well. The corrections tell the student what he has to do in order to achieve one of his goals. The teacher, however, needs to proceed with some caution in providing this punishing information. Children, like adults, can learn to hate an activity that results only in criticism. Paul Diederich, director of research in English for the Educational Testing Service, advises teachers who grade English themes to first find one thing, and preferably two or three things, that the student has done well or better than before; and then, if they must, find one thing, and preferably not more than one thing, that the student should try to improve on his next paper. This advice is consistent with the research finding of Stevenson, Weir, and Zigler (1959) who found that *mild* punishment resulted in improved performance by calling attention to incorrect responses that otherwise might be ignored.

Symonds (1949, pp. 108–10) has suggested the following additional positive values of punishment:

1. Punishment may be used in order to guard a child against impending danger. Punishment does temporarily deter the child and sometimes this temporary deterrent may save the life of the child. While a child may be trained in time to stay off a busy street without benefit of punishment, a parent may feel that he cannot afford this lengthy training period. Once is too often for a child to be run over by a car.

2. Punishment by a loving parent for unsocial behavior may be a way through which the child internalizes the social values of the parent. Through a process of identification, the child's superego develops. According to psychoanalytic theory, the child is first restrained from behaving in an antisocial manner by his parents, but eventually these external restraints become internalized and the superego becomes the punishing agent.

3. Punishment may have value in reducing feelings of guilt. The child knowing he has done wrong suffers. The tension created can only be relieved by external punishment.

4. To punish a child may be the lesser of two evils. The annoyed parent or teacher may continue his resentment over a long period. Possibly a venting of the resentment may be less damaging than the subdued warfare.

Having stated a case for punishment, we return now to some of its limitations in motivating behavior.

Severe punishment may have extremely injurious effects upon a child. Experiments with animals (e.g., Solomon and Wynne, 1954) have demonstrated that the emotional learning (fear and anxiety) produced by traumatic shocks is extraordinarily resistant to extinction. Masserman (1943) among others has produced neurotic behavior in animals through punishment. Clinical cases of humans indicate a comparable debilitating effect of traumatic punishment. No case can be built from the psychological literature to justify extremely severe physical punishment.

The effects of punishment are more variable and hence more difficult to predict than the effects of reward. Punishment may even be rewarding if the punished response becomes associated with some reward (Lohr, 1959). The parent or teacher who lavishes attention on a child after he has punished him runs the risk of having the child seek punishment. The boy, who learns that corporal punishment from his teacher is followed by admiration from his classmates, may seek corporal punishment.

Another reason why punishment leads to more variable behavior is that reward provides more complete information to the behaver than punishment. Reward tells a person what to do in order to gain satisfaction. Punishment tells only what not to do. After punishment, a person may still make wrong responses before discovering the rewarded response.

Learning Exercises

14. Which of the following statements are consistent with the findings of the three research studies reported on praise and reproof?
    (a) When a child practices a school task on successive days, criticism of his poor performance on the first day is likely to lead to poorer performance on the second day.
    (b) A child who has performed very poorly will strive to do better if he is praised for his poor performance.
    (c) Children confident of their own abilities are more apt to be motivated by reproof than children who lack confidence.
15. In which of the following is John's reward extrinsic?
    (a) John works hard at chemistry because he likes chemistry.
    (b) John plays golf because he likes to associate with his golf-playing friends.
16. Bob habitually copied his homework from other students. One day he was caught and punished by his teacher. On the basis of Estes' experiments, what prediction would you make about Bob's copying behavior:
    (a) Immediately after his punishment?
    (b) After completing a few homework assignments independently, each of which was graded as "unsatisfactory"?
17. Which of the three experiments reported in the section on "Praise and Reproof" support Diederich's advice on grading English themes?
18. From which of the following incidents would you expect the punishment described to have positive values?

(a) A boy, age twelve, habitually steals and sees nothing wrong in his behavior. One day he is caught stealing by his father (whom he does not respect) and is given a severe beating.

(b) Tom is ashamed of his unsportsmanlike conduct on the football field. His coach expresses disappointment and suspends him from the team for two weeks.

(c) Mary's loving mother expresses disapproval when Mary, age four, strikes her little brother.

Level of Aspiration

Success is said to breed success, and failure to breed failure. But success and failure cannot be objectively defined. What is success for one person may be failure for another. One student is disappointed to obtain a B in a course; another student is happy to get a C. What constitutes success or failure for a person depends upon his level of aspiration. The term "level of aspiration" refers to a standard by which a person judges his own performance as a success or a failure.

Why does one person set higher goals than another person? Put another way, what are the determinants of a person's level of aspiration? Lewin *et al.* (1944) have reviewed a number of experimental studies relevant to this question. In order to test the experimental findings in everyday life situations, Child and Whiting (1949) asked each of the 151 undergraduate men in an eastern university to write a description of three incidents in his life: (1) one involving complete frustration in which he never reached his goal, (2) one in which a period of frustration was followed by goal attainment, and (3) one of simple goal attainment without appreciable frustration. After writing the descriptions, each student filled out a questionnaire designed to get at the effects of each incident on his level of aspiration. Child and Whiting's results along with other experimental findings will be discussed under each of five generalizations that have been drawn primarily from Lewin's review.

1. *Success leads to a raising of the level of aspiration, and failure to a lowering* (Lewin *et al.* 1944, p. 337). This generalization is based on a number of research studies (e.g., Jucknat, 1937; Sears, 1940; Levin and Baldwin, 1958). Child and Whiting's data also bear out this generalization as indicated in Table 8–5.

2. *Failure is more likely than success to lead to withdrawal in the form of avoidance of setting a level of aspiration* (Lewin *et al.*, 1944, p. 340). Child and Whiting's data are only indirectly relevant to this generalization, although it may be noted in Table 8–5 that more than twice as many students reported no effect on level of aspiration for

incidents of complete frustration than for either of the other types of incidents.

That failure leads to a lessening of interest in an activity has been demonstrated in a number of studies (Gebhard, 1948; Sears and Levin, 1956; Israel, 1960).

TABLE 8–5

Shifts in Level of Aspiration Produced by
Each of Three Types of Incidents

Type of Incident	Percentage Shift in Level of Aspiration			
	N	Lowering	None	Rise
Complete frustration	140	47%	26%	27%
Frustration followed by goal attainment	125	12%	12%	76%
Simple goal attainment	141	2%	12%	86%

Adapted from Child and Whiting (1949).

3. *Effects of failure on level of aspiration are more varied than those of success.* In an experiment conducted by Sears (1940), the goal-setting characteristics of fourth- to sixth-grade pupils who were successful in school were compared to those of pupils who were unsuccessful. The pupils were given a number of tests in which they were asked to supply synonyms to simple words. After each test, each child was given his score and asked to tell what score he was going to try to get on his next trial. Successful pupils tended to set a goal slightly above their previous scores. Unsuccessful pupils tended to set a goal either well above or below their previous scores. Pupils who were successful in one subject but unsuccessful in another subject were found to set realistic goals in their successful subject but unrealistic goals (either much higher or much lower than previous performance) in their weak subject.

Child and Whiting's data indicate that most students reporting an incident of simple goal attainment and frustration followed by goal attainment raised their level of aspiration. The effects on level of aspiration of complete frustration were more varied. (See Table 8–5.)

4. *The stronger the success, the greater the probability of a rise in the level of aspiration; the stronger the failure, the greater the probability of a lowering* (Lewin et al., 1944, p. 338). This generalization is based on an experiment conducted by Jucknat (1937). A group of 500 eleven-year-old children were given a series of puzzles to solve; and after trying a puzzle, the child was asked to tell how rapidly he thought he could do the next puzzle. Some of the puzzles were easy so that the

children could succeed; others were insolvable, thus insuring failure. Jucknat distinguished different intensities of the feeling of success and failure. The children raised their level of aspiration much more frequently after success with a previous problem than after failure. The greater the strength of the success feeling, the larger the percentage of children who raised their aspiration level; and the greater degree of concern over failure, the smaller the percentage of children who raised their aspiration level. The findings in a more recent experiment by Martire (1956) are consistent with those of Jucknat's. Martire, investigating the relationship between level of aspiration and achievement motivation, found no general relationship. He did find, however, that students with strong achievement needs, and who were anxious about failure in a stressful achievement situation, had a significantly lower level of aspiration than other students. Child and Whiting's data, also tend to support the generalization. Upward shifts in level of aspiration occurred more frequently for success incidents where the goal to be attained was rated as important by the students. More negative shifts in level of aspiration occurred as a result of a failure incident when the goal was rated as important than when the goal was rated as of low importance. However, this effect of strength of failure was not statistically significant.

5. *Shifts in level of aspiration are in part a function of changes in the subject's confidence in his ability to attain goals.* Child and Whiting's data support this generalization. After each description of an incident, a student was questioned as to the effect of the outcome of the incident on both his confidence and his level of aspiration. For incidents involving an equal degree of success, students who reported the incident as raising their confidence tended also to report a rise in their level of confidence to attain similar future goals. Apparently whether or not a success experience results in raising the level of aspiration depends in part upon the effect of the success upon a person's confidence. One success or one failure does not necessarily change a person's confidence. However, once the confidence of a person has been built up, a raising of the level of aspiration may be expected to follow.

The effects of success and failure upon level of aspiration take on added significance during a period of history when social forces are pressuring schools to emphasize academic achievement. On this point, Travers (1963) writes:

In an age when the emphasis in education is upon the striving for excellence, whatever produces a gross lowering of the level of aspiration does not have a place in education, except under unusual circumstances. Any

dramatic failure may have this effect, and hence such failures should surely
be avoided, unless there is some really significant reason why the level of
aspiration should be lowered. [P. 171.]

Group Influences

The motivation of a student is often influenced by the group to
which he belongs. In Chapter 3, we noted, from studies of the social
structure of high schools (Gordon, 1957; Coleman, 1961), the importance to the adolescent of achieving social status among his peers.
Social goals were seemingly more important than academic goals.

Research studies conducted by Stern and others (e.g., Stern, Stein,
and Bloom, 1956; Stern, 1962; Pace and Stern, 1958; Thistlethwaite,
1959, 1962) suggest that personality variables and additional environmental forces need to be considered in evaluating the total impact of
the environment on the motivation of the college student.

For Stern, predicting performance in a particular role requires an
examination of the relationship between (1) the *presses* or the real and
felt demands of the situation, including the expectancies of others with
respect to role fulfillment; and (2) the *needs* or personality characteristics of the behaver that are relevant to the effective functioning of
the role (Stern, Stein, and Bloom, 1956). The demands of the situation
may be thought of as environmental *presses*. For presses to become
internalized, they must be compatible to the individual's needs. This
means, for example, that a person with a need for independence is more
likely to function effectively in a role in which he is expected to make
independent decisions than would a person with strong dependency
needs.

Stern (1958) has developed a needs inventory, called the *Activities
Index,* which is made up of 30 scales of 10 items each, with each scale
corresponding to one of the 30 needs listed by Murray (1938). A test
with 300 parallel items for identifying presses in a college environment,
called the *College Characteristics Index,* was subsequently constructed.
Pace and Stern (1958) illustrate the parallelism by quoting sample
items from corresponding Need and Press scales, thus:

A need for Order would be inferred from liking such activities as: "Arranging my clothes neatly before going to bed. Having a special place for
everything and seeing that everything is in its place. Keeping a calendar or
notebook of the things I have done or plan to do." What might such a
person like to find in a college environment or what features of a college
environment might be rewarding to such a need? The following items from
the Press scale for Order might be relevant: Faculty members and administration have definite and clearly posted office hours. In many classes stu-

dents have an assigned seat. Professors usually take attendance in class. [Pp. 270–71.]

Stern (1962) reports striking differences in the need and press characteristics between a representative sample of 32 American colleges. For example, 80 per cent of the 460 respondents from seven private liberal arts programs said it was *true* that "students are encouraged to criticize administrative policies and teaching practices"; 92 per cent of the 156 students from three business administrative programs said this was *false* at their colleges. Differences among colleges with respect to both the needs of the students and the environmental presses were found along three major dimensions: (1) dependency needs vs. autonomy; (2) emotional expression vs. control; and (3) intellectuality.

The following brief extracts from Stern's more detailed descriptions of a small liberal arts college for women and a women's denominational college may serve to illustrate points of similarity and differences in the needs of students and the presses prevailing in different colleges (Stern, 1962, pp. 719–23).

A Liberal Arts College

INTELLECTUALITY

Student Needs: "These students all like work that requires intense intellectual effort. They are as interested in doing experiments in the natural sciences as they are in the works of painters and sculptors. . . ." (P. 719.)

School Press: ". . . Long serious intellectual discussions are common here. . . . There is also much concern with values. . . . It [the school] has an excellent reputation for academic freedom. . . . Most courses are a real intellectual challenge. . . ." (P. 720.)

DEPENDENCY

Student Needs: "These students like striving for precision and clarity in their speech and writings, but they reject other external restric-

A Denominational College

". . . They are also interested in understanding themselves and others better. They are curious about the arts, and about the social problems and would like to play a part in community affairs. They set very high standards for themselves and work hard to achieve them. . . ." (P. 721.)

". . . Many students are concerned with developing their own personal and private system of values, and they also develop a strong sense of social and political responsibility. . . . Students set high standards for themselves. . . ." (P. 722.)

". . . These girls like following directions, particularly from an older person who will give them guidance and advice from his

A Liberal Arts College

tions on their conduct such as implied in going to parties where all activities are planned, shining their shoes or brushing their clothes each day, or working for someone who always tells them what to do and how to do it. . . ." (P. 720.)

School Press: ". . . Students are encouraged to be independent and individualistic, and there is a high degree of respect for Nonconformity and intellectual freedom; students are encouraged in many ways to criticize administrative policies and teaching practices. . . ." (Pp. 720–21.)

IMPULSE EXPRESSION

Student Needs: "These girls like doing whatever they are in the mood to do, without much deliberation. . . ." (P. 720.)

School Press: ". . . There are no social formalities or privileges here: there is no emphasis on tradition, proper social forms or manners, grooming, or various kinds of gracious living. . . ." (P. 721.)

A Denominational College

own experience. They would like to direct other people's work, but they want others to offer their opinions when they have to make a decision. . . ." (Pp. 721–22.)

"The girls quickly learn what is done and not done on the campus. Their needs for order and organization are re-enforced in the classrooms, where the course purposes are explained clearly, the presentation is well planned, assignments are clear and specific. . . . Student organizations are closely supervised. . . . The school helps everyone to get acquainted. . . ." (Pp. 722–23.)

"The girls here like being efficient and successful in practical things. . . . Although they like doing something crazy occasionally, like rearranging the furniture, they prefer routine and regularity. . . ." (P. 722.)

". . . Students generally show a good deal of caution and self-control in their behavior and there are few expressions of strong feelings or disruptiveness. . . ." (P. 723.)

The needs and presses of both institutions differ from that of a state university located in a small southern city. Students' responses on the Activities Index revealed few items concerned with intellectuality or dependency needs. In contrast to the two women's colleges, the students are rather critical of the faculty. The most important relationships appear to be between the students themselves. On impulse expression for this institution, Stern writes:

. . . They all agree that there is much to do at this school besides going to classes and studying. Every year there are carnivals, parades, and other festive events on campus. There are many fraternities and sororities, and receptions, teas, and formal dances occur frequently. Students give much thought to dressing appropriately. . . . [Stern, 1962, p. 725.]

The environmental presses on students in different elementary and high schools possibly vary as widely as those in different colleges, although comparable research evidence is lacking. Stern (1961) did find that the descriptions of high school press of freshmen in the same college but with different school backgrounds differed significantly.

In part, the environmental press within a school is a resultant of administrative and instructional policies and procedures and is therefore modifiable. There is some evidence that suggests that giving students social recognition for outstanding academic performance increases their motivation to attend college (Thistlethwaite, 1959). At the college level, Thistlethwaite (1962) has found that teachers who exert a press for *independence* tend to motivate men students in the social sciences and the humanities to seek advanced academic training. A press for independence is attained through such things as providing facilities and opportunities for creative activity, encouraging students to undertake independent projects, and emphasis on critical judgment even though it leads the student to conclusions contrary to those of his teacher.

Learning Exercises

19. In the section on "level of aspiration," five generalizations are listed. Which generalizations are illustrated in the following incident?

    At the beginning of a course in mathematics, Ada expected to earn an A grade in the course; Beth expected a C. Both girls earned a B on the mid-semester test. Ada was very disappointed; Beth was surprised but delighted. Ada lost and Beth gained confidence. Both girls now aspired to earn a B on the course.

20. Which of the following illustrates a *need,* and which illustrates a *press?*
    (a) At College A, a student can win respect from his peers by being able to discuss art and music intelligently.
    (b) At College B, Jean follows her high school pattern of behavior in that she strives to become a campus social leader.

SUMMARY

Two major conceptions of the motivational process have been examined in this chapter. We can think of the organism responding to external and internal stimuli in such a way as to maintain its equilibrium. The drive-reduction theory of motivation fits into this conception of motivation. The hunger drive serves as a model. Food deprivation results in a tissue deficiency that results in the drive state, and the organism is activated until the tissue deficiency is corrected. Primary drives can be identified as hunger, thirst, sex, elimination, and so forth. Through conditioning, other secondary drives are formed, such as fear, anxiety, and such things as the needs for affection, affiliation, and independence. A second conception of the motivational process views the organism as stimulated by the environment and as striving to act on the environment, often in ways that increase the environment's stimulation or excitement value. We seek mild excitement. We avoid monotony. The exploration and curiosity drives and the needs to master, to deal effectively with the environment, and to seek the novel—all fit into this second conception of motivation. According to Woodworth's *behavior-primacy* theory and White's competency theory, this second class of motives is of greater importance than our drive-reducing motives. The intense drive-reducing motives periodically interrupt the organism from its major business, i.e., the task of mastering the environment.

When we think of motivation as a process of purposeful planning, attention is focused on the intentional goal-seeking behavior of the individual. An individual's behavior is directed toward the achievement of multiple goals, some immediate and some distant. Goals may be programmed into a *plan* of action. The individual uses an over-all strategy in implementing his plan and specific tactics in achieving the more detailed aspects of the plan. The strategy and tactics used are a reflection or image of the individual's total accumulated, organized knowledge of himself and his world; and the execution of the plan involves a constant checking of the operations performed against the requirements of the image.

Some differences in performance of school children may be attributable to differences in achievement motivation. There is some evidence that people with a strong need to achieve, as measured by a projective technique, are motivated when they perceive a task as important; while individuals of low need achievement are motivated more by extrinsic rewards. Getting the job done well is reinforcing to the high need-achievers, whereas persons who have stronger need to affiliate are reinforced more by good interpersonal relationships. There is some evidence that the home background of the child is related to the strength of his need to achieve.

The social environment is a source of many motives. Praise is usually more motivating than reproof, although the confident individual may be motivated by criticism. Reward is usually more motivating than punishment. Punishment temporarily weakens rather than eliminates a response pattern. Punishment may under certain circumstances have positive value; but it may also have injurious effects, particularly if it is severe. Success and failure affect motivation. However, success and failure can only be meaningfully defined in terms of the level of aspiration of the individual.

Each group of individuals builds up a system of norms, i.e., ways they expect other members of the group to behave. These norms influence an individual's goals. To understand the motivation of school and college students, it is helpful to understand the environmental presses of the school or college.

Answer Cues

1. (a) The acquired drive, "fear," is associated with the primary drive, "escape from pain." (c) also fits—the tokens are secondary reinforcers. (b) and (d) do not fit. While it is possible to conceive of an exploratory drive, the physiological accompaniments of such a drive are not clear. And the need to seek variety does not seem to result in tension-reduction behavior.

2. John perceives himself as an A student in mathematics but does not perceive himself as a good student in French. Good performance in mathematics, but not good performance in French, contributes to John's sense of adequacy.

3. Maslow's. Belongingness needs would take precedence over esteem and self-actualization needs.

4. (a) Superiority. (b) Exhibition. (c) Achievement. (d) Autonomy. (e) Nurturance. (f) Aggression.

5. Functional autonomy.

6. (a) More immediate goal. (b) Distant goal. (c) Plan. (d) Image.

7. (a), (c), (e).

8. Yes. If the mean gains for both groups are distributed normally, then the gains for about two-thirds of the high group are 5.32 ± 3.89; and for the low group, 0.43 ± 4.81. Clearly, there is some overlap in the two distributions. (See Appendix.)

9. Several reasons. Table 8–3 does not provide data on a representative sample of *all* people. From the size of the standard deviations, it is clear that some officer candidates who scored low on n-achievement outperformed some candidates who scored high under "task motivation" conditions. Table 8–3 does provide evidence that *on the average*, the sample of the officer candidates in the high group outperformed those in the low group.

10. That some pupils may be motivated by feedback concerning the effectiveness of their achievement-directed activities, while other pupils may be motivated more by feedback concerning their skills in getting along well with others.

11. Mothers of high *n*-achievement boys.

12. With respect to independence training. Winterbottom found a relationship between the mothers' training for independence and *n*-achievement of the eight-year-old boys; Crandall *et al.* did not find such a relationship for their nursery school children.

13. No. In Rosen's study, only 23 per cent of the Class V boys were high *n*-achievers.

14. Only statement (c) is consistent.

15. (b).

16. (a) Decrease in copying behavior.   (b) A return to copying behavior.

17. Hurlock's, in that praise tends to increase motivation more than reproof; but most clearly Rosenfeld and Zander support Diederich's advice, i.e., good performance rewarded and poor performance criticized.

18. (b) Reducing feeling of guilt.   (c) Superego development.

19. Generalizations 1, 4, and 5.

20. (a) Press.   (b) Need.

9

TRANSFER, PERCEPTION, AND RETENTION

It is generally recognized that the past experience of a person influences his present behavior. Yet sometimes we find that a student is not able to cope with a learning task even though he appears to have all the necessary background experience. Past experience is not always utilized effectively in dealing with a learning task. Under what circumstances can we expect some previously established learning to affect performance on some new learning task? How similar do the two learning tasks have to be? This is the problem of *transfer of training*—the major concern in this chapter. As we examine this educationally important problem, we shall see that in order for transfer to take place, the learner must perceive in his present learning task the relevancy of his past learning. Therefore, we will also examine in this chapter the topic *perception*. Finally, to understand the problem of transfer, we will need to discuss the topic *retention,* because a child may fail in a present learning task merely because he has forgotten some important bit of information.

TRANSFER

In teaching, we try to organize learning experiences so that the learning from a first experience facilitates learning in a second learning task. We also try to provide learning experiences in the school that will transfer to out-of-school situations. In the final analysis, a program of formal education can best be justified if it can be shown that school learning has some beneficial effects on the out-of-school behavior of the learner. English courses, designed to develop literary appreciation, may be justified in terms of the quantity and quality of the reading of students after they leave school. Courses in social studies are expected to have some influence on the ways the student later discharges his civic responsibilities. Mathematical skills developed in schools are expected to enable the student to deal effectively with mathematical problems encountered in everyday life. It is true that we expect the education obtained in school to be of some immediate value. But its immediate value is its contribution to an on-going developmental process. Hence, customarily, we expect the training obtained in school to transfer to a wide variety of out-of-school situations.

The importance to educators of understanding how transfer of training occurs is apparent when we examine McGeoch and Irion's definition and discussion of the term.

Transfer of training occurs whenever the existence of a previously established habit has an influence upon the acquisition, performance, or relearning of a second habit. It is one of the most general phenomena of learning and, by means of its influence, almost all learned behavior is interrelated in various complex ways. Transfer serves to determine, in part, the ease of learning of a particular habit, and indeed, every new learning takes place in the context of all previously established habits. [McGeoch and Irion, 1952, p. 299.]

Transfer may be positive or negative. *Positive transfer* (or *proactive facilitation*[1]) occurs when the learning of one task facilitates the learning or performance of a second task. *Negative transfer* (or *proactive inhibition*) occurs when the learning of the first task interferes with the learning or performance of a second task. *Zero transfer* occurs if the first task neither facilitates nor interferes with the learning or performance of the second task, or if the positive and negative transfer effects cancel out.

Learning Exercise

1. Which of the following are examples of (1) positive transfer, (2) negative transfer, (3) zero transfer?
   (a) High school chemistry students given special instruction in the application of principles derived from the kinetic theory gained more on a test involving the application of other chemistry principles than did students who did not receive the special instruction (Babitz and Keys, 1939).
   (b) Winch (1911) found that practice in arithmetic computation did not improve pupils' arithmetic reasoning.
   (c) Archer (1930), in a study of transfer of training in spelling, found a

[1] *Proactive* may be thought of as *forward acting*. Thus, a proactive effect occurs if the processes involved in the performance of one task are activated in performing a subsequent task.

tendency for students who had learned to spell *create, creates,* and *created* to generalize their learning and spell *creating* as *createing*.

The Measurement of Transfer

In transfer experiments, a comparison is made of the performances of two or more groups of subjects on a learning task. One group is given prior practice on a different learning task, while another group is not. Thus, the performance on an English vocabulary test of students who have studied Latin might be compared to the vocabulary test performance of students who have not studied Latin. The *classical design* for a study of this type is as follows:

Group	Initial Test	Training	Final Test
Experimental	English Vocabulary	Course in Latin	English Vocabulary
Control	English Vocabulary	Inactivity or some unrelated activity	English Vocabulary

Assuming the experimental and control groups are initially comparable in ability, in initial performance on the vocabulary test, and in other relevant factors, then differences in final performances on the English vocabulary test can be attributed to the course in Latin. We have evidence of positive transfer of training if the experimental group performs better than the control group on the final vocabulary test. A poorer performance by the experimental group would constitute evidence of negative transfer. It should be noted, however, that the above design may not yield a pure measure of transfer. Part of the improvement in the final test scores may be due to the learning that took place during the initial testing procedure.

Another design that is frequently used in current studies on transfer is called the *proactive* design. In a typical proactive design, the experimental group learns Material A, while the control group does nothing. Later, both groups learn and are tested on Material B. Thus:

Group	First Learning	Test Situation
Experimental	Learn Material A	Learn Material B
Control	Rests	Learn Material B

The relative ease or difficulty of the two groups in learning Material B can be attributed to the proactive effects on the experimental group of learning Material A (assuming all other variables are under control).

A third commonly used experimental design for the study of transfer is known as the *retroactive* design, which takes the following form:

Group	First Learning	Second Learning	Test
Experimental	Learn Task A	Learn Task B	Test on Task A
Control	Learn Task A	Rests	Test on Task A

With adequate controls, this design permits an assessment of the extent to which the learning of Task B acts backward (retroactively) on the learning that took place on Task A. The learning of Task B may either result in an increase or a decrease in the performance of Task A. The retroactive design is particularly useful when Task A is of a kind that can be learned in one practice session to a defined level of performance. It is then possible to match experimental and control groups on degree of learning.

Learning Exercises

2. Why is it advisable to administer an initial test in English vocabulary in an investigation of the transfer effects of a course in Latin to the English vocabulary of students?

3. (a) What name is given to the following experimental design?

	First Learning	Test Situation
Experimental	$S_1 \longrightarrow R_1$	$S_2 \longrightarrow R_2$
Control	Rest or $S_x \longrightarrow R_x$	$S_2 \longrightarrow R_2$

    (b) Complete the following statement: The above design has been frequently used to investigate whether the learning of Response 1 to Stimulus 1 facilitates or interferes with the learning of _____ _____.

4. What question may be answered by an experiment using the following retroactive design?

	First Learning	Second Learning	Test
Experimental	$S_1 \longrightarrow R_1$	$S_2 \longrightarrow R_2$	$S_1 \longrightarrow R_1$
Control	$S_1 \longrightarrow R_1$	Rest or $S_x \longrightarrow R_x$	$S_1 \longrightarrow R_1$

Theories of Transfer

The Formal Discipline Theory. The formal discipline theory of transfer is based on the notion that memory, judgment, imagination, and other "faculties" of the mind can be disciplined through intellectual exercise in much the same way as a muscle of the body can be strengthened through physical exercise. According to this theory, the good curriculum is one that includes subjects that are good exercises for the various faculties of the mind. Thus, in the nineteenth century, the study of Latin was considered as excellent for training the powers of reasoning, observation, comparison, and synthesis. Geometry was a highly regarded discipline because geometry provided exercise in a special kind of reasoning. Toward the end of the nineteenth century and early in the twentieth century, scores of experiments were conducted to test the idea that mere exercise of a faculty produced a general improvement of that faculty.

A study conducted by Sleight (1911) will serve to illustrate the type of investigation in the field of memory that was stimulated by the formal discipline theory of transfer. In two series of experiments—one with school children and another with college students—Sleight equated one control group and three practice groups on the basis of their performance on ten memory tests. A wide range of memorization material was included in the ten tests—nonsense syllables, dates, poetry selections, prose selections, and letters. The tests were administered before and after each group was given a particular type of memory training. One experimental group practiced memorizing poetry; a second group practiced memorizing tables; and a third group practiced reproducing the substance of prose selections. The control group received no practice in memorizing between tests. Sleight's experiment produced varied and conflicting results, with sometimes an experimental group doing better than a control group and sometimes a control group doing better than a practice group. There was no indication that the practice in memorizing produced a *general* improvement of memory.

Thorndike (1924) sought to assess the effect on students' general mental ability of a year's high school course in various subjects such as English, history, geometry, Latin, biology, bookkeeping, and home economics. Tests of general mental ability were given to 8,564 high school students. One year later, other forms of the same test were readministered. Then, test gains of students who had taken different combinations of subjects were analyzed to find out if greater gains could be attributed to the disciplinary values of any particular subjects. Allowance was made for the practice effects of taking the initial tests and for the normal gains to be expected in mental test scores in one year. Thorndike found only small differences between the average gains of students who had taken different subjects. Greater gains were made by students who initially scored high. But one academic subject seemed to be nearly as good as any other when judged in terms of its contribution to growth in mental ability test scores. Other studies (e.g., Broyler *et al.*, 1927; Wesman, 1945) have confirmed Thorndike's original findings. West and Fruchter (1960) found that students who had taken much mathematics and foreign language in high school did no better in the first year in college than students of comparable ability who had taken little mathematics and foreign language.

From the hosts of transfer studies in the fields of memory, discrimination judgments, and so forth, little support can be found for the notion that the benefits accruing from instruction in any academic subject occur as a result of strengthening mental faculties via intellectual calisthenics. This does not mean that the subjects that were formerly claimed to be good exercises of the mind are useless. It is possible to justify a place in the curriculum for courses such as mathematics, grammar, logic, and Latin on the basis of a theory of transfer that can be supported by the accumulated experimental evidence on transfer. The formal discipline theory of transfer is not such a theory.

The Identical Elements Theory. The identical elements theory of transfer, as set forth in the writings of E. L. Thorndike (e.g., 1913), says that transfer of the learning from one task to the learning of a subsequent task occurs only to the extent that the two tasks have identical elements. Thus, learning to add benefits learning to multiply simply because many of the responses needed in adding are also needed in multiplying. Hence, in order to predict whether transfer is likely to occur from one learning to a second learning, it is necessary to search for identical elements in the two learning tasks. Exhaustive research data on transfer of training amassed over half a century do not fundamentally invalidate Thorndike's identical elements theory. What constitutes an "identical element" and some of the conditions favorable to positive transfer are, however, much better understood today.

The Generalization Theory. Proponents of practical education found in the identical elements theory of transfer a justification for attempting to make the classroom duplicate life situations. An experiment conducted by Charles Judd served to demonstrate that the identical element in two learning situations may be a generalization. Judd (1908) matched two groups of boys on the basis of their performance in throwing darts at a target placed under 12 inches of water. The experimental group was taught the principle of refraction of light; the control group was not. Then both groups were brought back to a new dart-throwing task in which the depth of the water was reduced to 4 inches. The experimental group outperformed the control group in this new task. Judd argued that the generalization concerning refraction of light transferred to the dart-throwing task. The design of the experiment may be summarized as follows:

	Pre-Test	Intervening Learning	Final Test
Experimental group	Dart-throwing	Refraction of light	Dart-throwing
Control group	Dart-throwing	–	Dart-throwing

Both the theory of identical elements and the theory of generalization have value to the educator. In attempting to assess the transfer potential of a learning experience, the identical elements theory cautions the educator to expect transfer only to situations that are similar to the original learning situation. The generalization theory reminds the educator that generalizations or general principles learned in one activity may be utilized by the learner in some new activity. Yet, the two theories, even when taken together, are incomplete. In what respects must two situations be identical for transfer to occur? Are certain characteristics of the learner of importance? Is the thoroughness of the original learning a factor in transfer? We will need to examine further experimental evidence to obtain answers to these questions.

Learning Exercise

5. What theory of transfer is most nearly reflected in each of the following statements:
   (a) We can expect transfer from classroom instruction to life situations only to the extent that we duplicate life situations within the classroom.
   (b) The major value of teaching logic in the school is that it exercises the student's reasoning faculty.
   (c) It is possible for children to learn to apply principles in situations they have not previously encountered.

Conditions of Transfer

Similarity Relations. Both the similarities existing among stimulus situations and among responsive behaviors affect transfer. Osgood (1953) discusses the direction and the degree of transfer effect to be expected for the three combinations of: (1) stimulus variation; (2) response variation; and (3) stimulus and response simultaneously varied.

1. *Stimulus variation:*

First learning: $S_1 \longrightarrow R_1$
Second learning: $S_2 \longrightarrow R_1$

This is simply the procedure used to measure *stimulus generalization.*
In the second learning, a previously learned response (R_1) is to be
learned to a new stimulus (S_2). In this case, we can expect *positive*
transfer. The degree of transfer effect will depend upon the degree of
similarity between S_1 and S_2. (Yum, 1931; Gibson, 1939; Hamilton,
1943.) For instance, a child who first learns to call a four-footed furry
animal that barks and wags its tail (S_1) a "dog" (R_1) is likely to find it
easier (positive transfer) to learn to call a second four-footed animal
that barks and wags its tail (S_2) a "dog" (R_1). And the more similar
the two dogs are in appearance, the easier it is for the child to attach
the name "dog" to the second animal.

Stimulus generalization takes place in all concept learning in the
school. A student learns to attach the term "triangle" (R_1) to two
differently shaped three-sided figures (S_1 and S_2); to recognize that a
description of the government of another country fits the definition of
a democracy, even though its government varies somewhat from that of
the United States; and to see that a mathematical problem can be
solved by using simultaneous equations, even though the problem
varies somewhat from problems previously solved.

Some caution is in order in applying laboratory research findings to
classroom learning. The finding that the extent of positive transfer is
related to the degree of stimulus similarity is based on relatively simple
learning tasks performed under well-controlled experimental conditions. Probably other factors need to be taken into account in predicting transfer effects in a school learning situation.

2. *Response variation:*

First learning: $S_1 \longrightarrow R_1$
Second learning: $S_1 \longrightarrow R_2$

Here, the learner is to learn a different response to an old stimulus.
Experimental evidence (e.g., Bruce, 1933; Gibson, 1941; Underwood,
1945) indicates that *negative* transfer may be expected. The first
learned response interferes with the acquisition of a new response to
the same stimulus. The amount of interference decreases, however, as
the degree of similarity of the responses increases (Osgood, 1946). In
some experiments, positive transfer has occurred when subjects were
required to learn a new response to an old stimulus. This may occur
when the common stimulus is complex and the first learning permits
the subject to become familiar with the intricacies of the stimulus.

However, unless the learning produces some practice effects of value in the second learning, negative transfer may be expected when a new response is to be learned to an old stimulus.

Often in daily living, we learn a new response to an old stimulus. For example, in driving a car to a new residence we may need to turn right (R_2) at the street corner when we previously turned left (R_1). The child in school finds that a new teacher expects him to do his schoolwork differently from the way he has learned from a former teacher. Ordinarily, we might expect some negative transfer to occur when the learner attempts to acquire a new response to an old stimulus.

3. *Stimulus and response simultaneously varied:*

$$\text{First learning: } S_1 \longrightarrow R_1$$
$$\text{Second learning: } S_2 \longrightarrow R_2$$

According to Osgood, the more S_1 and S_2 are similar, the more negative transfer can be expected. In teaching arithmetic, children often experience difficulty in distinguishing between problems that appear to be quite similar. For example:

$$\text{First learning: } (S_1) \; 40\% \text{ of } 50 = ? \longrightarrow (R_1) \; \frac{40}{100} \times 50 = 20$$

$$\text{Second learning: } (S_2) \; 40 \text{ is what per cent of } 50? \longrightarrow (R_2) \; \frac{40}{50} \times 100 = 80$$

Not all the experimental evidence supports Osgood's three generalizations on transfer (Bugelski, 1956; Deese, 1958; Travers, 1963). Under certain conditions, positive transfer is obtained where negative transfer would be predicted on the basis of Osgood's generalizations. More research is needed in order to develop generalizations that can be applied widely in predicting transfer effects.

Learning Exercise

6. Answer each of the following questions on the basis of Osgood's analysis of similarity relations:

(a) A child first learns to spell *receive*, noting particularly the *c-e-i* sequence of letters. Would you expect positive or negative transfer if the child next learns to spell *deceive* and *ceiling*? Would you expect greater transfer effect for *deceive* or *ceiling*?

(b) A child first learns to spell *to*. Would you expect positive or negative transfer if the child next learns to spell *two* and *too*? For which word—*two* or *too*—would you expect the greater transfer effect?

(c) A child first learns to spell *were*. Would you expect positive or negative transfer if the child next learns to spell *where* and *walk*? For which word—*where* or *walk*—would you expect the greater transfer effect?

Degree of Learning. The amount of transfer from previous learning depends upon how well the initial task is learned. We have noted that positive transfer may be expected in the learning of an old response to a new stimulus. The amount of positive transfer has been found to increase with an increase in the amount of practice on the first task (Jackson *et al.*, 1938; Underwood, 1951; Atwater, 1953). Under conditions that initially favor negative transfer (e.g., learning to make a new response to an old stimulus), an increase in the amount of practice on the first task results in a shift from negative to positive transfer (Siipola and Israel, 1933; Mandler, 1954). Thus, thorough learning promotes efficient transfer.

Task Difficulty. One of the most perplexing problems encountered by the teacher is that of organizing learning experiences so that one learning serves as a foundation for later learning. Simple rules such as proceeding "from the simple to the complex," "from the known to the unknown," or "from the concrete to the abstract" serve only as rough guides for the teacher. Sometimes these simple rules even seem to contradict other simple rules such as the rule of proceeding from "wholes" to "parts." And psychology at present does not provide a set of easily applied generalizations to guide the teacher in organizing learning experiences. The literature on transfer, for example, reveals that the relationships between transfer and the relative difficulty of Task 1 and Task 2 are quite complex. In some experiments, transfer from an easy task to a more difficult task has been found to be greater than transfer from a difficult to an easier task. In other experiments, the reverse has been found to be true.

Jones and Bilodeau (1952) found transfer to be greater from a hard motor task to an easy one. In both tasks, the subjects were required to keep a pointer on a moving target by manipulating hand controls. In the hard task, the target moved in a very complicated path, while in the easy task, the target moved in a relatively simple path. The investigators attributed the greater transfer from the difficult to the easy task to the fact that the difficult task included all the elements involved in the easy task. Practice on the hard task therefore included practice on the easier task.

In some situations, however, greater transfer may result from an easy task to a more difficult task. Lawrence (1952), in a study of discrimination learning in rats, found that more transfer occurred for the rats when given the easier discrimination problem first and the hard problem later.

Thus we see that the problem of the relationships of transfer to the relative difficulty of the tasks involved is not simple. Sometimes an easy task can be mastered economically in the course of mastering a more difficult task. Sometimes the easy task is sufficiently difficult to warrant separate teaching before the more difficult task is tackled. When the difficult task involves the coordination of a number of simple tasks (as is the case with many motor skills), then the more difficult task often may be presented first. When success on the difficult task depends primarily upon a thorough mastery of its separate elements rather than upon the coordination or putting together of the separate elements, then some preliminary attention to the development of the subskills involved would seem to be in order.

The problem of task difficulty in transfer is related to the problem of whole versus part learning. Early studies on this topic utilized school-type materials. For example, studies were conducted to find out whether it is more economical to memorize a poem as a whole (whole method) or to memorize the poem line by line (part method). Findings of these early investigations in general favored the whole method. Later investigations have modified somewhat this finding (Osgood, 1953). Orbison (1944) has supplied data on simple verbal learning that supports the hypothesis that the whole method is superior for a small amount of material, but the part method becomes superior as the amount of material learned is increased.

Ability and Transfer. There is some evidence that transfer occurs more readily for bright students than for students of lower intellectual ability. Ulmer (1939) investigated the amount of transfer occurring from a high school course in geometry to performance on a number of measures of logical reasoning. Three groups of students were included in this study. A control group received no instruction in geometry. A second group was taught a course in geometry by the conventional methods. A third group was taught geometry by a method designed to maximize practice in critical reasoning. All three groups were given a test on syllogistic reasoning at the beginning of the study and another form of the test at the end. The non-geometry controls showed the least amount of gain on mean test scores, 4.9; the conventional geometry group showed an average gain of 9.3 points; while the group taught geometry in a way designed to stress critical thinking gained on the average 26.7 points. In addition, Ulmer found that, while students of all levels of ability gained in the third group, more transfer occurred for superior students in both the second and third groups than for the average or inferior students.

Other studies have demonstrated a relationship between intelligence level and amount of transfer (e.g., Brooks, 1924; Pratt, 1938). Ray (1936) compared the efficiency in generalizing of bright (I.Q.'s of 117 to 137) and dull (I.Q.'s of 66 to 81) 12-year-old children. Ray found that the brighter children were able to discover generalizations more quickly and apply them more effectively.

The tendency of the bright child to form generalizations from his learning experiences and apply generalizations to other learning sometimes leads to negative transfer. Carroll (1930) found, for example, that the tendency of bright children to form phonetic generalizations led to a frequency of spelling errors such as "addvise" and "indicateing."

A study conducted by Klausmeier and Check (1962) suggests that the difficulty level of the initial learning is a critical factor in determining the amount of transfer and retention. Using arithmetic problems, Klausmeier and Check found no significant differences in transfer abilities among children of low, middle, and high intelligence when the difficulty of the arithmetic problems was at an appropriate level for each child.

Learning Sets. It is commonly believed that "experience is the best teacher." Certainly, our daily observations are sufficient to convince us of the importance of experience to the development of competencies. The engineer finds that with experience he increases in his efficiency in dealing with new engineering problems. The student who has taken many standardized achievement tests becomes "test wise." The person who learns a number of foreign languages finds it increasingly easy to learn an additional foreign language. Many college students learn how to study in the process of taking a number of courses in college. From experience in any line of endeavor, an individual virtually *learns how to learn*. With practice, an individual learns what to look for and what important discriminations to note in solving problems in a given area. In other words, the learner develops *learning sets* as he approaches problems in his area of competence.

That it is possible to learn how to learn has been demonstrated in numerous experimental studies. Ward (1937), for example, showed that as subjects memorized lists of nonsense syllables, their speed in learning increased with each new list. But improvement does not occur as a result of exercising some hypothetical memory muscle. Woodrow (1927) showed that instruction in how to memorize resulted in greater improvement in memorizing ability than did undirected practice. Woodrow administered a series of memorizing tests to three groups of subjects. The tests included: rote poetry; rote prose; a six-minute test in remembering facts from a dictionary of facts; Turkish-English vocabulary; historical dates; and memorizing span for consonants. Group 1 served as a control group. This group was not given practice in memorizing nor instruction in how to memorize. Group 2 was given over a period of four weeks a total of 90 minutes practice in memorizing rote poetry and 87 minutes practice in memorizing nonsense syllables. Group 3 was given a total of 76 minutes instruction on techniques of memorizing, 76 minutes practice in memorizing poetry, and 25 minutes practice in memorizing nonsense syllables. At the completion of training, the memorizing tests were readministered. Group 3 was found to be superior to both of the other two groups on the retest. Little difference was found in retest performance between Groups 1 and 2.

Harlow (1949, 1950) has reported a number of "learning how to learn" experiments. Monkeys, trained on a series of discrimination problems, finally learn to solve a new discrimination problem in one trial. In these studies, a monkey is offered a choice of two objects on a tray (e.g., a cube and a solid triangle). A food reward—a raisin—is placed under one of the objects and the monkey is permitted as many trials as necessary in order to learn the problem. The position of the reward object (to the right or to the left) is varied randomly, so that the monkey is required to discriminate between the cube and the triangle in order to make the right choice. When the monkey has mastered the first problem, a second problem is given (e.g., a red triangle and a blue triangle); then a third, a fourth, and so on for as many as 344 separate choice situations. The discriminating aspects of the objects are varied in color, shape, size, texture, and so on. As the problems continue, the monkey requires fewer and fewer trials in order to learn the discrimination, until, by the two hundredth problem, the monkey is able to solve a new problem in one trial.

In the Harlow experiments, the monkey appears to learn to search for a discriminating characteristic between the reward and the nonreward objects. We can speculate that the monkey learns from previous problems what discriminating characteristics he should observe. Harlow does not attempt to explain his findings except by labeling the results as a demonstration of "learning how to learn" or the "formation of learning sets."

Up to this point, our discussion of transfer has been pretty much restricted to an examination of the stimulus and response variables involved. Yet, it is clear that some intermediating perceptual process occurs within the organism when transfer occurs. We turn now to an examination of the perceptual process.

Learning Exercise

7. What conditions affecting transfer are illustrated in each of the following:
   (a) A person who is skilful in driving an American-make car experiences less negative transfer than the less skilful driver when he learns to drive a foreign-make car with a different gearshift.
   (b) Bill and Joe both study about levers in their science class. Bill, who is the brighter of the two, is better able to apply his newly acquired knowledge in out-of-school situations.
   (c) John's former natural science and social science teachers stressed the importance of defining problems before attempting to solve them. John quickly adapted to a similar requirement of his present English teacher.
   (d) Some students find it easier to learn the concept of standard deviation if they first are taught the simpler concept of *average deviation*.

PERCEPTION

The perceptual process may be defined as a "process of structuring stimulation" (Solley and Murphy, 1960, p. 26). Diagrammatically, we may represent this process as:

$$S \longrightarrow P \longrightarrow R$$

in which R represents an observable response that indicates that a perceptual process (P) has occurred through which the perceiver has structured the stimuli (S) in some way as to give it a meaning. Note that the perceptual process is inferred and is not directly observable. It is also a complex process. Allport captures the complexity inherent in the perceptual process when he writes:

. . . the concept of perception inevitably covers the energy from the stimulus, the receptor activity, a sensory core projected and organized through expectancy and intention, blended with subtle muscular adjustments and capped by a lightning process of categorization, made possible by bewilderingly swift associations with past experience—the whole baffling sequence occupying only a split second and resulting in a firm, well-configurated experience of objectified meaning. [Allport, 1960, pp. 299–300.]

Determinants of Perception

Allport's description of the perceptual process identifies a number of determinants of perception. We will discuss four of these:

1. The characteristics of the physical stimulus
2. The organizing tendencies of the perceiver
3. The past experiences of the perceiver
4. The influence of affective processes

Characteristics of the Stimulus. Obviously, the characteristics of the physical stimulus is one factor determining perception. Much of our environment is perceived in about the same way by most people. Some degree of communication is made possible because many auditory stimuli elicit approximately the same receptor activity and many printed words are structured fairly similarly from one individual to another. Discrimination between stimuli is made more difficult when the stimuli are similar. The child in learning to read, for example, encounters more difficulty in discriminating between "was" and "saw" than in discriminating between "cat" and "dog." Sometimes our senses play tricks on us and our perceptions do not correspond to physical reality. In the familiar Muller-Lyer illusion (Fig. 9–1), two equal lines appear unequal because of the surrounding arrowheads.

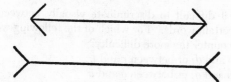

Fig. 9–1.   Muller-Lyer Illusion

Sometimes the object perceived is ambiguous, one person may see one thing and another person may see quite a different thing (Fig. 9–2).

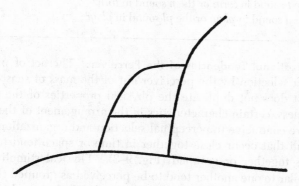

Fig. 9–2.   A Chair or a Hat?

Thus, physical stimuli may vary in clarity and the degree to which they can be differentiated from other stimuli. We perceive more accurately *intense* stimuli rather than weak ones; stimuli that *contrast* with the background than stimuli that blend into the background; and *repetitive* stimuli than unitary or stable stimuli.

Current methods of teaching reading assume that it is easier to teach a child first to see a word as a whole and then to note some of its distinguishing features. According to Vernon (1957), young children do tend to see things as a whole providing outlines are clear and not cluttered by a mass of details. Published reading readiness materials contain many practice exercises in recognizing letter shapes and words. Reading readiness materials also include what is called "ear training" exercises from which the child learns to discriminate more accurately between different sounds. Research findings indicate that, in general, initial consonants are the easiest to perceive, followed by final consonants, long vowels, short vowels, and consonant combinations (Harris, 1961).

Learning Exercises

8. Children find it difficult to discriminate visually between certain letters and between certain words. For which of the following would you expect children to encounter the more difficulty?
    (a) Between *b* and *d;* or between *r* and *t?*
    (b) Between *p* and *q;* or between *o* and *i?*
    (c) Between *s* and *l;* or between *m* and *n?*
    (d) Between *burn* and *born;* or between *blow* and *bell?*
9. Children also encounter difficulties in making auditory discriminations. For which of the following would you expect children to encounter the more difficulty:
    (a) The *t* sound in *torn;* or the *n* sound in *torn?*
    (b) The *a* sound in *play;* or the *pl* sound in *play?*

Organizational Tendencies of the Perceiver. The act of perceiving involves a selection by the perceiver out of the mass of sensory input. A percept does not duplicate the physical properties of the stimulus. Nevertheless, certain characteristics in the arrangement of the external stimuli are conducive to perceptual selection and organization. Physical stimuli that occur close together in time or space tend to be perceived as together or grouped (Fig. 9–3). Physical stimuli that are more similar to one another tend to be perceived as grouped (Fig. 9–4). Physical stimuli that form a good figure tend to be grouped (Fig. 9–5).

In Fig. 9–5a, we tend to see a circle with a straight line through it. In Fig. 9–5b, we tend to see a circle despite the break in the curve.

Fig. 9–3.   Proximity

OOOOXXXXOOOOXXXXOOOOXXXX

Fig. 9–4.   Similarity

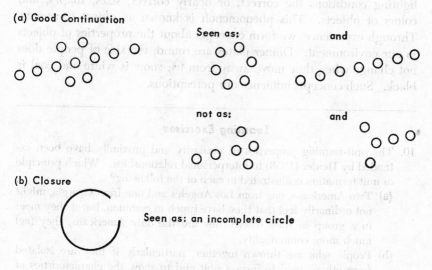

(a) Good Continuation

Seen as: and

not as: and

(b) Closure

Seen as: an incomplete circle

Fig. 9–5.   Good Figure

FIGURE-GROUND. When we view a scene, one part stands out in a distinctive way from the remainder. The part that stands out is technically called the *figure* while the remainder is called the *ground*. When you direct your attention to one person in a crowded room, that one person becomes the figure and the people in the background are the ground. The figure has form and stands out clearly whereas the ground is relatively vague and formless. Hebb (1949) has presented evidence that some kind of figure-ground organization is innate. However, a considerable body of research evidence indicates that *what* is figure and *what* is ground is learned. (Solley and Murphy, 1960, chap. 13.)

OBJECT CONSTANCY. What we visually perceive is not identical to the retinal image of a stimulus object. In some instances, perceptions yield more accurate information than we have any reason to expect. A small child standing ten feet away is perceived as smaller than a tall man standing twenty feet away even though the retinal image of the child is larger than the image of the man. A dinner plate is perceived as round when viewed from an angle even though the image of the plate on the retina of the eye is elliptical. A piece of coal in bright sunlight is perceived as black while a patch of snow at dusk appears white even though the amount of light reflected from the surface of the coal may be greater than that from the snow. We live in a stable environment in which we perceive from various distances, angles, and lighting conditions the correct, or nearly correct, sizes, shapes, and colors of objects. This phenomenon is known as *object constancy*. Through experience, we form concepts about the properties of objects in our environment. Dinner plates are round; the size of people does not change when they move away from us; snow is white and coal is black. Such concepts influence our perceptions.

Learning Exercises

10. The unit-forming properties of similarity and proximity have been extended by Heider (1958) to interpersonal relationships. Which principle of unit formation is illustrated in each of the following?
    (a) Two Americans, one from Los Angeles and one from Georgia, might not ordinarily feel that they have much in common, but if they meet in a group in Italy where they are the only Americans, they feel much more communality.
    (b) People who are thrown together, particularly if they are isolated from others, tend to form a unit and to show the characteristics of units.
11. At a large party, one may clearly hear the person with whom he is chatting and the rest of the talking forms a senseless babble. What tendency of the perceiver to organize sensory input does this illustrate?
12. Snyder and Snyder (1956) tape recorded selections from Rachel Carson's *The Sea Around Us*. Half of the selections were recorded with one voice and half with another. The experiment consisted of playing the recordings to a subject with the experimenter giving nickels to the subject while one voice was reading and taking nickels away from the subject while the other voice was reading. Then a test tape consisting of *both* voices reading simultaneously *different* sentences was played and the subject was required to reproduce all that he heard. Snyder and Snyder found that 31 out of the 41 subjects reproduced far more of the rewarded voice than the punished voice. What conclusion is supported

by this experiment concerning the learning of figure-ground relationships?

13. In the face of new information to the contrary, a person's image of an object remains relatively constant. Applying this constancy principle to people, we might expect that if a person has a well-formed image of Mr. Smith as an honorable man, and then receives information that Mr. Smith acted in a dishonorable fashion, then the person's image of Mr. Smith as an honorable man will _____.

ADAPTATION-LEVEL. Does the grade assigned a student on his composition theme depend in part upon the quality of other themes previously graded by his instructor? Adaptation-level theory of perception would suggest that the instructor's perceptual response (i.e., the grade assigned) is a function of the difference between a present stimulus (i.e., the paper the instructor is now grading) and a subjective standard derived from a polling of the effects of previous stimulations (i.e., the papers the instructor has previously graded).

The adaptation-level theory of perception has been advanced by Helson (1948). Helson has not tested the applicability of his theory on the way high school and college instructors assign grades. He has applied it to a variety of psychophysical problems during the past 15 years, and the theory has functioned as a precise predictive tool in many situations (Helson, 1959). For example, when subjects were asked to judge whether a weight was "light" or "heavy," and weights ranging from 400 to 600 grams were included in the series, a weight of about 475 grams turned out to be the adaptation-level. Weights below 475 grams tended to be judged as "light"; weights above 475 grams tended to be judged as "heavy." However, when a weight of 900 grams was introduced a single time, the adaptation-level rose to 550 grams. Some promising beginnings have been made in extending the theory to studies of the expression of attitudes (Helson et al., 1956).

SET. A perceptual set is a state of readiness, learned through experience, to perceive a given situation in a certain way. A person waiting for an important call readily identifies the sound of the telephone ringing. He may even misinterpret the sound of a door bell as the ringing of the telephone because of his set. The driver of a car has a set to respond to traffic lights to which his passengers pay little attention. A set has been described as a "perceptual expectancy" by Solley and Murphy (1960), and as a "hypothesis" by Postman (1951). The sound of someone beginning to open an outside door may lead to an expectancy or a hypothesis that you will see your roommate enter the room through the door. If the expectancy is fulfilled, the probability is increased that the set (expectancy or hypothesis) will occur again under similar circumstances. Postman, in developing his theory of perceptual learning, delineates the role of hypothesis in a perceptual act when he writes:

> Central to our analysis is the concept of *hypothesis*. By hypothesis we mean, in the most general sense, expectancies or predispositions of the organism (sets) which serve to select, organize, and transform the stimulus information that comes from the environment. A given sensory input has not only energy characteristics which trip off a series of organized reactions in the nervous system, but has cue or clue characteristics as well—it carries *information* about the environment. Thus, a hazy color has not only certain spectral and intensity values; it is also a cue or clue to distance and *qua* clue it is related to the organism's hypotheses about distance. [Postman, 1951, p. 249.]

Sets may be induced by external stimuli. In one study, children were asked to rate photographs of strangers on the degree of maliciousness they seemed to show. Then the children played a game of murder and were told hair-raising stories. Later, the children again were asked to rate the photographs. On the second rating, the photographs were perceived as more malicious than on the first rating. (Murray, 1933.)

A set may be induced by an instruction or suggestion on what to look for in an ambiguous stimulus. An experiment reported by Siipola (1935) is illustrative. By means of a tachistoscope, ten words were exposed and adult subjects were asked to write down the words they saw. Among the words were six nonsense words, as listed in Table 9–1.

TABLE 9–1

Influence of Instructions on Interpreting Ambiguous Words

	Most Frequent Response by Those Set for:	
Stimulus Word	Animals or Birds	Travel or Transportation
chack	chick	check
sael	seal	sail
wharl	whale	wharf
pasrort	parrot	passport
dack	duck	deck
pengion	penguin	pension

Each word was presented for 0.10 second. The 160 subjects were divided into two groups. Subjects of the first group were informed that the words appearing had to do with "animals or birds"; those in the second group were told the words had to do with travel or transportation. The group expecting "animals or birds" gave animal or bird responses 63 per cent of the time, and travel or transportation responses 14 per cent of the time. The group expecting words related to travel or transportation gave travel or transportation responses 74 per cent of the time, and "animal or bird" responses 11 per cent of the time. Thus, the ambiguous items tended to be interpreted according to the induced set.

Much of the behavior of pupils that occurs in the classroom constitutes ambiguous stimuli for the observing teacher. The warning: "Watch Johnny. He's a trouble-maker," given to a teacher at the beginning of the school year, may induce a set to perceive trouble-making behavior in all of Johnny's activities.

Learning Exercises

14. In a study conducted by Helson *et al.* (1956), students were asked to rate, on a seven-point scale, their agreement or disagreement with statements such as: "War brings out the bad qualities in men as well as the good ones." (On the scale, 1 meant "strongly disagree," 4 meant "neither agree nor disagree," and 7 meant "strongly agree.")

    The students heard each statement through earphones from a tape recording, and immediately after hearing a statement, the student heard voices (supposedly of other members of his group) give their ratings. Some students would hear judgments of 1,1,1,2 (indicating strong disagreement). Other students would hear judgments of 7,7,6,7 (indicating strong agreement).

    On the basis of Helson's adaption-level theory, how would you expect the supposed judgment of his peers to affect a student's own judgment?
15. Sells (1962, p. 195) identifies three types of sets: (1) set based on instructions, (2) set based on setting or context, and (3) set based on motives. To which type of set is each of the following related:
    (a) Siipola's experiment? (See above.)
    (b) A hungry person noticing restaurant signs?
    (c) + interpreted as a plus in mathematics but as a cross when seen in a church?

Influence of Past Learning and Experience. One theory of perception known as the "transactional approach" places a major emphasis on the part played in perception by past experience (Cantril, 1950; Ittelson and Cantril, 1954). Perception, according to the transactionalists is a process of interpreting present stimulus cues on the basis of expectations. These expectations have been built up as consequents of past experience. As expectations are confirmed or reinforced through later experiences, they become more and more stable and harder to alter. Perception is, from this point of view, not a passive "reaction to" stimuli in the environment, but rather an active transaction between the striving organism and its environment. Cantril writes:

Since our experience is concerned with purposive behavior, our perceptions are learned in terms of our purposes and in terms of what is important and useful to us.

Since the situations we are in seldom repeat themselves exactly and since change seems to be the rule of nature and of life, our perception is largely a matter of weighing probabilities, of guessing, of making hunches concerning the probable significance of meaning of "what is out there" and of what our reaction should be toward it, in order to protect or preserve ourselves and our satisfactions, or to enhance our satisfactions. This process of weighing the innumerable cues involved in any perception is, of course, a process that we are not generally aware of. [Cantril, 1959, p. 184.]

Some of the experiments conducted by the transactionalists have demonstrated cultural differences in perception. A few of these experiments have made use of an adapted version of the old-fashioned stereoscope. With such an apparatus, it is possible to create binocular rivalry since one picture may be viewed by the right eye while a different picture is viewed by the left eye. Bagby (1957) constructed pairs of slides consisting of one picture of an individual, object, or symbol that would be of particular interest to Mexicans; in the other, a picture of particular significance to Americans. For example, in one pair of slides a picture of a bullfighter was matched with a picture of a baseball player. When these pairs of pictures were shown to Mexican school teachers, most of them saw the Mexican symbol; when the same pictures were shown to American school teachers, most saw the American symbol. Thus, the culturally significant was perceived by the members of both groups.

Cultural differences in perception can create problems for the teacher who has children of varying backgrounds in his classroom. They also can make teaching exciting if reasonable freedom is given to children to express their different perceptions.

Influence of Affective Processes. It is commonly believed that when emotions are involved, people tend to hear what they wish to hear, see what they wish to see, and believe what they wish to believe. Psychological research lends some support concerning the influence of affective processes on perception (Jenkin, 1957).

Bodily needs determine, within limits, what is perceived. In one representative study (Levine, Chein, and Murphy, 1942), subjects deprived of food for one, three, six, and nine hours report on what they saw in pictures seen through a ground glass screen. The ground glass served to blur the pictures. Thirty of the pictures were ambiguous pictures of food; 30 were meaningless figures; and 20 were miscellaneous household articles. The main result of the study was that the number of food responses tended to increase with increased periods of food deprivation.

A number of studies have demonstrated that size judgments are influenced by the value attached to the object perceived (Jenkin, 1957). Bruner and Goodman (1947) had ten-year-old children estimate the size of coins by turning a knob that adjusted the size of a spot of light. The task of the child was to adjust the size of the spotlight to that of 1-, 5-, 10-, 25-, and 50-cent pieces. Members of the control group were given the task of adjusting the size of the spotlight to match the size of cardboard discs that were equal in sizes to the coins. The children were quite accurate in estimating the sizes of cardboard discs. But they overestimated the size of coins. Further, it was found that children coming from economically poor homes tended to overestimate the size of the coins—particularly the larger coins—more than did the children from the rich homes.

Some research points to a relationship between social attitudes and the perception of ambiguous stimuli. For some people, all situations are judged good or bad. Ambiguity cannot be tolerated in their social attitudes. Nor, apparently, in their perceptual processes. In one study (Frenkel-Brunswick, 1949), a group of people prejudiced toward minority groups was compared with a non-prejudiced group with respect to rigidity of perception. A picture of a dog was flashed on a screen followed by several other pictures in which the picture was gradually modified until it became a picture of a cat. The prejudiced group held to their interpretation, i.e., they continued to name the changing picture a "dog" longer than did the control group.

Learning Exercise

16. Which of the following statements are consistent with our discussion of "Influence of Past Learning and Experience" and "Influence of Affective Processes"?
   (a) New perceptions are dependent upon antecedent experiences.
   (b) Two men in the same geographic areas do not perceptually experience the same environment.
   (c) "Perception" means the same thing as "sensation."
   (d) Whether or not a child perceives a teacher as helpful and friendly depends in part upon the child's past experiences with authoritative figures.

(e) How accurately we perceive depends upon how accurately we need to perceive.

(f) Accuracy of perception is determined almost completely by the clarity of the stimulus.

Perception of People

Thus far, most of our examples of perceptual phenomena have dealt with perception of things. The topic "Perception of People," or as it is sometimes called, "social perception," is of even greater significance for the classroom teacher. However, the determinants of the perception of things and people are much alike. That is not to say there are no differences. The people we perceive also perceive us, whereas, except for the delightful world of early childhood, inanimate objects are not regarded as having the capacity to perceive back at their perceivers. There is a difference too in the nature of categories of our percepts of people. We see people as angry, sad, happy, pleased, favorably disposed toward us, etc. In short, we perceive the desires, pleasures, intentions, perceptions, abilities, and sentiments of another person.

The accuracy of perceptions of both things and people is dependent upon the degree of clarity of the stimulus object and its distinguishability from other stimulus objects. To what extent are emotions recognizable? In reviewing the literature on this question, Bruner and Tagiuri (1954) point out that some of the apparent contradictions of research findings are attributable to the nature of the discrimination demanded of the subject in the emotion-judging task. Obviously, to judge whether the emotion expressed by a person is one of happiness or one of disgust is an easier task than to judge whether the emotion is happiness or mirth. Woodworth (1938) constructed a six-step scale where the stimulus expression in posed pictures and the judges' responses fell into the following intervals: (a) love, happiness, and mirth; (b) surprise; (c) fear and suffering; (d) anger and determination; (e) disgust; (f) contempt; and (g) a residual category. In reanalyzing the published results of other researchers, Woodworth found that judgments seldom missed by more than one step.

Bruner and Tagiuri (1954, p. 636) point to research evidence indicating that the more information a person has about the situation in which an emotion is being expressed, the more accurate and reliable are judgments of the emotion. When a picture of a grimacing face is shown to a person with the information that the photograph was taken while the subject was viewing a hanging, the emotion perceived probably will be "disgust" or "anxiety." If the same picture were shown to another person with the information that the photograph was taken of the subject at the finishing line of a 100-yard dash, the perceived emotion likely would be "effort" or "determination." It may be noted that if information about a situation improves accuracy of perception, then we might expect misinformation to decrease accuracy of perception.

The phenomenon of perceptual constancy occurs in both the judging of emotions and in forming impressions of the personality of other people. We perceive the same presonality in another person in spite of changing conditions and in spite of the fact that the person behaves differently on different occasions. Probably, as Heider (1958) surmises, the constancy in social perception is less perfect than the constancy in thing perceptions. At least it is more difficult to describe constancy in social perception in terms of observables that can be measured.

Earlier, "set" was defined as a state of readiness, learned through experience, to perceive a given situation in a certain way. It is not difficult to find daily many examples of the influence of set on perception. When a friend greets us with a smile, we are prepared for cheerful talk, not sad news. Students in a classroom at the beginning of the class hour are prepared to hear their instructor begin lecturing, not singing. When events occur contrary to our expectations, they immediately attract our attention, although an unexpected event such as a traffic accident may find us ill prepared to make accurate observations.

Learning Exercises

17. What qualifications would you wish to make in the generalization, "Our perceptions of people are very inaccurate"?
18. Does additional information about a person in a situation increase the accuracy of our perception of the person?
19. A teacher has learned to regard a boy in her class as "impudent." The teacher continues to interpret the behavior of the boy as "being impudent" even after the boy has begun to strive to be courteous. What phenomenon concerning perception explains the teacher's misinterpretation of the boy's behavior?

RETENTION

Much that is learned in school is quickly forgotten. In one study by Greene (1931), university students were given in October the same zoology, psychology, and chemistry examinations that they had previously taken in June. The retention tests revealed that nearly half of the information acquired in the three courses was forgotten during the four-month period. Other studies at the elementary, high school, and college levels show roughly comparable losses in the retention of information.

Yet, we remember over long periods of time some early childhood experiences. Some skills in reading, writing, and arithmetic as well as many other intellectual and motor skills may be retained throughout life. Tyler (1933) administered a zoology test to university students prior to and after instruction and then again one year later. Students forgot over the one-year period all but 23 per cent of the facts about animal anatomy. However, the average retest score on questions dealing with the application of principles was just as high on the retention test as it was at the end of the course. Further, on a set of questions dealing with the interpretation of experimental results, students actually improved in their performance on the retention test. Problem-solving skills, once attained, are well retained.

Thus, the over-all picture on retention of school learning is not entirely bleak. Students forget much; but they also remember much. Further, some of what is forgotten may be quickly relearned or may be recalled with a little prompting.

Factors Affecting Retention

Much research effort has been spent by psychologists in an effort to identify the factors affecting retention. While a multiplicity of specific factors may be listed, research findings may be grouped under five headings:

1. The method of measurement
2. The nature of the materials learned
3. The conditions of the original learning
4. The activities intervening between learning and recall
5. The characteristics of the learner

Method of Measurement. The rate and extent of forgetting was first investigated by Ebbinghaus (1885). Ebbinghaus plotted the amount of retention of nonsense syllables over a period of several days to form a "curve of retention." The Ebbinghaus curve of retention for nonsense syllables falls rapidly from the completion of initial learning to his first measurement period (19 minutes) with only 58.2 per cent of the original learning time saved in relearning the nonsense syllables. From this point, the curve falls at a decelerating rate until, after 31 days, there is a saving in the time required to relearn of only 21 per cent (Fig. 9–6).

While retention curves for more meaningful materials and psychomotor skills do not show as much forgetting, the shape of the curves is

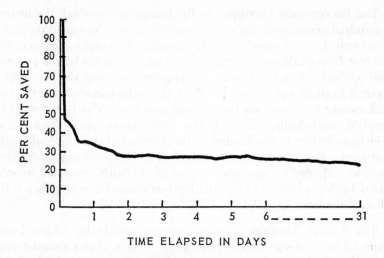

Fig. 9–6. Ebbinghaus Curve of Retention. (After Ebbinghaus, 1885.)

the same, with most forgetting occurring immediately after initial learning.

The amount of retention depends, in part, upon the method of measurement selected. Three of the more commonly employed methods of measuring retention are the recall method, the recognition method, and the saving method.

THE RECALL METHOD. In the recall method, the learner is retested over material once learned after a given interval, and the percentage of the amount of the original learning that is retained is computed. Thus, for a spelling test given before and after instruction and then one month later, the class average for each test might be:

Before Instruction	After Instruction	Retention Test	Per Cent Retained
20	45	35	60

In school, the essay and the completion tests are commonly used by teachers to find out how much pupils can recall. The essay test is an example of the *unaided recall* method. The pupil is presented with a topic and is required to reproduce previously learned material. The reproduction may be word for word (e.g., reciting a poem) or the pupil may be expected to express in his own words the substance of what he has learned. In *aided recall,* the pupil is given the same stimuli as on original learning, and is required to make the correct responses (e.g., a French-English vocabulary test).

THE RECOGNITION METHOD. In the recognition method, the learner is required to recognize the correct answers to questions or to recognize previously learned associations to stimuli. The multiple-choice and the true-false test items are examples of measurements by the recognition method. Two weaknesses are apparent in using the recognition method in studies of retention. First, the learner may obtain the correct answer to a question by guessing and hence this factor must be handled statistically. Second, the difficulty of recognition varies widely according to the fineness of the discriminations required by the test item. For example, the test item: The Declaration of Independence was adopted by representatives of the 13 North American colonies in (a) 1492; (b) 1607; (c) 1776; (d) 1919—is somewhat easier than if the alternatives were: (a) 1774; (b) 1776; (c) 1781; (d) 1789.

THE SAVINGS METHOD. In the savings method, the subject learns material to some standard of proficiency. Then, after a time interval, the subject relearns the same material to the same standard of proficiency and the percentage saving over the original learning is computed. Thus, if it took 20 trials to memorize a list of words correctly on 2 successive trials, and 5 trials to relearn the words after a three-hour interval, the per cent savings would be:

$$\frac{\text{No. trials to learn} - \text{No. trials to relearn}}{\text{No. trials to learn}} \times 100 = \frac{20 - 5}{20} \times 100 = 75\%$$

The savings method is a sensitive measure of retention because it shows some effects of past learning even when no evidence of retention is detected by other measures. Luh (1922) studied the form of retention curves under five methods of measurement. His subjects learned lists of 12 nonsense syllables up to a criterion of one perfect repetition. Over a two-day period of retention tests, Luh found the highest retention for the recognition method, the second highest for the savings method, and the lowest for what we are calling the recall method. Figure 9–7 shows the retention curves of the Luh study for the three methods of measurement we have discussed.

Learning Exercise

20. A teacher administered a multiple-choice science test at the beginning of the school year in order to assess how well his students recalled previously learned science. Would the test results reflect the amount of science knowledge recalled by the students?

Nature of Materials Learned. Retention varies according to the nature of the material learned. It is popularly believed that motor

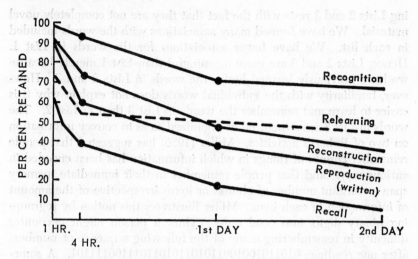

Fig. 9–7. Retention Curves Obtained by Five Different Methods of Measurement. (After Luh, 1922.)

skills are better retained than verbal materials. Osgood (1953) has pointed out a number of methodological problems in testing this notion. It may be that motor learning appears to be better retained because it is more thoroughly learned. Adequate comparisons between the retention of motor skills and verbal materials require comparability between the two in length, complexity, and degree of learning of the two types of learning. Some evidence indicates that when such conditions are equated, there is little difference in retention between these two types of learning (McGeoch and Melton, 1929).

Meaningful materials and those involving the discovery or understanding of a principle are better retained than nonsense syllables. Consider the following three lists of ten words:

List 1	List 2	List 3
req	book	Robert
jen	desk	finished
fom	lamp	his
kiv	pipe	homework
zaf	key	and
dix	pen	then
wap	plant	went
kib	chair	out
tal	case	to
nev	cup	play

List 3 is easier to learn and to remember than List 2. List 2, in turn, is easier to learn and remember than List 1. Part of the ease in learning Lists 2 and 3 rests with the fact that they are not completely novel material. We have formed many associations with the words included in each list. We have fewer associations for the words in List 1. Hence, Lists 2 and 3 are more meaningful than List 1 merely because we have previously learned better the words in Lists 2 and 3. However, familiarity with the individual words does not explain why it is easier to learn and remember the words in List 3 than in List 2. The words in List 3 are structured or organized so as to convey information on two of Robert's activities. Miller (1956) has suggested that people remember *chunks* of things in which information has been encoded in various ways; and that people remember in their immediate memory span a constant number of chunks or items irrespective of the amount of information in each item. Miller illustrates this notion by regrouping binary digits into octal units. Thus, a person might encounter difficulty in remembering many of the following sequence of numbers after one reading: 0101101001001101011010110111100111101. A somewhat better performance may be attained by reorganizing the numbers into groups of threes, thus: 010-110-100-100-110-101-101-, etc. Further efficiency may be attained by assigning the number 0 through 7 to groups of three, thus: 000 = 0; 001 = 1; 101 = 2; 011 = 3; 100 = 4; 101 = 5; 110 = 6; 111 = 7. The first series can then be read as: 264-465-533-475. Miller suggests that the storage of additional verbal items in memory is probably to a considerable extent a reorganization of items into new groups and that we finally reorganize the material into a small enough number of chunks so that we can remember the material in its entirety.

That reorganization of verbal material aids memory is well illustrated in an experiment conducted by Bousfield (1953). Subjects listened to a list of 60 words that fell in four categories: animals, names, professions, and vegetables. The words were presented in random order. After hearing the words, the subjects were asked to write down all the words they were able to recall. It was found that the subjects were able to recall more words than they could with lists of random words; and that they tended to recall words in the same category together.

We have noted previously in Tyler's study that complex cognitive abilities are retained better than specific facts (page 316). This finding also has been reported by West (1937), Frutchey (1937), and McDougall (1958). In McDougall's study, test items in educational psychology were constructed to measure educational objectives within four categories of Bloom's *Taxonomy of Educational Objectives*. The four categories in order of complexity were: knowledge, translation, interpretation, and extrapolation. Tests were given as a pretest, a test at the end of the course, and a retention test about four months later. On the retention test, about 79 per cent of the gains in interpretation and extrapolation abilities were retained. Gains in knowledge and translation were retained to a significantly lesser degree—about 73 per cent.

Learning Exercise

21. Katona (1940) gave two groups of subjects the task of learning the following series of numbers: 5812151922226293336404347. Group 1 was told that a principle underlay the sequence of numbers. Most subjects of Group 1 discovered that the principle consisted of adding alternately 3 and 4 (i.e., $5 + 3 = 8$; $8 + 4 = 12$; $12 + 3 = 15$, etc.). Group 2 learned the number by rote, although the experimenter suggested grouping the numbers (e.g., 581, 215, etc.).

    Both groups were tested shortly after initial learning and then three weeks later. Which group would you expect to do the better on the three-week retention test?

The Conditions of Original Learning. The degree of learning affects retention. Psychologists use the term *"overlearning"* when practice proceeds beyond the point where an act can just be performed at a required degree of mastery. Customarily, we overlearn much both in and out of school (e.g., our own names, the multiplication tables, certain phone numbers, etc.). It may be said that anything that is worth learning is worth overlearning. In school, teachers sometimes provide for overlearning when they schedule "drill" sessions. A better procedure is that of providing the additional practice within new activities. For example, overlearning in multiplication may occur as the child finds a use for multiplication facts in solving some of his daily problems.

Some students remember more than others of what they study simply because they study more efficiently. In an early study, Gates (1917) found that pupils remembered more material studied when a large part of their study time was spent in self-testing. For nonsense syllables, elementary school children who spent as much as 80 per cent of their time reciting and only 20 per cent reading remembered more than children who spent proportionally less time reciting. The proportion of study time that can be profitably spent in self-testing will vary according to the type of material studied. Recitation has been found to yield greater dividends for the less meaningful material. Yet, for difficult reading material, self-testing can result in an increase in meaningfulness if the student attempts to reorganize and state in his own words the material studied. And as McGeoch and Irion (1952) point out, recitation furnishes the student with knowledge of results which serve to motivate the student, eliminate wrong responses, and direct further study efforts.

It is commonly believed that we remember the pleasant better than the unpleasant, success experiences better than failures, and facts consistent with our belief system better than facts that do not fit into our beliefs. Extensive research efforts extending over a period of 40 years leave little doubt that emotional factors somehow affect retention. Freudian theory suggests that the unpleasant is repressed because it provokes anxiety. However, it is by no means clear *how* affective tone, motivation, ego involvement, and anxiety affect retention.[2] It is clear that when emotion interferes with the degree of initial learning, poorer retention can be expected. Levine and Murphy (1943) investigated the rates of both learning and forgetting of controversial material among pro-Communist and anti-Communist college students. During four weekly learning sessions, one pro-Communist and one anti-Communist prose selection were read over twice and then reproduced by the students. Five further weekly tests were given to find out how many ideas the students could remember from the selections. The results for the anti-Communist passage are shown in Fig. 9–8. Clearly, the pro-Communist students learned the anti-Communist passages more slowly. There was also a slight tendency for the pro-Communist students to forget the material more rapidly. The reverse was true for the pro-Communist articles, i.e., the pro-Communist students learned the articles more rapidly and forgot the content more slowly than did the anti-Communist students.

Some studies (e.g., Boswell and Foster, 1916; Karen, 1956) have demonstrated that retention is increased when students study material with the intention of remembering. Intention to remember seems to facilitate retention because of its influence on original learning. The student apparently studies material differently and probably learns it more thoroughly when he knows that he is to be tested at a later date. Ausubel, Schpoont, and Cukier (1957) designed a study to determine whether intent to remember influences retention when the intent to remember is induced *after* the original learning occurs. An experimental group of college students studied a reading on the history of opiate addiction for 25 minutes and then were tested on the material

[2] Critical analyses of research efforts to study the relationship of emotional factors and retention may be found in: Osgood, 1953, pp. 570–87; McGeoch and Irion, 1952, pp. 384–94; and Bugelski, 1956, pp. 332–36.

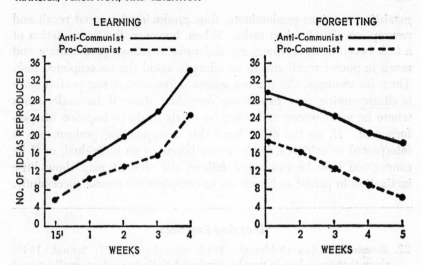

Fig. 9–8. Learning and Forgetting Curves on Anti-Communist Material for Pro- and Anti-Communist Students. (After Levine and Murphy, 1943.)

immediately afterwards by means of a multiple-choice test. *After* the test, an announcement was made that another test over the same material would be given two weeks later. A control group followed the same procedure except no announcement was made of a forthcoming retest. To minimize possibility of communication between groups, data for the control group was gathered in the Fall semester and data for the experimental group was gathered in the following Spring semester. No significant differences in the percentages of material retained was found between the two groups. Hence, teachers who wish to induce an intention to remember need to induce the intention at the beginning of a learning session.

An early investigation by Zeigarnik (1927) appeared to demonstrate that uncompleted tasks are remembered better than completed tasks. Subsequent investigations, designed to isolate the relevant variables, have yielded conflicting results. In some studies, the Zeigarnik effect has been verified; in other investigations, completed tasks have been better retained. Ego-involvement is one crucial factor. But difficulty is encountered in obtaining an objective measure of the degree to which a student is emotionally involved in a learning task.

The distinction made by Rosenzweig (1941, 1943) between "need-persistive" and "ego-defensive" motives may be of value to teachers. Under conditions of low stress, according to Rosenzweig, *need-*

persistive reactions predominate, thus producing increased recall and resumption of unfinished tasks. When, however, the incompletion of a task becomes threatening, *ego-defensive* reactions predominate and result in poorer recall and in an effort to avoid the uncompleted task. Thus, for example, the student whose mid-semester test performance is disappointing may experience only low stress if he understands where he went wrong and what he needs to do to improve his performance. If, on the other hand, his disappointing performance is interpreted as evidence of his unworthiness as an individual, or if he cannot see how he can avoid failure, the student may show little inclination to persist in his efforts to complete the course successfully.

Learning Exercises

22. Research studies (Ashbaugh, 1919; Brueckner, 1927; Stroud, 1940) show that some loss in poorly developed skills in reading, spelling, and arithmetic occurs over the summer for primary-grade pupils, while some gains in the same skills occur for intermediate-grade pupils. What factor probably explains this difference in retention?

23. Mary James claims that she does better on examinations when she studies with another person than when she studies alone. When she studies with another person, they both read a section of their notes and then question each other on what they have read before reading the next section. When Mary studies alone, she reads all of her notes over several times. Is it plausible that Mary actually does remember more of what she studies when she studies with another person? Why?

24. Gaier states: "The student cannot learn what he does not perceive or wish to perceive, and he cannot remember what he does not first acquire. Analogously, it is apparent that the intent to learn depends on just those factors of attitudes, value, need, interest, and experience responsible for selective perception." (Gaier, 1959.) What research study discussed in the preceding section supports Gaier's statement?

25. What procedure is suggested by Ausubel's study on how a teacher might increase the amount of learning and retention of students viewing a film?

26. Nowlis (1941) accompanied some interruptions of tasks with success-provoking statements and other interruptions with failure-provoking statements. On the basis of Rosenzweig's hypothesis, which tasks would you expect to be resumed?

Intervening Activities. The notion that forgetting occurs because of *disuse* or a lack of practice does not satisfactorily explain research data on forgetting. McGeoch (1932), in a classic paper, pointed out several limitations of the disuse explanation of forgetting. Forgetting does not occur merely as a result of the passage of time. Rather, forgetting occurs as a result of the nature of the activities that intervene between the initial learning and recall periods. Negative transfer, then, may be considered as one of the mechanisms of forgetting, and the previously discussed experimental designs for proactive inhibition and retroactive inhibition are appropriate for studying the effects of intervening activities on retention. The proactive design is appropriate for studying the interference or facilitating effects of initial learning upon the learning and retention of a new response. The retroactive design provides an appropriate measure of the interference or facilitating effects of learning a new response on the retention of a previously learned response. The interference theory of forgetting has been built upon the many experiments on proactive and retroactive inhibition.[3] The basic designs for the study of forgetting phenomena are as follows:

PROACTION

Group	First Learning	Second Learning	Retention Test
Experimental	Learn Task A	Learn Task B	Recalls Task B
Control	Rests	Learn Task B	Recalls Task B

The proactive effect of learning Task A upon the learning and retention of Task B can be assessed by comparing the performances of the experimental and control groups on the second learning and the retention test given some time after its original learning.

RETROACTION

Group	First Learning	Second Learning	Retention Test
Experimental	Learn Task A	Learn Task B	Measure retention of Task A
Control	Learn Task A	Rests	Measure retention of Task A

The retroactive effect of learning Task B on the retention of Task A is measured by comparing performances of the experimental and control groups on the retention test.

The amount of interference that occurs between the learning of two tasks is a function of (a) the degree of learning of the two tasks and (b) the degree of similarity of the two tasks. McGeoch and Irion (1952), after reviewing studies on degree of learning, conclude that less

[3] A summary of the issues and experiments associated with the interference theory of forgetting may be found in C. N. Cofer (ed.), *Verbal Learning and Verbal Behavior* (New York: McGraw-Hill Book Co., Inc., 1961), chap. 7.

interference occurs when either or both original and intervening materials are well learned. That similarity relationships affect amount of interference has been demonstrated for both proactive (e.g., Melton and Von Lackum, 1941) and retroactive (e.g., Britt, 1935) inhibition experiments. Robinson (1927) hypothesized that: "As similarity between interpolation and original memorization is reduced from near identity, retention falls away to a minimum and then rises again, but with decreasing similarity; it never reaches the level obtaining with maximum similarity." This hypothesis has become known as the Skaggs-Robinson Hypothesis.

Further experimental work has led Osgood (1949) to modify the Skaggs-Robinson hypothesis to take into account the degree of both stimulus and response similarity. As stimuli between tasks become more and more similar, the possibility for interference or facilitation increases. Facilitation is maximized to the degree that the response learned to S_1 resembles the response for S_2. Interference is maximized to the degree that the response learned to S_1 is dissimilar to the response for S_2.

Characteristics of the Learner. Both chronological age and I.Q. have been found to be related to amount of retention (Lahey, 1937). Older children tend to remember better than younger children, and the bright child better than the child who is not so bright.

The set of the learner can influence retention. The student who expects a multiple-choice test and is given an essay test may experience greater difficulty in recalling pertinent information than the student who expects an essay test. Lester (1932) established the following series of sets in his subjects: (1) expectation of recall; (2) expectation of interpolated material before recall; (3) information concerning the possible effects of learning interpolated materials; (4) an effort to avoid the detrimental effects of the interpolated materials. Most forgetting occurred when the subjects expected neither recall nor interpolated activity and were given both. Least forgetting occurred when an effort was made to counteract the effects of the interpolated materials.

SUMMARY

To a considerable extent, the teaching techniques that insure positive transfer of learning also insure retention of learning. The similarity relationships between two learning tasks affect both transfer and retention.

Retention and positive transfer are likely to occur when the responses to be learned in two tasks are functionally identical. Of course, if the two stimuli in the two learning tasks also are functionally identical, then the second learning task merely provides additional practice in the first task. However, if the two stimuli are similar (but not identical), then the teaching problem is that of aiding students to perceive the similarity in the two stimuli. This problem usually is not difficult for the bright child nor for the child who has learned the first task well. Thus, the child who has mastered the task of adding 4 + 3, finds little difficulty in learning the response "7" to a similar second stimulus "3 + 4." When one or both of the two tasks are difficult, the teacher needs his ingenuity and knowledge about perception in guiding the student to perceive the distinguishing features in two stimuli patterns.

Interference and negative transfer are likely to result when the correct responses differ for two tasks. The amount of interference and negative transfer increases as the degree of similarity of the two stimuli increase. Thus, for a child learning to read, if Task 1 is learning to recognize a *b* and Task 2 is learning to recognize a *d*, more interference and negative transfer may be expected than when the two tasks are learning to recognize a *b* and a *c*. When responses differ between two tasks but the stimuli are similar, the teaching problem involves: aiding the child to perceive differences in the two stimuli; attaching one response pattern to the one learning situation and a different response pattern to the second learning task; and remembering when to respond in the first way and when in the second way. Again, the ability of the learner, the degree of difficulty of each learning task, and the degree of mastery for both learnings will influence the amount of forgetting and negative transfer that occurs.

From our discussions on perception and the factors affecting transfer and retention, it is possible to identify a number of ways that teachers can help students to remember and apply what they learn. Some of these are:

1. Encourage the student to search for relationships between what he is currently learning and his past learning. Transfer possibilities increase as the student actively searches for points of similarity and difference in two or more situations. Retention is increased as the student reorganizes facts, concepts, and principles into a meaningful structure.

2. Provide reviews in which the student encounters previously learned material within new activities. Overlearning and the structuring of old learning in new situations aid both retention and transfer.

3. Provide well-distributed practice in problem-solving. Problem-solving is itself an exercise in transfer as the student strives to relate what he knows to a problem situation. And problem-solving skills once attained are well retained.

4. Relate materials learned in school to the abilities, needs, and interests of the learner. Several studies demonstrate the relationship between intelligence level and the amounts of transfer and retention. Students do tend to perceive and remember more accurately material in which they are interested.

5. Stress generalizations, but make certain the student understands the meaning and factual basis for each generalization taught.

6. Schedule frequent tests or in other ways create a "set" to remember.

7. Induce low stress by arranging for success or anticipation of success experiences in learning. Some evidence indicates that students tend to persist in low stress situations and become ego defensive in failure situations.

Answer Cues

1. (a) Positive. (b) Zero. (c) Negative.

2. To insure the initial comparability of the group receiving instruction in Latin to the group not receiving instruction in Latin. Then, significant differences between groups on the final test may be attributed to the transfer effect of the course in Latin.

3. (a) Proactive design. (b) R_2 to S_2.

4. Does the learning of R_2 to S_2 facilitate or interfere with the previous learning of R_1 to S_1?

5. (a) Identical elements. (b) Formal discipline. (c) Generalization.

6. (a) Positive. Greater transfer effect for *deceive*. (See "(1) stimulus variation.") (b) Negative. Assuming the degree of similarity between *to* and *too* is greater than between *to* and *two*, then, on the basis of Osgood's formulation, one would expect the greater negative transfer between *to* and *two*. Possibly, just the opposite would occur because of overlearning of *two*. (See response variation.) (c) Negative. Greater transfer effect for *where*. (See: Stimulus and response simultaneously varied.)

7. (a) Degree of learning. (b) Transfer occurs more readily for the brighter child. (c) Learning set—"When presented with a problem, first examine it carefully to be certain that you understand the nature of the problem." (d) Task difficulty is related to transfer. The concept of deviation from the mean is included in both *average deviation* and *standard deviation*.

8. (a) *b* and *d*. (b) *p* and *q*. (c) *m* and *n*. (d) *Burn* and *born*.

9. (a) n sound in torn (final consonant more difficult than initial). (b) pl sound in play (consonant combination more difficult).

10. (a) Similarity. (b) Proximity.

11. Figure-ground.

12. Reward and punishment affect what is learned as *figure* and what is learned as *ground*.

13. Remain relatively constant.

14. Students' ratings tended to move in the direction of what they thought were the judgments of their peers. However, students who scored high on a test designed to measure the trait of "ascendance" tended to deviate more from the supposed group opinions.

15. (a) Instructions. (b) Motives. (c) Context.

16. (a), (b), (d), (e).

17. Accuracy depends on *clarity* of the stimulus object and its *distinguishability* from other stimulus objects.

18. Yes. If the information is accurate.

19. Perceptual constancy.

20. No. The multiple-choice test would be a recognition measure of retention, and test scores would likely overestimate the amount of science information *recalled*.

21. The group that discovered the principle underlying the series. In this group, 23 per cent reproduced the series without error, while none in the "rote" group was able to do so. Only 15 per cent in the "understanding" group made 19 or more errors, compared to 74 per cent in the "rote" group.

22. Overlearning aids retention.

23. Yes, because she is using a large proportion of study time in testing herself on what she has read.

24. The Levine and Murphy study.

25. Announce that a test on the film content will be given at a later date.

26. The interrupted success tasks.

10

ACQUIRING INFORMATION
AND MOTOR SKILLS

This chapter is concerned with examining the teaching-learning process through which children acquire information and motor skills. The teaching-learning process involves:

1. What the teacher does in order to help pupils to learn;
2. What the pupil does in an effort to learn;
3. The environmental context or atmosphere in which the learning takes place;
4. Certain characteristics of the learner that may affect learning efficiency; and
5. Perceptual, cognitive, and motivational processes of the learner.

Analyzed in terms of stimulus, organismic, and response variables, the teaching-learning process may be represented diagrammatically as follows:

S	O	R
1. What the teacher does	1. Characteristics of the learner	1. Overt responses of the learner
2. Environmental context	2. Mediating processes within the learner	

A teaching procedure becomes effective when children are (1) motivated, (2) effectively guided, (3) given sufficient and well-distributed practice, and (4) reinforced for progress. The effectiveness of any teaching procedure depends upon certain readiness characteristics of the learner. Finally, an understanding of the cognitive processes occurring as the child learns may help the teacher to select appropriate learning experiences.

ACQUIRING INFORMATION

For many people, education is equated to the acquisition of information. The parent who asks his child, "What did you learn in school today?" usually expects the child to talk about information acquired. The child, too, tends to equate school learning to acquiring knowledge. And there is little doubt that a large portion of a teacher's time is devoted to this end.

In *Taxonomy of Educational Objectives* (Bloom *et al.*, 1956a), the "Knowledge" category includes all educational objectives that can be attained by the student *remembering* material taught.[1] The material taught includes such things as terminology, specific facts, classification systems, sequences of steps in performing a task, principles, generalizations, and theories. Progress in learning usually is measured by tests in which the pupil is called upon to *recall* the material learned. Hence, the section on "Retention" in Chapter 9 of this book is pertinent to our present discussion in guiding students to attain knowledge.

Factors Affecting Learning Efficiency

We have previously noted that efficiency in learning is dependent upon (1) the nature of the task to be learned, (2) the method of instruction, (3) certain characteristics of the learner, and (4) the environmental context in which the learning takes place. We shall examine the effect of the first two of these factors on efficiency in acquiring knowledge.

Task Variable. For objectives involving the acquisition of information, the *length, difficulty,* and *meaningfulness* of the material presented are important considerations. In rote learning, the length of time required to master a task increases much more rapidly than the length of a task (Kingsley and Garry, 1957). If a child can learn to spell 15 words in 10 minutes, we cannot expect him to learn 30 words in 20 minutes. More likely it will require at least 30 minutes. The length of task does not increase the difficulty of learning in a comparable manner for meaningful learning. Henmon (1917) found that in memorizing poetry, the number of repetitions required did not increase proportionally as great as the increase in length of the poem.

Krueger (1946) plotted learning curves for eight series of nonsense syllables of increasing difficulty. As one might expect, the rate of learning was most rapid for the easy series and became progressively slower for the more difficult series. Progress of primary grade children

[1] The terms "knowledge" and "information" are used synonymously throughout this chapter.

in reading is facilitated when the children are provided with "easy reading" (Fry, 1960). For the child who *can* read at the second-grade level, "easy reading" is reading materials at the first-grade level. Fry has developed a list of 300 commonest words that occur in the reading texts issued by three major publishers. Fry refers to these words as *instant words* because they must be recognized instantly by the child before he can develop real reading facility. These words, according to Fry, are not mastered by the average child until sometime in the third grade of school. Easy reading material usually contains a high proportion of these common words and hence provides recognition practice as well as contextual cues for the more difficult words. It is of interest to note that Fry's recommended procedures are consistent with conclusions reached by Hebb (1949) in exploring the neurological correlates of learning. Hebb suggests that sustained interest occurs most readily when the stimulus field is characterized by "difference-in-sameness." The new and more difficult learning material becomes easier to master when imbedded in older familiar materials.

We have noted that *meaningful* materials and those involving the discovery or understanding of a principle are more readily learned and better retained than less-meaningful material. But what is meant by the word "meaningfulness"? The term "meaning" can be defined in a number of ways. Osgood (1952, 1953, 1961) differentiates between two common meanings of "meaning"—*denotative meaning* and *connotative meaning*. The denotative meaning corresponds to a dictionary definition of a term. Osgood (1961) defines denotative meaning as "a conventional, habitual correlation between a nonlinguistic perceptual pattern, $\boxed{S}$, and some particular linguistic response, $\boxed{R}$ " (p. 102).[2] Thus, when two people both call a tool for driving nails a "hammer," we have denotative agreement. Connotative meaning involves a mediating interpretative process that occurs between the presentation of the stimulus and an observable response. Osgood (1961) defines connotative meaning as "that habitual symbolic process ($r_m \longrightarrow S_m$) that occurs in a sign user when a particular sign (perceptual or linguistic) is received or produced" (p. 103). Thus, the sign HAMMER may result in connotations such as *hard, cold, ugly,* and *threatening*.[3] The large

---

[2] Osgood distinguishes between the stimulus object Ṡ and the sign $\boxed{S}$, which is not S but evokes reactions relevant to S. Thus, the word "hammer" $\boxed{S}$ is the same stimulus as is the object "hammer" (Ṡ).

[3] Two stimuli with quite different denotative meanings may have quite similar connotative meanings. To quote Osgood (1961): "Take for example what is implied by the statement, 'A gourmet approaches his lamb chop as a lover approaches his mistress.' The only thing they have in common is their affectionate attitude. . . . We are not surprised to hear the gourmet murmur 'lover' tenderly to his lamb chop or to hear the lover murmur, equally tenderly, 'lamb chop' to his mistress." (P. 104.)

number of verbal metaphors found in everyday speech reflect the connotative meanings elicited by events. The happy man is said to feel "high"; the sad man, "low." Exciting music is termed "red-hot," and slow music is "heavy." Hope is "white," and despair is "black."

Osgood has developed a research technique, known as the Semantic Differential, to study individual's connotations of words or objects. A stimulus word such as "physician" is presented, and the subject is asked to rate the word on a seven-point scale with respect to pairs of descriptive polar terms (e.g., soft–hard). Figure 10–1 illustrates the application of a preliminary form of the Semantic Differential for two groups of 20 subjects differentiating the words "eager" and "burning."

A third conception equates "meaning" to all the verbal associative responses elicited by a given stimulus. Thus, in one study, when "table" was presented as a stimulus word and subjects were asked to list words that came to mind, the response "chair" occurred in about 84 per cent of the subjects (Russell and Jenkins, 1954). Forty-seven additional words were included in the remaining 16 per cent of the responses.

Brown and Berko (1960) studied the child's developing appreciation of English syntax by noting certain characteristics of word associations of children. An adult, given a stimulus word, tends to list words of the same parts of speech (e.g., table–chair). Children tend to list words of different parts of speech (e.g., table–eat). Given the stimulus "to send," children listed words such as "away," "letter," and "card." Adults listed "to receive," "to get," "to deliver," "to bring," "to mail," etc.

Bousfield (1961) explains the development of meaningful responses in terms of conditioning, in which words become associated, and a fraction of the response elicited by one word (UCS) is also elicited by another word (CS). Noble (1952) has developed a procedure for scaling meaningfulness based upon the average number of response associations made to a word in one minute. The 96 words in Noble's list ranged from common words like *kitchen* to makeup words like *gojey*. Noble then constructed three 12-word lists: one of low degree of meaningfulness, one of medium meaningfulness, and one of high meaningfulness. The number of trials required to memorize each list was determined using 72 college students as subjects. The smallest number of trials was required for the high meaningful list, and the largest number of trials for the low meaningful list.

Meaning also may be defined as that which is meant or *intended*. Viewed in this way, we need evidence concerning the intentions of the behaver in order to understand the meaning of a behavior. This fourth

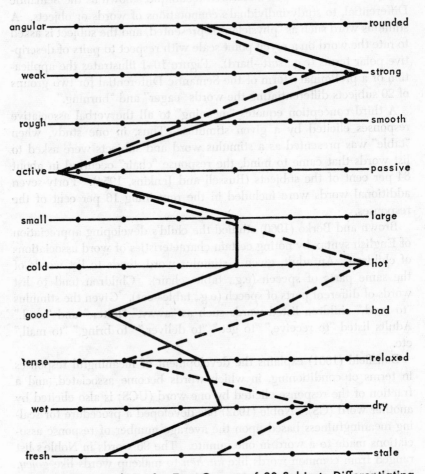

Fig. 10–1. Medians for Two Groups of 20 Subjects Differentiating "Eager" and "Burning" on Preliminary Form of the "Semantic Differential." (From Osgood, 1952, p. 229.)

meaning of meaning probably comes closest to the educator's use of the term. For the educator, a meaningful task is one in which:

1. The learner understands the requirements of the task and has the necessary background of knowledge and abilities to plan and execute a plan for the performance of the task.

2. The task to be performed is related to the needs and goals of the learner, and the learner sees the task as worthwhile performing.
3. The steps in performing the task are perceived by the learner as *logical* rather than a series of mechanical operations.
4. The learning of the task facilitates the later learning or performance of similar tasks.

For a pupil who views arithmetic as something worthwhile learning, a task performed meaningfully may be illustrated as follows:

$$\text{Task:} \quad \tfrac{3}{4} \div \tfrac{1}{2} = \, ?$$

Pupil's Intention	*Pupil's Response*
1. Clarification of problem	"This problem means, 'How many ½ units can I get out of ¾ units?'"
2. Drawing diagrams to aid in selecting correct procedure	(a)
3. "How many times can I take away ¾ units from ¾ units?"	(b)

$$\tfrac{3}{4} \div \tfrac{2}{4} = 3 \div 2 = 1\tfrac{1}{2}$$

Some learning tasks are inherently more meaningful than others. However, the meaningfulness of a task to a particular learner depends largely upon the teacher's method of presentation of the task and upon certain characteristics of the learner.

How important to the classroom teacher are the research findings on the relationship between (1) learning efficiency and (2) the length, difficulty, and meaningfulness of a learning task? Much of this research has involved learning by memorizing. Hence, the research findings are most clearly applicable to learning tasks that involve memorizing. How efficiently pupils memorize material depends in part upon its length, difficulty, and meaningfulness. Research findings do not provide a magical formula that insures the wisest selection of learning tasks of suitable length and difficulty for each pupil in a classroom. The teacher must rely largely upon informed opinion and his own good judgment. We can keep in mind the four meanings of meaning discussed above. At present, however, we do not have scales to measure the "meaningfulness" of the kinds of learning tasks school children are called up to perform.

Learning Exercises

1. If a student requires 15 minutes to memorize by rote 10 chemical formulas, would you expect him to take more than 30 minutes to memorize by rote 20 chemical formulas?
2. Fry has divided his list of 300 instant words into 12 groups of 25 words.

He describes two games designed to provide children with recognition practice. Which of the two following procedures would be the better?

   (a) Find what teaching technique—"easy reading," flash cards, games, etc.—is most effective; and then use the most effective technique exclusively.

   (b) Use a variety of techniques.

3. Boodish and Haller (1962) report an extensive effort on the part of the faculty of a Philadelphia high school to help their students to understand and appreciate the many racial, religious, and ethnic groups with whom they interact in their daily living. One of the goals developed for the home economics course of study was: "To respect the contributions which people of other cultures and races make to home and community living" (p. 70). Is this goal focused on improving denotative meanings or connotative meanings of the various racial, religious, and ethnic groups?

4. One of the principal products of country X is "livestock." Would you expect a farm boy to remember this fact better than a city boy (assuming that the farm boy can associate more words to the stimulus "livestock" than the city boy)?

5. Which of the following observations by a teacher constitute partial evidence that a task is meaningful to the student?

   (a) The student later made use of the information acquired in learning the task.

   (b) A student is asked whether she is prepared for a physics test. She replies, "I know it, but I don't believe it."

   (c) A student, who wishes to become a pilot, learns that it is necessary to be competent in mathematics to achieve his goal. He studies mathematics with increased enthusiasm.

Method Variables. Method variables may be classified in terms of the following factors: (1) motivation, (2) teacher-guidance, (3) practice, and (4) reinforcement. Instructional methods designed to forward the achievement of information will now be discussed in terms of these four factors.

Motivation. Motivation is essential to the acquisition of knowledge. Fortunately, children like to discover, to create, to construct, and to master. They are even willing to spend time memorizing uninteresting material in order to meet the expectations of parents, teachers, and other significant individuals in their lives. Some evidence suggests that compulsive students of college age will work effectively to attain distant vocational goals even when those goals are inconsistent with their measured interests (Frederiksen and Melville, 1954). There is no doubt that *extrinsic* motives stimulate learning. It is equally certain that *intrinsic* interests are even more generally effective in stimulating an effort to learn.

Bernstein (1954) reports a study in which 100 junior high school pupils were assigned two short stories of equal reading difficulty but varying greatly in interest value. An interest-rating scale was used in order to obtain a measure of the interest of pupils for each story. Objective and essay questions over the material in both stories provided measures of reading comprehension. The pupils obtained better reading comprehension scores over the more interesting reading material. Even though the two stories were equivalent in readability as measured by three reading-difficulty formulas, the pupils reported that they found the more interesting story easier to read.

Selecting learning materials of general interest to the learner is, then, one way by which the teacher can secure initial motivation. Research in the various subject areas offers some help to the teacher in identifying the interests of children. For example, from the research findings of the reading interests of elementary school children, Karlin (1960) draws the following conclusions:

1. Younger children prefer short stories of real animals and fairies.
2. Younger children enjoy realistic stories of children which contain elements of *surprise* and *humor*.
3. Older boys prefer books of adventure and mystery, fictionalized history and biography, science hobbies, and inventions.
4. Older girls prefer adventure (without grimness), mystery, sentimental stories of school and home life, romantic fiction.
5. The reading selections used in schools are favored by the older girls two to one.
6. There is need to find material for common reading which is more suited to both sexes.
7. The effect of "good teaching" is less important than the selection of good material for classroom reading. [P. 179.]

Teacher-pupil planning represents one way through which teachers strive to attain desirable initial motivation. It seems logical to expect pupils to be more enthusiastic about their work when they share in its planning. Good judgment, however, is needed on the part of the teacher in deciding when and how to bring pupils into the planning process. It takes time for pupils as a group to develop skills in selecting learning activities that are both interesting and educationally defensible. Nevertheless, the development of the ability to arrive at group decision is itself an important educational objective. Further, children enjoy a chance to talk, to exchange ideas, and express feelings.

Despite his best efforts, the teacher daily encounters the problem of creating interests in school tasks. The problem is not only one of relating subject matter to the needs and goals of the pupil. The teacher's task also involves aiding the pupil to develop new interests and to broaden his goals. That this is no easy task is well illustrated in a report by Rich (1962) of an effort made in two seventh-grade classes to create interest in current events. Initially, some pupils were interested in current events while other pupils were quite apathetic. A questionnaire administered to all the pupils revealed that the pupils who were more concerned over national and international affairs also seemed more interested in almost everything. They read more over a wider range of topics, belonged to more clubs, had a greater number and a wider range of hobbies, were more willing to speak before classmates, and in general demonstrated a greater eagerness for new experiences. Among the interested group of pupils, 80 per cent claimed that their parents discussed current events with them "frequently." Among the apathetic group, 10 per cent reported that they "frequently" engaged in this type of conversation with their parents. Rich found three approaches that yielded good results. These were:

1. Personal conferences with parents of the "apathetic" pupils. The importance of current events, the child's lack of interest, and possible methods for overcoming the difficulty were discussed. For some pupils, this approach seemed to work.
2. Remedial work in reading. Some pupils who lacked interest were deficient in reading ability. With remedial work in reading, utilizing materials found in newspapers and periodicals, some pupils became more interested in current events.
3. Identifying the type of news item that had at least some slight appeal for the apathetic pupil. By giving the pupil a share in reporting the news on the subject in which he had shown some interest, a beginning was made in developing an interest in current events.

Motivation is enhanced when the goals of a learning task are well defined. A reading assignment such as "Read the next chapter in the text" is altogether too vague. Efficiency in reading is promoted when the student understands clearly what he is supposed to learn from his reading. What a person learns from reading depends upon his purposes or "reading set."

Torrance and Harmon (1961) studied the effects of three textbook reading sets upon the test performance of 115 college students. The three sets were: read: (1) to *remember* everything read; (2) to *evaluate* critically the content; and (3) to *creatively apply*, i.e., to think about the many uses of the information contained in the reading material. Students were divided into three groups, and each group read for one week for each of the sets given. Each Friday the students were given a 20-minute test covering the reading assignment for that day. This test contained some items designed to test memory of content, some items calling for evaluation in decision-making situations, and other items on which the student needed to apply creatively the information in the reading. Analysis of the results indicated that the three reading sets produced differential effects on most of the tests for all three weeks. Students tended to perform relatively better on those test items that were consistent with his reading set.

Aiding the individual student to set appropriate learning goals is an important part of the problem of attaining good classroom motivation. An appropriate learning goal for a pupil is one that (1) is consistent with his needs and goals and is perceived by him as such, (2) is appropriate to his ability level, and (3) is clearly understood.

Numerous research studies have attempted to determine the motivating effects of incentives such as grades, gold stars, honors, and competition. There is little doubt that the hope for success and the fear of failure and the anticipation of gaining prestige and the desire to win over others do motivate people. However, such motivation is extrinsic to the task itself. Whenever the first motivation must be extrinsic, it is desirable that it be replaced as soon as possible by intrinsic motivation in which satisfaction is derived from the learning task itself.

Learning Exercises

6. Would you expect interest test scores to be useful in predicting the achievement of a non-compulsive student?
7. Why would you expect students to comprehend better some reading material than other material of comparable reading difficulty level?
8. From the following descriptions of a teacher's approach to a difficult teaching assignment, identify three teaching procedures that increased motivation.

"A group of high school students, holdovers who were all approaching 'retirement age,' were put into a special class with instructions to the teacher to 'try to keep them in school until the end of the year.' With no goal more noble than this, he set up a program called 'vital reading.' This was a label he used for all those tracts, documents, and forms which regardless of position or education, we are all required to deal with: job applications, leases, mortgages, insurance forms, license applications, drivers' manuals, loan applications, union contracts, appliance guarantees. The program was introduced with a discussion about the ways in which mistakes in these matters can be costly; how a misreading of the 'fine print' could be disastrous; how, even though the skill to drive was possessed, lack of simple literacy could mean no driver's license and, hence, no job. As one of the boys said of this program, 'You know, this is the first time this school taught me anything.'" (Gates and Jennings, 1961, p. 122.)

TEACHER-GUIDANCE. Teachers employ a variety of techniques in guiding learning in the classroom: explanations, demonstrations, audio-visual aids, reading, written and oral assignments, programmed learning, class discussions, etc. In this section, we will consider briefly: (1) learning through reading versus learning through listening; and (2) organizing learning experiences so as to facilitate learning.

The problem of whether students learn better through reading than through listening early attracted the attention of educational psychologists. From numerous experiments, it now appears clear that students in *general* learn about equally well through reading and listening, although *individual* students may learn better through one sense modality than another. Westover (1958), for example, administered during the course of a semester a series of seven 40-item objective tests to college students under two conditions. One form for each test was administered by the instructor reading the question aloud twice. The other form was administered by giving each student a mimeographed copy of the test. There were no group differences among students in their performances on tests administered by listening and by reading. However, some students performed better on the tests in which they listened to the questions, while others performed better on the tests in which they read the test items.

Teachers have long grappled with the problem of how learning experiences can best be organized so as to facilitate learning. This is the problem of organizing a series of learning experiences so that each new experience builds upon previous learning. The learner brings to any learning task a background of information and concepts that constitutes for the learner a *cognitive structure* for the assimilation of new information and ideas. In visiting a city for the first time, for example, we tend to note points of similarities and differences to previously visited cities. In reading about Buddhist doctrines, we may relate the new information acquired to more familiar previously learned concepts about Christian doctrines. Our past learning constitutes a reservoir of information, concepts, and strategies for structuring new learning material. The teacher, in introducing students to new materials, may facilitate learning by first reviewing familiar material that is related to the material to be learned. Ausubel and his co-workers (1957, 1960,

1961, 1962) call this familiar introductory material *advanced organizers* and have demonstrated their value in the learning and retention of meaningful verbal material.

In one study, Ausubel (1960) formed experimental and control groups of 40 college students equated on the basis of sex, field of specialization, and ability to learn unfamiliar scientific material. The learning task for Ausubel's experiment consisted of a 2,500-word passage dealing with the metallurgical properties of steel. Prior to the presentation of the learning task, the experimental subjects studied a 500-word passage containing *substantive* background material on the major similarities and differences between metals and alloys, their respective advantages and limitations, and the reasons for making and using alloys. This passage was on a higher level of generality, abstraction, and inclusiveness than the steel passage; but it did not contain information specifically helpful to answering questions based on the steel passage. The control group also was given an introductory passage to study. This passage contained *historical* material on the evolution of the methods used in processing iron and steel. The experiment consisted of having the students in both the experimental and the control groups study their introductory passages on two separate occasions—once 48 hours prior, and once immediately prior to their introduction to the steel passage. Both groups then studied the steel passage for 25 minutes, and three days later were tested over the information contained in the passage. On a 36-item multiple choice test, the experimental groups obtained a mean test score of 16.7 as compared to 14.1 for the control group. The difference between the means was significant at the .05 level of confidence. It is of interest to note that the introductory passage for both groups was related to the content in the steel passage. The substantive material studied by the experimental group apparently served better as an organizing structure for the information on the metallurgical properties of steel.

Ausubel stresses the importance of having the advanced organizers more general and abstract than the new material to be learned. For example, the student who first learns how the climate of *any* locale is influenced by such factors as latitude, altitude, nearness to large bodies of water, ocean currents, prevailing winds, and mountains is in a better position to assimilate information concerning the climate of different places. Given additional sets of advanced organizers relevant to geography (e.g., factors influencing development of industry in a region), a multitude of specific facts in geography begin to fit into a neat structure. The student knowing a few geographical features of a region is able to deduce a host of additional facts.

Learning Exercises

9. Some intelligence tests contain measures for both "verbal" and "non-verbal" abilities. Non-verbal tests require no reading or writing, although the child tested is required to listen and understand test directions. Suppose a classroom of pupils were given an intelligence test containing both verbal and non-verbal subtests. On the basis of research results on learning through reading and listening, would you expect each pupil to perform equally well on both subtests?

10. Miss Roberts, a high school English teacher, hopes to develop the ability of students to critically evaluate various novels that they read throughout the school year. Which of the following learning activities seems the more promising as an "advanced organizer"?
    (a) A discussion on the criteria that may be employed in evaluating the literary merits of a novel
    (b) A lecture on the history of the novel

PRACTICE. Brownell and Hendrickson (1950, p. 101) in discussing how children acquire information, state: "The fundamental method of *teaching* some factual material, most symbols, and arbitrary associations in general remains, as always, the administration of repetitive practice." This is particularly true when the factual material does not lend itself to some meaningful organization or is low in associative value. At all levels of education, the learner is required to learn arbitrary association. The word "book," not "boko," is arbitrarily assigned the object you now have at hand. That Ottawa is the capital of Canada is an arbitrary association for the learner. Hosts of isolated facts, names of places, persons, things, events, processes, etc., are learned by the child in school. These arbitrary associations are acquired by the child through repetitive practice. Errors are promptly corrected in order to avoid their fixation. Repetitive practice becomes less effective when meaningfulness is inherent or is injected into learning materials. Harap and Mapes (1934) found no relationship between the mastery by fifth-grade children of 26 concepts in fractions and denominators and the frequency of the repetitions of the various concepts in arithmetic projects. One experience that increases the meaningfulness of a concept contributes more to its ease of acquisition and retention than do many rote repetitions.

A teaching method that emphasizes problem solving may also be an effective method for teaching facts. Mark (1961) reports a study in which eleventh- and twelfth-graders were taught high school chemistry by two different methods. Students in six classes of the control group performed ten chemistry experiments according to the directions found in their laboratory manuals. The instructors for these classes discussed the experiments to be performed before each laboratory session. The experiments were written up by the students according to the instructions in the manual. In the experimental group, the same ten experiments were performed. The instructors first posed the problem involved in the experiment, and students discussed how an experiment could be devised to solve the problem. The students in the experimental group recorded the results of their experiment in the form of observations, equations, calculations, diagrams, and conclusions. Tests were administered at the beginning and end of the semester to measure progress in learning of the two groups. No significant difference between the experimental and the control groups was found with respect to the amount of knowledge attained. The experimental group did perform significantly better on test items that measured the ability of students to *interpret* chemistry knowledge. Thus, the students in the experimental classes improved their problem-solving abilities without sacrificing the amount of knowledge attained.

In Chapter 6, it was noted that experimental findings indicate that *distributed* practice generally yields better results than *massed* practice for verbal learning. Care needs to be exercised in applying this finding to classroom learning. The optimum length of a practice period probably varies from task to task and even from individual to individual. The teacher needs to be cognizant of the fact that too large doses of practice materials may result in inefficient learning and must exercise some judgment in pacing instruction.

REINFORCEMENT. The reinforcement of a student's response as he strives to acquire information serves two purposes: (1) it increases the probability that the student will increase his practice efforts; and (2) it provides the student with information as to the adequacy of the specific responses he has made in the learning task. For the learner, reinforcement is experienced as a consequence that is satisfying or that meets his expectations, e.g., praise, success, a feeling of accomplishment, or the attainment of some material or psychological goal. Various types of reinforcers may be used by the classroom teacher. Our present concern is to examine how the "knowledge of results" type of reinforcement forwards the acquisition of knowledge.

The learner requires some knowledge of results or feedback in order to benefit from practice. Thorndike (1927) asked blindfolded subjects to draw a line 4 inches long. No improvement on successive trials was observed when the experiment omitted informing his subjects as to their accuracy after each trial. Improvement does occur if, after each trial, the subject is informed whether his line is too long or too short and by how much (Trowbridge and Cason, 1932).

In school situations, knowledge of results is provided to pupils in a variety of ways. Returning to pupils their corrected test papers is one way. Some teachers give tests in order to motivate pupils to work harder. While there is some question as to whether the frequent use of tests is an effective means of maintaining motivation (Noll, 1939; Gable, 1936), there is no doubt that providing pupils with information as to the adequacy of their past learning is an effective first step in remedying faulty learning. In one study, pupils in one group received back their corrected test papers and were given 5 minutes to study their papers. The pupils in a second group did not have their papers returned. One week later the test was readministered. Pupils who received their test papers back performed much better than those who did not. (Plowman and Stroud, 1942.) To maximize the value of returned test papers, the corrections need to be in sufficient detail so that the pupil can see what he needs to do in order to improve his performance.

Learning Exercises

11. Facts, concepts, and generalizations may be thought of as occupying points on a continuum of meaningfulness; thus:

> Arbitrary Association . . . . . . Maximum Meaning
> (zero meaning)

Which one in each of the following pairs has the more meaning?
1. (a) The numeral "3" symbolizes "three."
> OR 1. (b) The concept "three."
2. (a) The "law of gravity" in physics.
> OR 2. (b) A particular river is named St. Lawrence.
3. (a) "To play" and "to have" are designated as "verbs."
> OR 3. (b) The ideals of "liberty," "justice," and "equality."

12. Which of the following procedures is the more promising in promoting learning?
    (a) Give a test each day. Do not return corrected test papers, but inform students as to their test scores.
    (b) Give four or five tests throughout the semester. Return corrected test papers and give pupils ample opportunity to study their papers.

PSYCHOMOTOR LEARNING

Psychomotor learning in the school covers a wide range of activities. Ragsdale (1950) classifies motor activities into three main categories:

1. *Object-motor activities*—directed toward manipulating objects such as tools and materials in industrial arts and home economics. In physical education, the objects to be manipulated may be other persons or one's own body.
2. *Language-motor activities*—in all forms of communication—movement of speech organs; eye movements in reading; movements involved in handwriting, typewriting, and commercial art.
3. *Feeling-motor activities*—in which inner feeling is expressed in action as in the graphic arts, sculpture, painting, and music.

A psychomotor act can be analyzed in terms of stimulus, organismic, and response variables. Let us consider, for example, a car stopped at a red traffic light. For the driver of the car, the light turning green serves as the stimulus or signal for action. Perceptual, motivational, and cognitive mediating processes intervene between the appearance of the stimulus and the car driver's response of putting the car in motion. The driver perceives the light as green. He completes an intent—to put the car in motion. The precise nature of the intent depends upon certain attitudes of the driver (e.g., attitude toward safe driving) and upon other goals that he has (e.g., to get to the office in a hurry). The driver utilizes his knowledge about driving a car in effecting his intent. The response is the sequence of motor acts that puts the car in motion. Diagrammatically, the psychomotor act may be represented thus:

$$S \longrightarrow O\text{—Mediating Process} \longrightarrow R$$

Green light   1. Perception—notices green light   The
           2. Motivation—the intent   motor
           3. Cognitive—knowledge of   act.
              strategies for realizing intent.

What is learned during the motor act? Certain consequences of the act are perceived. The process through which an individual perceives the consequence of a response or response pattern is known as *feedback*. The feedback information may change behavior in a number of ways. First, the individual learns to differentiate cues. In psychomotor learning, many of these are kinesthetic cues. These internal cues help in fashioning a smoothly coordinated sequence of responses for the skilled performer. The skilled performance literally "feels right." Second, the feedback information may modify the motivation of the behaver. For example, if a driver at the traffic light intends to put his car in motion at a high rate of speed just before the traffic light turns green, and this course of action leads to an accident, the driver may subsequently modify his motivation at traffic lights. The driver's intent has not led to a satisfying state of affairs. Third, feedback information may yield bits of knowledge that may be used by the behaver on future occasions. In summary, feedback information may modify perceptual, motivational, and/or cognitive processes; and these in turn may modify the overt response pattern of the learner.

Learning Exercises

13. Classify each of the following according to Ragsdale's categories of motor activities:
    (a) Developing skills in working with science laboratory apparatus
    (b) Learning to play a selection on the piano with expression
    (c) Learning to transmit a message in Morse code
14. How could the three types of feedback operate in learning to dive?

Characteristics of a Skilled Performance

A first task in guiding psychomotor learning is that of identifying the characteristics of a skilled performance. A skilled performance may be described in terms of (1) the mediating processes involved, (2) the feedback process involved, and (3) certain characteristics of the response pattern.

Mediating Processes. (1) A skilled performance is characterized by a rapid and accurate perception of the cues that guide action. As a skill develops, more cues are available but less cues are needed to guide action. The experienced defensive backfielder on a football team becomes sensitive to numerous cues in diagnosing the opposing team's plays. As his skill develops, he requires fewer and fewer cues in making his diagnosis. For many motor activities, the visual cues required by the beginner are supplanted by kinesthetic cues. This means that the instructor, in guiding motor learning, may point out to the beginner cues that are not required by the expert.

(2) The skilled performer increases in his ability to judge what is possible in an increasing number of situations. The beginning student in a clothing and textile course in home economics frequently selects a clothing construction project that is well beyond her abilities. With experience, plans are formed more realistically. The experienced out-

fielder in baseball learns when to try to catch a potential Texas leaguer and when to play the ball safely on the bounce. A major function of practice sessions in many motor activities is that of helping the participant to form more realistic intentions—to learn what is possible and what is not possible.

(3) A person increases his knowledge of ways of realizing his intentions as he develops skill in a motor activity. The skilled artist is not only able to visualize an end product, he knows and has mastered a number of techniques through which he can attain the desired effect. The dressmaker knows a variety of sewing techniques and therefore is able to select a technique that economically and efficiently solves a clothing construction problem. The professional baseball pitcher studies the strengths and weaknesses of each opposing ballplayer and plans how to pitch to each batter on the basis of this knowledge. Thus, part of the task of guiding motor learning is that of providing the information necessary to the performance of a skilled act.

Learning Exercise

15. What mediating processes may occur as a quarterback executes a forward pass?

The Feedback Process. Changes in mediating processes may occur as a result of what the teacher says or does, or they may occur as a result of the feedback that the learner obtains in practicing. The skilled performer utilizes feedback information more efficiently than the novice. Most motor activities include a series of responses. Hence, feedback can occur during the course of an activity as well as at the end of the activity. Even the skilled performer makes errors during the performance of an act. But the skilled performer notices and corrects errors more quickly than does the beginner. The expert car driver constantly makes small adjustments in steering as his car drifts slightly to the left or right. The baseball shortstop, in fielding a grounder, makes a series of responses. A single response in the series becomes part of the cue complex for the next response in the series. The observable change in the external stimulus field consequent to the first response in the series (e.g., a bad bounce of the ball) becomes another part of the cue complex for the succeeding response. The total cue complex thus consists of internal and external stimuli. The rapid series of responses with each single response, adjusted to the requirements of the changing stimulus complex, results in a well-coordinated performance.

Response Pattern. The observable characteristics of a skilled performance vary somewhat from one motor activity to another. However, most of the following factors are usually involved in some way: (1) accuracy, (2) coordination, (3) steadiness, (4) speed, (5) efficient use of cues, and (6) the maintenance of the skill under stress conditions.

Learning Exercises

16. Are kinesthetic cues external or internal?
17. Illustrate the characteristics of a skilled performance in:
    (a) Repairing a watch
    (b) Ballet dancing
    (c) Driving a truck at the end of a seven-hour run

Motivating Motor Learning

A complexity of motives are involved in the learning of a motor activity. The learner begins learning with certain distant goals. Some of these goals are congruent with those of the instructor and some are not. For example, a player on a football team and his coach may both wish to win games. Goals, here, are congruent. But the player may be motivated, in addition, to win personal glory; while the coach may be motivated to get his squad working together as a unit. Goals, here, are not congruent. Incongruency may exist in subgoals as well as in major goals. The coach may perceive mastery of fundamentals as a subgoal to be attained. The player may believe he has already mastered the fundamentals. For all types of motor learning, an important part of the instructional job is that of helping the learner to set desirable and realistic goals and to see the relationship between subgoals and major goals. The teacher has two approaches available in modifying the learner's goals. One approach is that of helping the student to understand the desirability of a goal through explanations. The second approach is that of reinforcing desirable goal-seeking behavior whenever it occurs.

The maintenance of motivation during the course of instruction is a problem in all forms of learning. Many students begin a course with good intentions only to slacken their efforts in the middle portion of a semester. The student may become discouraged because of unsatisfactory progress. Or competing activities may capture the undivided attention of the student. Or the student may become bored because the course has settled down to a routine. Whatever the reason, most teachers (including the football coach and the psychology instructor) find it difficult to maintain the motivation of all students for the entire semester.

There is no magic formula for maintaining motivation. The teacher finds it necessary to help students to form realistic goals and subgoals throughout the whole of the academic year—not just at the beginning of the year. How successful the teacher is in maintaining motivation depends also upon his skill in reinforcing the student's learning efforts. We shall return shortly to the problem of reinforcement.

Teacher-Guidance and Demonstration

Learning of motor-type activities is largely a matter of learning to perceive the appropriate cues and responding with an increasing speed and accuracy to those cues. The response patterns learned are built upon previously learned responses. Thus, the adolescent learning to drive a car experiences no difficulty in making each single response required. He has already learned to press a button or turn a key. He is able to turn a steering wheel or place his foot on a brake. Learning consists of combining a number of previously acquired responses into a sequence; becoming sensitive to visual, auditory, and kinesthetic cues; and responding promptly and without excess motion to these cues.

The importance of perception in motor learning is well illustrated in a study reported by Gates and Taylor (1923). One group of kindergarten children learned to write by *tracing* the letters a, b, c, d, e over transparent paper. A second matched group learned to write by *copying* from models the same letters. Thus, the motor aspect of the task to be performed was the same for both groups. But the cues to be perceived were different. When the two groups were given a copying test, the group that had learned by copying did much better than the tracing group. Also, it was found that the practice time spent by the tracing group helped the children very little in learning to *copy* a different set of letters (f, g, h, i, j). Practice in perceiving the appropriate cues is necessary in order to improve in a motor skill.

Teacher-guidance for all forms of learning is of particular importance during the initial stages of learning. It is here that the nature of the task to be performed is explained or demonstrated as simply as possible. In motor learning, initial instruction has additional importance because obvious visual and auditory cues guide responses during the earlier stages of learning. Later, these cues are often replaced by kinesthetic cues as the learner *feels* the right instant to make a specific response. Thus, in diving, one problem in learning a two-and-a-half forward somersault is that of timing the change from the spinning position to the entry position. To know initially that this response should be made some place between one and three-quarters to two spins serves as a rough guide to the learner as to what cues to observe. An instructor yelling "pop" at the appropriate instant serves as a useful additional cue during the early efforts. Later, this auditory cue is replaced by a kinesthetic cue as the diver feels in some complex fashion the cues that prompt the change in body position.

Learning Exercise

18. What fault can you find in the practice of using water wings in teaching a child to swim?

A demonstration is one way of drawing the students' attention to important cues. The demonstration is especially effective if it incorporates some means of insuring that the learner does perceive the right cues. This point is well illustrated in an experiment conducted by Thompson (1944) and reported by May (1946). The tasks chosen for learning from a demonstration were two mechanical puzzles—an easy one and a hard one. Children were taken from a classroom into a room one at a time. The demonstrator arranged the pieces of the puzzle in a certain order, then assembled them, then dissembled them, and then passed the pieces over to the child for his first trial. The child was given 30 seconds to assemble the easy puzzle and 60 seconds for the hard puzzle. This procedure was repeated until the child mastered the puzzle or until 25 trials were completed. The demonstration was conducted in six different ways. What the demonstrator did in addition to demonstrating was varied, as well as what the child did as he observed the demonstration. Some children merely looked on silently as the demonstrator worked. Some children counted aloud during the demonstration in order to prevent them from describing to themselves what the demonstrator was doing. Some children verbalized what the demonstrator was doing. The demonstrator helped the children in some groups by describing what she was doing, was silent with the children of other groups, and corrected errors in the perceptions of the children in still other groups. Table 10–1 outlines the experimental conditions and shows the average number of trials required for each experimental condition.

Learning Exercise

19. Why was Condition 2 in the Thompson experiment more effective for the easy puzzle than for the hard puzzle?

TABLE 10-1
Average Number of Trials Required by Children To Master Puzzles Under Six Demonstration Conditions

Group	Demonstration Conditions		Easy Puzzle		Hard Puzzle	
	Amount of Verbal Explanation of Demonstrator	What Child Did as He Observed	Number Who Learned It	Average Number of Trials	Number Who Learned It	Average Number of Trials
1	Silent	Counted to 100 by 2's	25	5.7	3	25+
2	Silent	Told what demonstrator was doing	25	3.1	22	22
3	Incomplete description	Silent	25	3.5	25	16.2
4	Complete description	Silent	25	3.2	25	14.1
5	Silent, except to correct child's verbal errors	Told what demonstrator was doing	25	2.2	25	12.4
6	Same as (5), except each block had a number on it; blocks were assembled in numerical order		25	2.8	25	9.5

Adapted from May (1946).

From Table 10–1 it is clear that the demonstration conditions where the child describes what the demonstrator is doing are superior to those conditions where the child is silent, particularly on the easy puzzle. It seems desirable, particularly on the harder tasks, for the demonstrator to either describe what she is doing or correct the observational errors of the child.

Practice with Reinforcement

In guiding motor learning, the teacher has two additional tasks: (1) guiding practice, and (2) evaluating progress. One important function of practice is to improve the learner's discrimination of task-relevant cues. The role of the teacher is that of selecting and programming practice that facilitates this perceptual learning. A second function of practice is that of attaching increasingly accurate responses to the task-relevant cues. Responses of the learner, initially, are diffused and include many movements extraneous to the task. For example, the beginning swimmer thrashes about in the water in his efforts to swim. As learning progresses, these extraneous movements drop out and accurate, well-timed, economical responses are made to cues. However, the skilled performer never achieves complete accuracy of responses. But an error response becomes a cue to prompt a corrective response. As previously noted, this phenomenon whereby a response produces a cue or stimulus for a later corrective response is sometimes called a *feedback* process. The role of the teacher for this second function of practice includes: (1) providing opportunities for the learner to modify his response patterns, and (2) evaluating and diagnosing the progress of the learner and suggesting modifications of his response patterns. But in the final analysis, only the learner can discover the less-obvious kinesthetic cues that lead to high-level performance.

The relative advantages of *massed versus distributed practice* and *whole versus part learning* are discussed in Chapter 6. In general, distributed practice and whole learning have been found to be superior, although the optimum length and frequency of practice session and the relative advantages of whole and part learning vary considerably from one learning task to another.

Failure of the instructor to provide reinforcement is possibly the most serious instructional deficiency in guiding motor learning. Reinforcement usually takes the form of providing knowledge of results. Some, but not all, motor acts have built-in knowledge of results. The boy who lands on his stomach on a dive from the high board does not need to be told that he has done something wrong. Almost immediate negative reinforcement is built in to his performance. However, for most motor acts, there is a need for an outside observer to point out what the performer is doing right and what he is doing wrong. Mere repetition of a motor act with no knowledge of results does not bring about improvement.

Learning Exercise

20. Which of the following illustrates built-in knowledge of results?
    (a) Running the 100-yard dash against competition
    (b) Running the 100-yard dash alone with the coach clocking you with a stopwatch

---

SUMMARY

Length, difficulty, and the *meaningfulness* of the material presented are important task variables affecting the efficiency of the child in acquiring information. The term "meaningfulness" has been assigned diverse definitions. Osgood differentiates between denotative meaning (the dictionary definition of a term) and connotative meaning (the personal thoughts and feelings elicited by a stimulus word). For many experimental psychologists, "meaning" is equated to all the verbal associative responses elicited by a given stimulus. Meaning also may be defined as the intent of the behaver. For the educator, a meaningful task is one in which the learner understands what he is supposed to do, has the abilities to perform the task, perceives the task as worthwhile performing, and one which can be performed by a series of logical operations, and one in which the learner develops abilities needed to perform other worthwhile similar tasks.

The efficiency of a method of teaching information can be examined in terms of (1) its motivational value, (2) the soundness of the teacher-guidance procedures used, (3) the adequacy of the practice pupils will obtain, and (4) its provision for reinforcement. Children acquire information more readily in material that interests them. Hence, a method of teaching may be assessed in terms of the extent to which (1) teaching materials are selected of intrinsic interest to pupils, and (2) the methods employed by the teacher to generate new interests.

A variety of teaching techniques are available to the teacher in guiding classroom learning, e.g., demonstrations, audio-visual aids, reading, written and oral assignments, projects, and field trips. Research has not clearly established the superiority of one technique over another. Probably the value of a particular teaching technique varies with certain characteristics of the learner and the complexity of the material taught. The way learning experiences are organized does influence how well children learn. The learner brings to any learning task a background of information, concepts, and experiences. In introducing new materials, the teacher may facilitate learning by reviewing familiar material and by providing the student with some organizational structure for the assimiliation of the new material.

Repetitive practice is important in acquiring information. But practice becomes most effective when the material to be learned is meaningful and well organized. While, in general, *distributed* practice is superior to *massed* practice, the optimum length of practice sessions varies from one task to another and from one individual to another.

Any teaching method to be effective should provide the student with periodic checks on the adequacy of his responses. Such reinforcement increases motivation and serves to guide the student in future practice.

The teacher's task of guiding psychomotor learning involves helping the learner (1) to set realistic goals and subgoals, (2) to perceive the appropriate cues, (3) to provide adequate practice sessions in which feedback is provided for each of the learner's trials, and (4) to maintain motivation by providing success experiences and reinforcing progress in learning.

Answer Cues

1. Yes. See Kingsley and Garry reference.

2. Use a variety of techniques to insure novelty or "difference in sameness."

3. Connotative meanings. On a Semantic Differential Scale, one would hope that, with constructive educational experiences, students would increasingly rate various racial, religious, and ethnic groups as "good," "worthy," "constructive," etc.

4. Yes. In Noble's study, words with many associations were learned easier than words with few associations.

5. (a) and (c).

6. On the basis of the Frederiksen and Melville study—yes. The non-compulsive student works hard only on what interests him. Frederiksen and Melville found interest test scores predicted achievement in engineering for the non-compulsive student but not for the compulsive student.

7. Bernstein's study indicates students comprehend better reading material in which they are interested.

8. (a) Selecting learning material of general interest to the learner (intrinsic interest). (b) Creating interest by showing relevancy of the reading material to problems of the learner. (c) Defining learning task clearly. Reading to find answers to real problems.

9. No. Some students might be expected to do about as well on each test. Some might be expected to do better on the non-verbal test that required no

reading, while other pupils might be expected to perform relatively better on the verbal test.

10. (a).

11. 1b, 2a, 3b.

12. (b).

13. (a) Object motor. (b) Feeling motor. (c) Language motor.

14. (a) The learner becomes sensitive to certain kinesthetic cues so that certain movements "feel right." (b) The learner picks up bits of information from his previous dives. This information leads the diver to conclusions as to what he has done right and what he has done wrong. (c) Original motivation may be conflictual—desire to perform the dive well and fear of painful consequences. If the diver cuts the water cleanly, he will likely be more confident that he can perform the dive well and not suffer injury.

15. Noticing numerous cues, such as the position on the field of potential receivers and opposing players; judgments as to what type of pass may be successful; and knowledge of what kind of passes have worked for him before in similar situations.

16. Internal.

17. (a) In repairing a watch, efficient use of cues and steadiness would appear to be of particular importance. (b) In ballet dancing, coordination and efficient responding to kinesthetic cues would be among the characteristics of vital importance. (c) Driving a truck after a tiring run perhaps best illustrates the maintenance of a skill under stress conditions.

18. Child does not learn the right cues.

19. Probably because the learner was able to observe the right cues without help from the instructor for the easy puzzle, but not for the hard puzzle.

20. (a).

11

ACQUIRING CONCEPTS

By the time a child enters the first grade of school, he has acquired literally thousands of concepts. One major task of the school is to extend, sharpen, and enrich the child's repertoire of concepts. The child learns new concepts in all school subjects. In arithmetic, for example, the child learns the concepts "addition," "multiplication," "fraction," "percentage," "decimal," etc. In social studies, the child acquires the concepts "government," "constitution," "justice," "citizen," etc. In science, the child learns the concepts "acid," "mass," "refraction," "cell," "ohm," etc. In each subject in the curriculum, hundreds of concepts are taught. Also, growing out of his interpersonal relationship experiences in the miniature society of the school, the child extends his concepts of "fairness," "kindness," "courage," "responsibility," and countless additional human characteristics.

CONCEPTS AS CATEGORIES

A concept cannot be observed. We infer that an individual has formed a concept when he exhibits *categorizing behavior*. A child who picks out apples from a pile of miscellaneous objects exhibits categorizing behavior even though the word "apple" is not in the child's vocabulary. The act of categorizing indicates that some meaning is attached to the objects placed in one class. The meaning that the child attaches to the class of objects may be quite incomplete or even erroneous. The fact that the child exhibits categorizing behavior is evidence that *concept formation* has occurred. Concept formation involves both *discrimination* and *generalization*. A child discriminates between apples and non-apples when he picks out apples from a variety of objects. The child generalizes when he places in the same category apples differing in size, color, and shape.

Concept attainment goes beyond concept formation. Bruner, Goodnow, and Austin (1956) define concept attainment as "the process of finding predictive defining attributes that distinguish exemplars from non-exemplars of the class one seeks to discriminate" (p. 22). An *attribute* is any discriminable feature of an object or an event that can vary from object to object or from event to event. Weight, color, size, and shape are attributes that permit discriminations between apples and non-apples. A single value or a range of values may serve to define all instances or exemplars of a category. For example, a range of color values (shades of red, green, or yellow) permit discriminations between apples and non-apples. When some discriminable feature in our environment is used to infer the identity of something, we refer to that discriminable feature as a *critical attribute*. Thus, color is one critical attribute used in attaining a concept of "apple."

Concept attainment is a decision-making process. A child may attain a concept of "kindness" as he observes events in which a person is characterized as "kind." Each exemplar of the concept is called an *instance*. Concept attainment occurs as the child abstracts from numerous instances the critical attributes that define the concept. The child himself may use the word "kind" in describing the behavior of others. The child's initial conception of kindness serves as a tentative hypothesis in deciding whether an observed behavior is an instance of kindness. Parents or teachers may confirm or correct the child's categorization of a behavior. The child learns the critical attributes that define "kindness" through the process of deciding whether an observed behavior is or is not an instance of kindness, and through information received as to the correctness of his decision.

Learning Exercises

1. Which of the following would you consider to be critical attributes defining a guitar?
   (a) Stringed instrument
   (b) Played by plucking strings
   (c) Color
   (d) Cost
   (e) Range of pitch
2. How many instances of the concept "noun" are in this sentence?

Category Types

Usually we categorize on the basis of several attributes exhibited by an instance. For example, abnormal body temperature may be one of several attributes that permit us to infer illness. Bruner *et al.* (1956) distinguish between three types of concepts on the basis of the ways we combine attributes. These are *conjunctive, disjunctive,* and *rela-*

tional concepts. Figure 11-1 may serve to illustrate each of these types of concepts. The array of eight instances provide three attributes with two values for each attribute. Thus:

Attribute	Value
Number	1 or 2
Sex	Male or female
Size	Big or small

Conjunctive Concepts. In a conjunctive concept, all of the attributes at appropriate values must be present at the same time. Defining the concept "boy" in terms of the three attributes included in Fig. 11-1, we find but one instance because an instance must have a *single, small, male* figure. Many concepts taught in school are of the conjunctive type. For example, for the concept "autobiography," two attributes are (1) mode of communication (written) and (2) subject (about one-self). To categorize something as an autobiography, the appropriate values (*written* and *about oneself*) for both attributes (*mode of communication* and *subject matter*) must be present.

Disjunctive Concepts. In a disjunctive concept, the appropriate values of attributes may vary from instance to instance. In Fig. 11-1, the concept "child" in one instance is *one, small, male* figure, and in a second instance, *one, small, female* figure. The concept "beautiful woman" is disjunctive, with a complexity of attributes involved and a variety of possible values for many of the attributes (e.g., *hair color:* blonde, brunette, redhead, etc.) characterizing specific instances of this intriguing concept. A disjunctive concept always contains an *either-or* element.

Relational Concepts. A relational concept is one defined by a speci-fiable relationship between defining attributes. In Fig. 11-1, we may define as a class all instances containing the same number of figures of the same sex (e.g., boy-man; girl-woman; 2 boys–2 men; 2 girls–2 women). In geometry, congruent triangles may be defined in terms of relationships of lengths of sides of one triangle to lengths of sides of a second triangle (i.e., SSS = SSS). In biology, the concept "homeosta-sis" is defined in terms of the maintenance of constancy of relations in the bodily processes. Map-reading in geography involves the rela-tional concepts of "distance" and "direction." There is some experi-mental evidence that subjects utilize conjunctive and relational con-cepts more frequently than disjunctive concepts even on tasks where all three types of concepts are relevant (Hunt and Hovland, 1960).

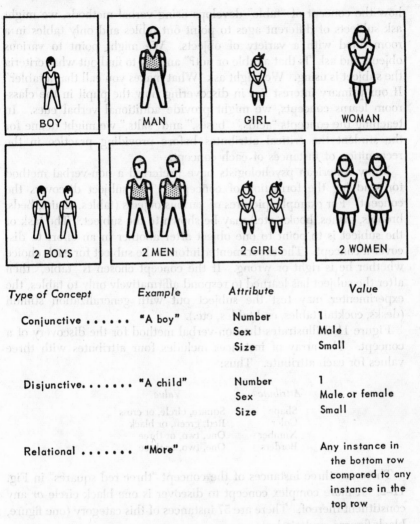

Fig. 11–1. An Array of Instances Combining Three Attributes (Number, Sex, and Child-Adult), Each with Two Values Illustrating Conjunctive, Disjunctive, and Relational Concepts

EXPERIMENTAL STUDY OF CONCEPT ATTAINMENT

The kind of tasks that subjects have been called upon to perform differ importantly from one concept attainment experiment to another. Both *verbal* and *non-verbal* methods have been used. In exploring how the concept of "table" develops using verbal methods, we might ask subjects of different ages to point out tables and only tables in a room filled with a variety of objects. We might point to various objects and ask "Is that a table or not?" and try to find out what criteria the subject is using. We might ask "What makes you call that a table?" If our primary interest lies in discovering how the pupil in the classroom learns concepts, we might provide additional verbal cues. In teaching the concepts "acids," "bases," and "salts," we might define for the student the critical attributes before providing practice in the recognition of instances of each concept.

Many American psychologists have preferred a non-verbal method for studying the formation of concepts. The subject discovers the concept. For example, pictures of various objects (tables, chairs, beds, brooms, dishes, books, etc.) may be shown to the subject. The task of the subject is to point to one object after another in an effort to discover a concept. The experimenter informs the subject for each choice whether he is right or wrong. If the concept chosen is "table," then after the subject has learned to respond affirmatively only to tables, the experimenter may test the subject out with generalization stimuli (desks, cocktail tables, end tables, etc.).

Figure 11–2 illustrates the non-verbal method for the discovery of a concept. The array of instances includes four attributes with three values for each attribute. Thus:

Attribute	Value
Shape	Square, circle, or cross
Color	Red, green, or black
Number	One, two, or three
Borders	One, two, or three

There are three instances of the concept "three red squares" in Fig. 11–2. A more complex concept to discover is one black circle *or* any constituent thereof. There are 57 instances of this category (one figure, black figures, and circles).

Bruner *et al.* (1956) have used an array of figures, such as found in Fig. 11–2 in order to study the variety of "strategies of decision-making" that subjects employ in acquiring, retaining, and utilizing information obtained in the process of discovering a concept. Differences have been identified in the strategies employed by different subjects. The "conservative" individual, having discovered a positive instance, would select as his next choice an instance that varied in but one attribute. The "gambling" individual would select as his next choice an instance that varied in two or more attributes. By varying

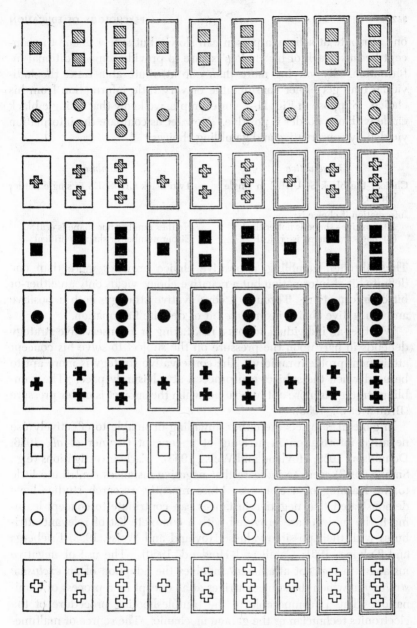

Fig. 11–2. An Array of Instances Comprising Combinations of Four
Attributes, Each Exhibiting Three Values. Plain figures are in green,
striped figures in red, solid figures in black. (Reprinted with permission from J. S. Bruner, J. J. Goodnow, and G. A. Austin, *A Study of
Thinking* [New York: John Wiley & Sons, Inc., 1956], p. 42.)

one attribute at a time, a person can slowly but surely define the concept because each of his choices is sure to provide some additional information. By varying more than one attribute at a time, the individual may get either considerable or very little information from his choice. Suppose in Fig. 11–2, for example, we know that a single black circle with one border is positive. Now let us compare the information yielded by conservative and gambling choices:

Conservative	*Gambling*
Choice: the black SQUARE in single border	Two black CROSSES in single border
Information if choice is:	
(a) positive—shape is not critical	Neither number nor shape is critical
(b) negative—shape is critical	Either number or shape is critical

Thus, through gambling, a positive choice provides more than one definite bit of information but a negative choice yields only an either-or bit of information. Through a conservative strategy, both a positive and a negative choice insure *one* bit of definite information.

Whether an individual adopts a risk-taking or a conservative strategy depends in part upon the pressure on the subject to solve his concept attainment problem rapidly. The conservative strategy is more apt to be used when the subject can proceed at a leisurely pace. The gambling strategy is more apt to be used when the subject is under pressure (Bruner *et al.*, 1956).

In general, subjects are either unwilling or unable to effectively use negative information in arriving at a concept (Bruner *et al.*, 1956; Donaldson, 1959; Hovland and Weiss, 1953). Early investigations (e.g., Smoke, 1933) seem to indicate that negative instances contribute little to the learning of a concept. More recently, research studies have demonstrated that negative instances can contribute to concept-learning if the subjects are provided with a complete list of relevant attributes with their possible values (Hovland and Weiss, 1953; Friebergs and Tulving, 1961; Cahill and Hovland, 1960). The use of negative instances in concept attainment involves the adoption of an *exclusive strategy* in which the subject arrives at a concept by a process of elimination. This is comparable to the troubleshooting procedure of the electronics technician or the garage mechanic. The source of malfunctioning is discovered by eliminating the subsystems that are intact until the malfunctioning subsystem is identified. Braley (1963) suggests that two processes are involved in concept-learning. One is the discrimination of actual cues, while the second is the strategy employed in searching out and testing cue information. The use of exclusion solutions is a higher level problem-solving strategy, more recently developed in an individual's learning history, and placing more strain on memory processes. Hence, a person is more likely to utilize information from negative instances when he perceives the number of relevant attributes as small or he has the defining attributes well specified for him in advance.

Learning Exercises

3. In Fig. 11–2, how many instances are there of the concept "two squares"?
4. Classify each of the following concepts represented in Fig. 11–2 into conjunctive, disjunctive, and relational.
   (a) "One bright-colored circle in a single border"
   (b) "Same number of figures as borders"
   (c) "Two crosses"
5. Classify each of the following concepts as conjunctive, disjunctive, or relational.
   (a) A "strike" in baseball
   (b) "Dog"
   (c) "Superior"

CONCEPTS AS EXPLANATIONS

Many of the child's concepts, even before school age, are revealed in his language development. It is not surprising, therefore, that much research on concept development and concept attainment has taken the form of analyses of children's verbal output. Concept attainment includes more than perceptual discriminations. Cognitive processes are also involved. Hunt (1962) includes, within his definition of concept-learning, the ability to present evidence that the categorizing behavior has occurred on the basis of some rule. To illustrate: A child's explanation as to why he classifies France as a "nation" may constitute one kind of evidence that the child understands the critical attributes of the concept "nation." A second kind of evidence on concept attainment is the child's ability to utilize a concept in problem-solving situations. This second kind of evidence has been used extensively by Piaget and his coworkers in Geneva, Switzerland, in their work on the intellectual development of children.

The development of children's concept of conservation has been investigated by Piaget and his colleagues in a series of studies. In one study, Piaget and Szeminska (1941) used, as part of their experiment, beakers of different dimensions to see how children developed the concept that the amount of liquid contained in a beaker did not change when the liquid is poured from one beaker into other different-sized beakers. The following report on a four-year-old, Clairette Blas, illustrates an absence of the concept of conservation of quantities of liquids. Verbal comments of Clairette are in italics. Figure 11–3 serves to illustrate the problems presented to Clairette.

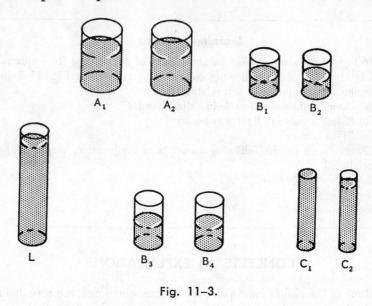

Fig. 11–3.

BLAS (4.0) Have you got a friend? — *Yes, Odette.* — Look, we're giving you, Clairette, a glass of orangeade (A_1, three-fourths full), and we're giving Odette a glass of lemonade (A_2, also three-fourths full). Has one of you more to drink than the other? — *The same.* — This is what Clairette does: she pours her drink into two other glasses (B_1 and B_2 which are thus half-full). Has Clairette the same amount as Odette? — *Odette has more.* — Why? — *Because we put less in* (she pointed to the levels of B_1 and B_2, without taking into account the fact that there were two glasses). — (Odette's drink was then poured into B_3 and B_4.) — *It's the same.* — And now (pouring Clairette's drink from B_1 and B_2 into L, a long thin tube which is almost full)? — *I've got more.* — Why? — *We poured it into that glass* (pointing to the level in L), *and here* (B_3 and B_4) *we haven't.* — But were they the same before? — *Yes.* — And now? — *I've got more.* Clairette's orangeade was then poured back from L into B_1 and B_2: "Look, Clairette has poured hers like Odette. So is all the lemonade (B_3 and B_4) and all the orangeade (B_1 and B_2) the same? — *It's the same* (said with conviction). — Now Clairette does this (pouring B_1 into C_1 which is then full, while B_2 remains half-full). Have you got the same amount to drink? — *I've got more.* — But where does the extra come from? — *From in there* (B_1). — What must we do so that Odette has the same? — *We must take that little glass* (pouring part of B_3 into C_2). — And is it the same now? Or has one of you got more? — *Odette has more.* — Why? — *Because we poured it into that little glass* (C_2). — But is there the same amount to drink, or has one got more than the other? — *Odette has more to drink.* — Why? — *Because she has three glasses* (B_3 almost empty, B_4 and C_2, while Clairette has C_1 full and B_2). [Piaget and Szeminska, 1941, p. 6.]

Clairette's criteria for each judgment is perceptual—the number of containers, the height of the liquid, the thinness or thickness of the beaker. She has not learned to correct appearances by logical thought processes or what Piaget terms *reversibility*. Her attention is centered on what she sees, and she does not think of reversing the pourings. Even when the experimenter reverses the pourings, she fails to see the implications of the reversals in terms of the "conservation of quantity."

The report on Clairette contrasts markedly with that of a boy aged six and a half years who seems to be on the verge of attaining the concept of conservation of quantity (see Fig. 11–4).

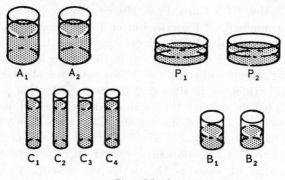

Fig. 11–4.

AES (6.6). A_1 and A_2 were ¾ filled, and then A_1 was poured into P_1 which was wide and low. "Is there still as much orange juice as there was in the other glass? — *There is less.* — (A_2 which is supposed to be his glass, was poured into P_2 (also wide and low . . .) Will you still have the same amount to drink now? — *Oh yes! It's the same, it just seems as if there's less because it's bigger* (= wider), *but it's the same.* — (P_1 and P_2 were poured back into A_1 and A_2, and A_1 was poured into B_1 plus B_2.) Has Roger got more than you now? — *He's got the same* (definitely stated). — And if I were to pour yours into four glasses (A_1 into $C_1 + C_2 + C_3 + C_4$)? — *It'll still be the same.* [Piaget and Szeminska, 1941, p. 17.]

According to Piaget's observations, the concept of conservation of quantity is typically attained by the seven- or eight-year-old child. The concept of conservation of weight is attained later, when the child is nine or ten; and the concept of conservation of volume usually appears when children are eleven or twelve. (Inhelder, 1953.)

Learning Exercises

6. Clairette initially judged amount of liquid by the level of the liquid in a glass. What criteria did Clairette use at the end of the experiment?
7. How does AES demonstrate greater progress than Clairette in attaining the concept of conservation of quantity?

PIAGET'S STAGES OF DEVELOPMENT

For more than 30 years, Piaget and his collaborators have been studying the intellectual development of children. Piaget's earlier work entailed observations of the language behavior of children in everyday situations. Much of this early work has been severely criticized (McCarthy, 1930; Curti, 1938; Huang, 1943). Russell (1956, pp. 160–62) has summarized the criticism of Piaget's methods, materials, and findings. Since the 1930's, Piaget has revised his method of observation and directed more attention to the child's overt behavior in manipulating objects and solving problems. At present, Piaget's work, although still criticized, is attracting increasing attention particularly from psychologists outside the field of developmental psychology. From his extremely detailed observations, Piaget has drawn inferences concerning the nature of the child's intellectual development. Development is viewed as a continuous development of new schemata and the integrations of each newly developed schema with existing schemata. A schema can be defined as "the structure common to all those acts which—from the subject's point of view—are equivalent." (Inhelder, 1962, p. 25.)

For Piaget, the structure of intelligence undergoes a continuous transformation as a result of interaction between maturational and experiential forces. Piaget's data seem to reveal that the child passes through the following identifiable periods:

1. Sensorimotor intelligence (birth to 1½ or 2 years)
2. Preconceptual thought (1½ or 2 to 4 years)
3. Intuitive thought (4 to 7 or 8 years)
4. Concrete operations (7 or 8 to 11 or 12 years)
5. Formal operations (11 or 12 to 15 or 16 years)

The Sensorimotor Period

Objects in the infant's immediate environment become the center of his attention during the sensorimotor period. Upon these objects, the infant brings to bear reflexes (e.g., grasping and sucking). These are the earliest perceptual-motor schemata. These schemata incorporate new elements to form schema of a higher order (e.g., thumb sucking by coordinating the movements of arm and hand with those of the mouth). Thus genuine habits are formed. Vision is coordinated with prehension (usually about four and a half months) and new behaviors appear that seem to represent a transition from a simple habit to intelligence. The infant in a cradle grasps a loose string to a series of rattles overhead. The surprising noise from the rattles appears to prompt the child to repeat the action, and the routine is repeated over and over again. Piaget cautions against interpreting this behavior of the infant as intelligent goal-directed behavior. New objects dangling above the head of the infant will elicit the string-pulling response, but so will the sight of something moving two or three yards from him (Piaget, 1947).

Progressively, perceptual-motor schemata are coordinated and brought under greater control. Means-ends relationships are explored. Characteristically, at about eight to ten months, the infant explores new objects by grasping, shaking, striking, rubbing, etc., as though to define the new in terms of his most recently acquired schemata. At about the end of the first year, the child manifests an interest in novelty for its own sake. The child gradually replaces groping trial and error by imitating unfamiliar models. (The child searches for an object that has disappeared.) This concept of permanency of external objects is necessary for the formation of concepts of space and of causality. Toward the middle of the second year, Piaget notes evidence of internalized schemata or thought processes partially replacing motor outputs. The child appears to rapidly imagine what would happen if he performed certain acts and then selects an appropriate response. In one of Piaget's observations, a stick was placed between a child and a desired out-of-reach object. After unsuccessful attempts to reach the object, the child looked at the desired object, then looked at the stick, then picked up the stick and drew the desired object to him (Piaget, 1936).

Preconceptual Thought

This is the period during which the child develops symbolic and preconceptual thought. For a child playing at eating, a pebble may represent or symbolize a sweet. As the child develops his language, a name becomes a symbol for the thing named. But the three-year-old has not developed the concept of "class." For example, the child walking through the woods does not know whether he sees a succession of different snails or whether the same snail keeps reappearing. For the child, the distinction does not exist; they are all "snail." Piaget uses the term "preconcepts" to these notions of the child that lie vaguely between the concept of an object and a concept of a class. Whereas adults reason deductively from the general to the particular, or inductively from the particular to the general, the child age two to four years reasons *trans*ductively from the particular to the particular. An incident recorded by Piaget (1945) is illustrative.

At 25 months and 13 days, Jacqueline wanted to see a little hunchback neighbor whom she used to meet on her walks. A few days earlier she had asked why he had a hump, and after I had explained she said: "*Poor boy, he's ill, he has a hump.*" The day before Jacqueline had wanted to see him, but he had influenza, which Jacqueline called "being ill in bed." We started out for our walk and on the way Jacqueline said: "*Is he still ill in bed?*" "No, I saw him this morning; he isn't in bed now." — *He hasn't a big hump now.* [1945, p. 231.]

For Jacqueline, eliminating the *illness of influenza* must also eliminate the *illness of hunchback.*

Learning Exercise

8. In which period—the sensorimotor or the preconceptual—would you expect the following behaviors to first appear?
   (a) A child pretends to drink out of a box and then holds the empty box to the mouth of others so that they can drink too.
   (b) A child searches the floor for an object he has dropped.
   (c) A child sees a shell and says "cup."
   (d) A child makes a noise with her saliva. An adult imitates the noise and the child imitates the adult in her turn.

Intuitive Thought

The reasoning of the child from four to seven is limited because it is perceptually dominated. The adult does not really believe that the magician creates the rabbit out of nothing or that the lady has been sawn in half. The adult places more reliance on his thought processes than his perceptions when the two come in conflict. The child at the intuitive stage is still dominated by his perceptions. We have seen this well illustrated in Piaget and Szeminska's report on Clairette as she centers attention first on the height of the liquid in beakers, then on the number of beakers, but never taking both into account simultaneously (see p. 364). The child of four or five who sees all the beads from one glass poured into a second taller and thinner glass typically judges that there are more beads in the second glass (because the level is higher) or that there are fewer (because the second glass is thinner).

Concrete Operations

Between the ages of seven and eleven, the child develops the ability to manipulate in thought, concepts previously developed through the manipulation of concrete objects. Three sorts of logical operations in the thought structures of the child begin to emerge at about the age of seven or eight or sometimes a little earlier. These are *classes, relations,* and *numbers.*

1. *Classes.* The concept of a "class" or the operation of "classifying" is a mental process equivalent of the motor act of placing together objects recognized as similar. The difference between intuitive thought and operational thought in dealing with classification problems is illustrated in an experiment reported by Piaget and Szeminska (1941). Children were presented with a box containing about 20 wooden beads. Most of the beads were brown but two of them were white. Children were asked whether the box contained *more wooden beads* or *more brown beads.* Children at the intuitive stage of development characteristically stated that there were *more brown beads.* These children seemed unable to think of the whole (wooden beads) and the parts (brown and white beads). With the attention centered on the parts, the child grasps only part-part relationships. Children at the concrete operations level of development encountered no difficulty with this problem and were able to conceptually move back and forth from whole to parts. That is, the children were able to think of brown beads as one class of wooden beads.

2. *Relations.* The operation of conceptually *ordering* objects or activities is developed during the concrete operations period. Prior to this, the child can arrange objects in order of size after some trial and error. But the child seems unable to visualize an ordered series before beginning actually to manipulate the objects. Piaget and Szeminska presented children with ten wooden dolls of varying heights and ten play walking sticks of varying lengths. Each child was then asked to arrange the dolls and sticks so that each doll could easily find his own stick. This task was not performed successfully by children of four or five years of age. Later, in the intuitive age period, children encountered some success after some trial and error by arranging both dolls and sticks in order of size. A child in the concrete operations stage typically appeared to visualize the whole series. He would pick out the tallest doll and the tallest stick and place them together; then proceed to the next tallest doll and stick, and so on.

3. *Numbers.* Number operations constitute a blending of classifying and ordering operations into a single operational whole. The number

8 is a classifying operation involving the grouping of any eight objects (eight dolls, eight marbles, eight tops, etc.) to form a class. The number 8 is also an ordering concept in which 8 is placed between 7 and 9 in a sequence of whole numbers. The preoperational child may have learned to count but numbers are still intuitive since they are bound by perceptual data. It is the abstract concept of number that emerges during the concrete operations stage of development.

Class, relation, and number operations may be grouped into systems of operations. For example, two distinct classes may be combined into a more comprehensive class (e.g., *all men and all women = all human adults. Texas is larger than Alabama; Alabama is larger than Rhode Island; therefore Texas is larger than Rhode Island.*) The child acquires a powerful problem-solving tool when he begins to realize that changes are reversible, i.e., two classes, two relations, or two numbers just combined may be intellectually separated again (e.g., $5 + 3 = 8$, but $8 - 3 = 5$). Piaget's studies seem to indicate that the principle of *reversibility* enables the child to attain the concept of conservation of quantity. A child, age five or six, may be fooled into thinking he is obtaining more candy when his single stick of candy is broken into several pieces. At a later age, the child is not fooled. He appears to reverse the breaking process by mentally putting the pieces back into a single stick. Reversibility permits the child to recognize reciprocal relationships (e.g., if Pierre is a foreigner in the United States, Peter is a foreigner in France).

From observations of children solving a variety of types of problems, Piaget has generated a number of principles (such as the principle of combinativity, the principle of reversibility, etc.). These principles explain how the child develops a system of logic that guides him in grouping operations. These principles serve as "search models" in the child's problem-solving behavior and also as criteria for judging the adequacy of his solutions.

Formal Thought

The development of the capacity for *abstract thought* is the major accomplishment during the period of formal operations (eleven or twelve to fifteen years). The eleven-year-old applies operational thinking to practical problems and concrete situations. The adolescent can manipulate ideas about ideas, or in Piaget's language, "perform operations upon operations." The adolescent can consider hypotheses which may or may not be true and reason out what would logically follow if they were true. The adolescent becomes a theorizer and a critic because he is able to see his environment as only one of many possible arrangements and to conceive of other arrangements that might be better. We have noted that the concrete problem of matching walking sticks of varying lengths to dolls of varying heights could be handled successfully by the seven-year-old child. Yet the formal relations problem of "Edith is fairer than Susan; Edith is darker than Lily—who is the darkest of the three?" is rarely solved by children before the age of twelve (Piaget, 1947).

Stages of Thought Illustrated

Much of Piaget's information on the formal operations period is derived from experiments conducted by Inhelder (Inhelder and Piaget, 1958), in which children were asked to discover elementary laws of physics using simple apparatus. In one experiment, for example, a child is presented with several buckets of water and a variety of objects. The child is asked to classify the objects on the basis of whether or not they will float on water. Then he is asked to explain the basis of his classification of each object. Next, the child experiments; and finally, he is asked to summarize his observations, and to look for a law.

Children at the intuitive stage of development fail to make a coherent classification. Wood stays on top because "it will swim anywhere." But "the little wood will sink." A pebble will sink "because it stays on the bottom." A candle will sink because it "doesn't belong in water." The child attributes various properties to identical objects but assigns quite different properties to analogous objects. Thus the child may predict that a piece of wire will sink to the bottom and that a piece of metal will float. The child searches for an explanation for each individual object rather than looking for common qualities of floating objects and common qualities of sinking objects. Thought processes are perceptually dominated and centered on one event at a time.

Children at the concrete operations level are successful in developing a classification system but not in formulating an explanatory law. Typically at this level, children base their classification system on whether an object is heavy or light. The child then discovers that the weight of an object is not an adequate basis for classifying. A large piece of wood is heavy, yet it floats; a needle is light, yet it sinks. Some nine- or ten-year-olds next develop a fourfold classification: small, light objects; small, heavy objects; large, light objects; and large, heavy objects. Inhelder's nine- and ten-year-old subjects were unable to take the next steps of relating weight to volume and the density of an object to the density of water. Attention was centered on the characteristics of the concrete objects under observation rather than on the relationship of the abstract concepts of weight and volume.

The following example illustrates most of the characteristics of the concrete operations period:

BAR (9 years): [Class 1] — Floating objects: ball, pieces of wood, corks, and an aluminum plate. [Class 2] — Sinking objects: keys, metal weights, needles, stones, large block of wood, and a piece of wax. [Class 3] — Objects which may either float or sink: covers. Later BAR sees a needle at the bottom of the water and says: *"Ah! They are too heavy for the water, so the water can't carry them."* — "And the tokens?" — *"I don't know; they are more likely to go under."* — "Why do these things float?" [Class 1]. *"Because they are quite light."* — "And the covers?" — *"They can go to the bottom because the water can come up over the top."* — "And why do these things sink?" [Class 2]. — *"Because they are heavy."* — "The big block of wood?" — *"It will go under."* "Why?" — *"There is too much water for it to stay up."* — "And the needles?" — *"They are lighter."* "So?" — *"If the wood were the same size as the needle, it would be lighter."* — "Put the candle in the water. Why does it stay up?" — *"I don't know."* — "And the cover?" — *"It's iron, that's not too heavy and there is enough water to carry it."* — "And now?" (it sinks). — *"That's because the water got inside."* — "And put the wooden block in." — *"Ah! Because it's wood that is wide enough not to sink."* — "If it were a cube?" — *"I think that it would go under."* — "And if you push it under?" — *"I think it would come back up."* — "And if you push this plate?" (aluminum). — *"It would stay at the bottom."* — "Why?" *"Because the water weighs on the plate."* — "Which is heavier, the plate or the wood?" — *"The piece of wood."* — "Then why does the plate stay at the bottom?" — *"Because it's a little lighter than the wood, when there is water on top there is less resistance and it can stay down. The wood has resistance and it comes back up."* — "And this little piece of wood?" — *"No, it will come back up because it is even lighter than the plate."* — "And if we begin again with this large piece of wood in the smallest bucket, will the same thing happen?" — *"No, it will come back up because the water isn't strong enough: there is not enough weight from the water."* [From *The Growth of Logical Thinking from Childhood to Adolescence* by Bärbel Inhelder and Jean Piaget. Trans. by Anne Parsons and Stanley Milgram. New York: Basic Books, 1958, p. 33.]

Children at the formal thought period revealed formal operations on the floating bodies problem in the way they (1) discard hypotheses, (2) construct new hypotheses, and (3) verify the hypotheses they construct.

Note in the following report how Fran, a twelve-year-old, discards hypotheses:

FRAN (12; 1) does not manage to discover the law, but neither does he accept any of the earlier hypotheses. He classifies correctly the objects presented but hesitates before the aluminum wire. "Why are you hesitating?"

— *"Because of the lightness, but no, that has no effect." — "Why?" — "The lightness has no effect. It depends on the sort of matter; for example, the wood can be heavy and it floats."* And for the cover: *"I thought of the surface." — "The surface plays a role?" — "Maybe, the surface that touches the water, but that doesn't mean anything."* Thus he discards all of his hypotheses without finding a solution. [Inhelder and Piaget, 1958, p. 37.]

Fran eliminates absolute weight as a factor by noting a negative instance that refutes his tentative hypothesis, "wood can be heavy and it floats." Crude hypotheses are discarded without experimentation as he mentally searches for a case where the hypothesized factor is associated with the opposite effect. The child at the concrete operations level of development centers his attention on the observable characteristics of each object in order to develop a classification system that permits a prediction of whether an object will float or sink. The child at the formal operations level is not so limited to the operation of perceptual processes. Cognitively, he abstracts a characteristic such as "weight" or "surface area" and then explores whether or not the abstracted characteristic is sufficient to explain all the observable phenomena. As Inhelder and Piaget (1958) put it: "The subject views the problem in terms of all combinations in such a way as to draw out their implications or nonimplications instead of noting the empirical links simply in order to draw tables of correspondences or classifications from them." (P. 39).

We have noted that children at the formal operations level are not as restricted to perceptual processes as are children at the concrete operations level. The increasing role of reasoning processes is revealed in the ways children at the formal operations level construct hypotheses and verify the hypotheses constructed. The following report on Mal, a twelve-year-old, is illustrative.

MAL (12; 2): *"The silver is heavy, that's why it sinks." —* "And if you take a tree?" — *"The tree is much heavier, but it is made of wood." —* "The silver is heavier than that water?" [bucket]. — *"No, you take the quantity of water for the size of the object; you take the same amount of water." —* "Can you prove that?" — *"Yes, with that bottle of water. If it were the same quantity of cork, it would float because the cork is less heavy than the same quantity of water."* And again: *"A bottle full of water goes to the bottom if it is full because it's completely filled without air, and that bottle stays at the surface if you only fill it halfway."* [Inhelder and Piaget, 1958, p. 38.]

Mal discards the comparison between the weight of the total volume of water in the bucket and the weight of an object and reasons that the amount of water weighed must be equal in volume to the object. Note that Mal cannot see a volume of water equal to the volume of an object. Nor can he see a relative weight. Moreover, the reasoning operations of Mal's verification procedures include the varying of a single factor while keeping all other things equal.

Learning Exercise

9. In an experiment reported by Inhelder and Piaget (1958), an apparatus resembling a billiard table is used. Balls are shot from a spring-plunger that can be pivoted and aimed in various directions around a fixed point. The ball is shot against a buffered projection wall and rebounds to the interior of the table. A target is placed successively at different points. The child is asked to aim, shoot, and afterwards report what he observes. The law that the child can discover is that the angle of incidence is equal to the angle of reflection.

At which one of the three stages—intuitive, concrete operations, or formal operations—is each of the following four subjects?

(a) "The subject is concerned with practical success or failure without consideration of means. Here are some of his comments: *'It always goes over there.'* But he does not succeed in adjusting his aim. *'Oh, it always goes there . . . it will work later.'*

(b) " *'The more I move the plunger this way* (to the left . . .) *the more the ball will go like that* (extremely acute angle), *and the more I put it like this* (inclined to the right) *the more the ball will go like that* (increasingly obtuse angle). . . .'

(c) " *'The rebound depends on the inclination* (of the plunger) . . . *Yes, it depends on the angle. I traced an imaginary line perpendicular* (to the buffer): *the angle formed by the target and the angle formed by the plunger with the imaginary line will be the same.'*

(d) " *'It's the corner* (the angle of the rebound) *that makes it turn; you change the contour* (the size of the angle) *when you change the plunger'* (inclination of the plunger). He demonstrates that the angle is extremely acute when the plunger is slightly inclined and extremely obtuse when it is sharply inclined. . . ." (Inhelder and Piaget, 1958, pp. 6–13.)

FACTORS AFFECTING CONCEPT ATTAINMENT

The problem of identifying the factors affecting concept learning is complicated by the variety of definitions of concept learning found in the current psychological literature. For Bruner, Goodnow, and Austin, concept attainment involves a new way of categorizing objects into sets so that a meaningful classification rule may be discovered.

For Piaget, concept attainment is demonstrated when a child is able to explain a phenomenon in terms of a rule or law. Thus, concept attainment may be viewed primarily as *categorizing* behavior or *explaining* behavior. Both types of behavior are of importance in school learning. In addition, teaching concepts in school includes the procedure of defining a concept for the pupils (i.e., stating the categorizing rule) and then providing children with practice in (1) recognizing instances of the concept and (2) applying the concept in the solving of problems or in explaining events.

Do certain characteristics of the learner make a difference to successful concept attainment? Piaget's extensive research indicates that age is an important factor in concept learning. The child advances through stages of cognitive development characterized by progressive changes in the processes by which the child characteristically adapts to his environment. Maturational, experiential, and motivational factors contribute to these progressive changes. Many (but not all) investigators who have experimentally examined some of Piaget's schemata have obtained results in general agreement with Piaget's classification of development (Peel, 1959; Woodward, 1959; Lovell, 1961; Case and Collinson, 1962). However, many differences between individual children have been found.

Case and Collinson (1962) extracted short passages from two history, one geography, and two literature texts. Subjects from ages seven to seventeen, after reading a passage, were asked three questions involving the interpretation of the material in the passage. The responses of each pupil were then scored on the basis of whether they reflected intuitive thinking, concrete operations, or formal operations. As each pupil was asked three questions on each of five passages, a total of 15 responses were available for each pupil. The average number of intuitive, concrete, and formal thought answers for children, by chronological age groups, is reported as follows:

Age	Intuitive	Concrete	Formal	Number of Pupils
7–10	5.9	4.9	4.2	10
11–14	2.49	4.39	8.12	41
15–17	.77	1.67	12.56	39

Clearly, Case and Collinson's data reveal a marked tendency for older children to use more mature thinking processes. And as might be expected, children with higher mental ages tended to use more mature thinking processes. Yet, Case and Collinson found that all pupils at all age levels answered at least one question at the formal thought level. Also, it was found that pupils tended to regress to a less mature level of thinking when presented with complex materials.

Efficiency in concept attainment is dependent upon the complexity and abstractness of the concept involved. For example, it is easier to learn the concept "apple" than the concept "conservation of weight." Both perceptual and cognitive processes are involved in learning a concept. Concept learning becomes increasingly a cognitive process as the learner supplants or replaces sensory data with information not contained in the immediate stimulus field. Wohlwill (1962) has identified three dimensions along which perception and conception can be related.

(1) *Redundancy:* As one proceeds from perception to conception, the amount of redundant information required decreases.
(2) *Selectivity:* As one proceeds from perception to conception, the amount of irrelevant information that can be tolerated without affecting the response increases.
(3) *Contiguity:* As one proceeds from perception to conception, the spatial and temporal separation over which the total information contained in the stimulus field can be integrated increases. [P. 98.]

Redundancy

Redundancy may be said to occur whenever more information is provided than is minimally required to identify an instance of a concept. The redundant information may take the form of (a) repeated presentation of the same instance or (b) the presentation of a new instance that does not yield additional information. Thus, for the child who is learning the concept of a "canoe," showing the same picture of a canoe more than once would be an example of the first form of redundancy. Showing a picture of a different canoe would be an example of the second form of redundancy if the second picture did not yield additional information concerning the defining attributes of a canoe.

Redundancy may facilitate concept attainment. Bourne and Haygood (1959) found that increases in redundant relevant information improved concept formation and that the amount of improvement increased with complexity.

Learning Exercise

10. In attempting to discover the concept "two circles" (see Fig. 11–2), a subject is told that the two green circles with a single border is an instance. The subject then makes the following series of choices. Identify the redundant choices:

Choice	Information (Is it an instance?)
(a) Two black circles in a single border	Yes
(b) Two red circles in a single border	Yes
(c) Two green circles with two borders	Yes
(d) Three green circles with a single border	No
(e) Two green squares with a single border	No
(f) Two black circles in a single border	Yes

Teaching concepts in the classroom is a more complex procedure than is the teaching of concepts in the experimental laboratory. Usually, the attributes that define a concept are pointed out to the student. For example, the concept "congruent triangles" may be initially defined for the student as two triangles with equal corresponding sides and angles. The student is then able to recognize exemplars of the "congruent triangles" concept if he is given 12 pieces of information, i.e., the length of the three corresponding sides and the size of the three corresponding angles of the two triangles. As learning progresses, the student acquires more information that permits him to recognize an exemplar of the concept with fewer pieces of information. Thus, knowing that there are 180° in a triangle permits the student to recognize an example of congruent triangles with 10 pieces of information. Knowing that two triangles are congruent when three sides of one are equal to the corresponding three sides of the other permits recognition of congruent triangles with but 6 pieces of information. As the student acquires more and more information, the ability to recognize instances of "congruent triangles" becomes decreasingly a perceptual process and increasingly a conceptual process. Pieces of information or cues that were necessary at one level of conceptual development become redundant at a higher level of development.

Learning Exercise

11. Following are 4 of the 48 frames from Set 15 of Holland and Skinner's programmed instruction on "The Analysis of Behavior" (1961, pp. 98–105). The concept "successive approximation" is the major concept treated in Set 15. The correct answer is left blank in Holland and Skinner's program, while below the correct answer is supplied within brackets.

Frame 8 — In training a high jumper, the coach reinforces *successive approximations* to good form by [raising] the crossbar a little, after a few successful jumps.

Frame 9 — Gradually shifting the criterion as to what form of response will be reinforced alters behavior through *successive ap-*

proximations. By requiring a slightly higher jump each time, behavior is gradually shaped through [successive approximations].

Frame 46 — When the instructor slowly raises his standards for saying "good," he is making [successive approximations] to the desired form.

Frame 48 — On the rifle range, we begin at close range and move to longer and longer ranges as we become more skilled. Moving to longer ranges applies the principle of [successive approximations].

Suppose we wished to supply additional information in Frames 46 and 48. Which of the following pieces of information would be *redundant* for a student who has completed the program up to Frame 46?

(a) Add a definition of "successive approximation" at the beginning of Frame 46.

(b) Include the length of the rifle range in Frame 48.

(c) Explain in Frame 46 that the word "good" may act as a reinforcer.

(d) In Frame 48 give an example of the application of "successive approximation" in teaching a motor skill.

Selectivity

In recognizing an instance of a concept, the learner must separate relevant from irrelevant information. In Fig. 11–2, for example, four attributes—number of figures, number of borders, shape, and color—are relevant while *position* of an instance on the chart is irrelevant. For the concepts children learn in school, relevant and irrelevant information may be inherent in both sensory stimuli and in the pupil's past learning. In recognizing an exemplar of the concept, the task of the pupil is to select the relevant and ignore the irrelevant out of all the information available. The difficulty of recognizing congruent triangles may be increased by imbedding congruent triangles in complex diagrams and supplying irrelevant information concerning the dimensions of the complex diagrams. Consider the following two problems in arithmetic:

1. John has 10 apples. John gives away 4 apples. How many apples has John left?

2. John has 10 apples. *Susan has 6 apples.* John gives away 4 apples. How many apples has John left?

The pupil's task of recognizing the second problem as one of simple subtraction is made more difficult by the irrelevant statement "Susan has 6 apples." A number of investigators have found that an increase in the amount of irrelevant information increases the difficulty encountered in attaining a concept (Kendler, 1961).

Contiguity

Spatial and temporal contiguity play two important roles in perception. First, we tend to group stimuli that are in close proximity. Thus, the following configuration of dots tends to be perceived as several pairs. We do not perceive the second and third dot as forming a pair.

. . . .

Second, learning is aided when a response we make is closely followed by an observable consequence. The response of turning on a light switch is closely followed by (or contiguous to) the light going on. We have noted in Piaget's work that the child at the earlier developmental levels is restricted in dealing conceptually with his environment by his immediate perceptions. Wohlwill (1960) reports a number of research studies showing that children as they grow older increase in their ability to relate objects in the stimulus field independent of their spatial or temporal contiguity.

Wohlwill (1957) differentiates between two processes involved in forming a concept. The first process is *abstraction*, which Wohlwill defines as a selective response to a given aspect of the stimulus. The second process is *conceptualization*, which he regards as a process of mediated generalization. The first process is primarily perceptual; the second is cognitive. At earlier levels of development, the child is more dependent upon the organization of the stimulus field.

Learning Exercise

12. Explain each of the following in terms of either the concept of "selectivity" or the concept of "contiguity."
    (a) Many psychologists conduct experiments with rats in the laboratory under well-controlled conditions. In the simplest type of experiment, only one condition is allowed to vary at a time and the behavior of the rats under the experimental conditions is observed.
    (b) Sometimes a well-planned experiment yields unexpected results. An experiment conducted by Michael Faraday in 1831 is a good illustration. Faraday wound a coil of wire around one part of an iron ring and a second wire around another part of the ring. He connected the first coil to a battery and the second coil to a galvanometer. He thought that the current through the first coil would create magnetic lines of force which would concentrate in the iron

ring which in turn would produce an electric current in the second coil. The experiment did not work as Faraday expected. But he noticed that *at the moment he turned on the current, the galvanometer needle jerked briefly and did the same thing in the opposite direction when he turned the current off.* This unexpected result led Faraday to the discovery of the principle (concept) of electrical induction.

Motivating and Reward Factors

In Chapter 9, the influence of affective processes on perception is discussed. To a considerable extent, we perceive what we wish to perceive. The needs of the learner thus constitute an important factor affecting the perceptual aspect of concept attainment. Research evidence also indicates that motivation operates on the mediating processes involved in concept attainment (Mednick, 1957; Romanow, 1958). For the teacher, this means that the relationship between motiviation and the effectiveness of concept attainment needs to be considered in planning learning experiences.

The teacher can facilitate the learning of concepts by reinforcing correct responses of pupils. Rhine and Silun (1958) found a positive relationship between consistency of reinforcement and efficiency of concept formation.

TEACHING CONCEPTS

It is neither possible nor desirable to teach thoroughly all the concepts that students encounter in one year's instruction in any school subject. There are too many concepts. The concepts encountered in any one subject vary in complexity, in their intrinsic and potential interest to students, in their breadth, and in their explanatory value. The level at which an individual attains mastery of a concept likewise varies. A child may be able to define a concept but only recognize its most obvious exemplars (Ojemann, 1957). A child may be able to identify numerous exemplars of a concept but be unable to use the concept in solving a problem. Some concepts introduced early in school are never completely mastered within a lifetime (e.g., the concepts of "justice" and "interdependence"). The research of Piaget and others show clearly that some concepts can be attained only after the child has sufficiently matured and gained the necessary background of experience.

It is abundantly apparent that the method of teaching a concept will vary according to certain characteristics of the learner, the concept to be taught, and the concept-attainment response to be learned. Nevertheless, it is possible to identify from research on concept attainment a number of implications relevant to the various decisions the teacher must make in teaching concepts.

Decision in Planning Instruction

Most concepts learned in school are taught within the context of some broad unit of study. For example, an analysis of current social trends such as presented by Dimond (1957) might suggest to a school faculty a unit of instruction on political, economic, and societal world trends. Within such a unit, new concepts would be related to student's past experiences and old concepts would be examined within a new context. In the teaching of such a unit, a major task of the teacher is that of identifying the major concepts to be taught. The decision on *what concepts to teach* represents the first in a series of decisions that the teacher makes in guiding students in their learning of concepts.

We have noted that the needs of the learner and the degree of striving of the learner are related to the effectiveness of concept attainment. Motivation may be assured through the selection of concepts to be taught. (Ojemann, 1957) points out that *concepts that deal with something of immediate concern to the child are mastered more readily than concepts of little immediate value.* The child in the primary grades wants to get along tolerably well with his peers. To do this, he must learn to exercise some control over his impulses. The concepts of "taking turns," of "sharing," and of "interdependence" are examples of concepts dealing with something of immediate concern to children in the primary grades.

Second, the teacher must decide *what student responses constitute concept attainment.* If the purpose in teaching the concept "natural resources" is to make the concept clearer and more exact, then instruction should be geared to this purpose. At the end of instruction, the student should be able to discriminate between exemplars and nonexemplars of the concept and be able to abstract the criterial attributes. If the purpose is to develop the ability of the student to utilize the concept of natural resources in an analysis of current world trends, then somewhat different teaching procedures would seem to be appropriate.

A third decision of the teacher is that of *selecting learning experiences.* Can the concept be developed most efficiently by the teacher's explaining it in class, by the student's reading about it, by class discussions, by the use of films, or by taking the class on a field trip? This decision needs to be made on the basis of the level of development of the student, the nature and complexity of the concept to be taught, and the past concept-related experiences of the students. In the light of Piaget's research, concrete experiences would seem to be particularly of value at the lower grade levels. For example, the concepts of "taking turns" and "sharing" are probably most effectively learned by the primary-grade child through his informal interactions with other children. Concrete experiences (or at least films) would appear appropriate when children lack experience related to the concept. A visit to a factory may aid a child attach meaning to the concept "automation." Children may attach only vague meaning to familiar words when used in describing places foreign to their experiences. Horn (1937) reports that the interpretations given by fifth-grade pupils of "many people" in the sentence "Many people are engaged in the fishing industry" varied from 50 to "as many people as Chicago has." Fourth-grade pupils varied in their estimates of the thickness of the "thick cap of ice and snow" covering Greenland from "one inch" to "thousands and thousands of feet."

A fourth decision concerns motivation. For many concepts that are taught in school, the initial motivation must be extrinsic. The problem of the teacher is somehow to relate the concept to be learned to the interests of the child. One method of eliciting interest is to *relate the concept to be learned to the past experiences of the child.* We have noted in Chapter 8 that sustained interest occurs most readily from a stimulus field characterized by "difference-in-sameness." The child is likely to be interested in something that has some degree of familiarity and some element of novelty. For example, the student who sees in his own community some of the effects of automation becomes interested in learning more about automation—particularly if he is afforded the opportunity to talk about what he already knows concerning automation.

Often the problem of maintaining motivation is more difficult in the classroom than the problem of eliciting initial interest. Many students begin each semester's work with good intentions. All students need to feel adequate, to develop competencies, to deal effectively with their environment. Many students find in school learning a means of fulfilling their needs. This means that for the student who is initially reasonably well motivated to learn, the major motivational problem of the teacher in fostering the development of concepts is that of, first, *selecting learning tasks that are appropriate to the student's level of development,* and second, *reinforcing appropriate responses when they occur.* A student's interest soon wanes when he is called upon to perform tasks beyond his abilities or when he sees no progress in attaining his goals.

A fifth decision concerns the *organization of learning experiences* to teach concepts. Learning experiences may be ordered from the easy to the more difficult, from the concrete to the abstract, or from the known to the unknown. Research on whether concepts can be attained more efficiently deductively or inductively has not resulted in clear-cut findings. Usually, both inductive and deductive processes are involved as a child learns a concept. For example, in teaching the concept "adverb," the teacher may first list a number of words that modify the meaning of verbs, then have the pupils tell what these words do. A negative instance may be inserted in the series. The teacher then may give the name "adverb" and ask the pupil to formulate a definition of an adverb. Up to this point, the organization of learning experiences calls for inductive thinking on the part of the child. He is called upon to proceed from the particular (instances of adverbs) to the general (a definition of adverb). Once the definition is well understood, the teacher may then ask the pupil to identify adverbs in a paragraph. This experience calls for deductive thinking. The pupil proceeds from the general (a definition of an adverb) to the particular (instances of adverbs).

In general, learning experiences should be organized in such a way as to encourage *searching* behavior on the part of the pupil (Della-Piana, 1957; Kittell, 1957). Initially, perceptual processes will play a large part, while later, conceptual processes will play an increasingly larger role in mastering a concept. Hence, Wohlwill's previously discussed three dimensions of *redundancy, selectivity,* and *contiguity* can be applied in ordering learning experiences. Consider, on the basis of Wohlwill's three dimensions, the comparative merits of the following two sets of practice exercises. Assume that one or the other set is to be given following a first lesson on adverbs.

DIRECTIONS: Underline the adverbs in the following sentences:

Set A	Set B
1. John ran quickly.	1. Certainly, John may come when he is ready.
2. I went yesterday.	2. Tom is brave.
3. Mary quickly arranged her books.	3. As of today, I have learned exactly nothing.
4. _____.	4. _____.

Set A is clearly superior if we assume that, in the early practice sessions, *redundancy* and *contiguity* are desirable and that the pupil should be aided in *selecting* by reducing non-exemplars to a minimum. In Set A, redundancy occurs—the adverb "quickly" is included twice in the list. Contiguity is attained by placing the adverb next to the verb in each sentence. Set B contains negative instances in that item 2 contains no adverb, and in item 3, the word "today" is used as a noun rather than as an adverb.

For succeeding practice sessions, the difficulty level may be increased by eliminating redundancy, providing fewer contiguous cues, and by including non-exemplars of adverbs that require finer discriminations. The use of non-exemplars may be of particular value by providing to the pupil additional information concerning the characteristics of the concept.

Learning Exercise

13. Werner and Kaplan (1950a, 1950b), in a study of concept formation among children from ages eight to thirteen, used a learning task in which the child was to discover the meaning of an artificial word by the way it was used in a series of six sentences. For example, one of the 12 sets used in the study was as follows:

    "1. The dinner was good, but the fruit we ate was soldeve.
    "2. When we were driving in the evening, we did not feel safe because things on the road seemed to soldeve.
    "3. The older you get, the sooner you will begin to soldeve.
    "4. People like a blossoming plant better than one that is soldeve.
    "5. Putting the dress on the sunny lawn made the color of the cloth soldeve.
    "6. Because the windshield was frozen things looked soldeve." (Werner and Kaplan, 1950b, p. 5.)

    The meaning assigned to *soldeve* was "wither" or "fade." Werner and Kaplan found a steady growth with age on a number of measures used to assess the child's understanding of the concept.
    Which of the following seems to best explain Werner and Kaplan's finding:
    (a) Concepts that deal with something of immediate concern to the child are mastered more readily than concepts of little immediate value.
    (b) The teacher can facilitate the learning of concepts by reinforcing correct responses.
    (c) Concept learning is facilitated by past experiences and previously acquired concepts.
    (d) Both deductive and inductive processes are involved in concept attainment.

SUMMARY

A child evidences conceptualizing behavior when he is able to classify objects or events into categories and demonstrates that his classification is based on the defining attributes of a concept. Both *discriminations* and *generalizations* are involved in forming a concept. A discrimination is made between an instance or exemplar of the concept and a non-exemplar. A generalization is made between one exemplar and another despite discriminable differences in irrelevant characteristics. Thus a trombone and a piano both may be classified as exemplars of the concept "musical instrument" while a television set and a dentist's drill may be classified as non-exemplars. In order to categorize, the child must *abstract* from instances the critical attributes.

Three types of concepts are distinguishable on the basis of the ways attributes are combined. These are *conjunctive, disjunctive,* and *relational.*

Attaining a concept *inductively* (i.e., without benefit of prior information as to the defining attributes) is somewhat like the game of "Twenty Questions." Suppose the concept to be discovered is "wind instruments." From an array of objects, the experimenter first shows the subject a positive instance (e.g., a trumpet). Then the subject makes a series of choices in order to discover the concept. After each choice, the experimenter tells the subject whether or not his choice is an example of the concept. Individuals differ in the strategies of decision-making through which they choose instances. One person may try to find out if an object that varies but slightly (e.g., a trombone) is a positive instance. Another person may choose an object that varies markedly (e.g., a piano) in order to test the boundaries of the concept. Each choice can provide additional information as to the defining attributes of the concepts. Positive instances permit inferences about the critical attributes; negative instances eliminate other attributes. Individual differences, of course, occur in the ability of persons to abstract relevant information from positive and negative instances and remember the information obtained from each choice. Research evidence indicates that subjects are not efficient in using information derived from negative instances.

For over 30 years, Jean Piaget and his colleagues in Geneva, Switzerland, have investigated the development of children's concepts. For Piaget, a child evidences grasp of a concept when he is able to apply the concept. Piaget has investigated the development of broad concepts (e.g., time, space, causality) and has identified stages in development that the child passes through. These are:

1. *Sensorimotor period* (birth to one and a half or two years). The child modifies and combines innate reflexes and, through trial and error, develops perceptual-motor schemata many of which involve eye-hand coordinations. Gradually, the child builds up a view that external objects (a) are distinct from himself, (b) exist even when out of sight, and (c) may be affected by his own responses.

2. *Preconceptual thought* (one and a half or two years to four years). Signs and symbols, particularly words and images, originate in this period. The child develops the capacity to imitate an increasing range of new responses. Words and the concepts for which they stand are used in social interaction, and the child discovers that through them he can influence and be influenced by others. The child, however, does not develop the concept of a class during this period.

3. *Intuitive thought* (four to seven or eight years). The reasoning of the child is limited because it is perceptually dominated. A stick of candy broken into two may be thought of by the child as more candy because it appears to be more. Further, the child centers on one aspect of an observable phenomenon at any one time. Beads poured into a tall, thin glass may appear to be more because the level of beads is higher, or less because the second glass is thinner.

4. *Concrete operations* (seven or eight to eleven or twelve years). Logical reasoning operations emerge during this period but are limited to internalized motor responses. But motor operations can be imagined as well as the *reversals* of these responses (e.g., mentally pulling two pieces of candy back together into one piece). Three sorts of logical operations in the thought structure of the child that emerge are *classes, relations,* and *numbers.*

5. *Formal thought* (eleven or twelve to fifteen or sixteen). The ability to abstract, to manipulate ideas about ideas, to scan systematically a large number of hypotheses, and to examine relationships—all emerge in this period.

The literature in psychology on concept learning has a number of implications for classroom teaching. Some implications are:

1. The method of teaching a concept needs to be geared to the developmental level of the child. At earlier age levels and for complex concepts at later age levels, concrete experiences are desirable.

2. As the course of concept attainment is marked by a transition from perceptual to conceptual processes, there is a need to take

into account, in the earlier phases of instruction, the limitations of perceptual processes. These limitations are discussed in this chapter in terms of three dimensions: *redundancy, selectivity,* and *contiguity.*

3. Motivation affects the concept attainment process. Hence, concepts that deal with something of immediate concern to the child are more readily attained.

4. The method of teaching a concept will vary according to what student responses are considered as evidence of concept attainment. If the student is expected to apply a concept in a problem situation, teaching procedures are called for different from those required where the student is expected only to recognize an example of the concept.

5. Concept learning is facilitated by past experiences and previously acquired concepts. This fact can be taken into account in selecting and organizing concepts in a teaching unit. New concepts can be related to the learner's past experiences and old concepts examined in a new context.

6. Relating new concepts to the past experiences of the student also serves to initiate interest on the part of the learner in materials taught.

7. If the concepts selected to be taught are geared to the learning ability and the needs of the student, motivation can be sustained by reinforcing appropriate responses when they occur.

8. Both deductive and inductive reasoning processes of the learner can be stimulated in guiding the student to attain a concept.

Answer Cues

1. (a), (b), (e).

2. Four—instances, concept, noun, sentence.

3. Nine.

4. (a) Disjunctive. (b) Relational. (c) Conjunctive.

5. (a) Disjunctive. (b) Conjunctive. (c) Relational.

6. The number of glasses.

7. AES recognizes after a demonstration that the amount of liquid does not change when poured into a beaker of a different shape.

8. (a) and (c) Preconceptual. (b) and (d) Sensorimotor.

9. (a) Intuitive. (b) Concrete operations. (c) Formal operations. (d) Concrete operations.

10. (b) Information obtained in choice (a) is that color is not a critical attribute. Choice (c) eliminated number of borders; choice (d) ascertained that "two" was critical; choice (e) that "circles" was critical. Hence, all information that is needed has been obtained after choice (e).

11. (a) and (d) are redundant.

12. (a) Principle of selectivity. By controlling conditions, irrelevant information can be eliminated. (b) Contiguity: turn current on—galvanometer needle *immediately* moves; turn current off—galvanometer needle *immediately* moves in opposite direction.

13. (c).

12

THINKING

The term "thinking" is used in everyday life in a variety of ways. It may be used to mean remembering something as when a student thinks of the right answer to a factual test question or a person thinks of mailing a letter. "Thinking" also may be synonymous to "believing" as when we say, "I think she is pretty."

Bartlett (1958) reserves the term "thinking" for cognitive processes that involve more than recall of information. The thinker does start with given information or recalled information. But this information or evidence must be manipulated cognitively in order to *fill gaps*. A series or succession of interconnected steps occur in the gap between the information given and accepted and some terminal point.

In this chapter, the term "thinking" is used to designate cognitive mediating processes that entail more than recall of information. Attention will be focused, first, on the general nature of cognitive mediating processes and, second, on ways of describing and classifying thinking in terms of an interaction between mediating processes and environmental factors.

MEDIATING COGNITIVE PROCESSES

The recent increase of interest by psychologists in mediating cognitive processes has been noted in Chapter 6.[1] The present author shares the view that: "Central to the activities of the teacher are the cognitive processes of the student, and it seems reasonable to conclude that the teacher's effectiveness depends to some extent on her understanding of these processes" (Harper *et al.*, 1964). Admittedly, much remains to be learned about higher mental processes. However, in recent years,

[1] A fine selection of research and theoretical papers on the many facets of higher thought processes may be found in R. J. C. Harper, C. C. Anderson, C. M. Christensen, and S. M. Hunka, *The Cognitive Processes: Readings* (Englewood Cliffs, N.J.: Prentice-Hall, Inc., 1964).

a beginning effort to understand central mediating processes has been made in a number of areas in psychology such as neuropsychology, information processing with electronic computers, and Piaget's observations of the development of intelligence. We now turn to a brief discussion of developments in these diverse areas of psychology.

The Nervous System and Learning

The efforts of psychologists to correlate theories of learning with knowledge of the structure of the nervous system has had a long history. Today, these efforts appear to be beginning to bear fruit. Improved techniques that permit the inspection of cell structure have led to advances in the understanding of the neurophysiology of the central nervous system. A growing body of experimental data on learning has led to more comprehensive theories of learning. Hence, today, speculations on the neurophysiological correlates of learning at least can be made in the light of an increasing body of experimental data. Before turning to one neurophysiological theory of thought, the functioning of the nerve cell in transmitting neural impulses will be briefly sketched.

The Nerve Cell. The nervous system can be conveniently thought of as a vast communication system. Energy received by the nervous system arises from the external environment and from within the body. This energy is transformed into nerve impulses by specialized *receptors,* transmitted to all parts of the body through *connectors,* and converted back into action by the *effectors.* Thus, the function of the communication system is to handle inputs of information from the senses and the output of responses. In short, mediating processes may be viewed in terms of the functioning of the nervous system.

The *neuron* (nerve cell) is the structural unit of the nervous system. The neuron consists of a mass of protoplasm bounded by a membrane. The neuron has three parts: a large cell-body containing the nucleus, the dendrites, and the axon. The *dendrites* are treelike fibers stemming from the large cell-body. The neuron may have more than one dendrite. The one *axon* usually has fewer branches than the dendrites and conducts nerve impulses away from the cell-body and toward the next cell. The *synapse* is the place where the axon of one neuron comes into contact with a dendrite or the cell-body of another neuron. A nerve cell in a state of activity transmits from one end to another. When thus active, the cell is said to be "fired."

The *neural impulse* is the fundamental process of neural transmission. Hebb (1958) summarizes important facts about neural impulses as follows:

(1) The impulse is a change, both electrical and chemical, that moves across the neuron at a fast but limited speed, the rate varying with the diameter of the fiber (up to 120 meters per second in large fibers, less than 1 m./sec. in the smallest); (2) this disturbance can set off a similar one in a second neuron, across the synapse, or when it reaches a gland or muscle cell can cause it to secrete or contract; (3) the neuron needs a definite time to "recharge" itself after firing in this way; (4) immediately after firing nothing can fire the neuron again, but a little later, before recharging is complete, the neuron can be fired by a supraliminal stimulation; and (5) when the neuron fires, its cell-body and axon fire completely—the all-or-none principle. [P. 90.]

Hebb's Neuropsychological Theory of Thought. Implicit within many concepts recognized by psychologists is the assumption that behavior is not completely dominated by the immediately preceding sensory stimulation. The concepts of attention, set, attitude, expectancy, and hypothesis, for example, imply an organism acting on, rather than reacting to, its environment. Hebb (1949, p. 5) assigns the term "autonomous central processes" to those processes that are relatively independent of afferent stimuli. Hebb presumes that these processes underlie perception, attention, perceptual learning, and (in short) thought. The problem of developing a neuropsychological theory of thought is one of finding "conceptions for dealing with such complexities of central neural action: conceptions that will be valid physiologically and at the same time 'molar' enough to be useful in the analysis of behavior" (Hebb, 1949, p. 11).

The "cell-assembly" and the "phase sequence" are the key concepts used by Hebb in theorizing on the neurophysiological basis for autonomous central processes. Hebb hypothesizes that "a mediating process consists of activity in a group of neurons, arranged as a set of closed pathways . . . which will be referred to as a *cell-assembly*, or a series of such activities, which will be referred to as a *phase sequence*" (1958, p. 103).

Hebb assumes that a cell-assembly is established, usually in infancy, as a result of a repetitive sensory event. Two neurons that are repeatedly active at the same time become functionally connected so as to reduce the resistance to a passage of impulses from one to another. This change in resistance may be due to an enlargement of the synaptic knob, or it may be due to some chemical change. When a neuron A fires another neuron B, some change occurs in A or B or both that increases A's future capacity to fire B. A stimulus that activates A and B simultaneously may activate a third cell, C. With the firing of C, impulses from C to A may be set off so as to reactivate A should it become inactive for any reason, thus strengthening the synaptic connection C-A. Similarly, the synapses A-B and B-C may be strengthened. Each neuron in this manner becomes more efficient at firing the next in the series, and eventually excitation of one of them alone may be sufficient to set off a reverberation A-B-C-A-B-C, and so on. The system, at this point, becomes capable of *autonomous* activity. The activity occurs with a particular stimulus event but can continue after the sensory stimuli has ceased. It is likely that one such circuit would excite a number of similar circuits. A single sensory event would involve probably millions of neurons in this circular chain reaction. The neurons fused in this neural firing chain are what is called the *cell-assembly*. Each assembly corresponds to a relatively simple sensory input such as a particular vowel sound.

A chain of cell-assemblies that fire each other in some order is called a *phase sequence*. The order need not necessarily be a fixed one. Each phase sequence corresponds to one current in a stream of thought. Hebb writes:

. . . each assembly activity in the series might be aroused (1) sensorily, (2) by excitation from other assemblies, or (3) in both ways. It is assumed that the last, (3), is what usually happens in an organized flow of behavior. Each assembly must establish connections with a number of other assemblies, at different times; which of these others it will arouse on any specific occasion will depend on what other activity, and especially what sensory activity, is going on at that moment. Assembly A tends to excite B, C, and D; sensory activity tends to excite D only, so A is followed by D. At each point in time, behavior would thus be steered both sensorily and centrally, jointly controlled by the present sensory input and immediately prior central activity. [1959, p. 629.]

Note that the stimulation that initiates the assembly may occur within the organism. A dry mouth or an empty stomach may initiate assemblies and phase sequences. Further, the neurons themselves are living things and may fire off by themselves because of nutritional or other conditions. Concerning this point, Bugelski (1960) writes:

We have just given the nervous system a license to act by itself. Since it does so anyway, giving the license may be a purely gratuitous act, but for many years psychologists have refused to grant this license and have restricted the operations of the nervous system to the function of connecting the outside world with the muscles. This limitation can no longer be tolerated. If a human has pellagra or too much alcohol, we can expect him to hallucinate. The pink elephants are not in the outside world and no amount of argument or postulation by the psychologist will put them there. They are the result of a physiological condition involving the brain. While the dietary deficiency can be blamed on the outside world, to be sure, and the alcohol came from a bottle, the pink elephants came from the brain. Because it might escape the notice of the student, we should point out that the license we have just given includes the privilege of having rather clever and ingenious behavior occur by virtue of the brain's action just as freely as bizarre activities have been licensed. Such action is presumably related to changes in the "internal environment" (oxygen, nutrition, etc.); it is not *uncaused* but we are unable to identify the specific factors involved. [Bugelski, 1960, p. 160.]

In his conceptual scheme, Hebb sees attention or set as evidence of the influence of ongoing mediating central processes. In a situation in which a number of different motor responses are possible, the response that occurs depends in part upon the assemblies that are already active when the receptor inputs from the situation arrive. Invention or insight is explained in terms of new combinations of the phase sequences available. Emotional disturbances are explained in terms of a conflict of two or more phase sequences.

Learning Exercises

1. What does Hebb consider to be the basic components of learned behavior?
2. The perception of an apex of a triangle may be explained in terms of cell-assemblies, but a whole series of neural events occur in seeing a triangle as a whole. What term does Hebb use to describe such a series of neural events?
3. Activity in the brain, initiated by a single sensory stimulus, may continue after the sensory stimulus ceases. How does Hebb explain this?
4. How does Hebb believe assembly activity is most frequently initiated?
5. What is meant by the contention that the nervous system is capable of acting by itself?

Information Processing in Electronic Computers

Modern electronic computers are sometimes referred to as *giant brains*. In many respects, the term is appropriate. "Computer programs now play chess and checkers, find proofs for theorems in geometry and logic, compose music, balance assembly lines, design electric motors and generators, memorize nonsense syllables, form concepts, and learn to read." (Simon and Newell, 1962, p. 137.) Further, on identical problems, Simon and Newell found striking similarities between the problem-solving processes of intelligent college students and their General Problem Solver (an informational processing system). The successful computer simulation of human thinking and problem solving has suggested a search for the counterpart of computer processing within neurophysiological processes. Newell, Shaw, and Simon (1958), for example, have inferred the following about neural processes:

> The broad class of theories usually labelled "associationist" share a general behavioristic viewpoint and a commitment to reducing mental functions to elementary, mechanistic neural events. . . .
>
> The picture of the nervous system to which our theory leads is a picture of a more complex and active system than that contemplated by most associationists. . . .
>
> . . . we postulate an information-processing system with large storage capacity that holds, among other things, complete strategies (programs) that may be evoked by stimuli. The stimulus determines what strategy or strategies will be evoked; the content of these strategies is already largely determined by the previous experience of the system. The ability of the system to respond in complex and highly selective ways to relatively simple stimuli is a consequence of this storage of programs and this "active" response to stimuli. The phenomena of set and insight that we have already described and the hierarchical structure of the response system are all consequences of this "active" organization of the central processes. [P. 63.]

Problem solving involves choosing an adequate path from a problem posed to a possible solution. A computer program provides a set of instructions for selecting such a path. A computing system that will invariably produce the correct answer for any problem in a set of possible problems is called an *algorithm*. A simple mathematical rule (e.g., to divide by a fraction, invert, and multiply) is an algorithm. Some problems do not lend themselves to algorithmic programming. In choosing the best move in a game of chess, each possible move has a number of implications. Each implication, in turn, has a number of implications, and so on. For the computer program to examine all possible implications of all possible choices for all possible chess situations might take years even with the fastest computer imaginable. Thus, for many problems algorithms are impractical.

An alternative type of computer system goes by the name of *heuristic*. A heuristic computing system does not invariably produce a correct solution to a problem, but it does provide rules that usually insure a solution in a reasonable time. Heuristic methods are characteristic of human problem solving. A baseball manager employs heuristics in managing his team. With the score tied in the late stages of a pitching duel and a runner on first and less than two out, the manager may instruct a batter to bunt. A left-handed pitcher is selected to pitch against a team with many left-handed hitters in the lineup. These maneuvres are heuristics—or rules of operation. They work more often than not, but they do not invariably produce an adequate solution to the problem at hand.

Simon and Newell (1962) use the puzzle of the Missionaries and Cannibals to illustrate the essential characteristics of information processing. Three missionaries and three cannibals are on the bank of a wide river and want to cross. There is a boat on the bank that will hold no more than two persons. All six know how to paddle it. It is somewhat important to carefully plan the order in which members of the party cross the river as the cannibals are partial to a diet of missionaries. If, even briefly, the number of cannibals exceeds the number of missionaries, the missionaries will be eaten. The problem is to find a sequence of boat trips that will get the whole party across the river without losing any missionaries.

What knowledge and abilities can be brought to bear in solving this problem? It is of little importance that we have had meagre experience with missionaries and cannibals. The three misisonaries can be treated as three objects and the three cannibals as three different objects. We have had vast experience with differences in location and modes of reducing these differences. We know that boats are useful for reducing differences of location on water. In short, stored in our memories we have knowledge and experience related to the problem and general problem-solving techniques that, at least, enable us to think about the problem.

The first step in solving a problem is one of *abstraction*. Abstracting consists of replacing objects, differences, and operations with new symbolic expressions that reduce a problem to its essentials while omitting unnecessary detail. In the Cannibal and Missionaries problem, three dimes may represent the three cannibals and three pennies, the three missionaries. The difference is between the initial situation and final solution, that is,

$$\underline{\hspace{4cm}} \qquad ccc \quad mmm$$
$$and$$
$$ccc \quad mmm \qquad \underline{\hspace{4cm}}$$

The operation is the sequences of crossings in order to transform the initial situation to a final solution.

The information processed by a computer, of course, must be translated into symbols that the computer program can handle. Simon and Newell (1962), in characterizing the program of the General Problem Solver, point out that symbols are used to represent objects (descriptions of the given, desired, and various intermediate possible situations), differences between pairs of objects, and operations that are capable of bringing about changes in the objects to which they are applied. The program includes methods that contribute to three types of goals:

1. *Transformation* goals: to transform object *a* (the given situation) into object *b* (the desired situation)
2. *Difference reducing* goals: to eliminate or reduce difference *d* between objects *a* and *b*
3. *Operator application* goals: to apply operation *q* to object *a*

Miller, Galanter, and Pribram's (1960) description of the mediating processes involved in problem solving resembles that of Newell, Shaw, and Simon (1958). Miller, Galanter, and Pribram use the term "image" to represent the goal to be attained and the resources the individual has available for reaching the goal. Goal-seeking behavior is directed by a "plan," i.e., some over-all "strategy" as well as some more detailed "tactics." In the execution of a plan, a constant feedback takes place in which the operations performed are checked against the requirements of the image. For Miller, Galanter, and Pribram, a plan consists of four stages: (1) a test to ascertain differences between the present and desired state of affairs, (2) an operation to reduce these differences, (3) a second test to re-evaluate the differences, and (4) an exit when the desired state of affairs has been attained. The entire sequence is called a TOTE unit (test, operate, test, exit). Problem solving may include several subordinate TOTE units within the total plan.

The TOTE sequence corresponds closely to the "similarity" and "matching" routines of Newell, Shaw, and Simon. Pribram (1960), in his review of theory in physiological psychology, shows that both conceptualizations of mediating processes correspond closely to neuro-behavioral theory.

Learning Exercises

6. What terms used by Hebb seem to be the equivalent of "information-processing strategies"?
7. Newell, Shaw, and Simon (1958) stored the axioms contained in *Principia Mathematica* (Whitehead and Russell, 1925) in the memory of a computer that was programmed to discover proofs in symbolic logic. Then the computer was given the task of deriving the 52 theorems in the second chapter of *Principia*. The computer succeeded in solving 38 of the theorems, some of which were solved in a few seconds, while others required extensive machine time. What clue in the above account suggests that the computer program of Newell *et al.* involved heuristic searching methods rather than algorithmic?
8. Which of the following is an algorithmic and which is a heuristic method of solving the problem of the Cannibals and Missionaries?

(a) List all possible combinations of trips. From these, select a solution that satisfies the requirements of the problem.

(b) Begin with sets of rules such as: "The solution cannot include a boat trip that leaves two cannibals and one missionary on one side of the river." Select a sequence of trips that will not lead to a violation of one of your rules.

9. In solving the problem $3x - 4 = x + 8$, identify from the following a transformation goal, a difference reducing goal, and an operator application goal:

(a) Get all the x's to one side of the equation.

(b) Solve for x.

(c) Change the sign of a term when you bring the term from one side of the equation to another.

10. What part or parts of a TOTE unit involves mediating processes?

Piaget's Development Studies

Hunt (1961) and Berlyne (1957, 1960) have noted the similarity between Piaget's general conceptions of cognitive mediating processes and the concepts developed by physiological psychologists, and researchers working on computer information processing. Hunt (1961) writes:

A conception of intelligence as problem-solving capacity based on a hierarchical organization of symbolic representations and information-processing strategies deriving to a considerable degree from past experience, has been emerging from several sources. These sources include observations of human behavior in solving problems, the programming of electronic computers, and neuropsychology. It is interesting, therefore, to find such a conception coming also from Piaget's observations of the development of intelligence in children. The various lines of evidence appear to be coalescing to flow in one direction, a direction that makes interaction between the environment and the organism continuous. Piaget's observations of the homely interactions of the child with his everyday environment demonstrate empirically the formation of a vertical hierarchy of operations for the processing of information to guide action. . . . [P. 109.]

The biological concept of "adaptation" is central in Piaget's description of intellectual development. The development of intelligence is seen as a process through which the organism develops increasingly complex *schemata* or repeatable, generalized ways of adapting to environmental forces. Adaptation is conceived as an interplay of two complementary processes—*assimilation* and *accommodation*. Assimilation occurs as the organism utilizes and incorporates something in the environment. At the psychological level, Piaget sees assimilation operating whenever the individual perceives something new in terms of something familiar; whenever the individual attaches familiarity, importance, or value to what he perceives; and whenever the individual acts in a new situation as he acted in similar situations in the past. Thus, assimilation seems to subsume what learning theorists refer to as *stimulus generalization* and *response generalization.* The term "accommodation" is used by Piaget for the process by which the organism develops new schemata or new ways of behaving to meet new environmental demands. The impact of new environmental events results in an interaction with and a modification of existing schemata. Through the dual adaptive processes of assimilation and accommodation, these schemata are transformed through differentiation and coordination into all the information-processing strategies subsumed under the term "intelligence." This continuous transformation in the structure of intelligence is viewed as developing through the sequence of stages discussed in Chapter 11.

Learning Exercises

11. What terms used by (a) Hebb, and by (b) Newell, Simon, and Shaw seem to be equivalent to Piaget's "schemata"?
12. Which of the following is an example of *assimilation,* and which is an example of *accommodation?*
    (a) Robert found it necessary to develop a new style of writing in order to receive a high grade on his composition theme from his new English teacher.
    (b) Mr. Jones recognized his old friend even though he had changed greatly.

FORMS OF THINKING

The term "thinking" includes many different forms of complex behavior. In this section, thinking will be considered from four points of view: (1) as a structuring process, (2) as a problem-solving process, (3) as a creating process, and (4) as a criticizing or evaluating process.

Structuring

It has been noted that *perception* involves an organization or structuring of sensory input by the perceiver. Comparably, thinking may be viewed as a structuring of information, concepts, and ideas by the thinker. The process through which an individual develops a *frame of reference* may be considered as a structuring process; and, as we have noted in Chapter 2, a frame of reference influences the further observations of an individual. Language development is facilitated as the child grasps the basic structure of a language (Chomsky, 1957). Many educators (e.g., Schwab, 1962; Johnson, 1962; Parker, 1962) consider a comprehension of the structure of a discipline as basic to a student's mastery of that discipline.

Many of the educational objectives quoted in Bloom's *Taxonomy of Educational Objectives* (1956a), particularly in the analysis category, represent subskills involved in structuring a communication. For example, objectives calling for the student to comprehend the interrelationship of ideas in a communication, to recognize unstated assumptions, to distinguish facts from hypotheses—all involve discovering the structure of a communication.

Bartlett (1958) classifies thinking into four categories: closed systems, experimental, everyday, and artistic. His "closed system" category illustrates well the structuring aspects of thinking processes.

Closed Systems. Closed systems are best exemplified with numerical, geometrical, and formal logical problems. A limited number of units, or items, or members, and the properties of the units are known at the outset and do not change as thinking proceeds. However, the units of the system may be arranged into a variety of orders or relations; and, as a result of rearranging, new properties of the orders may become evident. This reordering or restructuring of units so that new relationships become evident characterizes closed systems of thinking.

The following experiments conducted by Bartlett may serve to clarify the essential characteristics of closed system thinking.

1. Interpolation within a simple verbal system. Subjects are asked to fill in the gap between initial words and terminal words. Thus:

   A, BY,   HORRIBLE

This problem was given to subjects after they had completed several numerical gap-filling problems. In these problems, an orderly arrangement could be obtained by following some rule in developing a sequence of numbers. Thus, to fill the gap: 1, 3,   17, the rule "add 2" results in the orderly arrangement: 1, 3, 5, 7, 9, 11, 13, 15, 17.

For the word-gap problem, only two subjects out of more than two hundred employed two rules in filling the gap. A few more students employed two rules when an additional item of information was given, thus:

     A, BY, COW   HORRIBLE

The addition of the word DOOR after COW made a big difference. Many students then filled in the gap with words arranged in alphabetical order, each succeeding word having one letter more than its predecessor.

Learning Exercise

13. In what sense is the word series problem A, BY,   HORRIBLE an "open" system, and in what sense is it a "closed" system?

---

2. A verbal extrapolation problem. A subject is given a card listing the following words:

A, GATE, NO, I, DUTY, IN, CAT, BO, EAR
O, TRAVEL, ERASE, BOTH, GET, HO, FATE

E R A S E

F A T E

The subject is told to complete the vertical arrangement from the group of words at the top of the card. The subject is told that the word ERASE is the middle word in the column, and that not all words given need to be used.

Few subjects were successful in making a list that combined the applications of rules for alphabetical sequence and length of word sequence. Thus:

A
BO
CAT
DUTY
ERASE
FATE
GET
HO
I

Again, the number of subjects successful in discovering the structure increased as the amount of initial information increased. Slightly more subjects were successful when the word DUTY was included in the initial information, while most of the subjects were successful when the words CAT and GET were added.

Bartlett noticed that with extrapolation and other types of problems, subjects initially proceeded in a step-by-step manner of filling in gaps. Then, what appeared to be a flash of insight or intuition enabled the subject to glean a general structure of the elements of the problem. This phenomenon is akin to the experience of students who initially master the information in a school subject bit by bit, and then suddenly see the parts of the subject matter fitting together into a neat structure. How students can be aided in learning how to discover a structure for the elements of a problem or the material they learn is an important educational problem.

3. An arithmetic problem in disguise. A third class of situation in which information given has to be completed by bridging a gap is where all the information needed is initially presented to the subject, but the subject has to look at this information from a new point of view. The evidence that is presented to the student is in disguise. Bartlett's DONALD–GERALD problem is illustrative. The subject is given this simple disguised arithmetic problem:

$$
\begin{array}{l}
\text{D O N A L D} \\
\underline{\text{G E R A L D}} \\
\text{R O B E R T}
\end{array}
$$

Three facts are given: (1) $D = 5$, (2) every number from 1 to 10 has its corresponding letter, and (3) every letter is to be assigned a number different from that assigned to any other letter.

Students were asked to list the steps in the order used in solving the problem. A wide variation was found in the steps included by students and the order in which the steps were taken. Several students failed in the problem because they could not abandon their *set* of beginning their addition from the right-hand column and continuing to each succeeding column to the left. Success depended upon taking one key step that led to the discovery that $E = 9$. (Given $D = 5$, then $5 + 5 = T$. Therefore, $T = 0$; and as $0 + E = 0$, then E must equal 0 or 9. But $T = 0$. Therefore, $E = 9$.) The amount of trial-and-error guessing varied from subject to subject, as did the amount of intuitive or insightful grasping of relationships of elements of the problem.

Translating from or into a foreign language is an example of dealing with information in disguise. When there are no literal counterparts in one language for expressions in a second language, the translator must keep in mind the structure of both languages as he moves from one to the other.

Learning Exercise

14. Which of the following calls for a "closed" system of thinking, and which calls for an "open" system?
    (a) Solving a jigsaw puzzle
    (b) Writing a composition theme

Structuring in Problem Solving. Wertheimer (1959) in a series of problem-solving case studies delineates the part played by structuring in productive thinking. One of the problems Wertheimer used with children of different ages was that of finding the area of a parallelogram. Wertheimer reports the efforts of a five-and-a-half-year-old child as follows:

. . . Given the parallelogram problem, after she had been shown briefly how to get the area of a rectangle, she said, "I certainly don't know how to do *that!*" Then after a moment of silence: "This is *no good here,*" pointing to the region at the left end, "and *no good here,*" pointing to the region at the right.

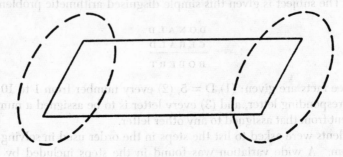

"It's troublesome, here and there." Hesitatingly she said: "I could make it right here . . . but . . ." Suddenly she cried out, "May I have a pair of scissors? What is bad there is just what is needed here. It fits." She took the scissors, cut the figure vertically, and placed the left end at the right. [Pp. 47, 48.]

A number of points are worthy of note in the above incident.

1. The instruction on finding the area of a rectangle provided the child with an initial structure, set, or search model.
2. The parallelogram did not fit the initial search model. A *gap* existed.
3. The troublesome structural features are located. "This is *no good here . . .* and *no good here.*"
4. The inner structural requirements of the problem are realized. "I could make it right here . . ."
5. The child sees a structural reorganization that results in a *fit* with her search model. "What is bad there is just what is needed here. It fits."

Learning Exercise

15. A teacher taught his class how to find the area of a parallelogram in the following manner:

(1) He showed the class how to find the area of a rectangle.

(2) He demonstrated how a parallelogram could be restructured into a rectangle.

(3) He presented a formula for finding the area of a parallelogram.

(4) He gave his class plenty of practice in finding the areas of parallelograms.

(5) He corrected the children's practice exercises and provided remedial practice.

Criticize the above teaching procedure as a method for developing the thinking abilities of children.

Problem Solving

The term "problem" is customarily used to describe a wide range of phenomena. A doctoral dissertation, an adolescent's acne, the behavior of a mother-in-law, a tantalizing blonde, a question in mathematics, a double-alternative temporal maze, and a mechanical puzzle —all may be classified as problems. All have in common a *gap* between an initial state of affairs and a desired state of affairs. The process of eliminating the gap involves more than just the recall of information. Before overtly responding to the problem situation, the problem-solver must cognitively manipulate or structure information in the process of selecting or inventing a strategy designed to eliminate the gap.

It is clear that a problem is an individual matter. What is a problem for one person may not be a problem for another. One person may experience a need to overcome an obstacle in a problem situation, while for another person the same situation is merely an uninteresting puzzle. A situation may be a real problem for one person because he is unable initially to see how the problem situation may be resolved. For a second person, the same situation may be no problem because he sees immediately what is required to overcome an obstacle. Problems may be of varying levels of complexity, ranging from those involving simple short-term goals (e.g., finding a misplaced book) to problems involving long-term goals and a host of subproblems (e.g., achieving a career goal).

Classical Viewpoints on Problem Solving. For many years, psychologists debated the relative merits of associationistic versus Gestalt theories of problem solving. While both types of theories have been greatly modified in recent years (with, as we have seen, a new emphasis on mediating processes), each has left its mark on present-day interpretations of the problem-solving process.

Associationistic theories place emphasis on the connection between stimulus elements of a problem and responses. The early experiments conducted by Thorndike (1898), in which cats learned to escape from a puzzle box, seemed to indicate that problem solving proceeds in a trial-and-error fashion. From this point of view, the problem-solving abilities of children in a classroom can best be developed by encouraging response variation in a problem situation, and then reinforcing correct responses when they occur.

Gestalt psychologists criticized Thorndike's trial-and-error interpretation of problem solving. Köhler (1925) conducted a series of experiments in which chimpanzees were presented with problems of obtaining food that was out of their reach. In one experiment, food was suspended from the roof of a chimpanzee's cage. The chimpanzee could reach the food only by making use of a box that was placed at the side of the cage. Köhler's chimpanzee did not acquire right responses and eliminate wrong responses gradually in a trial-and-error fashion in solving this problem. Rather, the solution appeared to be reached in a flash of *insight* as the chimpanzee perceived the relationships essential to the solution of the problem. For Gestalt psychologists, problem solving is viewed as a planning process in which the inner relationships of the problem are suddenly grasped by the problem-solver. From this point of view, the problem-solving abilities of children can best be developed by aiding children to perceive relationships between the crucial elements of a problem.

Under what conditions does insightful behavior occur? An experiment conducted by Birch (1945) points to the importance of background learning. Birch presented chimpanzees with a problem in which food was placed in front of the blade of a hoe. All the chimpanzee had to do was to rake in the food. Only two out of six chimpanzees were successful on this task. One appeared to solve the problem insightfully, and one by trial and error. Birch next provided the chimpanzees with sticks to play with. In the course of play, the animals developed some skill in using the sticks as functional extensions of their arms. With this play activity as a background, the chimpanzees were successful in solving a series of quite complex problems that required the use of sticks, hoes, and the like. Apparently, the acquisition of the subskills essential to the solving of a problem is prerequisite to insightful behavior.

What looks like trial-and-error behavior certainly seems to occur when a person is confronted with a complex and thoroughly confusing problem. Ordinarily, however, humans appear to be guided by hypotheses in solving problems. And these hypotheses are not randomly selected. Judson and Cofer (1956) presented subjects with four words with instructions to indicate the one word that was not related to the other three. This can be an easy problem if no ambiguity is introduced in the series of words. Thus, for ADD, SUBTRACT, MULTIPLY, PERCENT, the last word, PERCENT, is clearly of a different order than the first three. Judson and Cofer introduced ambiguity in their series of words and also varied the order of presentation of words in a series. For example, for the series ANGLE, RECTANGLE, SQUARE, CIRCLE, most subjects chose CIRCLE as the unrelated word—probably because the first three named figures are constructed by drawing straight lines. When the order of the words in the series was changed to CIRCLE, RECTANGLE, SQUARE, ANGLE, many subjects chose ANGLE as the unrelated word—probably because the first three represent enclosed figures. Judson and Cofer interpret their findings as evidence that verbal mediating processes can give direction to hypotheses formation in problem solving.

The importance of background learning is evidenced in another finding of the Judson and Cofer study. In a series of words consisting of SKYSCRAPER, TEMPLE, CATHEDRAL, and PRAYER, it was found that strongly religious subjects tended more than subjects with weak religious interests to include PRAYER and eliminate SKYSCRAPER.

Learning Exercise

16. Which of the following is most clearly exemplified in the Judson and Cofer study: (a) trial-and-error learning, (b) insight, (c) influence of set.

Logical Steps in Problem Solving. It has been amply demonstrated that people customarily do not follow a neat logical sequence of steps in solving problems. Even the psychologist may proceed in an opportunistic way in planning his research (Skinner, 1959). However, the educator has a legitimate interest in examining the logical sequence of steps involved in problem solving just as long as there is some hope that such a sequence of steps can be taught and will lead to more efficient problem solving.

Probably the analysis of problem solving that has most influenced educators is that presented by Dewey (1910) in a book entitled *How We Think*. Dewey believed that "the complete act of thought" includes the following stages:

1. *Becoming aware of the problem.* Dewey emphasized that a problem is a *felt* difficulty. A problem arises when an individual experiences some perplexity, confusion, or doubt.

2. *Clarifying and defining the problem.* One must locate the source of difficulty in order to solve his problem. What has to be done in order to solve the problem, what difficulties are likely to be encountered, and what constitutes a solution to the problem need to be determined in an initial clarification and definition of the problem.

3. *Searching for facts and formulating hypotheses.* The problem-solver gathers information relevant to his problem. He finds out what others have done in similar situations. He "thinks up" several alternative solutions to the problem.

4. *Evaluating proposed solutions.* Each alternative solution needs to be appraised in terms of its possible effectiveness in solving the problem. On the basis of this evaluation, a choice is made between the proposed solutions.

5. *Experimental verification.* Finally, the problem-solver acts on the one proposed solution. The rationally desired hypothesis is that certain consequences will follow the implementation of the proposed solution. This hypothesis needs to be checked experimentally, and revised if found deficient.

For the teacher, Dewey's analysis of problem solving has potential value in that it suggests questions the teachers need to raise in planning learning experiences. How can the teacher aid the pupil in becoming aware of a problem? Little improvement in the problem-solving skills of pupils may be expected unless pupils initially experience some perplexity, confusion, or doubt in working on a teacher-imposed task. However, as Bruner (1964a) points out, there is an optimal level of uncertainty needed to arouse a predisposition to tackle problems. Little uncertainty and curiosity are aroused by routine tasks. But confusion and anxiety may be aroused by tasks containing too much novelty and complexity. How much and what kind of guidance should the teacher provide for the pupil during the various stages of problem solving? Does the fact that problem solving is a "discovery" process mean that the pupil should be left entirely "on his own"? What practice should be provided in developing the subskills essential to solving a problem?

Each of Dewey's stages subsume a set of subskills that varies from one type of problem to another. Consider, for example, the high school student who is assigned the task of writing an essay on an occupation in which he is interested. Let us assume that this is a meaningful task for the student, that the problem of the student includes not only completing his assignment but that of obtaining information of value to him in selecting a career, that the student is considering a career in electrical engineering, and that he perceives the task of writing the essay as a step in making a vocational choice. Under this special set of circumstances, a few of the subskills that our student needs to solve his problem are (1) ability to locate information on electrical engineering; (2) ability to evaluate the accuracy of the information; (3) skills in the use of reference material; (4) ability to organize information; and (5) ability to relate information to job characteristics of importance to him, etc. For a different type of problem, quite a different constellation of subskills might be important.

For certain types of problems, Dewey's analysis of thinking does not provide an adequate vehicle for studying individual differences in problem-solving processes. Bloom and Broder (1950) taught college students to "think aloud" as they attempted to solve examination test items. Tape recordings were obtained of thinking-aloud sessions for six academically successful students and six academically unsuccessful students. The data so obtained did not fit well into Dewey's five stages. Bloom and Broder found that differences in problem-solving processes as revealed in their data could be summarized under four headings:

1. Understanding the nature of the problem
2. Understanding the ideas contained in the problem
3. General approach to the solution of the problem
4. Attitude toward the solution of problems

1. *Understanding the nature of the problem.* Successful problem-solvers were able to read the directions to a problem and almost immediately choose some word or phrase as a starting point from which to reason. The unsuccessful problem-solver rarely identified a key word in the directions to the problem and tended to skim over the directions without clarifying their meaning. Consequently, the unsuccessful problem-solvers often misinterpreted the problem. Sometimes they would achieve a good solution to a problem they were attempting to solve, but a poor solution to the actual problem posed.

2. *Understanding the ideas contained in the problem.* The major difference between successful and non-successful problem-solvers was *not* in the amount of information possessed that was relevant to the problem. Rather, the difference between the two groups was *"in the extent to which the two groups could bring the relevant knowledge they possessed to bear on the problem"* (p. 27). Successful problem-solvers attempted to translate unfamiliar or highly abstract terms into familiar concrete terms, e.g., corporate enterprise = Ford Motor Company. The non-successful problem-solvers gave up if they were not immediately able to relate the meaning of an abstract term to the

problem, even though, when questioned, they were able to supply examples of the abstract term.

The ability to understand the information contained in a problem may be contingent upon what Bruner (1964a, 1964b) terms the "mode of representation" of the problem. Bruner identifies three modes of representation: (1) enactive, (2) iconic, and (3) symbolic.

Enactive representation is "a mode of representing past events through appropriate motor responses" (Bruner, 1964b, p. 2). The child who adjusts his position on the seesaw is acting on the basis of the "principle" of the balance beam. Bruner illustrates the representation of problems in the enactive mode from an experiment in which eight-year-old children were taught to solve quadratic equations. Each child was supplied with large squares of wood, x units long and x units wide; oblong strips of wood, x units long and 1 unit wide; and small squares of wood, 1 unit long and 1 unit wide. The initial task of the children was to make a square bigger than the x by x square, using the material at hand. The easiest solution is to fit one oblong piece at the side, one oblong piece at the bottom, and one small square at the corner, making an $x^\square + 2x + 1$, thus:

Numerous manipulative problems of this kind were presented before proceeding to the next level of representation.

Iconic representation involves selective perception and the representation of information pertinent to a problem in the form of images. The child, described earlier who found the area of a parallelogram, literally imagined what would happen if one end of the parallelogram was cut off and fitted to the other end. Whenever we visualize the effect of a series of motor acts, we employ iconic representation of information.

Knowledge represented by "a set of symbolic or logical propositions drawn from a symbolic system that is governed by rules or laws for forming the transforming propositions" constitutes symbolic representation (Bruner, 1964a, p. 310). Language provides a medium through which experience can be represented and also transformed. A balance beam can be described verbally without the aid of diagrams or even can be described mathematically by reference to Newton's Law of Moments.

Bruner's analysis of mode of representation is suggestive of the way learning experiences may be sequenced so as to develop children's problem-solving abilities. We know that the usual course of intellectual development moves from the enactive through the iconic to symbolic representation. Possibly, the optimum instructional sequence proceeds in a similar fashion—at least for those subjects in the curriculum that lend themselves to alternative modes of representation.

3. *General approach to the solution of the problem.* In the Bloom and Broder study, one major difference between the successful and non-successful problem-solvers was in the extent of thought devoted to the problem posed. The non-successful problem-solver passively works on a problem. The successful problem-solver literally attacks the problem. The following two contrasting answers based on an essay-type problem are illustrative:

George H: Well, uh, I have to read the statement over, I haven't had any history for three years, and, uh, "Give the reasons which would have influenced the typical Virginia tobacco farmer to support the ratification of the Constitution in 1788 and reasons which would have influenced him to oppose ratification." Well, uh, to tell the truth I never had anything on the reasons of a Virginia tobacco farmer and at present I couldn't think of any.

Ralph R: (Reads the statement of the problem.) Tobacco farmers are quite wealthy, I imagine. He has to pay, ratification of the Constitution, well, what rights did the Constitution give him? Well, starting at the end, well, from the standpoint of money, which one would be more to his advantage? Well, prior to the Revolutionary War, he would have to pay taxes to England, but that isn't applying here. Support ratification of the Constitution. Well, as any other citizen of the colonies, I suppose he would approve of the Constitution, but as a Virginia tobacco planter, well, I think he would approve of it for patriotic reasons, and from the standpoint of money he wouldn't have to ship his tobacco to England or anything. Well, he wouldn't have to pay the taxes. [P. 29.]

Possibly, George has just as much knowledge about the Virginia tobacco farmer as Ralph. However, Ralph keeps working on the problem, examining one hypothesis after another, until some semblance of an answer is found.

Differences were also found between successful and non-successful problem-solvers in the care and system in thinking about the problem, and in the ability to follow through on a process of reasoning. The successful problem-solver attempted to break down a problem into simpler subproblems, search for key terms, and reconstruct the problem in ways in which he could attack it. The unsuccessful problem-solver plunged into the problem with no apparent plan for solution, was easily sidetracked, neglected important details, and failed to continue a line of reasoning to its fruitful conclusion.

4. *Attitude toward the solution of problems.* Three distinct kinds of attitudinal differences between successful and non-successful problem-solvers are identified by Bloom and Broder. First, successful problem-solvers seemed to believe that problems are amenable to reasoning; non-successful problem-solvers seemed to think that reasoning has little value, and either you know or you do not know the answer to a problem. Second, successful problem-solvers appeared to have confidence in their abilities to solve problems; non-successful problem-solvers were easily discouraged and made little effort to tackle problems that appeared complex or abstract. Third, successful problem-solvers did not permit personal biases to interfere with their efforts to solve problems; non-successful problem-solvers had difficulty in maintaining an objective attitude on certain problems.

Learning Exercises

17. Which is the first of the stages listed by Dewey that is not included in Bloom and Broder's analysis?
18. Which of the two characterizations of problem solving outlined in the above section represents a logical model for how to solve problems?
19. In which characterization of problem solving are the emotional responses of the problem-solver recognized as part of problem-solving efficiency?

Creative Thinking

Bruner (1962) describes creative thinking as an act that produces *effective surprise.* The effectiveness may be of three kinds: (1) predictive effectiveness, such as a scientific law; (2) formal effectiveness, in which elements are ordered in such a consistent, harmonious way as to reveal new relationships; and (3) metaphorical effectiveness, as in art where a single art expression communicates a wealth of experience and meaning. MacLeod (1962) suggests that the term "surprise" or "novelty" needs qualification. The novelty represents a newness to the thinker—a newness that is neither trivial nor accidentally produced.[2] Creative acts, defined in the above sense, may occur in the elementary school classroom. And possibly some methods of teaching are more conducive than others to the production of creative thinking.

---

[2] The qualification of *newness to the thinker* is not usually found as a criterion for critical thinking in the psychological literature. Rather, the reactions of other members of society to a product is taken as a criterion. See Maltzman (1960).

Various efforts have been made to analyze the course of creative thinking. The four stages in creative thought outlined by Wallas (1926) fit fairly well the self-reports of outstanding poets, artists, mathematicians, and scientists. These stages are:

1. *Preparation.* The background of knowledge that is prerequisite to the creative act is acquired.
2. *Incubation.* A period of no apparent progress. Even conscious thinking on the problem may be absent. The problem is, as it were, "in the back of the mind," as the thinker busies himself with other activities.
3. *Illumination.* The idea comes to the thinker suddenly, sometimes even when the person is dreaming or engaged in some trivial activity.
4. *Verification.* The idea is tried out and verified.

The Conditions of Creative Thinking. Henle (1962) draws upon the self-reports of creative thinkers such as Einstein, Newton, Goethe, Bacon, Mozart, Van Gogh, Picasso, Shaw, Poincaré, and others in examining the conditions under which creative thinking occurs. Henle points out a number of paradoxes. First, while we cannot get creative ideas by searching for them, yet we must be receptive to them if they are to occur. Nietzsche writes: "One hears—one does not seek; one takes—one does not ask who gives; a thought flashes out like lightning . . . Everything occurs without volition . . ." (Ghiselin, 1952.) A second paradox is that immersion in one's subject is prerequisite to the creative thought; yet our knowledge of current ideas in a field may blind us to new ones. Creative ideas can occur only if we devote time and energy in the one activity that makes their emergence most difficult. A third paradox is that a question asked is a first step in obtaining an answer to a problem; yet the mere act of asking a question limits creative thinking. A question narrows the range of the possible answers that may be obtained in a problem area. A fourth paradox pointed out by Henle is that, while a correct solution is the goal of problem solving, the utilization of errors is often the path to the goal. A disproven hypothesis yields new knowledge that points the way to new investigations. Finally, creative work demands a passionate devotion to one's work and yet a detachment that permits completely objective criticism.

The motives that impel a creative act are many and complex. Crutchfield (1962) differentiates between *intrinsic, task-involved and extrinsic, ego-involved* motivations for creativity. When the creative act is performed for its own sake, we have intrinsic, task-involved motivation. The person is inner-directed and is not susceptible to environmental pressures. Extrinsic, ego-involved motivation is exemplified by the person driven to create for material gain, self-enhancement, group acceptance, or other motives extraneous to the task itself. Crutchfield maintains that extraneous, ego-involved motivations, as contrasted with intrinsic, task-involved motivations, are more likely to interfere with creative behavior and produce conforming behavior. Torrance (1963) lists a number of ways in which the teacher can encourage creativity in the classroom. In part, Torrance's list represents an effort to encourage children to conform to an environmental pressure to be creative; e.g., ". . . make it clear that such [creative] thinking is expected and will be rewarded" (p. 20).

Characteristics of Creative Students. How does the creative thinker differ from the non-creative thinker? Apparently, the difference does not rest solely in intelligence. Getzels and Jackson (1962) identified distinctions between the cognitive styles of highly creative and highly intelligent secondary school students. Two groups of students were selected from 449 adolescents in a midwestern private secondary school. The highly intelligent group was made up of 28 students in the top 20 per cent in I.Q.'s, but not in the top 20 per cent in their performance on the five creativity tests administered. The highly creative group was made up of 26 students in the top 20 per cent on the creativity tests, but not in the top 20 per cent in I.Q. The highly creative student in the Getzels and Jackson study characteristically employed what Guilford (1959) has termed "divergent thinking." Given a problem, the creative student explored its multiple facets in divergent directions, thus leading to diversity and uniqueness of problem solutions. The highly intelligent student, on the other hand, corresponded more closely to Guilford's "convergent thinking" type. One direction is followed in patterning the facts of a problem to a single "right" answer.

Getzels and Jackson's group of "creative" students demonstrated an exuberant, carefree playfulness more than did their "intelligent" classmates. Students of both groups were shown a series of pictures and were asked to make up a story about each picture. One of the pictures showed a man in an airplane seat. The "intelligent" student typically told a story of a man returning from a successful business trip, happy to be reunited with his wife and three children. In contrast, one of the "creative" students made up and wrote in the four minutes time allotted the following story:

The man is flying back from Reno where he has just won a divorce from his wife. He couldn't stand to live with her anymore, he told the judge, because she wore so much cold cream on her face at night that her head would skid across the pillow and hit him in the head. He is now contemplating a new skid-proof face cream. [P. 39.]

Measuring Creativity. The type of items found in the conventional measure of intelligence appears to require convergent thinking. Each test question has a single correct answer. To test an individual's divergent thinking ability requires problems that have many possible solutions. The quality of responses then can be judged by the number and uniqueness of the solutions offered by the testee. A number of tests of this kind have been constructed by Guilford and his associates (Guilford, 1959) during the course of their factorial investigations of creativity.

One series of tests published by Guilford and his associates gets at different types of fluency. One test of *word fluency* is designed to measure the ability to produce rapidly words that fulfill specific requirements. For example, a person is asked to list words that begin with the prefix "con-," or to list words rhyming with a word such as "moon." In one study (Drevdahl, 1956), performance on word fluency tests of this kind was found to correlate positively with creative achievement of college students in science and art courses. A test on *ideational fluency* provides a measure of ability to produce many ideas in a situation containing few restrictions. For example, the subject is required to name things that are both solid and edible. Or the subject lists uses for a common brick. The total number of responses constitutes the score for the ideational fluency test. The *associational fluency* test gets at the ability to produce words from a restricted area of meaning. For example, the subject writes a number of synonyms in response to a word such as "soft," or writes adjectives to complete a simile, such as "As _____ as a fish." The *expressional fluency* test is designed to measure the ability to produce organized discourse. For example, the subject is required to write four connected words, the first letters of which are given. Thus, for "Y_____ c_____ g_____ n_____," a person might answer "You can go now." In another type of task included in the expressional fluency test, the subject is asked to complete a sentence such as "A woman's beauty is like the autumn, for it _____ _____ _____."

A great deal of research remains to be done before the value of the fluency tests can be properly assessed. Possibly, research may support Guilford's belief that:

> The fluency factors taken together must surely have much to do with ability to write successfully. Ideational fluency should give the writer something to write about. Expressional fluency should help him to put his ideas into organized discourse. Associational fluency should give him the word finding ability that he needs. [Pp. 385–86.]

Learning Exercises

20. Henle (1962) writes: ". . . the creative solutions, the creative idea, is one which the individual achieves by freeing himself from his own conceptual system, and by which he sees in a deeper or more comprehensive or clearer way the structure of the situation he is trying to understand" (p. 39).

    Which of Bruner's three kinds of effectiveness does Henle's comment correspond most clearly?

21. Two scientists independently make the same discovery. One scientist publishes his findings before the other. Has the second scientist been creative? Would a high school student be creative if, years later, he made the same discovery even though he started only with the facts that were initially available to the two scientists?

22. Mary Smith, an eleventh-grade student who excels in English, is writing a play for her class. In spite of her best efforts, Mary is unable to think of a satisfactory ending to her play. One day, while listening to a lecture in her history class, an idea comes to her. She goes home and completes her play and is well satisfied with her ending.

    How are Wallas' four stages of creative thinking illustrated in the above account?

23. George Bernard Shaw (1953), in his Postscript to *Back to Methuselah*, writes: "An author is an instrument in the grip of Creative Evolution. . . . When I am writing a play I never invent a plot: I let the play write itself and shape itself, which it always does even when up to the last moment I do not foresee the way out. Sometimes I do not see what the play was driving at until quite a long time after I have finished it; and even then I may be wrong about it just as any critical third party may be."

    Which of Henle's list of paradoxes does Shaw's comment illustrate?

24. "Brainstorming" is one frequently used technique used to encourage creative thinking. Students are encouraged to toss out ideas on a problem. Criticism of the ideas presented is to be withheld until all ideas are listed. Maltzman (1960), in reviewing the literature on the training of originality, identifies some research studies showing that brainstorming is effective in producing a greater number of unique ideas. Other experiments yielded negative results.

    Evaluate the potential value of brainstorming in terms of Crutchfield's differentiation between the two types of motivation for creativity.

25. Does brainstorming call for divergent or convergent thinking?

26. Are the creativity tests of Guilford and his associates examples of divergent thinking tests or convergent thinking tests?

27. Which type of Guilford's tests does the following test question exemplify?

    "Write as many words as you can that have a critical connotation?"

Critical Thinking

The development of critical thinking is commonly accepted as an important objective of the school. Despite the general recognition of the importance of critical thinking, there is little agreement as to its definition. Critical thinking is sometimes regarded as including all the response patterns subsumed under the term "problem solving" and is sometimes restricted to the kind of thinking involved in analyzing propaganda. Ennis (1962) defines critical thinking as the "correct assessment of statements." According to Ennis, three dimensions are involved in correctly assessing statements: (1) a logical dimension—judging alleged relationships between the meanings of words and statements, (2) a critical dimension—a knowledge of the criteria for judging statements, and (3) a pragmatic dimension—a consideration of the adequacy of the evidence for a statement in terms of the background purpose of the statement. Ennis identifies 12 aspects of critical thinking. Ennis' analysis has the merit of identifying the kind of behaviors of students subsumed under his definition of critical thinking. The analysis has further value in that it suggests the kind of learning experiences that should stimulate critical thinking and the type of test items needed to measure student's achievement on educational objectives involving critical thinking. The twelve aspects are:

1. *Grasping the meaning of a statement.* This includes understanding of what counts as evidence for and against a statement, what the implications are of the statement, and what implies the statement. Thus, grasping the meaning of the statement "Wood floats on water" includes understanding:

    a) What counts as evidence for, e.g., instances of wood floating on water;

    b) What counts as evidence against, e.g., any instance where wood does not float on water;

    c) What the implications are, e.g., a toy boat made of wood will float on water; and

    d) Conditions that imply the statement, e.g., (1) wood is lighter than water, and (2) anything lighter than water will float on water.

Learning Exercise

28. How could you test whether students have grasped the meaning of the statement, "Air exerts pressure upon all bodies with which it is in contact"?

---

2. *Judging whether there is ambiguity in a line of reasoning.* Ambiguity in a line of reasoning may occur when a term is applied with a meaning different from its initial definition. The following series of statements illustrate this type of ambiguity:

    a) Medication is anything intended for the prevention, cure, or alleviation of disease.

    b) Chlorination of water is medication (when medication is defined as above).

    c) Some people believe on religious grounds that medication is wrong (when medicine is defined as treatment of humans with medicine).

    d) Ambiguity in the line of reasoning results in the conclusions that: to chlorinate water is to violate some people's religious principles.

3. *Judging whether certain statements contradict each other.* This aspect is clearly in the logical dimension. The student is required to grasp and compare the meanings of two or more statements. In social studies, this subskill in critical thinking is revealed as the student examines two divergent statements on a social issue. For example, the debates in the Federal Convention of 1787 may be examined by the student in order to identify points of agreement and disagreement between the various speakers.

4. *Judging whether a conclusion follows necessarily.* A conclusion necessarily follows if its denial contradicts the premises upon which the conclusion is based. To illustrate:

Premise: All children who obtain low grades in school are feeble-minded.

               John, age eleven, obtains low grades in school.

Conclusion: John is feeble-minded.

In the above example, the conclusion necessarily follows if the premises are accepted.

5. *Judging whether a statement is specific enough.* How specific a statement should be depends upon the purposes that the statement serves. The statement "Education has disappeared from the schools" is too vague to be of help in revising a curriculum. The terms "education," "disappeared," and "schools" need clarification. The statement, however, is sufficiently specific to communicate what has happened to a country as a result of the ravages of war.

6. *Judging whether a principle establishes a statement that is alleged to be an application of it.* Caution is required in applying principles to specific situations. Principles, rules, generalizations, and laws have exceptions and limits. For example, the

economic law of supply and demand is applicable only to an economy free of government control and to a section of the economy that is free of monopolistic control. Hence, these limitations need to be kept in mind in judging whether the price of a specific commodity is likely to fall as a result of decreased demand.

7. *Judging whether an observation statement is reliable.* This aspect of critical thinking is crucial in the educational objective: "To develop the student's ability to assess sources of information." Accuracy of observation may be judged in terms of the qualifications of the observer, the method of observing, the adequacy of opportunity to observe, the absence of bias of the observer, corroborations of the observation, etc.

8. *Judging whether an inductive conclusion is warranted.* Three important considerations in judging whether a conclusion is warranted are: (*a*) the adequacy of sample of positive instances that support the conclusion, (*b*) the absence of negative instances, and (*c*) the consistency of the conclusion within a larger system of knowledge. Consider, for example, the conclusion of a teacher that "children from lower socioeconomic homes tend to achieve less adequately in school than children from middle class homes." To judge whether this conclusion is warranted requires some information concerning the relative performance of children from each socioeconomic class as well as knowledge of the research evidence concerning the relationship of socioeconomic class to academic achievement.

9. *Judging whether the problem has been identified.* Ennis identifies three different kinds of judgments under this aspect of critical thinking.

   a) Judging a want. The want may be one's own (e.g., "My problem is to find a good job") or someone else's want (e.g., "Robert wants to gain attention").

   b) Judging that a valuable goal has been selected (e.g., "The education provided in American schools should be improved").

   c) Judging that a means decision is adequate (e.g., "More financial support to our schools is necessary in order to improve the quality of education").

Critical thinking comes into play when inferences are drawn concerning the wants of others from observations of behavior, and when judgments are made concerning the adequacy of the means suggested for attaining a goal.

10. *Judging whether something is an assumption.* An assumption may be thought of as a *gap* in a logical argument. In the statement "Since the demand for children's toys has decreased, the

price of toys may be expected to decrease," the unstated assumption or gap is "When the demand for a commodity decreases, the price of that commodity will decrease." In the statement "The fiscal irresponsibility of the government has caused economic distress," the gaps or assumptions are evidences that the government has been fiscally irresponsible and that economic distress is prevalent. Thus, judging whether something is an assumption may take the form of distinguishing between fact and assumption.

11. *Judging whether a definition is adequate.* Judging the adequacy of a definition involves judging the adequacy of the concept defined and the explanatory value of the definition for its intended purpose. "Intelligence" may be defined in terms of the concept "innate ability" or in terms of the concept of a "learned aptitude." A judgment of the comparative worth of these two concepts may be involved in assessing the adequacy of any definition of intelligence. The explanatory value of a definition may be assessed in a number of ways: "Does the definition aid in precise communication with others?" "Does the definition represent a standard meaning for a term?" "If the definition is of a classificatory kind, does it aid in identifying members of the class?"

12. *Judging whether a statement made by an alleged authority is acceptable.* All of the above criteria may be applied in judging the content of a statement. The purpose of the statement needs to be taken into consideration in applying the criteria. In judging the alleged authority making the statement, his reputation, qualifications, and lack of bias are important considerations.

Learning Exercise

29. Some of the citizens of a large city became disturbed at the prospect of integration of their public schools. During the height of the emotional turmoil, one mother of five children was overheard discussing integration. The substance of her remarks was as follows: "Most Negroes are immoral. I have brought up my children to be moral and I don't want them to become immoral. I will take my children out of school rather than have them go to the same school as Negroes."
   (a) Identify the assumptions in the above statement.
   (b) Using Ennis' 12 aspects of critical thinking as a guide, identify the additional information you would require to assess the statement.

The variables that affect critical thinking are not clearly differentiated from the variables affecting general problem-solving behavior. It is of importance to note that the quality of critical thinking is affected by the emotional loading of the topic under consideration.

SUMMARY

An increased interest in mediating cognitive processes is being manifested among psychologists. Psychologists working within a stimulus-response framework have conducted ingenious experiments designed to shed light on the cognitive processes that intervene between the presentation of a stimulus and the appearance of a response. Advances in the understanding of the central nervous system have provided a sounder basis for correlating theories of learning with knowledge of the structure of the central nervous system. Hebb has introduced the terms "cell-assembly" and "phase sequence" in developing a neuropsychological theory of thought. Psychologists working with modern electronic computers have successfully simulated human thinking and developed a theory of thinking modelled upon their information-processing systems. Piaget's extensive developmental studies have yielded another conceptualization of cognitive mediating processes. As Hunt has pointed out, striking similarities may be found in the conceptualization of cognitive mediating processes that are emerging from these diverse sources.

A complex picture of the responses involved in thinking emerges from an examination of the writings of psychologists and educators. Four forms of thinking are discussed in this chapter. These four forms of thinking constitute alternate ways of viewing the thinking process rather than mutually exclusive categories. Thinking may be viewed as a structuring process. In so doing, attention is focused on the ways elements (information, concepts, and ideas) are combined or structured so that new relationships become evident. Thinking may be viewed as a problem-solving process. Here, attention is directed to the sequence of steps intervening between a felt need and the resolution of a problem. Creative thinking probably comes closest to a distinct type of thinking. Guilford has differentiated between convergent and divergent thinking, and has used measures of divergent thinking to assess creative abilities. Relatively little research has been conducted on critical thinking, although Ennis' analysis and parts of Bloom's *Taxonomy of Educational Objectives* provide the teacher with a description of a range of student responses indicative of critical thinking.

Answer Cues

1. Cell-assemblies and phase sequences.
2. Phase sequence.
3. A reverberation (e.g., A B C A B D C E B D C A F B C E—See Hebb, 1949, p. 73) results in the autonomous activity.
4. Interaction of sensory stimulation with other assembly activity.

5. Some behaviors, e.g., hallucinations of pink elephants, cannot be explained merely by examining the external stimuli or the condition of the organism. Some unique internal operation of the brain needs to be postulated.

6. Cell-assembly and phase sequence.

7. An algorithmic program invariably leads to a correct solution when given sufficient time; a heuristic program is time saving, but not always successful.

8. (a) Algorithmic. (b) Heuristic.

9. (a) Difference reducing. (b) Transformation. (c) Operator application.

10. All parts.

11. (a) Cell-assembly and phase sequence. (b) Information processing strategies.

12. (a) Accommodation. (b) Assimilation.

13. The words available for selection are left to the subject. In this sense, the problem represents an "open" system. But to arrive at an orderly structure, the subject is restricted to using two rules. In this sense, the problem represents a "closed" system.

14. (a) Closed. (b) Open.

15. No practice in structuring is provided. Hence, the children might experience difficulty in finding areas of figures that require some restructuring —such as the following:

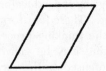 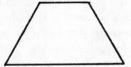 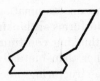

16. (c).

17. Becoming aware of the problem.

18. Dewey's is a logical model. Bloom and Broder identify actual differences found in the thought processes of successful and non-successful problem-solvers.

19. In Bloom and Broder, in the "attitude toward the solution of problems" category. The closest Dewey comes to emotional responses is in his "becoming aware of the problem" category.

20. Formal effectiveness (in the opinion of the present author). Possibly the reader might wish to read Bruner's and Henle's original articles and judge for himself.

21. Yes, in both cases, if the criteria for creativity does not include the reaction of other members of society.

22. Preparation: Mary's background in English and her initial work on the play

    Incubation: In history class with the play in the "back of Mary's mind"
    Illumination: The idea
    Verification: Working out the idea

23. We cannot get creative ideas by searching for them, but we must be receptive to them.

24. To the extent that creativity is stifled by the desire to conform, the withholding of criticism in brainstorming might be expected to increase the flow of ideas. If motivation to solve the problem is intrinsic, the value of brainstorming is not so clearly apparent.

25. Divergent.

26. Divergent.

27. Associational fluency.

28. See whether the students recognize that water forced up a straw by suction is evidence for the statement; that one implication of the statement is that air pressure is greater at sea level than on mountain tops; and that because air has weight and anything that has weight exerts pressure, the statement must be true.

29. (a) No evidence is presented that race is an important variable in the incidence of moral behavior. No evidence is presented that the mother's children are moral. Implicit in the argument is the assumption that the particular Negro children who will attend the same school as her children are immoral and that her children will become immoral if they attend the same classes as some immoral children. Hence, there is the further assumption that the mother's children have not, up to this time, attended a class containing immoral children. And so on. (b) A definition of morality is needed. What behaviors are counted as moral acts and what behaviors are counted as immoral acts? Does morality imply a stable resistance to act immorally? Is a person constantly in a process of becoming moral or becoming immoral; and, if so, what factors affect this *becoming* process? Answers to the above questions are needed in order to ascertain whether there are contradictions in the statement. In judging whether the observations of the mother are reliable, more information is needed concerning (1) her qualifications, (2) her methods of observing, (3) her opportunities to observe. The findings of social scientists on the variables affecting morality are relevant in assessing the statement.

13

AFFECTIVE LEARNING

Affective learning includes the learning of interests, appreciations, attitudes, values, and emotional-social adjustments.

An interest is a behavioral tendency that occurs when the behaver is free to choose. A child exhibits an interest in reading when he chooses to read even though he is free to do other things. An appreciation involves both feelings and cognitions. A child appreciates a novel when he enjoys reading the novel and understands and responds emotionally to the many qualities of the novel. Attitudes always include emotional and cognitive components and may also include a behavioral component. The child has a favorable attitude toward reading when he enjoys reading, has a number of beliefs about the values of reading, and therefore reads when given the opportunity. Values may be viewed as a system or complex of more specific attitudes.

In this chapter we will focus attention on the nature of attitudes and the ways in which attitudes are learned. Discussion of emotional-social adjustment, which is also a kind of affective learning, will be reserved for Chapter 15.

THE NATURE OF ATTITUDES

An attitude may be defined as "an individual's tendency or predisposition to evaluate an object or the symbol of that object in a certain way" (Katz and Stotland, 1959, p. 428). An attitude itself cannot be observed. It can only be inferred from observations of behavior. The schematic conception of attitudes, formulated by Rosenberg and Hovland (1960), provides a useful framework for describing the attitudes of an individual (see Fig. 13–1).

Attitude Objects

Attitudes are always related to some definite stimulus situation. The attitude object may be *concrete*, such as an automobile, apple pie, a

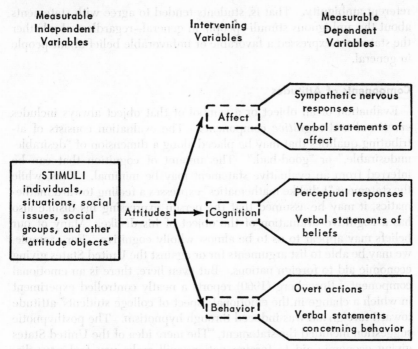

Fig. 13–1. Schematic Conception of Attitudes. (From Rosenberg and Hovland, 1960, p. 3.)

painting; *persons,* such as a teacher, sweetheart, father, president, the self; *group of people,* such as labor union members, Negroes, politicians, Englishmen; *institutions,* such as the school, church, club; *concepts, values,* or *customs,* such as the flag, equality, divorce; *social issues,* such as civil rights, foreign policy, a bond issue.

The object of an attitude for an individual may be *specific* or *general.* The attitude object may be one particular young lady or ladies in general; federal aid to education or all forms of governmental and individual action related to conservatism—liberalism; a specific church doctrine or churches in general.

The attitude object may be *definite* or *ambiguous.* Banta (1961) has demonstrated that the tendency to acquiesce to statements on an attitude questionnaire increases as the ambiguity of the attitude object increases. The direction of the attitude was experimentally controlled by including some statements favorable and some unfavorable to the attitude object. The attitude objects—President Eisenhower, college fraternities, and people in general—represented three levels on a definite-ambiguous continuum. Among students drawn from introductory psychology classes, degree of acquiescence was found to increase with referent ambiguity. That is, students tended to agree with statements about the ambiguous stimuli—people in general—regardless of whether the statement expressed a favorable or unfavorable belief about people in general.

Components of Attitudes

Evaluation of an object or a symbol of that object always includes *emotional* and *cognitive* components. The evaluation consists of attributing qualities that may be placed along a dimension of "desirable-undesirable," or "good-bad." The amount of cognition that can be inferred from an evaluative statement may be minimal. Thus, while the statement "I dislike mathematics" expresses a feeling toward mathematics, it may be assumed that the person expressing his dislike also has a cognitive evaluation of the object of his dislike. Many of our beliefs may appear to us to be almost wholly cognitive. For example, we may be able to list arguments for or against the United States giving economic aid to foreign nations. But even here, there is an emotional component. Rosenberg (1960) reports a neatly controlled experiment in which a change in the emotional aspect of college students' attitude toward foreign aid was induced through hypnotism. The posthypnotic suggestion included the statement, "The mere idea of the United States giving economic aid to foreign nations will make you feel very displeased and disgusted" (p. 38). For a week the experimental subjects responded with negative feeling to the idea of foreign aid. They also reorganized their thinking on the problem of foreign aid so that their arguments were consistent with their revised feelings. Thus, even many of our most objective intellectual beliefs may have an emotional component, and changing the emotional component may result in some reorganization of the intellectual component. Lest the reader be distressed at the thought of manipulating people's attitudes through hypnotism, it should be reported that Rosenberg's subjects all had returned to their original attitude when tested three days after amnesia removal.

An attitude may have a *behavioral* component in addition to emotional and cognitive components. The individual may take steps to approach, protect, aid, avoid, punish, or destroy the attitude object. This action-tendency is the behavioral component of an attitude.

In the measurement of attitudes, the emotional component may be inferred from measures of physiological variables such as blood pressure or galvanic response (e.g., Lawson and Stagner, 1957). More typically, the emotional component of attitudes are inferred from the subject's verbal statements as to his degree of liking or disliking of the attitude object. Items on attitude inventories may focus attention on the feelings, the beliefs, or the overt actions of the respondent and thus obtain information on the self-reported direction of the emotional, cognitive, and behavioral aspects of an individual's attitudes.

Learning Exercise

1. What component of an attitude—affect, cognition, or behavior—is more clearly evident in each of the following?
    (a) A coed experiences excitement when her team scores a touchdown.
    (b) Mr. Smith votes for the Democratic candidate.
    (c) College fans are more successful in detecting fouls committed by College Y players than those committed by College X players.

Structural Organization of Attitudes

Attitudes frequently become organized into larger structures or value systems. For example, an individual's attitudes toward big business, social welfare legislation, labor unions, the role of government in the economy, governmental policies of price support, etc., may be organized into a value system of progressivism versus conservatism.

The *Scale of Values* (Allport, Vernon, and Lindzey, 1960) represents one effort to measure the value system of an individual. Attitudes are appraised in the six fields that were originally described by Spranger (1928) as six basic types of men: theoretical, economic, aesthetic, social, political, and religious. The dominant interest of the theoretical man is the discovery of truth; the economic man values the useful and the practical; the aesthetic man values musical, artistic, literary, and naturalistic expressions of form and harmony; the social man values most highly love of people; the political man is interested primarily in seeking power; and the religious man seeks to comprehend the cosmos as a whole. The subject is asked to indicate preferences for activities or beliefs. For example, one item is: "When you visit a cathedral are you more impressed by a pervading sense of reverence and worship than by the architectural features and stained glass?" The first alternative might be expected to be the choice of the religious man; the second, of the aesthetic man. Throughout the test, one value is pitted against one or more other values in order to assess the relative strength of the six values.

The structural organization of attitudes may reflect the personality structure of an individual. The term *"authoritarian* personality" has been used to describe a syndrome of attitudes asociated with certain prejudices (Adorno *et al.*, 1950). According to Adorno and his associates, the authoritarian personality is a resultant of extreme rejection or domination in childhood. The authoritarian personality is marked by a rigid conformity to middle-class values; repressed hostility that finds expression in attacks on minority groups; a desire for power, that, if unsatisfied, may find expression through identifying with authoritarian "leaders"; and denial of sexual motives but projecting sexuality to others.

The F Scale (F stands for fascism), first published in *The Authoritarian Personality* (Adorno *et al.*, 1950), was designed to provide an indirect measure of prejudice without mentioning the names of any specific minority group. The F Scale has been found to correlate positively with measures of ethnocentrism, anti-Semitism, anti-Negro feeling, and political conservatism. However, as Rokeach (1960) points out, authoritarianism and intolerance is not confined to persons adhering to the political right wing. It may be found in persons falling along the whole range of the political spectrum from left to right. It may be found in religious and in antireligious groups, in the academic world, and, in short, in all walks of life. Rokeach has attempted to develop a measure of general intolerance, and to explore the relationships between cognitive behavior and measures of general intolerance.

Rokeach, in studying the structural organization of belief systems, distinguishes between the *open* and *closed* mind. For this purpose, Rokeach has developed two major measures: the *Dogmatic Scale* and the *Opinionation Scale*. Some of the characteristics of a closed belief-disbelief system may be gleaned by examining a few items in the Dogmatic Scale. The person with the closed belief-disbelief system would tend to agree with the following items (the characteristic measured is placed within brackets and is not a part of the scale):

1. The United States and Russia have just about nothing in common. [*Characteristic:* Accentuates differences between his own beliefs and alternative belief system.]
2. The highest form of government is a democracy and the highest form of democracy is a government run by those who are most intelligent. [*Characteristic:* Coexistence of contradictions within the belief system.]
3. There are certain "isms" which are really the same even though those who believe in these "isms" try to tell you they are different. [*Characteristic:* Unable to differentiate between alternative belief systems that differ from his own.]
4. Man on his own is a helpless and miserable creature. [*Characteristic:* Aloneness, isolation, and helplessness of man are emphasized.]
5. It is better to be a dead hero than to be a live coward. [*Characteristic:* Need for martyrdom.]

6. There are a number of people I have come to hate because of the things they stand for.
[*Characteristic:* Belief in positive and negative authority—the good guys and the bad guys.]

7. There are two kinds of people in this world: those who are for the truth and those who are against the truth.
[*Characteristic:* Intolerance toward the disbeliever.]

8. To compromise with our political opponents is dangerous because it usually leads to the betrayal of our own side.
[*Characteristic:* Belief in the one right cause.]

9. In the long run the best way to live is to pick friends and associates whose tastes and beliefs are the same as one's own.
[*Characteristic:* Avoiding contact with the belief-disbelief systems of others.]

Rokeach has conducted a number of studies in which students are presented with problems that can be solved only if the student rejects one or more of his beliefs. The performances of open- and closed-minded students (as measured by Dogmatic Scale) are compared. As might be expected the closed-minded individual experienced the more difficulty.[1] Ehrlich (1961) found that dogmatism, as measured by Rokeach's scale, was inversely related to the degree of classroom learning in a sociology course, and that the relationship was independent of academic aptitude.

Rokeach's concept of the open and closed mind suggests to the teacher that the problem of changing the attitudes of some students may be very difficult. The beliefs for some people remain unshaken even in the face of overwhelming evidence negating the beliefs.

[1] One of the problems used by Rokeach is called the Doodlebug problem. Joe Doodlebug, the hero, lives in a hypothetical world. This strange bug can jump in four directions: north, south, east, and west, but not diagonally. Once he starts in any direction, he must jump four times before he can change direction. His only mode of locomotion is jumping. He can jump very large or very small distances. He cannot turn around.

In one of the Doodlebug problems, the subject is told that food, larger in diameter than Joe, is placed three feet directly west of Joe. Joe stops in his tracks, facing north. Joe is smart and figures that he will have to jump four times to get to the food. The problem presented to the subject is to describe the circumstances that Joe must have been in to reach this conclusion.

To solve this problem, the subject must overcome three beliefs, replace these beliefs with new beliefs, and synthesize the new beliefs.

1. *The facing belief.* In everyday life, we face the food we eat. Joe doesn't have to. He can land on top of it.

2. *The direction belief.* In everyday life, we can change directions at will. Joe can't. He must forever face north. The only way he can change directions is by jumping sideways or backward or forward.

3. *The movement belief.* We can change directions if we wish. Joe can't. Once started in one direction, he must continue for four jumps.

Learning Exercises

2. Which of Spranger's six values appears to be reflected by the student who states that, for recreational reading, he prefers *Scientific Age* to *Arts and Decorations?*

3. One item on the California F Scale is: "What this country needs most, more than laws and political programs, is a few courageous, tireless, devoted leaders in whom the people can put their faith." Would you expect the authoritarian personality to agree with the above statement? Why?

4. Two of the following "beliefs" are part of Rokeach's Dogmatic Scale. With which statement would the closed-minded individual be least likely to agree?
   (a) Freedom of speech for all groups is a worthwhile democratic ideal.
   (b) Most people just don't give a "damn" for others.
   (c) Even though I have a lot of faith in the intelligence and wisdom of the common man I must say that the masses behave stupidly at times.

Types of Attitudes

Katz and Stotland (1959) classify attitudes into five types and point out that the motivational properties of attitudes vary according to type. The five types are (1) affective associations, (2) intellectual attitudes, (3) action-oriented attitudes, (4) balanced attitudes, and (5) ego-defensive attitudes.

Affective Associations. The association of an object in a pleasant or an unpleasant environment results in the affective association type of attitude. One pleasant experience with a foreigner may generate a favorable attitude toward all foreigners. The attitude can be long lasting if other experiences with foreigners are also pleasant or if the initial experience is sufficiently intense. A terrifying experience in deep water may result in a negative attitude toward deep water. The pupil rapped over his knuckles for the mistakes he makes in arithmetic may form a negative attitude toward arithmetic. Affective associations are the attitudes formed by a *spread* of the pleasant or unpleasant affect experienced in some goal-seeking endeavor *to* objects that happen to be present at the time.

The major source of affective attitudes is the past association of the attitude object with need satisfaction. But the object itself has not been instrumental in past satisfaction of needs. It merely was present while the need was satisfied. Hence, as long as the attitude remains at the affective association level, the individual does not need to do anything to the object except express his affectivity. Affective associations, thus, lack a behavioral component. As they also have few cognitive elements, they are difficult to change by presenting information and logical reasons for their change. Thus, the student who hates mathematics will not begin to enjoy mathematics just because he is provided with good reasons for liking mathematics. New positive associations (i.e., mathematics associated with pleasantness) are usually necessary in order to bring about a change in the affective attitude.

Intellectualized Attitudes. Many attitudes have a heavy cognitive component as well as an affective core. Such attitudes need not motivate a definite way of behaving. Thus, a person may accept the theory of evolution but not be motivated to behave in a specific way as a result of this acceptance.

Intellectualized attitudes develop out of the individual's need to understand and make sense out of the world around him. They may also arise out of a need for self-consistency. When the cognitive component of an attitude is inconsistent with newly acquired information, a person will either modify his attitudes or distort the new information so that it fits into his attitude. The modification of the attitude of many segregationists toward the Supreme Court after the Supreme Court's 1954 ruling against school segregation illustrates the maintenance of consistency through modifying the original attitude. Many studies have demonstrated how a perception that is inconsistent with a person's attitude may be distorted and thus leave the original attitude intact (Edwards, 1941; Levine and Murphy, 1943; Watson and Hartmann, 1939).

The cognitive component of an attitude also may arise out of its instrumental value in maintaining and defending one's self concept. The self concept "I am a Democrat" or "I am a Republican" may influence the acceptance or rejection of a statement made by a Democrat on foreign policy. The self concept "I appreciate good music" may impel the acceptance of beliefs about music that conform to the opinions of others who are deemed to be competent judges. The schoolboy's expressed attitudes toward poetry may be a function of what he perceives to be the expectations of his peers.

In summary, while the intellectual components of attitudes do arise out of a desire to understand, to see the world as logically consistent, they also are influenced by, and tend to be consistent with, other motivations of the individual.

Action-oriented Attitudes.   Society provides ready-made channels for satisfying many of our needs.   Action-oriented attitudes are those in which valued objects stimulate need-satisfying action tendencies with a minimum amount of cognitive activity.   Little cognitive activity is required, for example, in our attitudes toward food.   A positive action-oriented attitude is reinforced when satisfaction is derived from acting positively toward the attitude object.   Negative action-oriented attitudes (e.g., overt hostility to a minority group) are reinforced in a similar fashion.

Balanced Attitudes.   Balanced attitudes have an elaborated cognitive content, an action orientation, an affective core, and serve consciously recognized and accepted needs.   Economic and political attitudes often are of this variety.   For example, members of labor unions are favorably disposed to legislation designed to strengthen labor.   A manufacturer may favor high tariffs if he sees high tariffs as advantageous to his business.   Political parties customarily formulate their party platforms with these special interest attitudes in mind.   Balanced attitudes are learned in the process of goal-seeking behavior, reinforced to the extent they are need-satisfying, and elaborated with cognitive content to justify the course of action taken.

The pattern for many experiments on changing attitudes is to induce a change in the direction of an attitude and then note any subsequent change in behavior.   Another pattern is possible—a behavior change may result in a change in attitude.   A number of experiments indicate that subjects who are required to act contrary to their beliefs tend to modify their beliefs so as to make them consistent to their behavior (Brehm, 1960; Cohen, 1959; Festinger and Carlsmith, 1959; Rosenbaum and Franc, 1960).   Thus, one way of changing a balanced attitude is through gaining control of the individual's behavior toward the attitude object.

Ego-Defensive Attitudes.   Affective, cognitive, and behavioral components are present in ego-defensive attitudes.   They differ from balanced attitudes in that the needs they serve arise from internal conflict and the resulting behavior is directed at objects that cannot resolve this conflict.   Unfavorable attitudes toward minority groups may be of this variety.   Feelings of insecurity and hostility find expression in aggressive acts directed against some safe scapegoat.   External pressure may change the cognitive content of such attitudes but does not resolve the basic conflict.   The hostile and insecure individual merely finds a new scapegoat against whom he can safely direct his aggression.

Learning Exercise

5. Classify each of the following according to the Katz and Stotland typology:
   (a) Robert has felt kindly toward Polish people ever since a Polish farmer helped Robert when his car broke down.
   (b) Mr. Lax, who feels guilty about his own sexual motivations, believes that the sex morals in this country are now worse than in any other period in history.
   (c) Mary always treated animals kindly.
   (d) John became convinced that explorations in space are necessary after reading about possible future scientific advances.
   (e) Mr. and Mrs. Jones voted for higher school taxes because they believed in education and wanted good schools for their children.

The Principle of Consistency

An individual strives to attain some kind of consistency within himself. The student who believes that a college education is a good thing usually makes an effort to attend college. Most people attending a Shakespearean play have a favorable attitude toward Shakespeare. A teacher who believes that social progress can be achieved best through employing democratic procedures is likely to reflect this belief in his teaching. Usually, there is some consistency between what a person believes, what a person feels, and what he does.

Granted that consistency usually characterizes a person's thoughts, feelings, and actions, what about the many inconsistencies that we observe almost daily? The student knows that he should study, yet he fritters away his time in a round of social activities. To point out that the student achieves a psychological rather than a logical consistency evades the problem. A person strives to attain what he perceives to be a logical consistency between his thoughts, feelings, and actions. Thus, the student who spends more time on social activities than on his studies may rationalize that: (a) social activities are an important part of a college education; (b) he will make up for lost time in his studies next week; (c) he will study more when he takes courses that interest him. The important point is that inconsistencies between beliefs, feelings, and actions result in an effort on the part of a person to bring about a consistency.

A number of psychologists are currently concerned with the problem of how the multitude of attitudes of an individual are structured into some kind of cohesive and systematic organization. McGuire (1960) writes:

The "rational man" concept, long out of fashion in the behavioral sciences, is now undergoing a remarkable revival in the study of cognition. More and more, theory and research are being based on the postulate that a person's need to maintain harmony between his feelings, thoughts, and actions is a powerful determinant to his belief systems and of his gross behavior.[2] [P. 65.]

McGuire (1960) differentiates between two types of cognitive consistencies: (1) *logical thinking*—the tendency for a person's beliefs or expectations on related issues to become logically consistent; and (2) *wishful thinking*—the tendency for a person's beliefs on a given issue to become consistent with his desires on that issue.

Cognitive Dissonance and Consonance. To avoid the logical connotation of the terms "inconsistency" and "consistency," Festinger (1957) substitutes the terms *"dissonance"* and *"consonance."* For Festinger, "dissonance" and "consonance" refer to relations existing between pairs of elements. To illustrate, let us consider the case of a student who strongly opposes the integration of schools. *Consonant* with this element of the student's belief system is the fact that his parents and other individuals important in his life also are against integration and subscribe to a set of corollary beliefs that support segregation. *Dissonant* with the student's belief is the fact that other important individuals including the members of the Supreme Court and many religious leaders oppose segregation and support their opposition with a set of facts and corollary beliefs. Of course, other cognitions of our student (e.g., his opinion regarding the value of mathematics) are *irrelevant* elements. Thus, the three possible relations between pairs of elements are irrelevance, dissonance, and consonance.

Festinger states the following as basic hypotheses:

1. The existence of dissonance, being psychologically uncomfortable, will motivate the person to try to reduce the dissonance and achieve consonance.
2. When dissonance is present, in addition to trying to reduce it, the person will actively avoid situations and information which would likely increase the dissonance. [P. 3.]

---

[2] This process of maintaining harmony is labelled "tendency toward balance" by Heider (1958), "balanced structure" by Cartwright and Harary (1956), "balanced matrices" by Abelson and Rosenberg (1958), "stress toward symmetry" by Newcomb (1953), and "tendency toward increased congruity" by Osgood and Tannenbaum (1955). Perhaps the most systematic body of data is that reported by Festinger (1957) in his book *A Theory of Cognitive Dissonance.*

SOURCES OF DISSONANCE. Dissonance may stem from a variety of sources. Two beliefs that are logically inconsistent may result in dissonance once the inconsistency is perceived. Thus, to believe that man will reach the moon some time after 1970 is logically inconsistent with the belief that man will be destroyed by nuclear war before 1970. If the importance of these two beliefs is not great, then the magnitude of dissonance will be small. Consonance can be attained by modifying the less important belief.

A person may experience dissonance when he behaves contrary to his beliefs. A child who believes that he is kind to others may experience dissonance if he realizes that he has been unkind to one of his classmates. Here, consonance may easily be restored if the child changes the behavioral element—i.e., he becomes kind to his classmate—thus permitting him to retain the concept of himself as a kind child.

Dissonance may arise because an event turns out in an unexpected way. The high school student who believes that his school's football team is the best in the state will experience dissonance if his team suffers defeat. If the student's belief in his team is sufficiently strong, then consonance may be restored by finding good reasons why the team suffered defeat. There is a limit, however, to the total amount of resistance to changing a belief. If the student's team continues to lose game after game, then the student's belief in his team may weaken. However, the capacity of humans to deny reality is great, particularly if there is a sufficient amount of social support for the maintenance of a discredited belief. Sady's (1948) report on Japanese in relocation centers during World War II is illustrative. Some Japanese in relocation centers believed firmly that Japan would win the war, and therefore requested that they be repatriated at the end of the war. In so requesting, these Japanese renounced their United States citizenship. News of Japanese defeats was dismissed by these Japanese as American propaganda. Even the news of the Japanese surrender was not believed. When the Japanese were put on an American ship to be returned to Japan, they believed that Japan had won the war and that Japan was forcing United States to return them. Only when they arrived in Japan and viewed actual destruction and American occupation did these repatriated Japanese discard their belief that Japan had won the war.

Dissonance may occur because an act is not followed by the expected consequence. If a person turns the ignition key of his car and the car does not start, these two cognitions would be dissonant with one another. Adding new cognitive elements (e.g., the battery has run down) may eliminate the dissonance.

The few illustrations outlined above may serve to illustrate the meaning of the term "dissonance." In general, Festinger's theory of dissonance holds that: (1) "nonfitting" relations among cognitive elements produce dissonance; (2) dissonance gives rise to pressures to reduce the dissonance and to avoid increases in dissonance; and (3) these pressures may result in behavior changes, changes of cognitions or beliefs, and efforts to seek new information. In our discussion of how attitudes change, we will note some of the implications and applications of this theory.

Learning Exercises

6. How is dissonance created when a person listens to both sides of a debate?
7. Cognitive inconsistency may persist when a person maintains conflicting beliefs in "logic-tight" compartments. For example, a person may believe in freedom of speech, and yet also believe that extreme conservatives or extreme radicals should not be permitted to express their views in public. Does such compartmentalization produce dissonance?
8. Which of McGuire's two types of cognitive consistency is exemplified in Sady's study on Japanese in relocation centers?
9. Under what circumstances might the superego function so as to produce dissonance?

LEARNING ATTITUDES

The attitudes of each child in a classroom are attributable to a number of sources. The home is the major source for many of the child's attitudes. Other attitudes are learned by the child as he interacts with his age-mates and with other people. Some attitudes are learned through reading. In fact, all experiences of a child are potential sources for the development of attitudes.

The school is a major source for some of the child's attitudes. A favorable attitude toward a school subject is usually largely attributable to the child's experiences in school. The school may not wish to exert any influence on many of a child's attitudes. For example, public schools ordinarily are not concerned whether a child prefers one religious faith to another, and make no effort to modify a child's religious preference. The school may be chiefly concerned in developing other attitudes (e.g., the development of democratic ideals) and yet be only one of a number of sources shaping those attitudes. The school is concerned that the child develops a belief in the rights of the individual, an acceptance of principles of equality of privilege, a tolerance for the views of others, and a willingness to abide by the decisions of the majority. But home, church, and community, as well as the school, help to form democratic or undemocratic attitudes. Sometimes the teaching of the home and community runs contrary to the educational objective of the school.

How can the school modify the attitudes of children? Obviously, an educational objective such as "a willingness to accept social responsibilities" is not learned in the same way as a lesson in algebra. A child does not acquire a willingness to accept responsibility by trying to be willing. Rather, he learns social responsibility in the process of performing concrete tasks, and he may be completely unaware of any relationship between his task performance and the learning of an attitude. Attitudes emerge as a result of certain characteristics of a child's experiences. To identify what these characteristics are, it is necessary to look at some of the ways attitudes commonly develop in people.

Learning Exercise

10. Adolescents form attitudes concerning the regulation of their personal social life. For many adolescents, these attitudes constitute a code of behavior that is based upon ethical principles and yet leads to satisfying relations with their age-mates. What are the sources for such desirable attitudes?

Identification

Make-believe and other imaginative activities play an important part in a child's life. A little girl with her dolls, toy household furniture, appliances, and dishes can imitate the activities of her mother. She can do better than this. She can, in her imagination, be her mother. A little boy can put on his father's hat and, in his imagination, be his father returning from work. This make-believe behavior does not end in early childhood. The adolescent girl attends a movie and suffers all the trials and tribulations of the heroine. A boy, in his imagination, can be his favorite ballplayer as his hero steps up to the plate in a World Series game. And the adult imitates people whom he admires, and empathizes with persons who are dear to him.

Freud (1927) has used the term "*identification*" to describe this process through which a person molds himself after the fashion of one who has been taken as a *model*. For Freud, the superego is formed through the process of identification. The parent's "do's" and "don'ts" are initially externally enforced by the parents. Later, they become internalized. The little girl who enters first grade has learned a host of behaviors that are "right" to her and refrains from other acts that are "wrong." The little girl's conscience or superego helps her to act properly in many situations.

The term "identification" is given a variety of meanings in the literature of child development and mental hygiene. Sanford (1955) applies the term "identification" to situations in which "an individual may be observed to respond to the behavior of other people by imitating in fantasy or reality the same behavior himself" (p. 109). Identification is usually treated in the literature as an intervening mediating process, although Hill (1960) has endeavored to translate the behaviors and processes covered by the term "identification" into reinforcement learning processes. Kagan (1958) describes four types of identification:

1. *Imitative learning*—a person imitates and practices certain responses (gestures, speech patterns, dress, etc.) that are approved in his environment.
2. *Prohibition learning*—a person takes over the prohibitions of his parents or parent substitutes. The major motivation is claimed to be anxiety over the possible loss of love.
3. *Identification with the aggressor*—a person adopts behavior similar to that of an aggressive or threatening model. Bettleheim (1943) reports that prisoners in a German concentration camp during World War II adopted the mannerisms, attitudes, and values of their guards, and when given camp duties, they mistreated their fellow prisoners. Kagan attributes anxiety over anticipated aggression or domination by the threatening model as the motivation for this type of identification.
4. *Vicarious affective experience*—a person experiences the same positive or negative emotions as his model. A person experiences joy when his model is joyful and sorrow when his model is sorrowful.

Kagan (1958) suggests that, for the child especially, two important goal states motivate identification. These are the desires for: (a) a feeling of power and mastery over the environment and (b) love and affection.

Learning Exercise

11. Classify each of the following according to Kagan's four types of identification:
    (a) Mary usually tells the truth because her mother has taught her that it is wrong to lie.

(b) Mary weeps during a sad movie.
(c) John, who fears his father, is a bully on the playground.
(d) Sally copies the hairdo of her favorite actress.

Factors Influencing Identification. A teacher can influence the attitudes of children by serving as a model. But a child does not accept as a model each individual in his life; nor does he imitate all the behaviors of any one model.

Some of the factors influencing identification are:

1. *The sex of the model.* In our culture, certain ways of behaving are deemed appropriate only for males while other ways of behaving are considered suitable only for females. Identification with a member of like sex, therefore, is important in learning the appropriate sex role. This does not mean that a member of the opposite sex cannot influence the behavior of a child. Peck and Havighurst (1960), in their study of character development, found some boys who scored highest in maturity of character identified primarily with their mothers. On the basis of their data, Peck and Havighurst conclude that: "For both boys and girls, it seems that moral values may be learned equally well—or equally badly—from either parent" (p. 123).

2. *Social pressures.* Almost from birth to death, our society exerts pressure to insure that boys behave like boys and girls behave like girls. Taunts of "sissy" or "tomboy" plague the boys or girls who behave in ways judged to be inappropriate for their sex. The earliest pressures to assume an appropriate sex role come from the home. Both boys and girls form their first identifications with their mothers. Continued identification with the mother is appropriate for the girl, but not for the boy if he is to develop a normal masculine personality (Sears *et al.*, 1957). In one research study (Mussen and Distler, 1959) with five-year-old boys, it was found that masculine identification did not appear to be dependent upon one specific type of father-son relationship. Boys with strong identification with their fathers perceived their fathers as both rewarding and punishing figures. The major factor differentiating boys of a high level of masculine identification from boys of a low level seemed to be the *importance* of the father in the child's life.

Social pressures influence the child in his choice of models for all of his behaviors. The child is more apt to identify with a highly regarded person in his community than he is with a person who is poorly regarded by all the people of importance to the child.

3. *Affection accorded to the child.* The emotional relationship between a potential model and a child has a bearing upon the extent to

which identification occurs. Levin and Sears (1956) found that girls who were strongly identified with their mothers were very aggressive if their mothers were aggressive, but were non-aggressive if their mothers were non-aggressive. Payne and Mussen (1956) found that boys who had a favorable relationship with their fathers, displayed more masculine interests and attitudes than did boys with a less favorable relationship. Sears et al., (1957) found that the mothers of children rated high on conscience development had a warm relationship with their children but withdrew their love when their children behaved badly. Identification is most likely to occur when there is a bond of affection between two individuals but may occur when a bond of affection is lacking. Stoke (1950) distinguishes between *emotional* and *behavioral* identification and cites clinical cases to support his distinction. Mothers of adolescents were interviewed concerning their earlier home backgrounds as well as their present homes. Several of these women failed to make any emotional identification with their mothers, and actually expressed antagonism toward them. Yet, these women in their own homes displayed much of the same aggressive and domineering behavior to which they objected in their mothers. In other cases reported by Stoke, emotional identification occurred without behavioral identification. In one case, a man with a strong emotional identification with his puritanical father lived the carefree life of an irresponsible Lothario.

4. *Need fulfillment.* A child is more likely to identify with another individual when, by so doing, he satisfies important needs. In the home, the child finds it psychologically rewarding to adopt the attitudes, values, and standards of his parents. As the child grows up, he finds need for a variety of models to achieve his various goals. His parents continue to be models for many of his attitudes and behavior. Other classmates may serve as models in achieving a satisfactory peer-group adjustment. The teacher may be a model for tasks he performs in school and a source for many of his cognitive attitudes. Older children, young adults in his community, glamorous figures in the news, fictitious and imaginary characters—all may be models for some of the behaviors of the child and adolescent. Increasingly with age, the child perceives his ideal self as a composite of the qualities of a number of persons (Havighurst and MacDonald, 1955).

5. *Other factors.* The child must have sufficient contact with an adult for the adult to become an identifying figure. This fact constitutes a problem in many American homes—not only in fatherless homes, but also in homes where contacts with the father are brief or infrequent.

Teachers do have many contacts with children. However, the extent to which a teacher becomes an identifying figure for a child depends upon a number of factors. The teacher who helps the child meet needs is likely to be able to influence the attitudes and behavior of the child. The child must be capable of modeling his behavior after the teacher. The rugged football coach may serve as a model for physically well-developed boys, but not for boys with meager athletic abilities. The vivacious young lady teacher may serve as a model for many girls in the junior and senior high school, but not for the shy, timid girl. The intellectually stimulating science teacher may serve as a model for the intelligent boys and girls in his class, but not for children of low academic aptitude. The *capacity* and *temperament* of the child must be like the person with whom identification is attempted (Stoke, 1950). The child must have sufficient contact with such a person. And identification is more likely to occur when the child can meet his needs through identifying.

Models in Literature, Movies, Television, and Radio. It is difficult to conduct research on the influence of literature, movies, television, and radio on children's attitudes. Responses of children to these stimuli cannot be directly observed or adequately measured. Certainly, reading materials, films, and radio and television programs are sources of information. As we shall see later, information may function to form or modify attitudes when certain conditions prevail. The question of immediate concern to us is: Do the fictional or historical characters that children meet through the various communications media serve as models that affect the attitudes and behavior of children? Does, for example, reading a biography on Abraham Lincoln inspire a boy to emulate Lincoln? Does the viewing of violence on a television program adversely affect a boy's behavior? Is an adolescent girl's sex code influenced by sexy movies or books?

Unfortunately, definitive research evidence on the above questions is lacking. Insights of clinical psychologists into human personality do provide one basis for assessing the effects on the child of the communications media. Also, some research findings provide partial answers. Himmelweit, Oppenheim, and Vince (1958) have investigated the effects of television on children in England in two age groups, ten- and eleven-year-olds and thirteen- and fourteen-year-olds. These investigators matched on the basis of sex, age, intelligence, and social background, 927 television viewers with an equal number of non-viewers. The two groups were compared with respect to certain personality characteristics, interests, and habits. An over-all conclusion emerging from the comparison was that television is neither as detrimental as its detractors fear nor as beneficial as its advocates claim. The adverse effects of television in provoking neurotic disturbances and delinquent behavior, apparently, have been exaggerated. A similar but qualified conclusion is reached by Malm and Jamison (1952), who write: "No radio, television, or movie programs originate anxieties, unwholesome attitudes, bad habits or delinquent behavior in the boys or girls, but if the seed for these things already exists, some radio, television, and movie programs he hears and sees may stir them into action or give them emphases which are not wholesome." (P. 449.)

There is some evidence that boys who are moving in the direction of delinquency may identify with the bad man in a movie and learn techniques of crime (Forman, 1933). A similar possibility exists in learning desirable behavior patterns. The child who is already motivated to behave in some socially constructive manner may find in a book or movie a character with whom he can identify and learn from the model some technique of goodness. But, apparently, the desirable motivation must be present initially. Loban (1954) found that mere exposure to literature in which social sensitivity was exemplified did not bring about any apparent change in students rated low in social sensitivity. There are more possibilities of desirable effects when class discussion follows exposure to a desirable model. Taba (1955) found that the factual content of a story was the major learning when upper-elementary-grade pupils read a story. Discussion, in which the pupils interacted with the material in the story, permitted the pupils to achieve desirable insights that went beyond the facts of the story.

Learning Exercises

12. In which of the following cases would emotional identification be expected? In which would behavioral identification be expected?
    (a) Arthur's father is quiet, courteous, and interested in art and music. Arthur's playmates are boisterous, not particularly courteous, and have no interest in art and music. Arthur likes his father.
    (b) Bob's father is aggressive, frequently loses his temper when Bob irritates him, and shows Bob little affection. Bob dislikes his father.
13. Mr. Jones, a social science teacher manages to stimulate the interest of many class members in social sciences. Mr. Jones expects a high academic standard from all his students. Why might some of his students not identify with him?
14. How might a teacher increase the moral impact on his students of a novel dealing with an ethical issue?

Conditioning

An attitude elicits a feeling of pleasantness or unpleasantness. This feeling may be manifested behaviorally in an accepting or a rejecting act. The feeling tone aspect of an attitude may be explained in terms of classical conditioning. The acquisition of the behavioral component of an attitude may be explained in terms of instrumental conditioning.

Emotional Effects of Certain Experiences. The Watson and Rayner (1920) experiment reported in Chapter 5 illustrates the acquisition of fear by classical conditioning. The little boy who heard a painfully loud noise at the same time he was presented with a white rat learned to fear the white rat. Emotional conditioning of this kind frequently occurs in our daily living. Favorable attitudes may be formed toward certain foods when the foods are served in pleasant surroundings. Our attitudes toward a particular religious, racial, or national group are influenced by the over-all pleasantness or unpleasantness of our past associations with that group. A student's attitude toward a school subject is similarly affected by the pleasantness or unpleasantness of his learning experiences in that subject. A child forms a favorable attitude toward reading when reading is made an enjoyable task for him.

Contact between unfriendly groups is sometimes suggested as one means of modifying attitudes. Katz (1960) lists a number of studies reporting a reduction of racial prejudice resulting from increased contact. But some studies report an increase in racial prejudice following increased contact. The effectiveness of contact as a method of changing attitudes depends largely upon how satisfying the contact is. Mussen (1950) reports an experiment in which Negro and white boys of ages eight to fourteen camped together for four weeks. Tests to determine the prejudice of each boy were administered before and after the camping experience. During the camping experience, each boy's adjustment at the camp was assessed. At the end of the camping period, about 25 per cent of the boys obtained scores on the attitude test indicating less prejudice. About the same percentage of boys scored higher in prejudice. In personality structure, as measured by the Thematic Apperception Test, boys who increased their prejudice during the camping experience differed in a number of ways from the boys who decreased their prejudice. The increased prejudice group revealed more aggressive and dominance needs, more hostility toward their parents, and tended to view the world as a hostile place in which they were the victims of the aggression of others. Differences were found between the two groups in their adjustment to camp life. The boys who increased in prejudice were dissatisfied with their camping experience, whereas the boys who decreased in prejudice found the camping experience satisfying.

Two points in Mussen's study should be noted. First, the study illustrates the modification of attitudes by emotional conditioning. The pleasantness of a complete experience tends to induce a favorable attitude toward elements within the experience. Boys who enjoyed the total camping experience tended to form more favorable attitudes toward boys of a different race. The second point is that an experience that is enjoyable for one participant may not be enjoyable for another participant. Personality variables interact with situational variables in determining whether an experience is need satisfying for an individual.

It is sometimes assumed that experience in a foreign culture is an effective way of modifying attitudes toward the citizens of other countries and bringing about better international understanding. Some research evidence tends to support this assumption (Katz, 1960). The development of favorable attitudes is contingent, however, upon the specific conditions of the experiences in another culture. Positive outcomes occur when the cross-cultural experiences are need satisfying. Watson and Lippitt (1958) interviewed 29 Germans brought here by the State Department for advanced study. These visitors were interviewed while in the United States, shortly after they returned to Germany, and six months after their return. While in the United States, these students were eager to learn anything they thought would help them with their problems at home. Attitudes were learned that fit into their own value system. For example, many of the students initially had negative attitudes toward American child-rearing practices. At the same time, they placed a high value on individualism. Once they saw the relationship between American child-rearing practices and individualism, they developed favorable attitudes toward these practices.

Negative outcomes may also result from cross-cultural experiences. Morris (1956) found that when Americans assigned a lower status to the country of foreign students than did the foreign students themselves, unfavorable attitudes toward the United States tended to develop.

Learning Exercise

15. The students in the tenth-grade class at Riverside School enjoy school experiences in which they work together to plan a unit of instruction.

> How might Miss Murray, English teacher, capitalize upon the students' liking for group planning activities in developing the students' appreciation of Shakespeare?

TRAUMATIC EXPERIENCES. A single traumatic experience may dramatically change the attitude of an individual. A child may develop a fear of dogs from one experience of being bitten by a dog. While it is clear that traumatic experiences are effective in changing attitudes, the educational implications of this fact are not so obvious. Certainly, the psychological equivalents of dog bites would seem to be dangerous in a school classroom. The question is: Can teachers provide highly emotional experiences in the classroom that lead to desirable attitudinal changes? An experiment reported by Toch and Cantril (1957) is suggestive.

Toch and Cantril conducted a series of experiments designed to discover the kind of experiences that stimulated college students to re-examine their value systems. Ordinarily, students, like others, become involved in their daily routines and spend little time in thinking through a philosophy of life. "Lack of time" does not seem to be the reason for this. Toch and Cantril placed students in a soundproof room and asked them to occupy their minds with anything they wished for 15 minutes. The reported thoughts of the students were quite mundane. Students spent the time thinking of social dates, sports, their immediate study assignments, and the like. Apparently, some kind of stimulus material is required to spring a person loose from involvement in his daily routine. In one of Toch and Cantril's experiments, the following mimeographed letter was used as stimulus material:

DEAR MIKE:

Forgive me for not letting you know long before this how much I appreciated your kind note wishing me a speedy recovery. I was released from the hospital only yesterday, but unfortunately there is no question of a recovery. Their half-dozen lung men all agree that I have *at the most six weeks* left, although there is no danger for the next twenty days or so. They wouldn't tell me this at first and I had to pry it painfully out of the doctor. Now I almost wish I hadn't.

It is very, very difficult to get used to the idea, and I don't think I am quite convinced of it yet. Unfortunately, there is no way of getting around it, and I have to sit down and do some very serious thinking as to what to do with the infinitesimal time left me.

The one consolation I have is that my wife and children are provided for. With the insurance, the social security, and what I have managed to save, they should be able to get along. If things go well John might even get through college. I took care of the will this morning, so there is no worry on that score.

Ironically enough, I don't feel too badly. I will not be confined to bed and the Doc says to do anything I feel like doing.

But what am I to do Mike? Somehow I don't think I can just proceed as usual and pretend nothing is going to happen. Put yourself in my shoes, Mike. What would you do?

Yours,

Steve

[P. 148.]

The students in the experimental group were presented the above letter as stimulus material and given a half hour to think about it. Four students were placed singly in separate rooms; four students were grouped but were instructed not to discuss the letter among themselves; and four students were placed in a group with instructions to discuss the letter. Parallel control groups were given crossword puzzles to work prior to the half-hour contemplating sessions. The students in all of the experimental groups found their task highly satisfying and worthwhile. The evidence indicated that members in the experimental groups sensed some of the inadequacies of their daily routine and formulated conclusions as to the direction of desirable changes. Thus, inducing students to identify with a person experiencing an emotionally charged crisis may jolt students to re-examine seriously their life values.

Strong emotional conditioning may not result in the desired behavioral changes. Janis and Feshbach (1953) experimented with three types of communication designed to inform high school students about the consequences of failure to practice proper dental hygiene. The first group of students was shown pictures of a frightening character; the second group was shown less dramatic material; and the third group received similar information in a non-emotional fashion. The follow-up study indicated that the group subjected to the non-emotional appeal had most members changing to better practices. The group exposed to the maximum fear appeal apparently avoided the problem and had the fewest members following the suggestion about good dental care.

Learning Exercise

16. Sometimes people are emotionally moved by a dramatic movie, play, sermon, or a tragic news event. Can intense emotional experiences provided in the classroom change for the better the attitudes of students?

Behavioral Effects of Certain Experiences. The behavioral component of an attitude may be learned through instrumental conditioning. In the classroom, the child who tries arithmetic problems experiences success or failure. Success experiences with arithmetic problems are rewarding and tend to induce the child to seek further experiences in arithmetic. Frustration and failure consistently experienced by the child, on the other hand, would tend to generate an unfavorable attitude.

At home, at school, and on the playground, a child's verbal statements may be positively reinforced by approval or negatively reinforced through ignoring or disapproval. In this way, verbal expressions of attitudes may be learned. A child who is brought up in a home and a community that is prejudiced against another religion, nationality, or race will tend himself to become prejudiced. When he states an opinion that supports the prejudice, others agree with him. His statements that run contrary to the prejudice are met with disapproval. Because perception is selective, the child's prejudice can be further reinforced in his contacts with members of the other religion, nationality, or race. He will tend to find instances of the bad qualities he attributes to the objects of his prejudices and to overlook these same bad qualities in others.

In the classroom, a pupil's attitudes toward democratic procedures may be learned by trying out democratic procedures. Favorable attitudes toward democratic procedures are formed as pupils practice democratic procedures and find them more satisfying than undemocratic practices. These favorable attitudes may be further reinforced as important individuals in the life of the pupil express favorable attitudes toward democratic practices.

A number of studies have found that there is more similarity in attitudes among friends than among non-friends (Bonney, 1946; Loomis, 1946; Newcomb, 1956), that people of similar attitudes are attracted to each other (Byrne, 1961), and that there is a tendency over time for a person to ignore another whose opinion varies markedly from his own (Festinger et al., 1952; Schachter and Burdick, 1955). Hence, to change an attitude, the usual pattern of reinforcements obtained for the behavioral expression of the attitude must somehow be disrupted. Research evidence indicates a number of ways in which this may occur.

1. *Moving to a new environment in which new reference groups are found.* Newcomb's Bennington College study (1943) is illustrative. The girls included in this study came, for the most part, from homes in which the parents held conservative views on social issues. These girls entered Bennington College where the faculty and student body were

predominantly liberal in their outlook on social and political issues. Measurements were obtained on the attitudes of the girls toward a number of social issues, first as freshmen, and then through their sophomore, junior, and senior years. The majority of the students became increasingly liberal as they progressed through college. The freshmen girls reflected their parents' conservative attitudes. But the girls, for whom the college community became their reference group, found that liberal attitudes were reinforced while conservative attitudes were not reinforced. For those who did not change, the friends and family outside the campus continued to be their reference group. It is of interest to note that girls who were seeking emancipation from the home found in the college a congenial atmosphere in which they could express their independence. Some of the girls who did not change were overly dependent upon their parents. For these girls, rebellion against their parents' attitudes was too threatening.

A study reported by Sims and Patrick (1936) similarly shows that individuals tend to assimilate the attitudes prevailing in the culture in which they live. The attitudes of first-year northern whites toward Negroes in a southern university were found to be similar to that of northern students in northern universities. The attitudes toward Negroes of northern students who were in their third and fourth year in the southern university resembled that of southern students in the same southern university. The attitudes of second-year northern students were found to be about halfway between those of freshmen and upperclassmen.

2. *Gaining control of the individual's behavior.* We have noted that the individual strives to make consistent the behavioral, affective, and cognitive components of his attitudes. Hence, it would seem possible that the individual who is forced to change his behavior toward an attitude object would also change the accompanying affective and cognitive components of his attitude. Research evidence lends some support to this supposition. Harding and Hogrefe (1952) showed that department store clerks who had to work with Negroes tended to form more favorable attitudes toward Negroes. Brophy (1946) found that prejudice was reduced among white merchant seamen who shared common dangers with Negro crew members while being bombed and strafed in the South Pacific. Even without common dangers, common ties were formed through sharing of hardships on board ship and jointly participating in responsibilities on deck.

Festinger (1957) suggests that instances of "drastic change in ideology in an area that is highly resistant to change come about only after overt behavior that creates strong dissonance with the existing ideology has somehow been elicited." (Pp. 120–21.) The establishing of strong dissonance motivates the individual to reduce the dissonance. Festinger relates his theory of dissonance to the problem of implementing the United States Supreme Court ruling on desegregation of schools. Festinger writes:

The theory would imply that in those areas where compliance is obtained, that is, desegregation of schools is carried out, there would occur gradual opinion change toward favoring desegregation among the people. On the other hand, the theory similarly implies that in any area which does not comply, that is, successfully resists desegregation of its schools, attitudes would change in the opposite direction—toward greater favoring of segregation. [P. 122.]

Some support for Festinger's suggestion may be found in the Deutsch and Collins study (1951) of the changes in attitudes toward Negroes occurring during residence in an integrated housing project. Living in the project brought about contact of whites with Negroes. Ordinary rules of polite, neighborly behavior no doubt functioned to produce behavior dissonant with private beliefs. Deutsch and Collins report that their data support the conclusion that "once a change in behavior has occurred, a change in belief is likely to follow" (p. 142).

Attitudes may be modified even by role-playing in which a person assumes a role that is contrary to his attitudes. Culbertson (1957) found that more favorable attitudes toward Negroes were formed after subjects had been assigned the role of working out problems of Negro housing. Janis and King (1954) found that the task of making speeches led to changes in attitudes in line with the position taken in the speech.

Dissonance occurs whenever a person acts contrary to his beliefs in order to receive a reward or avoid a punishment. One way of reducing this dissonance is to modify one's beliefs. To illustrate, consider the case of a high school boy who believes it is wrong to cheat on a test, but who, nevertheless, cheated on a very important test. Here, the boy's behavior does not correspond to his belief about cheating. The boy will experience "dissonance." Under such circumstances, Festinger would predict that the boy's opinion about cheating is likely to be modified. Possibly, the boy might come to believe that cheating is justified under certain circumstances. How much dissonance the boy experiences depends upon the importance to him of his belief about cheating. If he is firmly convinced that cheating is wrong, then his deviate behavior will be greatly disturbing, i.e., the magnitude of his dissonance will be great. If he is not firmly committed in his belief, then the act of cheating may cause little dissonance. Festinger postulates that the greatest shifts in opinion result when maximum disso-

nance is experienced. Maximum dissonance occurs when the anticipated reward or punishment is just sufficient to produce the behavior
that is contrary to a person's belief. Too great a reward or punishment
will result in very little dissonance. For example, many people who
prefer Brand X soap would state that they prefer Brand Y soap if they
were offered several thousand dollars for so doing. Unless a person is
very firmly committed to a policy of honesty at all costs, little dissonance would be experienced. More dissonance would be experienced,
according to Festinger's theory, if the reward was reduced to an
amount just sufficient to produce the "little white lie."

The findings of an experiment conducted by Kelman (1953) are consistent with Festinger's theory of the relationship of the amount of
dissonance that exists after forced compliance and the magnitude of
the promised reward or threatened punishment that elicits the com-
pliant behavior. Kelman asked seventh-grade pupils whether they
preferred comic books of the "fantastic hero" type or the "jungle story"
type. One week later, the experimenter asked the pupils to write an
essay expressing their opinions on the two types of comic books. Incentives to write essays favoring one or the other type of books were
varied for three groups of pupils as follows:

1. *Moderate* incentive to write an essay favoring *fantastic hero
   stories.* Pupils in this group were informed that the publishers
   of the comic books would give a free copy of *Huckleberry Finn*
   to anyone writing an essay in favor of the fantastic hero stories.
2. *Low* incentive to write an essay favoring *jungle stories.* Pupils
   in this group were told that a free book awaited anyone who
   wrote in favor of fantastic hero stories, but a free pass to see a
   movie of *Huckleberry Finn* would be given to five of those who
   wrote a good essay favoring jungle stories. It had previously
   been determined that a pass to a movie was more attractive to
   the pupils than a free book. However, by writing an essay in
   favor of jungle stories, a pupil gave up a free book and was not
   sure that he would be one of the five lucky ones to receive a free
   movie pass.
3. *High* incentive to write an essay favoring *jungle stories.* Pupils
   in this group were promised a copy of *Huckleberry Finn* if they
   wrote an essay in favor of fantastic hero stories. Pupils were
   promised a free book, plus a pass to the movie, and permission
   to take time off from school to attend the movie if they wrote an
   essay favoring jungle stories.

After the experiment, pupils were asked again to express their preferences for the two types of books. Table 13–1 shows the mean

opinion change for pupils who wrote essays favoring each type of comic book.

TABLE 13–1

Mean Opinion Change in Each Experimental Condition

		Essay Favoring			
Degree of Incentive	Direction of Incentive	Jungle Stories	Number of Pupils	Fantastic Hero Stories	Number of Pupils
Moderate	Fantastic Hero	+2.62*	(29)	−4.57†	(14)
Low	Jungle	+5.49	(47)	+1.89	(9)
High	Jungle	+3.81	(52)	−5.00	(8)

* A positive sign indicates a change of opinion toward greater preference of jungle books.
† A negative sign indicates a change toward greater preference for fantastic hero stories.

The above data fit well into Festinger's theory of cognitive dissonance. For those pupils who wrote essays favoring jungle stories, the greatest change in opinion occurred under the low incentive conditions. Sources of dissonance for the 47 pupils in this group were (1) writing an essay contrary to their private opinion (for some of the 47 pupils), (2) giving up a free copy of *Huckleberry Finn*, and (3) running the risk of not receiving a free pass to the movie. This relatively great dissonance could be removed by a shift in their attitudes in favor of jungle stories.

Some of the 14 pupils who wrote essays in favor of fantastic hero stories, under a moderate degree of incentive, probably were expressing opinions that were contrary to their private opinions. Dissonance here might be expected to be great because the reward for so doing was not great. The 8 pupils who wrote essays favoring the fantastic hero stories were undoubtedly expressing their true opinions because, by so doing, they gave up a free pass to the movie. Yet dissonance for these 8 students might be expected to be great because of what they gave up through expressing their true opinion. This dissonance could be reduced by believing even more firmly that fantastic hero stories are better than jungle stories.

Learning Exercises

17. Why do people in the same group tend to develop similar attitudes?
18. Why might a student who leaves his hometown to go to college feel ill at ease with his old friends when he returns home for a vacation?

19. A student with an unfavorable attitude toward poetry may develop a favorable attitude as he studies poetry. Why?

20. A student with an unfavorable attitude toward the United Nations sees a film showing the good work performed by the United Nations. How can the student reduce the dissonance produced by viewing the film?

21. Which would be the more effective means of developing in a student a favorable attitude toward studying?
    (a) Apply just enough pressure (reward or punishment) to induce the student to study.
    (b) Make certain that the student does study by providing very strong incentives.

Exposure to Information

Commonly, people try to change the attitudes of others through verbal appeals. Advertisements are designed to create more favorable attitudes toward a multitude of commercial products. Politicians attempt to win votes by their speeches. The teacher tells one of his pupils why he should like school. Students are given reasons why democracy is the best form of government so that the students will form favorable attitudes toward democracy. Information in science courses is expected to dispel superstitious beliefs. From birth till death, the individual is subjected to a verbal barrage calculated to influence his beliefs and behavior.

It has long been established that communications can serve to form or to alter attitudes *under certain conditions.* Murphy, Murphy, and Newcomb's early survey (1937) reports numerous studies in which attitudes are shifted in the direction intended by a communication. Change is facilitated when the source of the communication is respected, when the communication reflects attitudes consistent to the needs of its receiver, and when the communication is acceptable to important reference groups of the receiver.

Learning Exercise

22. A student acquires a valuable educational objective when he is able to change his opinion on a controversial issue on the basis of evidence and arguments that reveal the inadequacies of his previous opinion. What additional conditions would make it easier for the student to change his opinion?

Interaction with a Communication. In the classroom, a mere presentation of a communication may result in little change of attitudes even under favorable conditions. Students need to interact with the communication if it is to affect their belief system. A classroom experiment reported by Bond (1940) illustrates the degree of interaction necessary if learning experiences are to influence students' beliefs. Bond prepared a unit in genetics as a vehicle for influencing the attitudes of college freshmen toward national groups, races, and imperialism. Students in the experimental group were encouraged to comment on national and social differences that they thought made certain groups inferior or difficult to assimilate. These differences were examined in the light of knowledge about genetics. Students drew their own generalizations from the evidence available. Differences that might reasonably be attributable to cultural rather than biological factors were identified. A control group of students were taught a unit in genetics in the traditional manner. They learned the same generalizations and were exposed to the same body of scientific information, but did not actively search for applications of the material in genetics to national and social problems. At the conclusion of the 15 hours of instruction, a series of tests, designed to measure the attitudes and understandings of the students, was administered to both groups. The experimental group was found to have more positive attitudes than the control group toward national groups, races, and imperialism.

Learning Exercise

23. How may Bond's results be explained in terms of the need of students to see the world as logically consistent (or the need for competencies)?

Motion picture films may influence the attitudes of viewers (Hovland *et al.*, 1949; Peterson and Thurstone, 1933; Raths and Trager, 1948). The film communication seems to exert a greater impact when viewers are given the opportunity to discuss its content. A study conducted by Mitnick and McGinnies (1958) suggests that personality variables operate as a factor influencing the amount of change in attitude induced by a film. These investigators first administered to 400 high school students in two schools a scale designed to measure ethnocentrism. (Ethnocentrism may be defined as the tendency to exalt the superiority of one's ethnic group and to judge outsiders adversely.) In each school, 27 students were selected from each extreme and the middle of the distribution of the ethnocentrism scores. At each level of ethnocentrism, 9 subjects in each of the two schools were assigned at random to each of the following experimental conditions: (1) film-discussion groups, (2) film-alone groups, and (3) control groups. Thus, a total of 18 groups, or 162 students, representing three levels of ethno-centricism, participated in the experiments. The film shown to the 12 experimental groups was *The High Wall,* a film in which group prejudice is treated as a communicable disease with origins in the family and the community. The 6 film-discussion groups were given 30 minutes to discuss the film after its showing. The 6 film-alone groups viewed the film but did not discuss it. The 6 control groups were not exposed to the film. Members of all groups filled out the ethnocentricism scale after the period in which the film was shown to the experimental groups. In addition, an information test covering factual material contained in the film was administered to the experi-mental groups. Both the ethnocentricism scale and the information test were readministered one month after the film showing as a meas-ure of retention. The major findings of the experiment were:

1. The film produced significant reduction in ethnocentricism in both the film-discussion and the film-alone groups. This reduc-tion in prejudice occurred for groups at all three levels of ethno-centricism. The discussion following the film did not result in a greater attitude change. In fact, the greatest attitude change of the 6 groups who were high in ethnocentricism occurred in the two film-alone groups.
2. The advantages of discussion following the film showed up on the retention tests. The members of film-discussion groups re-tained their attitude gains more than did the members of the film-alone groups.
3. Members of groups low in prejudice learned and retained more information from the film than did students who were high in prejudice.

The Mitnick and McGinnies study may be interpreted in terms of Festinger's theory of cognitive dissonance. For highly prejudiced stu-dents, we would expect the information contained in *The High Wall* film to produce dissonance. Festinger (1957) lists three ways by which dissonance may be reduced when subjects are involuntarily exposed to information: (1) the dissonant information is misperceived; (2) the sub-jects attempt to invalidate the dissonance-producing information; and (3) the subjects forget the dissonance-producing information.

Sleeper Effect of a Communication. Sometimes a communication exerts a greater influence over a period of time than it does immedi-ately after its reception. This has been referred to as the "sleeper effect" of a communication. Hovland, Lumsdaine, and Sheffield (1949) report an experiment in which the film *The Battle of Britain* was shown to two matched groups of American soldiers. The film was designed to strengthen confidence in America's ally, Britain. The group tested immediately after the showing of the film remembered better the factual content of the film, but the group tested after nine weeks revealed a greater favorable change in attitude toward Britain's war effort.

Influence of Anticipation. Unanticipated persuasive communications may be more effective in producing a change in attitude than anticipated persuasive communications. A person may be expected to avoid or build up his defenses against a communication containing dissonance-producing information. Allyn and Festinger (1961) had high school students, whose attitudes toward teen-age driving were known, listen to a lecture advocating strict control of young drivers. One group was given an orientation to attend to the speaker's opinions and was informed of the speaker's point of view. A second group was given an orientation of evaluating the speaker's personality and was not told about the speaker's topic nor about his point of view. It was found that students who were forewarned of the nature of the communication changed their attitudes less than the students who were not forewarned.

An earlier study reported by Ewing (1942) points to the influence of the anticipation of subjects to a persuasive communication. Subjects were given a communication to read that was highly unfavorable to Ford Motor Company. For one group of subjects, the persuasive communication was introduced thus: "Numerous people have pointed out that Ford represents 'Big Business' at its worst. However some of the following facts hardly justify this view." This introduction was designed to build up an anticipation of favorable content toward Ford. A second group was given exactly the same communication but introduced thus: "Numerous people have pointed out that Ford represents 'Big Business' at its best. However, some of the following facts hardly justify this view." This introduction was designed to elicit an expectation that the content of the forthcoming communication was unfavorable to Ford. Subjects in both groups indicated their opinion on the issue involved immediately before, immediately after, and two days after the reading of the communication. It was found that the subjects in the group who anticipated favorable comments about Ford, but actually received unfavorable comments, changed their opinion about Ford in an unfavorable direction more than did the group that expected unfavorable comments. Further, these unfavorable opinions persisted to the third measurement.

Kiesler and Kiesler (1964) compared the effects of a warning about the propagandistic communication given *before* the communication to the effects of a warning given *after* the communication. They found the temporal placement of the warning to be crucial. Warning before the communication tended to nullify the effect of the communication; warning after did not.

Immunizing Against Counterarguments. Teaching democratic attitudes is a major goal of our schools. The behavior of some prisoners of war during the Korean conflict seems to indicate that home, school, and army failed to teach democratic beliefs sufficiently well as to make them resistant to counterarguments. How can American ideals be taught so that they are not undermined when exposed to counterarguments? Two methods that have been suggested are the *supportive* method and the *refutational* method. In the supportive method, reasons for maintaining the ideals are taught. In the refutational method, counterarguments attacking the ideals are presented and the student is guided in answering the counterarguments. The relative immunizing value of these two methods has been investigated in a series of experiments conducted by McGuire (1961), McGuire and Papageorgis (1961), and Papageorgis and McGuire (1961).

Four health beliefs were selected as the issues in one study (McGuire and Papageorgis, 1961). These beliefs were: "Everyone should get a chest X-ray each year in order to detect any possible tuberculosis symptoms at an early stage." "The effects of penicillin have been, almost without exception, of great benefit to mankind." "Most forms of mental illness are not contagious." "Everyone should brush his teeth after each meal if at all possible." At the beginning of the experiment, 130 college students indicated on a 15-point scale the degree to which they subscribed to each belief. The average of 13.26 points revealed a high initial commitment of the students to the four beliefs.

The experiment included two sessions. In the first, or "immunizing," session, each student was given defensive treatment on two health beliefs. During the first 20 minutes, students were required to write an essay defending one of the health beliefs. In the second part of the immunizing session, the students were given a 1,000-word essay to read and then answered multiple-choice test items on the content of the essay. The conditions under which the students performed both the writing and reading assignments were also varied. In half of the treatments, students were presented with arguments supporting the health belief. In the other half of the treatment, students were exposed to possible counterarguments against the beliefs along with refutations of these counterarguments. As a final part of the immunizing session, students again indicated how strongly they subscribed to the four health beliefs. The following summarizes four of the immunizing conditions included in the experiment along with the average means of the health beliefs obtained after the immunizing treatment.

	Mean Belief Score
Immunizing Condition	
Writing: An essay to defend a health belief with the aid of:	
1. *Supportive material* made up of one-sentence synopses of each of four supporting arguments (number of students = 64)	14.28
or	
2. *Refutational material* made up of four two-sentence synopses each mentioning a counter-argument and an argument to refute it (number of students = 66)	13.58
Reading: A 1,000-word essay and answering questions covering the content of the essay. The essay consisted of:	
3. *Supportive material* made up of four supporting arguments for the belief (number of students = 64)	14.39
or	
4. *Refutational material* made up of four counter-arguments against the belief and a refutation of each counterargument (number of students = 66)	14.24

It is clear, from the above, that the immunizing material did further strengthen the beliefs of the students, even though the beliefs were initially at a high level (13.26). Both types of defense—the supportive and the refutational—had a significant strengthening effect on the beliefs for both the writing and the reading assignment. The supportive defense was slightly more effective although the difference was not significant.

The second experimental session took place 48 hours later and was designed to determine how effective each type of immunizing condition was in maintaining the beliefs in the face of strong counterarguments. Three 1,000-word essays were given the students to read. Each contained strong counterarguments against one health belief. Two of the health beliefs had previously been defended by the students in their immunizing session. The third belief had not been immunized. After reading each of the three passages, students were required to answer a series of multiple-choice test questions on the material. Finally, the belief scale was readministered.

The inclusion of one essay on a belief that was not included in the first immunizing session permitted an assessment of the vulnerability of a belief that is not immunized to strong counterarguments. Despite the fact that the four health beliefs are so generally accepted in our culture and despite the high initial level of the beliefs among the students, the non-immunized belief proved highly vulnerable to the strong counterarguments. The mean score was reduced from its initial level to 6.64 points. This point on a scale represents the lower end of the "uncertain" level. Table 13–2 shows the mean of belief scores for the four immunization conditions and the non-immunizing conditions.

TABLE 13–2
Beliefs After Both Immunization and Exposure to the Strong Counterarguments
(15 = absolute agreement; 1 = absolute disagreement)

Prior Immunization Condition	Number of Students	Weighted Mean
Writing-supportive	64	7.24
Writing-refutational	66	9.33
Reading-supportive	64	7.55
Reading-refutational	66	11.33
No immunization (strong counterarguments only)	130	6.64
Neither immunization nor counterarguments	130	12.62

Whereas supportive immunization was slightly superior to refutational in strengthening a belief, the refutational condition is clearly superior to the supportive in immunizing students against strong counterarguments ($p < .001$). Also, the reading assignment proved slightly more effective than the writing assignment although the difference has only borderline significance.

McGuire and Papageorgis point out a number of cautions in interpreting their research. The counterarguments occurred only 48 hours after the immunizing sessions. We do not know how long the immunizations would prove effective against strong counterarguments. On the other hand, possibly, repeated immunization sessions might prove effective against strong counterarguments over a long period of time. The subjects of the experiments were college students. We do not know whether the refutational technique would prove effective for subjects of lesser intellectual maturity. The subject matter of the belief may be a limiting factor, although we have research evidence on other beliefs where presenting both sides of an argument was more effective in changing opinions than one-sided arguments (Hovland *et al.*, 1949; Lumsdaine and Janis, 1953).

Learning Exercises

24. Bill Holmes, a candidate for president of the student body, hears an address by his opponent. His opponent outlines his own qualifications for the important school office. How might Bill reduce the dissonance produced by his opponent's address?

25. In Shakespeare's *Julius Caesar*, Mark Antony, in his speech to the Romans after the murder of Caesar, refers to Brutus as "an honorable man." At the beginning of Mark Antony's speech, the Roman populace was favorably disposed to Brutus. By the end of the speech, the Romans were bitterly opposed to Brutus. In what study dealing with the antici-pation of information do we find a technique of persuasion that is com-parable to Mark Antony's?

26. In an extensive poll taken of the opinions held by high school students, it was found that many students held beliefs more appropriate to a totalitarian state than to a democracy (Remmers and Radler, 1957). For example: 41 per cent disagreed with the idea of freedom of the press; 13 per cent questioned the idea of freedom of speech; 26 per cent be-lieved that police should be allowed to search a person or his home with-out a warrant. The Bill of Rights is apparently poorly taught in our schools. What procedures for teaching the Bill of Rights are suggested by the McGuire and Papageorgis study?

SUMMARY

Attitudes have affective, cognitive, and behavioral components. The young lady who states "I *enjoy* classical music" provides evidence about the affective component of her attitude toward classical music. Her *beliefs* about classical music constitute the cognitive component of her attitude. Her *action tendencies,* such as seeking out experiences related to classical music, constitute the behavioral component of her attitude.

Attitudes frequently become organized into larger structures or value systems. The young lady who enjoys classical music may also enjoy many other forms of artistic expression. Positive attitudes toward various expressions of art characterize the individual who has a high *esthetic value.* Economic, social, political, or religious values may be relatively more important in the life of another individual.

The structural organization of attitudes is influenced by the personality structure of the individual because attitudes function to satisfy needs. For example, the person who has experienced rejection and domination in childhood may satisfy feelings of hostility and relieve feelings of insecurity by identifying with a strong authoritarian figure who is hostile to a defenseless minority group. Because the person is insecure, he may conform rigidly to middle-class values. Because he is hostile, he may attack—if it is safe to do so—others who do not so conform.

Attitudes tend to become consistent with the instrumental and ego-defensive needs of an individual. They also tend to attain some internal consistency. A person strives to maintain harmony between his feelings, thoughts, and actions. To guard against the unpleasant truth, the individual may avoid dissonance-producing experiences, or he may distort information that would otherwise produce dissonance.

The process through which attitudes are learned and are modified may be described as: (1) an *identification* process in which attitudinal changes are a function of the relationships of an individual to other important individuals; (2) a *conditioning* process in which attitudinal changes are a function of certain characteristics of the experiences of an individual; and (3) as a function of the *information* received by an individual and the interaction of this information with his existing feelings, beliefs, and actions.

Identification is a process through which the behavior and feelings of one person are influenced by another person who serves as a model. Identification occurs when a person (a) imitates the behavior of a model, (b) is motivated *not* to do certain acts that are regarded as wrong by the model, (c) adopts the behavior of a threatening model, and (d) experiences the same emotions as his model. The parents of the child serve as his first model. As the child matures, he usually chooses models of like sex with whom he has warm emotional relationships and who exemplify behavior that can satisfy the needs of the child and win approval from others. Fictitious and real characters encountered by the child in his reading and in the movies may become models for the child if he is capable of imitating their behavior and if it is need satisfying to so do.

We tend to form favorable attitudes toward objects that happen to be present during a pleasant experience. Contact between unfriendly groups can result in improving the attitudes between the groups when the contact takes place within some need-satisfying experience. Prejudice can increase, however, when the experience is unpleasant. Attitudes may be modified dramatically during a highly emotional experience.

Attitudes are formed as a result of the consequences of behavior. For example, a boy forms a favorable attitude toward sports when he successfully competes in sports. Opinions expressed may be reinforced by others and thus strengthened. In this way, a particular set of attitudes tends to become acceptable within a group and tends to resist change. To move away to a new group can result in a modification of the attitudes if a different set of attitudes prevails within the new group. There is some possibility of modifying attitudes through gaining control of the behavior. Dissonance occurs when a person's behavior is not consonant with his feelings and beliefs. One way of reducing the dissonance is through modifying the feelings and beliefs. This occurs most readily when the anticipated rewards and punishments are just sufficient to produce the dissonant behavior.

Persuasive communications are commonly used as a method for changing attitudes. This method is frequently ineffective but can work under certain conditions. The opportunity to discuss the ideas contained in a communication seems to help bring about a change in attitudes. Unanticipated information has been found to be more effective in shifting attitudes when the information is at variance with existing attitudes. The problem of how to strengthen desirable attitudes to the extent that they are immunized against counterarguments is of major importance in today's school. There is some evidence that the procedure of presenting students with counterarguments against our cherished beliefs may result in immunization when the students later are helped to find answers to the counterarguments.

Answer Cues

1. (a) Affect. (b) Behavior. (c) Cognition (perceptual response).

2. Theoretical (rather than aesthetic).

3. Possibly, he would "agree." A person's response on one item means little. If a person's responses on other items indicated that he placed more faith on the strong leader than he did on sound legislation and the democratic processes, then one aspect of the authoritarian personality would be revealed.

4. (a). Note the coexistence of contradictions in (c).

5. (a) Affective association. (b) Ego-defensive. (c) Action oriented. (d) Intellectualized. (e) Balanced.

6. For the person who accepts the conclusions reached by the members of one debate team, the arguments of the other team can create dissonance.

7. No. The inconsistency must be perceived for the person to experience dissonance.

8. Wishful thinking.

9. When a person perceives his behavior or his wishes as contrary to his moral beliefs.

10. Many sources. Ethical principles are customarily learned in home,

church, and school. The adolescent may find among his age-mates models whose behavior is both consistent with ethical principles and acceptable to his peers.

11. (a) Prohibition learning. (b) Vicarious affective experiences. (c) Identification with the aggressor. (d) Imitative learning.

12. (a) Emotional identification. (b) Behavioral identification.

13. Some students may not be capable of modeling behavior after Mr. Jones.

14. By providing a learning experience in which students interact with the novel (e.g., a class discussion).

15. By utilizing some from of group activity in the study of Shakespeare. For example, in producing a Shakespearian play, the enjoyment of the group activity becomes associated with the play produced.

16. It is commonly assumed that they can. Many people can be found to testify that an intense emotional experience has influenced them for the better. There is some research evidence that dramatic films can change attitudes. The Toch and Cantril study illustrates how an emotional communication may stimulate students to examine their values. However, at present, psychologists and educators do not know under what conditions an emotional experience promotes a desirable attitudinal change.

17. Members of the group positively reinforce expressions of certain attitudes. Consequently, the expression of these attitudes increase among group members.

18. In the college environment, the student may be reinforced for expressing different attitudes than in his hometown. When he returns home, expressions of these attitudes may not be reinforced by his old friends.

19. The affective and cognitive components of an attitude tend to become consonant with the behavioral component. If the student dislikes reading poetry, then the reading of poetry is dissonant with his attitude. *One* way of reducing the dissonance is to modify the cognitive and affective components of the attitude (i.e., change beliefs about poetry and begin to like poetry).

20. He could dismiss the film as propaganda, question the truthfulness of the film, or forget the content of the film and thus maintain his unfavorable attitude toward the United Nations. Or he could revise his beliefs about the United Nations so that they are consonant with the content of the film.

21. (a) Maximum dissonance occurs when the anticipated reward or punishment is just enough to produce the desired behavior.

22. Some of the conditions that would make it easier are: (a) the source of the new evidence is respected; (b) the new opinion is consistent with his needs, and (c) the new opinion is acceptable to important reference groups.

23. To perceive himself as logical and to be regarded by others as logical are important goals of the student. The student who discovers the logical implications of evidence is therefore meeting an important need. To have others in the classroom recognize that his conclusions are logical also meets an important need. Hence, the expression of the more positive logically derived attitude is likely to be reinforced in the classroom.

24. By (1) misperceiving the information, (2) attempting to invalidate the information, or (3) forgetting the dissonance-producing information.

25. The Ewing study.

26. An examination by the students of the implications of the Bill of Rights. An exploration of the counterarguments against the Bill of Rights in which the students are guided in refuting the counterarguments. It would be important that the teacher be permissive in allowing the student to freely express his present opinions and have faith that the weight of historical and other evidence would create the dissonance necessary for a change of opinion.

14

EVALUATION OF LEARNING

Ideally, the total evaluation program of a school should involve an effort to assess the attainment by students of all the school's educational objectives. Hence, the program should include procedures for evaluating changes in children's attitudes, interests, appreciations, social and emotional adjustment, and psychomotor skills—as well as the more academic learning. However, the steps involved in constructing evaluative instruments are essentially the same for all types of educational objectives. These steps are: (1) defining the behavior to be measured, (2) selecting appropriate test situations, (3) planning the test, (4) constructing the test, (5) administering the test, (6) scoring the test, and (7) interpreting and reporting the test results. In this chapter, attention will be focused primarily on the application of these steps for educational objectives in the cognitive domain. First, we will examine the essential characteristics of any good test.

CHARACTERISTICS OF A GOOD TEST

Many kinds of tests are used in the schools today. For the teacher, the question of what constitutes a good test is pertinent to the tasks of selecting standardized tests, constructing achievement tests, and utilizing a wide variety of other evaluative devices. In general, the basic characteristics that need to be considered in either selecting or constructing a test or other evaluative device are: (1) validity, (2) reliability, (3) objectivity, and (4) practicality.

Validity

A test is *valid* if it measures what it sets out to measure. A geometry achievement test is valid if it may be used to measure the extent to which students have learned geometry. A reading test is valid to the extent that it measures certain reading competencies that the test was constructed to measure.

Various procedures are used in determining test validity, and different writers have described these procedures with various names. One classification that is gaining wide acceptance designates four types of validity. These are *content* validity, *predictive* validity, *concurrent* validity, and *construct* validity.

Content Validity. The procedure for determining content validity involves a systematic comparison of the test content to the specifications of the behaviors that the test is designed to measure. Content validity is usually of greatest importance in assessing achievement tests. A history teacher in constructing a test for his class strives to attain content validity by including a representative sample of questions from the important facts, concepts, and other important learnings of his course. The constructor of a standardized history test may examine a number of leading textbooks in the field and formulate questions that are covered by the various texts. Or the test constructor may examine statements of committees of history or social science teachers to ascertain what is considered to be the important educational objectives, and then construct a test designed to measure student attainment of those objectives.

A test that has content validity for one teacher may be deficient in content validity for a second teacher. For the science teacher who emphasizes in his classes the acquisition of scientific facts, a test covering facts in science may be valid. The same test may lack content validity for the teacher who tries to develop the ability of students to apply scientific principles in problem-solving situations. Content validity refers not only to a matching of the topics covered in a teacher's course and a text, but it also includes a matching of the type of behavior implied in the objective to the type of behavior measured by the test items.

Predictive Validity. Predictive validity refers to the effectiveness of a test in predicting some future performance. A college may administer an intelligence test to entering freshmen and later determine the extent to which the intelligence test scores predict later academic achievement. The predictive validity of a reading readiness test may be determined by administering the test to first-grade pupils and later determining whether the pupils who scored high on the test tended to advance more satisfactorily in learning to read than those pupils who scored low.

The most frequently used method for reporting the predictive validity of a test is through a correlation coefficient. The higher the correlation between the predicting test and a criterion, the more accurately the test predicts. However, no aptitude test predicts precisely. No aptitude test, for example, can predict whether a boy entering an engineering curriculum will land up fifth, fifteenth, or twenty-fifth in his class. Fortunately, in most situations, precise predictions are not necessary. Of necessity, we must settle for a test that predicts with some degree of accuracy a boy's chances of success in a particular school or occupation.

Concurrent Validity. Concurrent validity refers to the relation between the scores on a test and some criteria performance obtained at about the same time. Sometimes a test is used to diagnose existing status rather than predict some future performance. In such cases, information on concurrent validity is needed. For example, an adjustment inventory might be devised for the purpose of assessing the emotional adjustment of children. Users of the inventory would properly be interested in evidence on whether the test actually identified emotionally disturbed children. One kind of evidence would be the results of a concurrent validity study in which a group of clinically diagnosed emotionally disturbed children and a group of normal children were administered the inventory. If the clinically diagnosed emotionally disturbed children were identified as such by the adjustment inventory, this would constitute evidence on the concurrent validity of the adjustment inventory.

Construct Validity. Construct validity refers to the validity of inferences made from a test score about some characteristics of the person who took the test. Evidence that a so-called intelligence test really measures the construct "intelligence" would be evidence on the construct validity of the test. If a so-called "intelligence" test predicts some later achievement, we have evidence as to the test's predictive validity even though we have no evidence that the test really measures "intelligence." An "anxiety" test has construct validity if differences in test performances of individuals can be attributed to differences in the set of the behavioral characteristics we define as anxiety.

Content, predictive, and concurrent validity are all included in construct validity when construct validity is defined in terms of the operation required to establish it. To establish the construct validity of a particular intelligence test might involve a comparison of the test items included in the test to some theoretical definition of intelligence (content validity), evidence on how well the test predicts the kinds of achievement that we postulate as intellectual attainment (predictive validity), and the relationship between performance on the particular intelligence test and other tests and behaviors that require intelligence (concurrent validity)—see Table 14–1.

TABLE 14–1

Summary of Types of Validity and Typical Validity Studies

Type of Validity	Characteristic	Typical Validity Studies
I. *Content*	Representative sample of behaviors (important for achievement tests)	Comparing test content and objectives with course content and objectives
II. *Predictive*	Effectiveness in predicting later performance (important for aptitude tests)	Correlational studies between various types of tests and later achievement; studies of tests' ability to forecast later maladjustments
III. *Concurrent*	Agreement with another criterion measured at about the same time	Correlational studies between group versus individual tests, short versus longer tests, test diagnoses versus clinical diagnoses
IV. *Construct*	Inferences concerning a person made on the basis of his test performance	Includes all of the types of studies listed above, with an analysis of the organismic variables that the test measures

Learning Exercise

1. What type of validity is indicated by each of the following statements:
   (a) Scores on Intelligence Test A correlate +.71 with the Stanford Binet Intelligence Test.
   (b) The objectives measured by Science Achievement Test B are compared to the objectives for the science courses in Blair High School.
   (c) Scores on the C Mechanical Aptitude Test given at the beginning of the school year are correlated with physics grades obtained by students at the end of the school year.
   (d) Anxiety Test D is studied in a number of ways. Test items are examined in the light of a particular theory of anxiety. The scores of neurotics on the anxiety test are compared with the scores of normals. Scores on the test of two equated groups are compared. The one group is given the tranquilizing drug before taking the test; the other group is not given the drug.

Reliability

A test is reliable if it measures *accurately* or *consistently*. All measurements have some margin of error. In physical measurements, the error may be relatively small. If we were to measure the length of a room with a steel tape, the error in measurement probably would be smaller than if we used a yard stick and much smaller than it would be if we paced out the length. In psychological tests, the error in measurement of any given test is usually very large as compared to physical measurement. Suppose that an intelligence test is administered to each child in a class today and the same test is administered one week hence. The results of the two testings would not be in perfect agreement. Some children would obtain higher scores on the first test than on the second, and some children might obtain identical scores on the two tests. Obviously, the test does not measure perfectly accurately. Otherwise the results of the two testings would be in perfect agreement. To the extent that the results of the two testings differ, the test lacks reliability.

Coefficient of Stability. In the situation described above, administering the one test on two occasions separated by a short interval, we obtain a measure of *test-retest* reliability. The correlation between the scores made on the one test and the scores on the retest is referred to as a *coefficient of stability*. It is an estimate of the extent to which a testee stays within the same place within his group. If the test were perfectly reliable, the child who obtained the highest score on the first testing would obtain the highest score on the second testing; the child with the second highest score would again obtain the second highest score on the second testing; etc. Actually, what we obtain is an estimate of the extent to which the behavior, as measured by the test, varies over short time intervals.

Coefficient of Equivalence. A second source of unreliability rests within the test itself. The items included in any test constitute a sample drawn from all the items that could be made to measure the behavior in question. Thus, if in a fifth-grade class 700 spelling words have been taught during the school year, a sample of 70 words may be incorporated in a test as a measure of how well the pupils have learned to spell the 700 words. However, chance factors can make a difference in any given pupil's performance. Some children may misspell certain words but not have any trouble with equally difficult words that are misspelled by other pupils. A pupil's spelling score will depend to some extent on what words are selected to be included in the test.

We can obtain an estimate of this second source of unreliability by selecting two samples of test items, and then administering the two samples to a group of students. We then can determine whether the scores of pupils tend to correspond on the two parallel forms of the test. The correlation obtained through such a procedure is known as a *coefficient of equivalence*.

A coefficient of equivalence may be estimated on the basis of only one administration of a test. One way of doing this is to split the test into two halves and obtain a score for each pupil on each half of the test. Sometimes the test is split by obtaining a score for the odd numbered items on the test and another score for the even numbered items. This procedure is known as the *split-half method*. Other methods are available for estimating the equivalence of two tests.

Coefficient of Stability and Equivalence. Both the error in scores due to the variations in performance of individuals from one testing period to another and the error in test sampling may be estimated in one procedure. This procedure involves administering parallel forms of a test on two separate occasions. Correlating the test scores obtained from this procedure yields a *coefficient of stability and equivalence*. The fact that tests are given during two time intervals insures that variations in performance of students from day to day will be treated as error variance. By using parallel forms of the test, lack of equivalence between forms is treated as error variance.

Standard Error of Measurement. The foregoing procedures provide estimates of the over-all reliability of tests. Often, however, we wish to get some idea of the accuracy of a single score on a test. This may be done by computing the *standard error of measurement* of a test. The standard error of measurement is an estimate of the standard deviation of the scores obtained from testing the same individual numerous times. It may be calculated for a test from the standard deviation of the test and its reliability coefficient, using the formula:

$$\sigma_{\text{meas.}} = \sigma_1 \sqrt{1 - r_{11}}$$

where $\sigma_{\text{meas.}}$ is the standard error of measurement

σ_1 is the standard deviation of test scores

r_{11} is the reliability coefficient

Suppose the reliability of a test is .91 and the standard deviation is 10. Then the standard error of measurement is:

$$\sigma_{\text{meas.}} = 10\sqrt{1 - .91} = 10\sqrt{.09} = 3$$

If for this test a student obtains a score of 40, we can say that the chances are about 68 out of 100 that his true score lies between 37 and 43, i.e., between one $\sigma_{meas.}$ above and below his obtained score. Or going two $\sigma_{meas.}$'s above and below his obtained score, we can say that the probability is about 95 out of 100 that his true score lies between 34 and 46.

Learning Exercise

2. The reliability of Test A is .84. Its standard deviation is 5. Bob Little obtained 60 on this test.
   (a) What is the standard error of measurement for Test A?
   (b) The chances are about 68 out of 100 that Bob's true score lies between _____ and _____.
   (c) The chances are about 95 out of 100 that Bob's true score lies between _____ and _____.

Factors Affecting Estimates of Reliability. Certain factors need to be taken into consideration in comparing the reliabilities of two tests.

First, reliability is affected by the *range of individual differences* of the group upon which the reliability is computed. A high reliability for a test will be obtained when the reliability is computed using the scores of pupils who differ widely with respect to what is being measured. A measuring instrument does not need to be refined in order to discriminate gross differences. Two raters, merely by inspection, would come to perfect agreement in ranking the lengths of the following four lines:

```
          A _____

                      B _____

              C _____

                 D _____
```

If two raters each ranked the above lines as to length, from longest to shortest, as BDCA, then the interrater reliability of this inspection method of measuring would be $r = 1.00$. However, if the lengths of the four lines were almost equal, the chances are that two raters would disagree in their rankings, and hence a lower interrater reliability would be obtained. In a comparable manner, when the reliability of a reading test is computed from scores of pupils in grades 4–8, the obtained reliability for the test is likely to be higher than it would be if the reliability was computed from scores of pupils in a single grade. Hence, a reliability coefficient is affected by the degree of homogeneity of the group upon which it is based.

Second, for a speed test, the split-half method of computing reliability is inappropriate because the correlations would be spuriously high due to the fact that many students would not finish the test. Thus, for a 100-item test that depends *entirely* on speed, if individual A obtains a score of 62, he will have 31 odd numbered items correct and 31 even numbered items correct. Individual B with a score of 40 will have 20 odd and 20 even numbered items correct. Consequently, except for the occasional careless errors, the correlation between odd and even scores would be perfect. It is therefore important for the teacher in examining the reliabilities reported in manuals of standardized tests to discount the reported reliabilities of speeded tests when such reliabilities have been computed by some measure of internal consistency such as the split-half method.

Third, the reliability of a test depends upon the length of the test. A one-word vocabulary test would not be a reliable measure. Nor would a 12-item test. The student may guess 3 or 4 items correctly while another guesses 3 or 4 incorrectly. A test consisting of 50 or more items reduces the likelihood that luck in guessing will account for differences in scores of students. Usually, the reliability of a test can be improved by increasing its length. However, a test becomes too long when student's performance deteriorates because of fatigue. When this occurs, reliability will be reduced.

Fourth, the reliability of a test is affected by the average ability level of the students taking the test. Reliability is reduced by guessing. A test that yields satisfactory reliability for children of average intelligence at a particular age level may be much less reliable for younger and less-able groups of children because of an increase in guessing.

Objectivity

An achievement test has objectivity if two competent judges, independently scoring test papers, arrive at comparable scores for each paper graded. Obviously, the question of objectivity does not arise with objective tests. After a scoring key for the objective test has been made (and not before), all subjectivity in the grade assigned to a student has been eliminated. Subjective judgment can enter into the grades assigned on essay tests. Later we will see that there are techniques for reducing the subjectivity in grading essays. We can obtain an estimate of the objectivity of a test if we have two graders mark the same papers and then run a correlation between the two sets of scores. Such a correlation may be thought of as an *intergrader* reliability coefficient.

Practicality

Among the practical considerations to be taken into account in selecting tests for a school are the cost of a test per copy, the classroom time taken up in the administration of the test, the ease of scoring the test, and whether separate answer sheets are provided so as to permit the reuse of test booklets. However, validity and reliability are the two basic characteristics of a good standardized test. It is false economy to save a little money and time at the expense of selecting tests of inferior validity and reliability.

TEACHER-MADE ACHIEVEMENT TESTS

The process of constructing, administering, and scoring a test, and the interpretation of test results may be set forth as a logical sequence of steps. Certainly, the test constructor needs at the outset a set of educational objectives to guide him in constructing test items. And the more clearly these objectives are formulated, the better. Yet at all stages of the testing process, the test constructor finds a need to return to his initial task of defining objectives so that the objectives may be more clearly described. The very task of constructing a test item forces the test constructor to more clearly delineate an objective. And, after the test has been tried out on a group of students, the test constructor invariably discovers items that need revision. Hence, while we will describe the testing process as a logical sequence of steps, it should be remembered that the test constructor is likely to "shuttle back and forth" between the various steps involved in the process of constructing and using his test.

Defining Educational Objectives

The educational objectives, developed by the teacher (or by the teacher and pupils) in the process of planning learning activities, can serve the teacher as an initial guide in developing evaluative instruments.

The objectives of a course should be stated in terms of the changes in student behavior sought. The content aspect of the objectives also should be indicated. In order to keep clearly in mind the broad scope of the educational objectives of a course, it is useful to make a two-dimensional chart with the content aspects of the course listed along one dimension and the behavioral aspects listed along the other dimension. The illustration of this technique provided by Tyler (1947) is reproduced in Table 14–2. Note that seven types of behavior are included in the objectives of this biological science course. The course is clearly aimed at developing more than just the acquisition of information in the ten content areas listed. The chart indicates 70 possible educational objectives. The x's indicate the actual objectives identified by the instructor for the course.

The information contained in Table 14–2 is sufficient to suggest the kinds of evaluative devices needed for the biological science course. The objectives indicated in the first four columns could be most economically evaluated by means of a paper-and-pencil achievement test. Possibly, the teacher might wish to grade written assignments to evaluate column 5—ability to study and report results of study. Separate evaluative techniques would be required to determine whether the students developed broad and mature interests and the desired social attitudes during the course of instruction.

The information contained in Table 14–2 is not sufficiently detailed to suggest specific test questions. For example, the objectives indicated in column 4—ability to apply principles—do not indicate what principles are to be applied, nor the variety of ways in which they can be applied.

The test constructor, faced with the problem of developing test items measuring the ability of students to apply principles, would need to identify first, the principles to be applied, and second, the kinds of problems in which the students have learned to apply the principles. The objectives may be sufficiently specific for the teacher who has just completed teaching the course and who has in mind the principles to be applied and the range of situations to which they are to be applied. Often, however, it is useful for the teacher to analyze a broad educational objective into more clearly defined situations. For example, for the objective—"interest in principles and facts of food preparation"—the test constructor might list:

1. The student tries to gain more knowledge about the principles and facts of food preparation.
   a) She reads books and articles.
   b) She asks questions about food preparation both at home and at school.
   c) She attends clubs and views commercial programs from which she can gain knowledge about food preparation.
2. The student applies knowledge about the principles and facts of food preparation.

TABLE 14–2

Illustration of the Use of a Two-Dimensional Chart in Stating Objectives for High School Biological Science

Content Aspect	Behavioral Aspect						
	(1) Understanding of Important Facts and Principles	(2) Familiarity with Dependable Sources of Information	(3) Ability To Interpret Data	(4) Ability To Apply Principles	(5) Ability To Study and Report Results of Study	(6) Broad and Mature Interests	(7) Social Attitudes
A. Functions of human organisms							
1. Nutrition	x	x	x	x		x	x
2. Digestion	x		x	x		x	
3. Circulation	x		x	x		x	
4. Respiration	x		x	x		x	
5. Reproduction	x		x	x		x	
B. Use of plant and animal resources							
1. Energy relationships	x	x	x	x	x	x	x
2. Environmental factors conditioning plant and animal growth	x	x	x	x	x	x	x
3. Heredity and genetics	x	x				x	x
4. Land utilization	x	x	x	x		x	x
C. Evolution and development	x		x			x	x

SOURCE: R. W. Tylor, *Syllabus for Education 360. Basic Principles of Curriculum and Instruction* (mimeographed ed.; Chicago: University of Chicago Press, 1947), p. 28.

a) She prepares foods in new ways in the home.
b) She seeks new recipes.
c) She carries on food projects in home economics, agriculture, or other clubs.

No set rule can be given as to how detailed educational objectives should be stated. In general, objectives should be stated in sufficient detail to suggest the range of situations in which the behavior defined may take place.

Learning Exercise

3. Criticize the following as statements of educational objectives:
   (a) A teacher states that her objective for her next class period is "to give a lecture to her class on Hamlet."
   (b) A social science teacher states that his major objective is "to develop the ability of students to think."
   (c) An English teacher states that his major objective is "to develop the students' appreciation of literature."

Selecting Appropriate Test Situations

A second step in the test construction process is that of selecting test situations in which the student may display the competency described in the educational objective. An example provided by Furst (1958) will serve to illustrate.

Objective: the ability to detect political propaganda
Test Situations:

1. The students hear and see on television a speaker known to be biased. Students are instructed to analyze the speech for the presence or absence of propaganda and to describe the kind of devices used to achieve the propaganda effect.
2. Same as (1) except the students hear only a sound recording of the speech. Under these conditions, the students lack visual cues.
3. Same as (1) except the students read a reprint of the speech. Thus, they lack auditory cues.

The number of kinds of situations relevant to the detection of political propaganda can be greatly increased by adding variations in the type of stimulus material presented and different ways of asking questions about the stimulus materials.

It is *not* often economical to restrict the evidence on the attainment of an educational objective to the direct observation of behavior in a naturalistic situation. The strategy we usually employ is to control the situation so that we can stimulate the desired behavior at will. For example, to obtain evidence on spelling competency we:

Select a list of words for a spelling test, and then administer the test in one testing session	rather than	Keep a running count of all the errors students make in spelling on all their written work throughout the semester

In the interest of economy, the test situations we choose may vary somewhat from the behavior described in the objective. Proficiency in mathematics may be measured by a multiple-choice test even though the objective implies that students be able to work mathematical problems presented in free-response form. Apparently, a multiple-choice test in mathematics yields about the same results as the same test in a free-response form (College Entrance Examination Board, 1946; Loree, 1948). For educational objectives on certain other subjects, a multiple-choice test does not yield the same results as a test given in a free-response form.

A study reported by Tyler (1932) illustrates the point that performance on a multiple-choice test cannot always be interpreted as evidence of the student's ability on a free-response test. The educational objective of concern in Tyler's study was the "ability to formulate for oneself a reasonable generalization from specific experimental data (in botany and zoology)." In the original free-response test, students were presented with sets of experimental data that were new to them. Beneath each set, the students were asked to write generalizations that they thought could be most reasonably made from the data given. The scores obtained by students on this test were then correlated with scores on a test in which the same data were repeated, but this time with five suggested generalizations for each set. Students were asked to check the best generalization of each five. The coefficient of correlation between the two sets of scores was found to be only .38. Tyler then proceeded to construct a new test with the same data repeated, but this time the five generalizations were drawn from the generalizations actually proposed by students on the original free-response test. Students were asked to check the *best* and the *poorest* generalization. This new test correlated quite highly (.85) with the original free-response test.

Learning Exercise

4. Describe a test situation that might be appropriate to evaluate the student attainment of the educational objective, "the ability to participate effectively in a planned group discussion on a social science issue."

Planning the Test

Tests can be tailored to meet the specific purposes of the teacher of a course. Often, the purpose of a test is to measure the over-all achievement of students as a basis for assigning grades. For this purpose, it becomes important that the test adequately samples the objectives of the course. A chart similar to the one found in Table 14–2 is useful in planning a test designed to meet specific purposes. In place of the x's, the test constructor can decide the approximate percentage of test items he will need for each objective. Such a table would constitute a table of specifications for the test constructor. Table 14–3 presents one possible table of specifications for a test on a course in biological science. The percentage of items are entered.

TABLE 14–3

Table of Specifications for a Test in Biological Science

| | Behavior | | | | |
| | (1) Understanding Facts and Principles | (2) Familiarity with Sources of Information | (3) Interpretation of Data | (4) Application of Principles | Per Cent of Items |
Content					
A. Function of human organisms	20	2	10		32
B. Use of plant and animal resources	10	3	10	10	33
C. Evolution and development	20	5		10	35
Per Cent of Items	50	10	20	20	100

If in addition to assigning over-all grades, the teacher wished to identify specific strengths and weaknesses of students, then the test constructor would need to plan for part scores. A sufficient number of items need to be subsumed by a part score so as to insure its reliability. Consequently, there is a limitation in the number of reliable part scores that can be obtained from a single test. For the test in biological science detailed above, the teacher might wish to find out what students do fairly well on the factual-type items (columns 1 and 2) but do relatively poorly on the items calling for interpretation or application (columns 3 and 4). The teacher might also wish to communicate to his students their relative strengths in the three content areas. In short, the part scores that the teacher wishes to generate depends upon the specific purposes that the teacher expects the test to serve. These purposes need to be identified in the planning stage of test construction so that the test can be tailored to yield the required information.

Learning Exercise

5. What difference in the plans for a test are called for when a teacher wants to tell students their strengths and weaknesses rather than just determine fair grades?

Constructing Test Items

Advantages and Limitation of Essay and Objective Tests. Teacher-made tests may be divided into two broad categories: essay and objective tests. Both types of tests have their advantages and limitations. The skillful test constructor attempts to use each type of test in those situations where its advantages outweigh its disadvantages.

On logical grounds, the essay test is considered superior to the objective test for some types of educational objectives. For example, the essay would appear to be the more valid test for appraising writing abilities such as the ability to organize materials and the ability to treat a topic logically, clearly, and succinctly, yet comprehensively. Sims (1948, p. 17) has contended that the freedom permitted to the student by the essay test to attack a problem in his own way results in the student revealing "information regarding the structure, dynamics and functioning of [his] mental life as it has been modified by a particular set of learning experiences."

Experimental studies (e.g., Meyer, 1935; Terry, 1933) suggest that students study differently for essay tests than for objective tests. In preparing for an essay test, the student is more likely to focus attention on the important concepts of a course, to organize the materials of the course into some meaningful outline, and to search for applications and illustrative materials. In preparing for the kind of objective test constructed by most classroom teachers, the student is more apt to spend his time memorizing isolated facts.

The major limitation of the essay-type examination stems from certain difficulties encountered in grading. In one early study (Starch and Elliott, 1913), copies of the same geometry paper were marked by 116 high school mathematics teachers. The grades assigned to this paper ranged from 28 to 92. Falls (1928) had 100 English teachers mark a student's composition by assigning a percentage grade and indicating the school grade in which they would expect that quality of writing to be done. The percentages assigned ranged from 60 to 98, and the grade level ranged from the fifth grade to the junior year in college. Variations in the grade assigned an essay by two independent graders may occur even when some effort is made to insure comparability of grading standards. Stalnaker (1937) reports an experience of the College Entrance Examination Board in which English teachers from secondary schools and colleges graded essays written by 6,834 secondary school seniors. The students were required to choose one topic from seven presented and write a paper of some 350 words on the topic selected. Prior to marking the papers, the readers discussed how the essays should be graded, and had some practice sessions in applying the scale of values they had developed. Each paper was read twice independently on an eight-point scale. The second reader agreed with the grade assigned by the first reader in only 41 per cent of the cases.

Not only is variation in grading standards found between graders, but a number of studies have shown that the same grader may assign markedly different grades when he grades the same paper on two separate occasions. For example, Hulten (1925) had 28 experienced high school English teachers grade a composition theme supposedly written by an eighth-grade pupil, and then grade the same theme after an interval of two months. He found that 15 teachers who gave passing marks on the first marking failed the paper in the second marking, and 11 teachers who failed the paper the first time assigned a passing grade on the second time. These early studies on scorer unreliability served to stimulate the use of objective-type tests in the school. As we will see later, they also stimulated educators to seek ways of improving the essay test.

One of the major advantages of objective-type tests is that they permit extensive sampling of course content. The examiner can include in one test numerous items on the facts, information, and concepts included in a course. Hence, objective-type items are particularly well suited to testing educational objectives in the knowledge category.

Thinking skills and abilities can be tested with objective tests, although to do so requires considerable ingenuity on the part of the test constructor. Constructing objective test items designed to measure the student's ability to apply principles or to interpret data or to analyze a communication in a subject-material area is a frustrating but nevertheless intellectually rewarding task. Paul Diederich, who is highly skilled in constructing tests in the field of the humanities, reports that when he is asked whether he really understands a very difficult poem, like one of Eliot's *Four Quartets,* he has to answer, "I don't know. I haven't got around to making up a test on it." This is the typical experience of a highly skilled test constructor whenever he constructs penetrating test items on material that is worthy of testing. The amount of time, energy, and skill required to construct objective-type test items that measure "the higher mental processes" constitutes a limitation of objective-type tests. It should be added, however, that to adequately measure inductive and deductive thinking by means of an essay test is by no means an easy task, particularly when the test constructor faces the problem of developing a rational scoring key for his test.

Objective-type tests are obviously superior to essay tests with respect to objectivity of scoring. Subjectivity may enter into the construction of objective-type tests in the choice of test items and in keying the test; but once the key to the test has been agreed upon, two graders will assign identical scores to a test paper. As we have previously noted, the grades assigned to an essay may vary widely between graders.

Improving the Essay Test. There are two reasons for the lack of grader reliability for the essay test. The first reason rests in the actual preparation of the questions included in the essay test; the second reason rests in the marking practices.

It would seem obvious that a common task is desirable in order to compare the performances of several individuals. Yet an assignment such as "Write an essay on the body's functioning" lends itself to multiple interpretations for both the graders and the students. The grade received by a student on this assignment depends too much on the extent to which he has interpreted the assignment in the same way as the grader does. One major way in which an essay-type question can be improved is by making clear to the student the nature and scope of the answer desired. Usually, this will involve some delimitation of a broad topic. For a college course in biological science, the above topic might be reformulated as follows:

Prepare a sentence outline in which you present an organized view of the effects of muscle contraction and relaxation on the body's functioning. Try to reveal as much knowledge of the body's activities and their interrelations as you can. This outline should probably be two or more pages in length. Spend part of your time preparing a preliminary topical outline. While doing this preliminary work, check over all the aspects of the body's activity that we have studied to remind yourself of the part muscle activity plays in each aspect. Do not fail to include both direct and indirect effects on a function when both are prominent. Omit consideration of how muscles contract and how they are controlled. With your topical outline as a guide, write your sentence outline. (The main headings need not be complete sentences.) Your outline will be rated by the following criteria:

1. Number of significant points included
2. Insight into work of body revealed
3. Effectiveness of outline and statements[1]

More adequate sampling of course material is possible through including a large number of questions requiring brief answers than from a small number of questions requiring extended answers. Essay questions requiring extensive treatment are more appropriate when we wish to determine how well the student is able to select and organize significant material in dealing with some broad question.

In preparing essay questions, it is advisable for the examiner to prepare answers to each question. By so doing, the examiner often sees how he can revise and clarify his questions. Also, the examiner is taking a first step toward insuring objectivity in grading.

The extent to which it is possible to obtain adequate intergrader reliability in scoring essay examinations depends in large part on the kind of questions asked. Composition themes of about 400 words or more with scoring categories such as "material," "organization," and "style" are very difficult to grade objectively, particularly when a large number of themes are to be graded. Noyes, Sale, and Stalnaker (1945) report a reader reliability of only .58 in the grading of a well-constructed essay question even when detailed instructions for scoring and training of a selected group of readers were provided. On the other hand, Ross and Stanley (1954) review research studies in which a correlation coefficient as high as .98 has been obtained when careful grading procedures were followed. Sims (1931) has suggested the use of a technique in which the papers of students are sorted into five groups: very superior, superior, average, inferior, and very inferior—

[1] *Sample Questions. Illustrating the types of exercises used in Comprehensive Examinations* (Chicago: The University of Chicago, 1945), p. 5.

on the basis of a rapid, preliminary reading of the total examination. Then the papers are reread more carefully and shifted when the reader feels they have been misplaced. Sims suggests that about 10 per cent would be rated A, 20 per cent B, 40 per cent C, 20 per cent D, and 10 per cent F. Other suggestions that have been presented by various test specialists are:

1. Developing a scoring key that includes the number of marks to be assigned for each point or scoring category
2. Applying the tentative key to an assortment of answers as a preliminary check on its adequacy
3. Grading one question for all papers so as to reduce the number of points to be kept in mind and to reduce "halo" effect
4. Periodically rechecking papers that were graded earlier so as to insure that standards have not shifted

Learning Exercises

6. Which of the three types of tests—objective, short answer essay, extended answer essay—would be most situable for each of the following objectives?
   (a) The ability to recognize superior organization of furniture in a room of a home
   (b) To recall the major advantages and limitations of various types of tests and to judge which type would be most efficient to achieve a specific purpose
   (c) The ability to organize arguments on a social science issue
7. A teacher decides to test with an extended essay question, rather than use brief essay questions, for an educational objective involving the ability of the student to organize materials. In so doing, the teacher states, "I am willing to sacrifice some reliability in grading in order to achieve better validity." What does the teacher mean by this statement?

The Completion Item. The completion item is most commonly used for measuring recall of information and ideas. For example, a student's understanding of *conditioning* may be tested by having the student fill in the blanks in the following sentence (the correct responses are inserted in italics):

In classical conditioning, when the *conditioned* stimulus is followed by the *unconditioned* stimulus, the conditioned response is said to be *reinforced*.

Completion items are not usually suitable for appraising thinking abilities. However, a completion item is obviously suitable whenever it is possible to formulate a problem that requires reasoning and for which there is a unique answer. For instance, an arithmetic problem can be posed, leaving a blank for the student's answer.

A number of rules have been suggested for constructing completion items, such as:

1. Leave as the blanks to be filled in important words or phrases—not trivial details.
2. Try to word the statements so that there is only one correct response for each blank.
3. Try to formulate the test item so that it measures comprehension rather than rote memory. The practice of lifting statements from a text in constructing any type of objective-test item is likely to encourage rote learning.
4. Do not leave so many blanks in a statement that the student cannot know what specific meaning is intended. For example, the statement

> The _____ is computed by dividing the _____ by the _____

can be answered correctly by any one of many formulas (I.Q. MA, CA; rate, distance, time; etc.). The specific meaning that is intended is not clear.
5. Do not provide irrelevant cues, e.g., making blanks correspond to the length of the fill-in word; using "a" or "an" before a blank.

Learning Exercise

8. Which of the above rules is violated in each of the following completion-type items?
   (a) A psychological test _____.
   (b) In the United States _____ are elected for _____ and _____ for _____.
   (c) The capital of Louisiana is _____ _____, located on the _____ River.

The True-False Item. The true-false item probably is used more generally by teachers than any other type of objective-test item. This is unfortunate. Although the true-false item appears to be the easiest of all types to construct, it is really one of the most difficult to handle well. It is possible to construct true-false items that test well above the knowledge category in the *Taxonomy of Educational Objectives*. But it requires skill in constructing tests to do so.

The true-false item does have some advantages. It can be used for a wide range of subject matter. It is possible with true-false items to cover a wide sampling of subject matter in a relatively short testing time. And, of course, it can be scored objectively. The objection that guessing plays too large a part of a pupil's total score on a true-false test is overcome when a sufficient number of items are included. But the guessing factor usually does limit the usefulness of the true-false test as a diagnostic instrument.

In the usual form of true-false item, a statement is presented, and the student is required to judge whether the statement is true or false. Following are some examples based upon materials presented up to this point in this chapter.

T   F   1. Looking in the mirror to see if one's hat is on properly is a form of evaluation.
T   F   2. Educational objectives are defined in terms of what the teacher does in the classroom.
T   F   3. The test construction process involves a series of decisions on the part of the test constructor.
T   F   4. Research evidence indicates that students prepare differently for an essay examination than for an objective test.

The true-false item is only one way in which the student is called upon to select from two possible responses. Following are additional illustrations:

Directions: In the space provided to the right, mark the number of the correct word in each of the following sentences:

5. (^{1}Isn't ^{2}aren't) the boys in the room?   _____ 5
6. John is better than (^{1}I ^{2}me).   _____ 6

Directions: For each of the following pair of foods, write S if the two foods belong to the SAME food group; write D if the two foods belong to DIFFERENT food groups.

7. carrot   milk   _____ 7
8. tomato   orange   _____ 8

Many additional illustrations could be provided. A multiple-choice test item in which there may be more than one correct response really represents a series of true-false items. For each alternative, the student must decide whether it is right or wrong. The following item is illustrative:

Directions: Each of the following sentences is divided into five parts lettered A, B, C, D, and E. Look at each and decide which of the lettered parts have errors in grammar, punctuation, or spelling. Write the letters corresponding to the parts of the sentence containing errors in the space provided to the right.

9. Ain't you/ going to/ school/ with us/ this morning. _____ 9
   A   B   C   D   E

The true-false item may be modified in a number of ways. One suggestion is that of underlining portions of the statements given; and then, for those statements that the students mark "false," the student is asked to revise the statement so as to make it true. For example:

               Springfield
10. T *F* ~~Chicago~~ is the capital of Illinois.

Probably the true-false test can be improved most efficiently by including a sufficient number of items (50 or more), constructing each item carefully, and focusing the item upon an important objective of the course.

A number of rules have been suggested for the construction of true-false items. These rules may be grouped under three headings:

1. *Safeguards to insure that the item is clearly stated.*
    a) Keep the item reasonably short.
    b) Restrict the item to one single idea.
    c) Avoid statements that are partly true and partly false.
    d) Use language that is at the appropriate level of difficulty for the group to be tested.
    e) Exercise care in the use of vague qualifiers, such as many, much, little, few, small, seldom. Sometimes different, plausible interpretations of these qualifiers lead to different answers.
    f) Generally, avoid negative statements because they are often misread.
    g) Do not lift statements from text books. Often, such statements lose meaning when stated out of context.
    h) Avoid ambiguous statements.
    i) Avoid trick questions; e.g., Columbus discovered America in 1492 B.C.
2. *Safeguards to insure that irrelevant clues do not lead the examinee to the right answer to the item.*
    a) Caution should be exercised in the use of certain words that may serve as clues. Items containing the words "all," "always," "never," and "none" usually turn out to be false. Items containing the words "sometimes," "generally," "frequently," "usually" will usually turn out to be true.
    b) True items and false items should average the same length. There is a tendency for teachers to make true items longer.
    c) About the same number of true items as false items should be included in a test, and the items should be presented in a random order.
3. *Safeguards in constructing items that are focused on important*

aspects of the subject matter. Content validity is the most important criteria in judging any type of objective test. It is much easier to construct items on trivial details than on meaningful concepts. The test constructor in looking at a set of items needs to ask himself whether the items adequately sample the major learning outcomes expected from a course. The items as a whole need to be checked against his item specifications. For items designed to test above the knowledge category in the *Taxonomy of Educational Objectives,* some element of novelty should be introduced so that students will not arrive at correct answers through a process of rote memorization.

Rules for the construction of objective-test items serve only as a guide to the test constructor. An experienced test constructor may consciously violate many of the specific rules. For example, he may make a true-false item with the word "always" in it true. The important consideration is that the items he constructs are clearly stated and measure important facets of the educational objectives of a course.

Learning Exercise

9. Criticize the following true-false test items:
    (a) Overlearning pays because there is evidence to show that material that is 100 per cent overlearned is retained much more than 100 per cent better than material learned to the point where the correct word of a series is anticipated in 100 per cent of the cases (Source, Travers, 1950, p. 58).
    (b) It is always preferable to use an objective than an essay test.
    (c) It is not inadvisable to omit many words in a completion-test item.

The Multiple-Choice Item. The multiple-choice type of test item is the most versatile of all types of objective-test items. It consists of a statement of a problem contained in the *stem* of the item, followed by a series of suggested answers or *alternatives.* The incorrect alternatives are referred to as *distractors.* Some multiple-choice items call for the *correct* answer; others call for a *best* answer.

The multiple-choice item can be adapted to an unusually wide range of uses. Mosier, Myers, and Price (1945) suggest fourteen types of questions that may be asked in multiple-choice test items. Following are but a few of the questions that can be formulated in the stem of the item:

What purpose can be served by . . . . ?
What conclusion can be drawn from . . . . ?

What means the same as ....?
What is an important reason for ....?
Under which of the following conditions does .... occur?
If this is done what will happen? ....
What tends to occur in connection with ....?
What principle is violated when ....?
What is the best evaluation of .... (for a given purpose)?
Which is the best order to arrange .... to achieve ....?
All of the following except one are related to a common principle.
    Which one does not belong? ....

A number of multiple-choice test items can be based upon information provided to the examinee within the test. The following test situations are illustrative.

1. *Objective.* The ability to choose the foods to be bought for a family, taking into consideration family income and health.
    Test situation (basis for several items). A description of a family group with limited money to spend for food.
    Test items. *Stem*—Which of the following foods would best meet the nutritional needs of the family at the lowest cost?
    Alternatives—A list of foods or menus. The foods may be made equal in all respects except one: cost, nutrition value, particular health needs of family.

2. *Objectives.*
    (a) The ability to recognize the assumptions underlying a social science argument.
    (b) The ability to recognize implications of a social science argument.
    Test situation (basis for several test items). Two statements of three or four paragraphs each by two social scientists in which arguments are presented for and against a change in the foreign policy of the United States.
    Test items.
    (a) *Stem*—(A statement of an assumption) This assumption is consistent with:
        1. Author A but not Author B.
        2. Author B but not Author A.
        3. Both authors.
        4. Neither authors.
    (b) Same as above except the stem contains an implication.

Note: A wide range of educational objectives in the Comprehension and Analysis categories of the *Taxonomy of Educational Objectives* can be tested with the above type of test situation.

3. *Objective.* The ability to recognize form and pattern in musical works as a means of understanding their meaning.

Test situation (based on material presented by Diederich, 1958). Tape recordings in which a pianist plays snatches of 20 very familiar melodies. In most of the excerpts, the pianist inserts a definite but not too obvious error.

Test items. Stem—an excerpt from a musical selection.

    Alternatives. The excerpt contains:

      1. No error.
      2. An error in the melody.
      3. An error in the harmony.
      4. An error in the rhythm.
      5. An error in the expression or emphasis.

The multiple-choice test item can be adapted in many ways to measure quite complex educational objectives. The practice of jotting down the objective to be tested, the test situation, and the specifications for test items helps the test constructor generate test items. His work is by no means finished at this point. The task of constructing alternatives within the test item still remains, and this task requires skill.

A number of writers in the test construction field have listed rules for the construction of multiple-choice test items. Rules are formulated to insure (1) that all items represent an important aspect of the subject matter being tested, (2) that the problem is stated in such a way that the task that the examinee is called upon to perform is clear, and (3) that the examinee will not arrive at a correct choice through the use of clues within the item that are irrelevant to the objective tested. Following are some rules recommended by test constructors:

1. The item as a whole should provide the student with an opportunity to display a competency described in an educational objective.
2. The wording of the complete item is important. It should be at a level appropriate for the examinees to be tested, should not be lifted word for word from a textbook or other instructional materials, and should introduce some element of novelty if it is designed to measure more than rote memory.
3. The stem of the item should state a single problem clearly, succinctly, and accurately.
4. A problem should contain only material relevant to its solution unless the ability of the student to sift information is being tested.
5. It is usually preferable to state a problem in a positive form rather than in a negative form.
6. The distractors should represent the kinds of errors students commonly make on the problem presented.

7. The alternatives should be stated as briefly as possible.
8. Items should be reviewed to make certain that they do not contain grammatical, contextual, or other irrelevant clues.
9. The responses to items should be arranged so that the correct responses occur in a random order.

Learning Exercises

10. How can the difficulty level of a multiple-choice test item be changed by changing the distractors?
11. How might a multiple-choice test item be formulated to test the ability of students to recognize evidence for a theory? What would be included in the stem? What would be included in the alternatives?

Other Forms of Test Items. The true-false and the multiple-choice are the most common forms of test items constructed. However, it is possible to construct test items into many, many forms. The form of a test item usually emerges for a test constructor as he strives to clarify the educational objective he wishes to test. Often, a new form of test item developed by the test constructor turns out to be a variation of the multiple-choice type. The following set of items is illustrative.[2]

Objective: Ability to recognize the interrelationships of changes in contemporary economic society.

Directions: The following items deal with changes that occur at the beginning of a recession. For each item, *blacken* answer space.

A   if x and y move in the same direction, but x tends to
follow after y

B   if x and y move in the same direction, but y tends to
follow after x

C   if x and y move at the same time, but x tends to
move in the opposite direction from y

X	Y
135. Wage rates	Profits
137. Volume of employment	Business profits
138. Production of consumers' goods ..	Production of producers' goods
145. General price level	Value of money

The above set of items are really of a multiple-choice form. The stems for each of the four items are under the X and Y columns; and

[2] *Ibid.*, p. 121.

the A, B, and C alternatives constitute the alternatives for each of the four items.

The more familiar *matching* type item is also essentially a multiple-choice item. A matching test usually consists of two columns. Each item in the first column is to be paired with one item in the second column. Thus, the item in the first column is really the stem of the item with all items in the second column serving as suggested alternatives.

Learning Exercise

12. Revise stem 135 on wage rates and profits to the usual multiple-choice form.

Assembly, Administration, and Grading

Assembly. The most intellectually demanding portion of test construction is accomplished once the items to be included in a test are constructed. However, there still remains the task of reviewing the items, assembling the items into a single test, and reproducing the test.

A review of the test items, preferably by someone who has not constructed the items, invariably reveals some items that need clarification. It is desirable for the reviewers to independently work through the test and then check their answers with the keyed answers. The test as a whole needs to be checked for overlapping items and the distribution of the position of correct answers.

There are several ways of grouping items, and no one way is clearly superior to another. Items may be grouped according to (1) subject matter, (2) the objective tested, (3) order of difficulty, and (4) form of the item. In selecting a method of grouping items, both the functioning of the examinee and the later conveniences in scoring and interpretation of test performance need to be taken into consideration.

It is desirable to arrange the items in some uniform spatial pattern that permits the examinee to read the items with ease. Spaulding (1951) presents a thorough discussion of the layout and format of a test. In reproducing a test, the aim is to get a clear, attractive copy. A relatively small amount of time is needed to deal with these final details. Yet this attention to detail can affect not only the attractiveness of a test, but also the validity of the test results.

Administration. A number of decisions should be made preliminary to outlining the directions for a test. These decisions include, among other things, the amount of time to be allowed for the test and the extent to which the student should guess when he is not sure of an answer.

TIME LIMITS. A liberal time allotment is desirable for most achievement tests because time is not an important element for most educational objectives. Usually, the length of the testing period is set by the school's administration. Consequently, the problem of time allotment becomes one of deciding how many test items should be included in a test. We need to consider how the reliability of a test is affected by the number of items in a test before deciding to be extremely generous with the time allotted for a test.

Any test score is really made up of two parts—a true score and some error in measurement. A test has high reliability when the error in measurement is small compared to the true score. The error in measurement stems from a number of sources. Any test is made up of a sample of questions drawn from all the possible questions that could be asked. We are interested in measuring the student's competency on the total population of questions—not just on the sample. If we include only a few questions on a test, we might easily get a false picture of what the student could do on a test covering all possible questions. The student may just happen to know the few questions we ask, or the student might perform much better on other questions we might ask. By increasing the number of questions asked, chance factors are less likely to affect importantly a student's score. Within limits, therefore, the reliability of a test can be improved by lengthening the test. Of course, if we make a test too long for a time period, the student may be so rushed that he is not able to perform up to his capacity. In general, however, we can increase the reliability of a test by increasing the number of discriminating items.

In deciding how many test items to include for a set testing period, a compromise is usually called for. On the one hand, the examiner wants a test sufficiently short that all students can finish. But he also wants a reliable test. Test authors usually set the time limits so that between 80 and 90 per cent of the students can attempt all items (Traxler, 1950).

GUESSING. A student usually can raise the number of his correct responses by guessing on any test in which questions provide choices between two or more alternatives. A correction formula is sometimes applied to test scores to "correct" for guessing. One simple formula is

$$S = R - \frac{W}{n-1}$$

where S = score
R = the number of right responses
W = the number of wrong responses
n = the number of alternatives for item

Test specialists are not in complete agreement on whether such a correction formula should be applied or what instructions should be included in the directions of a test regarding guessing. The problem is complicated by the fact that all guesses are not pure guesses. Often, the student knows enough to eliminate one or more of the alternatives of a test item, and sometimes the student may be almost sure of the correct response. A second complicating factor is that students differ in their willingness to guess. Instructions not to guess fail to prevent some students from guessing, and instructions to guess will not induce other students to guess. One interesting variation of the correction formula is

$$S^1 = R + \frac{O}{n}$$

where S^1 = the corrected score
R = the number of correct responses
O = the number of omitted items
n = the number of alternatives per item

A case can be built for instructing the examinees to attempt every item in objective tests. If such instructions are followed, a scoring formula is unnecessary, because corrected scores would correlate perfectly with the number of correct responses. Teachers may object to such a procedure, however, on the basis that they are attempting to develop a respect for accuracy. Also, such a procedure will result in an increase in the error portion of a score and hence lower the reliability of the test.

One type of instruction that is commonly given is to tell the student to attempt a question even when not sure about the correct answer, but not to guess wildly. The student then may be informed that a formula is to be applied to scores to correct for guessing.

Grading. Scores on tests constitute measurements, not evaluations. Scores become evaluations only when they are translated into some form that reflects judgments as to their adequacy. The scores may be translated into a symbolic scale such as A, B, C, D, and F percentiles, etc. The points on the scale may be defined in terms of the position of a score in the group (e.g., A = top 7 per cent; B = next 24 per cent; C = middle 38 per cent; D = 24 per cent; F = lowest 7 per cent).

The points on the scale also may be defined in terms of the instructor's judgments concerning the students' level of achievement. For example, A, B, C, D, and F may be defined in terms of how well the student has attained the major and minor objectives of a course, or how well he is prepared for more advanced work, or how well the student is able to apply his learning in practical situations. The teacher may avoid the use of symbols in grading a student's work and restrict appraisals to verbal descriptions. In any case, grading is an evaluative procedure in which a value judgment is made concerning a student's performance.

The practice of reporting symbolic grades to students and parents has been criticized by a number of test specialists. Baron and Bernard (1958) contend that alternative practices—such as letters to parents, teacher-parent conferences in the home or school, self-appraisals, teacher-pupil conferences, teacher-pupil-parent conferences—offer the teacher greater opportunities to utilize evaluations as a means of fostering pupil growth. It should be noted that none of the alternative practices eliminates the basic problem of converting test scores into some form of evaluation. All of the alternatives do offer opportunities to report a more comprehensive and diagnostic evaluation of a student's achievement than is obtained in a simple letter grade. We will now turn to the problem of how the test performance of a class can be analyzed to yield information of value to the teacher in planning learning experiences.

Learning Exercises

13. What advantages can you see in arranging the items of a test according to: (a) order of difficulty, (b) subject matter.
14. Using the two correction formulas presented in the previous section, find corrected scores for a student who obtained 70 items right on a test, 20 wrong, and omitted 10 items. The test consisted of 100 five-choice items.

Analysis of Test Results

Any analysis of test results becomes worthwhile whenever it contributes to an improvement in the learning of an individual student. The improvement may come about as a result of the student reviewing his corrected test paper in order to note his errors and make plans to correct his weaknesses. Improved teaching practices may emerge as a result of the teacher noting the sections of the test in which the students did relatively well and the sections that were done poorly.

A process known as *item analysis* provides information on how well students have performed on each item of a test. Poor performance on an item may be due to inadequacy of student learning or to faulty construction of the item.

Item analysis procedures, as usually carried out, are based upon the assumption that the total test is a valid measure of student competency. If this assumption is made, the validity of each item on the test can be examined by comparing the performance on the item of the students who score high and the students who score low on the total test. The item contributes to whatever is measured by the whole test if a significantly higher proportion of the top group of students than of the bottom group of students get the item right.

In Fig. 14–1, Chauncey and Dobbin (1963) present a question (developed by Educational Testing Service) that is an example of a multiple-choice item that requires thought and insight. The statistical analysis that follows the test questions illustrates the kind of information obtained by item analysis.

The statistical analysis in Fig. 14–1 illustrates a number of features of item analysis. Two bits of information that can be obtained from item analysis are: (1) the *discriminating power* of the item, and (2) the *difficulty* of the item. A number of formulas are available for expressing indices of discriminating power and item difficulty.

Discrimination Power of an Item. The statistical analysis of the Educational Test Service item on European history and government reveals that the item discriminates quite well. Of the top fifth of students, 49 out of 60 selected the correct answer; while only 16 out of 60 of the poorer students did so. All the distractors, except response C, operated efficiently.

Note that the item analysis does not explain why 48 per cent of the college students failed to answer the item correctly. To answer the item, the student must be able to read the graph and note that the party system shown is essentially a two-party one. The student's knowledge of the form of government may lead him to eliminate certain alternatives. For example, the French National Assembly contains far more than three parties. The student's knowledge of political events may provide clues. For example, the suppression of political parties by Mussolini in Italy in 1938, or the defeat of the Conservative party in Britain by the Labor party following World War II. In general, failure to answer the item correctly may be attributable to lack of information or to lack of the ability to utilize information. A comparison of the statistical analysis of this item with that of other items on the test might provide clues as to the exact nature of student weaknesses.

Question 2

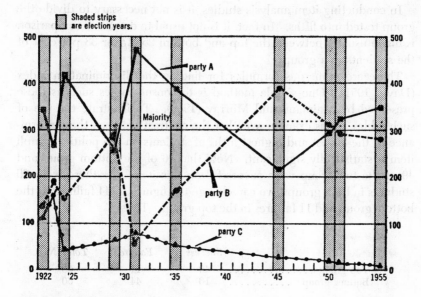

Shaded strips are election years.

party A

Majority

party B

party C

The graph above represents the political composition from 1922 to 1955 of which of the following?

(A) German Bundestag
(B) French National Assembly
(C) Italian Chamber of Deputies
(D) British House of Commons

Statistical Analysis

RESPONSES	Students Classified by Total Test Score				
	LOWEST FIFTH	NEXT LOWEST FIFTH	MIDDLE FIFTH	NEXT HIGHEST FIFTH	HIGHEST FIFTH
Omit	8	1	3	2	
A	5	4	5	4	2
B	25	28	14	11	3
C	6	5	6	5	6
*D	16	22	32	38	49
Total	60	60	60	60	60

Per cent of total group of 300 students answering correctly . . . 52%
Correlation between success on this question and total score on test .49

*Correct answer

Fig. 14–1. Item Analysis Data on a Problem-solving Type of Test Question. (Reprinted with permission from Henry Chauncey and John E. Dobbin, *Testing. Its Place in Education Today* [New York: Harper & Row, 1963], p. 190.)

494   PSYCHOLOGY OF EDUCATION

In conducting item analysis studies, it is not necessary to divide the group tested into fifths. In fact, it is not usual to do so. A comparison is made usually between the top and bottom 25, 27, or 33 per cent of the students in a group.

There are numerous formulas for finding the discrimination index (Davis, 1951). One simple method is to consult tables such as those presented by Mainland and Murray (1952). To illustrate the use of such tables, let us examine whether the contrast between the performance of the lowest and highest fifths of students on the political graph item is statistically significant. Note that 16 of the bottom group and 49 of the top group were successful on this item. As there were 60 students in both groups, we can change the figures to 44 failures in the bottom group and 11 failures in the top group. Thus:

	Success	Failure	Total (N)
Top group	49	11	60
Bottom group	16	44	60

TABLE 14–4

Minimum Contrasts Between Groups of Varying Size for
Significance at the 5 Per Cent Level

N	
10	0/5, 1/7, 2/8, 3/9, 4/10
12	0/5, 1/7, 2/8, 3/9, 4/10, 5/11, 6/12
15	0/5, 1/7, 2/9, 3/10, 4/11, 5/12, 6/13, 7/14
20	0/5, 1/7, 2/9, 3/10, 4/11, 5/13, 6/14, 7/15, 9/16, 10/17
30	0/6, 1/8, 2/9, 3/11, 4/12, 5/13, 6/15, 7/16, 8/17, 9/18, 10/19, . . . 15/24
50	0/6, 1/8, 2/10, 3/11, 4/13, 5/14, 6/15, 7/17, 8/18, 9/19, 10/20, 11/22, . . . 25/36
60	0/6, 1/8, 2/10, 3/11, 4/13, 5/14, 6/16, 7/17, 8/18, 9/20, 10/21, 11/22, 12/23, 13/24, 14/26, 15/27, . . . 30/42

Table 14–4 presents the minimum contrasts required between the top and bottom groups of students on a test item in order to be statistically significant at the 5 per cent level of confidence. Table 14–5 presents comparable data for the 1 per cent level of significance. The contrast in the failure column is 11/44. We note in Table 14–5 that, for an N of 60, a contrast of 11/25 is significant. This means that if 11 students of the top group fail the item, at least 25 students in the bottom group would need to fail the item for the discrimination to be significant.

The contrast, 11/44, easily meets this criteria; and hence the contrast is significant beyond the 1 per cent level.

TABLE 14–5
Minimum Contrasts Between Groups of Varying Size for Significance at the 1 Per Cent Level

N	
10	0/7, 1/8, 2/9, 3/10
12	0/7, 1/8, 2/10, 3/11, 4/11, 5/12
15	0/7, 1/9, . . . 7/15
20	0/7, 1/9, 2/11, 4/13, 5/15, 6/16, 7/16, . . . 10/19
30	0/8, 1/10, 2/12, 3/13, 4/15, . . . 10/21, . . . 15/26
50	0/8, 1/10, 2/12, 3/14, 4/15, 5/17, 6/18, 7/20, . . . 9/22, 10/24, . . . 25/39
60	0/8, 1/10, 2/12, 3/14, 4/16, 5/17, 6/19, 8/21, 9/23, 11/25, 12/27, 19/34, 20/36, 24/40, 25/41, 26/41, 30/45

In constructing an achievement test for the purpose of measuring growth, it is useful to analyze items by comparing the percentage of students marking the item correctly on a pretest with the percentage of students marking the item correctly on a test given after instruction. The desirable discriminating item would be, of course, the item in which students perform better after instruction than before instruction. The present writer, in an unpublished study, has analyzed in two ways the 50 items of a test administered before and after instruction to 201 students enrolled in eight sections of an educational psychology course.

1. The first method of analysis was to compare the performance on each item of *top* and *bottom* groups of students. The top group was composed of the 54 students who scored highest on the final test. The bottom group was composed of the 54 students who obtained the lowest scores on the final test.
2. The second method of analysis was to compare the proportion of students in the top and bottom groups who passed the item on the initial test to the proportion of the same students who passed the item on the *final* test.

Items were judged as discriminating on both methods of analysis if the contrast between the groups were significant at the 5 per cent level of confidence. For the top-bottom analysis that was based only on performance on the final test, an item was judged as unsatisfactory if its difficulty level fell outside of a range of 10–90 per cent. Thus, very easy items and very difficult items were rejected. Results of the two methods of analysis were:

Twenty-six items were satisfactory on the basis of both methods of analysis.

Seven items were unsatisfactory on the basis of both methods of analysis.

Nine items were satisfactory on the basis of comparison of top-bottom group comparisons, but were unsatisfactory on the basis of initial-final test comparisons.

Eight items were satisfactory on the basis of initial-final test comparisons, but were unsatisfactory on the basis of top-bottom group comparisons.

The following item is illustrative of the 26 items that yielded fairly comparable results for both methods of item analysis:

Item 2. Different answers to the question "Is it possible to improve a child's intelligence?" are arrived at when intelligence is regarded as:

1. A social rather than a perceptual concept
2. An organic concept rather than an innate potential
*3. A social concept rather than an innate potential
4. A behavioristic rather than a stimulus-response concept

Analysis of item 2:

| | Number Correct | |
	Initial Test	Final Test
Top 54 students	23	51
Bottom 54 students	8	19
Total	31	70

Note that for this item:

1. Few students were successful on the item on the initial test.
2. Instruction apparently resulted in a large increase in the number of top students getting the item right. Instruction was not so effective for the less-able student.

An item analysis that is based upon a comparison of top and bottom groups of students on a test given after instruction may result in eliminating good educational growth items. The following item is illustrative of the 8 items that turned out to be satisfactory on an initial-final test comparison, but which did not discriminate between top and bottom groups.

* Correct answer.

Item 15. An individual with an MA of 4 and a CA of 5 has an I.Q. of:

    *1. 80   4. 120
     2. 90   5. 125
     3. 108

Analysis of item 15:

	Number Correct	
	Initial Test	Final Test
Top 54 students	19	52
Bottom 54 students	15	46
Total	34	98

Item 15 is not an effective item for a test designed for the purpose of assigning grades. The item might very well be included in a test designed to measure the effects of instruction.

Item analysis conducted on the basis of comparisons of top and bottom groups of students on a posttest does not yield data that can be interpreted as evidence of the effectiveness of instruction. The following item is illustrative of the 9 items that were found to be satisfactory on the basis of top-bottom group-analysis but were not adequate growth items.

Item 7. I.Q. scores of children who come from other than middle class urban homes are difficult to interpret because:

   1. Their scores are usually lower.
  *2. Children may have lacked opportunity to develop verbal ability.
   3. The personality of the child may affect his intelligence test performance.
   4. Their scores may not be accurate.

Analysis of Item 7:

	Number Correct	
	Initial Test	Final Test
Top 54 students	42	39
Bottom 54 students	25	22
Total	67	61

The satisfactory discrimination between top and bottom groups on the final test merely reflects the equally satisfactory discrimination of the item on the pretest. Instruction did not have any apparent effect upon the students' learning of the point covered by the item.

* Correct answer.

Item Difficulty. The item difficulty may be expressed simply as the percentage of students who answer the item correctly. The optimum difficulty level of items in a test vary according to the purpose of the test. For the purpose of dividing a group equally into two segments of high and low achievers, items of 50 per cent difficulty are optimally efficient (Richardson, 1936). The difficulty level of items should be much greater if the purpose of the test is to select scholarship students out of all students of a grade. Items should be easy if the purpose of the test is to identify only the very most incompetent students. In the school situation where a test is used as a basis for assigning A, B, C, D, and F grades, the items on the test should cover a range of difficulty levels. For the type of achievement tests used in schools where items are fairly highly intercorrelated, the range of difficulty level of roughly 10 to 90 per cent is appropriate (Davis, 1951).

Teachers tend to construct excessively easy examinations (Wood, 1960). One reason for this is the naïve notion, shared by many teachers, that 70 per cent should be the "passing" score. Tests then are made easy to avoid failing the majority of students in a class. A second reason is the belief of some teachers that easy examinations somehow motivate students to work harder. Possibly an easy examination permits the student to experience a sense of achievement and thus encourages the student to work harder. On the other hand, a difficult examination may serve to persuade the student to work harder. There is little research evidence concerning the effects of either test difficulty or grading standards upon the motivation of students. Sax and Reade (1964) report one study in which one group of college students was given a "hard" mid-term examination while another group was given an "easy" examination. At the end of the term, comparisons were made of the groups on a final examination composed of items of medium difficulty. The students of above-average ability who had previously taken the "hard" mid-semester examination performed significantly better than the above-average students who had previously taken the "easy" examination. No significant differences in the performances of below-average students from the two groups were found.[3]

Item analysis is a time-consuming process, and this is perhaps the greatest limitation to its usefulness for the classroom teacher. How-

[3] The Sax and Reade study is neatly designed. Students for the two groups were randomly selected from a single class, thus controlling the teacher variable and lecture content. A test given one week before the final permitted the researchers to employ an analysis of covariance design and thus statistically control any initial differences in the students. Mid-semester examination papers were not returned, and evidence was obtained that students were unaware that the two mid-term tests differed in difficulty level.

ever, item analysis procedures do have potential value in increasing the teacher's understanding of the teaching-learning process in the classroom.

Learning Exercises

15. A test item was marked correctly by 40 of the top 50 students in a class, and by 25 of the bottom 50 students. What is the difficulty level of the item? Consult Tables 14–4 and 14–5 to determine whether the item discriminates satisfactorily.

16. On the basis of an analysis of student performance on the final test, item 15 on computing an I.Q. appears to be ineffective for two reasons. What are the two reasons?

STANDARDIZED ACHIEVEMENT TESTS

Standardized achievement tests differ from teacher-made tests in a number of ways.

1. The standardized test is based upon educational objectives that are common to many schools throughout the country. The teacher-made test is tailored to the specific objectives of the teacher.

2. The standardized test usually is constructed with great care and skill. Professional writers, reviewers, and editors scrutinize each item on the test. Items are refined on the basis of information obtained from item analysis. The teacher-made test is often poorly constructed.

3. The standardized test provides norms based on the performance of a representative sample of students throughout the country. The teacher-made test usually is administered to a single group.

4. Specific directions for administering and scoring of a standardized test are worked out and stated in detail. The procedures for administering and scoring a teacher-made test usually are not standardized.

Types of Achievement Tests

Reading. Reading involves a complexity of abilities, skills, and attitudes. Some reading abilities are of major concern in the primary grades, e.g., the ability to accurately perceive word forms. Other abilities are gradually added after the child acquires basic reading skills, e.g., inquiring as to the completeness, relevance, and accuracy of information presented; and integrating ideas acquired through reading with previous experiences. Some of the objectives of a reading program can be tested with objective tests; other objectives cannot.

In view of the complexity of the reading process, it is not surprising to find different standardized reading tests measuring quite different constellations of abilities. Reading tests may be of a *survey* type in which an effort is made to obtain assessments of a limited number of rather general reading objectives. Reading tests may also be of the *diagnostic* type in which an effort is made to obtain a diagnostic picture of the strengths and weaknesses of a student as a first step in remedial teaching.

Arithmetic. Standardized tests in arithmetic are also of a survey or a diagnostic nature. An arithmetic test of the survey variety may yield separate scores on a pupil's computational skills and on his problem-solving abilities, but it does not reveal the pupil's sources of difficulties in each area. A diagnostic arithmetic test will yield a larger number of subscores for the purpose of providing the teacher with information as to where the pupil needs help.

Standardized diagnostic tests in all subject areas would appear to be of greater potential value to the classroom teacher than survey tests. However, it should be remembered that the reliability of a test is dependent in part upon the number of items in the test. The subtest scores for many diagnostic tests are based upon too few items to attain a desirable level of reliability. The teacher may use subtest scores, even when they are not highly reliable, in analyzing the performance of the class as a whole. However, the value of unreliable scores in analyzing the performance of an individual in a classroom is quite questionable.

Learning Exercises

17. A sixth-grade teacher in a school attended by children from the higher socioeconomic homes administered a standardized reading test and found that most of her pupils scored well above the national average of sixth-grade pupils. The teacher concluded that the teachers in her school were doing a better-than-average job of teaching children to read. Criticize this conclusion.

18. What are some educational objectives of a school's reading program that could not be readily measured by standardized tests?

19. In which would you expect the larger number of subscores—a survey test or a diagnostic test?

20. A teacher item-analyzed an arithmetic test and found that only 10 out of her 30 pupils obtained the correct answer to one of the percentage problems. The teacher looked at the test item. She expected that nearly all of her pupils should have been able to answer the item cor-

rectly. The teacher decided that her class needed more work on percentage problems. Do you think the teacher's decision is defensible?

Achievement Batteries. A number of general achievement batteries
have been developed for measuring the educational achievement of
pupils in the basic skills and in the various subject areas. A few of the
more widely used achievement batteries are:

1. California Achievement Tests. California Test Bureau. Five
   levels: grades 1 to 2, 3 to 4, 4 to 6, 7 to 9, and 9 to 14. These tests
   are essentially surveys of achievement in reading, language, and
   arithmetic.
2. Iowa Tests of Basic Skills. Houghton Mifflin Co. Range: grades
   3 to 9. The battery yields 15 scores: vocabulary, reading comprehension, language (5 scores), work study skills (4 scores),
   arithmetic skills (3 scores), and total score.
3. The Iowa Tests of Educational Development. Science Research
   Associates. Range: grades 8.5 to 13.5. The battery yields 10
   scores: understanding of basic social concepts, general background in the natural sciences, correctness and appropriateness
   of expression, ability to do quantitative thinking, ability to interpret reading materials in the social sciences, ability to interpret reading materials in the natural sciences, ability to interpret
   literary materials, general vocabulary, the subtotal of these eight
   tests, and using sources of information.
4. Metropolitan Achievement Test. Harcourt, Brace & World, Inc.
   Five levels: grades 1.5 to 2.5, 2 to 3.5, 3 to 4, 5 to 6, and 7 to 9.
   Vocabulary, reading comprehension, and arithmetic skills are
   tested at all levels. Tests on word discrimination are included in
   the three lowest levels. Language skills are added at the grades
   3 to 4 level. Language study skills, social studies information,
   social studies study skills, and science are included in the tests
   in the upper two levels.
5. SRA Achievement Series. Science Research Associates. Three
   levels: grades 2 to 4, 4 to 6, 6 to 9. Vocabulary, reading comprehension, language, and arithmetic tests are included at all levels.
   At the higher levels, a test on study skills is added.
6. Stanford Achievement Tests. Harcourt, Brace & World, Inc.
   Four levels: grades 1.9 to 3.5, 3.0 to 4.9, 5 to 6, and 7 to 9. Reading, spelling, and arithmetic are included at all levels. A language test is included in the levels from grade 3 on. Tests on
   social studies, science, and study skills are added for the upper
   two levels.
7. Sequential Tests of Educational Progress (STEP). Cooperative
   Test Division, Educational Testing Service. Four levels: grades

4 to 6, 7 to 9, 10 to 12, and college freshmen and sophomores. STEP includes tests in the seven major fields of school and college instruction: reading, writing, listening, essay, social studies, mathematics, and science.

From the above brief descriptions, it may be seen that different batteries include somewhat different subject matter. A closer examination of each battery reveals further differences. While reading ability is measured in all tests, the relative amount of testing time varies from one battery to another. In the Metropolitan Achievement Tests, about 10 per cent of the testing time is devoted to a test on reading comprehension; in the California Achievement Tests, over 25 per cent of testing time is spent on reading comprehension. The specific objectives subsumed under tests of the same name differ from one test to another. Fortunately, the manuals of many standardized tests are becoming increasingly complete. The teachers of a school would need to study the manuals of various tests carefully (as well as the tests themselves) in order to decide which battery best reflects the educational objectives for their own school.

There are some advantages to a school in using a general achievement test battery rather than either standardized or teacher-made tests in separate subjects. The norms for the various subscores of the battery have been derived on the same population and are hence comparable. Therefore, the relative strengths and weaknesses of a pupil on the parts of the test battery can be determined. Further, if a pupil has taken a general achievement test at two different times in his academic career, the areas in which he has improved and the areas in which he has become relatively less proficient can be located. The fact that the test items are not directed specifically at material recently taught by a teacher means that the tests are more likely to measure permanent educational gains. Scores on teacher-made tests in contrast sometimes reflect the attainment of knowledge that is gained by "cramming" and is quickly forgotten. Teachers can learn much about test construction by studying standardized tests. Ingenious ways of testing important educational objectives may be found in many standardized tests. Some test items in standardized tests can serve as models for the teacher in constructing items for his own tests.

The limitations of general standardized achievement test batteries stem largely from their unwise use in the school. No battery can possibly cover all the important educational objectives of a school. Hence, important educational objectives may be overlooked when undue importance is attached to the results of standardized tests. A second limitation involves the use of the norms for the test. The norms for the test are usually established on pupils from a representative sample of schools. Rarely will the class of a teacher correspond to the ability level of the normative population. The norms for the test tell only how a representative sample of pupils throughout the country performed on the test. The norms do not tell how well any one particular class *should* perform. A third limitation is that the subscores of the test and the total scores contain errors in measurement. Teachers often tend to treat the scores of a pupil as though they were exact measurements.

Tests of Individual Subjects. Standardized tests are commercially available for all major subject areas taught in the schools. The value of these tests depends mainly upon the extent to which the subject-matter tests measure the same educational objectives as those of the classroom teacher.

Learning Exercises

21. Which of the standardized general achievement tests discussed contain sections in study skills?
22. Which of the batteries include tests of information in content areas (science and social studies)?
23. A teacher administered a chemistry test to his eleventh-grade class. The English teacher administered an English test, published by a different company, to the same class. The two teachers compared scores. They noted that one student scored at the 60th percentile in chemistry and the 50th percentile in English. They concluded that this student was better in chemistry than in English. Criticize this conclusion.

SUMMARY

The evaluation of student learning is a logical process. The defining of educational objectives in terms of content and in terms of behavior change is a first step in this process. The test constructor then seeks to think of test situations in which the student can exhibit the behavior defined by an objective. With objectives and ways of testing the objectives clearly in mind, the test constructor must make a series of decisions in planning a test. The purpose for evaluating the students' learning will always be an important consideration in deciding on the kind of evaluative device needed. The objective may be most efficiently measured through some form of observational technique, through the use of a teacher-made test, or through the use of some standardized test. At some stage in the test development process, decisions must be made regarding the administration, scoring of the test, and the interpreting and reporting of test results.

During the process of evaluating, the teacher should keep in mind the characteristics of a good test: validity, reliability, objectivity, and practicality. A test is valid if it measures what it sets out to measure. A test is reliable if measures consistently. Objectivity refers to agreement of competent judges as to the quality of a test performance. Practical considerations in the selection of a test include economy of money and time spent in administering, scoring, and interpreting the test.

Four types of validity have been discussed: content, predictive, concurrent, and construct. An achievement test attains content validity by including the important rather than the trivial and by including items measuring all the important objectives of a course. A test has predictive validity to the extent that a test predicts some later performance. Concurrent validity is demonstrated when a test identifies the current status with respect to some criteria performance. Construct validity refers to evidence that justifies the inferences that may be made from test results concerning some characteristic of the person tested.

There are a number of ways of estimating the reliability of a test. Administering one test on two different days and then correlating the test scores yields a coefficient of stability. This test-retest procedure provides an estimate of how much the test performance of individuals is likely to vary from day to day. A coefficient of equivalence may be obtained by administering parallel forms of a test or by splitting a test into two halves and correlating the two sets of scores so obtained.

The test interpreter often is interested in some estimate of the accuracy of a single test score. The standard error of measurement provides such an estimate.

A third characteristic of a good test, objectivity, is often assessed in terms of intergrader or interrater reliability. Finally, of necessity, certain practical considerations such as costs and ease of scoring are of importance in selecting a standardized test. However, these practical considerations should not be attained at the expense of validity and reliability.

In the construction of teacher-made achievement tests, the content aspect of an educational objective represents subject matter taught in a course. The behavioral aspect delineates what the student is expected to be able to do with the subject matter; e.g., memorize information, apply principles learned, interpret data, and analyze discussions on the subject matter. For teacher-made achievement tests, the selection of appropriate test situations is usually carried out in a series of steps: (1) a survey of the various ways the educational objective can be tested, (2) certain decisions concerning the most appropriate test form—essay or any number of types of objective-test items, and (3) the actual construction of test questions. Once a form of test question has been selected, the test constructor attempts to establish safeguards against the weaknesses inherent in the form. Rules for improving the essay test and various forms of objective tests are presented in this chapter. In general, these rules focus upon problems of (1) stating a problem clearly so that the task of the examinee is amply clear; (2) avoiding irrelevant clues that may lead the examinee to a correct response without employing the ability the question is designed to measure; (3) focusing the question on important aspects of subject matter rather than on the trivial; and (4) in the case of the essay test, insuring intergrader reliability.

Some problems concerning the assembly, administration, and grading of tests are discussed in the chapter. The overriding consideration in the assembly and administration of a test is to obtain a measure of maximum performance of the student. The major consideration in grading and reporting test results is that evaluations will be generated that enable the student to further his learning.

Teachers can benefit greatly from conducting item analysis on the tests they give. Weaknesses in test questions can be revealed through item analysis techniques. More important, the teacher can gain insight into the teaching-learning process by a study of the difficulty level and discrimination power of test items.

A wide variety of standardized achievement tests are commercially available. In order for a school to obtain real value through the use of a standardized achievement test, the staff of the school needs to study closely the educational objectives measured by a test and decide to what extent the test can yield data on the achievement of the objectives of the school. Testing becomes worthwhile only when test results suggest ways in which the teacher can better promote desirable learning on the part of individuals in the classroom.

Answer Cues

1. (a) Concurrent. (b) Content. (c) Predictive. (d) Construct.
2. (a) 2. (b) 58 and 62. (c) 56 and 64.
3. (a) Objective is not stated in terms of changes in student behavior. (b) Content aspect of the objective is not stated, and the behavioral aspect

is too general. (c) Objective needs to be more specific to be useful in developing evaluative devices.

4. Assign a group discussion topic (possibly with suggested readings on the topic). Develop an evaluative device to rate student's participation in a group discussion. Some of the major categories might be:

(1) The student has selected material relevant to the topic.
(2) The student listens to points presented by other members of the group and responds to them.
(3) The student aids the group in defining the problem under discussion.
(4) The student attempts to evaluate the implications of evidence presented by the group, etc.

5. A test that provides part-scores needs to be planned with a sufficient number of items on each part to insure reliability.

6. (a) Objective—the objective calls for an ability to recognize. (b) Short answer essay. (c) Extended essay.

7. The behavior measured is the ability to organize. To be valid, a test needs to measure this behavior. This can be done better by an extended essay question than by a series of short answer questions. Therefore, the teacher chooses the extended essay form of question even though short answer questions could be graded more reliably.

8. (a) Rule 2—one correct response. (b) Rule 4. (c) Rule 5.

9. (a) Item too long and is not clear. (b) Word "always" is a clue that the item is false. (c) Too many negatives.

10. Choosing distractors that are closer to the correct answer and that represent the kind of errors students commonly make on the problem presented will increase the difficulty level of an item.

11. *Stem:* Which of the following is the best evidence for the theory that . . . *Alternatives:* Possible evidence for the theory stated.

12. One possible revision is:

What changes may be expected to occur in wage rates and profits as a result of a recession?
A — Profits will fall first; then wage rates will fall.
B — Wage rates will fall first; then profits will fall.
C — Wage rates will fall and profits will rise, at about the same time.

13. (a) Students are not so apt to become discouraged by early failure on the test. The student who does not finish the test is not penalized as much. (b) Permits the student to organize his thinking around one topic at a time.

14. 65, 72.

15. .65; 10/24 is the minimum contrast for the 1 per cent level.

40 Right in top group; 25 Right in bottom group is the same as 10 Wrong in Top; 25 Wrong in Bottom or 10/25. Item discriminates at the 1 per cent level.

16. Does not discriminate adequately between top and bottom groups. The item is too easy.

17. Norms for standardized tests are based upon a cross-section of pupils from all socioeconomic classes. Children from middle and upper class homes have a better than average opportunity to develop reading skills in their own homes. Hence, the superiority of the teacher's sixth-grade class may not be attributable to superior teaching.

18. Ability to concentrate, increased interest in reading, more mature reading habits, an appreciation of good literature. In general, objectives in the affective domain and objectives involving action patterns.

19. A diagnostic test.

20. Yes. Even though the decision is based on one test item, the teacher has a sample of the performance of 30 pupils on the item. The poor performance of the class at least suggests further checking on the ability of the class to do percentage problems.

21. Iowa Tests of Basic Skills, Metropolitan, SRA, and Stanford.

22. Iowa Tests of Educational Development, Metropolitan (upper levels), Stanford (upper levels), and STEP.

23. The norms for the two tests would not be based on the same sample of pupils. Possibly the 50th percentile in English was just as good a performance as the 60th percentile in chemistry. Also, even if the two normative groups were comparable in ability, the difference might well be due to an error in measurement. Or the chemistry test might cover educational objectives that were comparable to the objectives of the chemistry teacher, while the English test may have tapped objectives not stressed by the English teacher.

15

PERSONALITY AND ADJUSTMENT[1]

This chapter will be used to present some of the major theoretical approaches to explaining personality. Much emphasis in the first section will be placed on what is meant by "personality," on how theories are developed, what rules may be used in evaluating theories, and on the major aspects of behavior customarily handled by personality theorists. In the second section, the focus of attention will shift to adjustment. Four ideas about conflict will be handled in an attempt to explain the necessity for the concept of psychological adjustment. This will be followed by a brief summary of the defense mechanisms, the use we make of defenses, and the possible consequences of using the various ego defense devices.

In the final section, your role as a teacher in relation to adjustment will be covered. This will be followed by a statement of a few of the major research problems encountered by personalogists and by a summary of areas expected to be of concern to personality theorists in the immediate future.

PERSONALITY THEORIES

The problems that arise in devising a theory of personality that adequately accounts for your behavior are not very different from the problems you have encountered in previous chapters of this book. This is not strange, for the methods used in psychology in general are the means by which the personality theorist is able to derive information necessary for the development of his theory and the testing of his hypotheses. Personality theory is not separate from psychology except

[1] By Kenneth M. Parsley, Jr., Associate Professor, Educational Psychology, University of Alabama.

to the extent that theory is emphasized and experimentation is often less prevalent.

Although a more complete definition appears later in this chapter, it might help you to realize that "persona," the root word upon which personality is based, means a mask, and refers to the masks worn by actors in Greek plays. This facade or mask is a fairly accurate description of our concept of personality today. Personality does not exist in the concrete sense; people do not *have* a personality as they have an arm. Numerous references will be made to aspects of the personality in this chapter. In no case should you see these as anything more than substitutes or shorthand symbols for more complex functions. The "ego" represents a function, not an object. This is also true of the "id," "superego," "shadow," and "archetype." Personality theorists are model builders. They build models of the operation of the variety of functions of personality just as theoretical physicists build models that describe the behavior of the atom, mu meson, nutrino, and so forth.

As many as 500 titles including articles and books are written on personality annually. It is apparent that a single chapter of a book will abridge theories, violate propositions, and unfairly develop streams of thinking in the field. For the student interested in an excellent review of a number of theories sampling a broad range of possible approaches to understanding the organization and consistency of human behavior, either Hall and Lindzey's *Theories of Personality* (1957) or Harper's *Psychoanalysis and Psychotherapy: 36 systems* (1959) are recommended. The chapters dealing with personality that appear in the *Annual Review of Psychology* are also helpful though difficult reading.

The absence of a formal foundation will force you to rely on your rather well-developed operational theory of personality. That is to say, since you were very young, you have been trying to predict the behavior of others—your parents, teachers, friends, and those with whom you have not been friendly. Much of your theory has been developed under emergency conditions, has been excessively personalized, and some has never been verbalized. You have tended to interpret what another person does in terms of what his behavior has done to you as well as what it would have meant had you done the same thing. From your study of perception in Chapter 9, you are now aware that you do not necessarily see things as others do. Thus, many of your actions toward others and conclusions about them have been based on false information. You are sufficiently sophisticated to read about and develop an approach as a teacher that might help you better understand the problems of others and help them solve those problems.

The individual approach to helping children work through their problems appears to be the most effective for you as a teacher, but you may also assume children have many problems and problem-solving approaches in common. This is one of the assumptions upon which theories of personality are based. The information that is used to formulate and to test the statements that emerge from a theory is generally gathered by personality theorists from the study of individuals (ideographic studies) or from the study of large groups of people (nomothetic studies). However, in either case, the aim is application of the results of studies to more than the individuals or groups from which the information was gathered. You will recall from the introduction to Chapter 2 the kinds of problems and safeguards statistical inferences produce and require. The theories that evolved are a set of conventions (Hall and Lindzey, 1957) and as such you cannot judge them in terms of truth or falsity. However, the proposals about how people behave may be judged on the basis of whether they work when you apply them. A detailed discussion of theory evaluation may be found in Feigl and Brodbeck's *Readings in the Philosophy of Science* (1953).

You and personality theorists make many assumptions about people. You should be familiar with some of the major assumptions, which are not considered facts, are neither true nor false, and frequently may not be very useful. Many of these have become central to our theories and to our beliefs about ourselves and others. Your readings about beliefs and attitudes in Chapter 13 probably helped you realize your beliefs and attitudes have a great deal to do with your selection or rejection of the new information you encounter. In this chapter, we will discuss a few of the beliefs or assumptions that have shaped theories about how we behave. These will be presented as assumptions, not as facts.

One assumption, for example, is *purpose*. Frequently, the consistency of the behavior we display is such that many people have said it is purposive, that you and I have a "free-will," that choices or decisions are up to us. Feigl and Brodbeck (1953) have pointed out that frequently the wording of an explanation can impart a sense of purpose. If you were to watch smoke rising from a pile of leaves burning at your curb you might say, "Look, the smoke is trying to reach the sky!" We all know there are physical laws relating to gases, and their actions may be fairly precisely predicted. It would be more accurate to say the smoke is rising because it is lighter than the surrounding gases, or it is less dense and as soon as the heat dissipates, the smoke will stop rising, but not that it *wants* to do anything. Feigl and Brodbeck (1953) further suggest there is a basis for believing that aspects of the biological and the physical sciences, together with some of their laws, will merge in ways we have not yet contemplated, or at least in ways some biologists do not foresee. You and I may behave according to many laws that are now applied only to non-living matter! You may say that man is different from smoke or plants or infrahuman animals. This may be true in many ways, but this is only an assumption upon which much of our work has been based—and our work is never completed. Neither all the assumptions nor all the propositions of our theories about man have been tested or perhaps formulated because we lack means of testing and because much more information must be gathered. We may *assume* man is purposive in his behavior, but this is an *opinion*. Man does appear to be purposive. Some computers have been programmed so that they "search" for particular bits of information (Newell, Shaw, and Simon, 1962). This searching methodology is called heuristics and is patterned after our "purposive" thinking. Does the machine have purpose? These assumptions are some of the matters you will cover in this chapter.

Learning Exercise

1. Comment on each of the following statements:
    (a) The reason so many people support Freud's psychoanalytic theory is that he appears to be right about much that he states in his writings.
    (b) A theory of personality is sufficient if it adequately describes one person.
    (c) One thing is nice about assumptions: they are at least always clearly stated.

Historical Background of Personality Theories

In the sequence S–O–R, personality theorists are concerned primarily with the "O"—the organism. If you were to read an historical review of the scientific and popular views of what we call personality, you would see in early descriptions that personality was located in specific organs: the emotions were in the stomach, the conative in the head, and courage and its related descriptive terms in the intestines or gut. Later, the fluids of the body were assigned a major role in the personality. A person could be described in terms of the dominance of certain fluids over other fluids. He could be sanguine (blood) and was considered warm of heart; or an excess of phlegm (phlegmatic) would mean he was slow and purposeless; too much black bile led to melancholia; and the choleric person was too easily upset and angered because he had too much yellow bile. Obviously, attempts at cures might involve the reduction of certain fluid levels in the body. Much later, we found the brain gaining in importance as a factor in personality theory. At one point, regions of the brain were assigned functions relating to personality types, and a search of the surface of the skull of a patient might reveal enlargements which were then used as a basis for diagnosis. This was the science of phrenology. Today, we tend to see the brain as the locus of personality variables in a sense, but we tend to see it as a total functioning organ rather than locally associated with different personal characteristics. We further tend to see it as a part of the body totality rather than as a functionally separate organ.

You would probably not be surprised to know that each of the theories discussed above is quite improbable in light of our present scientific evidence. Yet each theory contains insights supported by currently accepted experimental evidence. There are parts of the brain that have to do with certain functions, though these tend to be related to physiological functions rather than personality functions. We are able to stimulate parts of the brain and produce motion of a leg, arm, eyelid, etc. We are also able to stimulate small areas of the brain and produce memories under some conditions. For instance, Penfield (1958) found while conducting brain surgery that the accidental stimulation of a section of the brain resulted in a rather vivid recall of a part of the song "Marching Along Together" by a girl. He further was told by the patient that so long as the stimulation of the brain tissue was continued, the concert continued, but when he stopped the stimulation, the concert stopped and restimulation did not cause the concert to continue, rather, the music began at the beginning again, something like a tape recorder which rewinds when the current is cut off. So localization of some sort is possible, but not in the sense that all memories of music are in one area and all memories of food in another, etc.

So seemingly remote an explanation of personality as the humoral (fluid) theory has gained some credence through studies of the effect of chemicals secreted into the blood stream or endocrine secretions of a more general nature. For instance, a hungry dog's blood, when injected into a food-satisfied dog, will cause the latter to eat again (Luckhardt and Carlson, 1915). The blood is a major means of distribution of chemical substances throughout the body. Each of these early theories of personality is consistent with the then-known facts concerning the operation of the human organism. The logic has not necessarily been lacking, just the scientific knowledge and tools necessary for testing hypotheses, and frequently a clear statement of the assumptions. This is also true today. The logic that has been applied in the development of theories of personality is still not lacking as much as is the knowledge necessary for formulating a theory consistent with the operation of the human organism.

Definition

Perhaps one way of going about the process of familiarizing you with personality theory and the role of personality in psychology is to define what is meant by the term "personality." We will begin with a definition of personality that has quite wide acceptance in the field. Gordon W. Allport (1937) published as careful an historical study of the origins and development of the term "personality" as is available. He has also developed a definition that does violence to only a small group of psychological theories. Allport (1961) in a later, revised statement wrote: "Personality is the dynamic organization within the individual of those psychophysical systems that determine his characteristic behavior and thought." (P. 28.) This is a revision of the definition that has been popularly quoted since 1937, when it was first published. Allport expanded upon each of the terms in this definition meticulously and with such clarity and economy of space that the quotation is well worth including here:

Dynamic organization. We have seen that omnibus or ragbag definitions are not adequate. The central problem of psychology is mental organization (the forming of patterns or hierarchies of ideas and habits that dynamically direct activity). Integration and other organizational processes are necessary to account for the development and structure of personality. Hence "organization" must appear in the definition. The term implies also the reciprocal process of *disorganization,* especially in those abnormal personalities that are marked by progressive disintegration.

Psychophysical. This term reminds us that personality is neither exclusively mental nor exclusively neural (physical). Its organization entails the functioning of both "mind" and "body" in some inextricable unity.

Systems. A system (any system) is a complex of elements in mutual interaction. A habit is a system, so too a sentiment, a trait, a concept, a style of behaving. These systems are latent in the organism even when not active. Systems are our "potential for activity."

Determine. Personality *is* something and *does* something. The latent psychophysical systems, when called into action, either motivate or direct specific activity and thought. All the systems that comprise personality are to be regarded as *determining tendencies.* They exert a directive influence upon all the adjustive and expressive acts by which the personality comes to be known.

Characteristic. All behavior and thought are characteristic of the person, and, they are unique to him. Even the acts and concepts that we apparently "share" with others are at bottom individual and idiomatic. It is true that some acts and concepts are more idiosyncratic than others, but none can be found that lacks the personal flavor. In a sense, therefore, it is redundant to employ the term *characteristic* in our definition. Yet redundancy is not necessarily a bad thing; it helps to drive a point home.

Behavior and thought. These two terms are a blanket to designate anything whatsoever an individual may do. Chiefly what he does is to adjust to his environment. But it would be unwise to define personality only in terms of adjustment. We not only adjust to our environment but we reflect on it. Also, we strive to master it, and sometimes succeed. Behavior and thought, therefore, make both for survival and for growth. They are modes of adjustment and outreach elicited by the environmental situation we are in, always selected and directed by the psychophysical systems that comprise our personality. [From Gordon W. Allport, *Pattern and Growth in Personality,* copyright © 1961 by Holt, Rinehart & Winston, Inc., pp. 28–29. Reprinted by permission of the publishers.]

It would be difficult to make a more thoroughgoing investigation of the term "personality" than has been carried out by Allport. Each of us has a more or less enduring impression of what the word means, but none could fail to benefit from a quick perusal of the study Allport has made of the etymological, theological, philosophical, juristic, sociological, biosociological, and psychological meanings of the words (1937, pp. 24–54). There is no intention to suggest this definition is the best, only to offer it and Chapter 2 in Allport's book as an excellent opportunity for each of you to examine your own thinking and to expand the base of the term.

Allport's definition is sufficiently general to permit theorists from a number of camps to accept it. However, this may be more of a disadvantage than appears on the surface. The line between a definition and an explanation is sometimes fine, and to the extent a definition is acceptable to many of diverse viewpoints, it may lack explicitness. Theories may be viewed as definitions and perhaps it would be appropriate at this point to examine theories for a few moments.

Learning Exercises

2. What is the difference between dynamic and non-dynamic organization?
3. What useful distinction has the inclusion of both mind and body in the definition of personality?
4. Allport states behavior and thought are modes of adjustment and outreach the situation in which we find ourselves. What is the meaning of "outreaching"?

Evaluation of Theories

In a chapter such as this, while the intention may not be to recommend one particular theory over another, in fairness to the reader, some attempt at theory evaluation should be proposed. There are few "facts" that have universal superiority over others; no theory is a fact and there is no proposal that the reader accept one theory rather than another. Some theories are sufficiently broad to permit the inclusion of information from a wider variety of scientific fields. Others are not so broad. Some are better able to handle the information, for instance, from the field of neurology than are others and are more consistent with it. A global theory that includes the findings of all the various research fields relating to the human organism has not yet been devised. This is in part because we have an incomplete knowledge about ourselves. If we were to demand of an adequate master theory that it subsume, in the future, all possible information, we would place an improper evaluative restriction on theory.

Hall and Lindzey (1957) suggest a group of criteria to be used in evaluation of personality theories. They first point out that a theory is a set of conventions and that these are arbitrarily selected and organized and, further, that since they are not necessarily based on empirical (observable) relations, they cannot be judged as to truth or falsity. This may be hard for you to accept, but one way of looking at theories is to permit them this latitude. It is possible to evaluate them in terms of the accuracy of the statements that emerge from them. Most of the judgments you make about truth or falsity are related to the propositions generated from theories. You seldom deal with formal theories but have often been involved in discussions relating to propositions in religion or politics in which you were unable to resolve differences.

We can say a theory generates numbers of propositions, some of which are verifiable. If a theory generates propositions, then we can make use of it. Another basis on which a theory may be judged is on whether the assumptions upon which it is based are related to the empirical events with which it deals. Theories should also be both comprehensive and simple. The theory should deal with all aspects of the phenomenon with which it is concerned, and should do so in a manner that is economical. These are some of the bases on which theories may be evaluated.

Remember though, theories may not be measured in terms of their truth, only the propositions that they generate may be so evaluated. There is no pretense that one theory is more applicable than another, though in the minds of those who work with a specific theory, others are less convenient. The criterion of truth cannot be applied to theories. They are a set of conventions or rules and may be better judged on the basis of usefulness, simplicity, productivity of research, testability, and capacity to explain. It is possible and desirable that the propositions developed from a theory be testable and to this extent truth or falsity may be applied—but not to the theory, only to the propositions. Theory evaluation is a specialized field and the works of Cohen and Nagel (1934), Hempel (1952), and Feigl and Brodbeck (1953) are valuable sources of material in this area. There you may be able to see why it is that one religious view on the origin of man is no more true than another and why political arguments are not easily resolved. You may see why one theory is no less true than another. You may also find there are other theories about theory evaluation.

Learning Exercise

5. You believe man has a mind apart from, and in addition to, his flesh and blood. A close friend of yours believes all of our behavior may be accounted for by an information processing-storage-retrieval unit called the brain. You cannot agree.
   (a) Each of you subscribes to a theory, how can agreement be reached?
   (b) The two statements appear to be mutually exclusive. Is there somewhere to turn for theory evaluation? Would you trust a decision against you?
   (c) How do beliefs (Chapter 13) bear on this?

Classifying Theories

It would be very convenient if we could classify personality theories and then deal with the advantages and disadvantages of each of these. However, the process of classification tends to do some of the same violence to the individual theories as our classification of children in a school does to individual children. There are areas of emphasis in each of the theories that tend to make them distinctive in some particular ways, but there are also ways in which they are similar.

Rather than to enumerate the theories and their points of emphasis, you might gain more from a discussion of the major points which are somewhat common to theories. Hall and Lindzey (1957) suggest a number of major dimensions common to personality theories. Not all of these are characteristic of any one theory, but are variously present in two or more major contemporary theories.

Purpose. Man has been characterized as a purposeful animal by many and this is a popularly held point of view. The concept of "purpose" may be framed as social purpose, by saying that you are striving for social roles and goals, that the major determinants of your behavior are social in nature, and further, that direction and ends may be attributed to your activities. Others agree that you are purposeful but that biological needs are the mainspring for behavior and that all your activities are reducible to physiological needs such as food, water, warmth, and sex and that tissue balance is the goal of man. There are few psychologists who argue the point of purposivism. However, there may be other ways for accounting for the continuity of behavior than through purpose. Information theorists may frame purpose in a context of logical organization and feedback verification. Computer programmers may point to information-searching activities of computers and call this purpose.

Unconscious Determinants. Some theorists say your behavior may only be completely accounted for by considering motives of which you are unaware. Others contend that unconscious factors operate as a major determinant only in the abnormal individual. Few theorists deny the possibility of materials of some importance being stored in ways that make it unavailable to you. However, some feel a situation as you see it at a conscious level adequately accounts for the major determinants of your behavior. Whether or not you are able to divulge the information accurately is problematic. Some feel our statements may be accepted at face value; others feel, even if unconscious determinants are not a major factor in understanding our behavior, we may still be unable to identify all the conscious factors that led to our action. A major problem still lies in explaining the existence of unconscious material in brain circuitry.

The Centrality of Reward and Punishment. The concept of the Law of Effect has been discussed in previous chapters. For the past several hundred years, some aspect of the pleasure principle has been believed by some to influence man's behavior. Employing this principle to account for the acquisition of our behavior patterns is commonplace to most major theories today, though some theorists assign it secondary importance. *Contiguity* or association is a major construct in a number of theories but plays a minor role in others. Some means to account for why we retain some response patterns while dropping others seems a necessary part of theories of personality. This is one area in which the personality theorist has been given a great deal of support. Research in how we learn has been extensive. Some theorists place less emphasis on this aspect than others because of lack of interest or recognition that well-articulated theories of learning already exist.

Personality Structure. Some theorists place more emphasis on the form our personality takes; others appear to be more concerned with our dynamics or how we function. Many theorists feel naming imaginary parts to account for our behavior clouds the issues and makes an understanding of how we function less clear. There are few theorists today who propose an organ other than the brain that acts as a mediator for behavior. There are hypothetical constructs (the imaginary entity such as id, ego, or superego) that some theorists feel are legitimate tools of the theory builder. Historically, we have relied so heavily on physical explanations for personality that some theorists may be gun shy of the hypothesized model.

Hereditary Factors. The role of heredity is recognized by personality theorists. There is some variability in the reliance that theorists place on it. Freud believed the central factors that explain our behavior are inherited; others feel social factors are of central importance in explaining behavior because heredity factors cannot explain some variation in behavior. Jung relies heavily on the hereditary factors but adds the idea that we can gain abilities through our culture and transmit them genetically. You might, for instance, become a great pianist and then your genes would change, permitting transmission of this acquired characteristic to your children. This notion of the inheritance of acquired characteristics does not appear to be a fruitful approach to explaining behavior, and is not consistent with widely accepted genetic theory.

Role of Early Experiences. Some theorists feel the prototypes of behavior determined by environmental influences are acquired early in life and that it is necessary for us to travel back (through recall) to our childhood in order to gain an understanding of our present behavior. The typical route of psychoanalysis is backward through the memory sequences to significant events in childhood. Other theorists contend the significant elements in our behavior are in the present, and that we function in light of the here and now. The major issue is whether or not we can see the significant factors today in perspective without "returning" to the past. It is not so much a matter of what happened to us as what importance we attach to it and how it affects us now. Some theorists see what happened to you in the past as inappropriate to understanding you now, as you are more than an "extension of childhood or an older child." Adulthood and childhood do not appear to be completely continuous.

Other Factors. Consideration of you as a *total functioning unit* is emphasized by some theorists. The total functioning unit includes not only you but your environment (the psychological environment) as well. When all the factors some theorists propose as contributing to the total you are included, and all the relationships and individuality of them are considered, an individual, rather than a group study of the personality seems necessary. This is somewhat limiting to persons working with numbers of people as the teacher does, because it prevents generalizations and demands individual treatment of a nature impossible in the school situation.

The *self concept* or the *ego* is included in a majority of the theories. These concepts have been classed by Hall and Lindzey (1957) as the self-as-object or self-as-process. In the self-as-object, the individual has attitudes, feelings, perceptions, and evaluations of himself. In the self-as-process, he is a doer, a thinking, remembering, and perceiving organism. Some theorists, notably Rogers, see the self so centrally as to call their theories a *self theory*. Some excellent added reading on self and ego may be found in Freud (1946), Symonds (1951), Sarbin (1952), and Mead (1934).

The above exposition was provided in order that you gain some insight into the breadth of concerns of the personality theorists and to help you examine some of your own beliefs about personality.

Learning Exercises

6. A person who says "he will naturally be a good golfer, his father is" would probably subscribe to what belief with respect to heredity?
7. "The best way to attract flies is to use honey" expresses what psychological belief?
8. "He made his bed, let him lie on it" expresses what philosophy?

ADJUSTMENT

The term "adjustment" implies a change in response to *something*. In psychology, we are very much concerned with adjustment. It is a major concern not only of the clinician but of the teacher. Bills (1950) studied the effects of therapy with children classed as both emotionally disturbed and as retarded readers, and found significant improvement in reading ability after therapy. Bills was able to suggest that level of personal adjustment had a significant effect on academic functioning.

In this section, you will read about conflict of various types, the ways in which we distort our impressions of the world in order to make them fit what we want to perceive, and some ways in which you as teachers can assist students in their adjustment.

Conflict

We characteristically think of conflict as an important antecedent to adjustment. In the normal process of satisfying perceived needs, we are confronted with obstacles. These may be as simple as time or space gaps between ourselves and some goals we feel we must reach. The conflict may be very complicated, and involve a number of internal variables. There are a number of ways in which the idea of conflict may be represented. In this chapter, we will deal with (1) a topological approach, (2) a structural approach, (3) a role-playing approach, and (4) an information-processing approach. These may be outlined very briefly, and each is readily understandable.

Topological Approach

Lewin (1935) suggested a topological description of conflict that involves vectors representing both direction and strength of action. For instance, an *approach-approach* conflict might involve two positive goals presented at the same time in such a manner that the selection of one would exclude the selection of the other. The man who is about to decide on marriage between two beautiful women is in an approach-approach conflict in a monogamous culture. He must choose between them—normally. An *approach-avoidance* conflict involves a positive reward with the selection of one alternative but also a negative punishment with that same choice. A college student about to ask a girl for a date has the possibility of reward if she accepts his gambit and the possibility of punishment if she refuses it. This is commonly called an ambivalent situation. The *avoidance-avoidance* situation is one in which both alternatives are undesirable but inescapable. The choice between staying in a burning airplane and jumping from it are equally undesirable. Frequently in life, we are confronted with a multiple approach-avoidance situation. More than one course of action is available, but each alternative has desirable and undesirable features. The young man who if forced to choose between two job opportunities, each of which has its attractive and unattractive features, is in a *multiple approach-avoidance* situation.

In addition to describing the direction of action effectively, the topologist is able to present graphically the strength of response by means of the length of the vectors. Some interesting research has been done in the area of changes in the strength of approach and avoidance responses to cues. Brown (1948) and Miller (1959) have researched the matter of changes in the attractiveness of goals. They found that the closer you are to a negative goal, the more avoidance behavior you will display; the closer to a positive goal, the more approach behavior you will display; and that avoidance behavior increases in strength more than approach behavior as you come closer to a goal. In applied form, the closer the horse to the stable, the faster he will run; the closer the child to the paddle, the more slowly he will walk; and the boy will slow his pace in approaching the paddle before the horse will speed his pace when approaching the stable.

Thus, topology offers an explanation of the direction and strength of actions, and gives a neat graphic illustration of environment, goals, barriers, and intensity of interest.

Learning Exercise

9. A young man plans to get married in the near future. The prospect of marriage for the young man constitutes a conflictual state. On the positive side, it represents meeting the expectations of society, companionship, a home of his own, and sexual satisfaction. On the negative side, it represents loss of freedom, anxiety about the future, and increased responsibilities.
   (a) What type of conflict is this?
   (b) What predictions can be made concerning the relative strengths of the positive and negative feelings as the date of marriage approaches?

Psychoanalytic Approach. Conflict, from a psychoanalytic approach, may be explained in terms of the functioning of the id, the superego, and ego (see Chapter 2). The external demands of society are represented within the *superego*. These external demands are the rules of conduct which are not necessarily natural or logical, and which can run counter to the normal inclinations of the uncivilized organism. Herein is implied the necessity of an individual's conflict with the culture in which he lives. The "superego" (or some similar term) is used by some personality theorists as a label for this internal force that impels one to conform to cultural norms. The *id* represents the naturalistic function in Freudian personality theory. It is the biological aspect of personality and, in many theories of personality, is the hedonistic (pleasure-seeking) aspect which has the oomph! The id is obviously bound to come in conflict with the superego (cultural) values because man by nature is assumed to be contrary to the unnatural essence of culture. The *ego* represents the rational, logical, and conative aspects of the personality and acts as a moderator between the naturalistic, cultural, and realistic demands. The success with which the ego meets all of the demands placed upon it is a measure of adjustment. The ego is the resolver of conflicts. The psychoanalytic explanation of conflict is a type of conflict-of-interest formulation. A strong ego would be one that has enough skill and strength to handle the demands of the id and the superego in the commerce of the organism with the world.

Roles and Conflict. A conflict in role expectations may take a number of forms:

1. The conflict may be between two or more *perceived* expectations. For example, a teacher may *believe* that parents expect one type of behavior from her and that children expect another. In actuality, there may be no conflict in the expectations of the parents and the children.
2. The conflict in expectations may *actually* exist. For example, a judge appointed by his political boss is expected, not only to uphold the law, but also to serve the party interests.
3. The expectations may be perceived as *legitimate* or *illegitimate*, neither being necessarily less effective in producing the conflict than the other. For example, you as a teacher may have (a) a friend who expects you to treat her child differently than is your normal rule (an illegitimate expectation) and (b) a principal who expects you to treat every child in the classroom impartially (a legitimate expectation).

This may be a somewhat formal way of presenting the everyday feeling we have in our jobs. Many of you have been in role conflict and just did not know what to call it—now you do! As children, we are thrust into many types of conflicts. Our pals may expect one form of behavior on Halloween and our parents and teachers quite another. When our parents do something that we perceive as hostile and we are still expected to honor them, we are in role conflict. Role conflicts may be used to describe a wide variety of problems that require adjustment on the part of the individual involved in them. Further information about roles and conflict may be found in Gross, Mason, and McEachern's *Explorations in Role Analysis: Studies of the School Superintendency Role* (1958) which may have additional information of interest to you.

Information Processing Approach. You can readily imagine conflict in this framework by postulating two or more memory storage banks in which information is held. When you are confronted with a particular situation and must select a plan that will solve a problem, conflicting information may be retrieved.

In this case, you will be faced with a dilemma of choosing between alternatives. You will also be faced with the likelihood of information in non-retrievable storage that colors the choice on a non-rational basis. This latter situation could prevail if the information subtending the item on which you would have based the choice was not available or was secured in a non-rational manner. Your mother or father might have told you (under conditions of considerable threat) that you should not ride with strangers when you were quite young. The rational base was not there, but the information might be called up years later when you are presented the choice of accepting an offer of a ride as opposed to walking to a distant service station to get gas for your car that had stopped on the highway. The rule might remain and resist change despite the rational alternative, simply because it was not supported by a rational base. Under these circumstances, you might be expected to become quite anxious because of your inability to rationally resolve the conflict.

Learning Exercises

10. How is conflict related to adjustment?
11. Does one have to segment the personality in order to conceive of conflict?
12. Is it necessary and desirable to raise a child so that he experiences no conflict?
13. In what ways might you expect to see people adjusting to conflict?
    (a) By denying the desire exists
    (b) By substituting another goal
    (c) By rationally deducing that you do not need the desired object
    (d) a and c
    (e) a, b, and c

Personality Development

Chapter 3 covered the subject of development; therefore, little will be added here other than the specific application of the concept in the area of personality. We might start out with the following excerpt from Shakespeare, chosen because it reflects a popular conception of the nature of our lives.

> A man in his day plays many parts, his acts
> being seven ages. . . .

Is this an apt description of personality? Are there stages through which you progress, or is this a continuity that cannot be described well by the sequential concept? Do all people go through each of the stages, or is it possible to skip some? If there are differences in the rate and order of progress, what determines these? Are each of the animals on the earth committed to such steps? Are they different for each species?

Changes do occur in the "personality" over the years from infancy to adulthood. To what extent were the changes that occurred in you similar to those that took place in your friends and to what extent quite different? Though not stated, the study of development implies a note of continuity, and in the case of personality development, we are concerned with the extent to which the scope and sequence of one person's personality change resembles another's.

The reading you did in Chapter 3 on development will be helpful in providing a framework onto which you will be able to hang some of the concepts with which we will deal here. If some of the aspects of personality have genetic origins, we might well expect some regularity of growth of personality (assuming physical maturation will operate in the realm of personality because of the proposed genetic origins of aspects of personality), and we might also expect some similarity from person to person (since we have many gross physical similarities). Much speculation about the genetic origins of personality may be found in theories of Jung (1939) and Murphy (1947). We might also expect to see social factors emphasized and would expect to find, within the same culture, similarities in the appearance of certain personality characteristics. Most theorists include cultural factors; prominent among these theorists are Horney (1950), Sullivan (1953), Adler (1924, 1930), Murphy (1947), and Fromm (1941).

The controversy over environment and heredity, with which you are already familiar, is apparent in personality theory as well. The matter of emphasis is again in question. Efforts are made to identify elements or forces common to man in the shaping of personality and its development. These forces tend to emphasize possible similarities between individuals. Grouping in this way, for treatment and understanding, is one of the favorite pastimes of scientists as well as for armchair personologists. Theories are in part based on similarities, and it is small wonder that efforts have been made to isolate variables that would make generalizations feasible and appropriate.

Counter to this flow is a remarkably widespread acceptance of the idiosyncratic or unique features of each individual. Here the personality scientist is saying that there are important common factors in the make-up of our personality, but there are other factors that have sufficient influence to make prediction of an individual's behavior based on group factors impossible. This does not make the factors that are common to personality development meaningless. It does limit their usefulness in the prediction of individual events. Many theorists have thus turned from the use of such common factors as have been isolated and use an individual analytic approach to understanding the clients with whom they work. They are not taking the position that group factors are inoperative, but that the individual behavior patterns are related to factors so diverse that it is more practical to work on an individual basis.

You have previously read about Freud's psychosexual stages of development (oral, anal, phallic, latency, and genital). The concept that early years are significant in the formation of the personality and adjustment patterns is illustrated quite well by studies by Thompson and Heron (1954) and related data on the changes in patterns of behavior reported by Hebb (1955). In some of these studies, it was demonstrated that dogs reared in isolation but provided all necessary comforts and need satisfiers were oblivious to pain and did not learn as well as dogs reared under normal conditions. The effects of the isolation seemed to be relatively permanent and later efforts to modify the behavior of the dogs were unsuccessful. Apparently, at least with dogs, conditions of development during the early years are as important as Freud might contend, though the resistance to modification of these patterns is not as Freud might have predicted with human subjects.

There is considerable information that indicates that biological changes occur in a somewhat regularized pattern. Studies of children's thinking (Piaget, 1960) suggest there are qualitative differences in the thinking of children at different ages. Similar findings relating to the neurological tissue structure and behavioral manifestations are discussed by McGraw (1943) in her studies of neuromuscular maturation. Other studies of maturation by Gesell and Thompson (1941), Carmichael (1927), and Hebb (1955) are indicative of the areas in which maturation as a process has been partially explanatory. Here we are saying that your nervous system has changed since you were born, and that these changes have permitted walking to replace crawling, regularized speech to replace babbling, geometry to augment arithmetic, and Newton's, Einstein's, or Birkhoff's theory of gravitation to replace "It falls down" as an explanation of the descent of an apple. Some aspects of this pattern of change are attributable to factors common to all mankind and some to your particular ancestors, and some of the changes in you are due to your social background and the circumstances in which they occurred.

The concept of critical periods discussed quite thoroughly by Thompson (1962) also may be used to explain some of the changes. It is believed by many that the organism must be *ready* before it can benefit from experience. Some experiences may be helpful when they are timed properly, but others, poorly timed, may have no effect or may be quite harmful. The information about the stages, steps, or sequences appears meaningful. It is hoped that it will be possible to use this type of information in the design of institutional programs. Schools are one such institution, and we are already a long way toward having school programs that are keyed to such data.

The information gathered from studies of groups of people as well as individuals at different ages has yielded information that may be of assistance in working with both groups and individuals. However, our understanding of their behavior must be based on information about them. While we may be able to diagnose your problems from your behavior, if we merely name your problem as a neurosis or psychosis, we may be quite helpless to treat you. Your treatment will have to be individual, at least to the point of understanding the meaning of the diagnosis sufficiently to permit that treatment.

There appears to be much evidence to support the notion of a development process in personality. This may be the case only so long as we conceive of personality as having no reality apart from the organism. This is not to say that all is physical change. But physical change does contribute importantly to the developmental process in personality. Let us now view development within the framework of adjustment.

Learning Exercise

14. The idea that children are ready to read at the age of six years and six months is an embodiment of developmental stage concepts. If we changed the type of material or the mode of presentation, how would this affect the outcome?

Personality Adjustment

Personality adjustment refers to the way in which a person gets along with the world under the conditions in which he lives. This is not a very simple phenomenon and, in order to be understood, it must be viewed from a number of positions. The average person has a concept of adjustment that is different from the psychologist's, primarily because the professional is aware of the many factors entering into an appraisal of adjustment and because he is better able to detect subtle signs of maladjustment. For the teacher, adjustment to the classroom is most crucial; for the mother, adjustment at home; in the neighborhood, adjustment with other children; and at the police station, adjustment to the laws. In short, a child may have many situations to which he must adjust and he may be better adjusted to one situation than to another. Parents are frequently unbelieving when told of the behavior of their child in the classroom. How many times did you hear your mother express disbelief about your behavior? For some of you, this may have been a few years ago, but these memories tend to stay with us and are quite vivid. How often have you heard about a child or adult who has been arrested for something of which you thought him incapable?

We tend to know people in specific settings and generalize from these to all of the person's activities. Not long ago I was startled to pick up the paper and find that a woman whom I know as a secretary and as a kind and thoughtful person was arrested for embezzling nearly $100,-000. Parents are frequently brought to court to find that their son was involved in car theft or armed robbery; girls we know quite well have become pregnant out of wedlock; and public officials have evaded laws they helped draft. We usually respond to these experiences by saying we did not know them as well as we thought. This is true in a sense, but we should still expect them to act as we have always seen them act in the situations in which we know them. The secretary will still be a kind, thoughtful person in the office where she works; you are still the same person your mother knew and will continue to act toward her as you always have. In short, we may be different people in different situations. We usually recognize ourselves but are sometimes chagrined when others show amazement at our activities in other roles.

This is one way in which others may see adjustment varying. In part, it depends upon the situation. It also depends upon the level of skills of the observer. The professional is able to see areas of maladjustment that the average person is unable to see. You as a teacher are able to tell about the adjustment of children in the grade level at which you teach and make sound judgments about individuals in your class. Each teacher has learned to expect behavior within certain limits from children at her grade level. The mother of any of the individual children may not be able to make these judgments as accurately because she is not as familiar with the normal range of behavior as is the teacher. What are we saying? We are implying that children at certain ages behave differently than at other ages. There is a general band of behaviors that may be expected in nursery school that would be considered quite unusual at the seventh-grade level.

We would not expect to see a seventh-grader sucking his thumb, crying loudly when frustrated, or running to the window whenever a sound outside attracted his attention. Nor would we expect to see a woman of thirty giggling inanely at the attentions of a man. We might see them, but we would tend to think of the person as being "different." We have, then, an age-norm basis for judging behavioral adjustment.

In addition to situational and age variables associated with behavior, are there other measures? The psychologist might propose that there are ways of determining the extent to which the individual's behavior satisfies his internal demands. That is, to what extent does the way the individual characteristically behaves meet his inner demands for expression? The individual trained in the field of psychology uses many tools in addition to the interview as a means of determining the level of adjustment of people whom he contacts professionally. He is interested in the same things as the teacher, parent, minister, and employer but he is also interested in other signs than those easily seen under normal conditions. He is interested in the adjustment of the individual to himself, to the roles he normally finds himself in, all within the normal expectations of a person of his age, abilities, and environmental circumstances.

This gets to be a pretty tall order, and it is difficult to grasp unless one has some theory upon which to operate in evaluating behavior and adjustment. In order to do this, we shall look at one theory of personality in an attempt to indicate the possible factors present in the concept of adjustment.

The concept of adjustment implies conflict. Freud suggests the possibility of conflict in his representations of the personality—the id, ego, and superego. Freud believed that the infant is motivated by biological needs which are felt in the id as tension systems and are above the level of comfort for the organism. This accounts for the awareness of physical needs including chemical balance in the tissue, the endocrine system, and other body needs. The superego is a part of the personality structure postulated to account for the social demands of the environment but is connected to the id through the conceptualization that the id is the primary source of energy. The ego, you will recall, was cast in order to account for the commerce between man and the environment. Freud believed the id was unable to cope with reality and that the ego constituted the thinking, perceiving, cognitive element of the organism which again was tied to the id both as an extension of it and dependent upon it as a primary source of energy needed to deal with reality. The id operates on the pleasure principle; the ego, on the reality principle; and the superego might be said to operate according to the morality principle. In a rough way, the id represents the biological elements of personality; the ego, the psychological components; and the superego, the moral social elements. These three subsystems of the personality ordinarily operate together in achieving goals. One way of characterizing personality integration is to see the three systems functioning together.

When the biological needs or their derivatives are felt, and objects available in the environment satisfy the reality needs of the organism, and when the approval of the activity by the moral-valuing system is present, we have an integrated personal activity. The extent to which this is characteristic of the organism in major roles he is called upon to play is one measure of a well-adjusted person. If he has a major responsibility in which he is unable to meet the demands of the three structural components simultaneously, he may be maladjusted. This is, of course, a matter of degree. All of us are maladjusted in some role we play, but we are able to handle it so that we can continue to be effective people. The methods we use to handle situations in which adjustment is marginal are called defense mechanisms.

Learning Exercises

15. Identify the approximate roles played by the id, ego, and superego in Freud's formulation of personality structure.
16. Why would a major role conflict present a different level of adjustment than a minor role conflict?

The Ego Defense Mechanisms

Most theories of personality include a number of ways in which the individual handles those conflicts that arouse anxiety primarily through threatening the ego. Central to a number of theories is the concept of "I" or "self," the most pronounced of which is Rogers' self theory. Much is made of the individual's awareness of himself and apparently most theorists feel this is a stabilizing factor in the continuity of personality. At the expense of considerable rational thought, the individual appears to attempt to maintain a constancy of self appraisal. Whenever the self perception is threatened with alteration because of events perceived in the world that tend to work to the detriment of the self perception, adjustments are made in the perception so that the ego or self is either maintained or enhanced. Freud relies heavily upon the ego defense he developed.

Sarnoff (1962) points out that the main function of the ego is to maintain consciousness and to deal with threat in such a way that the intellective appraisal function of the ego is preserved. In order to accomplish this end, the individual develops a number of covert responses that emanate from his consciousness. If we cast it in other terms, we might say we can stand only so much pain in any form. Fear and anxiety are painful. Therefore, when the level becomes great enough, we have protective devices which insulate us from realizing the extent of the pain. This is necessary because it is believed the individual is able to anticipate the disorganizing effect of having too much pain. In fact, we are not able to function effectively under these circumstances and we use a number of mental gymnastics to keep pain down to a level that will still let us operate intelligently in appraising the environmental situations. These devices that protect us are called *ego defense mechanisms*. There are numbers of them, but we will cover only a few that are widely used and generally needed to account for the behavior you might need to understand.

It seems very likely that much of the intolerable fear reaction is attached to objects with which you came in contact in childhood. During this period, much of the relationship between events and outcomes is resolved using prelogical methods. Piaget (1960), Inhelder and Piaget (1955), and others have studied the problem-solving approaches of children and have demonstrated that changes in the thinking process occur with age. The methods you used as a very small child were quite primitive and perhaps led to erroneous conclusions. Consequently, much of the feedback you received failed to corroborate your hypotheses, and it is entirely possible that you not only felt quite helpless during those early years but that you also have retained some erroneous conclusions. If it is true that you committed to unconsciousness a great deal of the material that was extremely threatening to you, then it is rational to assume that these bits that you were unable to handle may not be recallable by you even now. However, they may still continue to influence your behavior and contribute elements of discord between that part of your actions you can account for and that part which is inexplicable. This is a basis for explanation of irrational fears in adults. Events occurring now may still trigger responses or response tendencies that produce fear beyond the limits of tolerance and may still be subject to the same defenses that were originally attached to them.

It should be remembered that all the mechanisms of defense have in common a distortion of the incoming stimuli such that you do not have to perceive the event as it is in the environment; you do not perceive yourself as you "really are"; and you do not accurately perceive yourself in the "real" relationship to the event. This is one of the reasons why many people argue that there is no reality. The only reality that exists is that which is perceived by the perceiver. You are not aware that you see a given event differently than it is (as it may be described by many others); you only see it as you see it. The effectiveness of the misperception would be lost and could no longer function as defense mechanisms if you were able to see the disturbing event both as it is (as others see it) and as you need to see it.

Now, in what ways do people distort the incoming stimuli in order to maintain or enhance their self perceptions? You must remember that the incoming stimulus is not the culprit. You are the one who has difficulty dealing with the effect the stimulus has on you.

One of the simplest defenses is direct *denial*. This may take the form of failure to admit that stimuli are present. One of the classic forms this takes is in *Aesop's Fables*. The fox, upon gazing at grapes which are out of reach, remarks that they are sour. He thus denies that he has an interest in the grapes. Another form is that of the smoker who fails to stop smoking though he is aware of some evidence that suggests it is detrimental to his health, on the grounds that he is one of the people who will not be affected.

Repression is a defense in which you are unable to admit that you are capable of certain acts foreign to your beliefs about yourself. In this case, a stimulus might trigger a response that is unacceptable to you, and in order to avoid admitting that the act is one you might carry out, you unconsciously reject the knowledge. You may, however, feel unaccountable anxiety. Also, you may still respond to the stimulus, but in other ways. Freud points out the inefficiency of suppression of the idea; he says this depletes our store of energy for constructive activities. Other defenses may be used. These are more constructive in that you are able to distort the direct response to the stimulus into some other type of action that is "ego-integrative" in nature.

Rationalization is a term used to describe the defense mechanism employed when we are confronted in some way, either by ourselves or others, with the fact that we have done something with which we are not in complete agreement. In this case, we are unable to accept the motivation that accounts for the behavior, so we manufacture a substitute explanation of the event.

Sublimation is a defense in which you might release your hostile aggressive feelings through your occupation. Boxers, wrestlers, and golfers may be doing this. Businessmen who are in a competitive market may siphon off considerable amounts of aggression into their work. The culture in which we live provides numerous opportunities for sublimation of aggressive feelings.

Identification as an ego-defensive action may take at least two general forms. You may identify with someone who is quite capable so that you may enjoy his successes as your own. Hero worship is an example of this. This is a satisfactory solution to the problem as long as the behavior is not a substitute for behavior that you could actually carry on successfully. However, it may become maladaptive if it reduces the possibility of your participating in some activity in which you would be perfectly adequate. Another form of identification is introjection of another who is threatening. In this case, you might internalize a parent or parent-figure who is threatening to you. You could then adopt his values in order to anticipate the disapproval he might demonstrate. Psychologists frequently view identification as the way in which the superego is formed. The child takes on the characteristics of the parent in order to avoid the punishment that will surely occur if he fails to behave as is expected of him. This Sarnoff (1962) indicates is identification with the aggressor.

Projection is a device in which we are able to misidentify the source of a desire, wish, urge, etc. We can relieve a great deal of pain by seeing someone else as the source of an unacceptable response. If you feel hostility toward someone, a way of avoiding guilt if you kill him is to say, "He tried to kill me, all I did was defend myself." This is relatively easy because the threat of punishment comes from the outside originally. *Reaction Formation* is another defense in which the reverse of what exists is expressed. In projection, you assign the unacceptable feelings you experience to others. In reaction formation, you reverse the feelings so that when you feel love toward someone you might express hate. The young adolescent may frequently clumsily conceal interest in an adolescent of the opposite sex by both negative comment and behavior. A person may prove to the world that he has no desire to drink by organizing an antialcohol league.

The concept of development discussed in Chapter 3 and in this chapter also appears in defenses. Two major types of defenses having to do with development and change are *fixation* and *regression*. Most of us recognize the risks that are involved in change. Though the present arrangement may not be perfect, many of you have experienced doubt about the future. Many would prefer the safety of the present or the past to the risks of the future. Fixation has to do with satisfaction with things as they are. A freezing of the present situation, though intolerable in some ways, is preferable to change to an unknown. Some of our political figures have been accused of fixation; others of regression. The idea behind regression is turning back the clock to the good old days. An adult who turns backward to childlike dependency may go to the extreme of playing the part of a two-year-old. A ten-year-old may resort to bed wetting or thumb-sucking behavior in an effort to regain the security of childhood. Usually, these people have been faced with situations involving advanced levels of adjustment that were anxiety producing. Avoidance of the entire situation may be had through a retreat. The extent of the retreat and its permanence are a measure both of the amount of the emotional shock and of the amount of satisfaction gained at the previous level of adjustment.

These are not all of the examples of defense mechanisms reported in the literature. They are representative of those proposed by Freud and contained in many theories of personality. The defenses may be seen as ways in which the individual is able to change the information about himself in relation to both the world of others and his own private world so that it will conform within tolerable limits to the behavior of which he thinks himself capable. In each of these defenses, there is an element of distortion, making possible the acceptance of the world as it is misperceived. The individual is not, however, aware of the distortion.

Learning Exercises

17. In the following examples, certain defense mechanisms will be illustrated. Choose from among the following, the mechanism you believe to be illustrated:

      sublimation   reaction formation   rationalization
      repression   projection   identification

    A girl has recently become engaged. She is separated from her fiancé by the summer vacation. During that period, she has a completely innocent date with a young man. She suffers considerable guilt over this. Some of her feelings were:
    (a) When she returned home from the date, she frequently suspected her fiancé of being unfaithful to her.
    (b) Later, when a friend spoke about people, who are engaged, dating, our girl defended a person's having a date while engaged on the grounds that this was a final test used by mature people. "After all, marriage is for a long period of time."
    (c) Her fiancé later asks her about dates she had during the summer. She said she hadn't been out. He knew a person who saw her with the boy that summer, but she was not able to recall going out at all.
18. Explain what the ego-defense mechanisms are guarding against.
19. The infant is not born with a complete system of defense mechanisms or, in all probability, an ego. Name two ways in which defense mechanism development could be explained.

20. What purpose or purposes do the ego-defenses serve?
21. What are the four general systems suggested in this chapter that may be conveniently used to explain conflict?
22. What is used in psychological theory to account for the central core or essence of a personality?

THE TEACHER'S ROLE IN ADJUSTMENT IN THE CLASSROOM

It has become increasingly apparent to professional psychologists that our society will never be able to train or support the number of competent persons necessary to handle mental illness of the numerical magnitude it presently produces. A study by Leighton (1955) indicates that 37 per cent of the population eighteen years old and over have symptoms of maladjustment sufficient to interfere with their everyday lives. Persons in all fields of psychology numbered 18,000 in 1960. Ogg (1955) indicates that only 38 per cent of these are in the clinical field. Based on a population of nearly 118,000,000 over eighteen years of age in the United States, the 44,000,000 persons (37 per cent) needing periodic help would demand the services of several hundred thousand therapists. Preventive psychological assistance appears to be the only practical solution at this time.

Many psychologists for this reason look to you teachers for assistance. Your specific training and responsibilities lie in the field of changing the behavior of children. You are charged with a great many responsibilities you may be loath to accept. However, you as a group are more likely than any other public employees to play a major role in the lives of most citizens of the United States. What assistance can a classroom teacher offer in the adjustment problems of youngsters?

There are some logical possibilities. (1) Those conflicts that exist between the individual and the environment can possibly be handled by you. It is possible for you to help a child either by manipulating some of the situations in the class or even in the home through parent conferences. It is also possible for you to help the child make limited reinterpretations of the school or home. Here it will be necessary for you to listen and watch to determine what he thinks the school or home is like. It is quite improbable you could guess the exact nature of the problem; and having done so, it would be of little value to you in changing his perceptions, though it could be of value in changing the actual environment. It would be most economical and most effective if you were to let the child have an opportunity to tell you his problems, then both perceptual and environmental manipulation would be more accurate. (2) Those conflicts within the child that he is able to express with mild encouragement may also be handled by you as teachers. You may recall these are frequently tied in with substantial anxiety; and when this is the case, you will not be sufficiently trained to handle the situation were you able to uncover the elements of which it is composed. Carl Rogers (1951) suggests a therapeutic approach that some psychologists feel teachers might use with discretion. It is not an aggressive form of therapy; and thus, with reasonable care, the patient seldom will get into a position where he will be unable to handle the anxiety that is aroused. This is not a suggestion that you as a teacher try to become a therapist, but the techniques employed in the Rogerian approach to therapy are sound advice to anyone interested in lending a friendly ear.

The areas in which you may be of assistance to a student, as described above, are in conflicts between the child and his environment, and conflicts between the child and his perception of the environment. You will, however, be of little help in dealing with internal conflict.

The typical approach of the teacher is explanatory or in a sense dictatorial. Teachers tend to tell people what the case is or is not. In therapy, this is a remarkably unsuccessful means of producing the desired change. At one time, hypnotism was used as a means of discovering the basis of a mental disturbance, and it was hoped this would be a quick way to resolving the problems. It was early discovered that this was only a means of diagnosis, that to tell the patient why he is troubled is useless, and that hypnosis has little general value to the patient. This appears to be the case today. Drugs and hypnosis are still used to unearth aspects of the problem, but telling the patient is of little value. You as a teacher might know exactly what is wrong with a student, but telling him what is wrong is not going to be any more successful for you than for professional therapists. Self-discovery through talking in a permissive atmosphere is still relied upon most heavily. Bills (1955) and Combs and Snygg (1959) relate methodologies that may be of help to you who are interested in becoming better informed about conflicts and their treatment. Manipulation of environmental variables is open to all, and often is successful when the source of an adjustment problem is primarily in the environment.

Learning Exercises

23. What are some of the ways in which the teacher is able to assist the student in his adjustment?
24. Why is "telling a person" an unsuccessful means of aiding adjustment?

25. Why is the training of professional therapists a doubtful means of reducing the number of adjustment problems in our culture?

RESEARCH IN PERSONALITY

There are many problems associated with attempting to conduct research in personality. In the S–O–R formulation, none of the three variables is determinable from the standpoint of the individual. The unobservable "O" part of the sequence is that which we are attempting to measure by controlling the "S" and observing the "R." But, while we can agree on the symbolic meaning of a particular stimulus, the complete personal meaning of a stimulus will differ from one individual to another. For instance, the word "horse" for you and for me is different because you, perhaps, have never ridden through the Rocky Mountains on horseback with only a horse as a friend. And even if you had our experiences on the same trail and on the same day, the experiences themselves would have had different meanings for us. Similarly, we may obtain an agreement between judges as to the symbolic meaning of a response, but the personal meaning of the response may vary from one judge to another. In short, one major difficulty in conducting research in personality is the fact that, in any experiences, the meanings of both the stimulus and the response are unique for an individual.

Another problem lies in the fact that the intervening processes (O) that occur between the stimulus and the responses are not available for direct observation. One cannot get "inside" the individual. Nor is it scientifically sound to interpret the responses to a specific stimulus as indicative of what goes on inside the brain. There is a certain amount of circularity in defining a process by means of changes in the stimulus-response sequence when we do not know either the meaning of the input or the output. In Chapter 12, it was noted that in the study of mediating thought processes, a similarity was found between the operations of large scale computers and the "thinking aloud" processes of college students. Possibly, processes of interest to personality theorists may be studied in a similar manner. Tompkins and Messick (1963) report that it is possible to program emotional responses in the computer. At the present time, however, research on personality is hampered by the fact that intervening mediating processes cannot be observed.

Research in personality, which stems from a therapeutically initiated theory, often takes a form similar to that of the anecdotal method.

The therapist records, with varying regularity, those events that appear significant in the therapeutic sessions. This has been criticized on the grounds of subjectivity. However, the therapist-theorist has quite legitimately countered with the argument that the more rigorous scientific methodologies of the physical sciences are fractional and when sufficient controls are maintained the results are not meaningful. This he states is because not all of the factors contributing to behavior are permitted to operate. In fact, the organism *as a whole* has not been honored, and the methodology of the physical scientists is inapplicable.

Another approach is to analyze the personality by counting frequency of a particular type of response. The individual is then described as primarily introverted, aggressive, submissive, etc. This may be done through information gained in therapy and other forms of observation or through tests in which the stimulus is controlled, as in the Thematic Apperception Test, or tests in which the stimulus is indeterminant, as in the Rorschach. The individual is asked to respond to the stimulus. These responses are assumed to be characteristic of the way he perceives the world. The affective clues gained from responses to both tests are also used to evaluate the importance of particular responses to the individual.

Still another means of validating a particular theory is through measurements of adjustment prior to and following the therapeutic session. In these, quite legitimately, the therapist feels able to assert that since the theory used in treating the patient resulted in improvement in his adjustment, then the theory is valid or at least useful. This of course may be questioned on the grounds that the treatment variables are only postulated to be associated with the activities engaged in during therapy. The rigorous scientists are more ready to apply their rules to results of research in personality theory but are less able to adapt their systems to research in which the total organism, with all of the postulated complex variables involved, is studied. Advances in the field of statistics and multivariate design plus computer technology necessary to handle such designs may make such research feasible in the future. The question again arises as to whether the responses and stimuli may be objectively evaluated. The researcher in the personality field must still make what amounts to value judgments about the meaning of the responses. Operational definitions that are often given to such things as anxiety responses and aggressive responses are not universally acceptable.

Research in this field is more frequently confined to the case study method or to examination of operational definitions, constructs, or functions, using methods that vary in scientific rigor.

NEW PROBLEMS FOR PERSONOLOGISTS

Discoveries in and out of the field of psychology are contributing information that is not readily integrated into many of the theories that now exist. One of the tests suggested for an adequate theory is its flexibility and capacity to explain information about that with which it is concerned. A few of the more recent findings that have not been dealt with by many of the theorists and may result in new directional changes are briefly mentioned in the following section.

Experiments in *stimulus deprivation* suggest the need of the organism for incoming information. When subjects are isolated from all forms of stimulation, they begin to hallucinate and manufacture their own stimuli. Experiments with human subjects indicate the necessity of an extension of the homeostatic concept to include stimulus seeking as well as stimulus reduction. The brain tissue may maintain a minimal level of activity and, failing to receive it from the external environment, may be auto-stimulated.

Some recent developments in the field of *computer simulation* of the brain suggest that the information processing and problem-solving abilities of the human are efficient at the sacrifice of absolute accuracy. Rather than checking every bit of information available, the brain may operate on a probabilistic basis. Teaching that requires absolute accuracy of responses may be inconsistent with the efficient operation of the brain. A probabilistic approach may better be substituted in which the individual responds with the first answer that occurs to him and then is given the opportunity to check it rather than having to respond accurately each time on the first try. At least, variation in method may be tolerated.

Newell, Shaw, and Simon (1962) tend to suggest that we are not far from producing machines that can think similarly to man. A machine can be programmed to play chess extremely efficiently. Wooldridge (1963) suggests that some of the cumbersome and inefficient characteristics of machines to date will be overcome when the scientist is able to produce neural protoplasm capable of the same programming characteristic as our own neural tissue. Major breakthroughs in the field of molecular biology suggest that this is not a remote dream. Breakthroughs in neurology and molecular biology also suggest the possibility that the nervous system of infrahumans are more, rather than less, similar in function to the human brain. Studies in chemotherapy and electrical stimulation of the brain suggest also that much more of our behavior is involuntary than was previously thought probable.

Further, studies of the changes in RNA production under conditions of learning suggest not only that chemical changes take place, but that it may be possible to transfer propensities to learn through chemical technologies.

Where does all of this leave us in the field of personality? This may mean that rather than to continue to justify the previously stated theories as we may have tended to do, it may be possible that a recasting will be done. This might take the form of an ecletic theory as is typified by Gardiner Murphy's biosocial theory (1947), or a new approach may be developed. Irrespective of the efficiency of one approach or the other, new discoveries will continue to require changes in existing theories, with the enunciation by theorists continuing to lag considerably behind the new developments.

SUMMARY

In this chapter, you had an opportunity to take a look at some of the more popular current views on personality theory. You also had an opportunity to realize that if you state some opinion about the relative merits of theories such as democracy, Christianity, redheads, or pansexualism, you might legitimately be asked to state your theory about these theories. Some people feel that the beliefs you have about religion, politics, women, and sex imply a theory or at least a number of assumptions that might be questionable or might lead to some other beliefs. Following the material on theory evaluation, you read about some of the major variables or dimensions with which personality theorists deal. The matter of whether man has purpose, whether the concept of self is necessary to understand personality, some of the more popular terms used in describing the various aspects of personality, the role of the unconscious material in behavior—all were discussed. That material was presented so that you could see the areas in which disagreement exists as well as to perhaps see some of your own and alternative points of view represented.

In the next major section, adjustment and conflicts were covered. The initial material set the stage by giving you a basis for seeing where conflict could arise. In this section, some of the major theories concerning conflict were presented. This gave you an opportunity not only to read about conflict, but permitted you to apply some of the principles covered in the earlier sections of this chapter and book. After using some of the theoretical positions to explain the concept of conflict, you then read about the resolution of conflict. The concept of adjustment was introduced, and it was followed immediately by material dealing with the major defense mechanisms we use in handling adjustment. These were a representative list, not a complete one. You will recall that distortion was common to all of the defenses; further, that some theorists feel the major elements present in ego defenses are denial and some form of identification or internalization of a feared object. No effort was made to relate defenses to information theory. It is possible to cast ego defenses in an information theory setting and perhaps make more economical use of them. This might be something for you to try on your own.

The concept of development in a personality setting was treated extremely briefly, not because it is unimportant, but because the material in Chapter 3 illustrated quite effectively the influences of time, physiology, neural anatomy, and the possible fruitfulnesss of this developmental approach. Personality, too, develops if the individual is viewed *as* a personality rather than as *having* a personality. In this sense, the previously introduced material is adequate.

Other matters covered in this chapter were your role as a teacher in pupil adjustment. In this connection, some of the reasons for asking that teachers be considerably trained in the field of psychology were covered. Particularly discussed were the widespread existence of mental disorders requiring early attention, the effect of mental health on learning characteristics of children judged to be retarded readers, and the lack of ability of our society to supply an adequate number of trained persons devoted solely to the field of psychotherapeutics. You also read about the role of research in personality theory and some of the problems that psychologists are having in dealing with theory-building and hypothesis-confirmation. The directions in which studies are presently directed and some of the possible problems not as yet met were also discussed.

This has been a rather brief study of personality and is therefore punctuated with reference material. It would be necessary to take a rather long look at some of these books and articles in order to become well informed. However, the experience might be gratifying and professionally advisable.

Answer Cues

1. (a) Since judgments as to the truth or falsity of a theory are not applicable according to one widely accepted theory of theory evaluation, right and wrong are not applicable either if you accept the metatheory proposed above. Freud is acceptable or unacceptable to many theorists upon other bases mentioned in this chapter. (b) Generally speaking, theories are more acceptable if they are applicable to a wide variety of situation that they are used to describe. A theory that applies only to one person would not usually

be acceptable. (c) Assumptions are not always stated. Some are tacit and others implicit; some, on the other hand, are explicit. "Arsenic is harmful to a person" contains an assumption that is unstated—that the individual wants to live. Arsenic is beneficial to the suicidal individual.

2. Dynamic implies change, and further, change that is causally related to preceding events. Non-dynamic would imply unchanging. The element of change and the factor of relatedness are both implied. A person may not be expected to be the same from day to day and the changes are partly from within.

3. "Mind" is a term that has persisted in theories about man and is firmly rooted in our culture. To exclude mind and subsume all of man's activity under physical function would do great violence to our beliefs. There is no scientific evidence of a "mind"; we only speculate that a mind exists, apparently.

4. Man might be termed reactive rather than active were this term not included. There appears reasonable evidence from stimulus deprivation experiments to suggest we are actively seeking to maintain a level of excitation, and we might either reduce stimulation if it is too great or increase if it is too small. Thus, there is some evidence for an outreaching of the situation in which we find ourselves. We are actively participating in living, not merely responding.

5. (a) Agreement must first be reached that each of your beliefs represents a theoretical position. It is necessary that each of you be able to accept the possibility of changing your own position. (b) Assuming your belief and that of your friend are mutually exclusive, then perhaps you can agree on a basis for evaluation. You would have to then apply these evaluative criteria. If you did not accept the outcome, you could both agree to examine, based on another theory (in this case one that deals with theories of theory evaluation), the evaluative criteria, and so on—metatheory, to metametatheory, to meta-metametatheory. (c) The evidence that some persons' beliefs remain intact despite evidence to the contrary might influence this situation. The possibility exists that an "open" or "closed" dimension could be introduced. There are other applications.

6. Doctrine of Acquired Characteristics.

7. Role of rewards and punishments.

8. Purposivism.

9. (a) Approach-avoidance. (b) Both approach and avoidance tendencies will increase, but avoidance tendencies will increase more than the approach tendencies. Happily, as Kimble and Garmezy (1963) point out, very few brides or grooms are left at the altar. The strength of the avoidance tendencies does not quite catch up to that of the approach tendencies. And parents and society conspire to insure that the engaged couple are firmly committed to the marriage plans.

10. In some frames of reference, conflict is necessary prior to the adjustment phase.

11. Some conflicts are between the world and the organism. In these, perhaps the total resources of the individual are pitted against the world, i.e., attack by a hostile animal. However, when formulating internal conflict

or ambivalence, there is a strong tendency to resort to partitioning. Since there is little evidence to support the position that we *have* a personality, it is necessary in whatever theoretical approach used to guard against physical concepts, but partitioning in the sense of systems of information in conflict appears rational.

12. First of all, it is highly improbable that conflict could be completely eliminated. Strong conflict, pressures that are extreme, are highly undesirable. They may be detected through sudden changes in behavior, though some of these changes may indicate the resolution of conflict. While in conflict, the organism appears less organized though some increase in direction less behavior may be seen, accompanied by increased anxiety and irritability. Efforts to shield a child from conflict usually result in an unrealistic perception of the world. Frequently, the "spoiled child" is characterized as one whose conflicts with the world have been handled by others. It may be that our so-called conflicts with the world are the basis for the solving of problems that are characterized later as inner conflicts.

13. (e).

14. The type of reading material will be a partial determinant of the age at which a child can master reading. When the experimenter states that readiness to read develops at six and a half years of age, generally the mode of presentation and material used are important limiting factors. One effective scientist has suggested that he can teach anything to anyone at any age. While this may be an overstatement, we have evidence to suggest that teaching complex geometrical concepts can take place at the age of two or three years of age.

15. The ego deals primarily with reality, the id with the biological needs of the organism, and the superego represents the social demands.

16. A major role conflict will tend to be more frequently encountered and is more central to the individual's self perception as reflected in his treatment by others.

17. (a) Projection. (b) Rationalization. (c) Repression.

18. It is believed that the ego-defense mechanisms are defenses against excessive anxiety that as being aroused by an unacceptable impulse.

19. There are several possible answers. One could postulate that the mechanisms are genetically determined in the sense that the organism is capable of certain thought processes, and these lead naturally to a limited system of possible distortions. It is possible to account for them as the result of copying the significant adults living in the child's world. A variation of the genetic determination might be a biological explanation of the order and timing of development of the mechanisms. The ego is postulated to be a function of age and experience. Ego-defenses may be a function of the system in the sense that an information processing system of the type we have may have means of maintaining stability through feedback control. Most studies to date have indicated some form of progressive change, though timing and sequence are violated in individual cases.

20. One was mentioned in the previous section. The individual, in order to maintain a tolerable level of anxiety, distorts the information in such a way as to permit interpretations consistent with the existing systems of informa-

tion. The defenses are also said to be ego-enhancing in use. This implies an advancement of some scheme or maintenance of continuity or advancement of a goal. The mechanisms are for minimizing anxiety and for enhancing the organism.

21. The structural approach, the role theory approach, information theory explanations, and topological approach. Each of the theories are able to account for conflict; however, these four are representative and are helpful in gaining an understanding. Adjustment and conflict are intimately related.

22. The concept of a self or an ego are helpful in suggesting a central core or theme continuity.

23. The manipulation of situations so that the child is able to adjust on a realistic level is one effective means. Helping the child to see the nature of his perceptions of the environment is another; this is done primarily though helping the child discover the nature of the conflict he is experiencing.

24. The knowledge of the conflict and the area in which adjustment is needed is historically established to be of little value. These may not be cognitive problems, and thus trying to use logic is not successful. The discovery of the problem on the part of the student is sometimes successful. This may also be a difficult role for the teacher to play.

25. This appears to be the case because we are not able to train the numbers necessary. It would require several million professional therapists. The teacher is one of the few public employees who is in a position to deal with some of the problems and may frequently be more successful in teaching in a role as a therapist than in that of a teacher (Bills, 1955).

Appendix

STATISTICAL CONCEPTS

Statistical concepts are becoming almost necessary tools for the modern teacher in order to think efficiently about educational problems, to read the professional literature, and to intepret test results and other quantitative data. The statistical concepts that we will present can be mastered by a student if he understands arithmetic processes taught in the elementary school. For the most part, to be able to add, subtract, multiply, and divide is all that is needed to grasp and be able to work with the concepts presented. Remember two things: First, understanding the statistical concepts presented in this section is a part of becoming a competent teacher. Second, many students who have thought of themselves as "hopeless" in mathematics have surprised and delighted themselves by mastering the concepts thoroughly.

METHODS FOR DESCRIBING DATA

Suppose that a teacher has administered a test in arithmetic to 25 children in grade 6 and obtained the following scores: 20, 18, 21, 19, 20, 24, 20, 22, 15, 19, 22, 17, 25, 20, 23, 13, 18, 26, 20, 17, 23, 21, 16, 19, 22. A clearer idea of the performance of any one pupil may be obtained by arranging the scores in a more organized fashion. Ordinarily, the teacher would tabulate the scores into what is called a *frequency distribution*.

Frequency Distribution

In making a frequency distribution, scores customarily are arranged in descending order. A tally is made for each score, and then the frequencies of the tallies are totalled. For the above series of scores the frequency distribution might be arranged as shown in Table A–1.

TABLE A–1

Frequency Distribution of 25 Sixth-Grade Pupils on Arithmetic Test

(ungrouped data)

Scores	Tallies	Frequency
26	1	1
25	1	1
24	1	1
23	11	2
22	111	3
21	11	2
20	↿↿↿↿	5
19	111	3
18	11	2
17	11	2
16	1	1
15	1	1
14		0
13	1	1
		N = 25

The frequency distribution in Table A–1 permits one to see at a glance the range in scores and to get a rough idea of average performance. With a larger number and greater range of scores, the teacher might wish to group the scores into score intervals. Tallies might be made for scores in the 13–14, 15–16, 17–18, etc., intervals. See Table A–2.

TABLE A–2

Frequency Distribution of Arithmetic Scores

(grouped data)

Score Interval	Tallies	Frequency
25–26	11	2
23–24	111	3
21–22	↿↿↿↿	5
19–20	↿↿↿↿ 111	8
17–18	1111	4
15–16	11	2
13–14	1	1
		N = 25

Broader intervals might be used when the range of scores is great. Usually, a class interval is chosen that will divide the total score range into about 15 groups. Thus, if scores ranged from a low of 20 to a high of 65, an interval of three (such as 64–66, 61–63, etc.) might be used. Ordinarily, with only 25 scores and with a small range in scores (13–26), we would not group the data as we have done in Table A–2.

Learning Exercises

1. From Table A–1, all but ten pupils obtained a score higher than ___.
2. How many pupils obtained scores of either 21 or 22?

Graphic Representations

It is sometimes helpful to make a graphic representation of a frequency distribution. One type of graphic representation is called a frequency polygon. Figure A–1 shows a frequency polygon of the scores obtained by the sixth-grade pupils. Scores are shown on the horizontal x-axis; the frequency of each score is shown on the vertical y-axis.

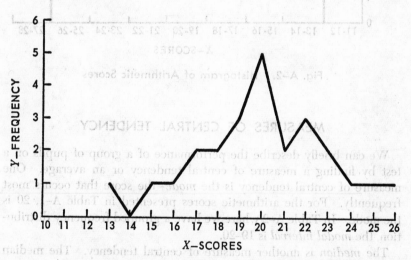

Fig. A–1. Frequency Polygon of Arithmetic Scores

Another type of graphic representation is called a *histogram*. Figure A–2 portrays the sixth-grade arithmetic scores. Frequencies for each score interval are shown by a piling up of small right angles.

Learning Exercises

3. How many pupils obtained a score of 22?
4. How many pupils obtained scores of either 19 or 20?

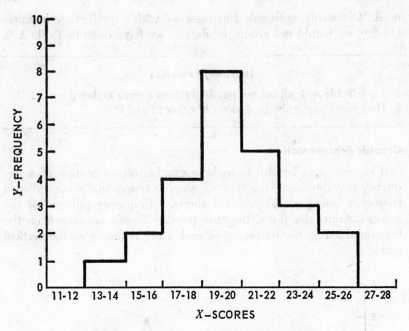

Fig. A–2.   Histogram of Arithmetic Scores

MEASURES OF CENTRAL TENDENCY

We can briefly describe the performance of a group of pupils on a test by finding a measure of central tendency or an average. One measure of central tendency is the *mode*—the score that occurs most frequently. For the arithmetic scores presented in Table A–1, 20 is the mode. In Table A–2 where we have a grouped frequency distribution, the *modal interval* is 19–20.

The *median* is another measure of central tendency. The median is the mid-point in a distribution. There are just as many scores above the median as below the median. For this series of five scores, 5, 6, 7, 8, and 9, the median is 7. For this set of four scores, 2, 3, 4, and 5, the median is 3½. When there is an even number of scores, the median is midway between the *two* middle scores.

The *mean* is a third and most frequently used measure of central tendency. The mean is what many people call the average. We obtain a mean by adding up a group of scores and dividing by the number of scores. Thus, for the series 2, 4, 7, 8, 9, the mean is $30 \div 5 = 6$. The symbol $\overline{X}$ is sometimes used to denote a mean. We can represent this simple process of obtaining a mean by a formula:

$$\text{Mean or } \bar{X} = \Sigma \frac{X}{N},$$

where Σ stands for *the summation of*
    X stands for each score
    N stands for the number of scores

Learning Exercise

5. For the following series of scores, find the mode, median, and mean.
    (a) 9, 9, 9, 8, 8, 7, 6, 5, 2.
    (b) 9, 8, 7, 5, 1.
    (c) 9, 8, 6, 5, 4, 3, 2, 2, 2, 1.
    (d) If 2 were added to each score in 5a, 5b, and 5c, how would this affect
        the means, medians, and modes?

PARTITION VALUES

We can give some notion of where a score lies in a frequency distribution by partitioning the distribution into groups of fourths, tenths, or
hundredths, and then indicating in which group a particular score lies.

Quartiles

Quartiles divide a frequency disrtibution into four quarters. For the
following eight scores:

$$
\begin{array}{c}
9 \\
8 \quad\quad Q_3 = 7.5 \\
\overline{7} \\
6 \quad\quad Q_2 = 5.5 \\
\overline{5} \\
4 \quad\quad Q_1 = 3.5 \\
\overline{3} \\
2
\end{array}
$$

a score of 9 or 8 is in the fourth quarter; a score of 7 or 6 is in the third
quarter, etc. Note that the value Q_2 is the same as the median. The
value Q_4 is not ordinarily computed as all scores would be below this
value. Note that we use the term "quarter" to designate a *group* of

scores and the term "quartile" to designate a *point* within a distribution.

Deciles

Deciles divide a frequency distribution into tenths. A value D_9 would be such as to divide the top tenth of the distribution from the remainder of the distribution. A value of D_5 would be at the median.

Percentiles

Percentiles divide a frequency distribution into hundredths. Thus, P_{40} or the 40th percentile (40 %-ile) would be a score that would exceed 40 per cent of the scores in a distribution. The 50 %-ile would correspond to the median.

Learning Exercises

6. (a) Bill Smith obtains a score on a test that is equivalent to P_{60} (for the normative population upon which the test was standardized). What percentage of the normative population does Bill's score exceed?
   (b) P_{10} means what?
   (c) To what percentile would the median be equivalent?
7. (a) A student scoring in the second quarter has a score between what percentiles?
   (b) Q_3 is equal to what percentile?
   (c) D_2 is equal to what percentile?

DISPERSION OF SCORES

A second type of information concerning a series of scores is how much the scores spread out from high to low. Two sets of scores may have the same mean or median and yet differ considerably in their variability.

Range

The *range* is one measure of variability or dispersion of scores. For the arithmetic scores reported in Table A–1, the lowest score is 13 and the highest score is 26. The range is $26 - 13 = 13$. Another class taking this same test might perform, on the average, the same as our sixth-grade class (Mean = 20) and yet have quite a different range. The lowest score may be 2 and the highest score 30. Thus, the range for this second class would be $30 - 2 = 28$.

The range is not a very satisfactory measure of the variability of a set of scores because it depends only upon the two extreme cases in the total group. Hence, the addition or omission of one extreme case can result in a sizable change in the range.

Semi-Interquartile Range

Semi-interquartile range is one-half the quantity obtained by subtracting Q_1 from Q_3. Thus, for the four scores 2, 4, 10, 12, the semi-interquartile range is $\dfrac{11-3}{2} = 4$. The scores between 3 and 11 make up 50 per cent of the four scores. For a longer series of test scores, we first count off 25 per cent of the scores from the low end of the scale. The mid-point between this score and the next highest score is called Q_1. Next, we count off 75 per cent of the scores from the low end of the distribution. Again, the mid-point between this score and the next highest score is called Q_3. Thus, a formula for finding the semi-interquartile range (Q) is:

$$Q = \frac{Q_3 - Q_1}{2}$$

The semi-interquartile range is usually used as the measure of variability when the median is the measure of central tendency.

Average Deviation

The *average deviation* (AD) is obtained by (1) subtracting the mean from each score in a series, (2) summing these deviations from the mean, and (3) dividing by the number of scores in the series. In the following example, the average deviation is computed for ten scores.

Score (X)	Deviation from Mean (x)
13	+4
11	+2
10	+1
10	+1
9	0
9	0
8	−1
7	−2
7	−2
6	−3
Total (ΣX) = 90	$\Sigma x = 16$

Mean $(\bar{X}) = 9$ 　　　　　 A.D. $= \dfrac{\Sigma x}{N} = \dfrac{16}{10} = 1.6$

Note that in finding the deviation from the mean for each score, plus and minus signs are disregarded. The average deviation tells us by how much, on the average, each score deviates from the mean. In the above example, the average deviation from the mean of the ten scores is 1.6.

Standard Deviation (σ)

The *standard deviation* (often denoted as S.D., or sigma, or s) is the most frequently used measure of variability. The standard deviation is computed by summing the squared difference of the mean from each score, dividing by the number of scores, and extracting the square root:

$$\text{S.D. or } \sigma = \sqrt{\frac{\Sigma x^2}{N}} = \sqrt{\frac{\Sigma(X-M)^2}{N}}$$

Following is an example of a procedure for finding the standard deviation from ungrouped data.

Score (X)	Deviation (x)	x^2
13	4	16
11	2	4
10	1	1
10	1	1
9	0	0
9	0	0
8	−1	1
7	−2	4
7	−2	4
6	−3	9
$\Sigma X = 90$		$x^2 = 40$

$$\bar{X} = 9 \qquad \text{S.D.} = \sigma = \sqrt{\frac{\Sigma x^2}{N}} = \sqrt{\frac{40}{10}} = \sqrt{4} = 2$$

The process of computing a standard deviation becomes somewhat more difficult with longer series of numbers and with grouped data. For our purposes, the above example will do as an aid in gleaning the meaning of a standard deviation. In order to see one important meaning of a standard deviation, we will need to discuss one type of distribution of scores known as the *normal* distribution.

Learning Exercises

8. (a) The range for a series of 30 test scores is 20. The lowest score is 11. What is the highest score?

    (b) The highest score a student obtained on a test was 80; the lowest score was 20. What is the range?

   (c) Is the range a measure of central tendency? If not, of what is the range a measure?

9. The manual for the Iowa Tests of Basic Skills lists the following mid-year norms for grade 3 on the Arithmetic Skills:

%-ile	Arithmetic Skills Score
90	38.7
75	36.7
50	34.7
25	32.4
10	30.4

Miss Smith administered the Arithmetic Skills test to the 28 pupils in her third-grade class at about mid-year. The scores of Miss Smith's class were: 43, 41, 40, 40, 39, 39, 38, 38, 37, 37, 37, 37, 35, 35, 34, 33, 32, 32, 31, 30, 30, 30, 29, 28, 28, 28, 27, 26. Comment on each of the following observations made by Miss Smith about the performance of her class. Explain in each case why you believe the observation is accurate or inaccurate.

   (a) MISS SMITH: "The average performance for my class is about the same as the average for the normative sample of boys and girls."

   (b) Miss Smith: "The semi-interquartile range for my class is about the same as that of the normative sample of third-grade pupils."

10. To find the average deviation you must compute the _____ and then subtract the _____ from each score (ignoring any minus signs).

11. Find the average deviation of each of the following sets of scores:
   (a) 4, 6, 8, 10
   (b) 6, 8, 8, 10
   (c) 5, 10, 15, 15, 30

12. Find the standard deviation for the following sets of scores:
   (a) 1, 2, 3, 5, 6, 7, 8, 9, 9, 10
   (b) 3, 4, 5, 7, 8, 9, 10, 11, 11, 12 (note that to get the (b) series of scores, 2 has been added to each of the scores in the (a) series)
   (c) 1, 3, 3, 5, 7, 7, 9, 9, 11, 15
   (d) 1, 2, 4, 5, 7, 7, 11, 12, 15, 16

THE NORMAL DISTRIBUTION

The normal distribution curve is bell shaped, with many cases piling up at the middle values and fewer and fewer cases occurring as we approach either extremes of the distribution. In a normal distribution, the mean, the median, and the mode will be identical. Many human characteristics are normally distributed. For example, a frequency distribution of the heights of twenty-year-old men would reveal many young men a few inches shorter than 6 feet but relatively few who were either 5 or 7 feet tall. Similarly, for many psychological tests, we find many scores that are average and relatively few that are extremely high or extremely low scores.

Figure A–3 represents a hypothetical ideal distribution of intelligence test scores. An actual distribution of intelligence test scores might look very much like this, but not quite so symmetrical.

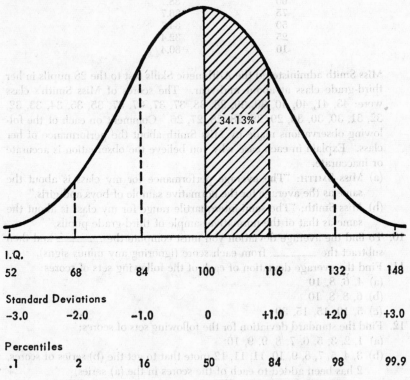

34.13%

I.Q.						
52	68	84	100	116	132	148

Standard Deviations

| –3.0 | –2.0 | –1.0 | 0 | +1.0 | +2.0 | +3.0 |

Percentiles

| .1 | 2 | 16 | 50 | 84 | 98 | 99.9 |

Fig. A–3.   An Idealized Distribution of I.Q. Scores

On the horizontal axis of Fig. A–3, three sets of scores are entered:
1. *I.Q. Scores.* Note that the mean of the distribution is 100 and that the greatest frequency (the highest point of the curve) is at 100. The standard deviation for this distribution is 16. Hence, an I.Q. score of 116 is one standard deviation above the mean; an I.Q. score of 132 is 2 standard deviations above the mean; and an I.Q. score of 148 is 3 standard deviations above the mean. Also, an I.Q. score of 84 (i.e., 100 minus 16) is one standard deviation below the mean; an I.Q. score of 68 is 2 standard deviations below the mean; and an I.Q. score of 52 is 3 standard deviations below the mean.
2. *Standard Deviation Scores.* We could express each score as a

standard deviation score. We shall see later that such scores are called *z-scores*. Thus, instead of saying that a person has an I.Q. of 132, we might say that he obtained a score that is 2 standard deviations above the mean.

3. *Percentile Scores.* In a normal distribution, the area of the curve between the mean and one standard deviation from the mean (the shaded area in Fig. A–3) always includes 34.13 per cent of the total area under the normal curve. This area is equivalent to the proportion of cases in the distribution. Thus, 34.13 per cent of the cases obtain scores between 100 and 116. As 50 per cent of the cases are below a score of 100, then 50 + 34.13 or 84.13 per cent (approximately 84 per cent) of the cases score 116 or below.

The standard deviation is a particularly meaningful statistic because of the exact mathematical relationship between the standard deviation and the proportion of cases falling below any standard deviation value for a normal distribution. In Fig. A–3, the approximate percentile score equivalent for certain standard score value is indicated. The relationships between various score values and percentile scores are shown in Table A–3.

TABLE A–3
Percentile Scores for Standard Deviation
Values for Normal Curve

Standard Deviation Value	Percentile Score	Standard Deviation Value	Percentile Score
3.0	99.9	−3.0	0.1
2.9	99.8	−2.9	0.2
2.8	99.7	−2.8	0.3
2.7	99.6	−2.7	0.4
2.6	99.5	−2.6	0.5
2.5	99.4	−2.5	0.6
2.4	99.2	−2.4	0.8
2.3	99	−2.3	1
2.2	99	−2.2	1
2.1	98	−2.1	2
2.0	98	−2.0	2
1.9	97	−1.9	3
1.8	96	−1.8	4
1.7	96	−1.7	4
1.6	95	−1.6	5
1.5	93	−1.5	7
1.4	92	−1.4	8
1.3	90	−1.3	10
1.2	88	−1.2	12
1.1	86	−1.1	14

TABLE A–3 (Cont.)

Standard Deviation Value	Percentile Score	Standard Deviation Value	Percentile Score
1.0	84	−1.0	16
0.9	82	−0.9	18
0.8	79	−0.8	21
0.7	76	−0.7	24
0.6	73	−0.6	27
0.5	69	−0.5	31
0.4	66	−0.4	34
0.3	62	−0.3	38
0.2	58	−0.2	42
0.1	54	−0.1	46
0.0	50	−0.0	50

Learning Exercises

13. What percentile corresponds to:
    (a) A score of 2 S.D. above the mean?
    (b) A score of 2 S.D. below the mean?
    (c) A score of 1.5 S.D. above the mean?
    (d) A score of 1.5 S.D. below the mean?
14. In a normal distribution, what is the relation between the:
    (a) Mean and the 50%-ile?
    (b) Mean and the median?
15. On a history test, the mean is 70 and the S.D. is 12. Assuming that the test scores are normally distributed, find the S.D. value and the corresponding percentile for each of the following history test scores:
    (a) 82
    (b) 58
    (c) 88
    (d) 52
16. For the history test mentioned in question 15, Albert obtained a score at the mean and Ada obtained a score one S.D. above the mean.
    (a) What scores did Albert and Ada obtain?
    (b) What are the percentile equivalents for the scores obtained by Albert and Ada?
17. For the history test mentioned in question 15, Bob obtained a score two S.D.'s above the mean and Betty obtained a score three S.D.'s above the mean.
    (a) What scores did Bob and Betty obtain?
    (b) What are the percentile equivalents for the scores obtained by Bob and Betty?

TYPES OF SCORES

Raw Scores

Most tests yield numerical scores on a person's performance. This score may be the number of questions answered correctly, the number of seconds taken to run 100 yards, or some similar measure. Such scores are termed "raw scores."

A raw score does not tell us much. Suppose John obtains a score of 75 on an arithmetic test and 60 on a history test, does this mean that John did better in arithmetic than in history? Not at all. John's score in arithmetic may have been one of the lowest in his class, and his score in history might have been one of the highest. A raw score can be interpreted only by comparing it to some standard.

Percentages

Percentage scores do not yield much more information than raw scores. A pupil may score zero on an arithmetic test and still know some arithmetic. Unlike physical measures, psychological measures do not have an absolute zero. Nor are the units of measurements equal. Hence, a pupil who obtains 80 per cent on an arithmetic test does not know twice as much arithmetic as a pupil who obtains 40 per cent on the test. Percentage scores taken by themselves yield no absolute information. To obtain 75 per cent on one test may be a poor performance, while on another test it may be a very creditable performance.

Grade and Age Scores

Most manuals of standardized tests include *norms* in the form of tables that show the performance of the standardization group. A table presenting *age norms* shows the average performance of children of different ages. *Grade norms* show the average performance of children of different grades. For example, the manual for the California Achievement Tests, Elementary Level (1963) presents various types of norms. Table A–4 illustrates the kind of information found in one table in the California Test.

Learning Exercise

18. Following are the reading, arithmetic, and language scores of three fifth-grade pupils on the California test. Find the grade equivalent and chronological age equivalent for each score.

	Reading	Arithmetic	Language
Art	46	62	40
Beth	100	47	106
Cora	76	54	89

Grade and age norms do provide familiar standards that may be used in assessing a pupil's test performance. However, grade and age norms do have some limitations. First, a year's growth is not a uniform unit, and the growth of one grade is not the same amount of growth at all grade levels. A year's growth for the later age levels is usually smaller than for the earlier age levels. Grade norms may be particularly deceptive because for many of the school subjects educational gains will depend upon the content and emphasis in school instruction.

Grade and age norms may easily be misinterpreted. A bright sixth-grade pupil who obtains a grade placement score of 11.5 on a standardized arithmetic achievement test is not ready to do eleventh-grade mathematics. He has performed as well on the test as the average eleventh-grade pupil. However, it is unlikely that the test administered adequately samples the mathematics taught from grades 6 to 11. Assuming that the test covers work in arithmetic taught in the first six grades, a grade placement score of 11.5 may best be interpreted as evidence that the pupil has learned well the work covered in arithmetic from grades 1 to 6.

Percentiles

A percentile score is a score representing the percentage of individuals in a given sample who fall below a given raw score. For example, if Mary scores at the 75 %-ile on a history test administered to 200 eighth-grade pupils, this means that Mary performed better than 75 per cent of the 200 eighth-grade pupils. The formula for computing the percentile at which a pupil scores is:

$$\text{Percentile} = \frac{\text{Number of pupils who scored below this pupil} \times 100}{\text{Total number of pupils}}$$

Percentile norms do provide a basis for comparing the performance of one pupil to others and can be easily explained to pupils and parents. A percentile rank is a useful interpretation of a test score providing it is based upon an appropriate norm group. The main deficiency of percentiles is that they represent unequal units of measurement. This is illustrated in Fig. A–4 representing a distribution of

TABLE A–4*

Grade Placement and Age Norms

	TEST			
Grade Placement	Reading	Arithmetic	Language	Age in Months
2.0	1–12	1	1–8	88
2.1	13–14	–	9–10	89–90
2.2	15	2	11–12	91
2.5	19	5	17–18	95
3.0	27	12–13	27–28	101
3.5	36–37	20–21	37–38	107
3.6	38–39	22–23	39–40	108
3.9	44–45	27	47–48	112
4.0	46–47	28–29	49–50	113
4.6	58–59	38–39	63–65	121
4.7	60–61	40–41	66–68	122
5.1	68–69	47	75–77	127
5.5	76–77	54	85–87	132
5.6	78	55–56	88–89	133
5.7	79–80	57–58	90–92	134
6.0	85	62–63	97–98	138
6.3	89–90	68–69	104–5	142
6.4	91	70–71	106–7	143
6.5	92–93	72–73	108–9	144
7.0	100	82	116–7	150
7.6	107	94–95	125	158
7.7	108–9	96–97	126	159
7.8	110	98–100	127	160
8.0	112	104–5	129	163
8.5	115	117–20	–	168
8.9	117	124	135	173
9.0	–	125	–	174

* Entries extracted from Table 21, *Manual California Achievement Tests, Elementary Level,* devised by E. W. Tiegs, and W. W. Clark (1963), p. 48.

test scores that has a mean of 50 and a standard deviation of 10. If John obtains 50 on this test and Henry 60, then John's percentile score is 50 and Henry's is 84—a difference of 34 percentile points. However, if Bill obtains 70 on the test, his percentile score is 98; and if Robert obtains 80, then his percentile score is 99.9—a difference of about 2

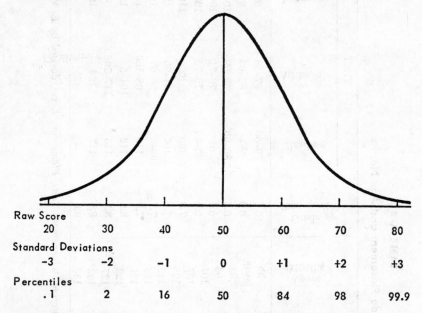

Raw Score						
20	30	40	50	60	70	80
Standard Deviations						
−3	−2	−1	0	+1	+2	+3
Percentiles						
.1	2	16	50	84	98	99.9

Fig. A–4. Normal Curve Showing Standard Deviations and Percentile Ranks

percentile points. Hence, a difference in two scores of 10 raw score points can mean a difference of 34 percentile points at one point on the scale and only 2 percentile points at another point on the scale. For normally distributed scores, small differences in raw score points at the middle of the distribution are reflected in large differences in percentiles, and large differences in raw score points at the extremes of the distribution are reflected in small differences in percentiles. Making use of Table A–3, you will note that a standard deviation value of .1 has a percentile score equivalent of 54, and a standard deviation value of −.1 has a percentile equivalent of 46. Thus, there would be 8 percentile points difference between −.1 and +.1. This would mean for the distribution represented in Fig. A–4 that 8 percentile points separate a score of 49 (SD score of −.1 = 46 %-ile) from a score of 51 (SD score of +.1 = 54 %-ile).

Learning Exercises

19. From Fig. A–4, find the standard deviation value equivalent to a raw score of (a) 50, (b) 70, (c) 20, (d) 45, (e) 65. (Note that 1 raw score point = .1 standard deviation.)
20. From Table A–3, find the percentile score equivalent for each of the scores listed in Exercise 19.

Standard Scores

Scores based upon standard deviation units are known as *standard scores*. A *z-score* is the simplest form of standard score. The z-score for any raw score in a series may be obtained by subtracting the mean of the series from the raw score and dividing by the standard deviation. The formula for finding a z-score is:

$$z = \frac{X - M}{\sigma}$$

For a series of test scores with a mean of 65 and a standard deviation of 5, the z-score equivalent for a raw score of 70 is:

$$z = \frac{70 - 65}{5} = \frac{5}{5} = 1$$

What we have been referring to as standard deviation scores in Figs. A–3 and A–4 and in Table A–3 are usually referred to as *z-scores*.

With z-scores we can readily compare the performances of one or more individuals on two or more tests. Suppose two tests have been given to a class. The means and standard deviations for the two classes are shown below, as are the scores made by two pupils in the class—Ava and Tom.

	Test 1	Test 2
Mean	60	45
Standard deviation	10	5
Ava's raw scores	70	50
Tom's raw scores	80	45

We can compare the performances of Ava and Tom on the two tests by transforming all scores into z-scores. Thus, Ava's score of 70 on Test 1 is 10 points above the mean and is equal to a z-score of +1.0 because the standard deviation of Test 1 is 10 ($z = \frac{70 - 60}{10} = 1$). Transforming the remaining raw scores into z-scores we have:

	Test 1	Test 2
Ava's z-scores	+1.0	+1.0
Tom's z-scores	+2.0	0

We see that Ava performed equally well on both tests, i.e., 1 standard deviation above the mean. Tom scored 2 standard deviations above the mean on one test, and just at the mean on the second test.

Assuming that the scores for the two tests are normally distributed, we can find the percentile equivalent for each score by referring to Table A–3. Thus:

	Test 1	Test 2
Ava's %-ile score	84	84
Tom's %-ile score	98	50

Learning Exercise

21. For Test 1 with a mean of 60 and a standard deviation of 10, find the z-score and percentile equivalent (assuming normal distribution) for each of the following raw scores: (a) 45, (b) 65, (c) 38.

Standard scores (z-scores) have some advantages over either raw scores or percentile scores. Differences in z-scores are proportional to differences in raw scores. This, as we have seen, does not hold true for percentile scores. A z-score yields information about a pupil's performance relative to other pupils in the normative group. Raw scores do not yield such information. Standard scores do have, however, two disadvantages. First, they are not so widely understood as are percentile scores. For this reason, percentile scores are retained in manuals for many tests. Second, the plus and minuses and the decimals are a little awkward. However, we can get rid of the decimal points by multiplying the standard deviation by some constant such as 10. And we can get rid of the minus signs by adding to each score a constant such as 50. Thus, Ava and Tom's z-score of 1.0 becomes $50 + 10 (1.0) = 60$. A standard score on a scale in which the standard deviation is *arbitrarily* set at 10 and the mean at 50 is known as a *T-score*.

Two useful formulas to understand are:

(1) $z\text{-score} = \dfrac{\text{raw score} - \text{mean}}{\text{standard deviation}}$

(2) $T\text{-score} = 50 + 10 \left(\dfrac{\text{raw score} - \text{mean}}{\text{standard deviation}} \right)$ or $T\text{-score} = 50 + 10z$

We can set the standard deviation and the mean at any quantities we wish. In Chapter 4, certain limitations of the ratio I.Q. are pointed out. More and more intelligence tests are supplanting the ratio I.Q. by what is termed the *deviation I.Q.* The deviation I.Q. is merely a standard score in which the mean is set at 100 and the standard deviation at 15 or 16. For example, on the latest edition of the Stanford-Binet Scale, the mean is set at 100 and the standard deviation at 16. A boy who obtained a score 1 standard deviation above the mean (z-score = 1.0) would have an I.Q. of 116.

Learning Exercises

22. Change each of the following z-scores to a scale that has a mean of 100 and a standard deviation of 16: (a) +1, (b) −1.0, (c) 0, (d) +2.5, (e) −3.

23. A test is administered to 50 students. The mean score on the test was found to be 40, and the standard deviation was computed to be 4. How many standard deviations *above* or *below* the means is each of the following scores?

(a) 44	(e) 46	(i) 41
(b) 36	(f) 34	(j) 49
(c) 48	(g) 42	(k) 40
(d) 32	(h) 38	(l) 30

24. Test 1 has a mean of 14 and a standard deviation of 3. Test 2 has a mean of 40 and a standard deviation of 4. Below are listed the scores obtained by five students on the two tests. For each student, tell whether the student did better on Test 1 than on Test 2; or better on Test 2 than Test 1; or equally well on both tests.

	Test 1	Test 2
Ada	20	32
Bob	17	48
Cindy	11	82
Don	17	44
Eva	14	40

25. Give the T-score equivalent for each of the following z-scores: (a) +2, (b) −2, (c) +1.5, (d) −1.3, (e) 0, (f) +2.7.

CORRELATION

Do college students who study the most tend to obtain the highest grades? Do students who score high on a test designed to measure rigidity also score high on a test designed to measure creativity? Each of these questions may be answered by obtaining measures on two variables—number of hours studied versus grades; rigidity test scores versus creativity test scores. It can be determined whether students who score high on one variable also score high on the second variable and whether students who score low on one variable also score low on the second variable. The relationship between two sets of test scores can be expressed mathematically by a *coefficient of correlation.* This correlation (designated as *r*) may vary from .00 to ±1.00. A plus correlation is known as a positive correlation; a minus correlation, as a negative correlation.

Product-Moment Correlation (r)

For purposes of illustration, let us consider the data of Table A–5, which consist of the scores of ten students on an arithmetic test and a science test. The arithmetic test score is denoted by X, and the science test score by Y.

TABLE A–5

Scores on Arithmetic and Science Tests

Student	Arithmetic (X)	Science (Y)
Ada	20	19
Bob	19	21
Charles	19	25
Dave	18	17
Edna	17	17
Frank	16	19
Gale	15	11
Helen	13	13
Ivy	12	15
John	11	13
	$\bar{X} = 16$	$\bar{Y} = 17$
	$\sigma x = 3$	$\sigma y = 4$
	$r = .75$	

You will notice there is a marked tendency for the student who scores high on arithmetic to score high on science and the student who scores low on arithmetic to score low on science. Note that Ada, who obtained the highest score on arithmetic (20) obtained one of the highest scores on science (19), while John, who scored lowest in arithmetic scored among the lowest in science. The scores on the two tests are in fairly close agreement. Actually, the correlation between the two sets of scores is .75. By graphing the data, as in Fig. A–5, we can see more clearly the degree of relationship between the two sets of scores. Such a graph is termed a "scatter diagram."

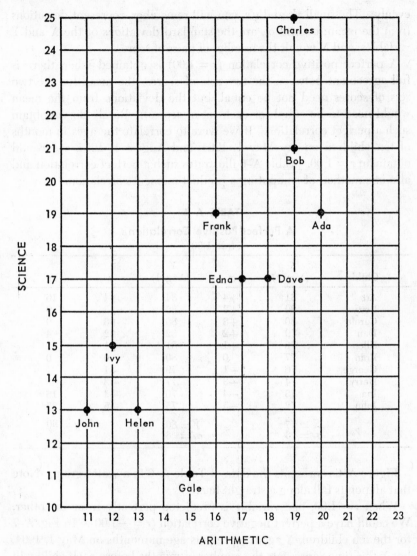

Fig. A–5. Scatter Diagram of Arithmetic and Science Test Scores Made by a Class of Ten Students

There are a number of formulas that may be used to compute a correlation. The formula that defines what is called a *product-moment correlation,* $r = \dfrac{\Sigma xy}{N\sigma_x\sigma_y}$, is convenient only in those rare cases when the means and standard deviations for the two variables work out evenly. The small x's and y's, you will remember, represent deviations from the mean; σ_x and σ_y are the standard deviations of the X and Y variables; and N equals the number of pairs of scores.

A perfect positive correlation ($r = 1.00$) is obtained when there is full agreement between the two sets of scores (the mean for the two sets of scores need not be equal, but the deviations from the mean would need to be equal for each set of scores). Rarely do we obtain such a perfect correlation. If we were to correlate the ages in months of ten children on say May 1, 1964, and August 1, 1964, we would obtain an $r = 1.00$. Table A–6 illustrates such a perfect correlation and also one method of computing a product-moment correlation.

TABLE A–6

A Perfect Positive Correlation
($r = 1.00$)

Child	X (May 1)	x	Y (Aug. 1)	y	xy
Art	81	+4	84	+4	16
Betty	80	+3	83	+3	9
Carole	80	+3	83	+3	9
Dan	79	+2	82	+2	4
Ellen	78	+1	81	+1	1
Fran	77	0	80	0	0
George	76	−1	79	−1	1
Harry	74	−3	77	−3	9
Ina	73	−4	76	−4	16
John	72	−5	75	−5	25
	$\bar{X} = 77$		$\bar{Y} = 80$		$\Sigma xy = 90$
	$\sigma_x = 3$		$\sigma_y = 3$		

Figure A–6 represents the data of Table A–6 in a scattergram. Note that all points fall along a straight line.

When $r = 1.00$, one variable is predicted perfectly from the other. We could have a perfect negative correlation ($r = -1.00$). In Fig. A–7 for the ten children, X again represents age in months on May 1, 1964, but Y this time represents the number of months before each child will reach age ninety months.

Learning Exercise

26. Revise the Y, y and xy columns of Table A–6 by letting Y equal the number of months before each child will be 90 months of age. Compute the product-moment correlation.

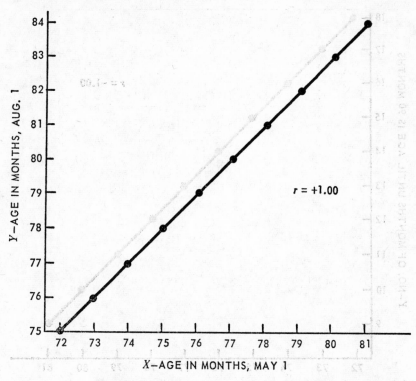

Fig. A–6.   Scattergram Illustrating Perfect Positive Correlation

When $r = +1.00$ or -1.00, all the points on the scattergram will fall on a straight line. Prediction will be perfect. Knowing the score on one variable, one can predict a score on the other variable exactly. It is possible to predict the score on one variable from the score on the other variable when the correlation is high (either plus or minus), but there will be some error in prediction. Perfect correlation is rarely, if ever, found between psychological variables. But when two variables are correlated, one can be predicted from the other; and the amount of error in prediction will depend upon the size (but not the sign) of the coefficient. For example, an r of $-.60$ will allow more precise prediction than will a coefficient of $+.50$. If the correlation is .00, then knowing the score on one variable will not help in predicting the score on a second variable. A correlation coefficient, then, yields information as to how well the scores on one variable can be predicted from the scores on a second variable.

The fact that two variables tend to increase or decrease together should not be interpreted as evidence of a causal relationship. Both

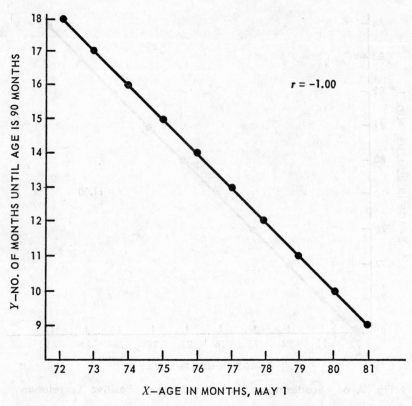

Fig. A–7. Scattergram Illustrating Perfect Negative Correlation

variables may be influenced by other variables. Several examples of non-causal correlations may be cited. The softness of asphalt paving in the streets of a city and the mortality rate of infants are positively correlated. A third variable, heat, is responsible for the relationship. Over a period of years, the correlation coefficient between teachers' salaries and the consumption of liquor has been reported as .98. During the period studied, a steady rise in wages and salaries throughout the country exerted a common effect on the two variables.

Rank Order Correlation Coefficient

Sometimes sets of data are obtained by their rank order only. For example, scholarship candidates may be ranked by two teachers in order from most deserving to least deserving. In such a situation, the rank order correlation coefficient ρ (the Greek letter *rho*) may be

Learning Exercise

27. Following is a distribution of scores:

Student	Test X	Test Y
1	14	15
2	13	15
3	13	17
4	12	16
5	12	18
6	12	15
7	11	16
8	11	19
9	11	15
10	11	17
11	10	18
12	10	18
13	10	14
14	10	12
15	10	14
16	9	14
17	9	15
18	9	13
19	9	14
20	8	15
21	8	14
22	8	13
23	7	12
24	7	11
25	6	15

The mean for Test X is 10 and the standard deviation is 2; the mean for Test Y is 15 and the standard deviation is 2.

Compute for yourself the product-moment correlation. (See Table A–6 for an example of the computational procedure.)

---

used to determine whether the two teachers tend to agree in ranking the candidates.

This formula is

$$\rho = 1 - \frac{6\Sigma d^2}{N(N^2 - 1)}$$

where N is the number of pairs of ranks

d is the difference in the rank assigned.

Following are rankings of the two teachers for five scholarship students:

	Teacher A's Rating	Teacher B's Rating	Difference in Rating (d)	d^2
Ada	1	2	1	1
Bob	2	1	1	1
Clara	3	4	1	1
Dave	4	3	1	1
Eve	5	5	0	
				$\Sigma d^2 = 4$

$$\rho = 1 - \frac{6 \ d^2}{N(N^2 - 1)}$$

$$\rho = 1 - \frac{6 \times 4}{5(25 - 1)}$$

$$\rho = 1 - \frac{24}{120}$$

$$\rho = 1 - .20$$

$$\rho = .80$$

Ranks are averaged in computing rho when two individuals are tied. For example, two pupils tied for third place would each be assigned a rank of 3.5, which is the average of ranks 3 and 4.

Learning Exercise

28. Following are the scores of nine students on two tests:

	Raw Scores		Ranks		Difference in Ranks	
Student	X	Y	X	Y	d	d^2
1	40	25				
2	36	23				
3	32	21				
4	32	21				
5	30	22				
6	29	18				
7	28	16				
8	26	20				
9	21	12				

Compute rho.

TESTS OF SIGNIFICANCE

In interpreting research studies and in interpreting test results, it is necessary to distinguish between a *population* and a *sample* drawn from the population. The term "population" refers to any group who are alike on at least one specified characteristic. All children in grade 8 in the United States would constitute a population. A sample is any number of cases less than the total number of cases in the total specified population. Grade 8 pupils from ten schools in the United States would be a sample. It is rarely possible that a researcher can test the total population. The investigator hopes to learn something about the behavior of a population by testing a sample from that population. Commonly, an effort is made to secure a sample that is representative of the total population by obtaining a *random* sample. A sample is random when each individual in the population has an equal chance of being selected for the sample.

Standard Error of the Mean

Suppose we wished to find the average achievement in reading for all children of a given grade in a very large school system, and that it is impractical to administer the test to all the children. We can select a sample and compute the mean for the sample. The obtained M will be only an approximation of the true M. If we tested successive random samples we would obtain a distribution of M's, and these M's would fall into a normal distribution. The M of all these samples would be our best estimate of the true M. We could compute the standard deviation for our distribution of M's, and we could say that the chances were about 68 out of 100 that the mean for any additional sample of scores would fall between $+1\sigma$ and -1σ.

Fortunately, we do not have to measure a series of samples to estimate how much the means will vary. We can base our estimate upon a single sample. This estimate is called the standard error of the mean (σ_M). It is an estimate of the standard deviation of a random sample of the means of successive random samples of a population. The formula for estimating the standard error of the mean is quite simple:

$$\sigma_M = \frac{\sigma}{\sqrt{N-1}}$$

Thus, if we obtained a mean of 60 for 37 reading test scores, and the standard deviation (σ) for the 37 scores was 9, then the standard error of the mean would be:

$$\sigma_M = \frac{9}{\sqrt{37-1}} = \frac{9}{\sqrt{36}} = \frac{9}{6} = 1.5$$

This statistic tells us that if we were to select another random sample of pupils and administered the reading test to them, the chances would be about 68 out of 100 that the obtained mean for this new sample would be 60 ± 1.5, i.e., between 58.5 and 61.5.

Traditionally, two confidence intervals are used most frequently with research data—the .01 level and the .05 level. A deviation of $2.58\sigma_M$ units above and below the mean includes 99 per cent of the cases in a normal distribution. In our example with the $\sigma_M = 1.5$, then $2.58 \times 1.5 = 3.87$ or, to round off, 4 points. Thus, as the mean is equal to 60, we might expect only 1 time in 100 that the true mean would lie outside of the interval—56 to 64. A deviation of $1.96\sigma_M$ units above and below the mean includes 95 per cent of the cases in a normal distribution. In our example with the $\sigma_M = 1.5$, then $1.96 \times 1.5 = 2.94$, or 3 points. Thus, we might expect only 5 times in 100 that the true mean would lie outside the interval 57–63.

Learning Exercise

29. An arithmetic test was given to a random sample of 37 sixth-grade pupils in a city. The mean was found to be 40, and the standard deviation was 12.
    (a) What is the standard error of the mean?
    (b) What is the 1 per cent confidence interval for the true mean?
    (c) What is the 5 per cent confidence interval for the true mean?

Standard Error of Differences in Means

Suppose an arithmetic test was given to two random samples, each sample containing 37 sixth-grade pupils in a city. One sample of pupils, whom we shall designate as Group 1 was taught arithmetic with the aid of teaching machines; the second sample, Group 2, was taught without benefit of teaching machines. Suppose the mean arithmetic test score for Group 1 was 45, and the standard deviation for their distribution of scores was 9. Suppose the mean score obtained by Group 2 was 40, and the standard deviation for Group 2 was 12. The problem is: "What is the probability that a difference between their M's of as much as 5 points could be attributable to random sampling error?"

In the problem posed above, we have sufficient information to find the standard error of the mean for both Group 1 and Group 2. Remember, $\sigma_M = \dfrac{\sigma}{\sqrt{N-1}}$. For Group 1, $\sigma_{M_1} = \dfrac{9}{\sqrt{37-1}} = 1.5$. For Group 2,

$\sigma_{M_2} = \dfrac{12}{\sqrt{37-1}} = 2$.

What we need now is an estimate of the standard deviation of a large number of differences between the means of a large number of random samples, i.e., a *standard error of a difference* (σdiff.). The formula for finding σdiff. is:

$$\sigma\text{diff.} = \sqrt{\sigma_{M_1}^2 + \sigma_{M_2}^2}$$

where σ_{M_1} = standard error of the mean of one sample

σ_{M_2} = standard error of the mean of the second sample

In our problem, σ_{M_1}(Group 1) = 1.5; and σ_{M_2}(Group 2) = 2. Therefore,

$$\sigma\text{diff.} = \sqrt{1.5^2 + 2^2} = \sqrt{2.25 + 4} = \sqrt{6.25} = 2.5$$

In our example, the difference in the means of Groups 1 and 2 was 5. But suppose the true difference is zero; then how often, as a result of sampling errors, might we expect a difference as large as 5 between the means of the two groups? Diagrammatically we can represent this problem as in Figure A–8.

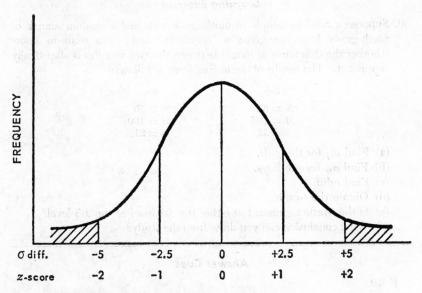

| σ diff. | –5 | –2.5 | 0 | +2.5 | +5 |
| z-score | –2 | –1 | 0 | +1 | +2 |

Fig. A–8. Mean of Differences in Means of Zero. σdiff. $= 2.5$.

The shaded portions in Fig. A–8 represent the proportion of times a difference in means of more than 5 might be expected. Actually we can translate the difference in means to z-scores, i.e., $\dfrac{X - M}{\sigma}$. For our problem, the equivalent z-score is $\dfrac{5-0}{2.5} = 2$. Such a translation is called a *t*-ratio, the formula for which is:

$$t = \frac{M_1 - M_2}{\sigma\text{diff.}}$$

For large samples, when the value of *t* is 2.58 or more, then we can say that the obtained difference in means is statistically significant at the .01 level of confidence. When the value of *t* falls between 1.96 and 2.58, then the obtained difference in means is statistically significant at the .05 level of confidence. For our problem, $t = 2.00$ $(t = \dfrac{5-0}{2.5} = 2)$, is significant at the .05 level of confidence. When a difference between means is found to be significant at the .05 level, this indicates that the observed difference could be expected to occur by chance only 5 times out of 100.

Learning Exercise

30. Suppose a random sample of ninth-grade girls and a random sample of ninth-grade boys are given a "creativity" test. We wish to know whether the difference in means between the two samples is statistically significant. The results of the testing were as follows:

Girls	Boys
$N = 65$	$N = 50$
$M = 108$	$M = 100$
$\sigma = 32$	$\sigma = 21$

(a) Find σ_M for the girls.
(b) Find σ_M for the boys.
(c) Find σdiff.
(d) Obtain the *t*-ratio.
(e) Is the *t*-ratio significant at either the .01 level or the .05 level?
(f) What conclusion can you draw from the study?

Answer Cues

1. 19.
2. Five.
3. Three.
4. Eight.
5. (a) 9, 8, 7. (b) No mode, 7, 6. (c) 2, 3.5, 4.2. (d) Adding any quantity to each score ordinarily increases all three measures by the quantity added.
6. (a) 60. (b) 10th percentile. (c) 50 %-ile.

7. (a) 25–50. (b) 75 %-ile. (c) 20 %-ile.

8. (a) 31. (b) 60. (c) No. Dispersion, or variability, of scores.

9. Accurate. Median or 50 %-ile is 34.5. (b) No; $\dfrac{Q_3 - Q_1}{2} = \dfrac{36.7 - 32.4}{2}$

= 2.15 on norms, and $\dfrac{38 - 30}{2} = 4$ for Miss Smith's class.

10. Mean, mean.

11. (a) 2. (b) 1. (c) 6.

12. (a) 3. (b) 3. (c) 4. (d) 5.

13. (a) 98. (b) 2. (c) 93. (d) 7.

14. (a) Same. (b) Same.

15. (a) 1.0, 84. (b) −1.00, 16. (c) 1.5, 93. (d) −1.5, 7.

16. (a) 70, 82. (b) 50, 84.

17. (a) 94, 106. (b) 98, 99.9.

18.

	Reading	Arithmetic	Language
Art	4.0, 113	6.0, 138	3.6, 108
Beth	7.0, 150	5.1, 127	6.4, 143
Cora	5.5, 132	5.5, 132	5.6, 133

19. (a) 0. (b) +2. (c) −3. (d) −.5. (e) +1.5.

20. (a) 50. (b) 98. (c) .1. (d) 31. (e) 93.

21. (a) −1.5, 7. (b) .5, 69. (c) −2.2, 1.

22. (a) 116. (b) 84. (c) 100. (d) 140. (e) 52.

23. (a) +1. (b) −1. (c) +2. (d) −2. (e) 1.5. (f) −1.5. (g) +.5. (h) −.5. (i) +.25. (j) +2.25. (k) 0. (l) −2.5.

24. Ada and Cindy did better on Test 1; Bob did better on Test 2; and Don and Eva did equally well on both tests.

25. (a) 70. (b) 30. (c) 65. (d) 37. (e) 50. (f) 77.

26. $r = -1.00$.

27. $r = .52$.

28. $\rho = .90$.

29. (a) 2. (b) 34.84 to 45.16 or 34 to 46. (c) 36.08 to 43.92.

30. (a) 4. (b) 3. (c) 5. (d) 1.6. (e) No. (f) Obtained difference is not statistically significant. The difference could have occurred as a result of random sampling errors.

REFERENCES

ABELSON, R. P., and ROSENBERG, M. J. (1958). Symbolic psycho-logic: a model of attitudinal cognition. *Behav. Sci.*, 3:1–13.

ADLER, A. (1924). *The practice and theory of individual psychology.* New York: Harcourt.

ADLER, A. (1930). Individual psychology. In C. Murchison (ed.), *Psychologies of 1930.* Worcester, Mass.: Clark University Press. Pp. 395–405.

ADORNO, T. W., FRENKEL-BRUNSWIK, E., LEVINSON, D. J., and SANFORD, R. N. (1950). *The authoritarian personality.* New York: Harper.

ALLISON, S. G., and ASH, P. (1951). Relationship of anxiety to learning from films. Pennsylvania State University, Human Engineering Report SDC 269–7–24.

ALLPORT, G. W. (1937). *Personality: a psychological interpretation.* New York: Holt.

ALLPORT, G. W. (1955). *Becoming: basic considerations for a psychology of personality.* New Haven: Yale University Press.

ALLPORT, G. W. (1960). *Personality and social encounter: selected essays.* Boston: Beacon Press.

ALLPORT, G. W., VERNON, P. E., LINDZEY, G. (1960). *A study of values,* rev. ed., Boston: Houghton Mifflin.

ALLPORT, G. W. (1961). *Pattern and growth in personality.* New York: Holt.

ALLYN, J., and FESTINGER, L. (1961). The effectiveness of unanticipated persuasive communications. *J. abnorm. soc. Psychol.*, 62:35–40.

ANASTASI, ANNE (1958). Heredity, environment, and the question "How?" *Psychol. Rev.*, 65:197–208.

ANASTASI, ANNE, COHEN, N., and SPATZ, D. (1948). A study of fear and anger in college students through the controlled diary method. *J. genet. Psychol.*, 73: 243–49.

ANDERSON, C. M. (1950). *Saints, sinners, and psychiatry.* Philadelphia: Lippincott.

ANDERSON, R. C. (1959). Learning in discussions: a résumé of the authoritarian-democratic studies. *Harvard educ. Rev.*, 29:201–15.

ANGELINO, H., DOLLINS, J., and MECH, E. V. (1956). Trends in the fears and worries of school children as related to socio-economic status and age. *J. genet. Psychol.*, 89:263–76.

ARCHER, C. P. (1930). Transfer of training in spelling. *Univer. Iowa Stud. Educ.*, 5:1–62.

ARNOLD, M. B. (1960). *Emotion and personality.* New York: Columbia University Press.

ASHBAUGH, E. J. (1919). Variability of children in spelling. *Sch. & Soc.*, 9:93–98.

ATKINSON, J. W., and REITMAN, W. R. (1956). Performance as a function of motive strength and expectancy of goal-attainment. *J. abnorm. soc. Psychol.*, 53:361–66.

ATWATER, S. K. (1953). Proactive inhibition and associate facilitation as affected by degree of prior learning. *J. exp. Psychol.*, 46:400–5.

AUSUBEL, D. P. (1960). The use of advance organizers in the learning and retention of meaningful verbal material. *J. educ. Psychol.*, 51:267–72.

AUSUBEL, D. P., and FITZGERALD, D. (1961). The role of discriminability in meaningful verbal learning and retention. *J. educ. Psychol.*, 52:266–74.

AUSUBEL, D. P., and FITZGERALD, D. (1962). Organizer, general background, and antecedent learning variables in sequential verbal learning. *J. educ. Psychol.*, 53:243–49.

AUSUBEL, D. P., ROBBINS, LILLIAN C., and BLAKE, E. (1957). Retroactive inhibition and facilitation in the learning of school materials. *J. educ. Psychol.*, 48: 334–43.

AUSUBEL, D. P., SCHPOONT, S. H., and CUKIER, L. (1957). The influence of intention on the retention of school materials. *J. educ. Psychol.*, 48:87–92.

AX, A. F. (1953). The physiological differentiation between fear and anger in humans. *Psychosom. Med.*, 15:433–42.

BABITZ, M., and KEYS, N. (1939). An experiment in teaching pupils to apply scientific principles. *Science Educ.*, 23:367–70.

BAGBY, J. W. (1957). A cross-cultural study of perceptual predominance in binocular rivalry. *J. abnorm. soc. Psychol.*, 54:331–34.

BALDWIN, A. L. (1949). The effect of home environment on nursery school behavior. *Child Develpm.*, 20:49–61.

BALDWIN, A. L. (1955). *Behavior and development in childhood.* New York: Holt.

BALDWIN, A. L., KALHORN, J., and BREESE, F. H. (1945). Patterns of parent behavior. *Psychol. Monogr.*, 58, No. 268.

BALDWIN, A. L., KALHORN, J., and BREESE, F. H. (1949). The appraisal of parent behavior. *Psychol. Monogr.*, 63, No. 299.

BANTA, T. J. (1961). Social attitudes and response styles. *Educ. Psychol. Measmt*, 21:543–57.

BARNARD, J. W., ZIMBARDO, P. G., and SARASON, S. B. (1961). Anxiety and verbal behavior in children. *Child Develpm.*, 32:379–92.

BARON, D., and BERNARD, H. W. (1958). *Evaluation techniques for classroom teachers.* New York: McGraw-Hill.

BARTLETT, F. (1958). *Thinking.* New York: Basic Books.

BATESON, G., and MEAD, MARGARET (1942). *Balinese character: a photographic analysis.* New York: New York Academy of Sciences.

BAYLEY, NANCY (1955). On the growth of intelligence. *Amer. Psychologist*, 10:805–18.

BAYLEY, NANCY (1956). Individual patterns of development. *Child Develpm.*, 27:45–74.

BAYLEY, NANCY, and ODEN, M. H. (1955). The maintenance of intellectual ability in gifted adults. *J. Geront.*, 10:91–107.

BENEDICT, RUTH (1934). *Patterns of culture.* New York: Mentor Books.

BENNETT, G. K., SEASHORE, H. G., and WESMAN, A. G. (1959). *Manual for the differential aptitude tests*, 3d ed. New York: Psychological Corporation.

BERKOWITZ, L. (1953). Sharing leadership in small, decision-making groups. *J. abnorm. soc. Psychol.*, 48:231–38.

BERLYNE, D. E. (1960). *Conflict, arousal, and curiosity.* New York: McGraw-Hill.

BERNSTEIN, M. R. (1954). Improved reading through interest. *Sch. Rev.*, 62:40–44.

BETTELHEIM, B. (1943). Individual and mass behavior in extreme situations. *J. abnorm. soc. Psychol.*, 38:417–52.

BEXTON, W. H., HERON, W., and SCOTT, T. H. (1954). Effects of decreased variation in the sensory environment. *Canad. J. Psychol.*, 8:70–76.

BILLS, R. E. (1950). Non-directive play therapy with retarded readers. *J. consult. Psychol.*, 14:140–49.

BILLS, R. E. (1955). About people and teaching. *Bull. Bur. Sch. Serv.*, Univer. Kentucky, 28, No. 2.

BINGHAM, W. V. (1951). Expectancies. *Année Psychol.*, 50:549–55.

BIRCH, H. G. (1945). The relation of previous experience to insightful problem-solving. *J. comp. Psychol.*, 38:367–83.

BLOCK, V. L. (1937). Conflicts of adolescents with their mothers. *J. abnorm. soc. Psychol.*, 32:192–206.

BLOOM, B. S. (ed.) (1956a). *Taxonomy of educational objectives. Handbook: I. Cognitive domain.* New York: McKay.

BLOOM, B. S. (1956b). The 1955 normative study of the tests of general educational development. *Sch. Rev.*, 64:110–24.

BLOOM, B. S. (1964). *Stability and change in human characteristics.* New York: Wiley.

BLOOM, B. S., and BRODER, LOIS (1950). Problem-solving processes of college students. *Suppl. educ. Monogr.*, No. 73. Chicago: The University of Chicago Press.

BLOOM, B. S., and BRODER, LOIS (1950). *Problem solving processes of college students.* Chicago: The University of Chicago Press.

BOGARDUS, E. S. (1925). Measuring social distance. *J. appl. Sociol.*, 9:299–308.

BOND, A. D. (1940). An experiment in the teaching of genetics. *Teachers College Contributions to Education*, No. 797. New York: Teachers College, Bureau of Publications, Columbia University Press.

BOND, E. A. (1940). *Tenth grade abilities and achievements.* New York: Teachers College, Bureau of Publications, Columbia University.

BONNEY, M. E. (1943). Personality traits of socially successful and socially unsuccessful children. *J. educ. Psychol.*, 34:449–72.

BONNEY, M. E. (1944). Relationships between social success, family size, socioeconomic home background, and intelligence among school children in grades III to V. *Sociometry*, 7:26–39.

BONNEY, M. E. (1946). A sociometric study of the relationship of some factors to mutual friendships on the elementary, secondary, and college levels. *Sociometry*, 9:21–47.

BONNEY, M. E. (1947). Sociometric study of agreement between teacher judgments and student choices. *Sociometry*, 10:133–46.

BOODISH, H. M., and HALLER, M. (1962). The teachers' page. *Social Studies*, 53:66–71; 109–14.

BOSWELL, F. P., and FOSTER, W. S. (1916). On memorizing with the intention permanently to retain. *Amer. J. Psychol.*, 27:420–26.

BOURNE, L. E., JR., and HAYGOOD, R. C. (1959). The role of stimulus redundancy in concept identification. *J. exp. Psychol.*, 58:232–38.

BOUSFIELD, W. A. (1953). The occurrence of clustering in the recall of randomly arranged associates. *J. genet. Psychol.*, 49:229–40.

BOUSFIELD, W. A. (1961). The problem of meaning in verbal learning. In C. N. COFER (ed.), *Verbal learning and verbal behavior.* New York: McGraw-Hill. Pp. 81–91.

BRALEY, L. S. (1963). Strategy selection and negative instances in concept learning. *J. educ. Psychol.*, 54:154–59.

BREHM, J. W. (1960). A dissonance analysis of attitude discrepant behavior. In C. I. HOVLAND and M. J. ROSENBERG (eds.), *Attitude organization and change.* New Haven: Yale University Press. Pp. 164–97.

BRIDGES, K. M. B. (1930). A genetic theory of the emotions. *J. genet. Psychol.*, 37:514–27.

BRIDGES, K. M. B. (1932). Emotional development in early infancy. *Child Develpm.*, 3:324–41.

BRITT, S. H. (1935). Retroactive inhibition: a review of the literature. *Psychol. Bull.*, 32:381–440.

BROOKS, F. D. (1924). The transfer of training in relation to intelligence. *J. educ. Psychol.*, 15:413–22.

BROPHY, I. N. (1946). The luxury of anti-Negro prejudice. *Publ. Opin. Quart.*, 10:456–66.

BROWN, H. L. (1959). Are the public schools doing their jobs? Yes. *The Saturday Evening Post,* September 21, 1957.

BROWN, J. S. (1948). Gradients of approach and avoidance responses and their relation to level of motivation. *J. comp. physiol. Psychol.*, 41:450–65.

BROWN, R., and BERKO, J. (1960). Word association and the acquisition of grammar. *Child Develpm.*, 31:1–14.

BROWNELL, W. A., and HENDRICKSON, G. (1950). How children learn information, concepts, and generalizations. In *Learning and instruction.* 49th Yearb. Nat. Soc. Stud. Educ., Part I, 92–128.

BROYLER, C. R., THORNDIKE, E. L., and WOODYARD, ELLA (1927). A second study of mental discipline in high school studies. *J. educ. Psychol.*, 18:377–404.

BRUCE, R. W. (1933). Conditions of transfer of training. *J. exp. Psychol.*, 16:343–61.

BRUECKNER, L. J. (1927). Certain arithmetic abilities of second grade pupils. *Elem. Sch. J.*, 27:433–43.

BRUNER, J. S. (1960). *The process of education.* Cambridge: Harvard University Press.

BRUNER, J. S. (1962). The conditions of creativity. In H. E. GRUBER, G. TERRELL, and M. WERTHEIMER (eds.), *Contemporary approaches to creative thinking.* New York: Atherton Press. Pp. 1–30.

BRUNER, J. S. (1964a). Some theorems on instruction illustrated with reference to mathematics. In E. R. HILGARD (ed.), *Theories of learning and instruction.* 63d Yearb. Nat. Soc. Stud. Educ., Part I, 306–35.

BRUNER, J. S. (1964b). The course of cognitive growth. *Amer. Psychologist.* 19:1–15.

BRUNER, J. S., and GOODMAN, C. C. (1947). Value and need as organizing factors in perception. *J. abnorm. soc. Psychol.*, 42:33–44.

BRUNER, J. S., GOODNOW, J. J., and AUSTIN, G. A. (1956). *A study of thinking.* New York: Wiley.

BRUNER, J. S., and TAGIURI, R. (1954). The perception of people. In G. LINDZEY (ed.), *Handbook of social psychology.* Cambridge: Addison-Wesley.

BUGELSKI, B. R. (1956). *The psychology of learning.* New York: Holt.

BUGELSKI, B. R. (1960). *An introduction to the principles of psychology.* New York: Holt.

BURT, C., and HOWARD, M. (1956). The multifactorial theory of inheritance and its application to intelligence. *Brit. J. statist. Psychol.*, 9:95–131.

BUSWELL, G. T. (1922). Fundamental reading habits: a study of their development. *Suppl. educ. Monogr.*, No. 21. Chicago: University of Chicago Press.

BUTLER, R. A., and HARLOW, H. F. (1957). Discrimination learning and language sets to visualize exploration incentives. *J. gen. Psychol.*, 57:257–64.

BYRNE, D. (1961). Interpersonal attraction and attitude similarity. *J. abnorm. soc. Psychol.*, 62:713–15.

CAHILL, H. E., and HOVLAND, C. I. (1960). The role of memory in the acquisition of concepts. *J. exp. Psychol.*, 59:137–44.

CALVIN, A. D., McGUIGAN, F. J., and SULLIVAN, M. W. (1957). A further investigation of the relationship between anxiety and classroom examination performance. *J. educ. Psychol.*, 48:240–44.

CAMPBELL, D. T., and STANLEY, J. C. (1963). Experimental and quasi-experimental designs for research on teaching. In N. L. GAGE (ed.), *Handbook of research on teaching*. Chicago: Rand McNally. Pp. 171–246.

CAMPBELL, R. E., and HORROCKS, J. E. (1961). A note on relationships between student and parent Minnesota Teacher Attitude Inventory scores. *J. educ. Psychol.*, 52:199–200.

CANTONI, L. J. (1955). High school tests and measurements as predictors of occupational status. *J. appl. Psychol.*, 39:253–55.

CANTRIL, H. (1950). *The "why" of man's experience*. New York: Macmillan.

CANTRIL, H. (1959). Perception and interpersonal relations. In A. E. KUENZLI (ed.), *The Phenomenological problem*. New York: Harper. Pp. 182–98.

CARMICHAEL, L. (1927). A further study of the development of behavior in vertebrates experimentally removed from the influence of external stimulation. *Psychol. Rev.*, 34:34–47.

CARROLL, H. A. (1930). Generalization of bright and dull children: a comparative study with special reference to spelling. *J. educ. Psychol.*, 21:489–99.

CARTWRIGHT, D., and HARARY, F. (1956). Structural balance: a generalization of Heider's theory. *Psychol. Rev.*, 63:277–93.

CASE, D., and COLLINSON, J. M. (1962). The development of formal thinking in verbal comprehension. *Brit. J. educ. Psychol.*, 32:103–11.

CASTANEDA, A., McCANDLESS, B. R., and PALERMO, D. S. (1956). The children's form of the Manifest Anxiety Scale. *Child Develpm.*, 27:317–26.

CASTANEDA, A., PALERMO, D. S., and McCANDLESS, B. R. (1956). Complex learning and performance as a function of anxiety in children and task difficulty. *Child Develpm.*, 32:327–32.

CATTELL, R. B. (1950). *Personality: a systematic, theoretical, and factual study*. New York: McGraw-Hill.

CATTELL, R. B. (1957). *Personality and motivation structure and measurement*. New York: Harcourt.

CHAUNCEY, H., and DOBBIN, J. E. (1963). *Testing: its place in education to-day*. New York: Harper.

CHILD, I. L., and WHITING, J. W. M. (1949). Determinants of level of aspiration. Evidence from everyday life. *J. abnorm. soc. Psychol.*, 44:303–14.

CHOMSKY, N. (1957). *Syntactic structures*. The Hague: Mouton.

COFER, C. N. (1961). *Verbal learning and verbal behavior*. New York: McGraw-Hill.

COHEN, A. R. (1959). Communication discrepancy and attitude change: a dissonance theory approach. *J. Pers.*, 27:386–96.

COHEN, M. R., and NAGEL, E. (1934). *An introduction to logic and scientific method*. New York: Harcourt.

COLEMAN, J. S. (1961). *The adolescent society*. New York: Free Press of Glencoe.

COLLEGE ENTRANCE EXAMINATION BOARD (1946). 46th annual report of the executive secretary. New York: The Board.

COMBS, A. W., and SNYGG, D. (1959). *Individual behavior*, rev. ed. New York: Harper.

COOK, W. W. (1948). Individual differences and curriculum practice. *J. educ. Psychol.*, 39:141–48.

COURTIS, S. A. (1933). Growth and development in children. *Report of the Seventh Annual Health Conference*. Ann Arbor: American Health Education Conference.

CRANDALL, V. J., PRESTON, A., and RABSON, A. (1960). Maternal reactions and the developmnet of independence and achievement behavior in young children. *Child Develpm.*, 31:243–51.

CRONBACH, L. J. (1960). *Essentials of psychological testing*, 2d ed. New York: Harper.

CROWDER, N. A. (1960). Automatic tutoring by intrinsic programming. In A. A. LUMSDAINE and R. GLASER (eds.), *Teaching machines and programmed learning: a source book.* Washington, D.C.: National Education Association. Pp. 286–98.

CRUTCHFIELD, R. S. (1962). Conformity and creative thinking. In H. E. GRUBER, G. TERRELL, and M. WERTHEIMER (eds.), *Contemporary approaches to creative thinking.* New York: Atherton Press. Pp. 120–40.

CULBERTSON, F. M. (1957). Modification of an emotionally held attitude through role playing. *J. abnorm. soc. Psychol.,* 54:230–33.

CURTI, MARGARET W. (1938). *Child psychology,* 2d ed. New York: McKay.

DAVE, R. H. (1963). The identification and measurement of environmental process variables that are related to educational achievement. Unpublished doctor's dissertation, The University of Chicago.

DAVIDSON, K. S., and SARASON, S. B. (1961). Test anxiety and classroom observations. *Child develpm.,* 32:199–210.

DAVIS, A. (1941). American status systems and the socialization of the child. *Amer. Sociol. Rev.,* 6:345–56.

DAVIS, A. (1948). *Social class influences on learning.* Cambridge: Harvard University Press.

DAVIS, A. (1951). Socioeconomic influences upon children's learning. *Understanding the child,* 20:10–16.

DAVIS, A., GARDNER, B. B., GARDNER, M. R. (1941). *Deep South.* Chicago: The University of Chicago Press.

DAVIS, F. B. (1951). Item selection techniques. In E. F. LINDQUIST (ed.), *Educational measurement.* Washington, D.C.: American Council on Education. Pp. 266–328.

DEESE, J. E. (1958). *The psychology of learning,* 2d ed. New York: McGraw-Hill.

DELLA-PIANA, G. M. (1957). Searching orientation and concept learning. *J. educ. Psychol.,* 48:245–53.

DEUTSCH, M., and COLLINS, M. E. (1951). *Interracial housing: a psychological evaluation of a social experiment.* Minneapolis: University of Minnesota Press.

DEWEY, J. (1910). *How we think.* Boston: Heath.

DICKS, H. V. (1952). Observations on contemporary Russian behavior. *Human Relat.,* 5:111–75.

DIEDERICH, P. B. (1958). Exercise writing in the field of the humanities. *Proceedings, 1957. Invitational conference on testing problems.* Princeton: Educational Testing Service. Pp. 36–44.

DIMOND, S. E. (1957). Current social trends and their implications for the social-studies program. In *Social studies in the elementary school.* 56th Yearb. Nat. Soc. Stud. Educ., Part II, 48–75.

DOBZHANSKY, T. (1956). *The biological basis of human freedom.* New York: Columbia University Press.

DOLGER, L., and GINANDES, J. (1946). Children's attitudes toward discipline as related to socio-economic status. *J. exp. Educ.,* 15:161–65.

DOLLARD, J., and MILLER, N. E. (1950). *Personality and psychotherapy.* New York: McGraw-Hill.

DONALDSON, M. (1959). Positive and negative information in matching problems. *Brit. J. Psychol.,* 50:253–62.

DONNELLY, H. E. (1935). The growth of word recognition skills in grade one. *Education,* 56:40–43.

DOUVAN, ELIZABETH (1956). Social status and success strivings. *J. abnorm. soc. Psychol.,* 52:219–23.

DOWNING, J. A. (1963). *Experiments with Pitman's Initial Teaching Alphabet in British schools.* New York: Initial Teaching Alphabet Publications, Inc.

DREVDAHL, J. E. (1956). Factors of importance for creativity. *J. clin. Psychol.*, 12:21–26.

DUGDALE, R. L. (1877). *The Jukes: a study in crime, pauperism, disease, and heredity.* New York: Putnam's.

DUNKEL, H. B., and PILLET, R. A. (1957). A second year of French in the elementary school. *Elem. Sch. J.*, 58:143–51.

DUNNINGTON, M. J. (1957). Behavioral differences of sociometric status groups in a nursery school. *Child Develpm.*, 28:103–11.

DYMOND, R. F., HUGHES, A. S., and RAABE, V. L. (1952). Measurable changes in empathy with age. *J. consult. Psychol.*, 16:202–6.

EBBINGHAUS, H. (1885). *Über das Gedächtnis: Untersuchungen zur experimentellen Psychologie.* Leipzig: Dunker and Humblot.

EDWARDS, A. L. (1941). Political frames of reference as a factor in influencing recognition. *J. abnorm. soc. Psychol.*, 36:34–50.

EELLS, K., DAVIS, A., HAVIGHURST, R., HERRICK, V., and TYLER, R. (1951). *Intelligence and cultural differences.* Chicago: The University of Chicago Press.

EHRLICH, H. J. (1961). Dogmatism and learning. *J. abnorm. soc. Psychol.*, 62: 148–49.

EHRMANN, W. W. (1952). Dating behavior of college students. *Marriage & Family Living*, 14:322–26.

EMMERICH, W. (1964). Continuity and stability in early social development. *Child Develpm.*, 35:311–32.

ENGLISH, H. B., and ENGLISH, AVA C. (1958). *A comprehensive dictionary of psychological and psychoanalytical terms.* New York: McKay.

ENNIS, R. H. (1962). A concept of critical thinking. *Harv. educ. Rev.*, 32:81–111.

ERIKSON, E. H. (1950). *Childhood and society.* New York: Norton.

ERIKSON, E. H. (1959). Identity and the life cycle. *Psychol. Issues*, 1, No. 1.

ESTES, K. W. (1944). An experimental study of punishment. *Psychol. Monogr.* 57, No. 263.

EWING, T. A. (1942). A study of certain factors involved in changes of opinion. *J. soc. Psychol.*, 16:63–88.

EYSENCK, H. J. (1953). *The structure of human personality.* New York: Wiley.

FALES, E. (1944). Genesis of level of aspiration in children from one and one-half to three years of age. Reported in K. LEWIN *et al.*, Level of aspiration. In J. McV. HUNT (ed.), *Personality and the behavior disorders.* New York: Ronald Press. Vol. I, pp. 333–78.

FALLS, J. D. (1928). Research in secondary education. *Kentucky Sch. J.*, 6:42–46.

FEIGL, H., and BRODBECK, MAY. (1953). *Readings in the philosophy of science.* New York: Appleton-Century-Crofts.

FESTINGER, L. (1957). *A theory of cognitive dissonance.* Evanston, Ill.: Row, Peterson.

FESTINGER, L., and CARLSMITH, J. M. (1959). Cognitive consequences of forced compliance. *J. abnorm. soc. Psychol.*, 58:203–10.

FESTINGER, L., GERARD, H. B., HYMOVITCH, B., KELLY, H. H., and RAVEN, B. H. (1952). The influence process in the presence of extreme deviates. *Hum. Relat.*, 5:327–46.

FLANAGAN, J. C. (1964). The implications of research for the improvement of secondary education. *Amer. educ. Res. J.*, 1:1–9.

FLANDERS, N. A. (1960). Diagnosing and utilizing social structures in classroom learning. In *The dynamics of instructional groups.* 59th Yearb. Nat. Soc. Stud. Educ., Part II, 187–217.

FLEEGE, U. H. (1945). *Self-revelation of the adolescent boy.* Milwaukee: Bruce.

FORMAN, H. J. (1933). *Our movie made children.* New York: Macmillan.

FORTUNE SURVEY (1940). *The people of the U.S.A.—a self portrait. Fortune*, 27: 14–28, 133–36.

FRANK, LAWRENCE K. (1944). The adolescent and the family. In NELSON B. HENRY (ed.), 43d Yearbook, *Nat. Soc. Stud. Educ.* Part I, 244–45.

FRANZBLAU, R. N. (1935). Race differences in mental and physical traits studied in different environments. *Arch. Psychol.*, No. 177.

FREDERIKSEN, N. O., and MELVILLE, S. D. (1954). Differential predictability in the use of test scores. *Educ. psychol. Measmt*, 14:647–56.

FRENCH, ELIZABETH G. (1955). Some characteristics of achievement motivation. *J. exp. Psychol.*, 50:232–36.

FRENCH, ELIZABETH G. (1958). Effects of the interaction of motivation and feedback on task performance. In J. W. ATKINSON (ed.), *Motives in fantasy, action, and society.* Princeton, N.J.: Van Nostrand. Chap. 29.

FRENCH, T. M. (1937). Reality and the unconscious. *Psychoanal. Quart.*, 6:23–61.

FRENCH, W. (1957). *Behavioral goals of general education in high school.* New York: Russell Sage Foundation.

FRENKEL-BRUNSWIK, E. (1949). Intolerance of ambiguity as an emotional and perceptual personality variable. *J. Pers.*, 18:108–43.

FREUD, ANNA (1946). *Ego and mechanisms of defense.* International Universities Press.

FREUD, S. (1926). *The problem of anxiety.* Translation, 1936. New York: Norton.

FREUD, S. (1927). *The ego and the id.* London: Hogarth Press.

FREUD, S. (1943). *A general introduction to psychoanalysis.* Garden City, N.Y.: Doubleday.

FRIEBERGS, V., and TULVING, E. (1961). The effect of practice on utilization of information from positive and negative instances in concept identification. *Canad. J. Psychol.*, 15:101–6.

FRIEDENBERG, E. Z. (1959). *The vanishing adolescent.* Boston: Beacon Press.

FROMM, E. (1941). *Escape from freedom.* New York: Holt.

FRUTCHEY, F. P. (1937). Retention in high school chemistry. *J. higher Educ.*, 8:217–18.

FRY, E. (1960). Teaching a basic reading vocabulary. *Elem. English*, 37:38–42.

FRY, E. B. (1960). A study of teaching machine response modes. In A. A. LUMSDAINE and R. GLASER (eds.), *Teaching machines and programmed learning: a source book.* Washington, D.C., Department of Audio-Visual Instruction, National Education Association.

FURST, E. J. (1958). *Constructing evaluation instruments.* New York: McKay.

GABLE, SISTER FELICITA (1936). The effect of two contrasting forms of testing upon learning. *Johns Hopk. Univer. Stud. Educ.*, No. 25.

GAIER, E. L. (1952). The relationship between selected personality variables and the thinking of students in discussion classes. *Sch. Rev.*, 60:404–11.

GAIER, E. L. (1959). Cognitive learning. In M. R. LOREE (ed.), *Educational psychology: readings.* New York: Ronald Press.

GALTON, F. (1869). *Hereditary genius.* London: Macmillan.

GAMOW, G. (1955). Information transfer in the living cell. *Sci. Amer.*, 193:70–79.

GATES, A. I. (1917). Recitation as a factor in memorizing. *Arch. Psychol.*, 6, No. 40.

GATES, A. I., and JENNINGS, F. G. (1961). The role of motivation. In N. B. Henry (ed.), *Development in and through reading.* 60th Yearb. Nat. Soc. Stud. Educ., Part I, 109–26.

GATES, A. I., and TAYLOR, G. A. (1923). The acquisition of motor control in writing by preschool children. *Teach. Coll. Rec.*, 24:459–68.

GEBHARD, MILDRED E. (1948). The effect of success and failure upon the attractiveness of activities as a function of experience, expectation, and need. *J. exp. Psychol.*, 38:371–88.

GESELL, A., and ILG, F. L. (1943). *Infant and child in the culture of today.* New York: Harper.

GESELL, A., and ILG, F. L. (1946). *The child from five to ten.* New York: Harper.

GESELL, A., ILG, F. L., and AMES, L. B. (1956). *Youth: the years from ten to sixteen.* New York: Harper.

GESELL, A., and THOMPSON, H. (1941). Twins T and C from infancy to adolescence: a biogenetic study of individual differences by the method of co-twin control. *Genet. Psychol. Monogr.,* 24:3–121.

GETZELS, J. W., and JACKSON, P. W. (1962). *Creativity and intelligence.* New York: Wiley.

GHISELIN, B. (ed.) (1952). *The creative process.* Berkeley: University of California Press.

GHISELLI, E. E. (1955). The measurement of occupational aptitude. *Univer. Calif. Publ. Psychol.,* 8:101–216.

GIBBONS, C. C. (1938). A comparison of Kuhlman-Anderson test scores and teachers' estimates. *Sch. & Soc.,* 47:710–12.

GIBSON, E. J. (1939). Sensory generalization with voluntary reactions. *J. exp. Psychol.,* 24:237–53.

GIBSON, E. J. (1941). Retroactive inhibition as a function of degree of generalization between tasks. *J. exp. Psychol.,* 28:93–115.

GNAGEY, W. J. (1960). Effects on classmates of a deviant student's power and response to a teacher-exerted control technique. *J. educ. Psychol.,* 51:1–9.

GOLDBECK, R. A. (1960). *The effect of response mode and learning material difficulty on automated instruction.* Tech. Report No. 1. Nonr-3077(00). Pittsburgh: American Institute for Research.

GOODENOUGH, F. L. (1931). Anger in young children. *Univer. Minn. Inst. Child Welf. Monogr. Ser.,* No. 9.

GORDON, C. W. (1957). *The social system of the high school.* New York: The Free Press of Glencoe.

GORDON, W. M., and BERLYNE, D. E. (1954). Drive-level and flexibility in paired-associate nonsense-syllable learning. *Quart. J. exp. Psychol.,* 6:181–85.

GREEN, E. G. (1962). *The learning process and programmed instruction.* New York: Holt.

GREENE, E. B. (1931). The retention of information learned in college courses. *J. educ. Res.,* 24:262–73.

GREENE, H. A., and GRAY, W. S. (1946). The measurement of understanding in the language arts. In *The measurement of understanding.* 45th Yearb. Nat. Soc. Stud. Educ., Part I, 175–200.

GREENSPOON, J. (1954). The effect of two nonverbal stimuli on the frequency of members of two verbal response classes. *Amer. Psychologist,* 9:384.

GRONLUND, N. E. (1951). The accuracy of teachers' judgments concerning sociometric status of sixth-grade pupils. *Sociometry Monogr.,* No. 25.

GRONLUND, N. E., and WHITNEY, A. P. (1958). The relation between teachers' judgments of pupils' sociometric status and intelligence. *Elem. Sch. J.,* 58:264–68.

GROSS, N., MASON, W. S., and McEACHERN, A. W. (1958). *Explorations in role analysis: studies of the school superintendency role.* New York: Wiley.

GUETZKOW, H., KELLY, E. L., and McKEACHIE, W. J. (1954). An experimental comparison of recitation, discussion, and tutorial methods in college teaching. *J. educ. Psychol.,* 45:193–207.

GUILFORD, J. P. (1959). *Personality.* New York: McGraw-Hill.

GUILFORD, J. P. (1964). Zero correlations among tests of intellectual abilities. *Psychol. Bull.,* 61:401–4.

HAGGARD, E. A. (1957). Socialization, personality, and academic achievement in gifted children. *Sch. Rev.,* 65:388–414.

HAGMAN, E. R. (1932). A study of fears of children at preschool age. *J. exp. Educ.,* 1:110–30.

HALL, C. S. (1954). *A primer of Freudian psychology.* Cleveland: World Publishing Co.

HALL, C. S., and LINDZEY, G. (1957). *Theories of personality.* New York: Wiley.

HAMILTON, R. J. (1943). Retroactive facilitation as a function of degree of generalization between tasks. *J. exp. Psychol.,* 32:363–76.

HARAP, H. K., and MAPES, C. E. (1934). The learning of fundamentals in an arithmetic-activity program. *Elem. Sch. J.,* 34:515–25.

HARDING, J., and HOGREFE, R. (1952). Attitudes toward Negro co-workers in an Eastern urban department store. *J. soc. Issues,* 8:18–28.

HARLOW, H. F. (1949). The formation of learning sets. *Psychol. Rev.,* 56:51–65.

HARLOW, H. F. (1950). Performance of catarrhine monkeys on a series of discrimination reversal problems. *J. comp. physiol. Psychol.,* 43:231–39.

HARLOW, H. F. (1953). Motivation as a factor in the acquisition of new responses. In J. S. BROWN (ed.), *Current theory and research in motivation.* Lincoln, Neb.: University of Nebraska Press. Pp. 24–49.

HARLOW, H. F., HARLOW, M. K., and MEYER, D. R. (1950). Learning motivated by a manipulative drive. *J. exp. Psychol.,* 40:228–34.

HARPER, J. C., ANDERSON, C. C., CHRISTENSEN, C. M., and HUNKA, S. M. (1964). *The cognitive processes: readings.* Englewood Cliffs, N.J.: Prentice-Hall.

HARPER, R. A. (1959). *Psychoanalysis and psychotherapy: 36 systems.* Englewood Cliffs, N.J.: Prentice-Hall.

HARRELL, T. W., and HARRELL, M. S. (1945). AGCT scores for civilian occupations. *Educ. Psychol. Measmt,* 5:229–39.

HARRIS, A. J. (1961). Reading and human development. In *Development in and through reading.* 60th Yearb. Nat. Soc. Stud. Educ., Part I.

HARTMANN, H., and KRIS, E., and LOEWENSTEIN, R. M. (1947). Comments on the formation of psychic structure. In ANNA FREUD *et al.* (eds.), *Psychoanalytic studies of the child,* Vol. 2. New York: International Universities Press.

HARTSON, L. D. (1945). Influence of level of motivation on the validity of intelligence tests. *Educ. Psychol. Measmt,* 5:273–83.

HARTSON, L. D., and SPROW, A. J. (1941). Value of intelligence quotients obtained in secondary schools for predicting scholarship. *Educ. psychol. Measmt,* 1:387–98.

HATTWICK, LaBERTA A. (1937). Sex difference in behavior of nursery school children. *Child Develpm.,* 8:323–55.

HAVIGHURST, R. J. (1950). *Developmental tasks and education.* New York: McKay.

HAVIGHURST, R. J. (1953). *Human development and education.* New York: McKay. Pp. 57, 58, 59.

HAVIGHURST, R. J., and MacDONALD, D. V. (1955). Development of the ideal self in New Zealand and American children. *J. educ. Res.,* 49:263–73.

HAVIGHURST, R. J., and NEUGARTEN, B. L. (1957). *Society and education.* Rockleigh, N.J.: Allyn.

HEBB, D. O. (1949). *Organization of behavior.* New York: Wiley.

HEBB, D. O. (1955). The mammal and his environment. *Amer. J. Psychiat.,* 111:828–31.

HEBB, D. O. (1958). *A textbook of psychology.* Philadelphia: Saunders.

HEBB, D. O. (1959). A neuropsychological theory. In S. KOCH (ed.), *Psychology: a study of a science.* New York: McGraw-Hill. Vol. I, pp. 622–43.

HEIDER, F. (1958). *The psychology of interpersonal relations.* New York: Wiley.

HELSON, H. (1948). Adaptation-level as a basis for a quantitative theory of frames of reference. *Psychol. Rev.,* 55:297–313.

HELSON, H. (1959). Adaptation-level theory. In S. KOCH (ed.), *Psychology: a study of a science,* Vol. I. New York: McGraw-Hill.

HELSON, H., BLAKE, R. R., MOUTON, J. S., and OLMSTEAD, J. A. (1956). Attitudes as adjustments to stimulus, background, and residual factors. *J. abnorm. soc. Psychol.*, 52:314–22.

HEMPEL, C. G. (1952). *Fundamentals of concept formation in empirical science.* Chicago: The University of Chicago Press.

HEMPHILL, H. K. (1949). Situational factors in leadership. *Ohio State Univer. educ. Res. Monogr.*, No. 32.

HENLE, MARY (1962). The birth and death of ideas. In H. E. GRUBER, G. TERRELL, and M. WERTHEIMER (eds.), *Contemporary approaches to creative thinking.* New York: Atherton Press. Pp. 31–62.

HENMON, V. A. C. (1917). The relation between learning and retention and the amount to be learned. *J. exp. Psychol.*, 2:476–84.

HENRY, J. (1949). Cultural objectification of the case history. *Amer. J. Orthopsychiat.*, 19:655–73.

HICKS, J. A., and HAYES, M. (1938). Study of the characteristics of 250 junior high school children. *Child Develpm.*, 9:219–42.

HILL, W. F. (1956). Activity as an autonomous drive. *J. comp. physiol. Psychol.*, 49:15–19.

HILL, W. F. (1960). Learning theory and the acquisition of values. *Psychol. Rev.*, 67:317–31.

HIMMELWEIT, H. T., OPPENHEIM, A. N., and VINCE, P. (1958). *Television and the child.* London: Oxford University Press.

HOHMAN, L. B., and SHAFFNER, B. (1947). The sex lives of unmarried men. *Amer. J. Sociol.*, 52:501–7.

HOLLAND, J. G., and SKINNER, B. F. (1961). *The analysis of behavior.* New York: McGraw-Hill.

HOLLINGSHEAD, A. B. (1949). *Elmtown's youth; the impact of social classes on adolescents.* New York: Wiley.

HOMANS, G. C. (1950). *The human group.* New York: Harcourt.

HONZIK, MARJORIE P., MACFARLANE, JEAN W., and ALLEN, LUCILE (1948). The stability of mental test performance between two and eighteen years. *J. exp. Educ.*, 17:309–24.

HORACE MANN–LINCOLN INSTITUTE OF SCHOOL EXPERIMENTATION (1947). *How to construct a sociogram.* New York: Teachers College, Bureau of Publications, Columbia University.

HORN, E. (1937). *Methods of instruction in the social studies.* New York: Scribner.

HORNEY, K. (1937). *The neurotic personality of our time.* New York: Norton.

HORNEY, K. (1942). *Self-analysis.* New York: Norton.

HORNEY, K. (1945). *Our inner conflicts.* New York: Norton.

HORNEY, K. (1950). *Neurosis and human growth.* New York: Norton.

HOVLAND, C. I. (1951). Human learning and retention. In S. S. STEVENS (ed.), *Handbook of experimental psychology.* New York: Wiley. Pp. 613–89.

HOVLAND, C. I., LUMSDAINE, A. A., and SHEFFIELD, F. D. (1949). *Experiments on mass communications.* Princeton, N.J.: Princeton University Press.

HOVLAND, C. I., and WEISS, W. (1953). Transmission of information concerning concepts through positive and negative instances. *J. exp. Psychol.*, 45:175–82.

HUANG, I. (1943). Children's conception of physical causality: a critical summary. *J. genet. Psychol.*, 63:71–121.

HULL, C. L. (1930). Knowledge and purpose as habit mechanisms. *Psychol. Rev.*, 37:511–25.

HULL, C. L. (1934). The concept of habit-family hierarchy and maze learning. *Psychol. Rev.*, 41:33–54, 134–52.

HULL, C. L. (1943). *Principles of behavior.* New York: Appleton-Century-Crofts.

HULL, C. L. (1952). *A behavior system.* New Haven: Yale University Press.

HULTEN, C. E. (1925). The personal element in teachers' marks. *J. educ. Res.*, 12:49–55.

HUNT, E. B. (1962). *Concept learning.* New York: Wiley.

HUNT, E. B., and HOVLAND, C. I. (1960). Order of consideration of different types of concepts. *J. exp. Psychol.*, 59:220–25.

HUNT, J. McV. (1960). Experience and the development of motivation: some reinterpretations. *Child Develpm.*, 31:489–504.

HUNT, J. McV. (1961). *Intelligence and experience.* New York: Ronald Press. Chaps. 4, 5, and 8.

HUNTER, W. S. (1912). The delayed reaction in animals and children. *Behav. Monogr.*, 2:1–85.

HUNTER, W. S. (1918). The temporal maze and kinaesthetic sensory processes in the white rat. *Psychobiol.*, 2:339–51.

HUNTER, W. S. (1924). The symbolic process. *Psychol. Rev.*, 31: 478–97.

HURLOCK, E. B. (1924). The value of praise and reproof as incentives for children. *Arch. Psychol.*, 11, No. 71.

HURLOCK, E. B. (1925). An evaluation of certain incentives used in school work. *J. educ. Psychol.*, 16:145–59.

HURLOCK, E. B. (1955). *Adolescent development,* 2d ed. New York: McGraw-Hill.

INHELDER, BÄRBEL (1953). Criteria of the stages of mental development. In J. M. TANNER and BARBEL INHELDER (eds.), *Discussions on child development.* New York: International Universities Press.

INHELDER, BÄRBEL (1962). Some aspects of Piaget's genetic approach to cognition. *Monogr. Soc. Res. Child Develpm.*, 27:19–40.

INHELDER, B., and PIAGET, J. (1958). *The growth of logical thinking from childhood to adolescence.* Trans. ANNE PARSONS and S. MILGRAM. New York: Basic Books.

INKELES, A., and LEVINSON, D. J. (1954). National character: the study of modal personality and sociocultural systems. In G. LINDZEY (ed.), *Handbook of social psychology.* Cambridge: Addison-Wesley. Vol. II, chap. 26.

ISRAEL, J. (1960). The effect of positive and negative self evaluation on the attractiveness of a goal. *Hum. Relat.*, 13:33–47.

ITTELSON, W. H., and CANTRIL, H. (1954). *Perception: a transactional approach.* Garden City, N.Y.: Doubleday.

JACKSON, T. A., STONEX, E., LANE, E., and DOMINGUEZ, K. (1938). Studies in the transposition of learning by children: I. Relative vs. absolute response as a function of amount of training. *J. exp. Psychol.*, 23:578–600.

JANIS, I. L., and FESHBACH, S. (1953). Effects of fear-arousing communication. *J. abnorm. soc. Psychol.*, 48:78–92.

JANIS, I. L., and KING, B. T. (1954). The influence of role playing on opinion change. *J. abnorm. soc. Psychol.*, 49:211–18.

JENKIN, N. (1957). Affective processes in perception. *Psychol. Bull.*, 54:100–27.

JENNESS, A. (1962). Personality dynamics. In PAUL R. FARNSWORTH, OLGA McNEMAR, and QUINN McNEMAR (eds.), *Annual review of psychology.* Palo Alto, Calif.: Annual Reviews, Inc. Vol. XIII.

JERSILD, A. T. (1954). Emotional development. In L. CARMICHAEL (ed.), *Manual of Child Psychol.*, 2d ed. New York: Wiley.

JERSILD, A. T., GOLDMAN, B., and LOFTUS, J. J. (1941). A comparative study of the worries of children in two school situations. *J. exp. Educ.*, 9:323–26.

JERSILD, A. T., and HOLMES, F. B. (1935). Children's fears. *Child Develpm. Monogr.*, No. 20.

JERSILD, A. T., and MARKEY, F. V. (1935). Conflicts between preschool children. *Child Develpm. Monogr.*, No. 21.

JERSILD, A. T., MARKEY, F. V., and JERSILD, C. L. (1933). Children's fears, dreams, wishes, daydreams, likes, dislikes, pleasant and unpleasant memories. *Child Develpm. Monogr.*, No. 12.

JOHN, E. M. (1941). A study of the effects of evacuation and air raids on children of preschool age. *Brit. J. educ. Psychol.*, 11:173–82.

JOHNSON, D. M. (1948). Application of the standard-score I.Q. to the social statistics. *J. soc. Psychol.*, 27:217–27.

JOHNSON, E. S. (1962). The concept of structure in the social sciences. *Educ. Rec.*, 43:206–9.

JOHNSON, G. R. (1937). High school survey, *Publ. Sch. Messenger*, 35:1–34.

JONES, E. I., and BILODEAU, E. A. (1952). Differential transfer of training between motor tasks of different difficulty. *U.S.A.F. Hum. Resour. Res. Bull.*, No. 52-35.

JONES, EDWINA, MORGAN, EDNA, and STEVENS, GLADYS (1957). *Methods and materials in elementary physical education.* New York: Harcourt.

JONES, H. E., and CONRAD, H. S. (1933). The growth and decline of intelligence; a study of a homogeneous group between the ages of ten and sixty. *Genet. Psychol. Monogr.*, 13:223–94.

JONES, M. C., and BAYLEY, N. (1950). Physical maturing among boys as related to behavior, *J. educ. Psychol.*, 41:129–48.

JOSSELYN, IRENE M. (1948). *The psychoanalytic development of children.* New York: Family Service Association of America.

JOST, H., and SONTAG, L. W. (1944). The genetic factors in automatic nervous system. *Psychosom. Med.*, 6:308–10.

JUCKNAT, MARAGARETE (1937). Leistung, Anspruchsniveau und Selbstbewusstsein. *Psychol. Forsch.*, 22:87–179.

JUDD, C. H. (1908). The relation of special training to general intelligence. *Educ. Rev.*, 36:28–42.

JUDSON, A. J., and COFER, C. N. (1956). Reasoning as an associative process: I. "Direction" in a simple verbal problem. *Psychol. Rep.*, 2:469–76.

JUNG, C. G. (1939). *The integration of personality.* New York: Farrar and Rinehart.

KAGAN, J. (1958). The concept of identification. *Psychol. Rev.*, 65:296–305.

KAGAN, J., and BERKUN, M. (1954). The reward value of running activity. *J. comp. physiol. Psychol.*, 47:108.

KAGAN, J., and MOSS, H. A. (1959). Stability and validity of achievement fantasy. *J. abnorm. soc. Psychol.*, 58:357–64.

KALLMANN, F. J. (1946). The genetic theory of schizophrenia. *Amer. J. Psychiat.* 103:309–22.

KALLMANN, F. J. (1953). *Heredity in health and mental disorder.* New York: Norton.

KARDINER, A. (1945). *The psychological frontiers of society.* New York: Columbia University Press.

KAREN, R. L. (1956). Recognition as a function of meaningfulness and intention to learn. *Amer. J. Psychol.*, 69:650–52.

KARLIN, R. (1960). Research in reading. *Elem. Eng.*, 37:177–83.

KATONA, G. (1940). *Organizing and memorizing.* New York: Columbia University Press.

KATZ, D. (1960). The functional approach to the study of attitudes. *Public Opinion Quart.*, 24:163–204.

KATZ, D., and STOTLAND, E. (1959). A preliminary statement to a theory of attitude structure and change. In S. KOCH (ed.), *Psychology: a study of a science. Formulations of the person and the social context.* New York: McGraw-Hill. Vol. III, pp. 423–75.

KEARNEY, N. C. (1953). *Elementary school objectives.* New York: Russell Sage Foundation.

KEISTER, M. E., and UPDEGRAFF, R. (1937). A study of children's reactions to failure and an experimental attempt to modify them. *Child Develpm.*, 8:241–48.

KELMAN, H. (1953). Attitude change as a function of response restriction. *Hum. Relat.*, 6:185–214.

KENDLER, T. S. (1961). Concept formation. *Annu. Rev. Psychol.*, 12:447–72.

KIESLER, C. A., and KIESLER, S. B. (1964). Role of forewarning in persuasive communications. *J. abnorm. soc. Psychol.*, 68:547–49.

KIMBLE, G. A. (1961). *Hilgard and Marquis' Conditioning and learning*, 2d ed. New York: Appleton-Century-Crofts.

KIMBLE, G. A., and GARMEZY, N. (1963). *Principles of general psychology*, 2d ed. New York: Ronald Press.

KINGSLEY, H. L., and GARRY, R. (1957). *The nature and conditions of learning*, 2d ed. Englewood Cliffs, N.J.: Prentice-Hall.

KINSEY, A. C., POMEROY, W. B., and MARTIN, C. E. (1948). *Sexual behavior in the human male*. Philadelphia: Saunders.

KINSEY, A. C., POMEROY, W. B., MARTIN, C. E., and GEBHARD, P. H. (1953). *Sexual behavior in the human female*. Philadelphia: Saunders.

KIRKENDALL, L. A. (1944). Health, sex, and human relations in education. *NEA Bulletin of Secondary School Principals*, 28:94–100.

KIRKENDALL, L. A., and OSBORNE, R. F. (1949). *Dating days*. Chicago Science Research Associates.

KITTELL, J. E. (1957). An experimental study of the effect of external direction during learning on transfer and retention of principles. *J. educ. Psychol.*, 48:391–405.

KLAUSMEIER, H. J., and CHECK, J. (1962). Retention and transfer in children of low, average, and high intelligence. *J. educ. Res.*, 55:319–22.

KLINEBERG, O. (1935). *Negro intelligence and selective migration*. New York: Columbia University Press.

KNEZEVICH, S. J. (1946). The constancy of the I.Q. of the secondary school pupil. *J. educ. Res.*, 39:506–16.

KOCH, H. L. (1956). Sissiness and tomboyishness in relation to sibling characteristics. *J. genet. Psychol.*, 88:231–44.

KOCH, H. L. (1957). The relation in young children between characteristics of their playmates and certain attributes of their siblings. *Child Develpm.*, 28:175–202.

KÖHLER, W. (1925). *The mentality of apes*. New York: Harcourt.

KOUNIN, J. S., and GUMP, P. V. (1958). The ripple effect in discipline. *Elem. Sch. J.*, 59:158–62.

KOUNIN, J. S., and GUMP, P. V. (1961). The comparative influence of punitive and nonpunitive teachers upon childrens' [sic] concepts of school misconduct. *J. educ. Psychol.*, 52:44–49.

KOUNIN, J. S., GUMP, P. V., and RYAN, J. J. (1961). Explorations in classroom management. *J. Teacher Educ.*, 12:235–46.

KRASNER, L. (1958). Studies of the conditioning of verbal behavior. *Psychol. Bull.*, 55:148–70.

KRATHWOHL, D. R., BLOOM, B. S., and MASIA, B. B. (1964). *A taxonomy of educational objectives: affective domain*. New York: McKay.

KRAUS, R. (1957). *Play activities for boys and girls*. New York: McGraw-Hill.

KRECHEVSKY, I. (1932). "Hypotheses" versus "chance" in the pre-solution period in sensory discrimination-learning. *Univer. Calif. Publ. Psychol.* 6:27–44.

KRUEGER, W. C. F. (1946). Rate of progress as related to difficulty of assignment. *J. educ. Psychol.*, 37:247–49.

KRUMBOLTZ, J. D. (1961). Meaningful learning and retention: practice and reinforcement variables. *Rev. educ. Res.*, 31:535–46.

KRUMBOLTZ, J. D., and WEISMAN, R. G. (1962a). The effect of overt vs. covert responding to programmed instruction on immediate and delayed retention. *J. educ. Psychol.*, 53:89–92.

KRUMBOLTZ, J. D., and WEISMAN, R. G. (1962b). The effect of intermittent confirmation in programmed instruction. *J. educ. Psychol.*, 53:250–53.

KUHLEN, R. G., and LEE, B. J. (1943). Personality characteristics and social acceptability in adolescence. *J. educ. Psychol.*, 34:321–40.

LACHMAN, S. J. (1960). *The foundations of science*, 2d ed. New York: Vantage Press.

LAHEY, M. F. (1937). Retroactive inhibition as a function of age, intelligence, and the duration of the interpolated activity. *J. exp. Educ.*, 6:61–67.

LANE, J. M. (1963). A study of two modes of reinforcement in programmed and block arithmetic learning materials. Unpublished doctor's dissertation, University of Alabama.

LAWRENCE, D. H. (1952). The transfer of a discrimination along a continuum. *J. comp. physiol. Psychol.*, 45:511–16.

LAWSON, E. D., and STAGNER, R. (1957). Group pressure, attitude change, and autonomic involvement. *J. soc. Psychol.*, 45:299–312.

LECKY, P. (1945). *Self-consistency. A theory of personality.* New York: Island Press.

LEE, E. S. (1951). Negro intelligence and selective migration: a Philadelphia test of the Klineberg hypothesis. *Amer. sociol. Rev.*, 16:227–33.

LEEDS, C. H. (1954). Teacher behavior liked and disliked by pupils. *Education*, 75:29–36.

LEIGHTON, D. C. (1955). *Distribution of symptoms in a small town.* Mimeographed paper read to American Psychiatric Association, May.

LESTER, O. P. (1932). Mental set in relation to retroactive inhibition. *J. exp. Psychol.*, 15:681–99.

LEUBA, C. (1955). Toward some integration of learning theories: the concept of optimal stimulation. *Psychol. Rep.*, 1:27–33.

LEVIN, H., and BALDWIN, A. L. (1958). The choice to exhibit. *Child Develpm.*, 29:373–80.

LEVIN, H., and SEARS, R. R. (1956). Identification with parents as a determinant of doll play aggression. *Child Develpm.*, 27:135–53.

LEVINE, J. M., and MURPHY, G. (1943). The learning and forgetting of controversial material. *J. abnorm. soc. Psychol.*, 38:507–17.

LEVINE, R., CHEIN, I., and MURPHY, G. (1942). The relation of the intensity of a need to the amount of perceptual distortion: a preliminary report. *J. Psychol.*, 13:283–93.

LEWIN, K. (1935). *A dynamic theory of personality.* New York: McGraw-Hill.

LEWIN, K. (1939). The effects of social climate. *Harvard educ. Rev.*, 9:21–32.

LEWIN, K., DEMBO, T., FESTINGER, L., and SEARS, P. S. (1944). Level of aspiration. In J. McV. HUNT (ed.), *Personality and the behavior disorders.* New York: Ronald Press. Vol. I, pp. 333–78.

LEWIN, K., LIPPITT, R., and WHITE, R. K. (1939). Patterns of aggressive behavior in experimentally created "social climates." *J. soc. Psychol.*, 10:271–99.

LEWIS, W. D. (1943). Some characteristics of very superior children. *J. genet. Psychol.*, 62:301–9.

LIGHTHALL, F. F., RUEBUSH, B., SARASON, S. B., and ZWEIBELSON, I. (1959). Change in mental ability as a function of test anxiety and type of mental test. *J. consult. Psychol.*, 23:34–38.

LINDSLEY, D. B. (1951). Emotion. In S. S. STEVENS (ed.), *Handbook of experimental psychology.* New York: Wiley.

LIPPITT, ROSEMARY (1941). Popularity among preschool children. *Child Develpm.*, 12:305–32.

LIPPITT, R., and WHITE, R. K. (1958). An experimental study of leadership and group life. In ELEANOR E. MACCOBY, T. M. NEWCOMB, and E. L. HARTLEY (eds.), *Readings in social psychology*, 3d ed. New York: Holt.

LISS, E. (1944). Examination anxiety. *Amer. J. Orthopsychist.*, 14:345–49.

LOBAN, W. (1954). *Literature and social sensitivity.* Champaign, Ill.: National Council of Teachers of English.

LOHR, T. F. (1959). The effect of shock on the rat's choice of a path to food. *J. exp. Psychol.*, 58:312–18.

LOOMIS, C. P. (1946). Political and occupational cleavages in a Hanoverian village, Germany: a sociometric study. *Sociometry*, 9:316–33.

LOREE, M. R. (1948). A study of a technique for improving tests. Unpublished doctor's dissertation, The University of Chicago.

LOREE, M. R. (ed.) (1959). *Educational psychology: readings, supplementary text and study questions.* New York: Ronald Press.

LOREE, M. R., and KOCH, MARGARET B. (1960). Use of verbal reinforcement in developing group discussion skills. *J. educ. Psychol.*, 51:164–68.

LORGE, I. (1945). Schooling makes a difference. *Teachers Coll. Rec.*, 46:483–92.

LORGE, I., FOX, D., DAVITZ, J., and BRENNER, M. (1958). A survey of studies contrasting the quality of group performance and individual performance 1920–1957. *Psychol. Bull.*, 55:337–72.

LOVELL, K. (1961). A follow-up study of Inhelder and Piaget's "The growth of logical thinking." *Brit. J. Psychol.*, 52:143–53.

LOWELL, E. L. (1950). A methodological study of projectively measured achievement motivation. Unpublished master's thesis, Wesleyan University.

LOWELL, E. L. (1952). The effect of need for achievement on learning and speed of performance. *J. Psychol.*, 33:31–40.

LUCAS, J. D. (1952). The interactive effects of anxiety, failure, and intra-serial duplication. *Amer. J. Psychol.*, 65:59–66.

LUCKHARDT, A. B., and CARLSON, A. J. (1915). Contributions to the physiology of the stomach, XVII, on the chemical control of the gastric hunger contractions. *Amer. J. Physiol.*, 36:37–46.

LUH, C. W. (1922). The conditions of retention. *Psychol. Monogr.*, 31, No. 142.

LUMSDAINE, A. A. (1963). Instruments and media of instruction. In N. L. GAGE (ed.), *Handbook of research in teaching.* Chicago: Rand McNally. Pp. 583–682.

LUMSDAINE, A. A., and GLASER, R. (eds.) (1960). *Teaching machines and programmed learning: a source book.* Washington, D.C.: National Education Association.

LUMSDAINE, A. A., and JANIS, I. L. (1953). Resistance to "counterpropaganda" produced by one-sided and two-sided "propaganda" presentations. *Publ. Opin. Quart.*, 17:311–18.

LYNN, R. (1957). Temperamental characteristics related to disparity of attainment in reading and arithmetic. *Brit. J. educ. Psychol.*, 27:62–67.

McCANDLESS, B. R., and CASTANEDA, A. (1956). Anxiety in children, school achievement and intelligence. *Child Develpm.*, 27:379–82.

McCANDLESS, B. R., CASTANEDA, A., and PALERMO, D. S. (1956). Anxiety in children and social status. *Child Develpm.*, 27:385–91.

McCANDLESS, B. R., and MARSHALL, H. R. (1957a). A picture sociometric technique for preschool children and its relation to teacher judgments of friendship. *Child Develpm.*, 28:139–47.

McCANDLESS, B. R., and MARSHALL, H. R. (1957b). Sex differences in social acceptance and participation of preschool children. *Child Develpm.*, 28:421–25.

McCARTHY, DOROTHEA (1930). The language development of the preschool child. *Inst. Child. Welf. Monogr. Ser.*, No. 4. Minneapolis: University of Minnesota Press.

McCLELLAND, D. C., ATKINSON, J. W., CLARK, R. A., and LOWELL, E. L. (1953). *The achievement motive.* New York: Appleton-Century-Crofts.

McCURDY, H. G., and LAMBERT, W. E. (1952). The efficiency of small human groups in the solution of problems requiring genuine cooperation. *J. Pers.,* 20:478–94.

McDOUGALL, W. P. (1958). Differential retention of course outcomes in educational psychology. *J. educ. Psychol.,* 49:53–60.

McGEOCH, J. A. (1932). Forgetting and the law of disuse. *Psychol. Rev.,* 39:352–70.

McGEOCH, J. A., and IRION, A. L. (1952). *The psychology of human learning,* 2d ed. New York: McKay.

McGEOCH, J. A., and MELTON, A. W. (1929). The comparative retention values of maze habits and of nonsense syllables. *J. exp. Psychol.,* 12:392–414.

McGRAW, M. B. (1943). *Neuromuscular maturation of the human infant.* New York: Columbia University Press.

McGUIRE, W. J. (1960). A syllogistic analysis of cognitive relationships. In C. I. HOVLAND and M. J. ROSENBERG (eds.), *Attitude organization and change.* New Haven: Yale University Press. Pp. 65–111.

McGUIRE, W. J. (1961). Resistance to persuasion conferred by active and passive prior refutation of the same and alternative counterarguments. *J. abnorm. soc. Psychol.,* 63:326–32.

McGUIRE, W. J., and PAPAGEORGIS, D. (1961). Immunization against persuasion. *J. abnorm. soc. Psychol.,* 62:327–37.

McKEACHIE, W. J., POLLIE, D., and SPEISMAN, J. (1955). Relieving anxiety in classroom examinations, *J. abnorm. soc. Psychol.,* 50:93–98.

MacLEOD, R. B. (1962). Retrospect and prospect. In H. E. GRUBER, G. TERRELL, and M. WERTHEIMER (eds.), *Contemporary approaches to creative thinking.* New York: Atherton Press. Pp. 175–212.

MAINLAND, D., and MURRAY, I. M. (1952). Tables for use in fourfold contingency tests. *Science.,* 116:591–94.

MALM, M., and JAMISON, O. G. (1952). *Adolescence.* New York: McGraw-Hill.

MALTZMAN, I. (1960). On the training of originality. *Psychol. Rev.,* 67:229–42.

MANDLER, G. (1954). Transfer of training as a function of degree of response over learning. *J. exp. Psychol.,* 47:411–17.

MARK, S. J. (1961). Experimental study involving the comparison of two methods of performing experiments in high school chemistry. *Science Educ.,* 45:410–12.

MARTIN, W. E., and STENDLER, C. B. (1959). *Child behavior and development,* rev. ed. New York: Harcourt.

MARTIRE, J. G. (1956). Relationships between the self concept and differences in the strength and generality of achievement motivation. *J. Pers.,* 24:364–75.

MASLOW, A. H. (1954). *Motivation and personality.* New York: Harper.

MASSERMAN, J. H. (1943). *Behavior and neurosis.* Chicago: The University of Chicago Press.

MAY, M. A. (1946). The psychology of learning from demonstration films. *J. educ. Psychol.,* 37:1–12.

MEAD, G. H. (1934). *Mind, self and society.* Chicago: The University of Chicago Press.

MEANS, M. H. (1936). Fears of one thousand college women. *J. abnorm. soc. Psychol.,* 31:291–311.

MEDNICK, M. T. (1957). Mediated generalization and the incubation effect as a function of manifest anxiety. *J. abnorm. soc. Psychol.,* 55:315–21.

MEEK, L. H. (1940). The personal-social development of boys and girls with implications for secondary education. New York: Progressive Education Association.

MELTON, A. W., and VON LACKUM, W. J. (1941). Retroactive and proactive inhibition in retention: evidence for a two-factor theory of retroactive inhibition. *Amer. J. Psychol.*, 54:157–73.

MELTZER, H. (1936). Economic security and children's attitude to parents. *Amer. J. Orthopsychiat.*, 6:590–608.

MEYER, G. (1935). An experimental study of the old and new types of examinations: II. Methods of study. *J. educ. Psychol.*, 26:30–40.

MEYER, SUSAN R. (1960). Report on the initial test of a junior high school vocabulary program. In A. A. LUMSDAINE and R. GLASER (eds.), *Teaching machines and programmed learning: a source book*. Washington, D.C.: National Education Association. Pp. 229–46.

MILLER, G. A. (1956). The magical number seven, plus or minus two, some limits on our capacity for processing information. *Psychol. Rev.*, 63:81–97.

MILLER, G. A., GALANTER, E., and PRIBRAM, K. H. (1960). *Plans and the structure of behavior*. New York: Holt.

MILLER, N. E. (1948). Studies of fear as an acquirable drive: I. Fear as motivation and fear-reduction as reinforcement in the learning of new responses. *J. exp. Psychol.*, 38:89–101.

MILLER, N. E. (1959). Liberalization of the basic S–R concepts: extensions to conflict behavior, motivation and social learning. In S. KOCH (ed.), *Psychology: a study of a science*. New York: McGraw-Hill. Vol. II, pp. 196–292.

MILLER, N. E., and DOLLARD, J. (1941). *Social learning and imitation*. New Haven: Yale University Press.

MILLS, C. W. (1951). *White collar*. Fair Lawn, N.J.: Oxford University Press.

MITNICK, L. L., and McGINNIES, E. (1958). Influencing ethnocentrism in small discussion groups through a film communication. *J. abnorm. soc. Psychol.*, 56:82–90.

MOORE, J. W., and SMITH, W. I. (1961). Knowledge of results in self-teaching spelling. *Psychol. Rep.*, 9:717–26.

MORENO, J. L. (1934). *Who shall survive?* A new approach to the problem of human interrelations. Washington, D.C.: Nervous and Mental Diseases Publishing Co.

MORRIS, R. T. (1956). National status and attitudes of foreign students. *J. soc. Issues*, 12:20–25.

MOSIER, C. I., MYERS, C., and PRICE, H. G. (1945). Suggestions for the construction of multiple-choice test items. *Educ. psychol. Measmt*, 5:261–71.

MOWRER, O. H. (1947). On the dual nature of learning, a reinterpretation of conditioning and problem-solving. *Harv. educ. Rev.*, 17:102–48.

MOWRER, O. H. (1950). *Learning theory and personality dynamics*. New York: Ronald Press.

MUNROE, R. L. (1955). *Schools of psychoanalytic thought*. New York: Holt.

MURPHY, G. (1947). *Personality: a biosocial approach to origins and structure*. New York: Harper.

MURPHY, G., MURPHY, L. B., and NEWCOMB, T. M. (1937). *Experimental social psychology*. New York: Harper.

MURPHY, LOIS B. (1937). *Social behavior and child personality: an exploratory study of some roots of sympathy*. New York: Columbia University Press.

MURRAY, H. A. (1933). The effect of fear upon estimates of the maliciousness of other personalities. *J. soc. Psychol.*, 4:310–39.

MURRAY, H. A. (1938). *Explorations in personality*. Fair Lawn, N.J.: Oxford University Press.

MUSSEN, P. (1950). Some personality and social factors related to changes in children's attitudes toward Negroes. *J. abnorm. soc. Psychol.*, 45:423–41.

MUSSEN, P., and DISTLER, L. (1959). Masculinity, identification, and father-son relationships. *J. abnorm. soc. Psychol.*, 59:350–56.

NEFF, W. S. (1938). Socioeconomic status and intelligence: a critical survey. *Psychol. Bull.*, 35:727–57.

NEWCOMB, T. M. (1943). *Personality and social change.* New York: Holt.

NEWCOMB, T. M. (1953). An approach to the study of communicative acts. *Psychol. Rev.*, 60:393–404.

NEWCOMB, T. M. (1956). The prediction of interpersonal attraction. *Amer. Psychologist*, 11:575–86.

NEWELL, A., SHAW, J. C., and SIMON, H. A. (1958). Elements of a theory of human problem solving. *Psychol. Rev.*, 65:151–66.

NEWELL, A., SHAW, J. C., and SIMON, H. A. (1962). The process of creative thinking. In HOWARD E. GRUBER, GLENN TERRELL, and MICHAEL WERTHEIMER (eds.), *Contemporary approaches to creative thinking.* New York: Atherton Press.

NEWMAN, H. H., FREEMAN, F. N., and HOLZINGER, K. J. (1937). *Twins: a study of heredity and environment.* Chicago: The University of Chicago Press.

NOBLE, C. E. (1952). The role of stimulus meaning (m) in serial verbal learning. *J. exp. Psychol.*, 43:437–46.

NOBLE, G. V., and LUND, S. E. T. (1951). High school pupils report their fears. *J. educ. Sociol.*, 25:97–101.

NOLL, V. H. (1939). The effect of written tests upon achievement in college classes: an experiment and a summary of evidence. *J. educ. Res.*, 32:345–58.

NORTHWAY, M. L. (1943). Children's social development: a summary of the Toronto studies. *Bull. Canad. Psychol. Ass.*, 3:3–5.

NORTHWAY, M. L. (1944). Outsiders: a study of the personality patterns of children least acceptable to their age mates. *Sociometry*, 7:10–25.

NOWLIS, H. H. (1941). The influence of success and failure on the resumption of an interrupted task. *J. exp. Psychol.*, 28:304–25.

NOYES, E. S., SALE, W. M., JR., and STALNAKER, J. M. (1945). *Report on the first six tests in English composition.* Princeton, N.J.: College Entrance Examination Board.

OGG, E. (1955). Psychologists in action. *Public Affairs Pamphlet.* Public Affairs Committee, Inc.

OJEMANN, R. H. (1957). Social studies in light of knowledge about children. In *Social studies in the elementary school.* 56th Yearb. Nat. Soc. Stud. Educ., Part II, 76–119.

OLSON, W. C. (1959). *Child Development*, 2d ed. Boston: Heath.

ORBISON, W. D. (1944). The relative efficiency of whole and part methods of learning paired-associates as a function of the length of list. Unpublished doctor's dissertation, Yale University.

OSGOOD, C. E. (1946). Meaningful similarity and interference in learning. *J. exp. Psychol.*, 36:277–301.

OSGOOD, C. E. (1949). The similarity paradox in human learning: a resolution. *Psychol. Rev.*, 56:132–43.

OSGOOD, C. E. (1952). Nature and measurement of meaning. *Psychol. Bull.*, 49:197–237.

OSGOOD, C. E. (1953). *Method and theory in experimental psychology.* Fair Lawn, N.J.: Oxford University Press.

OSGOOD, C. E. (1961). Comments on Professor Bousfield's paper. In C. N. COFER (ed.), *Verbal learning and verbal behavior.* New York: McGraw-Hill. Pp. 91–106.

OSGOOD, C. E., and TANNENBAUM, P. H. (1955). The principle of congruity in the prediction of attitude change. *Psychol. Rev.*, 62:42–55.

OWENS, W. A., JR. (1953). Age and mental abilities: a longitudinal study. *Genet. Psychol. Monogr.*, 48:3–54.

PACE, C. R., and STERN, G. G. (1958). An approach to the measurement of psychological characteristics of college environments. *J. educ. Psychol.*, 49:269–77.

PAPAGEORGIS, D., and McGUIRE, W. J. (1961). The generality of immunity to persuasion produced by pre-exposure to weakened counterarguments. *J. abnorm. soc. Psychol.*, 62:475–81.

PARKER, W. K. (1962). The concept of structure in English. *Educ. Rec.*, 43:210–16.

PAYNE, D. E., and MUSSEN, P. (1956). Parent-child relations and father identification among adolescent boys. *J. abnorm. soc. Psychol.*, 52:358–62.

PEARSON, G. H. J. (1954). *Psychoanalysis and the education of the child.* New York: Norton.

PECK, R. F. (1958). Family patterns correlated with adolescent personality structure. *J. abnorm. soc. Psychol.*, 57:347–50.

PECK, R. F., and HAVIGHURST, R. J. (1960). *The psychology of character development.* New York: Wiley.

PEEL, E. S. (1959). Experimental examination of some of Piaget's schemata concerning children's perception and thinking and a discussion of their educational significance. *Brit. J. educ. Psychol.*, 29:89–103.

PENFIELD, W. (1958). *The excitable cortex in conscious man.* Liverpool, Eng.: University Press of Liverpool.

PENNINGTON, L. A. (1938). The function of the brain in auditory localization. IV. Method of training and control experiments. *J. comp. Psychol.*, 25:129–211.

PETERSON, K. M. (1938). Sex information and its influence on later sex concepts. Unpublished master's thesis, University of Colorado.

PETERSON, R. C., and THURSTONE, L. L. (1933). *Motion pictures and the social attitudes of children.* New York: Macmillan.

PETTIGREW, T. F. (1964). *A profile of the Negro American.* Princeton, N.J.: Van Nostrand.

PIAGET, J. (1936). *The origins of intelligence in children.* Trans. MARGARET COOK. New York: International Universities Press, 1952.

PIAGET, J. (1945). *Play dreams, and imitation in childhood.* Trans. of C. GATTEGNO and F. M. HODGSON, La formation du symbole chez l'enfant. New York: Norton, 1951.

PIAGET, J. (1947). *The psychology of intelligence.* Trans. M. PIERCY and D. E. BERLYNE. London: Routledge & Kegan Paul, 1950.

PIAGET, J. (1960). *The child's conception of physical causality.* Paterson, N.J.: Littlefield, Adams.

PIAGET, J., and SZEMINSKA, A. (1941). *The child's conception of number.* Trans. C. GATTEGNO and F. M. HODGSON. New York: Humanities Press, 1952.

PITMAN, SIR JAMES (1963). *The future of the teaching of reading.* Address presented at the 28th Educational Conference by the Educational Records Bureau in New York, November 1, 1963.

PLOWMAN, LETHA F., and STROUD, J. B. (1942). Effect of informing pupils of the correctness of their responses to objective test questions. *J. educ. Res.*, 36:16–20.

POPE, B. (1953). Socio-economic contrasts in children's peer culture prestige values. *Genet. Psychol. Monogr.*, 48:157–220.

PORTER, D. (1959). Some effects of year long teaching machine instruction. In E. GALANTER (ed.), *Automatic teaching.* New York: Wiley. Pp. 85–102.

POSTMAN, L. (1951). Toward a general theory of cognition. In J. H. ROHRER and M. SHERIF (eds.), *Social psychology at the crossroads.* New York: Harper.

PRATT, K. C. (1938). Intelligence as a determinant of the "functional" value of curricular content. *J. educ. Psychol.*, 29:44–49.

PRESSEY, S. L. (1926). A simple apparatus which gives tests and scores—and teaches. *Sch. & Soc.*, 23:373–76.

PRESSEY, S. L. (1963). Teaching machine (and learning theory) crisis. *J. appl. Psychol.*, 47:1–6.

PRIBRAM, K. H. (1960). A review of theory in physiological psychology. *Annu. Rev. Psychol.*, 11:1–40.

PULLIAS, E. V. (1937). Masturbation as a mental hygiene problem—a study of the beliefs of seventy-five young men. *J. abnorm. soc. Psychol.*, 32:216–22.

PUNKE, H. H. (1943). High school youth and family quarrels. *School and Society*, 58:507–11.

RADKE, MARIAN J. (1946). The relation of parental authority to children's behavior and attitudes. *Univer. Minn. Inst. Welf. Monogr.*, No. 22.

RAGSDALE, C. E. (1950). How children learn the motor types of activities. In *Learning and instruction*. 49th Yearb. Nat. Soc. Stud. Educ., Part I, pp. 69–91.

RAMSEY, G. V. (1943). The sexual development of boys. *Amer. J. Psychol.*, 56: 217–33.

RATH, G., ANDERSON, NANCY S., and BRAINERD, R. C. (1959). The IBM Research Center Teaching Machine Project. In E. GALANTER (ed.), *Automatic teaching: the state of the art.* New York: Wiley. Pp. 117–30.

RATHS, L. E., and TRAGER, F. N. (1948). Public opinion and crossfire. *J. educ. Soc.*, 21:345–68.

RAY, J. J. (1936). The generalizing ability of dull, bright, and superior children. *Peabody Contr. Educ.*, No. 175.

REMMERS, H. H., and RADLER, D. H. (1957). *The American teenager.* Indianapolis: Bobbs-Merrill.

RHINE, R. J., and SILUN, B. A. (1958). Acquisition and change of a concept attitude as a function of consistency of reinforcement. *J. exp. Psychol.*, 55:524–29.

RICH, J. M. (1962). Creating interest in current events. *Social Studies*, 53:167–68.

RICHARDS, T. W. (1951). Mental test performance as a reflection of the child's current life situation: a methodological study. *Child Develpm.*, 22:221–33.

RICHARDSON, M. W. (1936). The relation between the difficulty and the differential validity of a test. *Psychometrika*, 1:33–49.

RICKETTS, A. F. (1934). A study of the behavior of young children in anger. *Univer. Iowa Stud. Child Welf.*, 9, No. 3:159–71.

ROBINSON, E. S. (1927). The "similarity" factor in retroaction. *Amer. J. Psychol.*, 39:297–312.

ROGERS, C. R. (1951). *Client-centered therapy: its current practice implications and theory.* Boston: Houghton Mifflin.

ROGERS, C. R. (1961). *On becoming a person: a therapist's view of psychotherapy.* Boston: Houghton Mifflin.

ROKEACH, M. (1960). *The open and closed mind.* New York: Basic Books.

ROMANOW, C. V. (1958). Anxiety level and ego involvement as factors in concept formation. *J. exp. Psychol.*, 56:166–73.

ROSEN, B. C. (1958). The achievement syndrome. In J. W. ATKINSON (ed.), *Motives in fantasy, action, and society.* Princeton, N.J.: Van Nostrand. Chap. 35.

ROSEN, B. C., and D'ANDRADE, R. (1959). The psychosocial origins of achievement motivation. *Sociometry*, 22:185–218.

ROSENBAUM, M. E., and FRANC, D. E. (1960). Opinion change as a function of external commitment and amount of discrepancy from the opinion of another. *J. abnorm. soc. Psychol.*, 61:15–20.

ROSENBERG, M. J. (1960). An analysis of affective-cognitive consistency. In C. I. HOVLAND and M. J. ROSENBERG (eds.), *Attitude organization and change.* New Haven: Yale University Press. Pp. 15–64.

ROSENBERG, M. J., and HOVLAND, C. I. (1960). Cognitive, affective, and behavioral components of attitudes. In C. I. HOVLAND and M. J. ROSENBERG (eds.), *Attitude organization and change.* New Haven: Yale University Press. Pp. 1–14.

ROSENFELD, H., and ZANDER, A. (1961). The influence of teachers on aspirations of students. *J. educ. Psychol.*, 52:1–11.

ROSENZWEIG, S. (1941). Need-persistive and ego-defensive reactions to frustration as demonstrated by an experiment on repression. *Psychol. Rev.*, 48:347–49.

ROSENZWEIG, S. (1943). An experimental study of "repression" with special reference to need-persistive and ego-defensive reactions to frustration. *J. exp. Psychol.*, 32:64–74.

ROSS, C. C., and STANLEY, J. C. (1954). *Measurement in today's schools.* Englewood Cliffs, N.J.: Prentice-Hall.

ROSS, R. T. (1950). Measures of the sex behavior of college males compared with Kinsey's results. *J. abnorm. soc. Psychol.*, 45:753–55.

RUEBUSH, B. K. (1960). Interfering and facilitating effects of test anxiety. *J. abnorm. soc. Psychol.*, 60:205–12.

RUSSELL, D. (1956). *Children's thinking.* Boston: Ginn.

RUSSELL, W. A., and JENKINS, J. J. (1954). The complete Minnesota norms for responses to 100 words from the Kent-Rosanoff word association test. Technical Report No. 11. *Studies in the role of language in behavior.* Office of Naval Research (N8 ONR–66216).

SADY, R. R. (1948). The function of rumors in relocation centers. Unpublished doctor's dissertation, The University of Chicago.

SANDIFORD, P. (1938). *Foundations of educational psychology.* New York: McKay.

SANFORD, N. (1955). The dynamics of identification. *Psychol. Rev.*, 62:106–18.

SANFORD, R. N., ADKINS, M. M., MILLER, R. B., COBB, E. A., et al. (1943). Physique, personality and scholarship: a cooperative study of school children. *Soc. Res. Child Develpm. Monogr.*, 8, No. 1.

SARASON, S. B., DAVIDSON, K. S., LIGHTHALL, F. F., WAITE, R. R., and RUEBUSH, B. K. (1960). *Anxiety in elementary school children.* New York: Wiley.

SARBIN, T. R. (1952). A preface of a psychological analysis of the self. *Psychol. Rev.*, 59:11–22.

SARBIN, T. R. (1954). Role theory. In G. LINDZEY (ed.), *Handbook of social psychology.* Cambridge: Addison-Wesley. Vol. I, chap. 6.

SARNOFF, I. (1962). *Personality, dynamics and development.* New York: Wiley.

SAX, G., and READE, M. (1964). Achievement as a function of test difficulty level. *Amer. educ. res. J.*, 1:22–25.

SCHACHTER, S., and BURDICK, H. (1955). A field experiment on rumor transmission and distortion. *J. abnorm. soc. Psychol.*, 50:363–71.

SCHEINFELD, A. (1950). *The new you and heredity.* Philadelphia: Lippincott.

SCHLOSBERG, H. (1937). The relationship between success and the laws of conditioning. *Psychol. Rev.*, 44:379–94.

SCHWAB, S. J. (1962). The concept of the structure of a discipline. *Educ. Rec.*, 43:197–205.

SEARS, PAULINE S. (1940). Levels of aspiration in academically successful and unsuccessful children. *J. abnorm. soc. Psychol.*, 35:498–536.

SEARS, PAULINE S., and LEVIN, H. (1956). Levels of aspiration in preschool children. *Child Develpm.*, 28:317–26.

SEARS, R. R. (1943). Survey of objective studies of psychoanalytic concepts. *Soc. Sci. Res. Council.*, No. 51.

SEARS, R. R. (1950). Personality. *Annu. Rev. Psychol.*, 1:105–18.

SEARS, R. R., and MACCOBY, E. E., and LEVIN, H. (1957). *Patterns of child rearing.* Evanston, Ill.: Row, Peterson.

SEARS, R. R., WHITING, J. W. M., NOWLIS, V., and SEARS, P. S. (1953). Some child-rearing antecedents of aggression and dependency in young children. *Genet. Psychol. Monogr.*, 47:135–234.

SEARS, R. R., and WISE, G. W. (1950). Relation of cup feeding in infancy to thumb sucking and the oral drive. *Amer. J. Orthopsychiat.*, 20:123–38.

SEASHORE, H. G. (1951). Differences between verbal and performance I.Q.'s on the Wechsler Intelligence Scale for children, *J. consult. Psychol.*, 15:62–67.

SELLS, S. B. (1962). *Essentials of psychology.* New York: Ronald Press.

SHAFFER, L. F. (1947). Fear and courage in aerial combat. *J. consult. Psychol.*, 11:137–43.

SHANE, H. G. (1959). Can we be proud of the facts? In C. W. SCOTT, C. M. HILL, and H. W. BURNS (eds.), *The great debate. Our schools in crises.* Englewood Cliffs, N.J.: Prentice-Hall. Pp. 132–39.

SHAW, G. B. (1953). *The complete plays of George Bernard Shaw.* London: Odhams Press.

SHAY, C. B. (1961). Relationship of intelligence to step size on a teaching machine program. *J. educ. Psychol.*, 52:98–103.

SHELDON, W. H., and STEVENS, S. S. (1942). *The varieties of temperament: a psychology of constitutional differences.* New York: Harper.

SHERMAN, M. (1927). The differentiation of emotional responses in infants. *J. comp. Psychol.*, 7:265–84, 335–51.

SIIPOLA, E. M. (1935). A group study of some effects of preparatory set. *Psychol. Monogr.*, 46, No. 210.

SIIPOLA, E. M., and ISRAEL, H. E. (1933). Habit interference as dependent upon stage of training. *Amer. J. Psychol.*, 45:205–27.

SILBERMAN, H. F. (1962). Self teaching devices and programmed materials. *Rev. educ. Res.*, 32:179–93.

SIMON, H. A., and NEWELL, A. (1962). Computer simulation of human thinking and problem solving. *Monogr. Soc. Child Develpm.*, 27, No. 2: 137–50.

SIMS, V. M. (1931). The objectivity, reliability, and validity of an essay examination graded by rating. *J. educ. Res.*, 24:216–23.

SIMS, V. M. (1948). The essay examination is a projective technique. *Educ. psychol. Measmt*, 8:15–31.

SIMS, V. M., and PATRICK, J. R. (1936). Attitude toward the Negro of northern and southern college students. *J. soc. Psychol.*, 7:192–204.

SKINNER, B. F. (1938). *The behavior of organisms.* New York: Appleton-Century-Crofts.

SKINNER, B. F. (1953). *Science and human behavior.* New York: Macmillan.

SKINNER, B. F. (1954). The science of learning and the art of teaching. *Harv. educ. Rev.*, 24, No. 2: 86–97.

SKINNER, B. F. (1959). A case history in scientific method. *Cumulative Rec.* New York: Appleton-Century-Crofts. Pp. 76–100.

SLEIGHT, W. G. (1911). Memory and formal training. *Brit. J. Psychol.*, 4:386–457.

SMOCK, C. D. (1958). Perceptual rigidity and closure phenomenon as a function of manifest anxiety in children. *Child Develpm.*, 29:237–47.

SMOKE, K. L. (1933). Negative instances in concept learning. *J. exp. Psychol.*, 16:583–88.

SNYDER, F. W., and SNYDER, C. W. (1956). The effects of monetary reward and punishment on auditory perception. *J. Psychol.*, 41:177–84.

SOLLEY, C. M., and MURPHY, G. (1960). *Development of the perceptual World.* New York: Basic Books.

SOLOMON, R. L., and WYNNE, L. C. (1954). Traumatic avoidance learning: the principles of anxiety conservation and partial irreversibility. *Psychol. Rev.*, 61:353–85.

SPAULDING, G. (1951). Reproducing the test. In E. F. LINDQUIST (ed.), *Educational Measurement.* Washington: American Council on Education. Pp. 417–54.

SPRANGER, E. (1928). *Types of men; synthetic psychology and ethics of personality.* Halle: Niemeyer.

STALNAKER, J. M. (1937). Question VI, the essay. *English J.* (Coll. ed.), 26:133–40.

STARCH, D., and ELLIOTT, E. C. (1913). Reliability of grading work in mathematics. *Sch. Rev.*, 21:254–59.

STEPHENS, J. M. (1934). The influence of punishment on learning. *J. exp. Psychol.*, 17:536–55.

STERN, C. (1949). *Principles of human genetics.* San Francisco: Freeman.

STERN, G. G. (1958). Preliminary manual: Activities Index and College Characteristics Index. Syracuse: Syracuse Univer. Psychological Research Center.

STERN, G. G., STEIN, M. I., and BLOOM, B. S. (1956). *Methods in personality assessment.* New York: The Free Press of Glencoe.

STERN, G. G. (1961). Continuity and contrast in the transition from school to college. In N. F. BROWN (ed.), *Orientation to college learning.* Washington, D.C.: American Council on Education.

STERN, G. G. (1962). Environments for learning. In N. SANFORD (ed.), *The American College.* New York: Wiley.

STERN, G. G. (1963). Measuring noncognitive variables in research on teaching. In N. L. GAGE (*ed.*), *Handbook of research on teaching.* Chicago: Rand McNally. Pp. 398–447.

STEVENSON, H. W., WEIR, M. W., and ZIGLER, E. F. (1959). Discrimination learning in children as a function of motive-incentive conditions. *Psychol. Rep.*, 5:95–98.

STOKE, S. M. (1950). An inquiry into the concept of identification. *J. genet. Psychol.*, 76:163–89.

STOLUROW, L. M. (1961). *Teaching by machines.* Cooperative Research Monograph No. 6. Washington, D.C.: U.S. Office of Education, Government Printing Office.

STOLZ, H. R., and STOLZ, L. M. (1951). *Somatic development of adolescent boys.* New York: Macmillan.

STOVALL, T. F. (1958). Lecture vs. discussion. *Phi Delta Kappan*, 39:255–58.

STRODTBECK, F. L. (1958). Family interaction, values, and achievement. In D. C. MCCLELLAND, A. L. BALDWIN, U. BRONFENBRENNER, and F. L. STRODTBECK. *Talent and society.* Princeton, N.J.: Van Nostrand. Chap. 4.

STROUD, J. B. (1940). Experiments on learning in school situations. *Psychol. Bull.*, 37:777–807.

SULLIVAN, H. S. (1953). *The interpersonal theory of psychiatry.* New York: Norton.

SUPER, D. E. (1949). *Appraising vocational fitness.* New York: Harper.

SYMONDS, P. M. (1949). *Dynamic psychology.* New York: Appleton-Century-Crofts.

SYMONDS, P. M. (1951). *The ego and the self.* New York: Appleton-Century-Crofts.

TABA, H. (1955). *With perspective on human relations.* Washington, D.C.: American Council on Education.

TAYLOR, JANET A. (1953). A personality scale of manifest anxiety. *J. abnorm. soc. Psychol.*, 48:285–90.

TAYLOR, JANET A. (1956). Drive theory and manifest anxiety. *Psychol. Bull.*, 53:303–20.

TAYLOR, J. H. (1960). Chromosome reproduction and the problem of coding and transmitting of the genetic heritage. *Amer. Scientist*, 48:365–82.

TERMAN, L. M. (1954). Scientists and nonscientists in a group of 800 gifted men. *Psychol. Monogr.*, 68 No. 378.

TERMAN, L. M. (ed.), et al. (1925). *Genetic studies of genius*, Vol. I: *Mental and physical traits of a thousand gifted children.* Stanford: Stanford University Press.

TERMAN, L. M., and MERRILL, M. A. (1937). *Measuring intelligence.* Boston: Houghton Mifflin.

TERMAN, L. M., and MERRILL, M. A. (1960). *Stanford-Binet intelligence scale.* Boston: Houghton Mifflin.

TERMAN, L. M., and ODEN, M. H. (1940). Status of the California gifted group at the end of sixteen years; correlates of adult achievement in the California gifted group. In *Intelligence: its nature and nurture.* 39th Yearb. Nat. Stud. Educ., Part I, 67–84.

TERMAN, L. M., and ODEN, M. H. (1947). *Genetic studies of genius,* Vol. IV: *The Gifted child grows up.* Stanford: Stanford University Press.

TERRY, P. W. (1933). How students review for objective and essay tests. *Elem. Sch. J.,* 33:592–603.

THISTLETHWAITE, D. L. (1959). Effects of social recognition upon the educational motivation of talented youth. *J. educ. Psychol.,* 50:111–16.

THISTLETHWAITE, D. L. (1962). Fields of study and development of motivation to seek advanced training. *J. educ. Psychol.,* 53:53–64.

THOMPSON, G. G. (1962). *Child psychology: growth trends in psychological adjustment;* 2d ed. Boston: Houghton Mifflin.

THOMPSON, G. G., and HUNNICUTT, C. W. (1944). The effect of repeated praise or blame on the work achievement of "introverts" and "extroverts." *J. educ. Psychol.,* 35:257–66.

THOMPSON, L. (1944). *The role of verbalization in learning from demonstration.* Unpublished doctor's dissertation, Yale University.

THOMPSON, W. R., and HERON, W. (1954). The effects of restricting early experience on the problem solving capacity of dogs. *Canad. J. Psychol.,* 8:17–31.

THORNDIKE, E. L. (1898). *Animal intelligence. Psychol. Monogr.,* 2, No. 8.

THORNDIKE, E. L. (1911). *Animal intelligence,* New York: Macmillan.

THORNDIKE, E. L. (1913). *Educational Psychology,* Vol. II: *The psychology of learning.* New York: Teachers College, Bureau of Publications, Columbia University Press.

THORNDIKE, E. L. (1924). Mental discipline in high school studies. *J. educ. Psychol.,* 15:1–22, 83–98.

THORNDIKE, E. L. (1927). The law of effect. *Amer. J. Psychol.,* 39:212–22.

THORNDIKE, E. L. (1932). *The fundamentals of learning.* New York: Teachers College, Bureau of Publications, Columbia University.

THORNDIKE, R. L., and HAGEN, ELIZABETH (1961). *Measurement and evaluation in psychology and education,* 2d ed. New York: Wiley.

THURSTONE, L. L. (1935). *The vectors of mind.* Chicago: The University of Chicago Press.

THURSTONE, L. L. (1938). Primary mental abilities. *Psychometrika Monogr. Series,* No. 1. Chicago: The University of Chicago Press.

TOCH, H., and CANTRIL, H. (1957). A preliminary inquiry into the learning of values. *J. educ. Psychol.,* 48:145–56.

TOLMAN, E. C. (1932). *Purposive behavior in animals and men.* New York: Appleton-Century-Crofts.

TOMPKINS, S. S., and MESSICK, S. J. (1963). *Computer simulation of personality.* New York: Wiley.

TORRANCE, E. P. (1963). *Creativity.* What Research Says Series, No. 28. Washington, D.C.: American Educational Research Association, National Education Association.

TORRANCE, E. P., and HARMON, J. A. (1961). Effects of memory, evaluative, and creative reading sets on test performance. *J. educ. Psychol.,* 52:207–14.

TRAVERS, R. M. W. (1950). *How to make achievement tests.* New York: Odyssey Press.

TRAVERS, R. M. W. (1963). *Essentials of learning.* New York: Macmillan.

TRAXLER, A. E. (1950). Administering and scoring the objective test. In E. F. LINDQUIST (ed.), *Educational measurement*. Washington, D.C.: American Council on Education. Pp. 329–416.

TROWBRIDGE, M. H., and CASON, H. (1932). An experimental study of Thorndike's theory of learning. *J. gen. Psychol.*, 7:245–58.

TYLER, F. T. (1964). Issues related to readiness to learn. In E. R. HILGARD (ed.), *Theories of learning and instruction*. 63d Yearb. Nat. Soc. Stud. Educ., Part I, 210–39.

TYLER, LEONA (1956). *The psychology of human differences*, 2d ed. New York: Appleton-Century-Crofts.

TYLER, R. W. (1932). Ability to use scientific method. *Educ. Res. Bull.*, 11:1–9.

TYLER, R. W. (1933). Permanence of learning. *J. Higher Educ.*, 4:203–5.

TYLER, R. W. (1947). Syllabus for education 360. *Basic principles of curriculum and instruction*. Mimeographed edition. Chicago: The University of Chicago Press.

TYLER, R. W. (1948). Educability and the schools. *Elem. Sch. J.*, 49:200–212.

TYLER, R. W. (1957). *The curriculum—then and now. Proceedings, 1956, Invitational conference on testing problems*. Princeton, N.J.: Educational Testing Service. Pp. 79–94.

ULMER, G. (1939). Teaching geometry to cultivate reflective thinking: an experimental study with 1239 high school pupils. *J. exp. Educ.*, 8:18–25.

UNDERWOOD, B. J. (1945). The effect of successive interpolations on retroactive and proactive inhibition. *Psychol. Monogr.*, 59, No. 273.

UNDERWOOD, B. J. (1949). *Experimental psychology*. New York: Appleton-Century-Crofts.

UNDERWOOD, B. J. (1951). Associative transfer in verbal learning as a function of response similarity and degree of first list learning. *J. exp. Psychol.*, 42:44–53.

UNDERWOOD, B. J. (1957). *Psychological research*. New York: Appleton-Century-Crofts.

VERNON, M. (1957). *Backwardness in reading: a study of its nature and origin*. London: Cambridge University Press.

VERPLANCK, W. S. (1955). The control of the content of conversation: reinforcement of statements of opinion. *J. abnorm. soc. Psychol.*, 51:668–76.

WALLAS, G. (1926). *The art of thought*. New York: Harcourt.

WALLEN, N. E., and TRAVERS, R. M. W. (1963). Analysis and investigation of teaching methods. In N. L. GAGE (ed.), *Handbook of research on teaching*. Chicago: Rand McNally. Pp. 448–505.

WARD, L. B. (1937). Reminiscence and rote learning. *Psychol. Monogr.*, 49, No. 220.

WARNER, W. L., MEEKER, M., and EELLS, K. (1949). *Social class in America*. Chicago: Science Research Associates.

WATSON, J. B. (1919). *Psychology from the standpoint of a behaviorist*. Philadelphia: Lippincott.

WATSON, J., and LIPPITT, R. (1958). Cross-culture experiences as a source of attitude change. *J. Conflicting Resolution*, 2:61–66.

WATSON, J. B., and RAYNER, R. (1920). Conditioned emotional reactions. *J. exp. Psychol.*, 3:1–14.

WATSON, R. I. (1959). *Psychology of the child*. New York: Wiley.

WATSON, W. S., and HARTMANN, G. W. (1939). The rigidity of a basic attitudinal frame. *J. abnorm. soc. Psychol.*, 34:314–35.

WECHSLER, D. (1955). *Wechsler adult intelligence scale, manual*. New York: Psychological Corporation.

WERNER, H., and KAPLAN, E. (1950a). Development of word meaning through verbal context: an experimental study. *J. Psychol.*, 29:251–57.

WERNER, H., and KAPLAN, E. (1950b). The acquisition of word meanings: a developmental study. *Soc. Res. Child Develpm. Monogr.*, 15, No. 1.

WERTHEIMER, M. (1959). *Productive thinking,* rev. ed. New York: Harper.

WESMAN, A. G. (1945). A study of transfer of training from high school subjects to intelligence. *J. educ. Res.,* 39:254–64.

WEST, J. (1945). *Plainville, U.S.A.* New York: Columbia University Press.

WEST, J. E. (1937). Twin examination assumptions. *J. higher Educ.,* 8:136–40.

WEST, J. V., and FRUCHTER, B. (1960). A longitudinal study of the relationship of high school foreign language and mathematics study to freshman grades. *J. educ. Res.,* 54:105–10.

WESTOVER, F. L. (1958). A comparison of listening and reading as a means of testing. *J. educ. Res.,* 52:23–26.

WHITE, R. W. (1959). Motivation reconsidered: the concept of competence. *Psychol. Rev.,* 66:297–333.

WHITEHEAD, A. N., and RUSSELL, B. (1925). *Principia Mathematica,* 2d ed. Cambridge, Eng.: Cambridge University Press.

WHITING, J. W. M. (1954). The cross-cultured method. In G. LINDZEY (ed.), *Handbook of social psychology.* Cambridge: Addison-Wesley. Vol. I, chap. 4.

WHITING, J. W. M., and CHILD, I. L. (1953). *Child training and personality: a cross-cultural study.* New Haven: Yale University Press.

WILLIAMS, M. J. (1949). Personal and familiar problems of high school youths and their bearing upon family education needs. *Social Forces,* 27:279–85.

WINCH, W. H. (1911). Further work on numerical accuracy in school children: does improvement in numerical accuracy transfer? *J. educ. Psychol.,* 2:262–71.

WINTERBOTTOM, MARION R. (1958). The relation of need for achievement to learning experiences in independence and mastery. In J. W. ATKINSON (ed.), *Motives in fantasy, action, and society.* Princeton, N.J.: Van Nostrand. Chap. 33.

WIRT, R. D., and BROEN, W. E. (1956). The relation of the Children's Manifest Anxiety Scale to the concept of anxiety as used in the clinic. *J. consult. Psychol.,* 20:482.

WISPE, L. G. (1951). Evaluating section teaching methods. *J. educ. Res.,* 45:161–86.

WOHLWILL, J. F. (1957). The abstraction and conceptualization of form, color, and number. *J. exp. Psychol.,* 53:304–9.

WOHLWILL, J. F. (1960). Developmental studies of perception. *Psychol. Bull.,* 57:249–88.

WOHLWILL, J. F. (1962). From perception to inference: a dimension of cognition development. *Monogr. Soc. Res. Child Develpm.,* 27, No. 2: 87–112.

WOLF, R. M. (1963). The identification and measurement of environmental process variables related to intelligence. Unpublished doctor's dissertation in progress, University of Chicago.

WOLFE, J. B. (1936). Effectiveness of token-rewards for chimpanzees. *Comp. Psychol. Monogr.,* 12, No. 60.

WOLFLE, D. (1951). Training. In S. S. STEVENS (ed.), *Handbook of experimental psychology.* New York: Wiley. Pp. 1267–86.

WOOD, B. D., and FREEMAN, F. N. (1932). *An experimental study of the educational influences of the typewriter in the elementary school classroom.* New York: Macmillan.

WOOD, DOROTHY A. (1960). *Test Construction.* Columbus, Ohio: Merrill Books, Inc.

WOODROW, H. (1927). The effect of type of training upon transference. *J. educ. Psychol.,* 18:159–72.

WOODWARD, MARY (1959). The behavior of idiots interpreted by Piaget's theory of sensori-motor development. *Brit. J. educ. Psychol.,* 29:60–71.

WOODWORTH, R. S. (1938). *Experimental psychology.* New York: Holt.

WOODWORTH, R. S. (1958). *Dynamics of behavior.* New York: Holt.

WOOLDRIDGE, D. E. (1963). *The machinery of the brain.* New York: McGraw-Hill.

WRIGHT, BEATRICE A. (1942). Altruism in children and the perceived conduct of others. *J. abnorm. soc. Psychol.,* 37:218–33.

YERKES, R. M. (ed.) (1921). Psychological examining in the United States Army. *Mem. Nat. Acad. Sci.,* 15.

YOUNG, P. T. (1961). *Motivation and emotion.* New York: Wiley.

YUM, K. S. (1931). An experimental test of the law of assimilation. *J. exp. Psychol.,* 14:68–82.

ZEIGARNIK, B. (1927). Das Behalten erledigter und unerledigter Handlungen. *Psychol. Forsch.,* 9:1–85.

ZWEIBELSON, I. (1956). Test anxiety and intelligence test performance. *J. consult. Psychol.,* 20:479–81.

NAME INDEX

Abelson, R. P., 432
Adkins, M. M., 93
Adler, A., 524
Adorno, T. W., 425, 426
Allen, Lucile, 134
Allison, S. G., 252
Allport, G. W., 84, 261, 262, 304, 305, 425, 513, 514
Allyn, J., 453
Ames, L. B., 180
Anastasi, A., 97, 159
Anderson, C. C., 389
Anderson, C. M., 251
Anderson, Nancy, 228
Anderson, R. C., 239, 240
Angelino, H., 159
Archer, C. P., 292
Arnold, M. B., 154
Ash, P., 252
Ashbaugh, E. J., 324
Atkinson, J. W., 266, 267, 271
Atwater, S. K., 300
Austin, G. A., 356, 357, 358, 360, 361, 362, 374
Ausubel, D. P., 322, 323, 340, 341
Ax, A. F., 156

Babitz, M., 292
Bagby, J. W., 312
Baldwin, A. L., 158, 172, 174, 191, 281
Banta, T. J., 423
Barnard, J. W., 249
Baron, D., 491
Bartlett, F., 389, 399–401
Bateson, G., 78
Bayley, N., 100, 101, 129, 188, 189
Benedict, Ruth, 79
Bennett, G. K., 142–46
Berko, J., 333
Berkowitz, L., 237

Berkun, M., 258
Berlyne, D. E., 245, 259, 397
Bernard, H. W., 491
Bernstein, M. R., 337, 354
Bettelheim, B., 436
Bexton, W. H., 263
Bills, R. E., 519, 535, 543
Bilodeau, E. A., 300
Binet, A., 117
Bingham, W. V., 22
Birch, H. G., 404
Blake, E., 340, 341
Blake, R. R., 309, 311
Block, V. L., 166
Bloom, B. S., 92, 196, 197, 198, 222, 263, 284, 331, 399, 407–10, 419, 420, 481, 484, 485
Bogardus, E. S., 178
Bond, A. D., 451
Bond, E. A., 136
Bonney, M. E., 178, 187, 188, 445
Boodish, H. M., 336
Boswell, F. P., 322
Bourne, L. E., Jr., 376
Bousfield, W. A., 320, 323
Brainerd, R. C., 228
Braley, L. S., 362
Breese, F. H., 172, 174
Brehm, J. W., 430
Brenner, M., 3
Bridges, K. M. B., 153, 154
Britt, S. H., 326
Brodbeck, May, 510, 511, 516
Broder, Lois, 263, 407–10, 420
Broen, W. E., 245, 246
Brooks, F. D., 302
Brophy, I. N., 446
Brown, H. L., 221
Brown, J. S., 520
Brown, R., 333

Brownell, W. A., 342
Broyler, C. R., 296
Bruce, R. W., 298
Brueckner, L. J., 324
Bruner, J. S., 77, 313, 314, 356, 357,
    358, 360, 361, 362, 374, 406, 408,
    409, 410, 414
Bugelski, B. R., 299, 392, 393
Burdick, H., 445
Burt, C., 96
Buswell, G. T., 19
Butler, R. A., 258
Byrne, D., 445

Cahill, H. E., 362
Calvin, A. D., 14
Campbell, D. T., 221
Campbell, R. E., 18
Cantoni, L. J., 139
Cantril, H., 311, 312, 443, 444, 460
Carlsmith, J. M., 430
Carlson, A. J., 512
Carmichael, L., 525
Carroll, H. A., 302
Cartwright, D., 432
Case, D., 375, 376
Cason, H., 344
Castaneda, A., 245, 249, 252
Cattell, R. B., 261
Chauncey, H., 492, 493
Check, J., 302
Chein, I., 312, 313
Child, I. L., 80–81, 281, 282
Chomsky, N., 399
Christensen, C. M., 389
Clark, R. A., 266, 267, 271
Cobb, E. A., 93
Cofer, C. N., 405
Cohen, A. R., 430
Cohen, M. R., 516
Cohen, N., 159
Coleman, J. S., 87, 284
Collins, M. E., 447
Collinson, J. M., 375, 376
Combs, A. W., 52, 53, 54, 103, 252,
    260, 264, 535
Conrad, H. S., 128
Cook, W. W., 78
Courtis, S. A., 100
Crandall, V. J., 270, 271, 274, 290
Cronbach, L. J., 119, 136
Crowder, N. A., 228, 229
Crutchfield, R. S., 411, 412, 414
Cukier, L., 322, 323
Culbertson, F. M., 447
Curti, Margaret W., 366

d'Andrade, R., 271, 290
Davidson, K. S., 246–51
Davis, A., 90–91, 93, 132
Davis, F. B., 494, 498
Davitz, J., 3
Deese, J. E., 299
Della-Piana, G. M., 383
Dembo, T., 281, 282
Deutsch, M., 447
Dewey, J., 405–7, 410, 420
Dicks, H. V., 82
Diederich, P. B., 279, 280, 478, 486
Dimond, S. E., 381
Distler, L., 437
Dobbin, J. E., 492, 493
Dobzhansky, T., 73
Dolger, L., 93
Dollard, J. C., 45, 194, 201, 202, 205,
    217
Dollins, J., 159
Dominguez, K., 300
Donaldson, M., 362
Donnelly, H. E., 76
Douvan, Elizabeth, 273
Downing, J. A., 77
Drevdahl, J. E., 413
Dugdale, R. L., 96
Dunkel, H. B., 77, 106
Dunnington, M. J., 187
Dymond, R. F., 181, 187

Ebbinghaus, H., 316, 317
Edwards, A. L., 429
Eells, K., 88–90, 132
Ehrlich, H. J., 427
Ehrmann, W. W., 183
Elliott, E. C., 477
Emmerich, W., 174
English, Ava C., 10, 79, 169, 213
English, H. B., 10, 79, 169, 213
Ennis, R. H., 415–19
Erikson, E. H., 60–65, 67, 82
Estes, K. W., 278
Ewing, T. A., 453, 461

Fales, E., 186
Falls, J. D., 477
Feigl, H., 510, 511, 516
Feshbach, S., 444
Festinger, L., 259, 281, 282, 430, 432,
    434, 445–49, 452, 453
Fitzgerald, D., 340, 341
Flanagan, J. C., 76, 146
Flanders, N. A., 237
Fleege, U. H., 159
Forman, H. J., 440

Foster, W. S., 322
Fox, D., 3
Franc, D. E., 430
Frank, Lawrence K., 184
Franzblau, R. N., 131
Frederiksen, N. O., 336, 354
Freeman, F. N., 76–77, 96–97, 106
French, Elizabeth G., 267, 268, 269, 273
French, T. M., 59
French, W., 199
Frenkel-Brunswik, E., 313, 425, 426
Freud, S., 56, 57, 60, 63, 244, 245, 435, 518, 519, 521, 525, 528, 529, 540
Friebergs, V., 362
Friedenberg, E. Z., 87
Fromm, E., 524
Frutcher, B., 296
Frutchey, F. P., 320
Fry, E., 332, 335
Fry, E. B., 233
Furst, E. J., 473

Gable, Sister Felicita, 344
Gaier, E. L., 249, 324
Galanter, E., 262, 263, 396
Galton, F., 95
Gamow, G., 73
Gardner, B. B., 90–91, 93
Gardner, M. R., 90–91, 93
Garmezy, N., 42, 43, 541
Garry, R., 331, 354
Gates, A. I., 321, 340, 349
Gebhard, Mildred, 282
Gebhard, P. H., 184
Gerard, H. B., 445
Gesell, A., 75, 76, 99, 100, 106, 180, 181, 525
Getzels, J. W., 412, 413
Ghiselin, B., 411
Ghiselli, E. E., 139
Gibbons, C. C., 137
Gibson, E. J., 298
Ginandes, J., 93
Glaser, R., 230
Gnagey, W. J., 241, 242
Goldbeck, R. A., 234
Goldman, B., 158, 159
Goodenough, F. L., 166, 167
Goodman, C. C., 313
Goodnow, J. J., 356, 357, 358, 360, 361, 362, 374
Gordon, C. W., 85–87, 284
Gordon, W. M., 245
Green, E. G., 211
Greene, E. B., 315, 316

Greenspoon, J., 203, 205
Gronlund, N. E., 137, 178
Gross, N., 522
Guetzkow, H., 237
Guilford, J. P., 114–16, 261, 412, 413, 414, 419
Gump, P. V., 241, 242, 243
Guthrie, F., 52

Haggard, E. A., 252
Hagman, E. R., 162
Hall, C. S., 66, 509, 510, 515, 516, 519
Haller, M., 336
Hamilton, R. J., 298
Harap, H. K., 342
Harary, F., 432
Harding, J., 446
Harlow, H. F., 258, 263, 277, 303
Harlow, M. K., 263
Harmon, J. A., 338, 339
Harper, R. A., 509
Harper, R. J. C., 389
Harrell, M. S., 138, 139
Harrell, T. W., 138, 139
Harris, A. J., 306
Hartmann, G. W., 429
Hartmann, H., 65–66
Hartson, L. D., 137
Hattwick, LaBerta, 182
Havighurst, R. J., 58–59, 60, 87, 103–4, 170, 437, 438
Hayes, M., 166
Haygood, R. C., 376
Hebb, D. O., 113, 116, 156, 157, 265, 307, 332, 390–93, 398, 419, 525
Heider, F., 308, 315, 432
Helson, H., 309, 311
Hempel, C. G., 516
Hemphill, H. K., 237
Hendrickson, G., 342
Henle, Mary, 411, 414, 420
Henmon, V. A. C., 331
Henry, J., 79
Heron, W., 263, 525
Hicks, J. A., 166
Hill, W. F., 258, 436
Himmelweit, H. T., 439
Hogrefe, R., 446
Hohman, L. B., 183
Holland, J. G., 377, 378
Hollingshead, A. deB., 92, 93–95
Holmes, F. B., 157, 163
Holzinger, K. J., 96–97
Homans, G. C., 168
Honzik, Marjorie P., 134
Horn, E., 382

Horney, Karen, 243, 244, 524
Horrocks, J. E., 18
Hovland, C. I., 214, 358, 362, 422, 423, 451, 452, 457
Howard, M., 96
Huang, I., 366
Hughes, A. S., 181, 187
Hull, C. L., 194, 208, 214
Hulten, C. E., 477
Hunka, S. M., 389
Hunnicutt, C. W., 275, 276
Hunt, E. B., 358, 363
Hunt, J. McV., 113, 135, 194, 257, 259, 397, 419
Hunter, W. S., 194
Hurlock, E. B., 159, 274, 275, 290
Hymovitch, B., 445

Ilg, Frances L., 99, 100, 180
Inhelder, B., 366, 371, 372, 373, 374, 530
Inkeles, A., 80, 82
Irion, A. L., 215, 292, 322, 325, 326
Israel, H. E., 300
Israel, J., 282
Ittelson, W. H., 311, 312

Jackson, P. W., 412, 413
Jackson, T. A., 300
Jamison, O. G., 100–101, 159, 440
Janis, I. L., 444, 447, 457
Jenkin, N., 312, 313
Jenkins, J. J., 333
Jennings, F. G., 340
Jersild, A. T., 157–59, 163, 167, 181
Jersild, C. I., 158
John, E., 162
Johnson, D. M., 131
Johnson, E. S., 399
Johnson, G. R., 128
Jones, Edwina, 19, 300
Jones, H. E., 128
Jones, M. C., 101, 188, 189
Josselyn, Irene, 59
Jost, H., 97
Jucknat, Margarete, 281, 282, 283
Judd, C. H., 296, 297
Judson, A. J., 405
Jung, C. G., 518, 524

Kagan, J., 258, 271, 436
Kalhorn, J., 172, 174
Kallmann, F. J., 97
Kaplan, E., 384
Kardiner, A., 80
Karen, R. L., 322

Karlin, R., 337
Katona, G., 321
Katz, D., 422, 428, 441, 442
Kearney, N. C., 33, 195, 199
Keister, M. E., 168
Kelly, E. L., 237
Kelly, H. H., 445
Kelman, H., 448, 449
Kendler, T. S., 379
Keys, N., 292
Kiesler, C. A., 454
Kiesler, S. B., 454
Kimble, G. A., 41, 42, 43, 44, 45, 207, 244, 541
King, B. T., 447
Kingsley, H., 331, 354
Kinsey, A. C., 93, 183, 184
Kirkendall, Lester A., 93, 184
Kittell, J. E., 383
Klausmeier, H. J., 302
Klineberg, O., 131
Knezevich, S. J., 134
Koch, H. L., 182
Koch, Margaret B., 204, 205
Köhler, W., 404
Kounin, J. S., 241, 242, 243
Krasner, L., 203
Krathwohl, D. R., 197, 198
Kraus, R., 19
Krechevsky, I., 194, 195
Kris, E., 65–66
Krueger, W. C. F., 331
Krumboltz, J. D., 233, 234
Kuhlen, R. G., 188

Lachman, S. J., 3, 4–6
Lahey, M. F., 326
Lambert, W. E., 237
Lane, E., 300
Lane, J. M., 231
Lawrence, D. H., 300, 301
Lawson, E. D., 424
Lecky, P., 39
Lee, B. J., 188
Lee, E. S., 131
Leeds, C. H., 236
Leighton, D. C., 534
Lester, O. P., 326
Leuba, C., 265
Levin, H., 172, 173, 281, 282, 437, 438
Levine, J. M., 322, 323, 429
Levine, R., 312, 313
Levinson, D. J., 80, 82, 425, 426
Lewin, K., 238, 239, 281, 282, 520
Lewis, W. D., 137
Lighthall, F. F., 246–50

Lindsley, D. B., 154, 156
Lindzey, G., 425, 509, 510, 515, 516, 519
Lippitt, R., 238, 239, 442
Lippitt, Rosemary, 187
Liss, E., 159
Loban, W., 440
Loewenstein, R. M., 65–66
Loftus, J. J., 158, 159
Lohr, T. F., 280
Loomis, C. P., 445
Loree, M. R., 204, 205, 474, 495–97
Lorge, I., 3, 134, 135
Lovell, K., 375
Lowell, E. L., 266, 267, 269, 271, 273
Lucas, J. D., 245
Luckhardt, A. B., 512
Luh, C. W., 318, 319
Lumsdaine, A. A., 230, 451, 452, 457
Lund, S., 159
Lynn, R., 252

McCandless, B. R., 187, 245, 249, 252
McCarthy, Dorothea, 366
McClelland, D. C., 266, 267, 271
Maccoby, Eleanor, 172, 173, 437, 438
McCurdy, H. G., 237
MacDonald, D. V., 438
McDougall, W. P., 320, 321
McEachern, A. W., 522
Macfarlane, Jean W., 134
McGeoch, J. A., 215, 292, 319, 322, 324, 325, 326
McGinnies, E., 451, 452
McGraw, M. B., 525
McGuigan, F. J., 13, 14
McGuire, W. J., 432, 434, 454, 455, 456, 457
McKeachie, W. J., 12–15, 17, 237
MacLeod, R. B., 410
Mainland, D., 494
Malm, M., 100, 101, 159, 440
Maltzman, I., 410, 414
Mandler, G., 300
Mapes, C. E., 342
Mark, S. J., 342, 343
Markey, F. V., 158, 181
Marshall, H. R., 187
Martin, C. E., 93, 183, 184
Martin, W. E., 91
Martire, J. G., 283
Masia, B. B., 197, 198
Maslow, A. H., 260, 289
Mason, W. S., 522
Masserman, J. H., 279, 280
May, M. A., 350, 351, 352

Mead, G. H., 519
Mead, Margaret, 78
Means, M. H., 159
Mech, E. V., 159
Mednick, M. T., 380
Meek, L. H., 94
Meeker, M., 88–90
Melton, A. W., 319, 326
Meltzer, H., 93
Melville, S. D., 336, 354
Merrill, M. A., 117, 127, 133, 140
Messick, S. J., 536
Meyer, D. R., 263
Meyer, G., 476
Meyer, Susan R., 233
Miller, G. A., 262, 263, 320, 396
Miller, N. E., 45, 161, 162, 194, 201, 202, 205, 217, 244, 258, 520
Miller, R. B., 93
Mills, C. W., 88
Mitnick, L. L., 451, 452
Moore, J. W., 232
Moreno, J. L., 177
Morgan, Edna, 19
Morris, R. T., 442
Mosier, C. I., 484, 485
Moss, H. A., 271
Mouton, J. S., 309, 311
Mowrer, O. H., 44
Munroe, Ruth L., 62
Murphy, G., 304, 307, 309, 312, 313, 322, 323, 429, 450, 524, 539
Murphy, L. B., 180, 181, 450
Murray, H. A., 260, 261, 264, 266, 284, 310
Murray, I. M., 494
Mussen, P. H., 437, 438, 441, 442
Myers, C., 484, 485

Nagel, E., 516
Neff, W. S., 92
Neugarten, B. L., 87
Newcomb, T. M., 432, 445, 446, 450
Newell, A., 393–96, 398, 511, 538
Newman, H. H., 96–97
Noble, C. E., 333, 354
Noble, G. V., 159
Noll, V. H., 344
Northway, M. L., 187
Nowlis, H. H., 19, 324
Nowlis, V., 19
Noyes, E. S., 479

Oden, M. H., 129, 138
Ogg, E., 534
Ojemann, R. H., 380, 381

Olmstead, J. A., 309, 311
Olson, W. C., 75
Oppenheim, A. N., 439
Orbison, W. D., 301
Osborne, R. F., 93
Osgood, C. E., 194, 195, 297, 298, 299, 301, 319, 326, 328, 332, 333, 334, 432
Owens, W. A., Jr., 129

Pace, C. R., 284
Palermo, D. S., 245, 249, 252
Papageorgis, D., 454, 455, 456, 457
Parker, W. K., 399
Parsley, K. M., 508–43
Patrick, J. R., 446
Paulsen, G. B., 22
Pavlov, I., 41–42, 47
Payne, D. E., 438
Pearson, G. H. J., 43
Peck, R. F., 58–59, 174, 175, 191, 437
Peel, E. S., 375
Penfield, W., 512
Peterson, K. M., 184
Peterson, R. C., 451
Pettigrew, T. F., 131
Piaget, J., 363–75, 379, 385, 386, 390, 397, 398, 419, 525, 530
Pillet, R. A., 77, 106
Pitman, J., 77
Plowman, Letha F., 344
Pollie, D., 12–15, 17
Pomeroy, W. B., 93, 183, 184
Pope, B., 188
Porter, D., 231, 232, 233
Postman, L., 309, 310
Pratt, K. C., 302
Pressey, S. L., 227, 235
Preston, A., 270, 271, 274, 290
Pribram, K. H., 262, 263, 396
Price, H. G., 484, 485
Pullias, E. V., 183
Punke, H. H., 187

Raabe, V. L., 181, 187
Rabson, A., 270, 271, 274, 290
Radke, Marian J., 175, 176, 191
Radler, D. H., 457
Ragsdale, C. E., 345
Ramsey, G. V., 183
Rath, G., 228
Raths, L. E., 451
Raven, B., 445
Ray, J. J., 302
Rayner, R., 160, 164, 441

Reade, M., 498
Reitman, W. R., 267
Remmers, H. H., 457
Rhine, R. J., 380
Rich, J. M., 338
Richards, T. W., 102, 132–33
Richardson, M. W., 498
Ricketts, A. F., 165, 166
Robbins, Lillian C., 340, 341
Robinson, E. S., 326
Rogers, C. R., 519, 529, 534, 535
Rokeach, M., 426, 427, 428
Romanow, C. V., 380
Rosen, B. C., 271, 272, 273, 290
Rosenbaum, M. E., 430
Rosenberg, M. J., 422–24, 432
Rosenfeld, H., 275, 290
Rosenzweig, S., 323, 324
Ross, C. C., 479
Ross, R. T., 183
Ruebush, B. K., 246–50
Russell, B. A. W., 396
Russell, D., 366
Russell, W. A., 333
Ryan, J. J., 241, 242

Sady, R. R., 443
Sale, W. M., 479
Sandiford, P., 95
Sanford, R. N., 93, 425, 426, 436
Sarason, S. B., 246–51
Sarbin, T. R., 83, 84, 519
Sarnoff, I., 529, 532
Sax, G., 498
Schachter, S., 445
Schaffner, B., 183
Schlosberg, H., 44
Schpoont, S. H., 322, 323
Schwab, S. J., 399
Scott, T. H., 263
Sears, Pauline S., 19, 281, 282
Sears, R. R., 19, 80–81, 172, 173, 437, 438
Seashore, H. G., 119, 142–46
Sells, S. B., 311
Shaffer, L. F., 156
Shaffner, B., 183
Shane, H. G., 222
Shaw, G. B., 414
Shaw, J. C., 394, 396, 398, 511, 538
Shay, C. B., 16, 17
Sheffield, F. D., 451, 452, 457
Siipola, E. M., 300, 310, 311
Silberman, H. F., 230, 231, 233, 234
Silun, B. A., 380

Simon, H. A., 393, 394, 395, 396, 398, 511, 533
Simon, T., 117
Sims, V. M., 446, 476, 479, 480
Skinner, B. F., 7, 8, 9, 44, 206, 207, 227, 228, 377, 378, 405
Sleight, W. G., 295
Smith, W. I., 232
Smock, C. D., 246
Smoke, K. L., 362
Snyder, C. W., 308
Snyder, F. W., 308
Snygg, D., 52, 53, 54, 103, 252, 260, 264, 535
Solley, C. M., 304, 307, 309
Solomon, R. L., 279
Sontag, G. W., 97
Spatz, D., 159
Spaulding, G., 488
Spearman, C., 114
Speisman, J., 12–15, 17
Spranger, E., 425
Stagner, R., 424
Stalnaker, J. M., 477, 479
Stanley, J. C., 221, 479
Starch, D., 477
Stein, M. I., 284
Stendler, C. B., 91
Stephens, J. M., 278
Stern, C., 97
Stern, G. G., 239, 284, 285, 286, 287
Stevens, Gladys, 19
Stevenson, H. W., 279
Stoke, S. M., 438, 439
Stolurow, L. M., 227
Stolz, H. R., 100
Stolz, L. M., 100
Stonex, E., 300
Stotland, E., 422, 428
Stovall, T. F., 239
Strodtbeck, F. L., 271
Stroud, J. B., 324, 344
Sullivan, H. S., 524
Sullivan, M. W., 14
Super, D. E., 135
Symonds, P. M., 279, 519
Szeminska, A., 363–65, 368–70, 385

Taba, Hilda, 440
Tagiuri, R., 314
Tannenbaum, P. H., 432
Taylor, G. A., 349
Taylor, J. H., 73
Taylor, Janet A., 245
Terman, L. M., 117, 127, 133, 137, 138, 140, 148

Terry, P. W., 476
Thistlethwaite, D. L., 284, 287
Thompson, G. G., 275, 276, 526
Thompson, H., 75, 76, 106, 525
Thompson, L., 350, 351
Thompson, W. R., 525
Thorndike, E. L., 44, 68, 114, 277, 278, 295, 296, 343, 344, 404
Thurstone, L. L., 114, 451
Toch, H., 443, 444, 460
Tolman, E. C., 194, 195
Tompkins, S. S., 536
Torrance, E. P., 338, 339, 412
Trager, F., 451
Travers, R. M. W., 224, 225, 226, 283, 284, 299, 484
Traxler, A. E., 489
Trowbridge, M. H., 344
Tulving, E., 362
Tyler, F. T., 77, 78
Tyler, Leona, 131
Tyler, R. W., 26, 138, 316, 320, 471, 472, 474

Ulmer, G., 301, 302
Underwood, B. J., 13, 25, 298, 300
Updegraff, R., 168

Vernon, M. D., 306
Vernon, P. E., 425
Verplanck, W. S., 203, 204, 205
Vince, P., 439
Von Lackum, W. J., 326

Waite, R. R., 246–50
Wallas, G., 411, 414
Wallen, N. E., 224, 225, 226
Ward, L. B., 302
Warner, W. L., 88–90
Watson, J., 442
Watson, J. B., 153, 160, 164, 441
Watson, R. I., 185
Watson, W. S., 429
Wechsler, D., 129
Weir, M., 279
Weisman, R. G., 233, 234
Weiss, W., 362
Werner, H., 384
Wertheimer, M., 402
Wesman, A. G., 142–46, 296
West, J., 88
West, J. E., 320
West, J. V., 296
Westover, F. L., 340
White, R. K., 238, 239
White, R. W., 259, 265, 266, 273, 288

Whitehead, A. N., 396
Whiting, J. W. M., 19, 80, 81, 281, 282, 283
Whitney, A. P., 137
Williams, M. J., 187
Winch, W. H., 292
Winterbottom, Marion R., 269, 270, 273, 274
Wirt, R. D., 245, 246
Wise, G. W., 80–81
Wispe, L. G., 237
Wohlwill, J. F., 376–79, 383
Wolf, R. M., 92
Wolfe, J. B., 45, 263
Wolfle, D., 203
Wood, B. D., 76–77, 106
Wood, Dorothy A., 498

Woodrow, H., 302, 303
Woodward, Mary, 375
Woodworth, R. S., 265, 288, 314
Woodyard, Ella, 296
Wooldridge, D. E., 538
Wright, Beatrice A., 180
Wynne, L. C., 279

Yerkes, R. M., 130
Young, P. T., 259
Yum, K. S., 298

Zander, A., 275, 290
Zeigarnik, B., 323
Zigler, E. F., 279
Zimbardo, P. G., 249
Zweibelson, I., 248

SUBJECT INDEX

Ability and transfer, 301–2
Abstracting, 357, 370, 379, 395
Academic aptitude tests, 108; see also
    Intelligence tests
  uses in school, 108–12
Accommodation, 397
Achievement
  batteries, 501–3
  and home background, 269–73
  need for, 266–74
  tests, 108, 470–503
Action pattern, 35, 199
Activities Index, 284
Adaptation, 397
  level, 309
Adjustment, 519–34
Adolescence
  cognitive development, 370–74
  developmental tasks, 104, 186–87
  and ego identity, 64–65, 186
  emotional development, 159, 166–67
  heterosexual relationships, 93, 103,
      182–84
  and the home, 174–75, 187
  and peer approval, 85–87, 94, 188
  physical maturity, 100–101, 188
  and social class, 91–95, 272–73
Advanced organizers, 340–41
Affiliation, need for, 268–69
Age scores, 557
Aggression, 19, 39, 61, 82, 169, 175,
    181, 239, 438, 441
Algorithm, 394
Anal stage, 61–62
Analysis, 196, 249
Anecdotal records, 178–79, 536–37
Anger, 165–69
  modification of, 167–69
  nature and development of, 165–67
Anticipation and regression, 179–80

Anxiety, 13, 62, 243–52, 530; see also
    Test anxiety
  measurement of, 245–47
  relation to other variables, 247–52
  and school learning, 251–52
  types of, 244
Application, 196, 249
Appreciations, 422
Approach-approach conflict, 520
Approach-avoidance conflict, 520
Aptitude, 141
  test, 108, 141–47
Arbitrary associations, 342, 344
Aspiration, level of, 281–84
Assimilation, 397
Associative responses, 333, 404, 428–29
Attitude objects, 422–24
Attitudes, 422–61
  action oriented, 430
  balanced, 430
  ego-defensive, 430
  influence of information, 450–57
  influence of literature, television, and
      radio, 438–40, 451–53
  intellectualized, 429
  nature of, 422–34
  and perception, 313
  and problem solving, 410
  social class differences in, 93, 94–95
  toward teaching, 18
Attribute, 357–61
  critical, 357
Authoritarian-democratic studies, 238–
    40
Authoritarianism, 426
Average deviation, 551
Avoidance-avoidance conflict, 520
Avoidance training, 45–46, 200

Basic personality structure, 80–82
Behavior-primacy, 265

Behaviorial norms, 32, 86–87; *see also* Norms, cultural
social class differences in, 91–95
Beliefs, 424, 426–28, 431–34, 447–57

California Achievement Tests, 501
California Short-Form Tests of Mental Maturity, 124, 141
Case study, 20–21
Categorizing behavior, 356–63, 369–71
Cell-assembly, 391–92
Central tendency, measures of, 548
Cephalocaudal direction, 99
Child care practices, developmental influences of, 46, 78, 80; *see also* Home
Children's Manifest Anxiety Scale, 245–46
Class consciousness, 90–91
Classical conditioning, 41–45, 47, 160–62, 200, 300, 441–42, 444
Classroom
learning climate, 31–32, 235–40
motivation, 30, 33, 212–13, 223, 263, 336–40, 348–49, 381, 382
Clinical methods, 20–21
Cliques, 94, 177
Coefficient
of equivalence, 466–67
of stability, 466–67
College Characteristics Index, 284–85
College Entrance Examination Board, 474
Communications
anticipation of, 453–54
effect on attitudes of, 450–57
sleeper effect of, 452–53
Competence, need for, 264–66
Completion item, 480–81
Comprehension, 196
Concepts
attainment of, 356–57, 359–63, 374–80
as categories, 356–59
critical attributes of, 357–63
discovery of, 360–63
exemplar of, 357–60
experimental study of, 359–63
as explanations, 363–66
factors affecting, 374–81
formation of, 356
stages of development, 366–74
teaching of, 380–84
Concrete operations, 369–70, 371–72, 375

Conditioning, 41–52; *see also* Classical conditioning; Counter-conditioning; Instrumental conditioning
in acquiring drives, 161–62, 258
in learning fears, 160–62, 244
of verbal behavior, 203–5
Conflict, 83–84, 87, 520–23
conceptual, 259
psychoanalytic approach to, 521–22, 528–29
topological approach to, 520–21
Conformity, 58, 59, 67, 79, 87
Conjunctive concept, 357–59
Connotative meaning, 332–33
Conservation concept, 363–66
Consistency
need for, 429
principle of, 431–32
self-, 39, 40, 431–32
Consonance, 432
Contiguity, 376, 379, 383–84
Continuous reinforcement, 207
Control group, 11
Convergent thinking, 115, 412
Correction formula for guessing, 489–90
Correlation, 21, 135, 464, 563–70
Counter-conditioning, 164
Creative thinking, 410–14
Critical thinking, 415–18
Cross-cultural studies, 78–82, 312, 442
Cross-sectional studies, 19–20
Cue, 162, 201–3, 205, 345–47, 349–50, 352
Culture, 78–95, 521, 524

Deciles, 22, 550
Decision-making, strategies of, 360–63
Defense mechanisms, 66, 528–33
Demonstration, 349–52
Denial, 531
Denotative meaning, 332
Dependency, 19, 176, 185–87, 249–50, 259, 446
Dependent variable, 11, 12–13, 17
Development
intellectual, 366–74
principles of, 98–104
Developmental tasks, 103–4
Diagnostic tests, 500
Differential
abilities, 141–47
Aptitude Test, 142–46
research method, 17–19
Differentiation, 53, 398
of emotions, 153–54
Discipline, 240–43

Discovering, 360–63, 383, 384
Discrimination, 49, 51, 303, 356–57
   index, 492–97
Disintegrative behavior, 155–57
Disjunctive concept, 357–59
Dissonance, 259, 432–34, 446–49, 452
Divergent thinking, 115, 412
Dogmatic Scale, 426–27
Drive, 45, 161–62, 186, 201, 203, 244,
   257–59
   primary and secondary, 201, 258, 264
   reduction, 258–59, 264

Ebbinghaus curve, 316–17
Educational psychologist, 2
Educational psychology defined, 1–2
Effectance motivation, 266
Effective surprise, 410
Ego, 57–60, 175, 519, 521, 528–29
   identity, 64, 87
   span, 59–60
Elementary school child
   and anxiety, 246–52
   cognitive development of, 368–72
   developmental tasks of, 104
   emotional development of, 157–58,
      166–67, 168–69
   and the home, 171–76, 269–71
   in the latency period, 63–64
   and readiness, 76–78
   and social class, 92, 93
   social development of, 170, 180–82,
      185–88
   and the teacher, 236, 242, 274–76,
      282–83, 337, 342
Emotion
   as a component of attitudes, 424
   definition of, 153
   differentiation of, 153–54
   effect on retention, 322
   judging expressions of, 314
Emotional behavior, observing, 154–55
Emotional climate
   of the classroom, 31–32, 235–40
   of the home, 163, 172–76, 437–38
Emotional development, 153–69
Emotional maturity, 59, 60, 67
Enactive representation, 408
Environmental process variable, 92; see
   also Presses
Environmental status variable, 92
Environmental variable; see also Anxiety, and school learning; Classroom, learning climate; Teacher-
   pupil relationships
   in adjustment, 534–35

   in development, 95–98, 113, 524–25
   in school learning, 11, 31–32, 235–40
Escape training, 46, 200
Essay tests, 476–80
Evaluation
   as an educational objective, 196
   of learning, 29, 224, 462–507
Exemplars; see Instances
Expectancy, 69, 194
   table, 21–22
Experiences, effect on personality, 518,
   523–26; see also Child care prac-
   tices; Development; Home
Experimental group, 11
Experimental method, 11–17
Extinction, 48, 51, 164, 200, 207–9
Extrinsic motivation, 277, 336, 339,
   382, 411–12

Faculty psychology, 25
Fears, 156–65
   and anxiety, 243, 530
   modification of, 163–64
   nature and development of, 156–63
Feedback, 31, 268–69, 345–46, 347,
   352, 396
Figure-ground, 53, 56, 307
Fixation, 65–66, 532
Fluency tests, 413
Forced compliance, 446–49
Formal thought, 370–71, 373–74, 375
Fortune Survey, 91
Frame of reference, 40, 398
   phenomenological, 52–56
   psychoanalytic, 56–68
   reinforcement, 41–52
Frequency distribution, 545–46
Frequency polygon, 547
Frustration, 39, 59–60, 61, 65–66, 165,
   168, 281–83
Functional autonomy, principle of, 262

General Anxiety Scale for Children, 246
General factor, 114, 116
Genes, 73–74
Gestalt psychology, 404
Gifted children, 137–38
Goals, 33, 212–13, 262–63, 336–40,
   348–49, 396; see also Motivation
Grade scores, 557
Grader reliability; see Objectivity
Grading, 490–91
Group
   factor, 114
   influences, 284–87

Group (*Continued*)
  intelligence tests, 120–26
  norms, 83
  versus independent study, 3–4
Guess Who, 177–78
Guiding learning, 28–29, 30–35, 205–6, 210–16, 220–56, 348–53
Guilt, 58, 59, 60, 62–63, 82, 163, 175, 183, 279

Habit-family hierarchy, 208–10
Harmony-disharmony, 236–37
Height, 96, 99–101
Heredity
  and acquired characteristics, 74
  and environment, 97–98, 113
  and family histories, 95–96
  and family resemblances, 96–97
  and mental illness, 97
  and personality, 518, 524
Heuristic computing, 394, 538
Home, influence on development, 61, 78, 80, 91–95, 163, 171–76, 269–71, 338
Horace Mann–Lincoln Institute, 178
Hypothesizing, 13–14, 370, 372–74, 404–6, 409

Iconic representation, 408
Id, 57, 59–60, 521, 528–29
Identification, 62, 435–40, 532
Identity diffusion, 64–65
Image, 262; *see also* TOTE units
Immunization, 454–57
Incubation, 410
Independence, 176, 185–87, 259, 446
Independent variable, 11, 12–13, 17, 422
Index of Status Characteristics, 88–90
Individual differences, 32, 39–40, 100–101, 224; *see also* Learner, characteristics of
  in abilities, 76–77, 109–12, 127–28
  in emotional and social development, 150–53, 159, 163, 170, 188
  in home background, 171–76, 269–71
  in motives, 269–73
  and psychoanalytic theory, 67
  and reward training, 49–51
  and science of psychology, 32, 39–40, 536–37
  in self concept, 56
  and social class, 91–95, 272–73
Information processing, 393–97, 398
Insight, 404

Instances
  of a concept, 357–63
  negative, 362
Instrumental conditioning, 44–52, **200,** 208–10, 445–49
Integrative behavior, 155–57
Intelligence
  and anxiety, 247–50
  and creativity, 412
  distribution of, 127–28
  growth of, 128–29, 366–74
  nature of, 113–17
Intelligence Quotient, 118–19
  deviation, 118, 119, 122, 124, 125
  ratio, 118, 122
  reliability and stability of, 133–35
  and retention, 326
  and size of step, 16–17
  and transfer, 302
  and type of home, 174
Intelligence test performance
  factors affecting, 129–33
  reliability and stability of, 133–35
Intelligence tests, 21–22, 92, 108–40
Intent to remember, 322–23
Interests, 180, 212, 213, 224, 336–38, 422; *see also* Motivation
Internalization, 58, 59, 198, 279
Intervening variable, 10–11, 15, 423
Intrinsic motivation, 277, 336, 339, 411–12
Introjection, 62
Intuitive thought, 368, 371, 375
Iowa Tests of Basic Skills, 501
Iowa Tests of Educational Development, 501
Item analysis, 492–99

Knowledge, 196, 249, 331–44, 478, 481
  of results, 31, 50, 203, 204, 215–16, 232–33, 343–44, 352–53

Laboratory versus natural setting research, 15, 27, 30
Latency
  as a developmental stage, 63–64
  as a time interval, 48
Law of effect, 68
Learner, characteristics of, 32–34, 212, 375
Learning
  action patterns, 35, 199
  and anxiety, 251–52
  of attitudes, 434–57
  definitions, 41, 193
  expectancies, 194

of fears, 159–65
by imitation, 162, 205
and the nervous system, 390–93
Learning experiences, 27–28, 210–16, 223–24, 381–83
Learning set, 302–4
Learning to learn, 302–3
Level of aspiration, 281–84
Libido, 60–65
Listening, 340
Longitudinal studies, 19–20
Lorge-Thorndike Intelligence Tests, 124–25, 140

Manifest Anxiety Scale, 245
Massed versus distributed practice, 214–15, 343, 352
Maturation, 74–75, 103–4, 193, 366, 525
Mean, 548
Meaningfulness, 319, 331–35, 342
Measurement of transfer, 293–94
classical design, 293
proactive design, 293, 325
retroactive design, 294, 325
Median, 548
Mediating processes, 10, 32, 34–35, 194–95, 262, 263, 345, 346–47, 389–98, 436, 536
Mental abilities, organization of, 113–17; see also Intelligence
Mental age, 117–18
Method variable, 11, 15–17, 30–31, 211–16, 224–26, 336–44; see also Classroom, motivation; Practice; Teacher as a reinforcer; Teacher-guidance
Metropolitan Achievement Test, 501
Mode, 548
Motivation, 30, 33, 212–13, 257–90, 336–39, 345, 348–49, 380, 381, 382, 516–17
Motives, 51, 262
social, 274–87
Multiple-choice, 474, 482, 486–87

Needs, 45, 259–62; see also Motivation
influence on attitudes, 430, 438
influence on perception, 312–13
viscerogenic and psychogenic, 260
Negative transfer, 292, 298–99, 325
Nerve cell, 390–91
Nervous system, 390–93
Neuropsychological theory of thought, 391–93
Nominating technique, 178

Non-verbal test, 121, 123, 125, 126
Normal distribution, 553–56
Norms; see also Behavioral norms; Group, norms
cultural, 79–80, 522
statistical, 557–62
Novelty, need for, 265, 266, 332, 382

Object constancy, 308
Objective tests, 12–15, 476–78, 480–88
Objectives, educational, 25–27, 35, 196–99, 223, 236, 381, 463, 470–73
Objectivity, 5, 469–70, 477–80
Omission training, 46
Omnibus test, 121, 123–24
Open and closed mind, 426–27
Operant response, 8, 9
Opinionation Scale, 426
Oral stage, 60–61
Organism, 6, 511–13
Organismic variables, 7–8, 15–19, 21, 32–35, 77, 153, 157, 225, 330, 345
Otis Quick-Scoring Mental Ability Tests, 122–24
Overachiever, 110, 111
Overlearning, 321

Parent-child relationships, 172–76; see also Home
Part versus whole, 215, 301
Partial reinforcement, 207
Pavlov experiment, 42
Peer approval, 50, 63, 86–87, 94, 103, 159, 171, 180, 187–89, 259
Percentiles, 550, 558–60
Perception, 304–15
and adjustment, 535
and affective processes, 312, 313
and conception, 365, 368, 371, 376–80
and defense mechanisms, 529–33
and emotion, 155, 156–57
in motor learning, 181, 345–46, 349–52
and past experience, 311, 312
of people, 314–15
of self, 54–56
and self-consistency, 431
Perceptual field, 52–54, 56
Personality, 508–19
adjustment, 526–29
definition of, 513–14
development, 523–26
research in, 536–37
theories of, 56–60, 514–19

Phallic stage, 62–63
Phase sequence, 391–92
Phenomenal field, 54–55; *see also* Perceptual field
Phenomenal self, 54–55
Phenomenology, 52–56, 260
Physiological processes during fear, 156
Pintner-Cunningham Primary Test, 121–23
Plan, 262; *see also* TOTE units
Pleasure principle, 57, 521
Population, 571
Positive transfer, 292, 298
Practice, 31, 204, 212, 213–15, 342–43, 352–53, 384
Praise, 50, 186, 237, 268–69
and reproof, 274–76
Preconceptual thought, 367–68
Predictive studies, 21–23, 463–64
Prejudice, 418, 421, 425–26, 441–42, 445–47, 451–52
and perception, 313
Preschool child
cognitive development of, 366–68
developmental tasks of, 104
fears of, 157–58, 242
and the home, 172–76, 270–71
and maturation, 75–76
psychosexual stages of, 60–63
social development of, 180, 182, 186, 187
sources of anger of, 165–66
Presses, environmental, 284–87; *see also* Environmental process variable
Proactive facilitation, 292
Proactive inhibition, 292, 325
Problem solving, 342–43, 403–10
and anxiety, 248–50
computer simulation of, 393–97
logical steps in, 405–10
mode of representation in, 408
theories of, 403–5
Product-moment correlation, 564–68
Program, 16
Programmed instruction, 16–17, 226–35; *see also* Teaching machine programs
characteristics of, 229–30
experimental findings on, 230–35
Projection, 532
Propositions, 515–16
Proximodistal, 99, 104
Psychological research, methods of, 10–23
Psychology
explanation in, 23–25

research, 6–25
as a science, 3–6
Psychomotor learning, 99, 345–53
classification of, 345
guiding learning of, 348–53
skilled performance, 346–47
Psychosexual development, 60–66
Psychosocial crises
autonomy versus shame or doubt, 62
ego identity, 64
industry versus inferiority, 63
initiative versus guilt, 62
trust versus mistrust, 61
Punishment, 19, 63, 66, 163, 172–76, 277–80, 517
Pure stimulus act, 194–95
Purposive behavior, 510–11, 516–17

Quartiles, 549

Race
and intelligence test performance, 130–31
and prejudice, 429, 430, 441–42, 446, 451–52
Range, 550–51
Rationalization, 531
Raw scores, 557
Reaction formation, 532
Reactive inhibition, 214
Readiness, 33–34, 76–78, 526
Reading, 76, 136, 205–6, 252, 306, 332, 337–39, 340, 499–500
Reality principle, 56, 521
Redundancy, 376–78, 383–84
Reference group, 83, 446
Regression, 65–66, 532
Reinforcement, 31, 41, 44–45, 47–48, 51, 68–69, 168, 202–3, 205–7, 212, 215–16, 227, 229, 232, 278, 343–44, 352–53, 380, 382, 430, 445
Reinforcer, 41, 45, 50–51, 205
Rejection, 176
Relational concept, 357–59
Reliability, 466–69, 476
of test scores, 133–35
Reminiscence, 214
Repression, 66, 531
Research on teaching methods, 221–34
Response, 6, 8, 202–3, 330
attitudinal, 423
conditioned, 42–51, 200
generalization, 49, 51, 398
individual meaning of, 536
respondent and operant, 8–9

variables, 8–9, 12–17, 18–19, 21–23, 35, 77, 153, 157, 225, 253, 330, 345, 348, 537–38
variation in transfer, 298–99
Retention, 315–26
  factors affecting, 316–26, 342
  methods of measuring, 316–21
  of school learning, 315–16
  teaching for, 327–28
  and unfinished tasks, 323–24
Retroactive inhibition, 325
Reversibility, 365, 370
Reward, 162, 276–77, 517
  extrinsic versus intrinsic, 277, 336
Reward training, 44–45, 48–52, 161–62
Rho, 569–70
Role, 83–85, 237
  conflict in, 522

Sample, 571
Scale of Values, 425
Scatter diagram, 565, 567, 568
Schemata, 366, 367, 397–98
School and College Ability Tests, 109–12, 126
School success, prediction of, 135–37
Science, operating conceptions of, 3–6
Secondary reinforcement, 201
Secondary reward training, 45, 200
Selecting learning experiences; see Learning experiences
Selecting test situations, 473–75
Selectivity, 376, 378, 383–84
Self concept, 51, 54–56, 64, 103, 171, 181, 260, 430, 519, 529
Self-testing, 321–22
Semantic Differential Scale, 333–34
Semi-interquartile range, 551
Sensorimotor intelligence, 366–67
Set, 198, 302–4, 309–11, 315, 326, 338, 401
Sex
  and fears, 159
  and libido, 60–65
  and maturity, 100–101
  problems of, 183–84
  and social class, 93, 183
Sex role, 181–82
Sex standards, 93
Sign learning, 194–95
Size of step, 16–17, 234
Social class, 87–94
  and achievement motivation, 272–73
  and intelligence test performance, 131–32
  and popularity, 188

Social development, 169–88
  developmental trends, 179–89
  home influence on, 163, 171–76
  measuring, 177–79
Social distance scale, 178
Social sanctions, 81–82, 86–87, 437
Social structure of a school, 84–87
Socialization, 169
Sociogram, 177
Specific factor, 114
Spontaneous recovery, 48, 51, 200, 208–9
S.R.A. Achievement Series, 501
Standard deviation, 552
Standard error
  of differences in mean, 572–73
  of mean, 571–72
  of measurement, 133, 467–68
Standard scores, 561–63
Standardized achievement tests, 499–503
Stanford Achievement Tests, 501
Stanford-Binet Scale, 117–19, 127–28, 140
Status, 83–86
Status striving, 85–86, 101
STEP, 109–11, 501–2
Stimulative-restrictive, 237–38
Stimulus, 6–7, 211
  an attitude object, 423
  conditioned and unconditioned, 42–44, 200
  deprivation, 538
  as a drive source, 45
  objects and signs, 194–95
  and perception, 305–6, 536
  variation in transfer, 298–99
Stimulus generalization, 49, 51, 160–61, 200, 298, 356, 398
Stimulus variables, 6, 12–17, 30–32, 35, 153, 157, 225, 253, 330, 345; see also Environmental variable; Learning experiences; Method variable; Task variable
Strategies of decision-making, 360–63
Structuring, 320, 340–41, 398–403
  as problem solving, 402–3
Sublimation, 531
Success and failure; see Level of aspiration
Successive approximation, 205–7, 378
Superego, 56–62, 173–75, 279, 434, 435, 521, 528–29, 532
Survey tests, 500
Symbolic representation, 408

Sympathy, 180–81
Synthesis, 196, 249

Task variable, 11, 12–15, 31, 300–301, 331–36
Taxonomy of educational objectives
   affective domain, 197–98
   cognitive domain, 196–97, 320, 331, 399, 481, 485
Teacher as a reinforcer, 31, 41, 50, 168, 204, 205–6, 212, 215–16, 274–77, 342–43, 352–53, 380, 382, 445
Teacher-guidance, 31, 205–6, 212–13, 253, 254, 327–28, 340–42, 349–52, 534–35
Teacher-pupil planning, 212, 236–37, 337
Teacher-pupil relationships, 235–42, 251–52
Teaching machine programs, 227–29
   branching versus linear, 228, 234–35
   knowledge of results, 232–33
   response modes in, 233–34
   scrambled book, 229
   size of step in, 16–17, 234
Teaching machines, 15–16, 227–29
Test anxiety, 13–15, 246–52
Test Anxiety Scale for Children, 246–52
Test construction, 470–99
Test-retest reliability, 466
Tests
   academic aptitude, 108–12
   of anxiety, 244–47
   characteristics of good, 462–70
   of creativity, 413
   differential aptitude, 141–47
   fear of, 159
   intelligence, 113–26
   of significance, 570–74
   sociometric, 177–78
   standard achievement, 499–503
   teacher-made achievement, 470–99
Then versus Now studies, 221–26

Theories, 5–6, 14, 25
   of personality, 508–19
   of transfer, 294–97
Therapy, 534–35
Thinking, 389–421
   abilities, 114–16
   closed systems of, 399–401
   computer simulation of, 393–97
   as creativity, 410–14
   as critical judgment, 415–18
   Piaget's stages of development, 366–74
   as problem solving, 403–10
   as structuring, 398–403
Threat; see Conflict
TOTE units, 396
Traditional versus modern, 222–25
Transfer of training, 291–304
   and ability, 301–2
   conditions of, 297–301
   measurement of, 293–94
   teaching for, 327–28
   theories of, 294–97
Transfer theories, 294–97
   formal discipline, 294–96
   generalization, 297–98
   identical elements, 296
Trial-and-error, 404–5
True-false, 481–84

Unconscious motivation, 57, 67, 517
Underachiever, 24, 25, 110, 111

Validity, 462–65
Values, 197–98, 422, 425, 433–44
   and social class, 272–73
   social class differences in, 91
Verbal tests, 121, 123, 125
Vocational attainment, prediction of, 138–40

Warmth in home, 172–76
Wechsler Intelligence Scales, 119–20, 129